THIRD EDITION

High Performance MySQL

Good Luck with MySQL

M. [signature]

Baron Schwartz, Peter Zaitsev, and Vadim Tkachenko

O'REILLY®

Beijing · Cambridge · Farnham · Köln · Sebastopol · Tokyo

High Performance MySQL, Third Edition

by Baron Schwartz, Peter Zaitsev, and Vadim Tkachenko

Published by O'Reilly Media, Inc., 1005 Gravenstein Highway North, Sebastopol, CA 95472.

O'Reilly books may be purchased for educational, business, or sales promotional use. Online editions
are also available for most titles (*http://my.safaribooksonline.com*). For more information, contact our
corporate/institutional sales department: (800) 998-9938 or *corporate@oreilly.com*.

Editor: Andy Oram
Production Editor: Holly Bauer
Proofreader: Rachel Head

Indexer: Jay Marchand
Cover Designer: Karen Montgomery
Interior Designer: David Futato
Illustrator: Rebecca Demarest

March 2004: First Edition.
June 2008: Second Edition.
March 2012: Third Edition.

Revision History for the Third Edition:
    2012-03-01   First release
See *http://oreilly.com/catalog/errata.csp?isbn=9781449314286* for release details.

ISBN: 978-1-449-31428-6

[LSI]

1330629570

Table of Contents

Foreword

I've been a fan of this book for years, and the third edition makes a great book even better. Not only do world-class experts share that expertise, but they have taken the time to update and add chapters with high-quality writing. While the book has many details on getting high performance from MySQL, the focus of the book is on the process of improvement rather than facts and trivia. This book will help you figure out how to make things better, regardless of changes in MySQL's behavior over time.

The authors are uniquely qualified to write this book, based on their experience, principled approach, focus on efficiency, and commitment to improvement. By *experience*, I mean that the authors have been working on MySQL performance from the days when it didn't scale and had no instrumentation to the current period where things are much better. By *principled approach*, I mean that they treat this like a science, first defining problems to be solved and then using reason and measurement to solve those problems.

I am most impressed by their focus on *efficiency*. As consultants, they don't have the luxury of time. Clients getting billed by the hour want problems solved quickly. So the authors have defined processes and built tools to get things done correctly and efficiently. They describe the processes in this book and publish source code for the tools.

Finally, they continue to get better at what they do. This includes a shift in concern from throughput to response time, a commitment to understanding the performance of MySQL on new hardware, and a pursuit of new skills like queueing theory that can be used to understand performance.

I believe this book augurs a bright future for MySQL. As MySQL has evolved to support demanding workloads, the authors have led a similar effort to improve the understanding of MySQL performance within the community. They have also contributed directly to that improvement via XtraDB and XtraBackup. I continue to learn from them and hope you take the time to do so as well.

—Mark Callaghan, Software Engineer, Facebook

Preface

We wrote this book to serve the needs of not just the MySQL application developer but also the MySQL database administrator. We assume that you are already relatively experienced with MySQL. We also assume some experience with general system administration, networking, and Unix-like operating systems.

The second edition of this book presented a lot of information to readers, but no book can provide complete coverage of a topic. Between the second and third editions, we took notes on literally thousands of interesting problems we'd solved or seen others solve. When we started to outline the third edition, it became clear that not only would full coverage of these topics require three to five thousand pages, but the book *still* wouldn't be complete. After reflecting on this problem, we realized that the second edition's emphasis on deep coverage was actually self-limiting, in the sense that it often didn't teach readers *how to think* about MySQL.

As a result, this third edition has a different focus from the second edition. We still convey a lot of information, and we still emphasize the same goals, such as reliability and correctness. But we've also tried to imbue the book with a deeper purpose: we want to teach the principles of why MySQL works as it does, not just the facts about how it works. We've included more illustrative stories and case studies, which demonstrate the principles in action. We build on these to try to answer questions such as "Given MySQL's internal architecture and operation, what practical effects arise in real usage? Why do those effects matter? How do they make MySQL well suited (or not well suited) for particular needs?"

Ultimately, we hope that your knowledge of MySQL's internals will help you in situations beyond the scope of this book. And we hope that your newfound insight will help you to learn and practice a methodical approach to designing, maintaining, and troubleshooting systems that are built on MySQL.

How This Book Is Organized

We fit a lot of complicated topics into this book. Here, we explain how we put them together in an order that makes them easier to learn.

A Broad Overview

Chapter 1, *MySQL Architecture and History* is dedicated to the basics—things you'll need to be familiar with before you dig in deeply. You need to understand how MySQL is organized before you'll be able to use it effectively. This chapter explains MySQL's architecture and key facts about its storage engines. It helps you get up to speed if you aren't familiar with some of the fundamentals of a relational database, including transactions. This chapter will also be useful if this book is your introduction to MySQL but you're already familiar with another database, such as Oracle. We also include a bit of historical context: the changes to MySQL over time, recent ownership changes, and where we think it's headed.

Building a Solid Foundation

The early chapters cover material we hope you'll reference over and over as you use MySQL.

Chapter 2, *Benchmarking MySQL* discusses the basics of benchmarking—that is, determining what sort of workload your server can handle, how fast it can perform certain tasks, and so on. Benchmarking is an essential skill for evaluating how the server behaves under load, but it's also important to know when it's not useful.

Chapter 3, *Profiling Server Performance* introduces you to the response time–oriented approach we take to troubleshooting and diagnosing server performance problems. This framework has proven essential to solving some of the most puzzling cases we've seen. Although you might choose to modify our approach (we developed it by modifying Cary Millsap's approach, after all), we hope you'll avoid the pitfalls of not having any method at all.

In Chapters 4 through 6, we introduce three topics that together form the foundation for a good logical and physical database design. In Chapter 4, *Optimizing Schema and Data Types*, we cover the various nuances of data types and table design. Chapter 5, *Indexing for High Performance* extends the discussion to indexes—that is, physical database design. A firm understanding of indexes and how to use them well is essential for using MySQL effectively, so you'll probably find yourself returning to this chapter repeatedly. And Chapter 6, *Query Performance Optimization* wraps the topics together by explaining how MySQL executes queries and how you can take advantage of its query optimizer's strengths. This chapter also presents specific examples of many common classes of queries, illustrating where MySQL does a good job and how to transform queries into forms that use its strengths.

Up to this point, we've covered the basic topics that apply to any database: tables, indexes, data, and queries. Chapter 7, *Advanced MySQL Features* goes beyond the basics and shows you how MySQL's advanced features work. We examine topics such as partitioning, stored procedures, triggers, and character sets. MySQL's implementation of these features is different from other databases, and a good understanding of them can open up new opportunities for performance gains that you might not have thought about otherwise.

Configuring Your Application

The next two chapters discuss how to make MySQL, your application, and your hardware work well together. In Chapter 8, *Optimizing Server Settings*, we discuss how you can configure MySQL to make the most of your hardware and to be reliable and robust. Chapter 9, *Operating System and Hardware Optimization* explains how to get the most out of your operating system and hardware. We discuss solid-state storage in depth, and we suggest hardware configurations that might provide better performance for larger-scale applications.

Both chapters explore MySQL internals to some degree. This is a recurring theme that continues all the way through the appendixes: learn how it works internally, and you'll be empowered to understand and reason about the consequences.

MySQL as an Infrastructure Component

MySQL doesn't exist in a vacuum. It's part of an overall application stack, and you'll need to build a robust overall architecture for your application. The next set of chapters is about how to do that.

In Chapter 10, *Replication*, we discuss MySQL's killer feature: the ability to set up multiple servers that all stay in sync with a master server's changes. Unfortunately, replication is perhaps MySQL's most troublesome feature for some people. This doesn't have to be the case, and we show you how to ensure that it keeps running well.

Chapter 11, *Scaling MySQL* discusses what scalability is (it's not the same thing as performance), why applications and systems don't scale, and what to do about it. If you do it right, you can scale MySQL to suit nearly any purpose. Chapter 12, *High Availability* delves into a related-but-distinct topic: how to ensure that MySQL stays up and functions smoothly. In Chapter 13, *MySQL in the Cloud*, you'll learn about what's different when you run MySQL in cloud computing environments.

In Chapter 14, *Application-Level Optimization*, we explain what we call *full-stack optimization*—optimization from the frontend to the backend, all the way from the user's experience to the database.

The best-designed, most scalable architecture in the world is no good if it can't survive power outages, malicious attacks, application bugs or programmer mistakes, and other disasters. That's why Chapter 15, *Backup and Recovery* discusses various backup and recovery strategies for your MySQL databases. These strategies will help minimize your downtime in the event of inevitable hardware failure and ensure that your data survives such catastrophes.

Miscellaneous Useful Topics

In the last chapter and the book's appendixes, we delve into several topics that either don't fit well into any of the earlier chapters, or are referenced often enough in multiple chapters that they deserve a bit of special attention.

Chapter 16, *Tools for MySQL Users* explores some of the open source and commercial tools that can help you manage and monitor your MySQL servers more efficiently.

Appendix A introduces the three major unofficial versions of MySQL that have arisen over the last few years, including the one that our company maintains. It's worth knowing what else is available; many problems that are difficult or intractable with MySQL are solved elegantly by one of the variants. Two of the three (Percona Server and MariaDB) are drop-in replacements, so the effort involved in trying them out is not large. However, we hasten to add that we think most users are well served by sticking with the official MySQL distribution from Oracle.

Appendix B shows you how to inspect your MySQL server. Knowing how to get status information from the server is important; knowing what that information means is even more important. We cover SHOW INNODB STATUS in particular detail, because it provides deep insight into the operations of the InnoDB transactional storage engine. There is a lot of discussion of InnoDB's internals in this appendix.

Appendix C shows you how to copy very large files from place to place efficiently—a must if you are going to manage large volumes of data. Appendix D shows you how to really use and understand the all-important EXPLAIN command. Appendix E shows you how to decipher what's going on when queries are requesting locks that interfere with each other. And finally, Appendix F is an introduction to Sphinx, a high-performance, full-text indexing system that can complement MySQL's own abilities.

Software Versions and Availability

MySQL is a moving target. In the years since Jeremy wrote the outline for the first edition of this book, numerous releases of MySQL have appeared. MySQL 4.1 and 5.0 were available only as alpha versions when the first edition went to press, but today MySQL 5.1 and 5.5 are the backbone of many large online applications. As we completed this third edition, MySQL 5.6 was the unreleased bleeding edge.

We didn't rely on a single version of MySQL for this book. Instead, we drew on our extensive collective knowledge of MySQL in the real world. The core of the book is focused on MySQL 5.1 and MySQL 5.5, because those are what we consider the "current" versions. Most of our examples assume you're running some reasonably mature version of MySQL 5.1, such as MySQL 5.1.50 or newer or newer. We have made an effort to note features or functionalities that might not exist in older releases or that might exist only in the upcoming 5.6 series. However, the definitive reference for mapping features to specific versions is the MySQL documentation itself. We expect that you'll find yourself visiting the annotated online documentation (*http://dev.mysql.com/doc/*) from time to time as you read this book.

Another great aspect of MySQL is that it runs on all of today's popular platforms: Mac OS X, Windows, GNU/Linux, Solaris, FreeBSD, you name it! However, we are biased toward GNU/Linux[1] and other Unix-like operating systems. Windows users are likely to encounter some differences. For example, file paths are completely different on Windows. We also refer to standard Unix command-line utilities; we assume you know the corresponding commands in Windows.[2]

Perl is the other rough spot when dealing with MySQL on Windows. MySQL comes with several useful utilities that are written in Perl, and certain chapters in this book present example Perl scripts that form the basis of more complex tools you'll build. Percona Toolkit—which is indispensable for administering MySQL—is also written in Perl. However, Perl isn't included with Windows. In order to use these scripts, you'll need to download a Windows version of Perl from ActiveState and install the necessary add-on modules (`DBI` and `DBD::mysql`) for MySQL access.

Conventions Used in This Book

The following typographical conventions are used in this book:

Italic
> Used for new terms, URLs, email addresses, usernames, hostnames, filenames, file extensions, pathnames, directories, and Unix commands and utilities.

`Constant width`
> Indicates elements of code, configuration options, database and table names, variables and their values, functions, modules, the contents of files, or the output from commands.

`Constant width bold`
> Shows commands or other text that should be typed literally by the user. Also used for emphasis in command output.

`Constant width italic`
> Shows text that should be replaced with user-supplied values.

 This icon signifies a tip, suggestion, or general note.

---

1. To avoid confusion, we refer to Linux when we are writing about the kernel, and GNU/Linux when we are writing about the whole operating system infrastructure that supports applications.

2. You can get Windows-compatible versions of Unix utilities at *http://unxutils.sourceforge.net* or *http://gnuwin32.sourceforge.net*.

This icon indicates a warning or caution.

Using Code Examples

This book is here to help you get your job done. In general, you may use the code in this book in your programs and documentation. You don't need to contact us for permission unless you're reproducing a significant portion of the code. For example, writing a program that uses several chunks of code from this book doesn't require permission. Selling or distributing a CD-ROM of examples from O'Reilly books *does* require permission. Answering a question by citing this book and quoting example code doesn't require permission. Incorporating a significant amount of example code from this book into your product's documentation *does* require permission.

Examples are maintained on the site *http://www.highperfmysql.com* and will be updated there from time to time. We cannot commit, however, to updating and testing the code for every minor release of MySQL.

We appreciate, but don't require, attribution. An attribution usually includes the title, author, publisher, and ISBN. For example: "*High Performance MySQL, Third Edition*, by Baron Schwartz et al. (O'Reilly). Copyright 2012 Baron Schwartz, Peter Zaitsev, and Vadim Tkachenko, 978-1-449-31428-6."

If you feel your use of code examples falls outside fair use or the permission given above, feel free to contact us at *permissions@oreilly.com*.

Safari® Books Online

Safari Books Online (*www.safaribooksonline.com*) is an on-demand digital library that delivers expert content in both book and video form from the world's leading authors in technology and business. Technology professionals, software developers, web designers, and business and creative professionals use Safari Books Online as their primary resource for research, problem solving, learning, and certification training.

Safari Books Online offers a range of product mixes and pricing programs for organizations, government agencies, and individuals. Subscribers have access to thousands of books, training videos, and prepublication manuscripts in one fully searchable database from publishers like O'Reilly Media, Prentice Hall Professional, Addison-Wesley Professional, Microsoft Press, Sams, Que, Peachpit Press, Focal Press, Cisco Press, John Wiley & Sons, Syngress, Morgan Kaufmann, IBM Redbooks, Packt, Adobe Press, FT Press, Apress, Manning, New Riders, McGraw-Hill, Jones & Bartlett, Course Technology, and dozens more. For more information about Safari Books Online, please visit us online.

How to Contact Us

Please address comments and questions concerning this book to the publisher:

O'Reilly Media, Inc.
1005 Gravenstein Highway North
Sebastopol, CA 95472
800-998-9938 (in the United States or Canada)
707-829-0515 (international or local)
707-829-0104 (fax)

We have a web page for this book, where we list errata, examples, and any additional information. You can access this page at:

http://shop.oreilly.com/product/0636920022343.do

To comment or ask technical questions about this book, send email to:

bookquestions@oreilly.com

For more information about our books, conferences, Resource Centers, and the O'Reilly Network, see our website at:

http://www.oreilly.com

Find us on Facebook: *http://facebook.com/oreilly*

Follow us on Twitter: *http://twitter.com/oreillymedia*

Watch us on YouTube: *http://www.youtube.com/oreillymedia*

You can also get in touch with the authors directly. You can use the contact form on our company's website at *http://www.percona.com*. We'd be delighted to hear from you.

Acknowledgments for the Third Edition

Thanks to the following people who helped in various ways: Brian Aker, Johan Andersson, Espen Braekken, Mark Callaghan, James Day, Maciej Dobrzanski, Ewen Fortune, Dave Hildebrandt, Fernando Ipar, Haidong Ji, Giuseppe Maxia, Aurimas Mikalauskas, Istvan Podor, Yves Trudeau, Matt Yonkovit, and Alex Yurchenko. Thanks to everyone at Percona for helping in dozens of ways over the years. Thanks to the many great bloggers[3] and speakers who gave us a great deal of food for thought, especially Yoshinori Matsunobu. Thanks also to the authors of the previous editions: Jeremy D. Zawodny, Derek J. Balling, and Arjen Lentz. Thanks to Andy Oram, Rachel Head, and the whole O'Reilly staff who do such a classy job of publishing books and running conferences. And much gratitude to the brilliant and dedicated MySQL team inside

---

3. You can find a wealth of great technical blogging on *http://planet.mysql.com*.

Oracle, as well as all of the ex-MySQLers, wherever you are, and especially to SkySQL and Monty Program.

Baron thanks his wife Lynn, his mother, Connie, and his parents-in-law, Jane and Roger, for helping and supporting this project in many ways, but most especially for their encouragement and help with chores and taking care of the family. Thanks also to Peter and Vadim for being such great teachers and colleagues. Baron dedicates this edition to the memory of Alan Rimm-Kaufman, whose great love and encouragement are never forgotten.

Acknowledgments for the Second Edition

Sphinx developer Andrew Aksyonoff wrote Appendix F. We'd like to thank him first for his in-depth discussion.

We have received invaluable help from many people while writing this book. It's impossible to list everyone who gave us help—we really owe thanks to the entire MySQL community and everyone at MySQL AB. However, here's a list of people who contributed directly, with apologies if we've missed anyone: Tobias Asplund, Igor Babaev, Pascal Borghino, Roland Bouman, Ronald Bradford, Mark Callaghan, Jeremy Cole, Britt Crawford and the HiveDB Project, Vasil Dimov, Harrison Fisk, Florian Haas, Dmitri Joukovski and Zmanda (thanks for the diagram explaining LVM snapshots), Alan Kasindorf, Sheeri Kritzer Cabral, Marko Makela, Giuseppe Maxia, Paul McCullagh, B. Keith Murphy, Dhiren Patel, Sergey Petrunia, Alexander Rubin, Paul Tuckfield, Heikki Tuuri, and Michael "Monty" Widenius.

A special thanks to Andy Oram and Isabel Kunkle, our editor and assistant editor at O'Reilly, and to Rachel Wheeler, the copyeditor. Thanks also to the rest of the O'Reilly staff.

From Baron

I would like to thank my wife, Lynn Rainville, and our dog, Carbon. If you've written a book, I'm sure you know how grateful I am to them. I also owe a huge debt of gratitude to Alan Rimm-Kaufman and my colleagues at the Rimm-Kaufman Group for their support and encouragement during this project. Thanks to Peter, Vadim, and Arjen for giving me the opportunity to make this dream come true. And thanks to Jeremy and Derek for breaking the trail for us.

From Peter

I've been doing MySQL performance and scaling presentations, training, and consulting for years, and I've always wanted to reach a wider audience, so I was very excited when Andy Oram approached me to work on this book. I have not written a book before, so I wasn't prepared for how much time and effort it required. We first started talking about updating the first edition to cover recent versions of MySQL, but we wanted to add so much material that we ended up rewriting most of the book.

This book is truly a team effort. Because I was very busy bootstrapping Percona, Vadim's and my consulting company, and because English is not my first language, we all had different roles. I provided the outline and technical content, then I reviewed the material, revising and extending it as we wrote. When Arjen (the former head of the MySQL documentation team) joined the project, we began to fill out the outline. Things really started to roll once we brought in Baron, who can write high-quality book content at insane speeds. Vadim was a great help with in-depth MySQL source code checks and when we needed to back our claims with benchmarks and other research.

As we worked on the book, we found more and more areas we wanted to explore in more detail. Many of the book's topics, such as replication, query optimization, InnoDB, architecture, and design could easily fill their own books, so we had to stop somewhere and leave some material for a possible future edition or for our blogs, presentations, and articles.

We got great help from our reviewers, who are the top MySQL experts in the world, from both inside and outside of MySQL AB. These include MySQL's founder, Michael Widenius; InnoDB's founder, Heikki Tuuri; Igor Babaev, the head of the MySQL optimizer team; and many others.

I would also like to thank my wife, Katya Zaytseva, and my children, Ivan and Nadezhda, for allowing me to spend time on the book that should have been Family Time. I'm also grateful to Percona's employees for handling things when I disappeared to work on the book, and of course to Andy Oram and O'Reilly for making things happen.

From Vadim

I would like to thank Peter, who I am excited to have worked with on this book and look forward to working with on other projects; Baron, who was instrumental in getting this book done; and Arjen, who was a lot of fun to work with. Thanks also to our editor Andy Oram, who had enough patience to work with us; the MySQL team that created great software; and our clients who provide me the opportunities to fine-tune my MySQL understanding. And finally a special thank you to my wife, Valerie, and our sons, Myroslav and Timur, who always support me and help me to move forward.

From Arjen

I would like to thank Andy for his wisdom, guidance, and patience. Thanks to Baron for hopping on the second edition train while it was already in motion, and to Peter and Vadim for solid background information and benchmarks. Thanks also to Jeremy and Derek for the foundation with the first edition; as you wrote in my copy, Derek: "Keep 'em honest, that's all I ask."

Also thanks to all my former colleagues (and present friends) at MySQL AB, where I acquired most of what I know about the topic; and in this context a special mention for Monty, whom I continue to regard as the proud parent of MySQL, even though his company now lives on as part of Sun Microsystems. I would also like to thank everyone else in the global MySQL community.

And last but not least, thanks to my daughter Phoebe, who at this stage in her young life does not care about this thing called "MySQL," nor indeed has she any idea which of The Wiggles it might refer to! For some, ignorance is truly bliss, and they provide us with a refreshing perspective on what is really important in life; for the rest of you, may you find this book a useful addition on your reference bookshelf. And don't forget your life.

Acknowledgments for the First Edition

A book like this doesn't come into being without help from literally dozens of people. Without their assistance, the book you hold in your hands would probably still be a bunch of sticky notes on the sides of our monitors. This is the part of the book where we get to say whatever we like about the folks who helped us out, and we don't have to worry about music playing in the background telling us to shut up and go away, as you might see on TV during an awards show.

We couldn't have completed this project without the constant prodding, begging, pleading, and support from our editor, Andy Oram. If there is one person most responsible for the book in your hands, it's Andy. We really do appreciate the weekly nag sessions.

Andy isn't alone, though. At O'Reilly there are a bunch of other folks who had some part in getting those sticky notes converted to a cohesive book that you'd be willing to read, so we also have to thank the production, illustration, and marketing folks for helping to pull this book together. And, of course, thanks to Tim O'Reilly for his continued commitment to producing some of the industry's finest documentation for popular open source software.

Finally, we'd both like to give a big thanks to the folks who agreed to look over the various drafts of the book and tell us all the things we were doing wrong: our reviewers. They spent part of their 2003 holiday break looking over roughly formatted versions of this text, full of typos, misleading statements, and outright mathematical errors. In no particular order, thanks to Brian "Krow" Aker, Mark "JDBC" Matthews, Jeremy "the other Jeremy" Cole, Mike "VBMySQL.com (*http://vbmysql.com*)" Hillyer, Raymond "Rainman" De Roo, Jeffrey "Regex Master" Friedl, Jason DeHaan, Dan Nelson, Steve "Unix Wiz" Friedl, and, last but not least, Kasia "Unix Girl" Trapszo.

From Jeremy

I would again like to thank Andy for agreeing to take on this project and for continually beating on us for more chapter material. Derek's help was essential for getting the last 20–30% of the book completed so that we wouldn't miss yet another target date. Thanks for agreeing to come on board late in the process and deal with my sporadic bursts of productivity, and for handling the XML grunt work, Chapter 10, Appendix F, and all the other stuff I threw your way.

I also need to thank my parents for getting me that first Commodore 64 computer so many years ago. They not only tolerated the first 10 years of what seems to be a lifelong obsession with electronics and computer technology, but quickly became supporters of my never-ending quest to learn and do more.

Next, I'd like to thank a group of people I've had the distinct pleasure of working with while spreading the MySQL religion at Yahoo! during the last few years. Jeffrey Friedl and Ray Goldberger provided encouragement and feedback from the earliest stages of this undertaking. Along with them, Steve Morris, James Harvey, and Sergey Kolychev put up with my seemingly constant experimentation on the Yahoo! Finance MySQL servers, even when it interrupted their important work. Thanks also to the countless other Yahoo!s who have helped me find interesting MySQL problems and solutions. And, most importantly, thanks for having the trust and faith in me needed to put MySQL into some of the most important and visible parts of Yahoo!'s business.

Adam Goodman, the publisher and owner of *Linux Magazine*, helped me ease into the world of writing for a technical audience by publishing my first feature-length MySQL articles back in 2001. Since then, he's taught me more than he realizes about editing and publishing and has encouraged me to continue on this road with my own monthly column in the magazine. Thanks, Adam.

Thanks to Monty and David for sharing MySQL with the world. Speaking of MySQL AB, thanks to all the other great folks there who have encouraged me in writing this: Kerry, Larry, Joe, Marten, Brian, Paul, Jeremy, Mark, Harrison, Matt, and the rest of the team there. You guys rock.

Finally, thanks to all my weblog readers for encouraging me to write informally about MySQL and other technical topics on a daily basis. And, last but not least, thanks to the Goon Squad.

From Derek

Like Jeremy, I've got to thank my family, for much the same reasons. I want to thank my parents for their constant goading that I should write a book, even if this isn't anywhere near what they had in mind. My grandparents helped me learn two valuable lessons, the meaning of the dollar and how much I would fall in love with computers, as they loaned me the money to buy my first Commodore VIC-20.

I can't thank Jeremy enough for inviting me to join him on the whirlwind book-writing roller coaster. It's been a great experience and I look forward to working with him again in the future.

A special thanks goes out to Raymond De Roo, Brian Wohlgemuth, David Calafrancesco, Tera Doty, Jay Rubin, Bill Catlan, Anthony Howe, Mark O'Neal, George Montgomery, George Barber, and the myriad other people who patiently listened to me gripe about things, let me bounce ideas off them to see whether an outsider could understand what I was trying to say, or just managed to bring a smile to my face when I needed it most. Without you, this book might still have been written, but I almost certainly would have gone crazy in the process.

## CHAPTER 1

MySQL Architecture and History

MySQL is very different from other database servers, and its architectural characteristics make it useful for a wide range of purposes as well as making it a poor choice for others. MySQL is not perfect, but it is flexible enough to work well in very demanding environments, such as web applications. At the same time, MySQL can power embedded applications, data warehouses, content indexing and delivery software, highly available redundant systems, online transaction processing (OLTP), and much more.

To get the most from MySQL, you need to understand its design so that you can work with it, not against it. MySQL is flexible in many ways. For example, you can configure it to run well on a wide range of hardware, and it supports a variety of data types. However, MySQL's most unusual and important feature is its storage-engine architecture, whose design separates query processing and other server tasks from data storage and retrieval. This separation of concerns lets you choose how your data is stored and what performance, features, and other characteristics you want.

This chapter provides a high-level overview of the MySQL server architecture, the major differences between the storage engines, and why those differences are important. We'll finish with some historical context and benchmarks. We've tried to explain MySQL by simplifying the details and showing examples. This discussion will be useful for those new to database servers as well as readers who are experts with other database servers.

MySQL's Logical Architecture

A good mental picture of how MySQL's components work together will help you understand the server. Figure 1-1 shows a logical view of MySQL's architecture.

The topmost layer contains the services that aren't unique to MySQL. They're services most network-based client/server tools or servers need: connection handling, authentication, security, and so forth.

The second layer is where things get interesting. Much of MySQL's brains are here, including the code for query parsing, analysis, optimization, caching, and all the

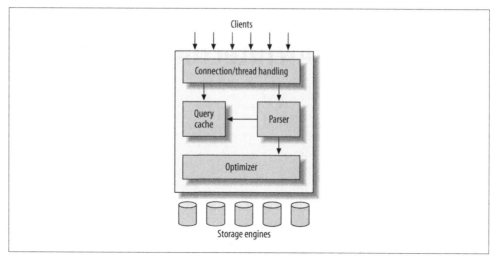

Figure 1-1. A logical view of the MySQL server architecture

built-in functions (e.g., dates, times, math, and encryption). Any functionality provided across storage engines lives at this level: stored procedures, triggers, and views, for example.

The third layer contains the storage engines. They are responsible for storing and retrieving all data stored "in" MySQL. Like the various filesystems available for GNU/Linux, each storage engine has its own benefits and drawbacks. The server communicates with them through the *storage engine API*. This interface hides differences between storage engines and makes them largely transparent at the query layer. The API contains a couple of dozen low-level functions that perform operations such as "begin a transaction" or "fetch the row that has this primary key." The storage engines don't parse SQL[1] or communicate with each other; they simply respond to requests from the server.

Connection Management and Security

Each client connection gets its own thread within the server process. The connection's queries execute within that single thread, which in turn resides on one core or CPU. The server caches threads, so they don't need to be created and destroyed for each new connection.[2]

When clients (applications) connect to the MySQL server, the server needs to authenticate them. Authentication is based on username, originating host, and password.

---

1. One exception is InnoDB, which does parse foreign key definitions, because the MySQL server doesn't yet implement them itself.

2. MySQL 5.5 and newer versions support an API that can accept thread-pooling plugins, so a small pool of threads can service many connections.

X.509 certificates can also be used across an SSL (Secure Sockets Layer) connection. Once a client has connected, the server verifies whether the client has privileges for each query it issues (e.g., whether the client is allowed to issue a SELECT statement that accesses the Country table in the world database).

Optimization and Execution

MySQL parses queries to create an internal structure (the parse tree), and then applies a variety of optimizations. These can include rewriting the query, determining the order in which it will read tables, choosing which indexes to use, and so on. You can pass hints to the optimizer through special keywords in the query, affecting its decision-making process. You can also ask the server to explain various aspects of optimization. This lets you know what decisions the server is making and gives you a reference point for reworking queries, schemas, and settings to make everything run as efficiently as possible. We discuss the optimizer in much more detail in Chapter 6.

The optimizer does not really care what storage engine a particular table uses, but the storage engine does affect how the server optimizes the query. The optimizer asks the storage engine about some of its capabilities and the cost of certain operations, and for statistics on the table data. For instance, some storage engines support index types that can be helpful to certain queries. You can read more about indexing and schema optimization in Chapter 4 and Chapter 5.

Before even parsing the query, though, the server consults the query cache, which can store only SELECT statements, along with their result sets. If anyone issues a query that's identical to one already in the cache, the server doesn't need to parse, optimize, or execute the query at all—it can simply pass back the stored result set. We write more about that in Chapter 7.

Concurrency Control

Anytime more than one query needs to change data at the same time, the problem of concurrency control arises. For our purposes in this chapter, MySQL has to do this at two levels: the server level and the storage engine level. Concurrency control is a big topic to which a large body of theoretical literature is devoted, so we will just give you a simplified overview of how MySQL deals with concurrent readers and writers, so you have the context you need for the rest of this chapter.

We'll use an email box on a Unix system as an example. The classic *mbox* file format is very simple. All the messages in an *mbox* mailbox are concatenated together, one after another. This makes it very easy to read and parse mail messages. It also makes mail delivery easy: just append a new message to the end of the file.

But what happens when two processes try to deliver messages at the same time to the same mailbox? Clearly that could corrupt the mailbox, leaving two interleaved messages at the end of the mailbox file. Well-behaved mail delivery systems use locking to prevent corruption. If a client attempts a second delivery while the mailbox is locked, it must wait to acquire the lock itself before delivering its message.

This scheme works reasonably well in practice, but it gives no support for concurrency. Because only a single process can change the mailbox at any given time, this approach becomes problematic with a high-volume mailbox.

Read/Write Locks

Reading from the mailbox isn't as troublesome. There's nothing wrong with multiple clients reading the same mailbox simultaneously; because they aren't making changes, nothing is likely to go wrong. But what happens if someone tries to delete message number 25 while programs are reading the mailbox? It depends, but a reader could come away with a corrupted or inconsistent view of the mailbox. So, to be safe, even reading from a mailbox requires special care.

If you think of the mailbox as a database table and each mail message as a row, it's easy to see that the problem is the same in this context. In many ways, a mailbox is really just a simple database table. Modifying rows in a database table is very similar to removing or changing the content of messages in a mailbox file.

The solution to this classic problem of concurrency control is rather simple. Systems that deal with concurrent read/write access typically implement a locking system that consists of two lock types. These locks are usually known as *shared locks* and *exclusive locks*, or *read locks* and *write locks*.

Without worrying about the actual locking technology, we can describe the concept as follows. Read locks on a resource are shared, or mutually nonblocking: many clients can read from a resource at the same time and not interfere with each other. Write locks, on the other hand, are exclusive—i.e., they block both read locks and other write locks—because the only safe policy is to have a single client writing to the resource at a given time and to prevent all reads when a client is writing.

In the database world, locking happens all the time: MySQL has to prevent one client from reading a piece of data while another is changing it. It performs this lock management internally in a way that is transparent much of the time.

Lock Granularity

One way to improve the concurrency of a shared resource is to be more selective about what you lock. Rather than locking the entire resource, lock only the part that contains the data you need to change. Better yet, lock only the exact piece of data you plan to change. Minimizing the amount of data that you lock at any one time lets changes to a given resource occur simultaneously, as long as they don't conflict with each other.

The problem is locks consume resources. Every lock operation—getting a lock, checking to see whether a lock is free, releasing a lock, and so on—has overhead. If the system spends too much time managing locks instead of storing and retrieving data, performance can suffer.

A locking strategy is a compromise between lock overhead and data safety, and that compromise affects performance. Most commercial database servers don't give you much choice: you get what is known as row-level locking in your tables, with a variety of often complex ways to give good performance with many locks.

MySQL, on the other hand, does offer choices. Its storage engines can implement their own locking policies and lock granularities. Lock management is a very important decision in storage engine design; fixing the granularity at a certain level can give better performance for certain uses, yet make that engine less suited for other purposes. Because MySQL offers multiple storage engines, it doesn't require a single general-purpose solution. Let's have a look at the two most important lock strategies.

Table locks

The most basic locking strategy available in MySQL, and the one with the lowest overhead, is *table locks*. A table lock is analogous to the mailbox locks described earlier: it locks the entire table. When a client wishes to write to a table (insert, delete, update, etc.), it acquires a write lock. This keeps all other read and write operations at bay. When nobody is writing, readers can obtain read locks, which don't conflict with other read locks.

Table locks have variations for good performance in specific situations. For example, READ LOCAL table locks allow some types of concurrent write operations. Write locks also have a higher priority than read locks, so a request for a write lock will advance to the front of the lock queue even if readers are already in the queue (write locks can advance past read locks in the queue, but read locks cannot advance past write locks).

Although storage engines can manage their own locks, MySQL itself also uses a variety of locks that are effectively table-level for various purposes. For instance, the server uses a table-level lock for statements such as ALTER TABLE, regardless of the storage engine.

Row locks

The locking style that offers the greatest concurrency (and carries the greatest overhead) is the use of *row locks*. Row-level locking, as this strategy is commonly known, is available in the InnoDB and XtraDB storage engines, among others. Row locks are implemented in the storage engine, not the server (refer back to the logical architecture diagram if you need to). The server is completely unaware of locks implemented in the storage engines, and as you'll see later in this chapter and throughout the book, the storage engines all implement locking in their own ways.

Transactions

You can't examine the more advanced features of a database system for very long before *transactions* enter the mix. A transaction is a group of SQL queries that are treated *atomically*, as a single unit of work. If the database engine can apply the entire group of queries to a database, it does so, but if any of them can't be done because of a crash or other reason, none of them is applied. It's all or nothing.

Little of this section is specific to MySQL. If you're already familiar with ACID transactions, feel free to skip ahead to "Transactions in MySQL" on page 10.

A banking application is the classic example of why transactions are necessary. Imagine a bank's database with two tables: checking and savings. To move $200 from Jane's checking account to her savings account, you need to perform at least three steps:

1. Make sure her checking account balance is greater than $200.
2. Subtract $200 from her checking account balance.
3. Add $200 to her savings account balance.

The entire operation should be wrapped in a transaction so that if any one of the steps fails, any completed steps can be rolled back.

You start a transaction with the START TRANSACTION statement and then either make its changes permanent with COMMIT or discard the changes with ROLLBACK. So, the SQL for our sample transaction might look like this:

```
1    START TRANSACTION;
2    SELECT balance FROM checking WHERE customer_id = 10233276;
3    UPDATE checking SET balance = balance - 200.00 WHERE customer_id = 10233276;
4    UPDATE savings  SET balance = balance + 200.00 WHERE customer_id = 10233276;
5    COMMIT;
```

But transactions alone aren't the whole story. What happens if the database server crashes while performing line 4? Who knows? The customer probably just lost $200. And what if another process comes along between lines 3 and 4 and removes the entire checking account balance? The bank has given the customer a $200 credit without even knowing it.

Transactions aren't enough unless the system passes the *ACID test*. ACID stands for Atomicity, Consistency, Isolation, and Durability. These are tightly related criteria that a well-behaved transaction processing system must meet:

Atomicity
> A transaction must function as a single indivisible unit of work so that the entire transaction is either applied or rolled back. When transactions are atomic, there is no such thing as a partially completed transaction: it's all or nothing.

Consistency

> The database should always move from one consistent state to the next. In our example, consistency ensures that a crash between lines 3 and 4 doesn't result in $200 disappearing from the checking account. Because the transaction is never committed, none of the transaction's changes are ever reflected in the database.

Isolation

> The results of a transaction are usually invisible to other transactions until the transaction is complete. This ensures that if a bank account summary runs after line 3 but before line 4 in our example, it will still see the $200 in the checking account. When we discuss isolation levels, you'll understand why we said *usually* invisible.

Durability

> Once committed, a transaction's changes are permanent. This means the changes must be recorded such that data won't be lost in a system crash. Durability is a slightly fuzzy concept, however, because there are actually many levels. Some durability strategies provide a stronger safety guarantee than others, and nothing is ever 100% durable (if the database itself were truly durable, then how could backups increase durability?). We discuss what durability *really* means in MySQL in later chapters.

ACID transactions ensure that banks don't lose your money. It is generally extremely difficult or impossible to do this with application logic. An ACID-compliant database server has to do all sorts of complicated things you might not realize to provide ACID guarantees.

Just as with increased lock granularity, the downside of this extra security is that the database server has to do more work. A database server with ACID transactions also generally requires more CPU power, memory, and disk space than one without them. As we've said several times, this is where MySQL's storage engine architecture works to your advantage. You can decide whether your application needs transactions. If you don't really need them, you might be able to get higher performance with a nontransactional storage engine for some kinds of queries. You might be able to use LOCK TABLES to give the level of protection you need without transactions. It's all up to you.

Isolation Levels

Isolation is more complex than it looks. The SQL standard defines four isolation levels, with specific rules for which changes are and aren't visible inside and outside a transaction. Lower isolation levels typically allow higher concurrency and have lower overhead.

Each storage engine implements isolation levels slightly differently, and they don't necessarily match what you might expect if you're used to another database product (thus, we won't go into exhaustive detail in this section). You should read the manuals for whichever storage engines you decide to use.

Let's take a quick look at the four isolation levels:

READ UNCOMMITTED

In the READ UNCOMMITTED isolation level, transactions can view the results of uncommitted transactions. At this level, many problems can occur unless you really, really know what you are doing and have a good reason for doing it. This level is rarely used in practice, because its performance isn't much better than the other levels, which have many advantages. Reading uncommitted data is also known as a *dirty read*.

READ COMMITTED

The default isolation level for most database systems (but not MySQL!) is READ COMMITTED. It satisfies the simple definition of isolation used earlier: a transaction will see only those changes made by transactions that were already committed when it began, and its changes won't be visible to others until it has committed. This level still allows what's known as a *nonrepeatable read*. This means you can run the same statement twice and see different data.

REPEATABLE READ

REPEATABLE READ solves the problems that READ UNCOMMITTED allows. It guarantees that any rows a transaction reads will "look the same" in subsequent reads within the same transaction, but in theory it still allows another tricky problem: *phantom reads*. Simply put, a phantom read can happen when you select some range of rows, another transaction inserts a new row into the range, and then you select the same range again; you will then see the new "phantom" row. InnoDB and XtraDB solve the phantom read problem with multiversion concurrency control, which we explain later in this chapter.

REPEATABLE READ is MySQL's default transaction isolation level.

SERIALIZABLE

The highest level of isolation, SERIALIZABLE, solves the phantom read problem by forcing transactions to be ordered so that they can't possibly conflict. In a nutshell, SERIALIZABLE places a lock on every row it reads. At this level, a lot of timeouts and lock contention can occur. We've rarely seen people use this isolation level, but your application's needs might force you to accept the decreased concurrency in favor of the data stability that results.

Table 1-1 summarizes the various isolation levels and the drawbacks associated with each one.

Table 1-1. ANSI SQL isolation levels

Isolation level	Dirty reads possible	Nonrepeatable reads possible	Phantom reads possible	Locking reads
READ UNCOMMITTED	Yes	Yes	Yes	No
READ COMMITTED	No	Yes	Yes	No
REPEATABLE READ	No	No	Yes	No
SERIALIZABLE	No	No	No	Yes

Deadlocks

A *deadlock* is when two or more transactions are mutually holding and requesting locks on the same resources, creating a cycle of dependencies. Deadlocks occur when transactions try to lock resources in a different order. They can happen whenever multiple transactions lock the same resources. For example, consider these two transactions running against the StockPrice table:

Transaction #1

```
START TRANSACTION;
UPDATE StockPrice SET close = 45.50 WHERE stock_id = 4 and date = '2002-05-01';
UPDATE StockPrice SET close = 19.80 WHERE stock_id = 3 and date = '2002-05-02';
COMMIT;
```

Transaction #2

```
START TRANSACTION;
UPDATE StockPrice SET high = 20.12 WHERE stock_id = 3 and date = '2002-05-02';
UPDATE StockPrice SET high = 47.20 WHERE stock_id = 4 and date = '2002-05-01';
COMMIT;
```

If you're unlucky, each transaction will execute its first query and update a row of data, locking it in the process. Each transaction will then attempt to update its second row, only to find that it is already locked. The two transactions will wait forever for each other to complete, unless something intervenes to break the deadlock.

To combat this problem, database systems implement various forms of deadlock detection and timeouts. The more sophisticated systems, such as the InnoDB storage engine, will notice circular dependencies and return an error instantly. This can be a good thing—otherwise, deadlocks would manifest themselves as very slow queries. Others will give up after the query exceeds a lock wait timeout, which is not always good. The way InnoDB currently handles deadlocks is to roll back the transaction that has the fewest exclusive row locks (an approximate metric for which will be the easiest to roll back).

Lock behavior and order are storage engine–specific, so some storage engines might deadlock on a certain sequence of statements even though others won't. Deadlocks have a dual nature: some are unavoidable because of true data conflicts, and some are caused by how a storage engine works.

Deadlocks cannot be broken without rolling back one of the transactions, either partially or wholly. They are a fact of life in transactional systems, and your applications should be designed to handle them. Many applications can simply retry their transactions from the beginning.

Transaction Logging

Transaction logging helps make transactions more efficient. Instead of updating the tables on disk each time a change occurs, the storage engine can change its in-memory copy of the data. This is very fast. The storage engine can then write a record of the change to the transaction log, which is on disk and therefore durable. This is also a relatively fast operation, because appending log events involves sequential I/O in one small area of the disk instead of random I/O in many places. Then, at some later time, a process can update the table on disk. Thus, most storage engines that use this technique (known as *write-ahead logging*) end up writing the changes to disk twice.

If there's a crash after the update is written to the transaction log but before the changes are made to the data itself, the storage engine can still recover the changes upon restart. The recovery method varies between storage engines.

Transactions in MySQL

MySQL provides two transactional storage engines: InnoDB and NDB Cluster. Several third-party engines are also available; the best-known engines right now are XtraDB and PBXT. We discuss some specific properties of each engine in the next section.

AUTOCOMMIT

MySQL operates in AUTOCOMMIT mode by default. This means that unless you've explicitly begun a transaction, it automatically executes each query in a separate transaction. You can enable or disable AUTOCOMMIT for the current connection by setting a variable:

```
mysql> SHOW VARIABLES LIKE 'AUTOCOMMIT';
+---------------+-------+
| Variable_name | Value |
+---------------+-------+
| autocommit    | ON    |
+---------------+-------+
1 row in set (0.00 sec)
mysql> SET AUTOCOMMIT = 1;
```

The values 1 and ON are equivalent, as are 0 and OFF. When you run with AUTOCOMMIT =0, you are always in a transaction, until you issue a COMMIT or ROLLBACK. MySQL then starts a new transaction immediately. Changing the value of AUTOCOMMIT has no effect on nontransactional tables, such as MyISAM or Memory tables, which have no notion of committing or rolling back changes.

Certain commands, when issued during an open transaction, cause MySQL to commit the transaction before they execute. These are typically Data Definition Language (DDL) commands that make significant changes, such as ALTER TABLE, but LOCK TABLES and some other statements also have this effect. Check your version's documentation for the full list of commands that automatically commit a transaction.

MySQL lets you set the isolation level using the SET TRANSACTION ISOLATION LEVEL command, which takes effect when the next transaction starts. You can set the isolation level for the whole server in the configuration file, or just for your session:

```
mysql> SET SESSION TRANSACTION ISOLATION LEVEL READ COMMITTED;
```

MySQL recognizes all four ANSI standard isolation levels, and InnoDB supports all of them.

Mixing storage engines in transactions

MySQL doesn't manage transactions at the server level. Instead, the underlying storage engines implement transactions themselves. This means you can't reliably mix different engines in a single transaction.

If you mix transactional and nontransactional tables (for instance, InnoDB and MyISAM tables) in a transaction, the transaction will work properly if all goes well.

However, if a rollback is required, the changes to the nontransactional table can't be undone. This leaves the database in an inconsistent state from which it might be difficult to recover and renders the entire point of transactions moot. This is why it is really important to pick the right storage engine for each table.

MySQL will not usually warn you or raise errors if you do transactional operations on a nontransactional table. Sometimes rolling back a transaction will generate the warning "Some nontransactional changed tables couldn't be rolled back," but most of the time, you'll have no indication you're working with nontransactional tables.

Implicit and explicit locking

InnoDB uses a two-phase locking protocol. It can acquire locks at any time during a transaction, but it does not release them until a COMMIT or ROLLBACK. It releases all the locks at the same time. The locking mechanisms described earlier are all implicit. InnoDB handles locks automatically, according to your isolation level.

However, InnoDB also supports explicit locking, which the SQL standard does not mention at all:[3]

- SELECT ... LOCK IN SHARE MODE
- SELECT ... FOR UPDATE

---

3. These locking hints are frequently abused and should usually be avoided; see Chapter 6 for more details.

MySQL also supports the LOCK TABLES and UNLOCK TABLES commands, which are implemented in the server, not in the storage engines. These have their uses, but they are not a substitute for transactions. If you need transactions, use a transactional storage engine.

We often see applications that have been converted from MyISAM to InnoDB but are still using LOCK TABLES. This is no longer necessary because of row-level locking, and it can cause severe performance problems.

 The interaction between LOCK TABLES and transactions is complex, and there are unexpected behaviors in some server versions. Therefore, we recommend that you never use LOCK TABLES unless you are in a transaction and AUTOCOMMIT is disabled, no matter what storage engine you are using.

Multiversion Concurrency Control

Most of MySQL's transactional storage engines don't use a simple row-locking mechanism. Instead, they use row-level locking in conjunction with a technique for increasing concurrency known as *multiversion concurrency control* (MVCC). MVCC is not unique to MySQL: Oracle, PostgreSQL, and some other database systems use it too, although there are significant differences because there is no standard for how MVCC should work.

You can think of MVCC as a twist on row-level locking; it avoids the need for locking at all in many cases and can have much lower overhead. Depending on how it is implemented, it can allow nonlocking reads, while locking only the necessary rows during write operations.

MVCC works by keeping a snapshot of the data as it existed at some point in time. This means transactions can see a consistent view of the data, no matter how long they run. It also means different transactions can see different data in the same tables at the same time! If you've never experienced this before, it might be confusing, but it will become easier to understand with familiarity.

Each storage engine implements MVCC differently. Some of the variations include *optimistic* and *pessimistic* concurrency control. We'll illustrate one way MVCC works by explaining a simplified version of InnoDB's behavior.

InnoDB implements MVCC by storing with each row two additional, hidden values that record when the row was created and when it was expired (or deleted). Rather than storing the actual times at which these events occurred, the row stores the system version number at the time each event occurred. This is a number that increments each time a transaction begins. Each transaction keeps its own record of the current system version, as of the time it began. Each query has to check each row's version numbers against the transaction's version. Let's see how this applies to particular operations when the transaction isolation level is set to REPEATABLE READ:

SELECT
> InnoDB must examine each row to ensure that it meets two criteria:
>
> a. InnoDB must find a version of the row that is at least as old as the transaction (i.e., its version must be less than or equal to the transaction's version). This ensures that either the row existed before the transaction began, or the transaction created or altered the row.
>
> b. The row's deletion version must be undefined or greater than the transaction's version. This ensures that the row wasn't deleted before the transaction began.
>
> Rows that pass both tests may be returned as the query's result.

INSERT
> InnoDB records the current system version number with the new row.

DELETE
> InnoDB records the current system version number as the row's deletion ID.

UPDATE
> InnoDB writes a new copy of the row, using the system version number for the new row's version. It also writes the system version number as the old row's deletion version.

The result of all this extra record keeping is that most read queries never acquire locks. They simply read data as fast as they can, making sure to select only rows that meet the criteria. The drawbacks are that the storage engine has to store more data with each row, do more work when examining rows, and handle some additional housekeeping operations.

MVCC works only with the REPEATABLE READ and READ COMMITTED isolation levels. READ UNCOMMITTED isn't MVCC-compatible[4] because queries don't read the row version that's appropriate for their transaction version; they read the newest version, no matter what. SERIALIZABLE isn't MVCC-compatible because reads lock every row they return.

MySQL's Storage Engines

This section gives an overview of MySQL's storage engines. We won't go into great detail here, because we discuss storage engines and their particular behaviors throughout the book. Even this book, though, isn't a complete source of documentation; you should read the MySQL manuals for the storage engines you decide to use.

MySQL stores each database (also called a *schema*) as a subdirectory of its data directory in the underlying filesystem. When you create a table, MySQL stores the table definition

---

4. There is no formal standard that defines MVCC, so different engines and databases implement it very differently, and no one can say any of them is wrong.

in a *.frm* file with the same name as the table. Thus, when you create a table named MyTable, MySQL stores the table definition in *MyTable.frm*. Because MySQL uses the filesystem to store database names and table definitions, case sensitivity depends on the platform. On a Windows MySQL instance, table and database names are case insensitive; on Unix-like systems, they are case sensitive. Each storage engine stores the table's data and indexes differently, but the server itself handles the table definition.

You can use the SHOW TABLE STATUS command (or in MySQL 5.0 and newer versions, query the INFORMATION_SCHEMA tables) to display information about tables. For example, to examine the user table in the mysql database, execute the following:

```
mysql> SHOW TABLE STATUS LIKE 'user' \G
*************************** 1. row ***************************
           Name: user
         Engine: MyISAM
     Row_format: Dynamic
           Rows: 6
 Avg_row_length: 59
    Data_length: 356
Max_data_length: 4294967295
   Index_length: 2048
      Data_free: 0
 Auto_increment: NULL
    Create_time: 2002-01-24 18:07:17
    Update_time: 2002-01-24 21:56:29
     Check_time: NULL
      Collation: utf8_bin
       Checksum: NULL
  Create_options:
        Comment: Users and global privileges
1 row in set (0.00 sec)
```

The output shows that this is a MyISAM table. You might also notice a lot of other information and statistics in the output. Let's look briefly at what each line means:

Name
: The table's name.

Engine
: The table's storage engine. In old versions of MySQL, this column was named Type, not Engine.

Row_format
: The row format. For a MyISAM table, this can be Dynamic, Fixed, or Compressed. Dynamic rows vary in length because they contain variable-length fields such as VARCHAR or BLOB. Fixed rows, which are always the same size, are made up of fields that don't vary in length, such as CHAR and INTEGER. Compressed rows exist only in compressed tables; see "Compressed MyISAM tables" on page 19.

Rows
: The number of rows in the table. For MyISAM and most other engines, this number is always accurate. For InnoDB, it is an estimate.

Avg_row_length

How many bytes the average row contains.

Data_length

How much data (in bytes) the entire table contains.

Max_data_length

The maximum amount of data this table can hold. This is engine-specific.

Index_length

How much disk space the index data consumes.

Data_free

For a MyISAM table, the amount of space that is allocated but currently unused. This space holds previously deleted rows and can be reclaimed by future INSERT statements.

Auto_increment

The next AUTO_INCREMENT value.

Create_time

When the table was first created.

Update_time

When data in the table last changed.

Check_time

When the table was last checked using CHECK TABLE or *myisamchk*.

Collation

The default character set and collation for character columns in this table.

Checksum

A live checksum of the entire table's contents, if enabled.

Create_options

Any other options that were specified when the table was created.

Comment

This field contains a variety of extra information. For a MyISAM table, it contains the comments, if any, that were set when the table was created. If the table uses the InnoDB storage engine, the amount of free space in the InnoDB tablespace appears here. If the table is a view, the comment contains the text "VIEW."

The InnoDB Engine

InnoDB is the default transactional storage engine for MySQL and the most important and broadly useful engine overall. It was designed for processing many short-lived transactions that usually complete rather than being rolled back. Its performance and automatic crash recovery make it popular for nontransactional storage needs, too. *You should use InnoDB for your tables unless you have a compelling need to use a different engine.* If you want to study storage engines, it is also well worth your time to study

InnoDB in depth to learn as much as you can about it, rather than studying all storage engines equally.

InnoDB's history

InnoDB has a complex release history, but it's very helpful to understand it. In 2008, the so-called InnoDB plugin was released for MySQL 5.1. This was the next generation of InnoDB created by Oracle, which at that time owned InnoDB but not MySQL. For various reasons that are great to discuss over beers, MySQL continued shipping the older version of InnoDB, compiled into the server. But you could disable this and install the newer, better-performing, more scalable InnoDB plugin if you wished. Eventually, Oracle acquired Sun Microsystems and thus MySQL, and removed the older codebase, replacing it with the "plugin" by default in MySQL 5.5. (Yes, this means that now the "plugin" is actually compiled in, not installed as a plugin. Old terminology dies hard.)

The modern version of InnoDB, introduced as the InnoDB plugin in MySQL 5.1, sports new features such as building indexes by sorting, the ability to drop and add indexes without rebuilding the whole table, and a new storage format that offers compression, a new way to store large values such as BLOB columns, and file format management. Many people who use MySQL 5.1 don't use the plugin, sometimes because they aren't aware of it. If you're using MySQL 5.1, please ensure that you're using the InnoDB plugin. It's much better than the older version of InnoDB.

InnoDB is such an important engine that many people and companies have invested in developing it, not just Oracle's team. Notable contributions have come from Google, Yasufumi Kinoshita, Percona, and Facebook, among others. Some of these improvements have been included into the official InnoDB source code, and many others have been reimplemented in slightly different ways by the InnoDB team. In general, InnoDB's development has accelerated greatly in the last few years, with major improvements to instrumentation, scalability, configurability, performance, features, and support for Windows, among other notable items. MySQL 5.6 lab previews and milestone releases include a remarkable palette of new features for InnoDB, too.

Oracle is investing tremendous resources in improving InnoDB performance, and doing a great job of it (a considerable amount of external contribution has helped with this, too). In the second edition of this book, we noted that InnoDB failed pretty miserably beyond four CPU cores. It now scales well to 24 CPU cores, and arguably up to 32 or even more cores depending on the scenario. Many improvements are slated for the upcoming 5.6 release, but there are still opportunities for enhancement.

InnoDB overview

InnoDB stores its data in a series of one or more data files that are collectively known as a *tablespace*. A tablespace is essentially a black box that InnoDB manages all by itself. In MySQL 4.1 and newer versions, InnoDB can store each table's data and indexes in separate files. InnoDB can also use raw disk partitions for building its tablespace, but modern filesystems make this unnecessary.

InnoDB uses MVCC to achieve high concurrency, and it implements all four SQL standard isolation levels. It defaults to the REPEATABLE READ isolation level, and it has a *next-key locking* strategy that prevents phantom reads in this isolation level: rather than locking only the rows you've touched in a query, InnoDB locks gaps in the index structure as well, preventing phantoms from being inserted.

InnoDB tables are built on a *clustered index*, which we will cover in detail in later chapters. InnoDB's index structures are very different from those of most other MySQL storage engines. As a result, it provides very fast primary key lookups. However, *secondary indexes* (indexes that aren't the primary key) contain the primary key columns, so if your primary key is large, other indexes will also be large. You should strive for a small primary key if you'll have many indexes on a table. The storage format is platform-neutral, meaning you can copy the data and index files from an Intel-based server to a PowerPC or Sun SPARC without any trouble.

InnoDB has a variety of internal optimizations. These include predictive read-ahead for prefetching data from disk, an adaptive hash index that automatically builds hash indexes in memory for very fast lookups, and an insert buffer to speed inserts. We cover these later in this book.

InnoDB's behavior is very intricate, and we highly recommend reading the "InnoDB Transaction Model and Locking" section of the MySQL manual if you're using InnoDB. There are many subtleties you should be aware of before building an application with InnoDB, because of its MVCC architecture. Working with a storage engine that maintains consistent views of the data for all users, even when some users are changing data, can be complex.

As a transactional storage engine, InnoDB supports truly "hot" online backups through a variety of mechanisms, including Oracle's proprietary MySQL Enterprise Backup and the open source Percona XtraBackup. MySQL's other storage engines can't take hot backups—to get a consistent backup, you have to halt all writes to the table, which in a mixed read/write workload usually ends up halting reads too.

The MyISAM Engine

As MySQL's default storage engine in versions 5.1 and older, MyISAM provides a large list of features, such as full-text indexing, compression, and spatial (GIS) functions. MyISAM doesn't support transactions or row-level locks. Its biggest weakness is undoubtedly the fact that it isn't even remotely crash-safe. MyISAM is why MySQL still has the reputation of being a nontransactional database management system, more than a decade after it gained transactions! Still, MyISAM isn't all that bad for a nontransactional, non-crash-safe storage engine. If you need read-only data, or if your tables aren't large and won't be painful to repair, it isn't out of the question to use it. (But please, don't use it by default. Use InnoDB instead.)

Storage

MyISAM typically stores each table in two files: a data file and an index file. The two files bear *.MYD* and *.MYI* extensions, respectively. MyISAM tables can contain either dynamic or static (fixed-length) rows. MySQL decides which format to use based on the table definition. The number of rows a MyISAM table can hold is limited primarily by the available disk space on your database server and the largest file your operating system will let you create.

MyISAM tables created in MySQL 5.0 with variable-length rows are configured by default to handle 256 TB of data, using 6-byte pointers to the data records. Earlier MySQL versions defaulted to 4-byte pointers, for up to 4 GB of data. All MySQL versions can handle a pointer size of up to 8 bytes. To change the pointer size on a MyISAM table (either up or down), you must alter the table with new values for the MAX_ROWS and AVG_ROW_LENGTH options that represent ballpark figures for the amount of space you need. This will cause the entire table and all of its indexes to be rewritten, which might take a long time.

MyISAM features

As one of the oldest storage engines included in MySQL, MyISAM has many features that have been developed over years of use to fill niche needs:

Locking and concurrency
> MyISAM locks entire tables, not rows. Readers obtain shared (read) locks on all tables they need to read. Writers obtain exclusive (write) locks. However, you can insert new rows into the table while select queries are running against it (concurrent inserts).

Repair
> MySQL supports manual and automatic checking and repairing of MyISAM tables, but don't confuse this with transactions or crash recovery. After repairing a table, you'll likely find that some data is simply gone. Repairing is slow, too. You can use the CHECK TABLE mytable and REPAIR TABLE mytable commands to check a table for errors and repair them. You can also use the *myisamchk* command-line tool to check and repair tables when the server is offline.

Index features
> You can create indexes on the first 500 characters of BLOB and TEXT columns in MyISAM tables. MyISAM supports full-text indexes, which index individual words for complex search operations. For more information on indexing, see Chapter 5.

Delayed key writes

MyISAM tables marked with the `DELAY_KEY_WRITE` create option don't write changed index data to disk at the end of a query. Instead, MyISAM buffers the changes in the in-memory key buffer. It flushes index blocks to disk when it prunes the buffer or closes the table. This can boost performance, but after a server or system crash, the indexes will definitely be corrupted and will need repair. You can configure delayed key writes globally, as well as for individual tables.

Compressed MyISAM tables

Some tables never change once they're created and filled with data. These might be well suited to compressed MyISAM tables.

You can compress (or "pack") tables with the *myisampack* utility. You can't modify compressed tables (although you can uncompress, modify, and recompress tables if you need to), but they generally use less space on disk. As a result, they offer faster performance, because their smaller size requires fewer disk seeks to find records. Compressed MyISAM tables can have indexes, but they're read-only.

The overhead of decompressing the data to read it is insignificant for most applications on modern hardware, where the real gain is in reducing disk I/O. The rows are compressed individually, so MySQL doesn't need to unpack an entire table (or even a page) just to fetch a single row.

MyISAM performance

Because of its compact data storage and low overhead due to its simpler design, MyISAM can provide good performance for some uses. It does have some severe scalability limitations, including mutexes on key caches. MariaDB offers a segmented key cache that avoids this problem. The most common MyISAM performance problem we see, however, is table locking. If your queries are all getting stuck in the "Locked" status, you're suffering from table-level locking.

Other Built-in MySQL Engines

MySQL has a variety of special-purpose storage engines. Many of them are somewhat deprecated in newer versions, for various reasons. Some of these are still available in the server, but must be enabled specially.

The Archive engine

The Archive engine supports only `INSERT` and `SELECT` queries, and it does not support indexes until MySQL 5.1. It causes much less disk I/O than MyISAM, because it buffers data writes and compresses each row with *zlib* as it's inserted. Also, each `SELECT` query requires a full table scan. Archive tables are thus best for logging and data acquisition, where analysis tends to scan an entire table, or where you want fast `INSERT` queries.

Archive supports row-level locking and a special buffer system for high-concurrency inserts. It gives consistent reads by stopping a SELECT after it has retrieved the number of rows that existed in the table when the query began. It also makes bulk inserts invisible until they're complete. These features emulate some aspects of transactional and MVCC behaviors, but Archive is not a transactional storage engine. It is simply a storage engine that's optimized for high-speed inserting and compressed storage.

The Blackhole engine

The Blackhole engine has no storage mechanism at all. It discards every INSERT instead of storing it. However, the server writes queries against Blackhole tables to its logs, so they can be replicated or simply kept in the log. That makes the Blackhole engine popular for fancy replication setups and audit logging, although we've seen enough problems caused by such setups that we don't recommend them.

The CSV engine

The CSV engine can treat comma-separated values (CSV) files as tables, but it does not support indexes on them. This engine lets you copy files into and out of the database while the server is running. If you export a CSV file from a spreadsheet and save it in the MySQL server's data directory, the server can read it immediately. Similarly, if you write data to a CSV table, an external program can read it right away. CSV tables are thus useful as a data interchange format.

The Federated engine

This storage engine is sort of a proxy to other servers. It opens a client connection to another server and executes queries against a table there, retrieving and sending rows as needed. It was originally marketed as a competitor to features supported in many enterprise-grade proprietary database servers, such as Microsoft SQL Server and Oracle, but that was always a stretch, to say the least. Although it seemed to enable a lot of flexibility and neat tricks, it has proven to be a source of many problems and is disabled by default. A successor to it, FederatedX, is available in MariaDB.

The Memory engine

Memory tables (formerly called HEAP tables) are useful when you need fast access to data that either never changes or doesn't need to persist after a restart. Memory tables can be up to an order of magnitude faster than MyISAM tables. All of their data is stored in memory, so queries don't have to wait for disk I/O. The table structure of a Memory table persists across a server restart, but no data survives.

Here are some good uses for Memory tables:

- For "lookup" or "mapping" tables, such as a table that maps postal codes to state names

- For caching the results of periodically aggregated data
- For intermediate results when analyzing data

Memory tables support HASH indexes, which are very fast for lookup queries. Although Memory tables are very fast, they often don't work well as a general-purpose replacement for disk-based tables. They use table-level locking, which gives low write concurrency. They do not support TEXT or BLOB column types, and they support only fixed-size rows, so they really store VARCHARs as CHARs, which can waste memory. (Some of these limitations are lifted in Percona Server.)

MySQL uses the Memory engine internally while processing queries that require a temporary table to hold intermediate results. If the intermediate result becomes too large for a Memory table, or has TEXT or BLOB columns, MySQL will convert it to a MyISAM table on disk. We say more about this in later chapters.

 People often confuse Memory tables with temporary tables, which are ephemeral tables created with CREATE TEMPORARY TABLE. Temporary tables can use any storage engine; they are not the same thing as tables that use the Memory storage engine. Temporary tables are visible only to a single connection and disappear entirely when the connection closes.

The Merge storage engine

The Merge engine is a variation of MyISAM. A Merge table is the combination of several identical MyISAM tables into one virtual table. This can be useful when you use MySQL in logging and data warehousing applications, but it has been deprecated in favor of partitioning (see Chapter 7).

The NDB Cluster engine

MySQL AB acquired the NDB database from Sony Ericsson in 2003 and built the NDB Cluster storage engine as an interface between the SQL used in MySQL and the native NDB protocol. The combination of the MySQL server, the NDB Cluster storage engine, and the distributed, shared-nothing, fault-tolerant, highly available NDB database is known as MySQL Cluster. We discuss MySQL Cluster later in this book.

Third-Party Storage Engines

Because MySQL offers a pluggable storage engine API, beginning around 2007 a bewildering array of storage engines started springing up to serve special purposes. Some of these were included with the server, but most were third-party products or open source projects. We'll discuss a few of the storage engines that we've observed to be useful enough that they remain relevant even as the diversity has thinned out a bit.

OLTP storage engines

Percona's XtraDB storage engine, which is included with Percona Server and MariaDB, is a modified version of InnoDB. Its improvements are targeted at performance, measurability, and operational flexibility. It is a drop-in replacement for InnoDB with the ability to read and write InnoDB's data files compatibly, and to execute all queries that InnoDB can execute.

There are several other OLTP storage engines that are roughly similar to InnoDB in some important ways, such as offering ACID compliance and MVCC. One is PBXT, the creation of Paul McCullagh and Primebase GMBH. It sports engine-level replication, foreign key constraints, and an intricate architecture that positions it for solid-state storage and efficient handling of large values such as BLOBs. PBXT is widely regarded as a community storage engine and is included with MariaDB.

TokuDB uses a new index data structure called Fractal Trees, which are cache-oblivious, so they don't slow down as they get larger than memory, nor do they age or fragment. TokuDB is marketed as a Big Data storage engine, because it has high compression ratios and can support lots of indexes on large data volumes. At the time of writing it is in early production release status, and has some important limitations around concurrency. This makes it best suited for use cases such as analytical datasets with high insertion rates, but that could change in future versions.

RethinkDB was originally positioned as a storage engine designed for solid-state storage, although it seems to have become less niched as time has passed. Its most distinctive technical characteristic could be said to be its use of an append-only copy-on-write B-Tree index data structure. It is still in early development, and we've neither evaluated it nor seen it in use.

Falcon was promoted as the next-generation transactional storage engine for MySQL around the time of Sun's acquisition of MySQL AB, but it has long since been canceled. Jim Starkey, the primary architect of Falcon, has founded a new company to build a cloud-enabled NewSQL database called NuoDB (formerly NimbusDB).

Column-oriented storage engines

MySQL is row-oriented by default, meaning that each row's data is stored together, and the server works in units of rows as it executes queries. But for very large volumes of data, a column-oriented approach can be more efficient; it allows the engine to retrieve less data when full rows aren't needed, and when each column is stored separately, it can often be compressed more effectively.

The leading column-oriented storage engine is Infobright, which works well at very large sizes (tens of terabytes). It is designed for analytical and data warehousing use cases. It works by storing data in blocks, which are highly compressed. It maintains a set of metadata for each block, which allows it to skip blocks or even to complete queries simply by looking at the metadata. It has no indexes—that's the point; at such huge sizes, indexes are useless, and the block structure is a kind of quasi-index. Infobright requires a customized version of the server, because portions of the server have to be rewritten to work with column-oriented data. Some queries can't be executed by the storage engine in column-oriented mode, and cause the server to fall back to row-by-row mode, which is slow. Infobright is available in both open source–community and proprietary commercial versions.

Another column-oriented storage engine is Calpont's InfiniDB, which is also available in commercial and community versions. InfiniDB offers the ability to distribute queries across a cluster of machines. We haven't seen anyone use it in production, though.

By the way, if you're in the market for a column-oriented database that isn't MySQL, we've also evaluated LucidDB and MonetDB. You can find benchmarks and opinions on the MySQL Performance Blog, although they will probably become somewhat out-dated as time passes.

Community storage engines

A full list of community storage engines would run into the scores, and perhaps even to triple digits if we researched them exhaustively. However, it's safe to say that most of them serve very limited niches, and many aren't known or used by more than a few people. We'll just mention a few of them. We haven't seen most of these in production use. *Caveat emptor*!

Aria
> Aria, formerly named Maria, is the original MySQL creator's planned successor to MyISAM. It's available in MariaDB. Many of the features that were planned for it seem to have been deferred in favor of improvements elsewhere in the MariaDB server. At the time of writing it is probably best to describe it as a crash-safe version of MyISAM, with several other improvements such as the ability to cache data (not just indexes) in its own memory.

Groonga
> This is a full-text search storage engine that claims to offer accuracy and high speed.

OQGraph
> This engine from Open Query supports graph operations (think "find the shortest path between nodes") that are impractical or impossible to perform in SQL.

Q4M
> This engine implements a queue inside MySQL, with support for operations that SQL itself makes quite difficult or impossible to do in a single statement.

SphinxSE
> This engine provides a SQL interface to the Sphinx full-text search server, which we discuss more in Appendix F.

Spider
> This engine partitions data into several partitions, effectively implementing transparent sharding, and executes your queries in parallel across shards, which can be located on different servers.

VPForMySQL
> This engine supports vertical partitioning of tables through a sort of proxy storage engine. That is, you can chop a table into several sets of columns and store those independently, but query them as a single table. It's by the same author as the Spider engine.

Selecting the Right Engine

Which engine should you use? InnoDB is usually the right choice, which is why we're glad that Oracle made it the default engine in MySQL 5.5. The decision of which engine to use can be summed up by saying, "Use InnoDB unless you need a feature it doesn't provide, and for which there is no good alternative approach." For example, when we need full-text search, we usually prefer to use InnoDB in combination with Sphinx, rather than choosing MyISAM for its full-text indexing capabilities. Sometimes we choose something other than InnoDB when we don't need InnoDB's features and another engine provides a compelling benefit without downsides. For instance, we might use MyISAM when its limited scalability, poor support for concurrency, and lack of crash resilience aren't an issue, but InnoDB's increased space consumption is a problem.

We prefer not to mix and match different storage engines unless absolutely needed. It makes things much more complicated and exposes you to a whole new set of potential bugs and edge-case behaviors. The interactions between the storage engines and the server are complex enough without adding multiple storage engines into the mix. For example, multiple storage engines make it difficult to perform consistent backups or to configure the server properly.

If you believe that you do need a different engine, here are some factors you should consider:

Transactions
> If your application requires transactions, InnoDB (or XtraDB) is the most stable, well-integrated, proven choice. MyISAM is a good choice if a task doesn't require transactions and issues primarily either SELECT or INSERT queries. Sometimes specific components of an application (such as logging) fall into this category.

Backups
> The need to perform regular backups might also influence your choice. If your server can be shut down at regular intervals for backups, the storage engines are equally easy to deal with. However, if you need to perform online backups, you basically need InnoDB.

Crash recovery

If you have a lot of data, you should seriously consider how long it will take to recover from a crash. MyISAM tables become corrupt more easily and take much longer to recover than InnoDB tables. In fact, this is one of the most important reasons why a lot of people use InnoDB when they don't need transactions.

Special features

Finally, you sometimes find that an application relies on particular features or optimizations that only some of MySQL's storage engines provide. For example, a lot of applications rely on clustered index optimizations. On the other hand, only MyISAM supports geospatial search inside MySQL. If a storage engine meets one or more critical requirements, but not others, you need to either compromise or find a clever design solution. You can often get what you need from a storage engine that seemingly doesn't support your requirements.

You don't need to decide right now. There's a lot of material on each storage engine's strengths and weaknesses in the rest of the book, and lots of architecture and design tips as well. In general, there are probably more options than you realize yet, and it might help to come back to this question after reading more. If you're not sure, just stick with InnoDB. It's a safe default and there's no reason to choose anything else if you don't know yet what you need.

These topics might seem rather abstract without some sort of real-world context, so let's consider some common database applications. We'll look at a variety of tables and determine which engine best matches with each table's needs. We give a summary of the options in the next section.

Logging

Suppose you want to use MySQL to log a record of every telephone call from a central telephone switch in real time. Or maybe you've installed *mod_log_sql* for Apache, so you can log all visits to your website directly in a table. In such an application, speed is probably the most important goal; you don't want the database to be the bottleneck. The MyISAM and Archive storage engines would work very well because they have very low overhead and can insert thousands of records per second.

Things will get interesting, however, if you decide it's time to start running reports to summarize the data you've logged. Depending on the queries you use, there's a good chance that gathering data for the report will significantly slow the process of inserting records. What can you do?

One solution is to use MySQL's built-in replication feature to clone the data onto a second server, and then run your time- and CPU-intensive queries against the data on the replica. This leaves the master free to insert records and lets you run any query you want on the replica without worrying about how it might affect the real-time logging.

You can also run queries at times of low load, but don't rely on this strategy continuing to work as your application grows.

Another option is to log to a table that contains the year and name or number of the month in its name, such as `web_logs_2012_01` or `web_logs_2012_jan`. While you're busy running queries against tables that are no longer being written to, your application can log records to its current table uninterrupted.

Read-only or read-mostly tables

Tables that contain data used to construct a catalog or listing of some sort (jobs, auctions, real estate, etc.) are usually read from far more often than they are written to. This seemingly makes them good candidates for MyISAM—*if you don't mind what happens when MyISAM crashes*. Don't underestimate how important this is; a lot of users don't really understand how risky it is to use a storage engine that doesn't even try to get their data written to disk. (MyISAM just writes the data to memory and assumes the operating system will flush it to disk sometime later.)

 It's an excellent idea to run a realistic load simulation on a test server and then literally pull the power plug. The firsthand experience of recovering from a crash is priceless. It saves nasty surprises later.

Don't just believe the common "MyISAM is faster than InnoDB" folk wisdom. It is *not* categorically true. We can name dozens of situations where InnoDB leaves MyISAM in the dust, especially for applications where clustered indexes are useful or where the data fits in memory. As you read the rest of this book, you'll get a sense of which factors influence a storage engine's performance (data size, number of I/O operations required, primary keys versus secondary indexes, etc.), and which of them matter to your application.

When we design systems such as these, we use InnoDB. MyISAM might seem to work okay in the beginning, but it will absolutely fall on its face when the application gets busy. Everything will lock up, and you'll lose data when you have a server crash.

Order processing

When you deal with any sort of order processing, transactions are all but required. Half-completed orders aren't going to endear customers to your service. Another important consideration is whether the engine needs to support foreign key constraints. InnoDB is your best bet for order-processing applications.

Bulletin boards and threaded discussion forums

Threaded discussions are an interesting problem for MySQL users. There are hundreds of freely available PHP and Perl-based systems that provide threaded discussions. Many of them aren't written with database efficiency in mind, so they tend to run a lot of queries for each request they serve. Some were written to be database-independent, so their queries do not take advantage of the features of any one database system. They also tend to update counters and compile usage statistics about the various discussions. Many of the systems also use a few monolithic tables to store all their data. As a result, a few central tables become the focus of heavy read and write activity, and the locks required to enforce consistency become a substantial source of contention.

Despite their design shortcomings, most of these systems work well for small and medium loads. However, if a website grows large enough and generates significant traffic, it will become very slow. The obvious solution is to switch to a different storage engine that can handle the heavy read/write volume, but users who attempt this are sometimes surprised to find that the system runs even more slowly than it did before!

What these users don't realize is that the system is using a particular query, normally something like this:

```
mysql> SELECT COUNT(*) FROM table;
```

The problem is that not all engines can run that query quickly: MyISAM can, but other engines might not. There are similar examples for every engine. Later chapters will help you keep such a situation from catching you by surprise and show you how to find and fix the problems if it does.

CD-ROM applications

If you ever need to distribute a CD-ROM- or DVD-ROM-based application that uses MySQL data files, consider using MyISAM or compressed MyISAM tables, which can easily be isolated and copied to other media. Compressed MyISAM tables use far less space than uncompressed ones, but they are read-only. This can be problematic in certain applications, but because the data is going to be on read-only media anyway, there's little reason not to use compressed tables for this particular task.

Large data volumes

How big is too big? We've built and managed—or helped build and manage—many InnoDB databases in the 3 TB to 5 TB range, or even larger. That's on a single server, not sharded. It's perfectly feasible, although you have to choose your hardware wisely, practice smart physical design, and plan for your server to be I/O-bound. At these sizes, MyISAM is just a nightmare when it crashes.

If you're going really big, such as tens of terabytes, you're probably building a data warehouse. In this case, Infobright is where we've seen the most success. Some very large databases that aren't suitable for Infobright might be candidates for TokuDB instead.

Table Conversions

There are several ways to convert a table from one storage engine to another, each with advantages and disadvantages. In the following sections, we cover three of the most common ways.

ALTER TABLE

The easiest way to move a table from one engine to another is with an `ALTER TABLE` statement. The following command converts `mytable` to InnoDB:

```
mysql> ALTER TABLE mytable ENGINE = InnoDB;
```

This syntax works for all storage engines, but there's a catch: it can take a lot of time. MySQL will perform a row-by-row copy of your old table into a new table. During that time, you'll probably be using all of the server's disk I/O capacity, and the original table will be read-locked while the conversion runs. So, take care before trying this technique on a busy table. Instead, you can use one of the methods discussed next, which involve making a copy of the table first.

When you convert from one storage engine to another, any storage engine–specific features are lost. For example, if you convert an InnoDB table to MyISAM and back again, you will lose any foreign keys originally defined on the InnoDB table.

Dump and import

To gain more control over the conversion process, you might choose to first dump the table to a text file using the *mysqldump* utility. Once you've dumped the table, you can simply edit the dump file to adjust the `CREATE TABLE` statement it contains. Be sure to change the table name as well as its type, because you can't have two tables with the same name in the same database even if they are of different types—and *mysqldump* defaults to writing a `DROP TABLE` command before the `CREATE TABLE`, so you might lose your data if you are not careful!

CREATE and SELECT

The third conversion technique is a compromise between the first mechanism's speed and the safety of the second. Rather than dumping the entire table or converting it all at once, create the new table and use MySQL's `INSERT ... SELECT` syntax to populate it, as follows:

```
mysql> CREATE TABLE innodb_table LIKE myisam_table;
mysql> ALTER TABLE innodb_table ENGINE=InnoDB;
mysql> INSERT INTO innodb_table SELECT * FROM myisam_table;
```

That works well if you don't have much data, but if you do, it's often more efficient to populate the table incrementally, committing the transaction between each chunk so the undo logs don't grow huge. Assuming that id is the primary key, run this query repeatedly (using larger values of x and y each time) until you've copied all the data to the new table:

```
mysql> START TRANSACTION;
mysql> INSERT INTO innodb_table SELECT * FROM myisam_table
    -> WHERE id BETWEEN x AND y;
mysql> COMMIT;
```

After doing so, you'll be left with the original table, which you can drop when you're done with it, and the new table, which is now fully populated. Be careful to lock the original table if needed to prevent getting an inconsistent copy of the data!

Tools such as Percona Toolkit's *pt-online-schema-change* (based on Facebook's online schema change technique) can remove the error-prone and tedious manual work from schema changes.

A MySQL Timeline

It is helpful to understand MySQL's version history as a frame of reference when choosing which version of the server you want to run. Plus, it's kind of fun for old-timers to remember what it used to be like in the good old days!

Version 3.23 (2001)

This release of MySQL is generally regarded as the moment MySQL "arrived" and became a viable option for widespread use. MySQL was still not much more than a query language over flat files, but MyISAM was introduced to replace ISAM, an older and much more limited storage engine. InnoDB was available, but was not shipped in the standard binary distribution because it was so new. If you wanted to use InnoDB, you had to compile the server yourself with support for it. Version 3.23 introduced full-text indexing and replication. Replication was to become the killer feature that propelled MySQL to fame as the database that powered much of the Internet.

Version 4.0 (2003)

New syntax features appeared, such as support for UNION and multi-table DELETE statements. Replication was rewritten to use two threads on the replica, instead of one thread that did all the work and suffered from task switching. InnoDB was shipped as a standard part of the server, with its full feature set: row-level locking, foreign keys, and so on. The query cache was introduced in version 4.0 (and hasn't changed much since then). Support for SSL connections was also introduced.

Version 4.1 (2005)

More query syntax features were introduced, including subqueries and INSERT ON DUPLICATE KEY UPDATE. The UTF-8 character set was supported. There was a new binary protocol and prepared statement support.

Version 5.0 (2006)

A number of "enterprise" features appeared in this release: views, triggers, stored procedures, and stored functions. The ISAM engine was removed completely, but new storage engines such as Federated were introduced.

Version 5.1 (2008)

This release was the first under Sun Microsystems's ownership after its acquisition of MySQL AB, and was over five years in the making. Version 5.1 introduced partitioning, row-based replication, and a variety of plugin APIs, including the pluggable storage engine API. The BerkeleyDB storage engine—MySQL's first transactional storage engine—was removed and some others, such as Federated, were deprecated. Also, Oracle, now the owner of Innobase Oy,[5] released the InnoDB plugin storage engine.

Version 5.5 (2010)

MySQL 5.5 was the first release following Oracle's acquisition of Sun (and therefore MySQL). It focused on improvements to performance, scalability, replication, partitioning, and support for Microsoft Windows, but included many other improvements as well. InnoDB became the default storage engine, and many legacy features and deprecated options and behaviors were scrubbed. The PERFORMANCE _SCHEMA database was added, along with a first batch of enhanced instrumentation. New plugin APIs for replication, authentication, and auditing were added. A plugin for semisynchronous replication was available, and Oracle released commercial plugins for authentication and thread pooling in 2011. There were also major architectural changes to InnoDB, such as a partitioned buffer pool.

Version 5.6 (Unreleased)

MySQL 5.6 will have a raft of new features, including the first major improvements to the query optimizer in many years, more plugin APIs (e.g., one for full-text search), replication improvements, and greatly expanded instrumentation in the PERFORMANCE_SCHEMA database. The InnoDB team is also hard at work, with a huge variety of changes and improvements having been released in development milestones and lab previews. Whereas MySQL 5.5 seemed to be about firming up and fixing the fundamentals, with a limited number of new introductions, MySQL 5.6 appears to be focused on advancing server development and performance, using 5.5's success as a springboard.

Version 6.0 (Canceled)

Version 6.0 is confusing because of the overlapping chronology. It was announced during the 5.1 development years. There were rumors or promises of many new features, such as online backups and server-level foreign keys for all storage engines, subquery improvements, and thread pooling. This release was canceled, and Sun resumed development with version 5.4, which was eventually released as

---

5. Oracle also now owns BerkeleyDB.

version 5.5. Many of the features of the 6.0 codebase have been (or will be) released in versions 5.5 and 5.6.

We'd summarize MySQL's history this way: it was clearly a disruptive innovation[6] early in its lifecycle, with limited and sometimes second-class functionality, but its features and low price made it a killer application to power the explosion of the Internet. In the early 5.x releases, it tried to move into enterprise territory with features such as views and stored procedures, but these were buggy and brittle, so it wasn't always smooth sailing. In hindsight, MySQL 5.0's flood of bug fixes didn't settle down until around the 5.0.50 releases, and MySQL 5.1 didn't fare much better. The 5.0 and 5.1 releases were delayed, and the Sun and Oracle acquisitions made many observers fearful. But in our opinion, things are on track: MySQL 5.5 was the highest-quality release in MySQL's history, Oracle's ownership is making MySQL much more palatable to enterprise customers, and version 5.6 promises great improvements in functionality and performance.

Speaking of performance, we thought it would be interesting to show a basic benchmark of the server's performance over time. We decided not to benchmark versions older than 4.1, because it's very rare to see 4.0 and older in production these days. In addition, an apples-to-apples benchmark is very hard to produce across so many different versions, for reasons you'll read more about in the next chapter. We had lots of fun crafting a benchmark method that would work uniformly across the server versions that we did use, and it took many tries to get it right. Table 1-2 shows the results in transactions per second for several levels of concurrency.

Table 1-2. Readonly benchmarks of several MySQL versions

Threads	MySQL 4.1	MySQL 5.0	MySQL 5.1	MySQL 5.1 with InnoDB plugin	MySQL 5.5	MySQL 5.6[a]
1	686	640	596	594	531	526
2	1307	1221	1140	1139	1077	1019
4	2275	2168	2032	2043	1938	1831
8	3879	3746	3606	3681	3523	3320
16	4374	4527	4393	6131	5881	5573
32	4591	4864	4698	7762	7549	7139
64	4688	5078	4910	7536	7269	6994

[a] At the time of our benchmark, MySQL 5.6 was not yet released as GA.

This is a little easier to see in graphical form, which we've shown in Figure 1-2.

Before we interpret the results, we need to tell you a little bit about the benchmark itself. We ran it on our Cisco UCS C250 machine, which has two six-core CPUs, each with two hardware threads. The server contains 384 GB of RAM, but we ran the

6. The term "disruptive innovation" originated in Clayton M. Christensen's book *The Innovator's Dilemma* (Harper).

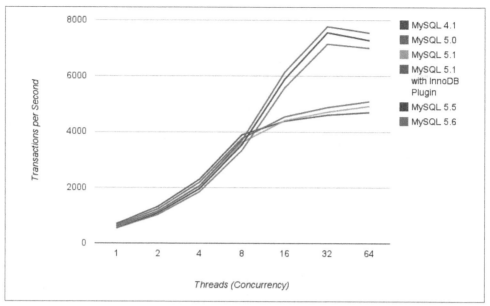

Figure 1-2. Readonly benchmarks of several MySQL versions

benchmark with a 2.5 GB dataset, so we configured MySQL with a 4 GB buffer pool. The benchmark was the standard SysBench read-only workload, with all data in InnoDB, fully in-memory and CPU-bound. We ran the benchmark for 60 minutes for each measurement point, measuring throughput every 10 seconds and using 900 seconds of measurements after the server warmed up and stabilized to generate the final results.

Now, looking at the results, two broad trends are clear. First, MySQL versions that include the InnoDB plugin perform much better at higher concurrency, which is to say that they are more scalable. This is to be expected, because we know older versions are seriously limited at high concurrency. Second, newer MySQL versions are slower than older versions in single-threaded workloads, which you might not have expected but is easily explained by noting that this is a very simple read-only workload. Newer server versions have a more complex SQL grammar, and lots of other features and improvements that enable more complex queries but are simply additional overhead for the simple queries we're benchmarking here. Older versions of the server are simpler and thus have an advantage for simple queries.

We wanted to show you a more complex read/write benchmark (such as TPC-C) over a broader range of concurrencies, but we found it ultimately impossible to do across such a diversity of server versions. We can say that in general, newer versions of the server have better and more consistent performance on more complex workloads, especially at higher concurrency, and with a larger dataset.

Which version should you use? This depends on your business more than on your technical needs. You should ideally build on the newest version that's available, but of course you might choose to wait until the first bugs have been worked out of a brand-new release. If you're building an application that's not in production yet, you might even consider building it on the upcoming release so that you delay your upgrade life-cycle as much as possible.

MySQL's Development Model

MySQL's development process and release model have changed greatly over the years, but now appear to have settled down into a steady rhythm. Oracle releases new development milestones periodically, with previews of features that will eventually be included in the next GA[7] release. These are for testing and feedback, not for production use, but Oracle's statement is that they're high quality and essentially ready to release at any time—and we see no reason to disagree with that. Oracle also periodically releases lab previews, which are special builds that include only a selected feature for interested parties to evaluate. These features are not guaranteed to be included in the next release of the server. And finally, once in a while Oracle will bundle up the features it deems to be ready and ship a new GA release of the server.

MySQL remains GPL-licensed and open source, with the full source code (except for commercially licensed plugins, of course) available to the community. Oracle seems to understand that it would be unwise to ship different versions of the server to the community and its paying customers. MySQL AB tried that, which resulted in its paying customers becoming the bleeding-edge guinea pigs, robbing them of the benefit of community testing and feedback. That policy was the reverse of what enterprise customers need, and was discontinued in the Sun days.

Now that Oracle is releasing some server plugins for paying customers only, MySQL is for all intents and purposes following the so-called open-core model. Although there's been some murmuring over the release of proprietary plugins for the server, it comes from a minority and has sometimes been exaggerated. Most MySQL users we know (and we know a lot of them) don't seem to mind. The commercially licensed, pay-only plugins are acceptable to those users who actually need them.

In any case, the proprietary extensions are just that: extensions. They do not represent a crippleware development model, and the server is more than adequate without them. Frankly, we appreciate the way that Oracle is building more features as plugins. If the features were built right into the server with no API, there would be no choice: you'd get exactly one implementation, with limited opportunity to build something that suited you better. For example, if Oracle eventually releases InnoDB's full-text search functionality as a plugin, it will be an opportunity to use the same API to develop a similar plugin for Sphinx or Lucene, which many people might find more useful. We

---

7. GA stands for generally available, which means "production quality" to pointy-haired bosses.

also appreciate clean APIs inside the server. They help to promote higher-quality code, and who doesn't want that?

Summary

MySQL has a layered architecture, with server-wide services and query execution on top and storage engines underneath. Although there are many different plugin APIs, the storage engine API is the most important. If you understand that MySQL executes queries by handing rows back and forth across the storage engine API, you've grasped one of the core fundamentals of the server's architecture.

MySQL was built around ISAM (and later MyISAM), and multiple storage engines and transactions were added later. Many of the server's quirks reflect this legacy. For example, the way that MySQL commits transactions when you execute an ALTER TABLE is a direct result of the storage engine architecture, as well as the fact that the data dictionary is stored in *.frm* files. (There's nothing in InnoDB that forces an ALTER to be nontransactional, by the way; absolutely everything InnoDB does is transactional.)

The storage engine API has its downsides. Sometimes choice isn't a good thing, and the explosion of storage engines in the heady days of the 5.0 and 5.1 versions of MySQL might have introduced too much choice. In the end, InnoDB turns out to be a very good storage engine for something like 95% or more of users (that's just a rough guess). All those other engines usually just make things more complicated and brittle, although there are special cases where an alternative is definitely called for.

Oracle's acquisition of first InnoDB and then MySQL brought both products under one roof, where they can be codeveloped. This appears to be working out well for everyone: InnoDB and the server itself are getting better by leaps and bounds in many ways, MySQL remains GPL'ed and fully open source, the community and customers alike are getting a solid and stable database, and the server is becoming ever more extensible and useful.

## CHAPTER 2

Benchmarking MySQL

Benchmarking is an essential skill for MySQL novices and power users alike. A benchmark, simply put, is a workload designed to stress your system. The usual goal is to learn about the system's behavior, but there are other worthwhile reasons for running benchmarks, such as reproducing a desired system state or burning in new hardware. In this chapter we'll explore reasons, strategies, tactics, and tools for benchmarking MySQL and MySQL-based applications. We'll focus especially on *sysbench*, because it's an excellent tool for MySQL benchmarking.

Why Benchmark?

Why is benchmarking so important? It's because benchmarking is uniquely convenient and effective for studying what happens when you give systems work to do. A benchmark can help you observe the system's behavior under load, determine the system's capacity, learn which changes are important, or see how your application performs with different data. Benchmarking lets you create fictional circumstances, beyond the real conditions you can observe. You can do these things and more with benchmarks:

- Validate your assumptions about the system, and see whether your assumptions are realistic.

- Reproduce a bad behavior you're trying to eliminate in the system.

- Measure how your application currently performs. If you don't know how fast it currently runs, you can't be sure any changes you make are helpful. You can also use historical benchmark results to diagnose problems you didn't foresee.

- Simulate a higher load than your production systems handle, to identify the scalability bottleneck that you'll encounter first with growth.

- Plan for growth. Benchmarks can help you estimate how much hardware, network capacity, and other resources you'll need for your projected future load. This can help reduce risk during upgrades or major application changes.

- Test your application's ability to tolerate a changing environment. For example, you can find out how your application performs during a sporadic peak in concurrency or with a different configuration of servers, or you can see how it handles a different data distribution.

- Test different hardware, software, and operating system configurations. Is RAID 5 or RAID 10 better for your system? How does random write performance change when you switch from ATA disks to SAN storage? Does the 2.4 Linux kernel scale better than the 2.6 series? Does a MySQL upgrade help performance? What about using a different storage engine for your data? You can answer these questions with special benchmarks.

- Prove that your newly purchased hardware is correctly configured. We can't count the number of times we've used benchmarks to burn in a new system and found misconfigurations or faulty hardware components. It's a good idea not to put a new server into production without benchmarking it first, and never to take a hosting provider or hardware vendor's word for what is installed and how fast it should perform. Testing is always a good idea, if possible.

You can also use benchmarks for other purposes, such as to create a unit test suite for your application, but we focus only on performance-related aspects here.

The problem with benchmarking is that it isn't real. The workload you use to stress the system is usually very simple in comparison with real-life workloads. There's a reason for that: real-life workloads are nondeterministic, varying, and too complex to understand readily. If you benchmarked your systems with real workloads, it would be harder to draw accurate conclusions from the benchmarks.

In what ways is a benchmark's workload unrealistic? There are many artificial dimensions to a benchmark—the data size, the distribution of data and queries—but perhaps the most important is that a benchmark usually runs as fast as it possibly can, loading the system so heavily that it behaves badly. In many cases we would like to tell benchmark tools to run as fast as possible within certain tolerances, throttling themselves as necessary to maintain good performance. This would be especially helpful for determining the system's maximum usable capacity. However, most benchmarking tools don't support such complexity. It's good to keep in mind that the tools limit the meaningfulness and usefulness of the results.

It's tricky to use benchmarks for capacity planning, too. It is often unrealistic to extrapolate from benchmark results. For example, suppose you want to know how much business growth you will be able to support with your new database server. You benchmark the existing server, then benchmark the new server and find that it can perform 40 times as many transactions per second. But that doesn't mean that your business will be able to grow 40-fold on the new server. By the time your revenue grows that much, the system will probably have more traffic, more users, more data, and more interconnections between related pieces of data. You should not expect any of those factors to grow only 40 times, especially the number of relationships. In addition, your application will almost certainly have changed by the time your revenue has grown by a factor of 40. You will have new features, some of which might impact the database far out of proportion to their apparent complexity. These changes in workload, data, relationships, and features are very hard to simulate, and their impacts are hard to guess.

As a result, we usually settle for approximations, with a goal of knowing whether there's still a decent amount of spare capacity in the system. It is possible to do more realistic load testing (as distinct from benchmarking), but it requires a lot of care in creating the dataset and workload, and in the end it's not really a benchmark. Benchmarks are simpler, more directly comparable to each other, and cheaper and easier to run. And despite their limitations, benchmarks are useful. You just need to be clear about what you're doing and in what ways the outcome is meaningful.

Benchmarking Strategies

There are two primary benchmarking strategies: you can benchmark the application as a whole, or isolate MySQL. We call these two strategies *full-stack* and *single-component* benchmarking, respectively. There are several reasons to measure the application as a whole instead of just MySQL:

- You're testing the entire application, including the web server, the application code, the network, and the database. This is useful because you don't care about MySQL's performance in particular; you care about the whole application.
- MySQL is not always the application bottleneck, and a full-stack benchmark can reveal this.
- Only by testing the full application can you see how each part's cache behaves.
- Benchmarks are good only to the extent that they reflect your actual application's behavior, which is hard to do when you're testing only part of it.

On the other hand, application benchmarks can be hard to create and even harder to set up correctly. If you design the benchmark badly, you can end up making bad decisions, because the results don't reflect reality.

Sometimes, however, you don't really want to know about the entire application. You might just need a MySQL benchmark, at least initially. Such a benchmark is useful if:

- You want to compare different schemas or queries.
- You want to benchmark a specific problem you see in the application.
- You want to avoid a long benchmark in favor of a shorter one that gives you a faster "cycle time" for making and measuring changes.

It's also useful to benchmark MySQL when you can repeat your application's queries against a real dataset. The data itself and the dataset's size both need to be realistic. If possible, use a snapshot of actual production data.

Unfortunately, setting up a realistic benchmark can be complicated and time-consuming, and if you can get a copy of the production dataset, count yourself lucky. It might even be impossible—for example, you might be developing a new application that has few users and little data. If you want to know how it'll perform when it grows very large, you'll have no option but to simulate the larger application's data and workload.

What to Measure

It's best to identify your goals before you start benchmarking—indeed, before you even design your benchmarks. Your goals will determine the tools and techniques you'll use to get accurate, meaningful results. Try to frame your goals as a questions, such as "Is this CPU better than that one?" or "Do the new indexes work better than the current ones?"

You sometimes need different approaches to measure different things. For example, latency and throughput might require different benchmarks.

Consider some of the following measurements and how they fit your goals:

Throughput

Throughput is defined as the number of transactions per unit of time. This is one of the all-time classics for benchmarking database applications. Standardized benchmarks such as TPC-C (see *http://www.tpc.org*) are widely quoted, and many database vendors work very hard to do well on them. These benchmarks measure online transaction processing (OLTP) throughput and are most suitable for interactive multiuser applications. The usual unit of measurement is transactions per second, although it is sometimes transactions per minute.

Response time or latency

This measures the total time a task requires. Depending on your application, you might need to measure time in micro- or milliseconds, seconds, or minutes. From this you can derive aggregate response times, such as average, maximum, minimum, and percentiles. Maximum response time is rarely a useful metric, because the longer the benchmark runs, the longer the maximum response time is likely to be. It's also not at all repeatable, because it's likely to vary widely between runs. For this reason, it's common to use *percentile response times* instead. For example, if the 95th percentile response time is 5 milliseconds, you know that the task finishes in 5 milliseconds or less 95% of the time.

It's usually helpful to graph the results of these benchmarks, either as lines (for example, the average and 95th percentile) or as a scatter plot so you can see how the results are distributed. These graphs help show how the benchmarks will behave in the long run. We will return to this point later in this chapter.

Concurrency

Concurrency is an important but frequently misused and misunderstood metric. For example, it's popular to say how many users are browsing a website at the same time, usually measured by how many sessions there are.[1] However, HTTP is stateless and most users are simply reading what's displayed in their browsers, so this doesn't translate into concurrency on the web server. Likewise, concurrency on the web server doesn't necessarily translate to the database server; the only thing it directly relates to is how much data your session storage mechanism must be able to handle. A more accurate measurement of concurrency on the web server is how many simultaneous requests are running at any given time.

You can measure concurrency at different places in the application, too. The higher concurrency on the web server might cause higher concurrency at the database level, but the language and toolset will influence this. Be sure that you don't confuse open connections to the database server with concurrency. A well-designed application might have hundreds of connections open to the MySQL server, but only a fraction of these should be running queries at the same time. Thus, a website with "50,000 users at a time" might require only 10 or 15 simultaneously running queries on the MySQL server!

In other words, what you should really care about benchmarking is the *working concurrency*, or the number of threads or connections doing work simultaneously. Measure whether throughput drops or response times increase when the concurrency increases; if so, your application probably can't handle spikes in load.

Concurrency is completely different from other metrics such as response time and throughput: it's usually not an *outcome*, but rather a *property* of how you set up the benchmark. Instead of measuring the concurrency your application achieves, you will usually instruct the benchmark tool to generate various levels of concurrency, and then measure the application's performance. However, you should measure concurrency at the database, too. When you tell *sysbench* to run with 32, 64, and 128 threads, check the database server during each run and record the value of the Threads_running status variable. In Chapter 11, you'll see why this is useful for capacity planning.

Scalability

Scalability measurements are useful for systems that need to maintain performance under a changing workload. We'll discuss scalability more formally in Chapter 11, but one short definition is that an ideal system should get twice as much work done (twice as much throughput) when you double the number of workers trying to complete tasks. A second angle on the same goal is that if you double the resources available (for example, twice as many CPUs), you should be able to achieve twice the throughput. In both cases, you also want to ensure that performance

1. Forum software, in particular, has miseducated countless website owners to believe they have tens of thousands of users at a time.

(response time) is acceptable. Most systems are not linearly scalable, and exhibit diminishing returns and degraded performance as you vary the parameters.

Scalability measurements are good for capacity planning, because they can show weaknesses in your application that other benchmark strategies won't show. For example, if you design your system to perform well on a response-time benchmark with a single connection (a poor benchmark strategy), your application might perform badly when there's any degree of concurrency. A benchmark that looks for consistent response times under an increasing number of connections would show this design flaw.

Some activities, such as batch jobs to create summary tables from granular data, just need fast response times, period. It's fine to benchmark them for pure response time, but remember to think about how they'll interact with other activities. Batch jobs can cause interactive queries to suffer, and vice versa.

In the final analysis, it's best to benchmark whatever is important to your users. Try to gather some requirements (formally or informally) about what acceptable response times are, what kind of concurrency you expect, and so on. Then try to design your benchmarks to satisfy all of the requirements, without getting tunnel vision and focusing on some things to the exclusion of others.

Benchmarking Tactics

With the general behind us, let's move on to the specifics of how to design and execute benchmarks. Before we discuss how to do benchmarks well, though, let's look at some common mistakes that can lead to unusable or inaccurate results:

- Using a subset of the real data size, such as using only one gigabyte of data when the application will need to handle hundreds of gigabytes, or using the current dataset when you plan for the application to grow much larger.
- Using incorrectly distributed data, such as uniformly distributed data when the real system's data will have "hot spots." (Randomly generated data is almost always unrealistically distributed.)
- Using unrealistically distributed parameters, such as pretending that all user profiles are equally likely to be viewed.[2]
- Using a single-user scenario for a multiuser application.
- Benchmarking a distributed application on a single server.
- Failing to match real user behavior, such as "think time" on a web page. Real users request a page and then read it; they don't click on links one after another without pausing.

---

2. Justin Bieber, we love you! Just kidding.

- Running identical queries in a loop. Real queries aren't identical, so they cause cache misses. Identical queries will be fully or partially cached at some level.

- Failing to check for errors. If a benchmark's results don't make sense—e.g., if a slow operation suddenly completes very quickly—check for errors. You might just be benchmarking how quickly MySQL can detect a syntax error in the SQL query! Always check error logs after benchmarks, as a matter of principle.

- Ignoring how the system performs when it's not warmed up, such as right after a restart. Sometimes you need to know how long it'll take your server to reach capacity after a restart, so you'll want to look specifically at the warmup period. Conversely, if you intend to study normal performance, you'll need to be aware that if you benchmark just after a restart many caches will be cold, and the benchmark results won't reflect the results you'll get under load when the caches are warmed up.

- Using default server settings. There's more on optimizing server settings in later chapters.

- Benchmarking too quickly. Your benchmark needs to last a while. We'll say more about this later.

Merely avoiding these mistakes will take you a long way toward improving the quality of your results.

All other things being equal, you should typically strive to make the tests as realistic as you can. Sometimes, though, it makes sense to use a slightly unrealistic benchmark. For example, say your application is on a different host from the database server. It would be more realistic to run the benchmarks in the same configuration, but doing so would add more variables, such as how fast and how heavily loaded the network is. Benchmarking on a single node is usually easier, and, in some cases, it's accurate enough. You'll have to use your judgment as to when this is appropriate.

Designing and Planning a Benchmark

The first step in planning a benchmark is to identify the problem and the goal. Next, decide whether to use a standard benchmark or design your own.

If you use a standard benchmark, be sure to choose one that matches your needs. For example, don't use TPC-H to benchmark an ecommerce system. In TPC's own words, "TPC-H is an ad-hoc, decision support benchmark." Therefore, it's not an appropriate benchmark for an OLTP system.

Designing your own benchmark is a complicated and iterative process. To get started, take a snapshot of your production dataset. Make sure you can restore this dataset for subsequent runs.

Next, you need queries to run against the data. You can make a unit test suite into a rudimentary benchmark just by running it many times, but that's unlikely to match how you really use the database. A better approach is to log all queries on your production system during a representative time frame, such as an hour during peak load or an entire day. If you log queries during a small time frame, you might need to choose several time frames. This will let you cover all system activities, such as weekly reporting queries or batch jobs you schedule during off-peak times.[3]

You can log queries at different levels. For example, you can log the HTTP requests on a web server if you need a full-stack benchmark. You can also enable MySQL's query log, but if you replay a query log, be sure to recreate the separate threads instead of just replaying each query linearly. It's also important to create a separate thread for each connection in the log, instead of shuffling queries among threads. The query log shows which connection ran each query.

Even if you don't build your own benchmark, you should write down your benchmarking plan. You're going to run the benchmark many times over, and you need to be able to reproduce it exactly. Plan for the future, too. You might not be the one who runs the benchmark the next time around, and even if you are, you probably will not remember exactly how you ran it the first time. Your plan should include the test data, the steps taken to set up the system, how you measured and analyzed the results, and the warmup plan.

Design some method of documenting parameters and results, and document each run carefully. Your documentation method might be as simple as a spreadsheet or notebook, or as complex as a custom-designed database. Keep in mind that you'll probably want to write some scripts to help analyze the results, so the easier it is to process the results without opening spreadsheets and text files, the better.

How Long Should the Benchmark Last?

It's important to run the benchmark for a meaningful amount of time. If you're interested in the system's steady-state performance, which you probably should be, then you need to observe the system in a steady state. This can take a surprisingly long time to achieve, especially on servers with a lot of data and a lot of memory. Most systems have some buffers that create burstable capacity—the ability to absorb spikes, defer some work, and catch up later after the peak is over. But if you pressure these mechanisms for a long time, they will fill up, and you will eventually see that the system can't sustain its short-term peak performance.

Sometimes you don't know how long your benchmark needs to run. If this is the case, you can just run the benchmark forever, and observe until you are satisfied that the system is starting to become stable. Here's an example of how we did this on a system we didn't know well. Figure 2-1 shows a time-series plot of the system's disk read and write throughput.

---

3. All this is provided that you want a perfect benchmark, of course. Real life usually gets in the way.

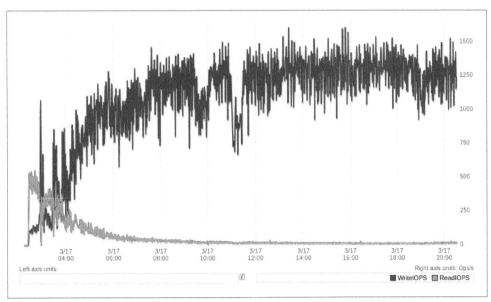

Figure 2-1. I/O performance during an extended benchmark

As the system warmed up, the read I/O activity settled into a steady line after three or four hours, but writes remained variable for at least eight hours, and then there were a few sharp notches in the plot of writes. After that, both reads and writes seemed to settle in.[4] A rule of thumb is to wait until the system looks like it's been steady for at least as long as the initial warmup appeared to take. We ended up running this benchmark for 72 hours to ensure that the system was exhibiting its typical long-term behavior.

A very common benchmarking mistake is to run a series of short benchmarks, such as 60-second runs, and conclude something about the system's performance from that. We hear a lot of comments such as "I tried benchmarking the new version of the server, and it wasn't faster than the old version." When we dig into the actual benchmark, we often find the benchmarks were conducted in a way that doesn't support the conclusions they're intended to generate. Sometimes people protest that they just don't have time to benchmark the server for 8 or 12 hours at 10 different levels of concurrency on two or three server versions. If you don't have the time to do the benchmarks right, any time you do spend is wasted; it is better to trust other people's results, instead of doing an incomplete benchmark and getting the wrong answers.

---

4. By the way, the graph of write I/O activity shows extremely bad behavior; this system's steady state is a performance catastrophe. Calling it a "steady state" is almost laughable, but our point is that it's indicative of how the server is going to behave over the long term.

Capturing System Performance and Status

It is important to capture as much information about the system under test (SUT) as possible while the benchmark runs. It's a good idea to make a benchmark directory with subdirectories for each run's results. You can then place the results, configuration files, measurements, scripts, and notes for each run in the appropriate subdirectory. If you can measure more than you think you're interested in, record the extra data anyway. It's much better to have unneeded data than to miss important data, and you might find the extra data useful in the future. Try to record status and performance metrics such as CPU usage, disk I/O, network traffic statistics, counters from SHOW GLOBAL STATUS; and so on.

Here is a sample shell script that you can use to gather data on MySQL during benchmarks:

```
#!/bin/sh

INTERVAL=5
PREFIX=$INTERVAL-sec-status
RUNFILE=/home/benchmarks/running
mysql -e 'SHOW GLOBAL VARIABLES' >> mysql-variables
while test -e $RUNFILE; do
    file=$(date +%F_%I)
    sleep=$(date +%s.%N | awk "{print $INTERVAL - (\$1 % $INTERVAL)}")
    sleep $sleep
    ts="$(date +"TS %s.%N %F %T")"
    loadavg="$(uptime)"
    echo "$ts $loadavg" >> $PREFIX-${file}-status
    mysql -e 'SHOW GLOBAL STATUS' >> $PREFIX-${file}-status &
    echo "$ts $loadavg" >> $PREFIX-${file}-innodbstatus
    mysql -e 'SHOW ENGINE INNODB STATUS\G' >> $PREFIX-${file}-innodbstatus &
    echo "$ts $loadavg" >> $PREFIX-${file}-processlist
    mysql -e 'SHOW FULL PROCESSLIST\G' >> $PREFIX-${file}-processlist &
    echo $ts
done
echo Exiting because $RUNFILE does not exist.
```

The shell script, simple as it is, is a solid framework for gathering performance and status data. There are a few things about it that we find useful, which you might not appreciate until you run large benchmarks across many servers and find it difficult to answer questions about system behavior:

- The iterations are timed so that it will run every time the clock is evenly divisible by 5 seconds. If you just insert "sleep 5" into the loop, the loop will take slightly longer than 5 seconds to run, and you won't have an easy time correlating any data captured by this script with any other scripts or graphs. And even if your loops somehow last exactly 5 seconds, it's annoying to have some data from one system with a timestamp of 15:32:18.218192 and another system at 15:32:23.819437. You can change 5 seconds to something else, such as 1, 10, 30, or 60 if you want; we usually use 5 or 10 seconds.

- Each file is named after the date and hour when the benchmark is run. When benchmarks last for days and the files grow large, you might find it handy to move previous files off the server and free up some disk space if needed, and get a head start on analyzing the full results. When you're looking for data about a specific point in time, it's also nice to be able to find it in a file named after the hour, rather than searching through a single file that has grown to gigabytes in size.

- Each sample begins with a distinctive timestamp line, so you can search through the files for samples related to specific times, and you can write little *awk* and *sed* scripts easily.

- The script doesn't preprocess or filter anything it gathers. It's a good idea to gather everything in its raw form, and process and filter it later. If you preprocess it, you'll surely find yourself wishing for the raw data later when you find an anomaly and need more data to understand it.

- You can make the script exit when the benchmark is done by removing the */home/ benchmarks/running* file in the script that executes your benchmark.

This is just a short code snippet, and probably won't meet your needs as-is, but it's an illustration of a good general approach to capturing performance and status data. As shown, the script captures only a few kinds of data on MySQL, but you can easily add more things to it. You can capture */proc/diskstats* to record disk I/O for later analysis with the *pt-diskstats* tool,[5] for example.

Getting Accurate Results

The best way to get accurate results is to design your benchmark to answer the question you want to answer. Have you chosen the right benchmark? Are you capturing the data you need to answer the question? Are you benchmarking by the wrong criteria? For example, are you running a CPU-bound benchmark to predict the performance of an application you know will be I/O-bound?

Next, make sure your benchmark results will be repeatable. Try to ensure that the system is in the same state at the beginning of each run. If the benchmark is important, you should reboot between runs. If you need to benchmark on a warmed-up server, which is the norm, you should also make sure that your warmup is long enough (see the previous section on how long to run a benchmark), and that it's repeatable. If the warmup consists of random queries, for example, your benchmark results will not be repeatable.

If the benchmark changes data or schema, reset it with a fresh snapshot between runs. Inserting into a table with a thousand rows will not give the same results as inserting into a table with a million rows! The data fragmentation and layout on disk can also

---

5. See Chapter 9 for more on the *pt-diskstats* tool.

make your results nonrepeatable. One way to make sure the physical layout is close to the same is to do a quick format and file copy of a partition.

Watch out for external load, profiling and monitoring systems, verbose logging, periodic jobs, and other factors that can skew your results. A typical surprise is a *cron* job that starts in the middle of a benchmark run, or a Patrol Read cycle or scheduled consistency check on your RAID card. Make sure all the resources the benchmark needs are dedicated to it while it runs. If something else is consuming network capacity, or if the benchmark runs on a SAN that's shared with other servers, your results might not be accurate.

Try to change as few parameters as possible each time you run a benchmark. If you must change several things at once, you risk missing something. Parameters can also be dependent on one another, so sometimes you can't change them independently. Sometimes you might not even know they are related, which adds to the complexity.[6]

It generally helps to change the benchmark parameters iteratively, rather than making dramatic changes between runs. For example, if you're trying to adjust a setting to create a specific behavior, use techniques such as divide-and-conquer (halving the differences between runs) to home in on the right value.

We see a lot of benchmarks that try to predict performance after a migration, such as migrating from Oracle to MySQL. These are often troublesome, because MySQL performs well on completely different types of queries than Oracle. If you want to know how well an application built on Oracle will run after migrating it to MySQL, you usually need to redesign the schema and queries for MySQL. (In some cases, such as when you're building a cross-platform application, you might want to know how the same queries will run on both platforms, but that's unusual.)

You can't get meaningful results from the default MySQL configuration settings either, because they're tuned for tiny applications that consume very little memory. Some of the biggest face-palm moments we've had were when someone published flawed benchmarks comparing MySQL to other relational database management systems (RDBMSs) with the default settings. Irritatingly, these novice benchmarks often seem to become headline news.

Solid-state storage (SSDs and PCIe cards) presents special challenges for benchmarking, which we address in Chapter 9.

Finally, if you get a strange result, don't simply dismiss it as a bad data point or say you don't understand. Investigate and try to find out what happened. You might find a valuable result, a huge problem, or a flaw in your benchmark design. It's not a good idea to publish benchmarks if you don't understand the results. We've seen more than

---

6. Sometimes, this doesn't really matter. For example, if you're thinking about migrating from a Solaris system on SPARC hardware to GNU/Linux on x86, there's no point in benchmarking Solaris on x86 as an intermediate step!

a few cases where benchmarks with odd results turned out to be completely meaning-less due to a silly mistake, and the benchmarker looked rather foolish in the end.[7]

Running the Benchmark and Analyzing Results

Once you've prepared everything, you're ready to run the benchmark and begin gathering and analyzing data.

It's a good idea to automate the benchmark runs. Doing so will improve your results and their accuracy, because it will prevent you from forgetting steps or accidentally doing things differently on different runs. It will also help you document how to run the benchmark.

Any automation method will do; for example, a Makefile or a set of custom scripts. Choose whatever scripting language makes sense for you: shell, PHP, Perl, etc. Try to automate as much of the process as you can, including loading the data, warming up the system, running the benchmark, and recording the results.

 When you have it set up correctly, benchmarking can be a one-step process. If you're just running a one-off benchmark to check something quickly, you might not want to automate it, but if you think you'll ever refer to the results in the future, do it anyway. If you don't, you'll never remember how you ran the benchmark or what parameters you used, and you won't be able to use the benchmark results later.

You'll usually run a benchmark several times. Exactly how many runs you need depends on how you score the results, and how important the benchmark is. If you need greater certainty, you need to run the benchmark more times. Common practices are to look for the best result, average all the results, or just run the benchmark five times and average the three best results. You can be as precise as you want. You might want to apply statistical methods to your results, find the confidence interval, and so on, but you often don't need that level of certainty.[8] If it answers your question to your satisfaction, you can simply run the benchmark several times and see how much the results vary. If they vary widely, either run the benchmark more times or run it for longer, which usually reduces variance.

Once you have your results, you need to analyze them—that is, turn the numbers into knowledge. The goal is to answer the question that frames the benchmark. Ideally, you'd like to be able to make a statement such as "Upgrading to four CPUs increases throughput by 50% with the same response time" or "The indexes made the queries faster." If you want to be more scientific, read up on the *null hypothesis* before

---

7. This has never, ever happened to any of the authors. Just in case you're wondering.

8. If you really need scientific, rigorous results, you should read a good book on how to design and execute controlled tests, because the subject is much larger than we can cover here.

benchmarking—but note that most people are unlikely to hold you to such strict standards.

How you "crunch the numbers" depends on how you collect the results. You should probably write scripts to analyze the results, not only to help reduce the amount of work required, but for the same reasons you should automate the benchmark itself: repeatability and documentation. Here is a very simple skeleton shell script that can help you extract time-series metrics from the data-gathering script we showed earlier. It accepts as its command-line options the filenames of the collected data:

```
#!/bin/sh

# This script converts SHOW GLOBAL STATUS into a tabulated format, one line
# per sample in the input, with the metrics divided by the time elapsed
# between samples.
awk '
    BEGIN {
        printf "#ts date time load QPS";
        fmt = " %.2f";
    }
    /^TS/ { # The timestamp lines begin with TS.
        ts       = substr($2, 1, index($2, ".") - 1);
        load     = NF - 2;
        diff     = ts - prev_ts;
        prev_ts  = ts;
        printf "\n%s %s %s %s", ts, $3, $4, substr($load, 1, length($load)-1);
    }
    /Queries/ {
        printf fmt, ($2-Queries)/diff;
        Queries=$2
    }
    ' "$@"
```

If you name this script *analyze* and run it against the status file generated by the earlier script, you might get something like the following:

```
[baron@ginger ~]$ ./analyze 5-sec-status-2011-03-20
#ts date time load QPS
1300642150 2011-03-20 17:29:10 0.00 0.62
1300642155 2011-03-20 17:29:15 0.00 1311.60
1300642160 2011-03-20 17:29:20 0.00 1770.60
1300642165 2011-03-20 17:29:25 0.00 1756.60
1300642170 2011-03-20 17:29:30 0.00 1752.40
1300642175 2011-03-20 17:29:35 0.00 1735.00
1300642180 2011-03-20 17:29:40 0.00 1713.00
1300642185 2011-03-20 17:29:45 0.00 1788.00
1300642190 2011-03-20 17:29:50 0.00 1596.40
```

The first line is the column headers, and you should ignore the second line, because it is before the benchmark really started to run. Subsequent lines have the Unix timestamp, date, time (notice the data points occur on the five-second clock ticks, as mentioned previously), system load average, and finally the QPS (queries per second) that the database server was executing. This is the bare minimum data you need to examine the system's performance. Next we'll show you how to plot this quickly and see what happened during the benchmark.

The Importance of Plotting

If you want to achieve world domination, you must plot continually, pun intended. But seriously, the single easiest and most rewarding thing you can do with your system performance metrics is plot them in a time series and look at them. You can spot problems on a chart instantly, when they could be difficult or impossible to see by examining the raw data. You should resist the temptation to simply look at the averages and other summary statistics your benchmark tool might print out. Averages are useless, because they obscure what is really happening. Fortunately, the output from the scripts we've written so far is custom-made for tools such as *gnuplot* or *R* to plot in the blink of an eye. We'll demonstrate using *gnuplot*, assuming you saved the data into a file called *QPS-per-5-seconds*:

```
gnuplot> plot "QPS-per-5-seconds" using 5 w lines title "QPS"
```

This instructs *gnuplot* to plot the fifth field in the file (the QPS field) with lines and title it "QPS" on the plot. Figure 2-2 shows the result.

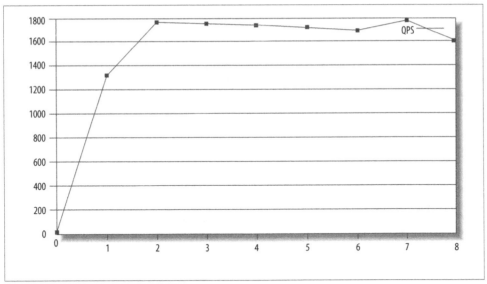

Figure 2-2. Plotting the benchmark's QPS

Now let's look at an example that will make the value of plotting more obvious. Suppose your system suffers from so-called "furious flushing" when it gets behind on checkpointing and blocks all activity until it catches up, causing sharp drops in the throughput. The 95th percentile and average response times will not show the drops, so the results will hide the problem. However, a graph will show periodic notches. This is illustrated in Figure 2-3.

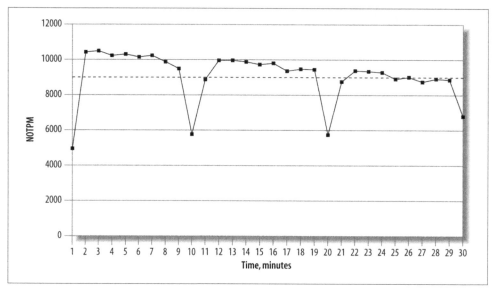

Figure 2-3. Results from a 30-minute dbt2 benchmark run

Figure 2-3 shows the throughput in new-order transactions per minute (NOTPM). This line shows significant drops, which the overall average (the dotted line) doesn't show at all. The first drop is because the server's caches are cold. The others show when the server spends time intensively flushing dirty pages to the disk. Without the graph, these aberrations are hard to see.

Such spiky behavior is very common in heavily loaded systems, and needs to be investigated. In this case, the behavior was because of the use of an older version of InnoDB, which had a poor flushing algorithm. But you can't take that for granted. You need to go back to your detailed statistics and look at them. What did SHOW ENGINE INNODB STATUS look like during these notches? What about the output of SHOW FULL PROCESS LIST? You might be able to see instantly that InnoDB was flushing, or that there were many threads in the process list with a status of "waiting on query cache lock," or something else similarly obvious. This is why it's helpful to capture very detailed data during your benchmarks, and then plot it so problems pop out.

Benchmarking Tools

You don't have to roll your own benchmarking system, and in fact you shouldn't unless there's a good reason why you can't use one of the available ones. We show you some of the available tools in the following sections.

Full-Stack Tools

Recall that there are two types of benchmarks: full-stack and single-component. Not surprisingly, there are tools to benchmark full applications, and there are tools to stress-test MySQL and other components in isolation. Testing the full stack is usually a better way to get a clear picture of your whole application's performance. Full-stack tools include:

ab

> *ab* is an Apache HTTP server benchmarking tool. It shows how many requests per second your HTTP server is capable of serving. If you are benchmarking a web application, this translates to how many requests per second the entire application can satisfy. It's a very simple tool, but its usefulness is limited because it just hammers one URL as fast as it can. More information on *ab* is available at *http://httpd .apache.org/docs/2.0/programs/ab.html*.

http_load

> This tool is similar in concept to *ab*; it is also designed to load a web server, but it's more flexible. You can create an input file with many different URLs, and *http_load* will choose from among them at random. You can also instruct it to issue requests at a timed rate, instead of just running them as fast as it can. See *http:// www.acme.com/software/http_load/* for more information.

JMeter

> JMeter is a Java application that can load another application and measure its performance. It was designed for testing web applications, but you can also use it to test FTP servers and issue queries to a database via JDBC.

> JMeter is much more complex than *ab* and *http_load*. For example, it has features that let you simulate real users more flexibly, by controlling such parameters as ramp-up time. It has a graphical user interface with built-in result graphing, and it offers the ability to record and replay results offline. For more information, see *http://jakarta.apache.org/jmeter/*.

Single-Component Tools

Here are some useful tools to test the performance of MySQL and the system on which it runs. We show example benchmarks with some of these tools in the next section:

mysqlslap

> *mysqlslap* (*http://dev.mysql.com/doc/refman/5.1/en/mysqlslap.html*) simulates load on the server and reports timing information. It is part of the MySQL 5.1 server distribution, but it should be possible to run it against MySQL 4.1 and newer servers. You can specify how many concurrent connections it should use, and you can give it either a SQL statement on the command line or a file containing SQL statements to run. If you don't give it statements, it can also autogenerate SELECT statements by examining the server's schema.

MySQL Benchmark Suite (sql-bench)

MySQL distributes its own benchmark suite with the MySQL server, and you can use it to benchmark several different database servers. It is single-threaded and measures how quickly the server executes queries. The results show which types of operations the server performs well.

The main benefit of this benchmark suite is that it contains a lot of predefined tests that are easy to use, so it makes it easy to compare different storage engines or configurations. It's useful as a high-level benchmark, to compare the overall performance of two servers. You can also run a subset of its tests (for example, just testing UPDATE performance). The tests are mostly CPU-bound, but there are short periods that demand a lot of disk I/O.

The biggest disadvantages of this tool are that it's single-user, it uses a very small dataset, you can't test your site-specific data, and its results might vary between runs. Because it's single-threaded and completely serial, it will not help you assess the benefits of multiple CPUs, but it can help you compare single-CPU servers.

Perl and DBD drivers are required for the database server you wish to benchmark. Documentation is available at *http://dev.mysql.com/doc/en/mysql-benchmarks .html/*.

Super Smack

Super Smack (*http://vegan.net/tony/supersmack/*) is a benchmarking, stress-testing, and load-generating tool for MySQL and PostgreSQL. It is a complex, powerful tool that lets you simulate multiple users, load test data into the database, and populate tables with randomly generated data. Benchmarks are contained in "smack" files, which use a simple language to define clients, tables, queries, and so on.

Database Test Suite

The Database Test Suite, designed by The Open Source Development Labs (OSDL) and hosted on SourceForge at *http://sourceforge.net/projects/osdldbt/*, is a test kit for running benchmarks similar to some industry-standard benchmarks, such as those published by the Transaction Processing Performance Council (TPC). In particular, the *dbt2* test tool is a free (but uncertified) implementation of the TPC-C OLTP test. We used to use it a lot, but we have developed purpose-built tools for MySQL that we now use instead.

Percona's TPCC-MySQL Tool

We have created a fair-usage implementation of a benchmark similar to the TPC-C test, with tools specifically designed for benchmarking MySQL. This is the tool we use most often for evaluating how MySQL behaves on nontrivial workloads. (For simpler benchmarks, we usually use *sysbench* instead.) The source code is available at *https://launchpad.net/perconatools*, and there is brief usage documentation in the source repository.

sysbench

> *sysbench* (*https://launchpad.net/sysbench*) is a multithreaded system benchmarking tool. Its goal is to get a sense of system performance, in terms of the factors important for running a database server. For example, you can measure the performance of file I/O, the OS scheduler, memory allocation and transfer speed, POSIX threads, and the database server itself. *sysbench* supports scripting in the Lua language (*http://www.lua.org*), which makes it very flexible for testing a variety of scenarios. It is our favorite all-around benchmarking tool for MySQL, operating system, and hardware performance.

MySQL's BENCHMARK() Function

MySQL has a handy `BENCHMARK()` function that you can use to test execution speeds for certain types of operations. You use it by specifying a number of times to execute and an expression to execute. The expression can be any scalar expression, such as a scalar subquery or a function. This is convenient for testing the relative speed of some operations, such as seeing whether `MD5()` is faster than `SHA1()`:

```
mysql> SET @input := 'hello world';
mysql> SELECT BENCHMARK(1000000, MD5(@input));
+--------------------------------+
| BENCHMARK(1000000, MD5(@input)) |
+--------------------------------+
|                              0 |
+--------------------------------+
1 row in set (2.78 sec)
mysql> SELECT BENCHMARK(1000000, SHA1(@input));
+---------------------------------+
| BENCHMARK(1000000, SHA1(@input)) |
+---------------------------------+
|                               0 |
+---------------------------------+
1 row in set (3.50 sec)
```

The return value is always `0`; you time the execution by looking at how long the client application reported the query took. In this case, it looks like `MD5()` is faster. However, using `BENCHMARK()` correctly is tricky unless you know what it's really doing. It simply measures how fast the server can execute the expression; it does not give any indication of the parsing and optimization overhead. And unless the expression includes a user variable, as in our example, the second and subsequent times the server executes the expression might be cache hits.[9]

Although it's handy, we don't use `BENCHMARK()` for real benchmarks. It's too hard to figure out what it really measures, and it's too narrowly focused on a small part of the overall execution process.

---

9. One of the authors made this mistake and found that 10,000 executions of a certain expression ran just as fast as 1 execution. It was a cache hit. In general, this type of behavior should always make you suspect either a cache hit or an error.

Benchmarking Examples

In this section, we'll show you some examples of actual benchmarks with tools we mentioned in the preceding sections. We can't cover each tool exhaustively, but these examples should help you decide which benchmarks might be useful for your purposes and get you started using them.

http_load

Let's start with a simple example of how to use *http_load*. We'll use the following URLs, which we saved to a file called *urls.txt*:

```
http://www.mysqlperformanceblog.com/
http://www.mysqlperformanceblog.com/page/2/
http://www.mysqlperformanceblog.com/mysql-patches/
http://www.mysqlperformanceblog.com/mysql-performance-presentations/
http://www.mysqlperformanceblog.com/2006/09/06/slow-query-log-analyzes-tools/
```

The simplest way to use *http_load* is to simply fetch the URLs in a loop. The program fetches them as fast as it can:

```
$ http_load -parallel 1 -seconds 10 urls.txt
19 fetches, 1 max parallel, 837929 bytes, in 10.0003 seconds
44101.5 mean bytes/connection
1.89995 fetches/sec, 83790.7 bytes/sec
msecs/connect: 41.6647 mean, 56.156 max, 38.21 min
msecs/first-response: 320.207 mean, 508.958 max, 179.308 min
HTTP response codes:
  code 200 - 19
```

The results are pretty self-explanatory; they simply show statistics about the requests. A slightly more complex usage scenario is to fetch the URLs as fast as possible in a loop, but emulate five concurrent users:

```
$ http_load -parallel 5 -seconds 10 urls.txt
94 fetches, 5 max parallel, 4.75565e+06 bytes, in 10.0005 seconds
50592 mean bytes/connection
9.39953 fetches/sec, 475541 bytes/sec
msecs/connect: 65.1983 mean, 169.991 max, 38.189 min
msecs/first-response: 245.014 mean, 993.059 max, 99.646 min
HTTP response codes:
  code 200 - 94
```

Alternatively, instead of fetching as fast as possible, we can emulate the load for a predicted rate of requests (such as five per second):

```
$ http_load -rate 5 -seconds 10 urls.txt
48 fetches, 4 max parallel, 2.50104e+06 bytes, in 10 seconds
52105 mean bytes/connection
4.8 fetches/sec, 250104 bytes/sec
msecs/connect: 42.5931 mean, 60.462 max, 38.117 min
msecs/first-response: 246.811 mean, 546.203 max, 108.363 min
```

```
HTTP response codes:
  code 200 - 48
```

Finally, we emulate even more load, with an incoming rate of 20 requests per second. Notice how the connect and response times increase with the higher load:

```
$ http_load -rate 20 -seconds 10 urls.txt
111 fetches, 89 max parallel, 5.91142e+06 bytes, in 10.0001 seconds
53256.1 mean bytes/connection
11.0998 fetches/sec, 591134 bytes/sec
msecs/connect: 100.384 mean, 211.885 max, 38.214 min
msecs/first-response: 2163.51 mean, 7862.77 max, 933.708 min
HTTP response codes:
  code 200 -- 111
```

MySQL Benchmark Suite

The MySQL Benchmark Suite consists of a set of Perl benchmarks, so you'll need Perl to run them. You'll find the benchmarks in the *sql-bench/* subdirectory in your MySQL installation. On Debian GNU/Linux systems, for example, they're in */usr/share/mysql/ sql-bench/*.

Before getting started, read the included *README* file, which explains how to use the suite and documents the command-line arguments. To run all the tests, use commands like the following:

```
$ cd /usr/share/mysql/sql-bench/
sql-bench$ ./run-all-tests --server=mysql --user=root --log --fast
Test finished. You can find the result in:
output/RUN-mysql_fast-Linux_2.4.18_686_smp_i686
```

The benchmarks can take quite a while to run—perhaps over an hour, depending on your hardware and configuration. If you give the *--log* command-line option, you can monitor progress while they're running. Each test logs its results in a subdirectory named *output*. Each file contains a series of timings for the operations in each benchmark. Here's a sample, slightly reformatted for printing:

```
sql-bench$ tail -5 output/select-mysql_fast-Linux_2.4.18_686_smp_i686
Time for count_distinct_group_on_key (1000:6000):
  34  wallclock secs ( 0.20 usr  0.08 sys +  0.00 cusr  0.00 csys =  0.28 CPU)
Time for count_distinct_group_on_key_parts (1000:100000):
  34  wallclock secs ( 0.57 usr  0.27 sys +  0.00 cusr  0.00 csys =  0.84 CPU)
Time for count_distinct_group (1000:100000):
  34  wallclock secs ( 0.59 usr  0.20 sys +  0.00 cusr  0.00 csys =  0.79 CPU)
Time for count_distinct_big (100:1000000):
  8   wallclock secs ( 4.22 usr  2.20 sys +  0.00 cusr  0.00 csys =  6.42 CPU)
Total time:
  868 wallclock secs (33.24 usr  9.55 sys +  0.00 cusr  0.00 csys = 42.79 CPU)
```

As an example, the count_distinct_group_on_key (1000:6000) test took 34 wall-clock seconds to execute. That's the total amount of time the client took to run the test. The other values (usr, sys, cursr, csys) that added up to 0.28 seconds constitute the overhead for this test. That's how much of the time was spent running the benchmark client code, rather than waiting for the MySQL server's response. This means that the figure we care about—how much time was tied up by things outside the client's control—was 33.72 seconds.

Rather than running the whole suite, you can run the tests individually. For example, you might decide to focus on the insert test. This gives you more detail than the summary created by the full test suite:

```
sql-bench$ ./test-insert
Testing server 'MySQL 4.0.13 log' at 2003-05-18 11:02:39

Testing the speed of inserting data into 1 table and do some selects on it.
The tests are done with a table that has 100000 rows.

Generating random keys
Creating tables
Inserting 100000 rows in order
Inserting 100000 rows in reverse order
Inserting 100000 rows in random order
Time for insert (300000):
    42 wallclock secs ( 7.91 usr  5.03 sys +  0.00 cusr  0.00 csys = 12.94 CPU)
Testing insert of duplicates
Time for insert_duplicates (100000):
    16 wallclock secs ( 2.28 usr  1.89 sys +  0.00 cusr  0.00 csys =  4.17 CPU)
```

sysbench

The *sysbench* tool can run a variety of "tests" (benchmarks). It was designed to test not only database performance, but also how well a system is likely to perform as a database server. In fact, Peter and Vadim originally designed it to run benchmarks specifically relevant to MySQL performance, even though they aren't actually all MySQL benchmarks. We'll start with some tests that aren't MySQL-specific and measure performance for subsystems that will determine the system's overall limits. Then we'll show you how to measure database performance.

We highly recommend getting familiar with *sysbench*. It is one of the most useful tools in a MySQL user's bag. And although there are many other tools that perform some of the functions it can do, those tools aren't always reliable and the results aren't always relevant to MySQL performance. For example, you can test I/O performance with *iozone*, *bonnie++*, and a number of other tools, but it requires a lot of care to make them test I/O in a similar fashion to the way InnoDB exercises the disks. On the other hand, *sysbench* behaves a lot like InnoDB, so its `fileio` test is relevant out-of-the-box.

The sysbench CPU benchmark

The most obvious subsystem test is the CPU benchmark, which uses 64-bit integers to calculate prime numbers up to a specified maximum. We run this on two servers, both running GNU/Linux, and compare the results. Here's the first server's hardware:

```
[server1 ~]$ cat /proc/cpuinfo
...
model name      : AMD Opteron(tm) Processor 246
stepping        : 1
cpu MHz         : 1992.857
cache size      : 1024 KB
```

And here's how to run the benchmark:

```
[server1 ~]$ sysbench --test=cpu --cpu-max-prime=20000 run
sysbench v0.4.8:  multithreaded system evaluation benchmark
...
Test execution summary:    total time:                      121.7404s
```

The second server has a different CPU:

```
[server2 ~]$ cat /proc/cpuinfo
...
model name      : Intel(R) Xeon(R) CPU          5130  @ 2.00GHz
stepping        : 6
cpu MHz         : 1995.005
```

Here's its benchmark result:

```
[server1 ~]$ sysbench --test=cpu --cpu-max-prime=20000 run
sysbench v0.4.8:  multithreaded system evaluation benchmark
...
Test execution summary:    total time:                      61.8596s
```

The result simply indicates the total time required to calculate the primes, which is very easy to compare. In this case, the second server ran the benchmark about twice as fast as the first server.

The sysbench file I/O benchmark

The `fileio` benchmark measures how your system performs under different kinds of I/O loads. It is very helpful for comparing hard drives, RAID cards, and RAID modes, and for tweaking the I/O subsystem. It emulates how InnoDB uses the disks in some important ways.

The first stage in running this test is to prepare some files for the benchmark. You should generate much more data than will fit in memory. If the data fits in memory, the operating system will cache most of it, and the results will not accurately represent an I/O-bound workload. We begin by creating a dataset:

```
$ sysbench --test=fileio --file-total-size=150G prepare
```

This creates files in the current working directory, which the run step will read and write. The second step is to run the benchmark. Several options are available to test different types of I/O performance:

seqwr

Sequential write

seqrewr

Sequential rewrite

seqrd

Sequential read

rndrd

Random read

rndwr

Random write

rndrw

Combined random read/write

The following command runs the random read/write access file I/O benchmark:

```
$ sysbench --test=fileio --file-total-size=150G --file-test-mode=rndrw/
--init-rng=on --max-time=300 --max-requests=0 run
```

Here are the results:

```
sysbench v0.4.8:  multithreaded system evaluation benchmark

Running the test with following options:
Number of threads: 1
Initializing random number generator from timer.

Extra file open flags: 0
128 files, 1.1719Gb each
150Gb total file size
Block size 16Kb
Number of random requests for random IO: 10000
Read/Write ratio for combined random IO test: 1.50
Periodic FSYNC enabled, calling fsync() each 100 requests.
Calling fsync() at the end of test, Enabled.
Using synchronous I/O mode
Doing random r/w test
Threads started!
Time limit exceeded, exiting...
Done.

Operations performed:  40260 Read, 26840 Write, 85785 Other = 152885 Total
Read 629.06Mb  Written 419.38Mb  Total transferred 1.0239Gb  (3.4948Mb/sec)
  223.67 Requests/sec executed

Test execution summary:
    total time:                          300.0004s
    total number of events:              67100
    total time taken by event execution: 254.4601
    per-request statistics:
        min:                             0.0000s
        avg:                             0.0038s
```

```
       max:                        0.5628s
       approx. 95 percentile:      0.0099s

Threads fairness:
    events (avg/stddev):     67100.0000/0.00
    execution time (avg/stddev):  254.4601/0.00
```

There's a lot of information in the output. The most interesting numbers for measuring the I/O subsystem are the number of requests per second and the total throughput. In this case, the results are 223.67 requests/sec and 3.4948 MB/sec, respectively. The timing information, especially the approximate 95th percentile, is also valuable. These values provide a good indication of disk performance.

When you're finished, you can run a cleanup to delete the files *sysbench* created for the benchmarks:

```
$ sysbench --test=fileio --file-total-size=150G cleanup
```

The sysbench OLTP benchmark

The OLTP benchmark emulates a simple transaction-processing workload. We show an example with a table that has a million rows. The first step is to prepare a table for the test:

```
$ sysbench --test=oltp --oltp-table-size=1000000 --mysql-db=test/
--mysql-user=root prepare
sysbench v0.4.8:  multithreaded system evaluation benchmark

No DB drivers specified, using mysql
Creating table 'sbtest'...
Creating 1000000 records in table 'sbtest'...
```

That's all you need to do to prepare the test data. Next, we run the benchmark in read-only mode for 60 seconds, with eight concurrent threads:

```
$ sysbench --test=oltp --oltp-table-size=1000000 --mysql-db=test --mysql-user=root/
--max-time=60 --oltp-read-only=on --max-requests=0 --num-threads=8 run
sysbench v0.4.8:  multithreaded system evaluation benchmark

No DB drivers specified, using mysql
WARNING: Preparing of "BEGIN" is unsupported, using emulation
(last message repeated 7 times)
Running the test with following options:
Number of threads: 8

Doing OLTP test.
Running mixed OLTP test
Doing read-only test
Using Special distribution (12 iterations,  1 pct of values are returned in 75 pct
cases)
Using "BEGIN" for starting transactions
Using auto_inc on the id column
Threads started!
Time limit exceeded, exiting...
```

```
(last message repeated 7 times)
Done.

OLTP test statistics:
    queries performed:
        read:                   179606
        write:                  0
        other:                  25658
        total:                  205264
    transactions:               12829   (213.07 per sec.)
    deadlocks:                  0       (0.00 per sec.)
    read/write requests:        179606  (2982.92 per sec.)
    other operations:           25658   (426.13 per sec.)

Test execution summary:
    total time:                 60.2114s
    total number of events:     12829
    total time taken by event execution: 480.2086

    per-request statistics:
        min:                    0.0030s
        avg:                    0.0374s
        max:                    1.9106s
        approx. 95 percentile:  0.1163s

Threads fairness:
    events (avg/stddev):        1603.6250/70.66
    execution time (avg/stddev): 60.0261/0.06
```

As before, there's quite a bit of information in the results. The most interesting parts are:

- The transaction count
- The rate of transactions per second
- The timing statistics (minimal, average, maximal, and 95th percentile time)
- The thread-fairness statistics, which show how fair the simulated workload was

The example we've given is applicable to version 4 of *sysbench*, which is available in prebuilt binaries from SourceForge.net. However, if you're willing to compile *sysbench* from the source code on Launchpad (it's easy and tastes great!), you can take advantage of a lot of improvements in version 5. You can run benchmarks against multiple tables instead of a single table, and you can observe throughput and response time at regular intervals, such as every 10 seconds. These metrics are very important for understanding system behavior.

Other sysbench features

The *sysbench* tool can run several other system benchmarks that don't measure a database server's performance directly:

memory
    Exercises sequential memory reads or writes.

---

threads

Benchmarks the thread scheduler's performance. This is especially useful to test the scheduler's behavior under high load.

mutex

Measures mutex performance by emulating a situation where all threads run concurrently most of the time, acquiring mutex locks only briefly. (A mutex is a data structure that guarantees mutually exclusive access to some resource, preventing concurrent access from causing problems.)

seqwr

Measures sequential write performance. This is very important for testing a system's practical performance limits. It can show how well your RAID controller's cache performs and alert you if the results are unusual. For example, if you have no battery-backed write cache but your disk achieves 3,000 requests per second, something is wrong, and your data is not safe.

In addition to the benchmark-specific mode parameter *(--test)*, *sysbench* accepts some other common parameters, such as *--num-threads, --max-requests*, and *--max-time*. See the documentation for more information on these.

dbt2 TPC-C on the Database Test Suite

The Database Test Suite's *dbt2* tool is a free implementation of the TPC-C test. TPC-C is a specification published by the TPC organization that emulates a complex online transaction-processing load. It reports its results in transactions per minute (tpmC), along with the cost of each transaction (Price/tpmC). The results depend greatly on the hardware, so the published TPC-C results contain detailed specifications of the servers used in the benchmark.

 The *dbt2* test is not really TPC-C. It's not certified by TPC, and its results aren't directly comparable with TPC-C results. Also note that the authors have created what we consider to be a better tool than *dbt2* for MySQL; see the next section.

Let's look at a sample of how to set up and run a *dbt2* benchmark. We used version 0.37 of *dbt2*, which is the most recent version we were able to use with MySQL (newer versions contain fixes that MySQL does not fully support). The following are the steps we took:

1. Prepare data.

   The following command creates data for 10 warehouses in the specified directory. The warehouses use a total of about 700 MB of space. The amount of space required will change in proportion to the number of warehouses, so you can change the -*w* parameter to create a dataset with the size you need:

```
# src/datagen -w 10 -d /mnt/data/dbt2-w10
warehouses = 10
districts = 10
customers = 3000
items = 100000
orders = 3000
stock = 100000
new_orders = 900

Output directory of data files: /mnt/data/dbt2-w10

Generating data files for 10 warehouse(s)...
Generating item table data...
Finished item table data...
Generating warehouse table data...
Finished warehouse table data...
Generating stock table data...
```

2. Load data into the MySQL database.

   The following command creates a database named dbt2w10 and loads it with the data we generated in the previous step (*-d* is the database name and *-f* is the directory with the generated data):

   ```
   # scripts/mysql/mysql_load_db.sh -d dbt2w10 -f /mnt/data/dbt2-w10/
   -s /var/lib/mysql/mysql.sock
   ```

3. Run the benchmark.

   The final step is to execute the following command from the *scripts* directory:

   ```
   # run_mysql.sh -c 10 -w 10 -t 300 -n dbt2w10/
   -u root -o /var/lib/mysql/mysql.sock-e
   **********************************************************************
   *                   DBT2 test for MySQL  started                    *
   *                                                                    *
   *              Results can be found in output/9 directory            *
   **********************************************************************
   *                                                                    *
   *  Test consists of 4 stages:                                        *
   *                                                                    *
   *  1. Start of client to create pool of databases connections       *
   *  2. Start of driver to emulate terminals and transactions generation *
   *  3. Test                                                           *
   *  4. Processing of results                                          *
   *                                                                    *
   **********************************************************************

   DATABASE NAME:                 dbt2w10
   DATABASE USER:                 root
   DATABASE SOCKET:               /var/lib/mysql/mysql.sock
   DATABASE CONNECTIONS:          10
   TERMINAL THREADS:              100
   SCALE FACTOR(WARHOUSES):       10
   TERMINALS PER WAREHOUSE:       10
   DURATION OF TEST(in sec):      300
   SLEEPY in (msec)               300
   ```

```
ZERO DELAYS MODE:              1

Stage 1. Starting up client...
Delay for each thread - 300 msec. Will sleep for 4 sec to start 10 database
connections
CLIENT_PID = 12962

Stage 2. Starting up driver...
Delay for each thread - 300 msec. Will sleep for 34 sec to start 100 terminal
threads
All threads has spawned successfuly.

Stage 3. Starting of the test. Duration of the test 300 sec

Stage 4. Processing of results...
Shutdown clients. Send TERM signal to 12962.
 Response Time (s)
 Transaction     %  Average :  90th %   Total  Rollbacks     %
 ------------  -----  -----------------  ------  ---------  -----
      Delivery  3.53   2.224 :   3.059    1603          0   0.00
     New Order 41.24   0.659 :   1.175   18742        172   0.92
  Order Status  3.86   0.684 :   1.228    1756          0   0.00
       Payment 39.23   0.644 :   1.161   17827          0   0.00
   Stock Level  3.59   0.652 :   1.147    1630          0   0.00

3396.95 new-order transactions per minute (NOTPM)
5.5 minute duration
0 total unknown errors
31 second(s) ramping up
```

The most important result is this line near the end:

```
3396.95 new-order transactions per minute (NOTPM)
```

This shows how many transactions per minute the system can process; more is better. (The term "new-order" is not a special term for a type of transaction; it simply means the test simulated someone placing a new order on the imaginary ecommerce website.)

You can change a few parameters to create different benchmarks:

-c

The number of connections to the database. You can change this to emulate different levels of concurrency and see how the system scales.

-e

This enables zero-delay mode, which means there will be no delay between queries. This stress-tests the database, but it can be unrealistic as real users need some "think time" before generating new queries.

-t

The total duration of the benchmark. Choose this time carefully, or the results will be meaningless. Too short a time for benchmarking an I/O-bound workload will give incorrect results because the system will not have enough time to warm the caches and start to work normally. On the other hand, if you want to benchmark a CPU-bound workload, you shouldn't make the time too long, or the dataset might grow significantly and become I/O-bound.

This benchmark's results can provide information on more than just performance. For example, if you see too many rollbacks, you'll know something is likely to be wrong.

Percona's TPCC-MySQL Tool

Although it's great for simple tests and comparisons, the workload that *sysbench* generates is not really relevant to any real-world application. The TPC-C benchmark is much better for that. Although the *dbt2* tool shown in the previous section is one fair-use implementation of that benchmark, it has some drawbacks. These prompted the authors of this book to create another TCP-C-like benchmark tool better suited to running a lot of very large benchmarks. The code is available through Launchpad at *https://code.launchpad.net/~percona-dev/perconatools/tpcc-mysql*, and there is a brief *README* file that explains how to build and use the tool. It is quite simple to use. For large numbers of warehouses, you might want to consider using the parallel data loading utility included with the tool, because otherwise it can take a long time to generate the dataset.

To use the tool, you need to create the database and table structures, load the data, and then execute the benchmark. The database and table structures are simple SQL scripts included with the source code, and the data loading is accomplished through the *tpcc_load* C program, which you must compile. This will run for a while and produce a great deal of output. (You should always redirect program output to files for documentation purposes, but here you really need to do so, or you might even lose your scrollback history.) Here is an example setup, creating a small (five warehouses) dataset in a database named tpcc5:

```
$ ./tpcc_load localhost tpcc5 username p4ssword 5
*************************************
*** ###easy### TPC-C Data Loader  ***
*************************************
<Parameters>
     [server]: localhost
       [port]: 3306
     [DBname]: tpcc5
       [user]: username
       [pass]: p4ssword
  [warehouse]: 5
TPCC Data Load Started...
Loading Item
.................................................. 5000
.................................................. 10000
.................................................. 15000

[output snipped for brevity]

Loading Orders for D=10, W= 5
.......... 1000
```

```
.......... 2000
.......... 3000
Orders Done.

...DATA LOADING COMPLETED SUCCESSFULLY.
```

Next, you need to execute the benchmark, which requires the *tpcc_start* C program. Again there is a lot of output, which should be redirected to a file. Here is a very short sample run that runs five threads against the five warehouses, warming up for 30 seconds and then benchmarking for 30 seconds:

```
$ ./tpcc_start localhost tpcc5 username p4ssword 5 5 30 30
***************************************
*** ###easy### TPC-C Load Generator ***
***************************************
<Parameters>
     [server]: localhost
       [port]: 3306
     [DBname]: tpcc5
       [user]: username
       [pass]: p4ssword
  [warehouse]: 5
 [connection]: 5
     [rampup]: 30 (sec.)
    [measure]: 30 (sec.)

RAMP-UP TIME.(30 sec.)

MEASURING START.

   10, 63(0):0.40, 63(0):0.42, 7(0):0.76, 6(0):2.60, 6(0):0.17
   20, 75(0):0.40, 74(0):0.62, 7(0):0.04, 9(0):2.38, 7(0):0.75
   30, 83(0):0.22, 84(0):0.37, 9(0):0.04, 7(0):1.97, 9(0):0.80

STOPPING THREADS.....

<RT Histogram>

1.New-Order
2.Payment
3.Order-Status
4.Delivery
5.Stock-Level

<90th Percentile RT (MaxRT)>
   New-Order : 0.37  (1.10)
     Payment : 0.47  (1.24)
Order-Status : 0.06  (0.96)
    Delivery : 2.43  (2.72)
 Stock-Level : 0.75  (0.79)

<Raw Results>
  [0] sc:221  lt:0  rt:0  fl:0
  [1] sc:221  lt:0  rt:0  fl:0
  [2] sc:23   lt:0  rt:0  fl:0
```

```
  [3] sc:22  lt:0  rt:0  fl:0
  [4] sc:22  lt:0  rt:0  fl:0
in 30 sec.

<Raw Results2(sum ver.)>
  [0] sc:221  lt:0  rt:0  fl:0
  [1] sc:221  lt:0  rt:0  fl:0
  [2] sc:23  lt:0  rt:0  fl:0
  [3] sc:22  lt:0  rt:0  fl:0
  [4] sc:22  lt:0  rt:0  fl:0

<Constraint Check> (all must be [OK])
 [transaction percentage]
        Payment: 43.42% (>=43.0%) [OK]
   Order-Status: 4.52% (>= 4.0%) [OK]
       Delivery: 4.32% (>= 4.0%) [OK]
    Stock-Level: 4.32% (>= 4.0%) [OK]
 [response time (at least 90% passed)]
      New-Order: 100.00%  [OK]
        Payment: 100.00%  [OK]
   Order-Status: 100.00%  [OK]
       Delivery: 100.00%  [OK]
    Stock-Level: 100.00%  [OK]

<TpmC>
          442.000 TpmC
```

The very last line is the benchmark result: the number of transactions per minute that the benchmark achieved.[10] If you see aberrant results in the lines immediately preceding this, such as the constraint check lines, you can examine the response-time histograms and other verbose output for clues about what was going wrong. Of course, you should have used scripts such as those we showed earlier in this chapter as well, so you should also have detailed diagnostic and performance data about what the server was doing during the benchmark run.

Summary

Everyone who uses MySQL has reasons to learn the basics of benchmarking it. Benchmarking is not just a practical activity for solving business problems, it's also highly educational. Learning how to frame a problem in such a way that a benchmark can help provide an answer is analogous to working from word problems to setting up equations in a math course. Phrasing the question correctly, choosing the right benchmark to answer the question, selecting the benchmark duration and parameters, running the benchmark, collecting the data, and analyzing the results will all make you a much better MySQL user.

---

10. We ran this benchmark on a laptop for demonstration purposes only. Real servers should perform much faster.

If you haven't done so yet, we recommend at least getting familiar with *sysbench*. Learn how to use its `oltp` and `fileio` benchmarks, if nothing else. The `oltp` benchmark is very handy for quickly comparing different systems. Filesystem and disk benchmarks, on the other hand, are invaluable for troubleshooting and isolating misbehaving components when there are system performance problems. We've used such benchmarks many times to prove that despite the administrator's claims, a SAN really did have a failed disk, or a RAID controller's cache policy wasn't actually configured as the utility claimed it was. And when you're benchmarking a single disk and it claims to be able to execute 14,000 random reads per second, you know that you've either made a mistake or something is seriously wrong or misconfigured.[11]

If you'll be benchmarking systems often, it's a good idea to make a discipline of it. Pick a few benchmark tools that suit your needs, and learn them well. Build up a library of scripts to help you set up benchmarks, capture the output and system performance and status information, and analyze it afterward. Get comfortable with a plotting utility such as *gnuplot* or *R*—don't waste your time on spreadsheets; they are far too cumbersome and slow. Plot early and plot often, to discover problems and failures in your benchmarks and systems. Your eyes are more sophisticated than any script or tool for discovering anomalies.

---

11. A single spinning disk can perform only a couple hundred operations per second, due to seek and rotation times.

## CHAPTER 3

Profiling Server Performance

The three most common performance-related requests we receive in our consulting practice are to find out whether a server is doing all of its work optimally, to find out why a specific query is not executing quickly enough, and to troubleshoot mysterious intermittent incidents, which users commonly call "stalls," "pileups," or "freezes." This chapter is a direct response to those three types of requests. We'll show you tools and techniques to help you speed up a server's overall workload, speed up a single query, or troubleshoot and solve a problem when it's hard to observe, and you don't know what causes it or even how it manifests.

This might seem like a tall order, but it turns out that a simple method can show you the signal within the noise. That method is to focus on measuring what the server spends its time doing, and the technique that supports this is called *profiling*. In this chapter, we'll show you how to measure systems and generate profiles, and we'll show you how to profile your whole stack, from the application to the database server to individual queries.

But you must empty your cup before you can fill it, so let's dispel a few common misconceptions about performance first. This gets a bit dense, so stay with us and we'll explain it all with examples later.

Introduction to Performance Optimization

Ask 10 people to define performance and you'll probably get 10 different answers, filled with terms such as "queries per second," "CPU utilization," "scalability," and so on. This is fine for most purposes, because people understand performance differently in different contexts, but we will use a formal definition in this chapter. Our definition is that performance is measured by the time required to complete a task. In other words, *performance is response time*. This is a very important principle. We measure performance by tasks and time, not by resources. A database server's purpose is to execute SQL statements, so the tasks we care about are queries or statements—the bread-and-butter SELECT, UPDATE, INSERT, and so on.[1] A database server's performance is measured by query response time, and the unit of measurement is time per query.

Now for another rhetorical question: what is optimization? We'll return to this later, but for now let's agree that *performance* optimization is the practice of reducing response time as much as possible[2] for a given workload.

We find that many people are very confused about this. If you think performance optimization requires you to reduce CPU utilization, for example, you're thinking about reducing resource consumption. But this is a trap. Resources are there to be consumed. Sometimes making things faster requires that you *increase* resource consumption. We've upgraded many times from an old version of MySQL with an ancient version of InnoDB, and witnessed a dramatic increase in CPU utilization as a result. This is usually nothing to be concerned about. It usually means that the newer version of InnoDB is spending more time doing useful work and less time fighting with itself. Looking at query response time is the best way to know whether the upgrade was an improvement. Sometimes an upgrade introduces a bug such as not using an index, which can also manifest as increased CPU utilization. CPU utilization is a symptom, not a goal, and it's best to measure the goal, or you could get derailed.

Similarly, if you thought that performance optimization was about improving queries per second, then you were thinking about throughput optimization. Increased throughput can be considered as a side effect of performance optimization.[3] Optimizing queries makes it possible for the server to execute more queries per second, because each one requires less time to execute when the server is optimized. (The unit of throughput is queries per time, which is the inverse of our definition of performance.)

So if the goal is to reduce response time, we need to understand why the server requires a certain amount of time to respond to a query, and reduce or eliminate whatever unnecessary work it's doing to achieve the result. In other words, we need to measure where the time goes. This leads to our second important principle of optimization: *you cannot reliably optimize what you cannot measure.* Your first job is therefore to measure where time is spent.

---

1. We don't distinguish between queries and statements, DDL and DML, and so on. If you send a command to the server, no matter what it is, you just care about how quickly it executes. We tend to use "query" as a catch-all phrase for any command you send.

2. We'll mostly avoid philosophical discussions about performance optimization, but we have two suggestions for further reading. There is a white paper called *Goal-Driven Performance Optimization* on Percona's website (http://www.percona.com), which is a compact quick-reference sheet. It is also very worthwhile to read Cary Millsap's book *Optimizing Oracle Performance* (O'Reilly). Cary's performance optimization method, Method R, is the gold standard in the Oracle world.

3. Some people define performance in terms of throughput, which is okay, but it's not the definition we use here. We think response time is more useful, although throughput is often easier to measure in benchmarks.

We've observed that many people, when trying to optimize something, spend the bulk of their time changing things and very little time measuring. In contrast, we aim to spend most of our time—perhaps upwards of 90%—measuring where the response time is spent. If we don't find the answer, we might not have measured correctly or completely. When we gather complete and properly scoped measurements about server activity, performance problems usually can't hide, and the solution often becomes trivially obvious. Measuring can be a challenge, however, and it can also be hard to know what to do with the results once you have them—measuring where the time is spent is not the same thing as understanding why the time is spent.

We mentioned proper scoping, but what does that mean? A properly scoped measurement is one that measures only the activity you want to optimize. There are two common ways that you can capture something irrelevant:

- You can begin and end your measurements at the wrong time.
- You can measure things in aggregate instead of specifically targeting the activity itself.

For example, a common mistake is to observe a slow query, and then look at the whole server's behavior to try to find what's wrong. If the query is slow, then it's best to measure the query, not the whole server. And it's best to measure from the beginning of the query to the end, not before or after.

The time required to execute a task is spent either executing, or waiting. The best way to reduce the time required to execute is to identify and measure the subtasks, and then do one or more of the following: eliminate subtasks completely, make them happen less often, or make them happen more efficiently. Reducing waiting is a more complex exercise, because waiting can be caused by "collateral damage" from other activities on the system, and thus there can be interaction between the task and other tasks that might be contending for access to resources such as the disk or CPU. And you might need to use different techniques or tools, depending on whether the time is spent executing or waiting.

In the preceding paragraph we said that you need to identify and optimize subtasks. But that's an oversimplification. Infrequent or short subtasks might contribute so little to overall response time that it's not worth your time to optimize them. How do you determine which tasks to target for optimization? This is why profiling was invented.

Optimization Through Profiling

Once you have learned and practiced the response time–oriented method of performance optimization, you'll find yourself profiling systems over and over.

Profiling is the primary means of measuring and analyzing where time is consumed. Profiling entails two steps: measuring tasks and the time elapsed, and aggregating and sorting the results so that the important tasks bubble to the top.

Profiling tools all work in pretty much the same way. When a task begins, they start a timer, and when it ends, they stop the timer and subtract the start time from the end time to derive the response time. Most tools also record the task's parent. The resulting data can be used to construct call graphs, but more importantly for our purpose, similar tasks can be grouped together and summed up. It can be helpful to do sophisticated statistical analysis on the tasks that were grouped into one, but at a minimum, you need to know how many tasks were grouped together, and the sum of their response times. The *profile report* accomplishes this. A profile report consists of a table of tasks, one line per task. Each line shows a name, the number of times the task executed, the total time consumed, the average time per execution, and what portion of the whole this task consumed. The profile report should be sorted in order of total time consumed, descending.

To make this clearer, let's look at a real profile of an entire server's workload, which shows the types of queries that the server spends its time executing. This is a top-level view of where the response time goes; we'll show others later. The following is from Percona Toolkit's *pt-query-digest* tool, which is the successor to Maatkit's *mk-query-digest*. We've simplified it slightly and included only the first few types of queries, to remove distractions:

```
Rank Response time     Calls R/Call Item
==== ================= ===== ====== =======
   1 11256.3618 68.1% 78069 0.1442 SELECT InvitesNew
   2  2029.4730 12.3% 14415 0.1408 SELECT StatusUpdate
   3  1345.3445  8.1%  3520 0.3822 SHOW STATUS
```

We've shown only the first few lines in the profile, ranked in order of total response time consumption, with the minimal set of columns that a profile ought to have. Each row shows the response time as a total and as a percent of the overall total, the number of times the query executed, the average response time per query, and an abstraction of the query. This profile makes it clear how expensive each of these types of queries is, relative to each other as well as to the whole. In this case, tasks are queries, which is probably the most common way that you'll profile MySQL.

We will actually discuss two kinds of profiling: *execution-time profiling* and *wait analysis*. Execution-time profiling shows which tasks consume the most time, whereas wait analysis shows where tasks get stuck or blocked the most.

When tasks are slow because they're consuming too many resources and are spending most of their time executing, they won't spend much time waiting, and wait analysis will not be useful. The reverse is true, too: when tasks are waiting all the time and not consuming any resources, measuring where they spend time executing won't be very helpful. If you're not sure which kind of time consumption is the problem, you might need to do both. We'll show some examples of that later.

In practice, when execution-time profiling shows that a task is responsible for a lot of elapsed time, you might be able to drill into it and find that some of the "execution time" is spent waiting, at some lower level. For example, our simplified profile above shows that a lot of time is consumed by a SELECT against the InvitesNew table, but at a lower level, that time might be spent waiting for I/O to complete.

Before you can profile a system, you need to be able to measure it, and that often requires *instrumentation*. An instrumented system has measurement points where data is captured, and some way to make the data available for collection. Systems that are well-instrumented are rather uncommon. Most systems are not built with a lot of instrumentation points, and those that are often provide only counts of activities, and no way to measure how much time those activities took. MySQL is an example of this, at least until version 5.5 when the first version of the Performance Schema introduced a few time-based measurement points.[4] Versions 5.1 and earlier of MySQL had practically no time-based measurement points; most of the data you could get about the server's operation was in the form of SHOW STATUS counters, which simply count how many times activities occur. That's the main reason we ended up creating Percona Server, which has offered detailed query-level instrumentation since version 5.0.

Fortunately, even though our ideal performance optimization technique works best with great instrumentation, you can still make progress even with imperfectly instrumented systems. It's often possible to measure the systems externally, or, failing that, to make educated guesses based on knowledge of the system and the best information available to you. However, when you do so, just be conscious that you're operating on

---

4. The Performance Schema in MySQL 5.5 doesn't provide query-level details; that is added in MySQL 5.6.

potentially flawed data, and your guesses are not guaranteed to be correct. This is a risk that you usually take when you observe systems that aren't perfectly transparent.

For example, in Percona Server 5.0, the slow query log can reveal a few of the most important causes of poor performance, such as waiting for disk I/O or row-level locks. If the log shows 9.6 seconds of disk I/O wait for a 10-second query, it's not important to find out where the remaining 4% of the response time went. The disk I/O is clearly the most important problem.

Interpreting the Profile

The profile shows you the most important tasks first, but what it doesn't show you can be just as important. Refer to the example profile we showed earlier. Unfortunately, there's a lot that it conceals, because all it shows is ranks, sums, and averages. Here's what's missing:

Worthwhile queries

> The profile doesn't automatically show you which queries are worth your time to optimize. This brings us back to the meaning of optimization. If you read Cary Millsap's book, you'll get a lot more on this topic, but we'll repeat two salient points. First, some tasks aren't worth optimizing because they contribute such a small portion of response time overall. Because of Amdahl's Law, a query that consumes only 5% of total response time can contribute only 5% to overall speedup, no matter how much faster you make it. Second, if it costs you a thousand dollars to optimize a task and the business ends up making no additional money as a result, you just deoptimized the business by a thousand dollars. Thus, optimization should halt when the cost of improvement outweighs the benefit.

Outliers

> Tasks might need to be optimized even if they don't sort to the top of the profile. If an occasional task is very slow, it might be unacceptable to users, even though it doesn't happen often enough to constitute a significant portion of overall response time.

Unknown unknowns[5]

> A good profiling tool will show you the "lost time," if possible. Lost time is the amount of wall-clock time not accounted in the tasks measured. For example, if you measure the process's overall CPU time as 10 seconds, but your profile of subtasks adds up to 9.7 seconds, there are 300 milliseconds of lost time. This can be an indication that you're not measuring everything, or it could just be unavoidable due to rounding errors and the cost of measurement itself. You should pay attention to this, if the tool shows it. You might be missing something important. If the profile doesn't show this, you should try to be conscious of its absence and

---

5. With apologies to Donald Rumsfeld. His comments were actually very insightful, even if they sounded funny.

include it in your mental (or real) notes about what information you're missing. Our example profile doesn't show lost time; that's just a limitation of the tool we used.

Buried details

The profile doesn't show anything about the distribution of the response times. Averages are dangerous because they hide information from you, and the average isn't a good indication of the whole. Peter often likes to say that the average temperature of patients in the hospital isn't important.[6] What if item #1 in the profile we showed earlier were really composed of two queries with one-second response times, and 12,771 queries with response times in the tens of microseconds? There's no way to know from what we're given. In order to make the best decisions about where to concentrate your efforts, you need more information about the 12,773 queries that got packed into that single line in the profile. It's especially helpful to have more information on the response times, such as histograms, percentiles, the standard deviation, and the index of dispersion.

Good tools can help you by automatically showing you some of these things. In fact, *pt-query-digest* includes many of these details in its profile, and in the detailed report that follows the profile. We simplified so that we could focus the example on the important basics: sorting the most expensive tasks to the top. We'll show examples of a richer and more useful profile report later in this chapter.

Another very important thing that's missing from our example profile is the ability to analyze interactions at a higher layer in the stack. When we're looking solely at queries in the server, we don't really have the ability to link together related queries and understand whether they were all part of the same user interaction. We have tunnel vision, so to speak, and we can't zoom out and profile at the level of transactions or page views. There are some ways to solve this problem, such as tagging queries with special comments indicating where they originated and then aggregating at that level. Or you can add instrumentation and profiling capabilities at the application layer, which is the subject of our next section.

Profiling Your Application

You can profile pretty much anything that consumes time, and this includes your application. In fact, profiling your application is generally easier than profiling your database server, and much more rewarding. Although we've started by showing a profile of a MySQL server's queries for the purposes of illustration, it's better to try to measure and profile from the top down.[7] This lets you trace tasks as they flow through

---

6. Blimey! (It's an inside joke. We can't resist.)

7. We'll show examples later where we have *a priori* knowledge that the problem originates at a lower level, so we skip the top-down approach.

the system from the user to the servers and back. It's often true that the database server is to blame for performance problems, but it's the application's fault at least as often. Bottlenecks can also be caused by any of the following:

- External resources, such as calls to web services or search engines
- Operations that require processing large amounts of data in the application, such as parsing big XML files
- Expensive operations in tight loops, such as abusing regular expressions
- Badly optimized algorithms, such as naïve search algorithms to find items in lists

Fortunately, it's easy to figure out whether MySQL is the problem. You just need an application profiling tool. (As a bonus, once you have it in place, it can help developers write efficient code from the start.)

We recommend that you include profiling code in *every* new project you start. It might be hard to inject profiling code into an existing application, but it's easy to include it in new applications.

Will Profiling Slow Your Servers?

Yes, it will make your application slower. No, it will make your application much faster. Wait, we can explain.

Profiling and routine monitoring add overhead. The important questions are how much overhead they add and whether the extra work is worth the benefit.

Many people who design and build high-performance applications believe that you should measure everything you can and just accept the cost of measurement as a part of your application's work. Oracle performance guru Tom Kyte was famously asked how costly Oracle's instrumentation is, and he replied that the instrumentation makes it possible to improve performance by at least 10%. We agree with this philosophy, and for most applications that wouldn't otherwise receive detailed performance evaluations every day, we think the improvement is likely to be much more than 10%. Even if you don't agree, it's a great idea to build in at least some lightweight profiling that you can enable permanently. It's no fun to hit a performance bottleneck you never saw coming, just because you didn't build your systems to capture day-to-day changes in their performance. Likewise, when you find a problem, historical data is invaluable. You can also use the profiling data to help you plan hardware purchases, allocate resources, and predict load for peak times or seasons.

What do we mean by "lightweight" profiling? Timing all SQL queries, plus the total script execution time, is certainly cheap. And you don't have to do it for every page view. If you have a decent amount of traffic, you can just profile a random sample by enabling profiling in your application's setup file:

```
<?php
$profiling_enabled = rand(0, 100) > 99;
?>
```

Profiling just 1% of your sessions should help you find the worst problems. It's extremely helpful to do this in production, because you'll find things that you'll never see elsewhere.

A few years ago, when we wrote the second edition of this book, good prefabricated tools for profiling applications in production weren't all that readily available for the popular web programming languages and frameworks, so we showed you a code example of baking your own in a simple but effective way. Today we're glad to say that great tools are available and all you have to do is open the box and start improving performance.

First and foremost, we want to tout the benefits of a software-as-a-service product called New Relic. We aren't paid to praise it, and we normally don't endorse specific companies or products, but this is a great tool. If you can possibly use it, you should. Our customers who use New Relic are able to solve their problems without our help much more often, and they can sometimes use it to identify problems correctly even when they can't find the solution. New Relic plugs into your application, profiles it, and sends the data back to a web-based dashboard that makes it easy to take a response time–oriented approach to application performance. You end up doing the right thing without having to think about it. And New Relic instruments a lot of the user experience, from the web browser to the application code to the database and other external calls.

What's great about tools like New Relic is that they let you instrument your code in production, all the time—not just in development, and not just sometimes. This is an important point because many profiling tools, or the instrumentation they need to function, can be so expensive that people are afraid to run them in production. You need to instrument in production because you'll discover things about your system's performance that you won't find in development or staging environments. If your chosen tools are really too expensive to run all the time, try to at least run them on one application server in the cluster, or instrument just a fraction of executions, as mentioned in the sidebar "Will Profiling Slow Your Servers?".

Instrumenting PHP Applications

If you can't use New Relic, there are other good options. For PHP in particular, there are several tools that can help you do profile your application. One of them is *xhprof* (*http://pecl.php.net/package/xhprof*), which Facebook developed for its own use and open sourced in 2009. It has a lot of advanced features, but for our purposes, the primary things to mention are that it's easy to install and use, it's lightweight and built for scale so it can run in production all the time even on a very large installation, and it generates a sensible profile of function calls sorted by time consumption. In addition to *xhprof*, there are low-level profiling tools such as *xdebug, Valgrind*, and *cachegrind* to help you inspect your code in various ways.[8] Some of these tools are not suitable for production use because of their verbosity and high overhead, but can be great to use in your development environment.

The other PHP profiling tool we'll discuss is one that we wrote ourselves, based partially on the code and principles we introduced in the second edition of this book. It is called *instrumentation-for-php* (IfP), and it's hosted on Google Code at *http://code .google.com/p/instrumentation-for-php/*. It doesn't instrument PHP itself as thoroughly as *xhprof* does, but it instruments database calls more thoroughly, and thus it's an extremely valuable way to profile your application's database usage when you don't have much access to or control over the database, which is often the case. IfP is a singleton class that provides counters and timers, so it's also easy to put into production without requiring access to your PHP configuration, which again is the norm for a lot of developers.

IfP doesn't profile all of your PHP functions automatically—just the most important ones. You have to start and stop custom counters manually when you identify things that you want to profile, for example. But it times the whole page execution automatically, and it makes it easy to instrument database and *memcached* calls automatically, so you don't have to start and stop counters explicitly for those important items. This means that you can profile three very valuable things in a jiffy: the application at the level of requests (page views), database queries, and cache queries. It also exports the counters and timers to the Apache environment, so you can get Apache to write the results out to the log. This is an easy and very lightweight way to store the results for later analysis. IfP doesn't store any other data on your systems, so there's no need for additional system administrator involvement.

To use it, you simply call start_request() at the very start of the page execution. Ideally, this should be the first thing your application does:

```
require_once('Instrumentation.php');
Instrumentation::get_instance()->start_request();
```

This registers a shutdown function, so you don't have to do anything further at the end of the execution.

IfP adds comments to your SQL queries automatically. This makes it possible to analyze the application quite flexibly by looking at the database server's query log, and it also makes it easy to know what's really going on when you look at SHOW PROCESSLIST and see some abusive query running in MySQL. If you're like most people, you'll have a hard time tracking down the source of a bad query, especially if it's a query that was cobbled together through string concatenation and so forth, so you can't just search for it in the source code. This solves that problem. It tells you which application host

---

8. Unlike PHP, many programming languages have some built-in support for profiling. For Ruby, use the *-r* command-line option; for Perl you can use *perl -d:DProf*, and so on.

sent the query, even if you're using a proxy or a load balancer. It tells you which application user is responsible, and you can find the page request, source code function, and line number, as well as key-value pairs for all of the counters you've created. Here's an example:

```
-- File: index.php Line: 118 Function: fullCachePage request_id: ABC session_id: XYZ
SELECT * FROM ...
```

How you instrument the calls to MySQL depends on which interface you use to connect to MySQL. If you're using the object-oriented *mysqli* interface, it's a one-line change: just replace the call to the *mysqli* constructor with a call to the automatically instrumented *mysqli_x* constructor instead. This constructor is a subclass provided by IfP, with instrumentation and query rewrites baked in. If you're not using the object-oriented interface, or you're using some other database access layer, you might need to rewrite a little bit of code. Hopefully you don't have database calls scattered haphazardly throughout your code, but if you do, you can use an integrated development environment (IDE) such as Eclipse to help you refactor it easily. Centralizing your database access code is a very good practice, for many reasons.

Analyzing the results is easy. The *pt-query-digest* tool from Percona Toolkit has functionality to extract the embedded name-value pairs from the query comments, so you can simply log the queries with the MySQL log file and process the log file. And you can use *mod_log_config* with Apache to set up custom logging with environment variables exported by IfP, along with the %D macro to capture request times in microseconds.

You can load the Apache log into a MySQL database with LOAD DATA INFILE and examine it with SQL queries easily. There is a PDF slideshow on the IfP website that gives examples of how to do all of these things and more, with sample queries and command-line arguments.

If you're resisting adding instrumentation to your application, or if you feel too busy, consider that it might be much easier than you think. The effort invested will pay you back many times over in time savings and performance improvements. There's no substitute for application instrumentation. Use New Relic, *xhprof*, IfP, or any of a number of other solutions for various application languages and environments; this is not a wheel you need to reinvent.

Profiling MySQL Queries

There are two broad approaches to profiling queries, which address two of the questions we mentioned in this chapter's introduction. You can profile a whole server, in terms of which queries contribute the most to its load. (If you've started at the top with application-level profiling, you might already know which queries need attention.) Then, once you've targeted specific queries for optimization, you can drill down to profiling them individually, measuring which subtasks contribute the most to their response times.

Profiling a Server's Workload

The server-wide approach is worthwhile because it can help you to audit a server for inefficient queries. Identifying and fixing these "bad" queries can help you improve the application's performance overall, as well as target specific trouble spots. You can reduce the overall load on the server, thus making all queries faster by reducing contention for shared resources ("collateral benefit"). Reducing load on the server can help you delay or avoid upgrades or other more costly measures, and you can discover and address poor user experiences, such as outliers.

MySQL is getting more instrumentation with each new release, and if the current trend is a reliable indicator, it will soon have world-class support for measuring most important aspects of its performance. But in terms of profiling queries and finding the most expensive ones, we don't really need all that sophistication. The tool we need the most has been there for a long time. It's the so-called *slow query log*.

Capturing MySQL's queries to a log

In MySQL, the slow query log was originally meant to capture just "slow" queries, but for profiling, we need it to log *all* queries. And we need high-resolution response times, not the one-second granularity that was available in MySQL 5.0 and earlier. Fortunately, those old limitations are a thing of the past. In MySQL 5.1 and newer versions, the slow query log is enhanced so that you can set the long_query_time server variable to zero, capturing all queries, and the query response time is available with microsecond resolution. If you are using Percona Server, this functionality is available in version 5.0, and Percona Server adds a great deal more control over the log's contents and capturing queries.

The slow query log is the lowest-overhead, highest-fidelity way to measure query execution times in current versions of MySQL. If you're worried about the additional I/O it might cause, put your mind at ease. We benchmarked it, and on I/O-bound workloads, the overhead is negligible. (It's actually *more* noticeable on CPU-bound workloads.) A more valid concern is filling up your disk. Make sure that you have log rotation set up for the slow query log, if you leave it on all the time. Or, just don't enable it all the time; leave it disabled, and turn it on only for a period of time to gather a workload sample.

MySQL has another type of query log, called the "general log," but it's not much use for analyzing and profiling a server. The queries are logged as they arrive at the server, so the log has no information on response times or the query execution plan. MySQL 5.1 and later also support logging queries to tables, but that too is a nonstarter for most purposes. The performance impact is huge, and although MySQL 5.1 prints query times with microsecond precision in the slow query log, it reverts to one-second granularity for logging slow queries to a table. That's not very helpful.

Percona Server logs significantly more details to the slow query log than MySQL does. There is valuable information on the query execution plan, locking, I/O activity, and much more. These additional bits of data were added slowly over time, as we faced different optimization scenarios that demanded more details about how queries actually executed and where they spent their time. We also made it much easier to administer. For example, we added the ability to control every connection's long_query_time threshold globally, so you can make them start or stop logging their queries when the application uses a connection pool or persistent connections and you can't reset their session-level variables. All in all, it is a lightweight and full-featured way to profile a server and optimize its queries.

Sometimes you don't want to log queries on the server, or you can't for some reason, such as not having access to the server. We encountered these same limitations, so we developed two alternative techniques and programmed them both into Percona Toolkit's *pt-query-digest* tool. The first tactic is watching SHOW FULL PROCESSLIST repeatedly with the *--processlist* option, noting when queries first appear and when they disappear. This is a sufficiently accurate method for some purposes, but it can't capture all queries. Very short-lived queries can sneak in and finish before the tool can observe them.

The second technique is capturing TCP network traffic and inspecting it, then decoding the MySQL client/server protocol. You can use *tcpdump* to save the traffic to disk, then use *pt-query-digest* with the *--type=tpcdump* option to decode and analyze the queries. This is a much higher-precision technique, and it can capture all queries. It even works with advanced protocol features such as the binary protocol used to create and execute server-side prepared statements, and the compressed protocol. You can also use MySQL Proxy with a logging script, but in practice we rarely do this.

Analyzing the query log

We suggest that at least every now and then you should use the slow query log to capture all queries executing on your server, and analyze them. Log the queries for some representative period of time, such as an hour during your peak traffic time. If your workload is very homogeneous, a minute or less might even be enough to find bad queries that need to be optimized.

Don't just open up the log and start looking at it directly—it's a waste of time and money. Generate a profile first, and if you need to, then you can go look at specific samples in the log. It's best to work from a high-level view down to the low level, or you could de-optimize the business, as mentioned earlier.

Generating a profile from the slow query log requires a good log analysis tool. We suggest *pt-query-digest*, which is arguably the most powerful tool available for MySQL query log analysis. It supports a large variety of functionality, including the ability to save query reports to a database and track changes in workload over time.

By default, you simply execute it and pass it the slow query log file as an argument, and it just does the right thing. It prints out a profile of the queries in the log, and then selects "important" classes of queries and prints out a detailed report on each one. The report has dozens of little niceties to make your life easier. We continue to develop this tool actively, so you should read the documentation for the most recent version to learn about its current functionality.

We'll give you a brief tour of the report *pt-query-digest* prints out, beginning with the profile. Here is an uncensored version of the profile we showed earlier in this chapter:

```
# Profile
# Rank Query ID           Response time     Calls R/Call V/M   Item
# ==== ================== ================= ===== ====== ===== =======
#    1 0xBFCF8E3F293F6466 11256.3618 68.1% 78069 0.1442  0.21 SELECT InvitesNew?
#    2 0x620B8CAB2B1C76EC  2029.4730 12.3% 14415 0.1408  0.21 SELECT StatusUpdate?
#    3 0xB90978440CC11CC7  1345.3445  8.1%  3520 0.3822  0.00 SHOW STATUS
#    4 0xCB73D6B5B031B4CF  1341.6432  8.1%  3509 0.3823  0.00 SHOW STATUS
# MISC 0xMISC               560.7556  3.4% 23930 0.0234   0.0 <17 ITEMS>
```

There's a little more detail here than we saw previously. First, each query has an ID, which is a hash of its "fingerprint." A fingerprint is the normalized, canonical version of the query with literal values removed, whitespace collapsed, and everything lower-cased (notice that queries 3 and 4 appear to be the same, but they have different fingerprints). The tool also merges tables with similar names into a canonical form. The question mark at the end of the InvitesNew table name signifies that there is a shard identifier appended to the table name, and the tool has removed that so that queries against tables with a similar purpose are aggregated together. This report is from a heavily sharded Facebook application.

Another bit of extra detail here is the variance-to-mean ratio, in the V/M column. This is also known as the *index of dispersion*. Queries with a higher index of dispersion have a more variable execution-time profile, and highly variable queries are generally good candidates for optimization. If you specify the *--explain* option to *pt-query-digest*, it will also add a column with a short representation of the query's EXPLAIN plan—sort of a "geek code" for the query. This, in combination with the V/M column, makes it a snap to see which queries are bad and potentially easy to optimize.

Finally, there's an additional line at the bottom, showing the presence of 17 other types of queries that the tool didn't consider important enough to report individually, and a summary of the statistics for all of them. You can use options such as *--limit* and *--outliers* to make the tool show more details instead of collapsing unimportant queries into this final line. By default, the tool prints out queries that are either in the top 10 time consumers overall, or whose execution time was over a one-second threshold too many times. Both of these limits are configurable.

Following the profile, the tool prints out a detailed report on each type of query. You can match the query reports to the profile by looking for the query ID or the rank. Here's the report for the #1 ranked query, the "worst" one:

```
# Query 1: 24.28 QPS, 3.50x concurrency, ID 0xBFCF8E3F293F6466 at byte 5590079
# This item is included in the report because it matches --limit.
# Scores: V/M = 0.21
# Query_time sparkline: |  _^_.^_  |
# Time range: 2008-09-13 21:51:55 to 22:45:30
# Attribute    pct   total     min     max     avg     95%  stddev  median
# ============ === ======= ======= ======= ======= ======= ======= =======
# Count         63   78069
# Exec time     68  11256s    37us      1s   144ms   501ms   175ms    68ms
# Lock time     85    134s       0   650ms     2ms   176us    20ms    57us
# Rows sent      8  70.18k       0       1    0.92    0.99    0.27    0.99
# Rows examine   8  70.84k       0       3    0.93    0.99    0.28    0.99
# Query size    84  10.43M     135     141  140.13  136.99    0.10  136.99
# String:
# Databases      production
# Hosts
# Users          fbappuser
# Query_time distribution
#   1us
#  10us  #
# 100us  ###################################################
#   1ms  ###
#  10ms  ###############
# 100ms  ###############################################################
#    1s  #
#  10s+
# Tables
#    SHOW TABLE STATUS FROM `production ` LIKE'InvitesNew82'\G
#    SHOW CREATE TABLE `production `.`InvitesNew82'\G
# EXPLAIN /*!50100 PARTITIONS*/
SELECT InviteId, InviterIdentifier FROM InvitesNew82 WHERE (InviteSetId = 87041469)
AND (InviteeIdentifier = 1138714082) LIMIT 1\G
```

The report contains a variety of metadata at the top, including how often the query executes, its average concurrency, and the byte offset where the worst-performing instance of the query was found in the log file. There is a tabular printout of the numeric metadata, including statistics such as the standard deviation.[9]

This is followed by a histogram of the response times. Interestingly, you can see that this query has a double-peak histogram, under `Query_time distribution`. It usually executes in the hundreds of milliseconds, but there's also a significant spike of queries that execute about three orders of magnitude faster. If this log were from Percona Server, we'd have a richer set of attributes in the query log, so we'd be able to slice and dice the queries to determine why that happens. Perhaps those are queries against specific values that are disproportionately common, so a different index is used, or perhaps they're query cache hits, for example. This sort of double-peak histogram shape is not unusual in real systems, especially for simple queries, which will usually have only a few alternative execution paths.

Finally, the report detail section ends with little helper snippets to make it easy for you to copy and paste commands into a terminal and examine the schema and status of the tables mentioned, and an EXPLAIN-ready sample query. The sample contains all of the literals and isn't "fingerprinted," so it's a real query. It's actually the instance of this query that had the worst execution time in our example.

After you choose the queries you want to optimize, you can use this report to examine the query execution very quickly. We use this tool constantly, and we've spent a lot of time tweaking it to be as efficient and helpful as possible. We definitely recommend that you get comfortable with it. MySQL might gain more sophisticated built-in instrumentation and profiling in the future, but at the time of writing, logging queries with the slow query log or *tcpdump* and running the resulting log through *pt-query-digest* is about as good as you can get.

Profiling a Single Query

After you've identified a single query to optimize, you can drill into it and determine why it takes as much time as it does, and how to optimize it. The actual techniques for optimizing queries are covered in later chapters in this book, along with the background necessary to support those techniques. Our purpose here is simply to show you how to measure what the query does and how long each part of that takes. Knowing this helps you decide which optimization techniques to use.

Unfortunately, most of the instrumentation in MySQL isn't very helpful for profiling queries. This is changing, but at the time of writing, most production servers don't have the newest profiling features. So for practical purposes, we're pretty much limited to

---

9. We're keeping it simple here for clarity, but Percona Server's query log will produce a much more detailed report, which could help you understand why the query is apparently spending 144 ms to examine a single row—that's a lot!

SHOW STATUS, SHOW PROFILE, and examining individual entries in the slow query log (if you have Percona Server—standard MySQL doesn't have any additional information in the log). We'll demonstrate all three techniques for a single query and show you what you can learn about the query execution from each.

Using SHOW PROFILE

The SHOW PROFILE command is a community contribution from Jeremy Cole that's included in MySQL 5.1 and newer, and some versions of MySQL 5.0. It is the only real query profiling tool available in a GA release of MySQL at the time of writing. It is disabled by default, but can be enabled for the duration of a session (connection) simply by setting a server variable:

```
mysql> SET profiling = 1;
```

After this, whenever you issue a statement to the server, it will measure the elapsed time and a few other types of data whenever the query changes from one execution state to another. The feature actually has quite a bit of functionality, and was designed to have more, but it will probably be replaced or superseded by the Performance Schema in a future release. Regardless, the most useful functionality of this feature is to generate a profile of the work the server did during statement execution.

Every time you issue a query to the server, it records the profiling information in a temporary table and assigns the statement an integer identifier, starting with 1. Here's an example of profiling a view included with the Sakila sample database:[10]

```
mysql> SELECT * FROM sakila.nicer_but_slower_film_list;
[query results omitted]
997 rows in set (0.17 sec)
```

The query returned 997 rows in about a sixth of a second. Let's see what SHOW PRO FILES (note the plural) knows about this query:

```
mysql> SHOW PROFILES;
+----------+------------+------------------------------------------------+
| Query_ID | Duration   | Query                                          |
+----------+------------+------------------------------------------------+
|        1 | 0.16767900 | SELECT * FROM sakila.nicer_but_slower_film_list |
+----------+------------+------------------------------------------------+
```

The first thing you'll notice is that it shows the query's response time with higher precision, which is nice. Two decimal places of precision, as shown in the MySQL client, often isn't enough when you're working on fast queries. Now let's look at the profile for this query:

---

10. The view is too lengthy to show here, but the Sakila database is available for download from MySQL's website.

```
mysql> SHOW PROFILE FOR QUERY 1;
+---------------------+----------+
| Status              | Duration |
+---------------------+----------+
| starting            | 0.000082 |
| Opening tables      | 0.000459 |
| System lock         | 0.000010 |
| Table lock          | 0.000020 |
| checking permissions| 0.000005 |
| checking permissions| 0.000004 |
| checking permissions| 0.000003 |
| checking permissions| 0.000004 |
| checking permissions| 0.000560 |
| optimizing          | 0.000054 |
| statistics          | 0.000174 |
| preparing           | 0.000059 |
| Creating tmp table  | 0.000463 |
| executing           | 0.000006 |
| Copying to tmp table| 0.090623 |
| Sorting result      | 0.011555 |
| Sending data        | 0.045931 |
| removing tmp table  | 0.004782 |
| Sending data        | 0.000011 |
| init                | 0.000022 |
| optimizing          | 0.000005 |
| statistics          | 0.000013 |
| preparing           | 0.000008 |
| executing           | 0.000004 |
| Sending data        | 0.010832 |
| end                 | 0.000008 |
| query end           | 0.000003 |
| freeing items       | 0.000017 |
| removing tmp table  | 0.000010 |
| freeing items       | 0.000042 |
| removing tmp table  | 0.001098 |
| closing tables      | 0.000013 |
| logging slow query  | 0.000003 |
| logging slow query  | 0.000789 |
| cleaning up         | 0.000007 |
+---------------------+----------+
```

The profile allows you to follow through every step of the query's execution and see how long it took. You'll notice that it's a bit hard to scan this output and see where most of the time was spent. It is sorted in chronological order, but we don't really care about the order in which the steps happened—we just care how much time they took, so we know what was costly. Unfortunately, you can't sort the output of the command with an ORDER BY. Let's switch from using the SHOW PROFILE command to querying the corresponding INFORMATION_SCHEMA table, and format to look like the profiles we're used to seeing:

```
mysql> SET @query_id = 1;
Query OK, 0 rows affected (0.00 sec)

mysql> SELECT STATE, SUM(DURATION) AS Total_R,
```

```
   ->      ROUND(
   ->        100 * SUM(DURATION) /
   ->          (SELECT SUM(DURATION)
   ->            FROM INFORMATION_SCHEMA.PROFILING
   ->            WHERE QUERY_ID = @query_id
   ->        ), 2) AS Pct_R,
   ->      COUNT(*) AS Calls,
   ->      SUM(DURATION) / COUNT(*) AS "R/Call"
   -> FROM INFORMATION_SCHEMA.PROFILING
   -> WHERE QUERY_ID = @query_id
   -> GROUP BY STATE
   -> ORDER BY Total_R DESC;
+----------------------+----------+-------+-------+---------------+
| STATE                | Total_R  | Pct_R | Calls | R/Call        |
+----------------------+----------+-------+-------+---------------+
| Copying to tmp table | 0.090623 | 54.05 |     1 | 0.0906230000  |
| Sending data         | 0.056774 | 33.86 |     3 | 0.0189246667  |
| Sorting result       | 0.011555 |  6.89 |     1 | 0.0115550000  |
| removing tmp table   | 0.005890 |  3.51 |     3 | 0.0019633333  |
| logging slow query   | 0.000792 |  0.47 |     2 | 0.0003960000  |
| checking permissions | 0.000576 |  0.34 |     5 | 0.0001152000  |
| Creating tmp table   | 0.000463 |  0.28 |     1 | 0.0004630000  |
| Opening tables       | 0.000459 |  0.27 |     1 | 0.0004590000  |
| statistics           | 0.000187 |  0.11 |     2 | 0.0000935000  |
| starting             | 0.000082 |  0.05 |     1 | 0.0000820000  |
| preparing            | 0.000067 |  0.04 |     2 | 0.0000335000  |
| freeing items        | 0.000059 |  0.04 |     2 | 0.0000295000  |
| optimizing           | 0.000059 |  0.04 |     2 | 0.0000295000  |
| init                 | 0.000022 |  0.01 |     1 | 0.0000220000  |
| Table lock           | 0.000020 |  0.01 |     1 | 0.0000200000  |
| closing tables       | 0.000013 |  0.01 |     1 | 0.0000130000  |
| System lock          | 0.000010 |  0.01 |     1 | 0.0000100000  |
| executing            | 0.000010 |  0.01 |     2 | 0.0000050000  |
| end                  | 0.000008 |  0.00 |     1 | 0.0000080000  |
| cleaning up          | 0.000007 |  0.00 |     1 | 0.0000070000  |
| query end            | 0.000003 |  0.00 |     1 | 0.0000030000  |
+----------------------+----------+-------+-------+---------------+
```

Much better! Now we can see that the reason this query took so long was that it spent over half its time copying data into a temporary table. We might need to look into rewriting this query so it doesn't use a temporary table, or perhaps do it more efficiently. The next biggest time consumer, "Sending data," is really kind of a catch-all state that could represent any number of different server activities, including searching for matching rows in a join and so on. It's hard to say whether we'll be able to shave any time off this. Notice that "Sorting result" takes up a very small portion of the time, not enough to be worth optimizing. This is rather typical, which is why we encourage people not to spend time on "tuning the sort buffers" and similar activities.

As usual, although the profile helps us identify what types of activity contribute the most to the elapsed time, it doesn't tell us *why*. To find out why it took so much time to copy data into the temporary table, we'd have to drill down into that state and produce a profile of the subtasks it executed.

Using SHOW STATUS

MySQL's SHOW STATUS command returns a variety of counters. There is a server-wide global scope for the counters, as well as a session scope that is specific to your own connection. The Queries counter, for example, starts at zero in your session and increases every time you issue a query. If you execute SHOW GLOBAL STATUS (note the addition of the GLOBAL keyword), you'll see a server-wide count of queries the server has issued since it was started. The scope of each counter varies—counters that don't have a session-level scope still appear in SHOW STATUS, masquerading as session counters—and this can be confusing. It's something to keep in mind as you use this command. As we discussed earlier, gathering properly scoped measurements is key. If you're trying to optimize something that you can observe occurring in your specific connection to the server, measurements that are being polluted by server-wide activity are not helpful. The MySQL manual has a great reference to all of the variables and whether they have session or global scope.

SHOW STATUS can be a helpful tool, but it isn't really profiling.[11] Most of the results from SHOW STATUS are just counters. They tell you how often various activities took place, such as reads from an index, but they tell you nothing about how much time was consumed. There is only one counter in SHOW STATUS that shows time consumed by an operation (Innodb_row_lock_time), and it has only global scope, so you can't use it to examine only the work you've done in your session.

Still, although SHOW STATUS doesn't provide timings, it can be helpful to look at it after you execute a query and examine the values for a few of the counters. You can form a guess about which types of expensive operations took place and how likely they were to contribute to the query time. The most important counters are the handler counters and the temporary file and table counters. We explain these in more detail in Appendix B. Here's an example of resetting the session status counters to zero, selecting from the same view we used in the previous section, and then looking at the counters:

```
mysql> FLUSH STATUS;
mysql> SELECT * FROM sakila.nicer_but_slower_film_list;
[query results omitted]
mysql> SHOW STATUS WHERE Variable_name LIKE 'Handler%'
        OR Variable_name LIKE 'Created%';
+----------------------------+-------+
| Variable_name              | Value |
+----------------------------+-------+
| Created_tmp_disk_tables    | 2     |
| Created_tmp_files          | 0     |
| Created_tmp_tables         | 3     |
| Handler_commit             | 1     |
| Handler_delete             | 0     |
| Handler_discover           | 0     |
| Handler_prepare            | 0     |
| Handler_read_first         | 1     |
```

11. If you own the second edition of this book, you'll notice that we're doing an about-face on this point.

```
| Handler_read_key              | 7483 |
| Handler_read_next             | 6462 |
| Handler_read_prev             | 0    |
| Handler_read_rnd              | 5462 |
| Handler_read_rnd_next         | 6478 |
| Handler_rollback              | 0    |
| Handler_savepoint             | 0    |
| Handler_savepoint_rollback    | 0    |
| Handler_update                | 0    |
| Handler_write                 | 6459 |
+-------------------------------+------+
```

It looks like the query used three temporary tables—two of them on disk—and did a lot of unindexed reads (Handler_read_rnd_next). If we didn't know anything about the view we just accessed, we might guess that the query is perhaps doing a join without an index, possibly because of a subquery that created temporary tables and then made it the right-hand input to a join. Temporary tables created to hold the results of subqueries don't have indexes, so this seems plausible.

When you use this technique, be aware that SHOW STATUS itself creates a temporary table, and accesses this table with handler operations, so the numbers you see in the output are actually impacted by SHOW STATUS. This varies between server versions. Given what we already know about the query's execution from SHOW PROFILES, it looks like the count of temporary tables might be overstated by 2.

It's worth noting that you can probably discover most of the same information by looking at an EXPLAIN plan for this query. But EXPLAIN is an estimate of what the server thinks it will do, and looking at the status counters is a measurement of what it actually did. EXPLAIN won't tell you whether a temporary table was created on disk, for example, which is slower than in memory. There's more on EXPLAIN in Appendix D.

Using the slow query log

What does the enhanced slow query log in Percona Server reveal about this query? Here's what it captured from the very same execution of the query that we demonstrated in the section on SHOW PROFILE:

```
# Time: 110905 17:03:18
# User@Host: root[root] @ localhost [127.0.0.1]
# Thread_id: 7  Schema: sakila  Last_errno: 0  Killed: 0
# Query_time: 0.166872  Lock_time: 0.000552  Rows_sent: 997  Rows_examined: 24861
   Rows_affected: 0  Rows_read: 997
# Bytes_sent: 216528  Tmp_tables: 3  Tmp_disk_tables: 2  Tmp_table_sizes: 11627188
# InnoDB_trx_id: 191E
# QC_Hit: No  Full_scan: Yes  Full_join: No  Tmp_table: Yes  Tmp_table_on_disk: Yes
# Filesort: Yes  Filesort_on_disk: No  Merge_passes: 0
#    InnoDB_IO_r_ops: 0  InnoDB_IO_r_bytes: 0  InnoDB_IO_r_wait: 0.000000
#    InnoDB_rec_lock_wait: 0.000000  InnoDB_queue_wait: 0.000000
#    InnoDB_pages_distinct: 20
# PROFILE_VALUES ... Copying to tmp table: 0.090623... [omitted]
SET timestamp=1315256598;
SELECT * FROM sakila.nicer_but_slower_film_list;
```

It looks like the query did create three temp tables after all, which was somewhat hidden from view in SHOW PROFILE (perhaps due to a subtlety in the way the server executed the query). Two of the temp tables were on disk. And we're shortening the output here for readability, but toward the end, the SHOW PROFILE data for this query is actually written to the log, so you can even log that level of detail in Percona Server.

As you can see, this highly verbose slow query log entry contains just about everything you can see in SHOW PROFILE and SHOW STATUS, and then some. This makes the log a very useful place to look for more detail when you find a "bad" query with *pt-query-digest*. When you're looking at a report from *pt-query-digest*, you'll see a header line such as the following:

```
# Query 1: 0 QPS, 0x concurrency, ID 0xEE758C5E0D7EADEE at byte 3214 _____
```

You can use the byte offset from the header to zoom right into that section of the log, like this:

```
tail -c +3214 /path/to/query.log | head -n100
```

And presto, you can look at all the details. By the way, *pt-query-digest* understands all the added name-value pairs in the Percona Server slow query log format, and automatically prints out a much more detailed report as a result.

Using the Performance Schema

At the time of writing, the Performance Schema tables introduced in MySQL 5.5 don't support query-level profiling. The Performance Schema is rather new and in rapid development, with much more functionality in the works for future releases. However, even MySQL 5.5's initial functionality can reveal interesting information. For example, here's a query that shows the top causes of waiting in the system:

```
mysql> SELECT event_name, count_star, sum_timer_wait
    -> FROM events_waits_summary_global_by_event_name
    -> ORDER BY sum_timer_wait DESC LIMIT 5;
+----------------------------------------+------------+------------------+
| event_name                             | count_star | sum_timer_wait   |
+----------------------------------------+------------+------------------+
| innodb_log_file                        | 205438     | 2552133070220355 |
| Query_cache::COND_cache_status_changed | 8405302    | 2259497326493034 |
| Query_cache::structure_guard_mutex     | 55769435   | 361568224932147  |
| innodb_data_file                       | 62423      | 347302500600411  |
| dict_table_stats                       | 15330162   | 53005067680923   |
+----------------------------------------+------------+------------------+
```

There are a few of things that limit the Performance Schema's use as a general-purpose profiling tool at present. First, it doesn't yet provide the level of detail on query execution stages and timing that we've been showing with existing tools. Second, it hasn't been "in the wild" for all that long, and the implementation has more overhead at present than many conservative users are comfortable with. (There is reason to believe this will be fixed soon.)

Finally, it's sometimes too complex and low-level to be accessible to most users in its raw form. The features implemented so far are mostly targeted toward the things we need to measure when modifying MySQL source code to improve the server's performance. This includes things like waits and mutexes. Some of the features in MySQL 5.5 are valuable to power users as opposed to server developers, but those still need some frontend tool development to make it convenient to use them and interpret the results. Right now the state of the art is writing complex queries against a large variety of metadata tables with lots and lots of columns. It's a pretty intimidating amount of instrumentation to navigate and understand.

When the Performance Schema gets more functionality in MySQL 5.6 and beyond, and there are nice tools to use it, it's going to be awesome. And it's really nice that Oracle is implementing it as tables accessible through SQL so that users can consume the data in whatever manner is most useful to them. For the time being, though, it's not quite a workable replacement for the slow query log or other tools that can help us immediately see how to improve server and query performance.

Using the Profile for Optimization

So you've got a profile of your server or your query—what do you do with it? A good profile usually makes the problem obvious, but the *solution* might not be (although it often is). At this point, especially when optimizing queries, you need to rely on a lot of knowledge about the server and how it executes queries. The profile, or as much of one as you can gather, points you in the right direction and gives you a basis for using further tools, such as EXPLAIN, to apply your knowledge and measure the results. That's a topic for future chapters, but at least you have the right starting point.

In general, although a profile with complete measurements ought to make determining the problem trivial, we can't always measure perfectly because the systems we're trying to measure don't support it. In the example we've been looking at, we suspect that temporary tables and unindexed reads are contributing most of the response time to the query, but we can't prove it. Sometimes problems are hard to solve because you might not have measured everything you need, or your measurements might be badly scoped. You might be measuring server-wide activity instead of looking specifically at what you're trying to optimize, for example, or you might be looking at measurements that count from a point in time before your query started to execute, rather than the instant the query began.

There's another possibility. Suppose you analyze your slow query log and find a simple query that took an unreasonably long time to execute a handful of times, although it ran quickly thousands of other times. You run the query again, and it is lightning fast, as it should be. You use EXPLAIN, and it is using an index correctly. You even try similar queries with different values in the WHERE clause to ensure you aren't just seeing cache hits, and they run quickly. Nothing seems to be wrong with this query. What gives?

If you have only the standard MySQL slow query log, with no execution plan or detailed timing information, you are limited to the knowledge that the query ran badly at the point that it was logged—you can't see why that was. Perhaps something else was consuming resources on the system, such as a backup, or perhaps some kind of locking or contention blocked the query's progress. Intermittent problems are a special case that we'll cover in the next section.

Diagnosing Intermittent Problems

Intermittent problems such as occasional server stalls or slow queries can be frustrating to diagnose, and the most egregious wastes of time we've seen have been results of phantom problems that happen only when you're not looking, or aren't reliably reproducible. We've seen people spend literally months fighting with such problems. In the process, some of them reverted to a trial-and-error troubleshooting approach, and sometimes made things dramatically worse by trying to change things such as server settings at random, hoping to stumble upon something that would help.

Try to avoid trial and error if you can. Trial-and-error troubleshooting is risky, because the results can be bad, and it can be frustrating and inefficient. If you can't figure out what the problem is, you might not be measuring correctly, you might be measuring in the wrong place, or you might not know the necessary tools to use. (Or the tools might not exist—we've developed a number of tools specifically to address the lack of transparency in various system components, from the operating system to MySQL itself.)

To illustrate the importance of trying to avoid trial and error, here are some sample resolutions we've found to some of the intermittent database performance problems we've been called in to solve:

- The application was executing *curl* to fetch exchange rate quotes from an external service, which was running very slowly at times.
- Important cache entries were expiring from *memcached*, causing the application to flood MySQL with requests to regenerate the cached items.
- DNS lookups were timing out randomly.
- The query cache was freezing MySQL periodically due to mutex contention or inefficient internal algorithms for deleting cached queries.
- InnoDB scalability limitations were causing query plan optimization to take too long when concurrency was over some threshold.

As you can see, some of these problems were in the database, and some of them weren't. Only by beginning at the place where the misbehavior could be observed and working through the resources it used, measuring as completely as possible, can you avoid hunting in the wrong place for problems that don't exist there.

We'll stop lecturing you now, and explain the approach and tools we use for solving intermittent problems.

Single-Query Versus Server-Wide Problems

Do you have any evidence of the problem? If so, try to determine whether the problem is with a single isolated query, or if it's server-wide. This is important to point you in the right direction. If everything on the server is suffering, and then everything is okay again, then any given query that's slow isn't likely to be the problem. Most of the slow queries are likely to be victims of some other problem instead. On the other hand, if the server is running nicely as a whole and a single query is slow for some reason, you have to look more closely at that query.

Server-wide problems are fairly common. As more powerful hardware has become available in the last several years, with 16-core and bigger servers becoming the norm, MySQL's scalability limitations on SMP systems have become more noticeable. Most of these problems are in older versions, which are unfortunately still widely used in production. MySQL still has some scalability problems even in newer versions, but they are much less serious, and much less frequently encountered, because they're edge cases. This is good news and bad news: good because you're much less likely to hit them, and bad because they require more knowledge of MySQL internals to diagnose. It also means that a lot of problems can be solved by simply upgrading MySQL.[12]

How do you determine whether the problem is server-wide or isolated to a single query? If the problem occurs repeatedly enough that you can observe it in action, or run a script overnight and look at the results the next day, there are three easy techniques that can make it obvious in most cases. We'll cover those next.

Using SHOW GLOBAL STATUS

The essence of this technique is to capture samples of SHOW GLOBAL STATUS at high frequency, such as once per second, and when the problem manifests, look for "spikes" or "notches" in counters such as Threads_running, Threads_connected, Questions, and Queries. This is a simple method that anyone can use (no special privileges are required) without impacting the server, so it's a great way to learn more about the nature of the problem without a big investment of time. Here's a sample command and output:

```
$ mysqladmin ext -i1 | awk '
    /Queries/{q=$4-qp;qp=$4}
    /Threads_connected/{tc=$4}
    /Threads_running/{printf "%5d %5d %5d\n", q, tc, $4}'
2147483647    136      7
    798    136      7
    767    134      9
    828    134      7
```

---

12. Again, don't do that without a good reason to believe that it's the solution.

683	134	7
784	135	7
614	134	7
108	134	24
187	134	31
179	134	28
1179	134	7
1151	134	7
1240	135	7
1000	135	7

The command captures samples of SHOW GLOBAL STATUS every second and pipes those into an *awk* script that prints out queries per second, Threads_connected, and Threads_running (number of queries currently executing). These three tend to be very sensitive to server-wide stalls. What usually happens is that, depending on the nature of the problem and how the application connects to MySQL, queries per second will drop and at least one of the other two will spike. Here the application is probably using a connection pool, so there's no spike of connected threads, but there's a clear bump in in-progress queries at the same time that the queries per second value drops to a fraction of its normal level.

What could explain this behavior? It's risky to guess, but in practice we've seen two common cases. One is some kind of internal bottleneck in the server, causing new queries to begin executing but to pile up against some lock that the older queries are waiting to acquire. This type of lock usually puts back-pressure on the application servers and causes some queueing there, too. The other common case we've seen is a spike of heavy queries such as those that can happen with a badly handled *memcached* expiration.

At one line per second, you can easily let this run for hours or days and make a quick plot to see if there are any areas with aberrations. If a problem is truly intermittent, you can let it run as long as needed and then refer back to the output when you notice the problem. In most cases this output will show the problem clearly.

Using SHOW PROCESSLIST

With this method, you capture samples of SHOW PROCESSLIST and look for lots of threads that are in unusual states or have some other unusual characteristic. For example, it's rather rare for queries to stay in the "statistics" state for very long, because this is the phase of query optimization where the server determines the best join order—normally very fast. Likewise, it's rare to see a lot of threads reporting the user as "Unauthenticated user," because this is a state that happens in the middle of the connection handshake when the client specifies the user it's trying to use to log in.

Vertical output with the \G terminator is very helpful for working with SHOW PROCESS LIST, because it puts each column of each row of the output onto its own line, making it easy to do a little *sort|uniq|sort* incantation that helps you view the count of unique values in any desired column easily:

```
$ mysql -e 'SHOW PROCESSLIST\G' | grep State: | sort | uniq -c | sort -rn
    744    State:
     67    State: Sending data
     36    State: freeing items
      8    State: NULL
      6    State: end
      4    State: Updating
      4    State: cleaning up
      2    State: update
      1    State: Sorting result
      1    State: logging slow query
```

Just change the *grep* pattern if you want to examine a different column. The `State` column is a good one for a lot of cases. Here we can see that there are an awful lot of threads in states that are part of the end of query execution: "freeing items," "end," "cleaning up," and "logging slow query." In fact, in many samples on the server from which this output came, this pattern or a similar one occurred. The most characteristic and reliable indicator of a problem was a high number of queries in the "freeing items" state.

You don't have to use command-line techniques to find problems like this. You can query the `PROCESSLIST` table in the `INFORMATION_SCHEMA` if your server is new enough, or use *innotop* with a fast refresh rate and watch the screen for an unusual buildup of queries. The example we just showed was of a server with InnoDB internal contention and flushing problems, but it can be far more mundane than that. The classic example would be a lot of queries in the "Locked" state. That's the unlovable trademark of MyISAM with its table-level locking, which quickly escalates into server-wide pileups when there's enough write activity on the tables.

Using query logging

To find problems in the query log, turn on the slow query log and set `long_query_time` to 0 globally, and make sure that all of the connections see the new setting. You might have to recycle connections so they pick up the new global value, or use Percona Server's feature to force it to take effect instantly without disrupting existing connections.

If you can't enable the slow query log to capture all queries for some reason, use *tcpdump* and *pt-query-digest* to emulate it. Look for periods in the log where the throughput drops suddenly. Queries are sent to the slow query log at completion time, so pileups typically result in a sudden drop of completions, until the culprit finishes and releases the resource that's blocking the other queries. The other queries will then complete. What's helpful about this characteristic behavior is that it lets you blame the first query that completes after a drop in throughput. (Sometimes it's not quite the first query; other queries might be running unaffected while some are blocked, so this isn't completely reliable.)

Again, good tools can help with this. You can't be looking through hundreds of gigabytes of queries by hand. Here's a one-liner that relies on MySQL's pattern of writing the current time to the log when the clock advances one second:

```
$ awk '/^# Time:/{print $3, $4, c;c=0}/^# User/{c++}' slow-query.log
080913 21:52:17 51
080913 21:52:18 29
080913 21:52:19 34
080913 21:52:20 33
080913 21:52:21 38
080913 21:52:22 15
080913 21:52:23 47
080913 21:52:24 96
080913 21:52:25 6
080913 21:52:26 66
080913 21:52:27 37
080913 21:52:28 59
```

There was a drop in throughput in that output, which was interestingly also preceded by a rush of queries completing. Without looking into the log around these timestamps it's hard to say what happened, but it's possible that the spike is related to the drop immediately afterward. In any case, it's clear that something odd happened in this server, and digging into the log around the timestamps in question could be very fruitful. (When we looked into this log, we found that the spike was due to connections being disconnected. Perhaps an application server was being restarted. Not everything is a MySQL problem.)

Making sense of the findings

Nothing beats visualization of the data. We've shown only small examples here, but in reality many of these techniques can result in thousands of lines of output. Get comfortable with *gnuplot* or *R* or another graphing tool of your choice. You can use them to plot things in a jiffy—much faster than a spreadsheet—and you can instantly zoom in on aberrations in a plot that you'll have a hard time seeing in a scrolling terminal, even if you think you're pretty good at Matrix-watching.[13]

We suggest trying the first two approaches—SHOW STATUS and SHOW PROCESSLIST—initially, because they're cheap and can be done interactively with nothing more than a little bit of shell scripting or running queries repeatedly. Analyzing the slow query log is much more disruptive and harder to do, and often shows what looks like funny patterns that disappear as you look closer. We've found that it's easy to imagine patterns where there are none.

When you find an aberration, what does it mean? It usually means that queries are queueing somewhere, or there's a flood or spike of a particular kind of query. Now the task is to find out why.

---

13. We haven't seen the woman in the red dress yet, but we'll let you know if we do.

Capturing Diagnostic Data

When an intermittent problem strikes, it's important to measure *everything* you possibly can, preferably for only the duration of the problem. If you do this right, you will gather a ton of diagnostic data. The data you don't collect often seems to be the data you really need to diagnose the problem.

To get started, you need two things:

1. A reliable and real-time "trigger"—a way to know when the problem happens
2. A tool to gather the diagnostic data

The diagnostic trigger

The trigger is very important to get right. It's the foundation for capturing the data when the problem happens. There are two common problems that cause this to go sideways: false positives and false negatives. If you have a false positive, you'll gather diagnostic data when nothing's wrong, and you'll waste time and get frustrated. False negatives will result in missed opportunities and more wasted time and frustration. Spend a little extra time making sure that your trigger indicates for sure that the problem is happening, if you need to. It's worth it.

What is a good criterion for a trigger? As shown in our examples, Threads_running tends to be very sensitive to problems, but pretty stable when nothing is wrong. A spike of unusual thread states in SHOW PROCESSLIST is another good indicator. But there can be many more ways to observe the problem, including specific output in SHOW INNODB STATUS, a spike in the server's load average, and so on. The key is to express this as something that you can compare to a definite threshold. This usually means a count. A count of threads running, a count of threads in "freeing items" state, and so on works well. The -c option to *grep* is your friend when looking at thread states:

```
$ mysql -e 'SHOW PROCESSLIST\G' | grep -c "State: freeing items"
36
```

Pick a threshold that's high enough that you won't hit it during normal operation, but not so high that you won't capture the problem in action. Beware, too, of setting the threshold too high to catch the problem when it begins. Problems that escalate tend to cause cascades of other problems, and if you capture diagnostic information after things have really gone down the toilet, you'll likely have a harder time isolating the original cause. You want to collect your data when things are clearly circling the drain, if possible, but before the loud flushing sound deafens you. For example, spikes in Threads_connected can go insanely high—we've seen it escalate from 100 to 5000 or more in the space of a couple minutes. You could clearly use 4999 as the threshold, but why wait for things to get that bad? If the application doesn't open more than 150 connections when it's healthy, start collecting at 200 or 300.

Referring back to our earlier example of Threads_running, it looks like the normal concurrency is less than 10. But 10 is not a good threshold—it is way too likely to produce false positives, and 15 isn't far enough away to definitely be out of the normal range of behavior either. There could be a mini-pileup at 15, but it's quite possible that it could not quite cross the tipping point, and the problem could clear right up before getting bad enough to be clearly diagnosable. We'd suggest setting 20 as the threshold in that example.

You probably also want to capture the problem as soon as it is clearly happening, but only after waiting briefly to ensure that it's not a false positive or short-term spike. So, our final trigger would be this: watch the status variables once per second, and if Threads_running exceeds 20 for more than 5 seconds, start gathering diagnostic data. (By the way, our example showed the problem going away after three seconds. That's a bit contrived to keep the example brief. A three-second problem is not likely to be easily diagnosable, and most problems we've seen last a bit longer.)

Now you need to set up some kind of tool to watch the server and take action when the trigger condition occurs. You could script this yourself, but we've saved you the trouble. There's a tool called *pt-stalk* in Percona Toolkit that is custom-built just for this. It has a lot of nice features whose necessity we've learned of through the school of hard knocks. For example, it looks at how much disk space is free, so it won't fill up your disk with the data it collects and crash your server. Not that we've ever done that, you understand!

The *pt-stalk* tool is really simple to use. You can configure the variable to watch, the threshold, the frequency of checks, and so forth. It supports a lot more fanciness than that if needed, but that's all you need to do for our example. Read the user's manual that comes with it before you use it. It relies on another tool for actually collecting the data, which we'll discuss next.

What kinds of data should you collect?

Now that you have determined a diagnostic trigger, you can use it to fire some process to collect data. But what kind of data should you collect? The answer, as mentioned previously, is everything you possibly can—but for only a reasonable amount of time. Gather operating system stats, CPU usage, disk utilization and free space, samples of *ps* output, memory usage, and everything you can from within MySQL, such as samples of SHOW STATUS, SHOW PROCESSLIST, and SHOW INNODB STATUS. You'll need all of these things, and probably more, to diagnose problems.

Execution time is spent doing work or waiting, as you'll recall. When an unknown problem happens, there are two types of causes, broadly speaking. The server could be doing a lot of work—consuming a lot of CPU cycles—or it could be stuck waiting for resources to become free. You need two different approaches to gather the diagnostic data to identify the causes of each of these types of problems: a profile when the system is doing too much work, and wait analysis when the system is doing too much waiting. But how do you know which of these to focus on when the problem is unknown? You don't, so it's best to collect data for both.

The primary profiling tool we rely on for server internals on GNU/Linux (as opposed to queries server-wide) is *oprofile*. We'll show examples of this a bit later. You can also profile the server's system calls with *strace*, but we have found this to be riskier on production systems. More on that later, too. For capturing queries to profile, we like to use *tcpdump*. It's hard to turn the slow query log on and off reliably at a moment's notice on most versions of MySQL, but you can get a pretty good simulation of it from TCP traffic. Besides, the traffic is useful for lots of other kinds of analysis.

For wait analysis, we often use GDB stack traces.[14] Threads that are stuck in a particular spot inside of MySQL for a long time tend to have the same stack trace. The procedure is to start *gdb*, attach it to the *mysqld* process, and dump stack traces for all threads. You can then use some short scripts to aggregate common stack traces together and do the *sort|uniq|sort* magic to show which ones are most common. We'll show how to use the *pt-pmp* tool for this a bit later.

You can also do wait analysis with data such as snapshots of SHOW PROCESSLIST and SHOW INNODB STATUS by observing thread and transaction states. None of these approaches is perfectly foolproof, but in practice they work often enough to be very helpful.

Gathering all of this data sounds like a lot of work! You probably anticipated this already, but we've built a tool to do this for you too. It's called *pt-collect*, and it's also part of Percona Toolkit. It's intended to be executed from *pt-stalk*. It needs to be run as *root* in order to gather most of the important data. By default, it will collect data for 30 seconds and then exit. This is usually enough to diagnose most problems, but not so much that it causes problems when there's a false positive.

The tool is easy to download and doesn't need any configuration—all of the configuration goes into *pt-stalk*. You will want to ensure that *gdb* and *oprofile* are installed on your server, and enable those in the *pt-stalk* configuration. You also need to ensure that *mysqld* has debug symbols.[15] When the trigger condition occurs, the tool will gather a pretty complete set of data. It will create timestamped files in a specified directory. At the time of writing, it's rather oriented toward GNU/Linux and will need tweaking on other operating systems, but it's still a good place to start.

Interpreting the data

If you've set up your trigger condition correctly and let *pt-stalk* run long enough to catch the problem in action a few times, you'll end up with a lot of data to sift through. What's the most useful place to start? We suggest looking at just a few things, with two

---

14. A caveat: using GDB is intrusive. It will freeze the server momentarily, especially if you have a lot of threads (connections), and can sometimes even crash it. The benefit still sometimes outweighs the risk. If the server becomes unusable anyway during a stall, it's not such a bad thing to double-freeze it.

15. Sometimes symbols are omitted as an "optimization," which really is not an optimization; it just makes diagnosing problems harder. You can use the *nm* tool to check if you have them, and install the *debuginfo* packages for MySQL to supply symbols.

purposes in mind. First, check that the problem really did occur, because if you have many samples to examine, you won't want to spend your time on false positives. Second, see if something obvious jumps out at you.

 It's very helpful to capture samples of how the server looks when it's behaving well, not just when it's in trouble. This will help you determine whether a particular sample, or even a portion of a sample, is abnormal or not. For example, when you're looking at the states of queries in the process list, you can answer questions such as "Is it normal for a lot of queries to be sorting their results?"

The most fruitful things to look at are usually query or transaction behavior, and server internals behavior. Query or transaction behavior shows you whether the problem was caused by the way the server is being used: badly written SQL, bad indexing, bad logical database design, and so on. You can see what the users are doing to the server by looking at places where queries and transactions appear: in the logged TCP traffic, in the SHOW PROCESSLIST output, and so on. Server internals behavior tells you whether the server is buggy or has built-in performance or scalability problems. You can see this in some of the same places, but also in *oprofile* and *gdb* output. This takes more experience to interpret.

If you don't know how to interpret what's wrong, you can tarball the directory full of collected data and submit it to a support provider for analysis. Any competent MySQL support professional will be able to interpret the data and tell you what it means. And they'll love you for sending such detailed data to peruse. You might also want to send the output of two other tools in Percona Toolkit: *pt-mysql-summary* and *pt-summary*. These show status and configuration snapshots of your MySQL instance and the operating system and hardware, respectively.

Percona Toolkit includes a tool designed to help you look through lots of samples of collected data quickly. It's called *pt-sift*, and it helps you navigate between samples, shows a summary of each sample, and lets you drill down into particular bits of the data if desired. It can save a lot of keystrokes.

We showed some examples of status counters and thread states earlier. We'll finish out this chapter by showing some examples of output from *oprofile* and *gdb*. Here's an *oprofile* report from a server that was having trouble. Can you find the problem?

```
samples  %        image name    app name    symbol  name
893793   31.1273  /no-vmlinux   /no-vmlinux  (no symbols)
325733   11.3440  mysqld        mysqld       Query_cache::free_memory_block()
117732   4.1001   libc          libc         (no symbols)
102349   3.5644   mysqld        mysqld       my_hash_sort_bin
76977    2.6808   mysqld        mysqld       MYSQLparse()
71599    2.4935   libpthread    libpthread   pthread_mutex_trylock
52203    1.8180   mysqld        mysqld       read_view_open_now
46516    1.6200   mysqld        mysqld       Query_cache::invalidate_query_block_list()
42153    1.4680   mysqld        mysqld       Query_cache::write_result_data()
```

```
37359  1.3011  mysqld      mysqld      MYSQLlex()
35917  1.2508  libpthread  libpthread  __pthread_mutex_unlock_usercnt
34248  1.1927  mysqld      mysqld      __intel_new_memcpy
```

If you said "the query cache," you were right. This server's query cache was causing far too much work and slowing everything down. This had happened overnight, a factor of 50 slowdown, with no other changes to the system. Disabling the query cache returned the server to its normal performance. This is an example of when server internals are relatively straightforward to interpret.

Another important tool for bottleneck analysis is wait analysis using stack traces from *gdb*. A single thread's stack trace normally looks like the following, which we've formatted a bit for printing:

```
Thread 992 (Thread 0x7f6ee0111910 (LWP 31510)):
#0  0x0000003be560b2f9 in pthread_cond_wait@@GLIBC_2.3.2 () from /libpthread.so.0
#1  0x00007f6ee14f0965 in os_event_wait_low () at os/os0sync.c:396
#2  0x00007f6ee1531507 in srv_conc_enter_innodb () at srv/srv0srv.c:1185
#3  0x00007f6ee14c906a in innodb_srv_conc_enter_innodb () at handler/ha_innodb.cc:609
#4  ha_innodb::index_read () at handler/ha_innodb.cc:5057
#5  0x00000000006538c5 in ?? ()
#6  0x0000000000658029 in sub_select() ()
#7  0x0000000000658e25 in ?? ()
#8  0x00000000006677c0 in JOIN::exec() ()
#9  0x000000000066944a in mysql_select() ()
#10 0x0000000000669ea4 in handle_select() ()
#11 0x00000000005ff89a in ?? ()
#12 0x0000000000601c5e in mysql_execute_command() ()
#13 0x000000000060701c in mysql_parse() ()
#14 0x000000000060829a in dispatch_command() ()
#15 0x0000000000608b8a in do_command(THD*) ()
#16 0x00000000005fbd1d in handle_one_connection ()
#17 0x0000003be560686a in start_thread () from /lib64/libpthread.so.0
#18 0x0000003be4ede3bd in clone () from /lib64/libc.so.6
#19 0x0000000000000000 in ?? ()
```

The stack reads from the bottom up; that is, the thread is currently executing inside of the pthread_cond_wait function, which was called from os_event_wait_low. Reading down the trace, it looks like this thread was trying to enter the InnoDB kernel (srv_conc_enter_innodb), but got put on an internal queue (os_event_wait_low) because more than innodb_thread_concurrency threads were already inside the kernel. The real value of stack traces is aggregating lots of them together, however. This is a technique that Domas Mituzas, a former MySQL support engineer, made popular with his "poor man's profiler" tool. He currently works at Facebook, and he and others there have developed a wide variety of tools for gathering and analyzing stack traces. You can find out more about what's available at *http://www.poormansprofiler.org*.

We have an implementation of the poor man's profiler in Percona Toolkit, called *pt-pmp*. It's a shell and *awk* program that collapses similar stack traces together and does the usual *sort|uniq|sort* to show the most common ones first. Here's what the full set of stack traces looks like after crunching it down to its essence. We're going to use the *-l 5* option to truncate the stack traces after five levels so that we don't get so many traces with common tops but different bottoms, which would prevent them from aggregating together and showing where things are really waiting:

```
$ pt-pmp -l 5 stacktraces.txt
    507 pthread_cond_wait,one_thread_per_connection_end,handle_one_connection,
        start_thread,clone
    398 pthread_cond_wait,os_event_wait_low,srv_conc_enter_innodb,
        innodb_srv_conc_enter_innodb,ha_innodb::index_read
     83 pthread_cond_wait,os_event_wait_low,sync_array_wait_event,mutex_spin_wait,
        mutex_enter_func
     10 pthread_cond_wait,os_event_wait_low,os_aio_simulated_handle,fil_aio_wait,
        io_handler_thread
      7 pthread_cond_wait,os_event_wait_low,srv_conc_enter_innodb,
        innodb_srv_conc_enter_innodb,ha_innodb::general_fetch
      5 pthread_cond_wait,os_event_wait_low,sync_array_wait_event,rw_lock_s_lock_spin,
        rw_lock_s_lock_func
      1 sigwait,signal_hand,start_thread,clone,??
      1 select,os_thread_sleep,srv_lock_timeout_and_monitor_thread,start_thread,clone
      1 select,os_thread_sleep,srv_error_monitor_thread,start_thread,clone
      1 select,handle_connections_sockets,main
      1 read,vio_read_buff,::??,my_net_read,cli_safe_read

      1 pthread_cond_wait,os_event_wait_low,sync_array_wait_event,rw_lock_x_lock_low,
        rw_lock_x_lock_func
      1 pthread_cond_wait,MYSQL_BIN_LOG::wait_for_update,mysql_binlog_send,
        dispatch_command,do_command
      1 fsync,os_file_fsync,os_file_flush,fil_flush,log_write_up_to
```

The first line is the characteristic signature of an idle thread in MySQL, so you can ignore that. The second line is the most interesting one: it shows that a lot of threads are waiting to enter the InnoDB kernel but are blocked. The third line shows many threads waiting on some mutex, but we can't see which one because we have truncated the deeper levels of the stack trace. If it is important to know which mutex that is, we would need to re run the tool with a larger value for the *-l* option. In general, the stack traces show that lots of things are waiting for their turn inside InnoDB, but why? That isn't clear at all. To find out, we probably need to look elsewhere.

As the preceding stack trace and *oprofile* reports show, these types of analysis are not always useful to those who aren't experts with MySQL and InnoDB source code, and you should ask for help from someone else if you get stuck.

Now let's move on to a server whose problems don't show up on either a profile or wait analysis, and need to be diagnosed differently.

A Case Study in Diagnostics

In this section we'll step you through the process of diagnosing a real customer's intermittent performance problem. This case study is likely to get into unfamiliar territory unless you're an expert with MySQL, InnoDB, and GNU/Linux. However, the specifics we'll discuss are not the point. Try to look for the method within the madness: read this section with an eye toward the assumptions and guesses we make, the reasoning-based and measurement-based approaches we take, and so on. We are delving into a specific and detailed case simply to illustrate generalities.

Before beginning to solve a problem at someone else's request, it's good to try to clear up two things, preferably taking notes to help avoid forgetting or omitting anything:

1. First, what's the problem? Try to be clear on that. It's surprisingly easy to go hunting for the wrong problem. In this case, the customer complained that once every day or two, the server rejected connections with a `max_connections` error. It lasted from a few seconds to a few minutes, and was highly sporadic.

2. Next, what has been done to try to fix it? In this case, the customer did not attempt to resolve the issue at all. This was extremely helpful, because few things are as hard to understand as another person's description of the exact sequence of events, changes they made, and effects thereof. This is especially true when they call in desperation after a couple of sleepless nights and caffeine-filled days. A server that has been subjected to unknown changes, with unknown effects, is much harder to troubleshoot, especially if you're under time pressure.

With that behind us, let's get started. It's a good idea not only to try to understand how the server behaves, but also to take an inventory of the server's status, configuration, software, and hardware. We did so with the *pt-summary* and *pt-mysql-summary* tools. Briefly, this server had 16 CPU cores, 12 GB of RAM, and a total of 900 MB of data, all in InnoDB, on a solid-state drive. The server was running GNU/Linux with MySQL 5.1.37 and the InnoDB plugin version 1.0.4. We'd worked with this customer previously on other unexpected performance problems, and we knew the systems. The database was never the problem in the past; it had always been bad application behavior. We took a look at the server and found nothing obviously wrong at a glance. The queries weren't perfect, but they were still running in less than 10 ms most of the time. So we confirmed that the server was fine under normal circumstances. (This is important to do; many problems that are noticed only sporadically are actually symptoms of chronic problems, such as failed hard drives in RAID arrays.)

 This case study might be a little tedious. We'll "play dumb" to show all of the diagnostic data, explain everything we see in detail, and follow several potential trains of thought to completion. In reality, we don't take such a frustratingly slow approach to every problem, and we're not trying to say that you should, either.

We installed our diagnostic toolkit and set it to trigger on `Threads_connected`, which was normally less than 15 but increased to several hundred during these problems. We'll present a sample of the data we collected as a result, but we'll hold our commentary until later. See if you can drink from the fire hose and pick out items that are likely to be important:

- The query activity ranged from 1,000 to 10,000 queries per second, with many of them being "garbage" commands such as pinging the server to see if it was alive. Most of the rest were SELECT commands—from 300 to 2,000 per second—and there were a very small number of UPDATE commands (about 5 per second).

- There were basically two distinct types of queries in SHOW PROCESSLIST, varying only in the values in the WHERE clauses. Here are the query states, summarized:

```
$ grep State: processlist.txt | sort | uniq -c | sort -rn
    161    State: Copying to tmp table
    156    State: Sorting result
    136    State: statistics
     50    State: Sending data
     24    State: NULL
     13    State:
      7    State: freeing items
      7    State: cleaning up
      1    State: storing result in query cache
      1    State: end
```

- Most queries were doing index scans or range scans—no full-table scans or cross joins.

- There were between 20 and 100 sorts per second, with between 1,000 and 12,000 rows sorted per second.

- There were between 12 and 90 temporary tables created per second, with about 3 to 5 of them on disk.

- There was no problem with table locking or the query cache.

- In SHOW INNODB STATUS, we observed that the main thread state was "flushing buffer pool pages," but there were only a few dozen dirty pages to flush (Innodb_buffer _pool_pages_dirty), there was practically no change in Innodb_buffer_pool _pages_flushed, and the difference between the log sequence number and the last checkpoint was very small. The InnoDB buffer pool wasn't even close to being full; it was much bigger than the data size. Most threads were waiting in the InnoDB queue: "12 queries inside InnoDB, 495 queries in queue."

- We captured *iostat* output for 30 seconds, one sample per second. This showed that there was essentially no read activity at all on the disks, but writes went through the roof, and average I/O wait times and queue length were extremely high. Here is the first bit of the output, simplified to fit on the page without wrapping:

```
 r/s     w/s rsec/s      wsec/s avgqu-sz  await svctm  %util
1.00  500.00   8.00   86216.00      5.05  11.95  0.59   29.40
0.00  451.00   0.00  206248.00    123.25 238.00  1.90   85.90
0.00  565.00   0.00  269792.00    143.80 245.43  1.77  100.00
0.00  649.00   0.00  309248.00    143.01 231.30  1.54  100.10
0.00  589.00   0.00  281784.00    142.58 232.15  1.70  100.00
0.00  384.00   0.00  162008.00     71.80 238.39  1.73   66.60
```

0.00	14.00	0.00	400.00	0.01	0.93	0.36	0.50
0.00	13.00	0.00	248.00	0.01	0.92	0.23	0.30
0.00	13.00	0.00	408.00	0.01	0.92	0.23	0.30

- The output of *vmstat* confirmed what we saw in *iostat* and showed that the CPUs were basically idle except for some I/O wait during the spike of writes (ranging up to 9% wait).

Is your brain full yet? This can happen quickly when you dig into a system in detail and you don't have (or you try to ignore) any preconceived notions, so you end up looking at *everything*. Most of what you'll look at is either completely normal, or shows the effects of the problem but doesn't indicate the source of the problem. Although at this point we have some good guesses about the cause of the problem, we'll keep going by looking at the *oprofile* report, and we'll begin to add commentary and interpretation as we throw more data at you:

```
samples   %        image name      app name        symbol name
473653    63.5323  no-vmlinux      no-vmlinux      /no-vmlinux
95164     12.7646  mysqld          mysqld          /usr/libexec/mysqld
53107     7.1234   libc-2.10.1.so  libc-2.10.1.so  memcpy
13698     1.8373   ha_innodb.so    ha_innodb.so    build_template()
13059     1.7516   ha_innodb.so    ha_innodb.so    btr_search_guess_on_hash
11724     1.5726   ha_innodb.so    ha_innodb.so    row_sel_store_mysql_rec
8872      1.1900   ha_innodb.so    ha_innodb.so    rec_init_offsets_comp_ordinary
7577      1.0163   ha_innodb.so    ha_innodb.so    row_search_for_mysql
6030      0.8088   ha_innodb.so    ha_innodb.so    rec_get_offsets_func
5268      0.7066   ha_innodb.so    ha_innodb.so    cmp_dtuple_rec_with_match
```

It's not at all obvious what most of these symbols represent, and most of the time is lumped together in the kernel[16] and in a generic *mysqld* symbol that doesn't tell us anything.[17] Don't get distracted by all of the ha_innodb.so symbols. Look at the percentage of time they contributed: regardless of what they do, they're burning so little time that you can be sure they're not the problem. This is an example of a problem that isn't going to yield results from this type of profile analysis. We are looking at the wrong data. When you see something like the previous sample, move along and look at other data to see if there's a more obvious pointer to the cause.

At this point, if you're interested in the wait analysis from *gdb* stack traces, please refer to the end of the preceding section. The sample we showed there is from the system we're currently diagnosing. If you recall, the bulk of stack traces were simply waiting to enter the InnoDB kernel, which corresponds to "12 queries inside InnoDB, 495 queries in queue" in the output from SHOW INNODB STATUS.

Do you see anything that points conclusively to a specific problem? We didn't; we saw possible symptoms of many different problems, and at least two potential causes of the

---

16. In theory, we need kernel symbols to understand what's going on inside the kernel. In practice, this can be a hassle to install, and we know from looking at *vmstat* that the system CPU usage was low, so we're unlikely to find much other than "sleeping" there anyway.

17. It looks like this was a bad build of MySQL.

problem based on intuition and experience. But we also saw something that didn't make sense. If you look at the *iostat* output again, in the `wsec/s` column you can see that for about six seconds, the server is writing hundreds of megabytes of data per second to the disks. Each sector is 512 bytes, so those samples show up to 150 MB of writes per second at times. Yet the entire database is only 900 MB, and the workload is mostly `SELECT` queries. How can this happen?

When you examine a system, try to ask yourself whether there are any things like this that simply don't add up, and investigate them further. Try to follow each train of thought to its conclusion, and try not to get sidetracked on too many tangents, or you could forget about a promising possibility. Write down little notes and cross them off to help ensure that you've dotted all the Ts.[18]

At this point, we could jump right to a conclusion, and it would be wrong. We see from the main thread state that InnoDB is trying to flush dirty pages, which generally doesn't appear in the status output unless flushing is delayed. We know that this version of InnoDB is prone to the "furious flushing" problem, also called a *checkpoint stall*. This is what happens when InnoDB doesn't spread flushing out evenly over time, and it suddenly decides to force a checkpoint (flush a lot of data) to make up for that. This can cause serious blocking inside InnoDB, making everything queue and wait to enter the kernel, and thus pile up at the layers above InnoDB in the server. We showed an example in Chapter 2 of the periodic drops in performance that can happen when there is furious flushing. Many of this server's symptoms are similar to what happens during a forced checkpoint, but it's not the problem in this case. You can prove that in many ways, perhaps most easily by looking at the `SHOW STATUS` counters and tracking the change in the `Innodb_buffer_pool_pages_flushed` counter, which, as we mentioned earlier, was not increasing much. In addition, we noted that the buffer pool doesn't have much dirty data to flush anyway—certainly not hundreds of megabytes. This is not surprising, because the workload on this server is almost entirely `SELECT` queries. We can therefore conclude that instead of blaming the problem on InnoDB flushing, we should blame InnoDB's flushing delay on the problem. It is a symptom— an effect—not a cause. The underlying problem is causing the disks to become saturated that InnoDB isn't having any luck getting its I/O tasks done. So we can eliminate this as a possible cause, and cross off one of our intuition-based ideas.

Distinguishing cause from effect can be hard sometimes, and it can be tempting to just skip the investigation and jump to the diagnosis when a problem looks familiar. It is good to avoid taking shortcuts, but it's equally important to pay attention to your intuition. If something looks familiar, it is prudent to spend a little time measuring the necessary and sufficient conditions to prove whether that's the problem. This can save a lot of time you'd otherwise spend looking through other data about the system and its performance. Just try not to jump to conclusions based on a gut feeling that "I've

---

18. Or whatever that phrase is. Put all your eggs in one haystack?

seen this before, and I am sure it's the same thing." Gather some evidence, if you can—especially evidence that could disprove your gut feeling.

The next step was to try to figure out what was causing the server's I/O usage to be so strange. We call your attention to the reasoning we used earlier: "The server writes hundreds of megabytes to disk for many seconds, but the database is only 900 MB. How can this happen?" Notice the implicit assumption that the database is doing the writing? What evidence did we have that it's the database? Try to catch yourself when you think unsubstantiated thoughts, and when something doesn't make sense, ask if you're assuming something. If you can, measure and remove the doubt.

We saw two possibilities: either the database was causing the I/O—and if we could find the source of that, we thought that it was likely that we'd find the cause of the problem—or, the database wasn't doing all that I/O, but rather something else was, and the lack of I/O resources could have been impacting the database. We're stating that very carefully to avoid another implicit assumption: just because the disks are busy doesn't guarantee that MySQL will suffer. Remember, this server basically has a read-only in-memory workload, so it is quite possible to imagine that the disks could stop responding for a long time without causing serious problems.

If you're following our reasoning, you might see that we need to go back and gut-check another assumption. We can see that the disk device was behaving badly, as evidenced by the high wait times. A solid-state drive shouldn't take a quarter of a second per I/O on average. And indeed, we can see that *iostat* claimed the drive itself was responding quickly, but things were taking a long time to get through the block device queue to the drive. Remember that this is only what *iostat* claims; it could be wrong.

What Causes Poor Performance?

When a resource is behaving badly, it's good to try to understand why. There are a few possibilities:

1. The resource is being overworked and doesn't have the capacity to behave well.
2. The resource is not configured properly.
3. The resource is broken or malfunctioning.

In the case we're examining, *iostat*'s output could point to either too much work, or misconfiguration (why are I/O requests queueing so long before reaching the disk, if it's actually responding quickly?). However, a very important part of deciding what's wrong is to compare the demand on the system to its known capacity. We know from extensive benchmarking that the particular SSD drive this customer was using can't sustain hundreds of megabytes of writes per second. Thus, although *iostat* claims the disk is responding just fine, it's likely that this isn't entirely true. In this case, we had no way to prove that the disk was slower than *iostat* claimed, but it looked rather likely to be the case. Still, this doesn't change our opinion: this could be disk abuse,[19] misconfiguration, or both.

After working through the diagnostic data to reach this point, the next task was obvious: measure what was causing the I/O. Unfortunately, this was infeasible on the version of GNU/Linux the customer was using. We could have made an educated guess with some work, but we wanted to explore other options first. As a proxy, we could have measured how much I/O was coming from MySQL, but again, in this version of MySQL that wasn't really feasible due to lack of instrumentation.

Instead, we opted to try to observe MySQL's I/O, based on what we know about how it uses the disk. In general, MySQL writes only data, logs, sort files, and temporary tables to disk. We eliminated data and logs from consideration, based on the status counters and other information we discussed earlier. Now, suppose MySQL were to suddenly write a bunch of data to disk temporary tables or sort files. How could we observe this? Two easy ways are to watch the amount of free space on the disk, or to look at the server's open filehandles with the *lsof* command. We did both, and the results were convincing enough to satisfy us. Here's what *df -h* showed every second during the same incident we've been studying:

```
Filesystem  Size  Used  Avail  Use%  Mounted  on
/dev/sda3   58G   20G   36G    36%   /
/dev/sda3   58G   20G   36G    36%   /
/dev/sda3   58G   19G   36G    35%   /
/dev/sda3   58G   19G   36G    35%   /
/dev/sda3   58G   19G   36G    35%   /
/dev/sda3   58G   19G   36G    35%   /
/dev/sda3   58G   18G   37G    33%   /
/dev/sda3   58G   18G   37G    33%   /
/dev/sda3   58G   18G   37G    33%   /
```

And here's the data from *lsof*, which for some reason we gathered only once per five seconds. We're simply summing the sizes of all of the files *mysqld* has open in */tmp*, and printing out the total for each timestamped sample in the file:

```
$ awk '
  /mysqld.*tmp/ {
    total += $7;
  }
  /^Sun Mar 28/ && total {
    printf "%s %7.2f MB\n", $4, total/1024/1024;
    total = 0;
  }' lsof.txt
18:34:38 1655.21 MB
18:34:43    1.88 MB
18:34:48    1.88 MB
18:34:53    1.88 MB
18:34:58    1.88 MB
```

Based on this data, it looks like MySQL is writing about 1.5 GB of data to temporary tables in the beginning phases of the incident, and this matches what we found in the SHOW PROCESSLIST states ("Copying to tmp table"). The evidence points to a storm of

19. Someone call the 1-800 hotline!

bad queries all at once saturating the disk. The most common cause of this we've seen (this is our intuition at work) is a cache stampede, when cached items expire all at once from *memcached* and many instances of the application try to repopulate the cache simultaneously. We showed samples of the queries to the developers and discussed their purpose. Indeed, it turned out that simultaneous cache expiration was the cause (confirming our intuition). In addition to the developers addressing the problem at the application level, we were able to help them modify the queries so they didn't use temporary tables on disk. Either one of these fixes might have prevented the problem, but it was much better to do both than just one.

Now, we'd like to apply a little hindsight to explain some questions you might have had as we went along (we certainly critiqued our own approach as we reviewed it for this chapter):

Why didn't we just optimize the slow queries to begin with?
> Because the problem wasn't slow queries, it was "too many connections" errors. Sure, it's logical to see that long-running queries cause things to stack up and the connection count to climb. But so can dozens of other things. In the absence of finding a good reason for why things are going wrong, it's all too tempting to fall back to looking for slow queries or other general things that look like they could be improved.[20] But this goes badly more often than it goes well. If you took your car to the mechanic and complained about an unfamiliar noise, and then got slapped with a bill for balancing the tires and changing the transmission fluid because the mechanic couldn't figure out the real problem and went looking for other things to do, wouldn't you be annoyed?

But isn't it a red flag that the queries were running slowly with a bad EXPLAIN?
> They were indeed—during the incidents. Was that a cause or an effect? It wasn't obvious until we dug into things more deeply. And remember, the queries seemed to be running well enough in normal circumstances. Just because a query does a filesort with a temporary table doesn't mean it is a problem. Getting rid of filesorts and temporary tables is a catch-all, "best practice" type of tactic.

> Generic "best practices" reviews have their place, but they are seldom the solution to highly specific problems. The problem could easily have been misconfiguration, for example. We've seen many cases where someone tried to fix a misconfigured server with tactics such as optimizing queries, which was ultimately a waste of time and just prolonged the damage caused by the real problem.

If cached items were being regenerated many times, wouldn't there be multiple identical queries?
> Yes, and this is something we did not investigate at the time. Multiple threads regenerating the same cached item would indeed cause many completely identical queries. (This is different from having multiple queries of the same general type,

---

20. Also known as the "when all you have is a hammer, everything looks like a nail" approach.

which might differ in a parameter to the WHERE clause, for example.) Noticing this could have stimulated our intuition and directed us to the solution more quickly.

There were hundreds of SELECT *queries per second, but only five* UPDATE*s. What's to say that these five weren't really heavy queries?*

They could indeed have been responsible for a lot of load on the server. We didn't show the actual queries because it would clutter things too much, but it's a valid point that the absolute number of each type of query isn't necessarily meaningful.

Isn't the "proof" about the origin of the I/O storms still pretty weak?

Yes, it is. There could be many explanations for why a small database would write a huge amount of data to disk, or why the disk's free space decreased quickly. This is something that's ultimately pretty hard to measure (though not impossible) on the versions of MySQL and GNU/Linux in question. Although it's possible to play devil's advocate and come up with lots of scenarios, we chose to balance the cost and potential benefit by pursuing what seemed like the most promising leads first. The harder it is to measure and be certain, the higher the cost/benefit ratio climbs, and the more willing we are to accept uncertainty.

We said "the database was never the problem in the past." Wasn't that a bias?

Yes, that was a bias. If you caught it, great—if not, well, then hopefully it serves as a useful illustration that we all have biases.

We'd like to finish this troubleshooting case study by pointing out that this issue probably could have been solved (or prevented) without our involvement by using an application profiling tool such as New Relic.

Other Profiling Tools

We've shown a variety of ways to profile MySQL, the operating system, and queries. We've demonstrated those that we think you'll find most useful, and of course, we'll show more tools and techniques for inspecting and measuring systems throughout this book. But wait, there's more!

Using the USER_STATISTICS Tables

Percona Server and MariaDB include additional INFORMATION_SCHEMA tables for object-level usage statistics. These were originally created at Google. They are extremely useful for finding out how much or little the various parts of your server are actually used. In a large enterprise, where the DBAs are responsible for managing the databases and have little control over the developers, they can be vital for measuring and auditing database activity and enforcing usage policies. They're similarly useful for multitenant applications such as shared hosting environments. When you're hunting for performance problems, on the other hand, they can be great for helping you figure out who's spending the most time in the database or what tables and indexes are most or least used. Here are the tables:

```
mysql> SHOW TABLES FROM INFORMATION_SCHEMA LIKE '%_STATISTICS';
+---------------------------------------------+
| Tables_in_information_schema (%_STATISTICS) |
+---------------------------------------------+
| CLIENT_STATISTICS                           |
| INDEX_STATISTICS                            |
| TABLE_STATISTICS                            |
| THREAD_STATISTICS                           |
| USER_STATISTICS                             |
+---------------------------------------------+
```

We don't have space for examples of all the queries you can perform against these tables, but a couple of bullet points won't hurt:

- You can find the most-used and least-used tables and indexes, by reads, updates, or both.

- You can find unused indexes, which are candidates for removal.

- You can look at the CONNECTED_TIME versus the BUSY_TIME of the replication user to see whether replication will likely have a hard time keeping up soon.

In MySQL 5.6, the Performance Schema adds tables that serve purposes similar to the aforementioned tables.

Using strace

The *strace* tool intercepts system calls. There are several ways you can use it. One is to time the system calls and print out a profile:

```
$ strace -cfp $(pidof mysqld)
Process 12648 attached with 17 threads - interrupt to quit
^CProcess 12648 detached
% time     seconds  usecs/call     calls    errors syscall
------ ----------- ----------- --------- --------- ----------------
 73.51    0.608908       13839        44           select
 24.38    0.201969       20197        10           futex
  0.76    0.006313           1     11233         3 read
  0.60    0.004999         625         8           unlink
  0.48    0.003969          22       180           write
  0.23    0.001870          11       178           pread64
  0.04    0.000304           0      5538           _llseek
[some lines omitted for brevity]
------ ----------- ----------- --------- --------- ----------------
100.00    0.828375                 17834        46 total
```

In this way, it's a bit like *oprofile*. However, *oprofile* will profile the internal symbols of the program, not just the system calls. In addition, *strace* uses a different technique for intercepting the calls, which is a bit more unpredictable and adds a lot of overhead. And *strace* measures wall-clock time, whereas *oprofile* measures where the CPU cycles are spent. As an example, *strace* will show when I/O waits are a problem because it measures from the beginning of a system call such as read or pread64 to the end of the call, but *oprofile* usually won't because the I/O system call doesn't actually do any CPU work—it just waits for the I/O to complete.

We use *oprofile* only when necessary, because it can have strange side effects on a big multithreaded process like *mysqld*, and while *strace* is attached, *mysqld* will run so slowly that it's pretty much unusable for a production workload. Still, it can be extremely useful in some circumstances, and there is a tool in Percona Toolkit called *pt-ioprofile* that uses *strace* to generate a true profile of I/O activity. This has been helpful in proving or disproving some hard-to-measure cases that we couldn't bring to a close otherwise. (If the server had been running MySQL 5.6, we'd have been able to do this with the Performance Schema instead.)

Summary

This chapter lays the foundation of thought processes and techniques you'll need to succeed in performance optimization. The right mental approach is the key to unlocking the full potential of your systems and applying the knowledge you'll gain in the rest of this book. Here are some of the fundamentals we tried to illustrate:

- We think that the most useful way to define performance is in terms of response time.

- You cannot reliably improve what you cannot measure, so performance improvement works best with high-quality, well-scoped, complete measurements of response time.

- The best place to start measuring is the application, not the database. If there is a problem in the lower layers, such as the database, good measurements will make it obvious.

- Most systems are impossible to measure completely, and measurements are always wrong. But you can usually work around the limitations and get a good outcome anyway, if you acknowledge the imperfection and uncertainty of the process you use.

- Thorough measurements produce way too much data to analyze, so you need a profile. This is the best tool to help you bubble important things to the top so you can decide where to start.

- A profile is a summary, which obscures and discards details. It also usually doesn't show you what's missing. It's unwise to take a profile at face value.

- There are two kinds of time consumption: working and waiting. Many profiling tools can only measure work done, so wait analysis is sometimes an important supplement, especially when CPU usage is low but things still aren't getting done.

- Optimization is not the same thing as improvement. Stop working when further improvement is not worth the cost.

- Pay attention to your intuition, but try to use it to direct your analysis, not to decide on changes to the system. Base your decisions on data, not gut feeling, as much as possible.

The overall approach we showed to solving performance problems is to first clarify the question, then choose the appropriate technique to answer it. If you're trying to see if you can improve the server's performance overall, a good way to start is to log all the queries and produce a system-wide profile with *pt-query-digest*. If you're hunting for bad queries you might not know about, logging and profiling will also help. Look for top time consumers, queries that are causing a bad user experience, and queries that are highly variable or have strange response-time histograms. When you find "bad" queries, drill into them by looking at the detailed report from *pt-query-digest*, using SHOW PROFILE, and using other tools such as EXPLAIN.

If the queries are performing badly for no discernible reason, you might be experiencing sporadic server-wide problems. To find out, you can measure and plot the server's status counters at a fine level of detail. If this reveals a problem, use the same data to formulate a reliable trigger condition, so you can capture a burst of detailed diagnostic data. Invest as much time and care as necessary to find a good trigger condition that avoids false positives and false negatives. If you capture the problem in action but you still don't understand the cause, gather more data, or ask for help.

You're working with systems you can't measure fully, but they're just state machines, so if you are careful, logical, and persistent, you will usually get results. Try not to confuse effects with causes, and try not to make changes until you have identified the problem.

The theoretically pure approach of top-down profiling and exhaustive measurement is the ideal toward which we aspire, but we often have to deal with real systems. Real systems are complex and inadequately instrumented, so we do the best we can with what we have. Tools such as *pt-query-digest* and the MySQL Enterprise Monitor's query analyzer aren't perfect, and often won't show conclusive proof of a problem's cause. But they are good enough to get the job done much of the time.

## CHAPTER 4

Optimizing Schema and Data Types

Good logical and physical design is the cornerstone of high performance, and you must design your schema for the specific queries you will run. This often involves trade-offs. For example, a denormalized schema can speed up some types of queries but slow down others. Adding counter and summary tables is a great way to optimize queries, but they can be expensive to maintain. MySQL's particular features and implementation details influence this quite a bit.

This chapter and the following one, which focuses on indexing, cover the MySQL-specific bits of schema design. We assume that you know how to design databases, so this is not an introductory chapter, or even an advanced chapter, on database design. It's a chapter on MySQL database design—it's about what is different when designing databases with MySQL rather than other relational database management systems. If you need to study the basics of database design, we suggest Clare Churcher's book *Beginning Database Design* (Apress).

This chapter is preparation for the two that follow. In these three chapters, we will explore the interaction of logical design, physical design, and query execution. This requires a big-picture approach as well as attention to details. You need to understand the whole system to understand how each piece will affect others. You might find it useful to review this chapter after reading the chapters on indexing and query optimization. Many of the topics discussed can't be considered in isolation.

Choosing Optimal Data Types

MySQL supports a large variety of data types, and choosing the correct type to store your data is crucial to getting good performance. The following simple guidelines can help you make better choices, no matter what type of data you are storing:

Smaller is usually better.
In general, try to use the smallest data type that can correctly store and represent your data. Smaller data types are usually faster, because they use less space on the

disk, in memory, and in the CPU cache. They also generally require fewer CPU cycles to process.

Make sure you don't underestimate the range of values you need to store, though, because increasing the data type range in multiple places in your schema can be a painful and time-consuming operation. If you're in doubt as to which is the best data type to use, choose the smallest one that you don't think you'll exceed. (If the system is not very busy or doesn't store much data, or if you're at an early phase in the design process, you can change it easily later.)

Simple is good.

Fewer CPU cycles are typically required to process operations on simpler data types. For example, integers are cheaper to compare than characters, because character sets and collations (sorting rules) make character comparisons complicated. Here are two examples: you should store dates and times in MySQL's built-in types instead of as strings, and you should use integers for IP addresses. We discuss these topics further later.

Avoid NULL if possible.

A lot of tables include nullable columns even when the application does not need to store NULL (the absence of a value), merely because it's the default. It's usually best to specify columns as NOT NULL unless you intend to store NULL in them.

It's harder for MySQL to optimize queries that refer to nullable columns, because they make indexes, index statistics, and value comparisons more complicated. A nullable column uses more storage space and requires special processing inside MySQL. When a nullable column is indexed, it requires an extra byte per entry and can even cause a fixed-size index (such as an index on a single integer column) to be converted to a variable-sized one in MyISAM.

The performance improvement from changing NULL columns to NOT NULL is usually small, so don't make it a priority to find and change them on an existing schema unless you know they are causing problems. However, if you're planning to index columns, avoid making them nullable if possible.

There are exceptions, of course. For example, it's worth mentioning that InnoDB stores NULL with a single bit, so it can be pretty space-efficient for sparsely populated data. This doesn't apply to MyISAM, though.

The first step in deciding what data type to use for a given column is to determine what general class of types is appropriate: numeric, string, temporal, and so on. This is usually pretty straightforward, but we mention some special cases where the choice is unintuitive.

The next step is to choose the specific type. Many of MySQL's data types can store the same kind of data but vary in the range of values they can store, the precision they permit, or the physical space (on disk and in memory) they require. Some data types also have special behaviors or properties.

For example, a DATETIME and a TIMESTAMP column can store the same kind of data: date and time, to a precision of one second. However, TIMESTAMP uses only half as much storage space, is time zone–aware, and has special autoupdating capabilities. On the other hand, it has a much smaller range of allowable values, and sometimes its special capabilities can be a handicap.

We discuss base data types here. MySQL supports many aliases for compatibility, such as INTEGER, BOOL, and NUMERIC. These are only aliases. They can be confusing, but they don't affect performance. If you create a table with an aliased data type and then examine SHOW CREATE TABLE, you'll see that MySQL reports the base type, not the alias you used.

Whole Numbers

There are two kinds of numbers: whole numbers and real numbers (numbers with a fractional part). If you're storing whole numbers, use one of the integer types: TINYINT, SMALLINT, MEDIUMINT, INT, or BIGINT. These require 8, 16, 24, 32, and 64 bits of storage space, respectively. They can store values from $-2^{(N-1)}$ to $2^{(N-1)}-1$, where N is the number of bits of storage space they use.

Integer types can optionally have the UNSIGNED attribute, which disallows negative values and approximately doubles the upper limit of positive values you can store. For example, a TINYINT UNSIGNED can store values ranging from 0 to 255 instead of from –128 to 127.

Signed and unsigned types use the same amount of storage space and have the same performance, so use whatever's best for your data range.

Your choice determines how MySQL *stores* the data, in memory and on disk. However, integer *computations* generally use 64-bit BIGINT integers, even on 32-bit architectures. (The exceptions are some aggregate functions, which use DECIMAL or DOUBLE to perform computations.)

MySQL lets you specify a "width" for integer types, such as INT(11). This is meaningless for most applications: it does not restrict the legal range of values, but simply specifies the number of characters MySQL's interactive tools (such as the command-line client) will reserve for display purposes. For storage and computational purposes, INT(1) is identical to INT(20).

 Third-party storage engines, such as Infobright, sometimes have their own storage formats and compression schemes, and don't necessarily use those that are common to MySQL's built-in storage engines.

Real Numbers

Real numbers are numbers that have a fractional part. However, they aren't just for fractional numbers; you can also use DECIMAL to store integers that are so large they don't fit in BIGINT. MySQL supports both exact and inexact types.

The FLOAT and DOUBLE types support approximate calculations with standard floating-point math. If you need to know exactly how floating-point results are calculated, you will need to research your platform's floating-point implementation.

The DECIMAL type is for storing exact fractional numbers. In MySQL 5.0 and newer, the DECIMAL type supports exact math. MySQL 4.1 and earlier used floating-point math to perform computations on DECIMAL values, which could give strange results because of loss of precision. In these versions of MySQL, DECIMAL was only a "storage type."

The server itself performs DECIMAL math in MySQL 5.0 and newer, because CPUs don't support the computations directly. Floating-point math is significantly faster, because the CPU performs the computations natively.

Both floating-point and DECIMAL types let you specify a precision. For a DECIMAL column, you can specify the maximum allowed digits before and after the decimal point. This influences the column's space consumption. MySQL 5.0 and newer pack the digits into a binary string (nine digits per four bytes). For example, DECIMAL(18, 9) will store nine digits from each side of the decimal point, using nine bytes in total: four for the digits before the decimal point, one for the decimal point itself, and four for the digits after the decimal point.

A DECIMAL number in MySQL 5.0 and newer can have up to 65 digits. Earlier MySQL versions had a limit of 254 digits and stored the values as unpacked strings (one byte per digit). However, these versions of MySQL couldn't actually use such large numbers in computations, because DECIMAL was just a storage format; DECIMAL numbers were converted to DOUBLEs for computational purposes,

You can specify a floating-point column's desired precision in a couple of ways, which can cause MySQL to silently choose a different data type or to round values when you store them. These precision specifiers are nonstandard, so we suggest that you specify the type you want but not the precision.

Floating-point types typically use less space than DECIMAL to store the same range of values. A FLOAT column uses four bytes of storage. DOUBLE consumes eight bytes and has greater precision and a larger range of values than FLOAT. As with integers, you're choosing only the storage type; MySQL uses DOUBLE for its internal calculations on floating-point types.

Because of the additional space requirements and computational cost, you should use DECIMAL only when you need exact results for fractional numbers—for example, when storing financial data. But in some high-volume cases it actually makes sense to use a BIGINT instead, and store the data as some multiple of the smallest fraction of currency

---

you need to handle. Suppose you are required to store financial data to the ten-thousandth of a cent. You can multiply all dollar amounts by a million and store the result in a BIGINT, avoiding both the imprecision of floating-point storage and the cost of the precise DECIMAL math.

String Types

MySQL supports quite a few string data types, with many variations on each. These data types changed greatly in versions 4.1 and 5.0, which makes them even more complicated. Since MySQL 4.1, each string column can have its own character set and set of sorting rules for that character set, or *collation* (see Chapter 7 for more on these topics). This can impact performance greatly.

VARCHAR and CHAR types

The two major string types are VARCHAR and CHAR, which store character values. Unfortunately, it's hard to explain exactly how these values are stored on disk and in memory, because the implementations are storage engine–dependent. We assume you are using InnoDB and/or MyISAM. If not, you should read the documentation for your storage engine.

Let's take a look at how VARCHAR and CHAR values are typically stored on disk. Be aware that a storage engine may store a CHAR or VARCHAR value differently in memory from how it stores that value on disk, and that the server may translate the value into yet another storage format when it retrieves it from the storage engine. Here's a general comparison of the two types:

VARCHAR

VARCHAR stores variable-length character strings and is the most common string data type. It can require less storage space than fixed-length types, because it uses only as much space as it needs (i.e., less space is used to store shorter values). The exception is a MyISAM table created with ROW_FORMAT=FIXED, which uses a fixed amount of space on disk for each row and can thus waste space.

VARCHAR uses 1 or 2 extra bytes to record the value's length: 1 byte if the column's maximum length is 255 bytes or less, and 2 bytes if it's more. Assuming the latin1 character set, a VARCHAR(10) will use up to 11 bytes of storage space. A VARCHAR(1000) can use up to 1002 bytes, because it needs 2 bytes to store length information.

VARCHAR helps performance because it saves space. However, because the rows are variable-length, they can grow when you update them, which can cause extra work. If a row grows and no longer fits in its original location, the behavior is storage engine–dependent. For example, MyISAM may fragment the row, and InnoDB may need to split the page to fit the row into it. Other storage engines may never update data in-place at all.

It's usually worth using VARCHAR when the maximum column length is much larger than the average length; when updates to the field are rare, so fragmentation is not a problem; and when you're using a complex character set such as UTF-8, where each character uses a variable number of bytes of storage.

In version 5.0 and newer, MySQL preserves trailing spaces when you store and retrieve values. In versions 4.1 and older, MySQL strips trailing spaces.

It's trickier with InnoDB, which can store long VARCHAR values as BLOBs. We discuss this later.

CHAR

CHAR is fixed-length: MySQL always allocates enough space for the specified number of characters. When storing a CHAR value, MySQL removes any trailing spaces. (This was also true of VARCHAR in MySQL 4.1 and older versions—CHAR and VAR CHAR were logically identical and differed only in storage format.) Values are padded with spaces as needed for comparisons.

CHAR is useful if you want to store very short strings, or if all the values are nearly the same length. For example, CHAR is a good choice for MD5 values for user passwords, which are always the same length. CHAR is also better than VARCHAR for data that's changed frequently, because a fixed-length row is not prone to fragmentation. For very short columns, CHAR is also more efficient than VARCHAR; a CHAR(1) designed to hold only Y and N values will use only one byte in a single-byte character set,[1] but a VARCHAR(1) would use two bytes because of the length byte.

This behavior can be a little confusing, so we'll illustrate with an example. First, we create a table with a single CHAR(10) column and store some values in it:

```
mysql> CREATE TABLE char_test( char_col CHAR(10));
mysql> INSERT INTO char_test(char_col) VALUES
    -> ('string1'), ('  string2'), ('string3 ');
```

When we retrieve the values, the trailing spaces have been stripped away:

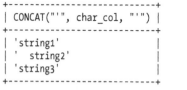

```
mysql> SELECT CONCAT("'", char_col, "'") FROM char_test;
+---------------------------+
| CONCAT("'", char_col, "'") |
+---------------------------+
| 'string1'                 |
| '  string2'               |
| 'string3'                 |
+---------------------------+
```

If we store the same values into a VARCHAR(10) column, we get the following result upon retrieval:

---

1. Remember that the length is specified in characters, not bytes. A multibyte character set can require more than one byte to store each character.

```
mysql> SELECT CONCAT("'", varchar_col, "'") FROM varchar_test;
+------------------------------+
| CONCAT("'", varchar_col, "'") |
+------------------------------+
| 'string1'                    |
| '  string2'                  |
| 'string3 '                   |
+------------------------------+
```

How data is stored is up to the storage engines, and not all storage engines handle fixed-length and variable-length data the same way. The Memory storage engine uses fixed-size rows, so it has to allocate the maximum possible space for each value even when it's a variable-length field.[2] However, the padding and trimming behavior is consistent across storage engines, because the MySQL server itself handles that.

The sibling types for CHAR and VARCHAR are BINARY and VARBINARY, which store binary strings. Binary strings are very similar to conventional strings, but they store bytes instead of characters. Padding is also different: MySQL pads BINARY values with \0 (the zero byte) instead of spaces and doesn't strip the pad value on retrieval.[3]

These types are useful when you need to store binary data and want MySQL to compare the values as bytes instead of characters. The advantage of byte-wise comparisons is more than just a matter of case insensitivity. MySQL literally compares BINARY strings one byte at a time, according to the numeric value of each byte. As a result, binary comparisons can be much simpler than character comparisons, so they are faster.

Generosity Can Be Unwise

Storing the value 'hello' requires the same amount of space in a VARCHAR(5) and a VARCHAR(200) column. Is there any advantage to using the shorter column?

As it turns out, there is a big advantage. The larger column can use much more memory, because MySQL often allocates fixed-size chunks of memory to hold values internally. This is especially bad for sorting or operations that use in-memory temporary tables. The same thing happens with filesorts that use on-disk temporary tables.

The best strategy is to allocate only as much space as you really need.

BLOB and TEXT types

BLOB and TEXT are string data types designed to store large amounts of data as either binary or character strings, respectively.

---

2. The Memory engine in Percona Server supports variable-length rows.

3. Be careful with the BINARY type if the value must remain unchanged after retrieval. MySQL will pad it to the required length with \0s.

In fact, they are each families of data types: the character types are TINYTEXT, SMALL
TEXT, TEXT, MEDIUMTEXT, and LONGTEXT, and the binary types are TINYBLOB, SMALLBLOB,
BLOB, MEDIUMBLOB, and LONGBLOB. BLOB is a synonym for SMALLBLOB, and TEXT is a synonym
for SMALLTEXT.

Unlike with all other data types, MySQL handles each BLOB and TEXT value as an object
with its own identity. Storage engines often store them specially; InnoDB may use a
separate "external" storage area for them when they're large. Each value requires from
one to four bytes of storage space in the row and enough space in external storage to
actually hold the value.

The only difference between the BLOB and TEXT families is that BLOB types store binary
data with no collation or character set, but TEXT types have a character set and collation.

MySQL sorts BLOB and TEXT columns differently from other types: instead of sorting the
full length of the string, it sorts only the first max_sort_length bytes of such columns.
If you need to sort by only the first few characters, you can either decrease the
max_sort_length server variable or use ORDER BY SUBSTRING(column, length).

MySQL can't index the full length of these data types and can't use the indexes for
sorting. (You'll find more on these topics in the next chapter.)

On-Disk Temporary Tables and Sort Files

Because the Memory storage engine doesn't support the BLOB and TEXT types, queries
that use BLOB or TEXT columns and need an implicit temporary table will have to use on-
disk MyISAM temporary tables, even for only a few rows. (Percona Server's Memory
storage engine supports the BLOB and TEXT types, but at the time of writing, it doesn't
yet prevent on-disk tables from being used.)

This can result in a serious performance overhead. Even if you configure MySQL to
store temporary tables on a RAM disk, many expensive operating system calls will be
required.

The best solution is to avoid using the BLOB and TEXT types unless you really need them.
If you can't avoid them, you may be able to use the SUBSTRING(column, length) trick
everywhere a BLOB column is mentioned (including in the ORDER BY clause) to convert
the values to character strings, which will permit in-memory temporary tables. Just be
sure that you're using a short enough substring that the temporary table doesn't grow
larger than max_heap_table_size or tmp_table_size, or MySQL will convert the table
to an on-disk MyISAM table.

The worst-case length allocation also applies to sorting of values, so this trick can help
with both kinds of problems: creating large temporary tables and sort files, and creating
them on disk.

Here's an example. Suppose you have a table with 10 million rows, which uses a couple of gigabytes on disk. It has a VARCHAR(1000) column with the utf8 character set. This can use up to 3 bytes per character, for a worst-case size of 3,000 bytes. If you mention this column in your ORDER BY clause, a query against the whole table can require over 30 GB of temporary space just for the sort files!

If the Extra column of EXPLAIN contains "Using temporary," the query uses an implicit temporary table.

Using ENUM instead of a string type

Sometimes you can use an ENUM column instead of conventional string types. An ENUM column can store a predefined set of distinct string values. MySQL stores them very compactly, packed into one or two bytes depending on the number of values in the list. It stores each value internally as an integer representing its position in the field definition list, and it keeps the "lookup table" that defines the number-to-string correspondence in the table's *.frm* file. Here's an example:

```
mysql> CREATE TABLE enum_test(
    ->     e ENUM('fish', 'apple', 'dog') NOT NULL
    -> );
mysql> INSERT INTO enum_test(e) VALUES('fish'), ('dog'), ('apple');
```

The three rows actually store integers, not strings. You can see the dual nature of the values by retrieving them in a numeric context:

```
mysql> SELECT e + 0 FROM enum_test;
+-------+
| e + 0 |
+-------+
|     1 |
|     3 |
|     2 |
+-------+
```

This duality can be terribly confusing if you specify numbers for your ENUM constants, as in ENUM('1', '2', '3'). We suggest you don't do this.

Another surprise is that an ENUM field sorts by the internal integer values, not by the strings themselves:

```
mysql> SELECT e FROM enum_test ORDER BY e;
+-------+
| e     |
+-------+
| fish  |
| apple |
| dog   |
+-------+
```

You can work around this by specifying ENUM members in the order in which you want them to sort. You can also use FIELD() to specify a sort order explicitly in your queries, but this prevents MySQL from using the index for sorting:

```
mysql> SELECT e FROM enum_test ORDER BY FIELD(e, 'apple', 'dog', 'fish');
+-------+
| e     |
+-------+
| apple |
| dog   |
| fish  |
+-------+
```

If we'd defined the values in alphabetical order, we wouldn't have needed to do that.

The biggest downside of ENUM is that the list of strings is fixed, and adding or removing strings requires the use of ALTER TABLE. Thus, it might not be a good idea to use ENUM as a string data type when the list of allowed string values is likely to change arbitrarily in the future, unless it's acceptable to add them at the end of the list, which can be done without a full rebuild of the table in MySQL 5.1.

Because MySQL stores each value as an integer and has to do a lookup to convert it to its string representation, ENUM columns have some overhead. This is usually offset by their smaller size, but not always. In particular, it can be slower to join a CHAR or VARCHAR column to an ENUM column than to another CHAR or VARCHAR column.

To illustrate, we benchmarked how quickly MySQL performs such a join on a table in one of our applications. The table has a fairly wide primary key:

```
CREATE TABLE webservicecalls (
    day date NOT NULL,
    account smallint NOT NULL,
    service varchar(10) NOT NULL,
    method varchar(50) NOT NULL,
    calls int NOT NULL,
    items int NOT NULL,
    time float NOT NULL,
    cost decimal(9,5) NOT NULL,
    updated datetime,
    PRIMARY KEY (day, account, service, method)
) ENGINE=InnoDB;
```

The table contains about 110,000 rows and is only about 10 MB, so it fits entirely in memory. The service column contains 5 distinct values with an average length of 4 characters, and the method column contains 71 values with an average length of 20 characters.

We made a copy of this table and converted the service and method columns to ENUM, as follows:

```
CREATE TABLE webservicecalls_enum (
    ... omitted ...
    service ENUM(...values omitted...) NOT NULL,
    method ENUM(...values omitted...) NOT NULL,
```

```
    ... omitted ...
) ENGINE=InnoDB;
```

We then measured the performance of joining the tables by the primary key columns. Here is the query we used:

```
mysql> SELECT SQL_NO_CACHE COUNT(*)
    -> FROM webservicecalls
    ->     JOIN webservicecalls USING(day, account, service, method);
```

We varied this query to join the VARCHAR and ENUM columns in different combinations. Table 4-1 shows the results.

Table 4-1. Speed of joining VARCHAR and ENUM columns

Test	Queries per second
VARCHAR joined to VARCHAR	2.6
VARCHAR joined to ENUM	1.7
ENUM joined to VARCHAR	1.8
ENUM joined to ENUM	3.5

The join is faster after converting the columns to ENUM, but joining the ENUM columns to VARCHAR columns is slower. In this case, it looks like a good idea to convert these columns, as long as they don't have to be joined to VARCHAR columns. It's a common design practice to use "lookup tables" with integer primary keys to avoid using character-based values in joins.

However, there's another benefit to converting the columns: according to the Data_length column from SHOW TABLE STATUS, converting these two columns to ENUM made the table about 1/3 smaller. In some cases, this might be beneficial even if the ENUM columns have to be joined to VARCHAR columns. Also, the primary key itself is only about half the size after the conversion. Because this is an InnoDB table, if there are any other indexes on this table, reducing the primary key size will make them much smaller, too. We explain this in the next chapter.

Date and Time Types

MySQL has many types for various kinds of date and time values, such as YEAR and DATE. The finest granularity of time MySQL can store is one second. (MariaDB has microsecond-granularity temporal types.) However, it can do temporal *computations* with microsecond granularity, and we'll show you how to work around the storage limitations.

Most of the temporal types have no alternatives, so there is no question of which one is the best choice. The only question is what to do when you need to store both the date and the time. MySQL offers two very similar data types for this purpose: DATE

TIME and TIMESTAMP. For many applications, either will work, but in some cases, one works better than the other. Let's take a look:

DATETIME

This type can hold a large range of values, from the year 1001 to the year 9999, with a precision of one second. It stores the date and time packed into an integer in YYYYMMDDHHMMSS format, independent of time zone. This uses eight bytes of storage space.

By default, MySQL displays DATETIME values in a sortable, unambiguous format, such as 2008-01-16 22:37:08. This is the ANSI standard way to represent dates and times.

TIMESTAMP

As its name implies, the TIMESTAMP type stores the number of seconds elapsed since midnight, January 1, 1970, Greenwich Mean Time (GMT)—the same as a Unix timestamp. TIMESTAMP uses only four bytes of storage, so it has a much smaller range than DATETIME: from the year 1970 to partway through the year 2038. MySQL provides the FROM_UNIXTIME() and UNIX_TIMESTAMP() functions to convert a Unix timestamp to a date, and vice versa.

MySQL 4.1 and newer versions format TIMESTAMP values just like DATETIME values, but MySQL 4.0 and older versions display them without any punctuation between the parts. This is only a display formatting difference; the TIMESTAMP storage format is the same in all MySQL versions.

The value a TIMESTAMP displays also depends on the time zone. The MySQL server, operating system, and client connections all have time zone settings.

Thus, a TIMESTAMP that stores the value 0 actually displays it as 1969-12-31 19:00:00 in Eastern Standard Time (EST), which has a five-hour offset from GMT. It's worth emphasizing this difference: if you store or access data from multiple time zones, the behavior of TIMESTAMP and DATETIME will be very different. The former preserves values relative to the time zone in use, while the latter preserves the textual representation of the date and time.

TIMESTAMP also has special properties that DATETIME doesn't have. By default, MySQL will set the first TIMESTAMP column to the current time when you insert a row without specifying a value for the column.[4] MySQL also updates the first TIMESTAMP column's value by default when you update the row, unless you assign a value explicitly in the UPDATE statement. You can configure the insertion and update behaviors for any TIMESTAMP column. Finally, TIMESTAMP columns are NOT NULL by default, which is different from every other data type.

---

4. The rules for TIMESTAMP behavior are complex and have changed in various MySQL versions, so you should verify that you are getting the behavior you want. It's usually a good idea to examine the output of SHOW CREATE TABLE after making changes to TIMESTAMP columns.

Special behavior aside, in general if you can use TIMESTAMP you should, because it is more space-efficient than DATETIME. Sometimes people store Unix timestamps as integer values, but this usually doesn't gain you anything. The integer format is often less convenient to deal with, so we do not recommend doing this.

What if you need to store a date and time value with subsecond resolution? MySQL currently does not have an appropriate data type for this, but you can use your own storage format: you can use the BIGINT data type and store the value as a timestamp in microseconds, or you can use a DOUBLE and store the fractional part of the second after the decimal point. Both approaches will work well. Or you can use MariaDB instead of MySQL.

Bit-Packed Data Types

MySQL has a few storage types that use individual bits within a value to store data compactly. All of these types are technically string types, regardless of the underlying storage format and manipulations:

BIT

Before MySQL 5.0, BIT is just a synonym for TINYINT. But in MySQL 5.0 and newer, it's a completely different data type with special characteristics. We discuss the new behavior here.

You can use a BIT column to store one or many true/false values in a single column. BIT(1) defines a field that contains a single bit, BIT(2) stores 2 bits, and so on; the maximum length of a BIT column is 64 bits.

BIT behavior varies between storage engines. MyISAM packs the columns together for storage purposes, so 17 individual BIT columns require only 17 bits to store (assuming none of the columns permits NULL). MyISAM rounds that to three bytes for storage. Other storage engines, such as Memory and InnoDB, store each column as the smallest integer type large enough to contain the bits, so you don't save any storage space.

MySQL treats BIT as a string type, not a numeric type. When you retrieve a BIT (1) value, the result is a string but the contents are the binary value 0 or 1, not the ASCII value "0" or "1". However, if you retrieve the value in a numeric context, the result is the number to which the bit string converts. Keep this in mind if you need to compare the result to another value. For example, if you store the value b'00111001' (which is the binary equivalent of 57) into a BIT(8) column and retrieve it, you will get the string containing the character code 57. This happens to be the ASCII character code for "9". But in a numeric context, you'll get the value 57:

```
mysql> CREATE TABLE bittest(a bit(8));
mysql> INSERT INTO bittest VALUES(b'00111001');
mysql> SELECT a, a + 0 FROM bittest;
```

```
+------+-------+
| a    | a + 0 |
+------+-------+
| 9    |    57 |
+------+-------+
```

This can be very confusing, so we recommend that you use BIT with caution. For most applications, we think it is a better idea to avoid this type.

If you want to store a true/false value in a single bit of storage space, another option is to create a nullable CHAR(0) column. This column is capable of storing either the absence of a value (NULL) or a zero-length value (the empty string).

SET

If you need to store many true/false values, consider combining many columns into one with MySQL's native SET data type, which MySQL represents internally as a packed set of bits. It uses storage efficiently, and MySQL has functions such as FIND_IN_SET() and FIELD() that make it easy to use in queries. The major drawback is the cost of changing the column's definition: this requires an ALTER TABLE, which is very expensive on large tables (but see the workaround later in this chapter). In general, you also can't use indexes for lookups on SET columns.

Bitwise operations on integer columns

An alternative to SET is to use an integer as a packed set of bits. For example, you can pack eight bits in a TINYINT and manipulate them with bitwise operators. You can make this easier by defining named constants for each bit in your application code.

The major advantage of this approach over SET is that you can change the "enumeration" the field represents without an ALTER TABLE. The drawback is that your queries are harder to write and understand (what does it mean when bit 5 is set?). Some people are comfortable with bitwise manipulations and some aren't, so whether you'll want to try this technique is largely a matter of taste.

An example application for packed bits is an access control list (ACL) that stores permissions. Each bit or SET element represents a value such as CAN_READ, CAN_WRITE, or CAN_DELETE. If you use a SET column, you'll let MySQL store the bit-to-value mapping in the column definition; if you use an integer column, you'll store the mapping in your application code. Here's what the queries would look like with a SET column:

```
mysql> CREATE TABLE acl (
    ->    perms SET('CAN_READ', 'CAN_WRITE', 'CAN_DELETE') NOT NULL
    -> );
mysql> INSERT INTO acl(perms) VALUES ('CAN_READ,CAN_DELETE');
mysql> SELECT perms FROM acl WHERE FIND_IN_SET('AN_READ', perms);
+---------------------+
| perms               |
+---------------------+
| CAN_READ,CAN_DELETE |
+---------------------+
```

If you used an integer, you could write that example as follows:

```
mysql> SET @CAN_READ    := 1 << 0,
    ->     @CAN_WRITE   := 1 << 1,
    ->     @CAN_DELETE  := 1 << 2;
mysql> CREATE TABLE acl (
    ->    perms TINYINT UNSIGNED NOT NULL DEFAULT 0
    -> );
mysql> INSERT INTO acl(perms) VALUES(@CAN_READ + @CAN_DELETE);
mysql> SELECT perms FROM acl WHERE perms & @CAN_READ;
+-------+
| perms |
+-------+
|     5 |
+-------+
```

We've used variables to define the values, but you can use constants in your code instead.

Choosing Identifiers

Choosing a good data type for an identifier column is very important. You're more likely to compare these columns to other values (for example, in joins) and to use them for lookups than other columns. You're also likely to use them in other tables as foreign keys, so when you choose a data type for an identifier column, you're probably choosing the type in related tables as well. (As we demonstrated earlier in this chapter, it's a good idea to use the same data types in related tables, because you're likely to use them for joins.)

When choosing a type for an identifier column, you need to consider not only the storage type, but also how MySQL performs computations and comparisons on that type. For example, MySQL stores ENUM and SET types internally as integers but converts them to strings when doing comparisons in a string context.

Once you choose a type, make sure you use the same type in all related tables. The types should match exactly, including properties such as UNSIGNED.[5] Mixing different data types can cause performance problems, and even if it doesn't, implicit type conversions during comparisons can create hard-to-find errors. These may even crop up much later, after you've forgotten that you're comparing different data types.

Choose the smallest size that can hold your required range of values, and leave room for future growth if necessary. For example, if you have a state_id column that stores US state names, you don't need thousands or millions of values, so don't use an INT. A TINYINT should be sufficient and is three bytes smaller. If you use this value as a foreign key in other tables, three bytes can make a big difference. Here are a few tips:

---

5. If you're using the InnoDB storage engine, you may not be able to create foreign keys unless the data types match exactly. The resulting error message, "ERROR 1005 (HY000): Can't create table," can be confusing depending on the context, and questions about it come up often on MySQL mailing lists. (Oddly, you can create foreign keys between VARCHAR columns of different lengths.)

Integer types

Integers are usually the best choice for identifiers, because they're fast and they work with `AUTO_INCREMENT`.

`ENUM` *and* `SET`

The `ENUM` and `SET` types are generally a poor choice for identifiers, though they can be okay for static "definition tables" that contain status or "type" values. `ENUM` and `SET` columns are appropriate for holding information such as an order's status, a product's type, or a person's gender.

As an example, if you use an `ENUM` field to define a product's type, you might want a lookup table primary keyed on an identical `ENUM` field. (You could add columns to the lookup table for descriptive text, to generate a glossary, or to provide meaningful labels in a pull-down menu on a website.) In this case, you'll want to use the `ENUM` as an identifier, but for most purposes you should avoid doing so.

String types

Avoid string types for identifiers if possible, because they take up a lot of space and are generally slower than integer types. Be especially cautious when using string identifiers with MyISAM tables. MyISAM uses packed indexes for strings by default, which can make lookups much slower. In our tests, we've noted up to six times slower performance with packed indexes on MyISAM.

You should also be very careful with completely "random" strings, such as those produced by `MD5()`, `SHA1()`, or `UUID()`. Each new value you generate with them will be distributed in arbitrary ways over a large space, which can slow `INSERT` and some types of `SELECT` queries:[6]

- They slow `INSERT` queries because the inserted value has to go in a random location in indexes. This causes page splits, random disk accesses, and clustered index fragmentation for clustered storage engines. More about this in the next chapter.

- They slow `SELECT` queries because logically adjacent rows will be widely dispersed on disk and in memory.

- Random values cause caches to perform poorly for all types of queries because they defeat locality of reference, which is how caching works. If the entire dataset is equally "hot," there is no advantage to having any particular part of the data cached in memory, and if the working set does not fit in memory, the cache will have a lot of flushes and misses.

If you do store UUID values, you should remove the dashes or, even better, convert the UUID values to 16-byte numbers with `UNHEX()` and store them in a `BINARY(16)` column. You can retrieve the values in hexadecimal format with the `HEX()` function.

---

6. On the other hand, for some very large tables with many writers, such pseudorandom values can actually help eliminate "hot spots."

Values generated by UUID() have different characteristics from those generated by a cryptographic hash function such as SHA1(): the UUID values are unevenly distributed and are somewhat sequential. They're still not as good as a monotonically increasing integer, though.

Beware of Autogenerated Schemas

We've covered the most important data type considerations (some with serious and others with more minor performance implications), but we haven't yet told you about the evils of autogenerated schemas.

Badly written schema migration programs and programs that autogenerate schemas can cause severe performance problems. Some programs use large VARCHAR fields for *everything*, or use different data types for columns that will be compared in joins. Be sure to double-check a schema if it was created for you automatically.

Object-relational mapping (ORM) systems (and the "frameworks" that use them) are another frequent performance nightmare. Some of these systems let you store any type of data in any type of backend data store, which usually means they aren't designed to use the strengths of any of the data stores. Sometimes they store each property of each object in a separate row, even using timestamp-based versioning, so there are multiple versions of each property!

This design may appeal to developers, because it lets them work in an object-oriented fashion without needing to think about how the data is stored. However, applications that "hide complexity from developers" usually don't scale well. We suggest you think carefully before trading performance for developer productivity, and always test on a realistically large dataset, so you don't discover performance problems too late.

Special Types of Data

Some kinds of data don't correspond directly to the available built-in types. A time-stamp with subsecond resolution is one example; we showed you some options for storing such data earlier in the chapter.

Another example is an IPv4 address. People often use VARCHAR(15) columns to store IP addresses. However, they are really unsigned 32-bit integers, not strings. The dotted-quad notation is just a way of writing it out so that humans can read it more easily. You should store IP addresses as unsigned integers. MySQL provides the INET_ATON() and INET_NTOA() functions to convert between the two representations.

Schema Design Gotchas in MySQL

Although there are universally bad and good design principles, there are also issues that arise from how MySQL is implemented, and that means you can make MySQL-specific mistakes, too. This section discusses problems that we've observed in schema designs with MySQL. It might help you avoid those mistakes and choose alternatives that work better with MySQL's specific implementation.

Too many columns

MySQL's storage engine API works by copying rows between the server and the storage engine in a row buffer format; the server then decodes the buffer into columns. But it can be costly to turn the row buffer into the row data structure with the decoded columns. MyISAM's fixed row format actually matches the server's row format exactly, so no conversion is needed. However, MyISAM's variable row format and InnoDB's row format always require conversion. The cost of this conversion depends on the number of columns. We discovered that this can become expensive when we investigated an issue with high CPU consumption for a customer with extremely wide tables (hundreds of columns), even though only a few columns were actually used. If you're planning for hundreds of columns, be aware that the server's performance characteristics will be a bit different.

Too many joins

The so-called entity-attribute-value (EAV) design pattern is a classic case of a universally bad design pattern that especially doesn't work well in MySQL. MySQL has a limitation of 61 tables per join, and EAV databases require many self-joins. We've seen more than a few EAV databases eventually exceed this limit. Even at many fewer joins than 61, however, the cost of planning and optimizing the query can become problematic for MySQL. As a rough rule of thumb, it's better to have a dozen or fewer tables per query if you need queries to execute very fast with high concurrency.

The all-powerful ENUM

Beware of overusing ENUM. Here's an example we saw:

```
CREATE TABLE ... (
    country enum('','0','1','2',...,'31')
```

The schema was sprinkled liberally with this pattern. This would probably be a questionable design decision in any database with an enumerated value type, because it really should be an integer that is foreign-keyed to a "dictionary" or "lookup" table anyway. But in MySQL, you can't add a new country to the list without an ALTER TABLE, which is a blocking operation in MySQL 5.0 and earlier, and even in 5.1 and newer if you add the value anywhere but at the end of the list. (We'll show some hacks to address this later, but they're just hacks.)

The ENUM *in disguise*

An ENUM permits the column to hold one value from a set of defined values. A SET permits the column to hold one or more values from a set of defined values. Sometimes these can be easy to confuse. Here's an example:

```
CREATE TABLE ...(
    is_default set('Y','N') NOT NULL default 'N'
```

That almost surely ought to be an ENUM instead of a SET, assuming that it can't be both true and false at the same time.

NULL *not invented here*

We wrote earlier about the benefits of avoiding NULL, and indeed we suggest considering alternatives when possible. Even when you do need to store a "no value" fact in a table, you might not need to use NULL. Perhaps you can use zero, a special value, or an empty string instead.

However, you can take this to extremes. Don't be too afraid of using NULL when you need to represent an unknown value. In some cases, it's better to use NULL than a magical constant. Selecting one value from the domain of a constrained type, such as using –1 to represent an unknown integer, can complicate your code a lot, introduce bugs, and just generally make a total mess out of things. Handling NULL isn't always easy, but it's often better than the alternative.

Here's one example we've seen pretty frequently:

```
CREATE TABLE ... (
    dt DATETIME NOT NULL DEFAULT '0000-00-00 00:00:00'
```

That bogus all-zeros value can cause lots of problems. (You can configure MySQL's SQL_MODE to disallow nonsense dates, which is an especially good practice for a new application that hasn't yet created a database full of bad data.)

On a related topic, MySQL does index NULLs, unlike Oracle, which doesn't include non-values in indexes.

Normalization and Denormalization

There are usually many ways to represent any given data, ranging from fully normalized to fully denormalized and anything in between. In a normalized database, each fact is represented once and only once. Conversely, in a denormalized database, information is duplicated, or stored in multiple places.

If you're not familiar with normalization, you should study it. There are many good books on the topic and resources online; here, we just give a brief introduction to the aspects you need to know for this chapter. Let's start with the classic example of employees, departments, and department heads:

EMPLOYEE	DEPARTMENT	HEAD
Jones	Accounting	Jones
Smith	Engineering	Smith
Brown	Accounting	Jones
Green	Engineering	Smith

The problem with this schema is that inconsistencies can occur while the data is being modified. Say Brown takes over as the head of the Accounting department. We need to update multiple rows to reflect this change, and that's a pain and introduces opportunities for error. If the "Jones" row says the head of the department is something different from the "Brown" row, there's no way to know which is right. It's like the old saying, "A person with two watches never knows what time it is." Furthermore, we can't represent a department without employees—if we delete all employees in the Accounting department, we lose all records about the department itself. To avoid these problems, we need to normalize the table by separating the employee and department entities. This process results in the following two tables for employees:

EMPLOYEE_NAME	DEPARTMENT
Jones	Accounting
Smith	Engineering
Brown	Accounting
Green	Engineering

and departments:

DEPARTMENT	HEAD
Accounting	Jones
Engineering	Smith

These tables are now in second normal form, which is good enough for many purposes. However, second normal form is only one of many possible normal forms.

 We're using the last name as the primary key here for purposes of illustration, because it's the "natural identifier" of the data. In practice, however, we wouldn't do that. It's not guaranteed to be unique, and it's usually a bad idea to use a long string for a primary key.

Pros and Cons of a Normalized Schema

People who ask for help with performance issues are frequently advised to normalize their schemas, especially if the workload is write-heavy. This is often good advice. It works well for the following reasons:

- Normalized updates are usually faster than denormalized updates.
- When the data is well normalized, there's little or no duplicated data, so there's less data to change.
- Normalized tables are usually smaller, so they fit better in memory and perform better.

- The lack of redundant data means there's less need for `DISTINCT` or `GROUP BY` queries when retrieving lists of values. Consider the preceding example: it's impossible to get a distinct list of departments from the denormalized schema without `DISTINCT` or `GROUP BY`, but if `DEPARTMENT` is a separate table, it's a trivial query.

The drawbacks of a normalized schema usually have to do with retrieval. Any nontrivial query on a well-normalized schema will probably require at least one join, and perhaps several. This is not only expensive, but it can make some indexing strategies impossible. For example, normalizing may place columns in different tables that would benefit from belonging to the same index.

Pros and Cons of a Denormalized Schema

A denormalized schema works well because everything is in the same table, which avoids joins.

If you don't need to join tables, the worst case for most queries—even the ones that don't use indexes—is a full table scan. This can be much faster than a join when the data doesn't fit in memory, because it avoids random I/O.

A single table can also allow more efficient indexing strategies. Suppose you have a website where users post their messages, and some users are premium users. Now say you want to view the last 10 messages from premium users. If you've normalized the schema and indexed the publishing dates of the messages, the query might look like this:

```
mysql> SELECT message_text, user_name
    -> FROM message
    ->    INNER JOIN user ON message.user_id=user.id
    -> WHERE user.account_type='premiumv
    -> ORDER BY message.published DESC LIMIT 10;
```

To execute this query efficiently, MySQL will need to scan the `published` index on the `message` table. For each row it finds, it will need to probe into the `user` table and check whether the user is a premium user. This is inefficient if only a small fraction of users have premium accounts.

The other possible query plan is to start with the `user` table, select all premium users, get all messages for them, and do a filesort. This will probably be even worse.

The problem is the join, which is keeping you from sorting and filtering simultaneously with a single index. If you denormalize the data by combining the tables and add an index on (`account_type, published`), you can write the query without a join. This will be very efficient:

```
mysql> SELECT message_text,user_name
    -> FROM user_messages
    -> WHERE account_type='premium'
    -> ORDER BY published DESC
    -> LIMIT 10;
```

A Mixture of Normalized and Denormalized

Given that both normalized and denormalized schemas have benefits and drawbacks, how can you choose the best design?

The truth is, fully normalized and fully denormalized schemas are like laboratory rats: they usually have little to do with the real world. In the real world, you often need to mix the approaches, possibly using a partially normalized schema, cache tables, and other techniques.

The most common way to denormalize data is to duplicate, or cache, selected columns from one table in another table. In MySQL 5.0 and newer, you can use triggers to update the cached values, which makes the implementation easier.

In our website example, for instance, instead of denormalizing fully you can store account_type in both the user and message tables. This avoids the insert and delete problems that come with full denormalization, because you never lose information about the user, even when there are no messages. It won't make the user_message table much larger, but it will let you select the data efficiently.

However, it's now more expensive to update a user's account type, because you have to change it in both tables. To see whether that's a problem, you must consider how frequently you'll have to make such changes and how long they will take, compared to how often you'll run the SELECT query.

Another good reason to move some data from the parent table to the child table is for sorting. For example, it would be extremely expensive to sort messages by the author's name on a normalized schema, but you can perform such a sort very efficiently if you cache the author_name in the message table and index it.

It can also be useful to cache derived values. If you need to display how many messages each user has posted (as many forums do), either you can run an expensive subquery to count the data every time you display it, or you can have a num_messages column in the user table that you update whenever a user posts a new message.

Cache and Summary Tables

Sometimes the best way to improve performance is to keep redundant data in the same table as the data from which it was derived. However, sometimes you'll need to build completely separate summary or cache tables, specially tuned for your retrieval needs. This approach works best if you can tolerate slightly stale data, but sometimes you really don't have a choice (for instance, when you need to avoid complex and expensive real-time updates).

The terms "cache table" and "summary table" don't have standardized meanings. We use the term "cache tables" to refer to tables that contain data that can be easily, if more slowly, retrieved from the schema (i.e., data that is logically redundant). When we say

---

"summary tables," we mean tables that hold aggregated data from GROUP BY queries (i.e., data that is not logically redundant). Some people also use the term "roll-up tables" for these tables, because the data has been "rolled up."

Staying with the website example, suppose you need to count the number of messages posted during the previous 24 hours. It would be impossible to maintain an accurate real-time counter on a busy site. Instead, you could generate a summary table every hour. You can often do this with a single query, and it's more efficient than maintaining counters in real time. The drawback is that the counts are not 100% accurate.

If you need to get an accurate count of messages posted during the previous 24-hour period (with no staleness), there is another option. Begin with a per-hour summary table. You can then count the exact number of messages posted in a given 24-hour period by adding the number of messages in the 23 whole hours contained in that period, the partial hour at the beginning of the period, and the partial hour at the end of the period. Suppose your summary table is called msg_per_hr and is defined as follows:

```
CREATE TABLE msg_per_hr (
    hr DATETIME NOT NULL,
    cnt INT UNSIGNED NOT NULL,
    PRIMARY KEY(hr)
);
```

You can find the number of messages posted in the previous 24 hours by adding the results of the following three queries. We're using LEFT(NOW(), 14) to round the current date and time to the nearest hour:

```
mysql> SELECT SUM(cnt) FROM msg_per_hr
    -> WHERE hr BETWEEN
    ->    CONCAT(LEFT(NOW(), 14), '00:00') - INTERVAL 23 HOUR
    ->    AND CONCAT(LEFT(NOW(), 14), '00:00') - INTERVAL 1 HOUR;
mysql> SELECT COUNT(*) FROM message
    -> WHERE posted >= NOW() - INTERVAL 24 HOUR
    ->    AND posted < CONCAT(LEFT(NOW(), 14), '00:00') - INTERVAL 23 HOUR;
mysql> SELECT COUNT(*) FROM message
    -> WHERE posted >= CONCAT(LEFT(NOW(), 14), '00:00');
```

Either approach—an inexact count or an exact count with small range queries to fill in the gaps—is more efficient than counting all the rows in the message table. This is the key reason for creating summary tables. These statistics are expensive to compute in real time, because they require scanning a lot of data, or queries that will only run efficiently with special indexes that you don't want to add because of the impact they will have on updates. Computing the most active users or the most frequent "tags" are typical examples of such operations.

Cache tables, in turn, are useful for optimizing search and retrieval queries. These queries often require a particular table and index structure that is different from the one you would use for general online transaction processing (OLTP) operations.

For example, you might need many different index combinations to speed up various types of queries. These conflicting requirements sometimes demand that you create a cache table that contains only some of the columns from the main table. A useful technique is to use a different storage engine for the cache table. If the main table uses InnoDB, for example, by using MyISAM for the cache table you'll gain a smaller index footprint and the ability to do full-text search queries. Sometimes you might even want to take the table completely out of MySQL and into a specialized system that can search more efficiently, such as the Lucene or Sphinx search engines.

When using cache and summary tables, you have to decide whether to maintain their data in real time or with periodic rebuilds. Which is better will depend on your application, but a periodic rebuild not only can save resources but also can result in a more efficient table that's not fragmented and has fully sorted indexes.

When you rebuild summary and cache tables, you'll often need their data to remain available during the operation. You can achieve this by using a "shadow table," which is a table you build "behind" the real table. When you're done building it, you can swap the tables with an atomic rename. For example, if you need to rebuild my_summary, you can create my_summary_new, fill it with data, and swap it with the real table:

```
mysql> DROP TABLE IF EXISTS my_summary_new, my_summary_old;
mysql> CREATE TABLE my_summary_new LIKE my_summary;
-- populate my_summary_new as desired
mysql> RENAME TABLE my_summary TO my_summary_old, my_summary_new TO my_summary;
```

If you rename the original my_summary table my_summary_old before assigning the name my_summary to the newly rebuilt table, as we've done here, you can keep the old version until you're ready to overwrite it at the next rebuild. It's handy to have it for a quick rollback if the new table has a problem.

Materialized Views

Many database management systems, such as Oracle or Microsoft SQL Server, offer a feature called *materialized views*. These are views that are actually precomputed and stored as tables on disk, and can be refreshed and updated through various strategies. MySQL doesn't support this natively (we'll go into details about its support for views in Chapter 7). However, you can implement materialized views yourself, using Justin Swanhart's open source Flexviews tools (*http://code.google.com/p/flexviews/*). Flexviews is more sophisticated than roll-your-own solutions and offers a lot of nice features that make materialized views simpler to create and maintain. It consists of a few parts:

- A Change Data Capture (CDC) utility that reads the server's binary logs and extracts relevant changes to rows
- A set of stored procedures that help define and manage the view definitions
- Tools to apply the changes to the materialized data in the database

In contrast to typical methods of maintaining summary and cache tables, Flexviews can recalculate the contents of the materialized view incrementally by extracting delta changes to the source tables. This means it can update the view without needing to query the source data. For example, if you create a summary table that counts groups of rows, and you add a row to the source table, Flexviews simply increments the corresponding group by one. The same technique works for other aggregate functions, such as SUM() and AVG(). It takes advantage of the fact that row-based binary logging includes images of the rows before and after they are updated, so Flexviews can see not only the new value of each row, but the delta from the previous version, without even looking at the source table. Computing with deltas is much more efficient than reading the data from the source table.

We don't have space for a full exploration of how to use Flexviews, but we can give an overview. You start by writing a SELECT statement that expresses the data you want to derive from your existing database. This can include joins and aggregations (GROUP BY). There's a helper tool in Flexviews that transforms your SQL query into Flexviews API calls. Then Flexviews does all the dirty work of watching changes to the database and transforming them into updates to the tables that store your materialized view over the original tables. Now your application can simply query the materialized view instead of the tables from which it was derived.

Flexviews has good coverage of SQL, including tricky expressions that you might not expect a tool to handle outside the server. That makes it useful for building views over complex SQL expressions, so you can replace complex queries with simple, fast queries against the materialized view.

Counter Tables

An application that keeps counts in a table can run into concurrency problems when updating the counters. Such tables are very common in web applications. You can use them to cache the number of friends a user has, the number of downloads of a file, and so on. It's often a good idea to build a separate table for the counters, to keep it small and fast. Using a separate table can help you avoid query cache invalidations and lets you use some of the more advanced techniques we show in this section.

To keep things as simple as possible, suppose you have a counter table with a single row that just counts hits on your website:

```
mysql> CREATE TABLE hit_counter (
    ->     cnt int unsigned not null
    -> ) ENGINE=InnoDB;
```

Each hit on the website updates the counter:

```
mysql> UPDATE hit_counter SET cnt = cnt + 1;
```

The problem is that this single row is effectively a global "mutex" for any transaction that updates the counter. It will serialize those transactions. You can get higher concurrency by keeping more than one row and updating a random row. This requires the following change to the table:

```
mysql> CREATE TABLE hit_counter (
    ->    slot tinyint unsigned not null primary key,
    ->    cnt int unsigned not null
    -> ) ENGINE=InnoDB;
```

Prepopulate the table by adding 100 rows to it. Now the query can just choose a random slot and update it:

```
mysql> UPDATE hit_counter SET cnt = cnt + 1 WHERE slot = RAND() * 100;
```

To retrieve statistics, just use aggregate queries:

```
mysql> SELECT SUM(cnt) FROM hit_counter;
```

A common requirement is to start new counters every so often (for example, once a day). If you need to do this, you can change the schema slightly:

```
mysql> CREATE TABLE daily_hit_counter (
    ->    day date not null,
    ->    slot tinyint unsigned not null,
    ->    cnt int unsigned not null,
    ->    primary key(day, slot)
    -> ) ENGINE=InnoDB;
```

You don't want to pregenerate rows for this scenario. Instead, you can use ON DUPLICATE KEY UPDATE:

```
mysql> INSERT INTO daily_hit_counter(day, slot, cnt)
    ->    VALUES(CURRENT_DATE, RAND() * 100, 1)
    ->    ON DUPLICATE KEY UPDATE cnt = cnt + 1;
```

If you want to reduce the number of rows to keep the table smaller, you can write a periodic job that merges all the results into slot 0 and deletes every other slot:

```
mysql> UPDATE daily_hit_counter as c
    ->    INNER JOIN (
    ->       SELECT day, SUM(cnt) AS cnt, MIN(slot) AS mslot
    ->       FROM daily_hit_counter
    ->       GROUP BY day
    ->    ) AS x USING(day)
    -> SET c.cnt = IF(c.slot = x.mslot, x.cnt, 0),
    ->       c.slot = IF(c.slot = x.mslot, 0, c.slot);
mysql> DELETE FROM daily_hit_counter WHERE slot <> 0 AND cnt = 0;
```

Speeding Up ALTER TABLE

MySQL's ALTER TABLE performance can become a problem with very large tables. MySQL performs most alterations by making an empty table with the desired new structure, inserting all the data from the old table into the new one, and deleting the old table. This can take a very long time, especially if you're short on memory and the table is large and has lots of indexes. Many people have experience with ALTER TABLE operations that have taken hours or days to complete.

MySQL 5.1 and newer include support for some types of "online" operations that won't lock the table for the whole operation. Recent versions of InnoDB[7] also support building indexes by sorting, which makes building indexes much faster and results in a compact index layout.

In general, most ALTER TABLE operations will cause interruption of service in MySQL. We'll show some techniques to work around this in a bit, but those are for special cases. For the general case, you need to use either operational tricks such as swapping servers around and performing the ALTER on servers that are not in production service, or a "shadow copy" approach. The technique for a shadow copy is to build a new table with the desired structure beside the existing one, and then perform a rename and drop to swap the two. Tools can help with this: for example, the "online schema change" tools from Facebook's database operations team (*https://launchpad.net/mysqlatfacebook*), Shlomi Noach's openark toolkit (*http://code.openark.org/*), and Percona Toolkit (*http://www.percona.com/software/*). If you are using Flexviews (discussed in "Materialized Views" on page 138), you can perform nonblocking schema changes with its CDC utility too.

Not all ALTER TABLE operations cause table rebuilds. For example, you can change or drop a column's default value in two ways (one fast, and one slow). Say you want to change a film's default rental duration from three to five days. Here's the expensive way:

```
mysql> ALTER TABLE sakila.film
    -> MODIFY COLUMN rental_duration TINYINT(3) NOT NULL DEFAULT 5;
```

---

7. This applies to the so-called "InnoDB plugin," which is the only version of InnoDB that exists anymore in MySQL 5.5 and newer versions. See Chapter 1 for the details on InnoDB's release history.

SHOW STATUS shows that this statement does 1,000 handler reads and 1,000 inserts. In other words, it copies the table to a new table, even though the column's type, size, and nullability haven't changed.

In theory, MySQL could have skipped building a new table. The default value for the column is actually stored in the table's *.frm* file, so you should be able to change it without touching the table itself. MySQL doesn't yet use this optimization, however; any MODIFY COLUMN will cause a table rebuild.

You can change a column's default with ALTER COLUMN,[8] though:

```
mysql> ALTER TABLE sakila.film
    -> ALTER COLUMN rental_duration SET DEFAULT 5;
```

This statement modifies the *.frm* file and leaves the table alone. As a result, it is very fast.

Modifying Only the .frm File

We've seen that modifying a table's *.frm* file is fast and that MySQL sometimes rebuilds a table when it doesn't have to. If you're willing to take some risks, you can convince MySQL to do several other types of modifications without rebuilding the table.

 The technique we're about to demonstrate is unsupported, undocumented, and may not work. Use it at your own risk. We advise you to back up your data first!

You can potentially do the following types of operations without a table rebuild:

- Remove (but not add) a column's AUTO_INCREMENT attribute.
- Add, remove, or change ENUM and SET constants. If you remove a constant and some rows contain that value, queries will return the value as the empty string.

The basic technique is to create a *.frm* file for the desired table structure and copy it into the place of the existing table's *.frm* file, as follows:

1. Create an empty table with *exactly the same layout*, except for the desired modification (such as added ENUM constants).
2. Execute FLUSH TABLES WITH READ LOCK. This will close all tables in use and prevent any tables from being opened.
3. Swap the *.frm* files.
4. Execute UNLOCK TABLES to release the read lock.

As an example, let's add a constant to the rating column in sakila.film. The current column looks like this:

---

8. ALTER TABLE lets you modify columns with ALTER COLUMN, MODIFY COLUMN, and CHANGE COLUMN. All three do different things.

```
mysql> SHOW COLUMNS FROM sakila.film LIKE 'rating';
+--------+-------------------------------------+------+-----+---------+-------+
| Field  | Type                                | Null | Key | Default | Extra |
+--------+-------------------------------------+------+-----+---------+-------+
| rating | enum('G','PG','PG-13','R','NC-17')   | YES  |     | G       |       |
+--------+-------------------------------------+------+-----+---------+-------+
```

We'll add a PG-14 rating for parents who are just a little bit more cautious about films:

```
mysql> CREATE TABLE sakila.film_new LIKE sakila.film;
mysql> ALTER TABLE sakila.film_new
    -> MODIFY COLUMN rating ENUM('G','PG','PG-13','R','NC-17', 'PG-14')
    -> DEFAULT 'G';
mysql> FLUSH TABLES WITH READ LOCK;
```

Notice that we're adding the new value *at the end of the list of constants*. If we placed it in the middle, after PG-13, we'd change the meaning of the existing data: existing R values would become PG-14, NC-17 would become R, and so on.

Now we swap the *.frm* files from the operating system's command prompt:

```
/var/lib/mysql/sakila# mv film.frm film_tmp.frm
/var/lib/mysql/sakila# mv film_new.frm film.frm
/var/lib/mysql/sakila# mv film_tmp.frm film_new.frm
```

Back in the MySQL prompt, we can now unlock the table and see that the changes took effect:

```
mysql> UNLOCK TABLES;
mysql> SHOW COLUMNS FROM sakila.film LIKE 'rating'\G
*************************** 1. row ***************************
Field: rating
 Type: enum('G','PG','PG-13','R','NC-17','PG-14')
```

The only thing left to do is drop the table we created to help with the operation:

```
mysql> DROP TABLE sakila.film_new;
```

Building MyISAM Indexes Quickly

The usual trick for loading MyISAM tables efficiently is to disable keys, load the data, and reenable the keys:

```
mysql> ALTER TABLE test.load_data DISABLE KEYS;
-- load the data
mysql> ALTER TABLE test.load_data ENABLE KEYS;
```

This works because it lets MyISAM delay building the keys until all the data is loaded, at which point it can build the indexes by sorting. This is much faster and results in a defragmented, compact index tree.[9]

Unfortunately, it doesn't work for unique indexes, because DISABLE KEYS applies only to nonunique indexes. MyISAM builds unique indexes in memory and checks the

---

9. MyISAM will also build indexes by sorting when you use LOAD DATA INFILE and the table is empty.

uniqueness as it loads each row. Loading becomes extremely slow as soon as the index's size exceeds the available memory.

In modern versions of InnoDB, you can use an analogous technique that relies on InnoDB's fast online index creation capabilities. This calls for dropping all of the non-unique indexes, adding the new column, and then adding back the indexes you dropped. Percona Server supports doing this automatically.

As with the ALTER TABLE hacks in the previous section, you can speed up this process if you're willing to do a little more work and assume some risk. This can be useful for loading data from backups, for example, when you already know all the data is valid and there's no need for uniqueness checks.

 Again, this is an undocumented, unsupported technique. Use it at your own risk, and back up your data first.

Here are the steps you'll need to take:

1. Create a table of the desired structure, but without any indexes.
2. Load the data into the table to build the .MYD file.
3. Create another empty table with the desired structure, this time including the indexes. This will create the .frm and .MYI files you need.
4. Flush the tables with a read lock.
5. Rename the second table's .frm and .MYI files, so MySQL uses them for the first table.
6. Release the read lock.
7. Use REPAIR TABLE to build the table's indexes. This will build all indexes by sorting, including the unique indexes.

This procedure can be much faster for very large tables.

Summary

Good schema design is pretty universal, but of course MySQL has special implementation details to consider. In a nutshell, it's a good idea to keep things as small and simple as you can. MySQL likes simplicity, and so will the people who have to work with your database:

- Try to avoid extremes in your design, such as a schema that will force enormously complex queries, or tables with oodles and oodles of columns. (An oodle is somewhere between a scad and a gazillion.)

- Use small, simple, appropriate data types, and avoid NULL unless it's actually the right way to model your data's reality.

- Try to use the same data types to store similar or related values, especially if they'll be used in a join condition.

- Watch out for variable-length strings, which might cause pessimistic full-length memory allocation for temporary tables and sorting.

- Try to use integers for identifiers if you can.

- Avoid the legacy MySQL-isms such as specifying precisions for floating-point numbers or display widths for integers.

- Be careful with ENUM and SET. They're handy, but they can be abused, and they're tricky sometimes. BIT is best avoided.

Normalization is good, but denormalization (duplication of data, in most cases) is sometimes actually necessary and beneficial. We'll see more examples of that in the next chapter. And precomputing, caching, or generating summary tables can also be a big win. Justin Swanhart's Flexviews tool can help maintain summary tables.

Finally, ALTER TABLE can be painful because in most cases, it locks and rebuilds the whole table. We showed a number of workarounds for specific cases; for the general case, you'll have to use other techniques, such as performing the ALTER on a replica and then promoting it to master. There's more about this later in the book.

## CHAPTER 5

Indexing for High Performance

Indexes (also called "keys" in MySQL) are data structures that storage engines use to find rows quickly. They also have several other beneficial properties that we'll explore in this chapter.

Indexes are critical for good performance, and become more important as your data grows larger. Small, lightly loaded databases often perform well even without proper indexes, but as the dataset grows, performance can drop very quickly.[1] Unfortunately, indexes are often forgotten or misunderstood, so poor indexing is a leading cause of real-world performance problems. That's why we put this material early in the book— even earlier than our discussion of query optimization.

Index optimization is perhaps the most powerful way to improve query performance. Indexes can improve performance by many orders of magnitude, and optimal indexes can sometimes boost performance about two orders of magnitude more than indexes that are merely "good." Creating truly optimal indexes will often require you to rewrite queries, so this chapter and the next one are closely related.

Indexing Basics

The easiest way to understand how an index works in MySQL is to think about the index in a book. To find out where a particular topic is discussed in a book, you look in the index, and it tells you the page number(s) where that term appears.

In MySQL, a storage engine uses indexes in a similar way. It searches the index's data structure for a value. When it finds a match, it can find the row that contains the match. Suppose you run the following query:

```
mysql> SELECT first_name FROM sakila.actor WHERE actor_id = 5;
```

---

1. This chapter assumes you're using conventional hard drives, unless otherwise stated. Solid-state drives have different performance characteristics, which we cover throughout this book. The indexing principles remain true, but the penalties we're trying to avoid aren't as large with solid-state drives as they are with conventional drives.

There's an index on the `actor_id` column, so MySQL will use the index to find rows whose `actor_id` is 5. In other words, it performs a lookup on the values in the index and returns any rows containing the specified value.

An index contains values from one or more columns in a table. If you index more than one column, the column order is very important, because MySQL can only search efficiently on a leftmost prefix of the index. Creating an index on two columns is not the same as creating two separate single-column indexes, as you'll see.

If I Use an ORM, Do I Need to Care?

The short version: yes, you still need to learn about indexing, even if you rely on an object-relational mapping (ORM) tool.

ORMs produce logically and syntactically correct queries (most of the time), but they rarely produce index-friendly queries, unless you use them for only the most basic types of queries, such as primary key lookups. You can't expect your ORM, no matter how sophisticated, to handle the subtleties and complexities of indexing. Read the rest of this chapter if you disagree! It's sometimes a hard job for an expert human to puzzle through all of the possibilities, let alone an ORM.

Types of Indexes

There are many types of indexes, each designed to perform well for different purposes. Indexes are implemented in the storage engine layer, not the server layer. Thus, they are not standardized: indexing works slightly differently in each engine, and not all engines support all types of indexes. Even when multiple engines support the same index type, they might implement it differently under the hood.

That said, let's look at the index types MySQL currently supports, their benefits, and their drawbacks.

B-Tree indexes

When people talk about an index without mentioning a type, they're probably referring to a *B-Tree index*, which typically uses a B-Tree data structure to store its data.[2] Most of MySQL's storage engines support this index type. The Archive engine is the exception: it didn't support indexes at all until MySQL 5.1, when it started to allow a single indexed `AUTO_INCREMENT` column.

We use the term "B-Tree" for these indexes because that's what MySQL uses in `CREATE TABLE` and other statements. However, storage engines might use different storage structures internally. For example, the NDB Cluster storage engine uses a T-Tree data

---

2. Many storage engines actually use a B+Tree index, in which each leaf node contains a link to the next for fast range traversals through nodes. Refer to computer science literature for a detailed explanation of B-Tree indexes.

structure for these indexes, even though they're labeled `BTREE`, and InnoDB uses B+Trees. The variations in the structures and algorithms are out of scope for this book, though.

Storage engines use B-Tree indexes in various ways, which can affect performance. For instance, MyISAM uses a prefix compression technique that makes indexes smaller, but InnoDB leaves values uncompressed in its indexes. Also, MyISAM indexes refer to the indexed rows by their physical storage locations, but InnoDB refers to them by their primary key values. Each variation has benefits and drawbacks.

The general idea of a B-Tree is that all the values are stored in order, and each leaf page is the same distance from the root. Figure 5-1 shows an abstract representation of a B-Tree index, which corresponds roughly to how InnoDB's indexes work. MyISAM uses a different structure, but the principles are similar.

A B-Tree index speeds up data access because the storage engine doesn't have to scan the whole table to find the desired data. Instead, it starts at the root node (not shown in this figure). The slots in the root node hold pointers to child nodes, and the storage engine follows these pointers. It finds the right pointer by looking at the values in the node pages, which define the upper and lower bounds of the values in the child nodes. Eventually, the storage engine either determines that the desired value doesn't exist or successfully reaches a leaf page.

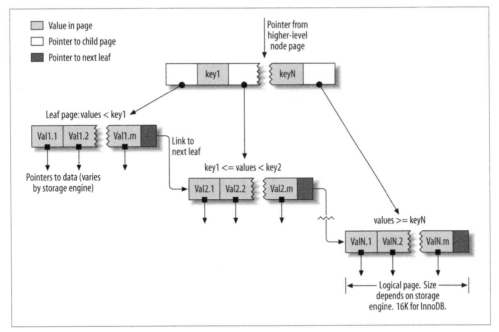

Figure 5-1. An index built on a B-Tree (technically, a B+Tree) structure

Leaf pages are special, because they have pointers to the indexed data instead of pointers to other pages. (Different storage engines have different types of "pointers" to the data.) Our illustration shows only one node page and its leaf pages, but there might be many levels of node pages between the root and the leaves. The tree's depth depends on how big the table is.

Because B-Trees store the indexed columns in order, they're useful for searching for ranges of data. For instance, descending the tree for an index on a text field passes through values in alphabetical order, so looking for "everyone whose name begins with I through K" is efficient.

Suppose you have the following table:

```
CREATE TABLE People (
    last_name   varchar(50)    not null,
    first_name  varchar(50)    not null,
    dob         date           not null,
    gender      enum('m', 'f')not null,
    key(last_name, first_name, dob)
);
```

The index will contain the values from the last_name, first_name, and dob columns for every row in the table. Figure 5-2 illustrates how the index arranges the data it stores.

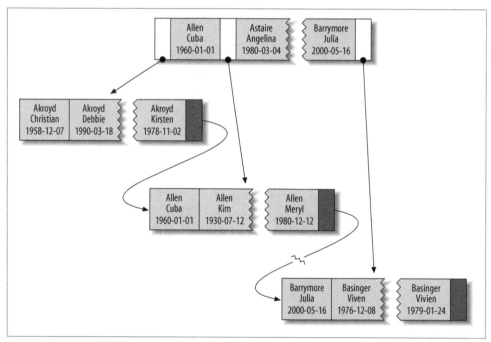

Figure 5-2. Sample entries from a B-Tree (technically, a B+Tree) index

Notice that the index sorts the values according to the order of the columns given in the index in the CREATE TABLE statement. Look at the last two entries: there are two people with the same name but different birth dates, and they're sorted by birth date.

Types of queries that can use a B-Tree index. B-Tree indexes work well for lookups by the full key value, a key range, or a key prefix. They are useful only if the lookup uses a leftmost prefix of the index.[3] The index we showed in the previous section will be useful for the following kinds of queries:

Match the full value
> A match on the full key value specifies values for all columns in the index. For example, this index can help you find a person named Cuba Allen who was born on 1960-01-01.

Match a leftmost prefix
> This index can help you find all people with the last name Allen. This uses only the first column in the index.

Match a column prefix
> You can match on the first part of a column's value. This index can help you find all people whose last names begin with J. This uses only the first column in the index.

Match a range of values
> This index can help you find people whose last names are between Allen and Barrymore. This also uses only the first column.

Match one part exactly and match a range on another part
> This index can help you find everyone whose last name is Allen and whose first name starts with the letter K (Kim, Karl, etc.). This is an exact match on last_name and a range query on first_name.

Index-only queries
> B-Tree indexes can normally support index-only queries, which are queries that access only the index, not the row storage. We discuss this optimization in "Covering Indexes" on page 177.

Because the tree's nodes are sorted, they can be used for both lookups (finding values) and ORDER BY queries (finding values in sorted order). In general, if a B-Tree can help you find a row in a particular way, it can help you sort rows by the same criteria. So, our index will be helpful for ORDER BY clauses that match all the types of lookups we just listed.

Here are some limitations of B-Tree indexes:

---

3. This is MySQL-specific, and even version-specific. Some other databases can use nonleading index parts, though it's usually more efficient to use a complete prefix. MySQL might offer this option in the future; we show workarounds later in the chapter.

- They are not useful if the lookup does not start from the leftmost side of the indexed columns. For example, this index won't help you find all people named Bill or all people born on a certain date, because those columns are not leftmost in the index. Likewise, you can't use the index to find people whose last name *ends* with a particular letter.

- You can't skip columns in the index. That is, you won't be able to find all people whose last name is Smith and who were born on a particular date. If you don't specify a value for the first_name column, MySQL can use only the first column of the index.

- The storage engine can't optimize accesses with any columns to the right of the first range condition. For example, if your query is WHERE last_name="Smith" AND first_name LIKE 'J%' AND dob='1976-12-23', the index access will use only the first two columns in the index, because the LIKE is a range condition (the server can use the rest of the columns for other purposes, though). For a column that has a limited number of values, you can often work around this by specifying equality conditions instead of range conditions. We show detailed examples of this in the indexing case study later in this chapter.

Now you know why we said the column order is extremely important: these limitations are all related to column ordering. For optimal performance, you might need to create indexes with the same columns in different orders to satisfy your queries.

Some of these limitations are not inherent to B-Tree indexes, but are a result of how the MySQL query optimizer and storage engines use indexes. Some of them might be removed in the future.

Hash indexes

A *hash index* is built on a hash table and is useful only for exact lookups that use every column in the index.[4] For each row, the storage engine computes a *hash code* of the indexed columns, which is a small value that will probably differ from the hash codes computed for other rows with different key values. It stores the hash codes in the index and stores a pointer to each row in a hash table.

In MySQL, only the Memory storage engine supports explicit hash indexes. They are the default index type for Memory tables, though Memory tables can have B-Tree indexes, too. The Memory engine supports nonunique hash indexes, which is unusual in the database world. If multiple values have the same hash code, the index will store their row pointers in the same hash table entry, using a linked list.

Here's an example. Suppose we have the following table:

```
CREATE TABLE testhash (
    fname VARCHAR(50) NOT NULL,
    lname VARCHAR(50) NOT NULL,
```

---

4. See the computer science literature for more on hash tables.

```
    KEY USING HASH(fname)
) ENGINE=MEMORY;
```

containing this data:

```
mysql> SELECT * FROM testhash;
+--------+-----------+
| fname  | lname     |
+--------+-----------+
| Arjen  | Lentz     |
| Baron  | Schwartz  |
| Peter  | Zaitsev   |
| Vadim  | Tkachenko |
+--------+-----------+
```

Now suppose the index uses an imaginary hash function called f(), which returns the following values (these are just examples, not real values):

```
f('Arjen')= 2323
f('Baron')= 7437
f('Peter')= 8784
f('Vadim')= 2458
```

The index's data structure will look like this:

Slot	Value
2323	Pointer to row 1
2458	Pointer to row 4
7437	Pointer to row 2
8784	Pointer to row 3

Notice that the slots are ordered, but the rows are not. Now, when we execute this query:

```
mysql> SELECT lname FROM testhash WHERE fname='Peter';
```

MySQL will calculate the hash of 'Peter' and use that to look up the pointer in the index. Because f('Peter') = 8784, MySQL will look in the index for 8784 and find the pointer to row 3. The final step is to compare the value in row 3 to 'Peter', to make sure it's the right row.

Because the indexes themselves store only short hash values, hash indexes are very compact. As a result, lookups are usually lightning fast. However, hash indexes have some limitations:

- Because the index contains only hash codes and row pointers rather than the values themselves, MySQL can't use the values in the index to avoid reading the rows. Fortunately, accessing the in-memory rows is very fast, so this doesn't usually degrade performance.

- MySQL can't use hash indexes for sorting because they don't store rows in sorted order.
- Hash indexes don't support partial key matching, because they compute the hash from the entire indexed value. That is, if you have an index on (A,B) and your query's WHERE clause refers only to A, the index won't help.
- Hash indexes support only equality comparisons that use the =, IN(), and <=> operators (note that <> and <=> are not the same operator). They can't speed up range queries, such as WHERE price > 100.
- Accessing data in a hash index is very quick, unless there are many collisions (multiple values with the same hash). When there are collisions, the storage engine must follow each row pointer in the linked list and compare their values to the lookup value to find the right row(s).
- Some index maintenance operations can be slow if there are many hash collisions. For example, if you create a hash index on a column with a very low selectivity (many hash collisions) and then delete a row from the table, finding the pointer from the index to that row might be expensive. The storage engine will have to examine each row in that hash key's linked list to find and remove the reference to the one row you deleted.

These limitations make hash indexes useful only in special cases. However, when they match the application's needs, they can improve performance dramatically. An example is in data-warehousing applications where a classic "star" schema requires many joins to lookup tables. Hash indexes are exactly what a lookup table requires.

In addition to the Memory storage engine's explicit hash indexes, the NDB Cluster storage engine supports unique hash indexes. Their functionality is specific to the NDB Cluster storage engine, which we don't cover in this book.

The InnoDB storage engine has a special feature called *adaptive hash indexes*. When InnoDB notices that some index values are being accessed very frequently, it builds a hash index for them in memory on top of B-Tree indexes. This gives its B-Tree indexes some properties of hash indexes, such as very fast hashed lookups. This process is completely automatic, and you can't control or configure it, although you can disable the adaptive hash index altogether.

Building your own hash indexes. If your storage engine doesn't support hash indexes, you can emulate them yourself in a manner similar to that InnoDB uses. This will give you access to some of the desirable properties of hash indexes, such as a very small index size for very long keys.

The idea is simple: create a pseudohash index on top of a standard B-Tree index. It will not be exactly the same thing as a real hash index, because it will still use the B-Tree index for lookups. However, it will use the keys' hash values for lookups, instead of the keys themselves. All you need to do is specify the hash function manually in the query's WHERE clause.

An example of when this approach works well is for URL lookups. URLs generally cause B-Tree indexes to become huge, because they're very long. You'd normally query a table of URLs like this:

```
mysql> SELECT id FROM url WHERE url="http://www.mysql.com";
```

But if you remove the index on the url column and add an indexed url_crc column to the table, you can use a query like this:

```
mysql> SELECT id FROM url WHERE url="http://www.mysql.com"
    ->     AND url_crc=CRC32("http://www.mysql.com");
```

This works well because the MySQL query optimizer notices there's a small, highly selective index on the url_crc column and does an index lookup for entries with that value (1560514994, in this case). Even if several rows have the same url_crc value, it's very easy to find these rows with a fast integer comparison and then examine them to find the one that matches the full URL exactly. The alternative is to index the full URL as a string, which is much slower.

One drawback to this approach is the need to maintain the hash values. You can do this manually or, in MySQL 5.0 and newer, you can use triggers. The following example shows how triggers can help maintain the url_crc column when you insert and update values. First, we create the table:

```
CREATE TABLE pseudohash (
    id int unsigned NOT NULL auto_increment,
    url varchar(255) NOT NULL,
    url_crc int unsigned NOT NULL DEFAULT 0,
    PRIMARY KEY(id)
);
```

Now we create the triggers. We change the statement delimiter temporarily, so we can use a semicolon as a delimiter for the trigger:

```
DELIMITER //

CREATE TRIGGER pseudohash_crc_ins BEFORE INSERT ON pseudohash FOR EACH ROW BEGIN
SET NEW.url_crc=crc32(NEW.url);
END;
//

CREATE TRIGGER pseudohash_crc_upd BEFORE UPDATE ON pseudohash FOR EACH ROW BEGIN
SET NEW.url_crc=crc32(NEW.url);
END;
//

DELIMITER ;
```

All that remains is to verify that the trigger maintains the hash:

```
mysql> INSERT INTO pseudohash (url) VALUES ('http://www.mysql.com');
mysql> SELECT * FROM pseudohash;
+----+----------------------+------------+
| id | url                  | url_crc    |
+----+----------------------+------------+
|  1 | http://www.mysql.com | 1560514994 |
+----+----------------------+------------+
mysql> UPDATE pseudohash SET url='http://www.mysql.com/' WHERE id=1;
mysql> SELECT * FROM pseudohash;
+----+-----------------------+------------+
| id | url                   | url_crc    |
+----+-----------------------+------------+
|  1 | http://www.mysql.com/ | 1558250469 |
+----+-----------------------+------------+
```

If you use this approach, you should not use SHA1() or MD5() hash functions. These return very long strings, which waste a lot of space and result in slower comparisons. They are cryptographically strong functions designed to virtually eliminate collisions, which is not your goal here. Simple hash functions can offer acceptable collision rates with better performance.

If your table has many rows and CRC32() gives too many collisions, implement your own 64-bit hash function. Make sure you use a function that returns an integer, not a string. One way to implement a 64-bit hash function is to use just part of the value returned by MD5(). This is probably less efficient than writing your own routine as a user-defined function (see Chapter 7), but it'll do in a pinch:

```
mysql> SELECT CONV(RIGHT(MD5('http://www.mysql.com/'), 16), 16, 10) AS HASH64;
+---------------------+
| HASH64              |
+---------------------+
| 9761173720318281581 |
+---------------------+
```

Handling hash collisions. When you search for a value by its hash, you must also include the literal value in your WHERE clause:

```
mysql> SELECT id FROM url WHERE url_crc=CRC32("http://www.mysql.com")
    ->     AND url="http://www.mysql.com";
```

The following query will *not* work correctly, because if another URL has the CRC32() value 1560514994, the query will return both rows:

```
mysql> SELECT id FROM url WHERE url_crc=CRC32("http://www.mysql.com");
```

The probability of a hash collision grows much faster than you might think, due to the so-called Birthday Paradox. CRC32() returns a 32-bit integer value, so the probability of a collision reaches 1% with as few as 93,000 values. To illustrate this, we loaded all the words in */usr/share/dict/words* into a table along with their CRC32() values, resulting in 98,569 rows. There is already one collision in this set of data! The collision makes the following query return more than one row:

```
mysql> SELECT word, crc FROM words WHERE crc = CRC32('gnu');
+---------+------------+
| word    | crc        |
+---------+------------+
| codding | 1774765869 |
| gnu     | 1774765869 |
+---------+------------+
```

The correct query is as follows:

```
mysql> SELECT word, crc FROM words WHERE crc = CRC32('gnu')AND word = 'gnu';
+------+------------+
| word | crc        |
+------+------------+
| gnu  | 1774765869 |
+------+------------+
```

To avoid problems with collisions, you must specify both conditions in the WHERE clause. If collisions aren't a problem—for example, because you're doing statistical queries and you don't need exact results—you can simplify, and gain some efficiency, by using only the CRC32() value in the WHERE clause. You can also use the FNV64() function, which ships with Percona Server and can be installed as a plugin in any version of MySQL. It's 64 bits long, very fast, and much less prone to collisions than CRC32().

Spatial (R-Tree) indexes

MyISAM supports spatial indexes, which you can use with partial types such as GEOME
TRY. Unlike B-Tree indexes, spatial indexes don't require your WHERE clauses to operate on a leftmost prefix of the index. They index the data by all dimensions at the same time. As a result, lookups can use any combination of dimensions efficiently. However, you must use the MySQL GIS functions, such as MBRCONTAINS(), for this to work, and MySQL's GIS support isn't great, so most people don't use it. The go-to solution for GIS in an open source RDBMS is PostGIS in PostgreSQL.

Full-text indexes

FULLTEXT is a special type of index that finds keywords in the text instead of comparing values directly to the values in the index. Full-text searching is completely different from other types of matching. It has many subtleties, such as stopwords, stemming and plurals, and Boolean searching. It is much more analogous to what a search engine does than to simple WHERE parameter matching.

Having a full-text index on a column does not eliminate the value of a B-Tree index on the same column. Full-text indexes are for MATCH AGAINST operations, not ordinary WHERE clause operations.

We discuss full-text indexing in more detail in Chapter 7.

Other types of index

Several third-party storage engines use different types of data structures for their indexes. For example, TokuDB uses fractal tree indexes. This is a newly developed data structure that has some of the same benefits as B-Tree indexes, without some of the drawbacks. As you read through this chapter, you'll see many InnoDB topics, including clustered indexes and covering indexes. In most cases, the discussions of InnoDB apply equally well to TokuDB.

ScaleDB uses Patricia tries (that's not a typo), and other technologies such as InfiniDB or Infobright have their own special data structures for optimizing queries.

Benefits of Indexes

Indexes enable the server to navigate quickly to a desired position in the table, but that's not all they're good for. As you've probably gathered by now, indexes have several additional benefits, based on the properties of the data structures used to create them.

B-Tree indexes, which are the most common type you'll use, function by storing the data in sorted order, and MySQL can exploit that for queries with clauses such as ORDER BY and GROUP BY. Because the data is presorted, a B-Tree index also stores related values close together. Finally, the index actually stores a copy of the values, so some queries can be satisfied from the index alone. Three main benefits proceed from these properties:

1. Indexes reduce the amount of data the server has to examine.
2. Indexes help the server avoid sorting and temporary tables.
3. Indexes turn random I/O into sequential I/O.

This subject really deserves an entire book. For those who would like to dig in deeply, we recommend *Relational Database Index Design and the Optimizers*, by Tapio Lahdenmaki and Mike Leach (Wiley). It explains topics such as how to calculate the costs and benefits of indexes, how to estimate query speed, and how to determine whether indexes will be more expensive to maintain than the benefit they provide.

Lahdenmaki and Leach's book also introduces a three-star system for grading how suitable an index is for a query. The index earns one star if it places relevant rows adjacent to each other, a second star if its rows are sorted in the order the query needs, and a final star if it contains all the columns needed for the query.

We'll return to these principles throughout this chapter.

Is an Index the Best Solution?

An index isn't always the right tool. At a high level, keep in mind that indexes are most effective when they help the storage engine find rows without adding more work than they avoid. For very small tables, it is often more effective to simply read all the rows in the table. For medium to large tables, indexes can be very effective. For enormous tables, the overhead of indexing, as well as the work required to actually use the indexes, can start to add up. In such cases you might need to choose a technique that identifies groups of rows that are interesting to the query, instead of individual rows. You can use partitioning for this purpose; see Chapter 7.

If you have lots of tables, it can also make sense to create a metadata table to store some characteristics of interest for your queries. For example, if you execute queries that perform aggregations over rows in a multitenant application whose data is partitioned into many tables, you can record which users of the system are actually stored in each table, thus letting you simply ignore tables that don't have information about those users. These tactics are usually useful only at extremely large scales. In fact, this is a crude approximation of what Infobright does. At the scale of terabytes, locating individual rows doesn't make sense; indexes are replaced by per-block metadata.

Indexing Strategies for High Performance

Creating the correct indexes and using them properly is essential to good query performance. We've introduced the different types of indexes and explored their strengths and weaknesses. Now let's see how to really tap into the power of indexes.

There are many ways to choose and use indexes effectively, because there are many special-case optimizations and specialized behaviors. Determining what to use when and evaluating the performance implications of your choices are skills you'll learn over time. The following sections will help you understand how to use indexes effectively.

Isolating the Column

We commonly see queries that defeat indexes or prevent MySQL from using the available indexes. MySQL generally can't use indexes on columns unless the columns are isolated in the query. "Isolating" the column means it should not be part of an expression or be inside a function in the query.

For example, here's a query that can't use the index on `actor_id`:

```
mysql> SELECT actor_id FROM sakila.actor WHERE actor_id + 1 = 5;
```

A human can easily see that the WHERE clause is equivalent to `actor_id = 4`, but MySQL can't solve the equation for `actor_id`. It's up to you to do this. You should get in the habit of simplifying your WHERE criteria, so the indexed column is alone on one side of the comparison operator.

Here's another example of a common mistake:

```
mysql> SELECT ... WHERE TO_DAYS(CURRENT_DATE) - TO_DAYS(date_col) <= 10;
```

Prefix Indexes and Index Selectivity

Sometimes you need to index very long character columns, which makes your indexes large and slow. One strategy is to simulate a hash index, as we showed earlier in this chapter. But sometimes that isn't good enough. What can you do?

You can often save space and get good performance by indexing the first few characters instead of the whole value. This makes your indexes use less space, but it also makes them less *selective*. Index selectivity is the ratio of the number of distinct indexed values (the *cardinality*) to the total number of rows in the table (*#T*), and ranges from 1/*#T* to 1. A highly selective index is good because it lets MySQL filter out more rows when it looks for matches. A unique index has a selectivity of 1, which is as good as it gets.

A prefix of the column is often selective enough to give good performance. If you're indexing BLOB or TEXT columns, or very long VARCHAR columns, you *must* define prefix indexes, because MySQL disallows indexing their full length.

The trick is to choose a prefix that's long enough to give good selectivity, but short enough to save space. The prefix should be long enough to make the index nearly as useful as it would be if you'd indexed the whole column. In other words, you'd like the prefix's cardinality to be close to the full column's cardinality.

To determine a good prefix length, find the most frequent values and compare that list to a list of the most frequent prefixes. There's no good table to demonstrate this in the Sakila sample database, so we derive one from the city table, just so we have enough data to work with:

```
CREATE TABLE sakila.city_demo(city VARCHAR(50) NOT NULL);
INSERT INTO sakila.city_demo(city) SELECT city FROM sakila.city;
-- Repeat the next statement five times:
INSERT INTO sakila.city_demo(city) SELECT city FROM sakila.city_demo;
-- Now randomize the distribution (inefficiently but conveniently):
UPDATE sakila.city_demo
   SET city = (SELECT city FROM  sakila.city ORDER BY RAND() LIMIT 1);
```

Now we have an example dataset. The results are not realistically distributed, and we used RAND(), so your results will vary, but that doesn't matter for this exercise. First, we find the most frequently occurring cities:

```
mysql> SELECT COUNT(*) AS cnt, city
    -> FROM sakila.city_demo GROUP BY city ORDER BY cnt DESC LIMIT 10;
+-----+----------------+
| cnt | city           |
+-----+----------------+
|  65 | London         |
|  49 | Hiroshima      |
|  48 | Teboksary      |
|  48 | Pak Kret       |
```

```
| 48 | Yaound        |
| 47 | Tel Aviv-Jaffa |
| 47 | Shimoga       |
| 45 | Cabuyao       |
| 45 | Callao        |
| 45 | Bislig        |
+-----+----------------+
```

Notice that there are roughly 45 to 65 occurrences of each value. Now we find the most
frequently occurring city name *prefixes*, beginning with three-letter prefixes:

```
mysql> SELECT COUNT(*) AS cnt, LEFT(city, 3) AS pref
    -> FROM sakila.city_demo GROUP BY pref ORDER BY cnt DESC LIMIT 10;
+-----+------+
| cnt | pref |
+-----+------+
| 483 | San  |
| 195 | Cha  |
| 177 | Tan  |
| 167 | Sou  |
| 163 | al-  |
| 163 | Sal  |
| 146 | Shi  |
| 136 | Hal  |
| 130 | Val  |
| 129 | Bat  |
+-----+------+
```

There are many more occurrences of each prefix, so there are many fewer unique prefixes than unique full-length city names. The idea is to increase the prefix length until
the prefix becomes nearly as selective as the full length of the column. A little experimentation shows that 7 is a good value:

```
mysql> SELECT COUNT(*) AS cnt, LEFT(city, 7) AS pref
    -> FROM sakila.city_demo GROUP BY pref ORDER BY cnt DESC LIMIT 10;
+-----+---------+
| cnt | pref    |
+-----+---------+
|  70 | Santiag |
|  68 | San Fel |
|  65 | London  |
|  61 | Valle d |
|  49 | Hiroshi |
|  48 | Teboksa |
|  48 | Pak Kre |
|  48 | Yaound  |
|  47 | Tel Avi |
|  47 | Shimoga |
+-----+---------+
```

Another way to calculate a good prefix length is by computing the full column's selectivity and trying to make the prefix's selectivity close to that value. Here's how to find
the full column's selectivity:

```
mysql> SELECT COUNT(DISTINCT city)/COUNT(*) FROM sakila.city_demo;
+------------------------------+
| COUNT(DISTINCT city)/COUNT(*) |
+------------------------------+
|                        0.0312 |
+------------------------------+
```

The prefix will be about as good, on average (there's a caveat here, though), if we target a selectivity near .031. It's possible to evaluate many different lengths in one query, which is useful on very large tables. Here's how to find the selectivity of several prefix lengths in one query:

```
mysql> SELECT COUNT(DISTINCT LEFT(city, 3))/COUNT(*) AS sel3,
    ->     COUNT(DISTINCT LEFT(city, 4))/COUNT(*) AS sel4,
    ->     COUNT(DISTINCT LEFT(city, 5))/COUNT(*) AS sel5,
    ->     COUNT(DISTINCT LEFT(city, 6))/COUNT(*) AS sel6,
    ->     COUNT(DISTINCT LEFT(city, 7))/COUNT(*) AS sel7
    -> FROM sakila.city_demo;
+--------+--------+--------+--------+--------+
| sel3   | sel4   | sel5   | sel6   | sel7   |
+--------+--------+--------+--------+--------+
| 0.0239 | 0.0293 | 0.0305 | 0.0309 | 0.0310 |
+--------+--------+--------+--------+--------+
```

This query shows that increasing the prefix length results in successively smaller improvements as it approaches seven characters.

It's not a good idea to look only at average selectivity. The caveat is that the *worst-case* selectivity matters, too. The average selectivity might make you think a four- or five-character prefix is good enough, but if your data is very uneven, that could be a trap. If you look at the number of occurrences of the most common city name prefixes using a value of 4, you'll see the unevenness clearly:

```
mysql> SELECT COUNT(*) AS cnt, LEFT(city, 4) AS pref
    -> FROM sakila.city_demo GROUP BY pref ORDER BY cnt DESC LIMIT 5;
+-----+------+
| cnt | pref |
+-----+------+
| 205 | San  |
| 200 | Sant |
| 135 | Sout |
| 104 | Chan |
|  91 | Toul |
+-----+------+
```

With four characters, the most frequent prefixes occur quite a bit more often than the most frequent full-length values. That is, the selectivity on those values is lower than the average selectivity. If you have a more realistic dataset than this randomly generated sample, you're likely to see this effect even more. For example, building a four-character prefix index on real-world city names will give terrible selectivity on cities that begin with "San" and "New," of which there are many.

Now that we've found a good value for our sample data, here's how to create a prefix index on the column:

```
mysql> ALTER TABLE sakila.city_demo ADD KEY (city(7));
```

Prefix indexes can be a great way to make indexes smaller and faster, but they have downsides too: MySQL cannot use prefix indexes for ORDER BY or GROUP BY queries, nor can it use them as covering indexes.

A common case we've found to benefit from prefix indexes is when long hexadecimal identifiers are used. We discussed more efficient techniques of storing such identifiers in the previous chapter, but what if you're using a packaged solution that you can't modify? We see this frequently with vBulletin and other applications that use MySQL to store website sessions, keyed on long hex strings. Adding an index on the first eight characters or so often boosts performance significantly, in a way that's completely transparent to the application.

 Sometimes suffix indexes make sense (e.g., for finding all email addresses from a certain domain). MySQL does not support reversed indexes natively, but you can store a reversed string and index a prefix of it. You can maintain the index with triggers; see "Building your own hash indexes" on page 154.

Multicolumn Indexes

Multicolumn indexes are often very poorly understood. Common mistakes are to index many or all of the columns separately, or to index columns in the wrong order.

We'll discuss column order in the next section. The first mistake, indexing many columns separately, has a distinctive signature in SHOW CREATE TABLE:

```
CREATE TABLE t (
  c1 INT,
  c2 INT,
  c3 INT,
  KEY(c1),
  KEY(c2),
  KEY(c3)
);
```

This strategy of indexing often results when people give vague but authoritative-sounding advice such as "create indexes on columns that appear in the WHERE clause." This advice is very wrong. It will result in one-star indexes at best. These indexes can be many orders of magnitude slower than truly optimal indexes. Sometimes when you can't design a three-star index, it's much better to ignore the WHERE clause and pay attention to optimal row order or create a covering index instead.

Individual indexes on lots of columns won't help MySQL improve performance for most queries. MySQL 5.0 and newer can cope a little with such poorly indexed tables by using a strategy known as *index merge*, which permits a query to make limited use of multiple indexes from a single table to locate desired rows. Earlier versions of MySQL could use only a single index, so when no single index was good enough to help, MySQL often chose a table scan. For example, the `film_actor` table has an index on `film_id` and an index on `actor_id`, but neither is a good choice for both WHERE conditions in this query:

```
mysql> SELECT film_id, actor_id FROM sakila.film_actor
    -> WHERE actor_id = 1 OR film_id = 1;
```

In older MySQL versions, that query would produce a table scan unless you wrote it as the UNION of two queries:

```
mysql> SELECT film_id, actor_id FROM sakila.film_actor WHERE actor_id = 1
    -> UNION ALL
    -> SELECT film_id, actor_id FROM sakila.film_actor WHERE film_id = 1
    ->    AND actor_id <> 1;
```

In MySQL 5.0 and newer, however, the query can use both indexes, scanning them simultaneously and merging the results. There are three variations on the algorithm: union for OR conditions, intersection for AND conditions, and unions of intersections for combinations of the two. The following query uses a union of two index scans, as you can see by examining the Extra column:

```
mysql> EXPLAIN SELECT film_id, actor_id FROM sakila.film_actor
    -> WHERE actor_id = 1 OR film_id = 1\G
*************************** 1. row ***************************
           id: 1
  select_type: SIMPLE
        table: film_actor
         type: index_merge
possible_keys: PRIMARY,idx_fk_film_id
          key: PRIMARY,idx_fk_film_id
      key_len: 2,2
          ref: NULL
         rows: 29
        Extra: Using union(PRIMARY,idx_fk_film_id); Using where
```

MySQL can use this technique on complex queries, so you might see nested operations in the Extra column for some queries.

The index merge strategy sometimes works very well, but it's more common for it to actually be an indication of a poorly indexed table:

- When the server intersects indexes (usually for AND conditions), it usually means that you need a single index with all the relevant columns, not multiple indexes that have to be combined.

- When the server unions indexes (usually for OR conditions), sometimes the algorithm's buffering, sorting, and merging operations use lots of CPU and memory resources. This is especially true if not all of the indexes are very selective, so the scans return lots of rows to the merge operation.

- Recall that the optimizer doesn't account for this cost—it optimizes just the number of random page reads. This can make it "underprice" the query, which might in fact run more slowly than a plain table scan. The intensive memory and CPU usage also tends to impact concurrent queries, but you won't see this effect when you run the query in isolation. Sometimes rewriting such queries with a UNION, the way you used to have to do in MySQL 4.1 and earlier, is more optimal.

When you see an index merge in EXPLAIN, you should examine the query and table structure to see if this is really the best you can get. You can disable index merges with the optimizer_switch option or variable. You can also use IGNORE INDEX.

Choosing a Good Column Order

One of the most common causes of confusion we've seen is the order of columns in an index. The correct order depends on the queries that will use the index, and you must think about how to choose the index order such that rows are sorted and grouped in a way that will benefit the query. (This section applies to B-Tree indexes, by the way; hash and other index types don't store their data in sorted order as B-Tree indexes do.)

The order of columns in a multicolumn B-Tree index means that the index is sorted first by the leftmost column, then by the next column, and so on. Therefore, the index can be scanned in either forward or reverse order, to satisfy queries with ORDER BY, GROUP BY, and DISTINCT clauses that match the column order exactly.

As a result, the column order is vitally important in multicolumn indexes. The column order either enables or prevents the index from earning "stars" in Lahdenmaki and Leach's three-star system (see "Benefits of Indexes" on page 158 earlier in this chapter for more on the three-star system). We will show many examples of how this works through the rest of this chapter.

There is an old rule of thumb for choosing column order: place the most selective columns first in the index. How useful is this suggestion? It can be helpful in some cases, but it's usually much less important than avoiding random I/O and sorting, all things considered. (Specific cases vary, so there's no one-size-fits-all rule. That alone should tell you that this rule of thumb is probably less important than you think.)

Placing the most selective columns first can be a good idea when there is no sorting or grouping to consider, and thus the purpose of the index is only to optimize WHERE lookups. In such cases, it might indeed work well to design the index so that it filters out rows as quickly as possible, so it's more selective for queries that specify only a prefix of the index in the WHERE clause. However, this depends not only on the selectivity (overall cardinality) of the columns, but also on the actual values you use to look up rows—the distribution of values. This is the same type of consideration we explored for choosing a good prefix length. You might actually need to choose the column order such that it's as selective as possible for the queries that you'll run most.

Let's use the following query as an example:

```
SELECT * FROM payment WHERE staff_id = 2 AND customer_id = 584;
```

Should you create an index on (staff_id, customer_id), or should you reverse the column order? We can run some quick queries to help examine the distribution of values in the table and determine which column has a higher selectivity. Let's transform the query to count the cardinality of each predicate[5] in the WHERE clause:

```
mysql> SELECT SUM(staff_id = 2), SUM(customer_id = 584) FROM payment\G
*************************** 1. row ***************************
     SUM(staff_id = 2): 7992
SUM(customer_id = 584): 30
```

According to the rule of thumb, we should place customer_id first in the index, because the predicate matches fewer rows in the table. We can then run the query again to see how selective staff_id is within the range of rows selected by this specific customer ID:

```
mysql> SELECT SUM(staff_id = 2) FROM payment WHERE customer_id = 584\G
*************************** 1. row ***************************
SUM(staff_id = 2): 17
```

Be careful with this technique, because the results depend on the specific constants supplied for the chosen query. If you optimize your indexes for this query and other queries don't fare as well, the server's performance might suffer overall, or some queries might run unpredictably.

If you're using the "worst" sample query from a report from a tool such as *pt-query-digest*, this technique can be an effective way to see what might be the most helpful indexes for your queries and your data. But if you don't have specific samples to run, it might be better to use the old rule of thumb, which is to look at the cardinality across the board, not just for one query:

```
mysql> SELECT COUNT(DISTINCT staff_id)/COUNT(*) AS staff_id_selectivity,
    > COUNT(DISTINCT customer_id)/COUNT(*) AS customer_id_selectivity,
    > COUNT(*)
    > FROM payment\G
*************************** 1. row ***************************
   staff_id_selectivity: 0.0001
customer_id_selectivity: 0.0373
               COUNT(*): 16049
```

customer_id has higher selectivity, so again the answer is to put that column first in the index:

```
mysql> ALTER TABLE payment ADD KEY(customer_id, staff_id);
```

As with prefix indexes, problems often arise from special values that have higher than normal cardinality. For example, we have seen applications treat users who aren't logged in as "guest" users, who get a special user ID in session tables and other places where user activity is recorded. Queries involving that user ID are likely to behave very

---

5. Optimizer geeks call this a "sarg," for "searchable argument." Now you're a geek, too!

differently from other queries, because there are usually a lot of sessions that aren't logged in. We've also seen system accounts cause similar problems. One application had a magical administrative account, which wasn't a real user, who was "friends" with every user of the whole website so that it could send status notices and other messages. That user's huge list of friends was causing severe performance problems for the site.

This is actually fairly typical. Any outlier, even if it's not an artifact of a poor decision in how the application is managed, can cause problems. Users who really do have lots of friends, photos, status messages, and the like can be just as troublesome as fake users.

Here's a real example we saw once, on a product forum where users exchanged stories and experiences about the product. Queries of this particular form were running very slowly:

```
mysql> SELECT COUNT(DISTINCT threadId) AS COUNT_VALUE
    -> FROM Message
    -> WHERE (groupId = 10137) AND (userId = 1288826) AND (anonymous = 0)
    -> ORDER BY priority DESC, modifiedDate DESC
```

This query appeared not to have a very good index, so the customer asked us to see if it could be improved. The EXPLAIN follows:

```
         id: 1
select_type: SIMPLE
      table: Message
       type: ref
        key: ix_groupId_userId
    key_len: 18
        ref: const,const
       rows: 1251162
      Extra: Using where
```

The index that MySQL chose for this query is on (groupId, userId), which would seem like a pretty decent choice if we had no information about the column cardinality. However, a different picture emerged when we looked at how many rows matched that user ID and group ID:

```
mysql> SELECT COUNT(*), SUM(groupId = 10137),
    -> SUM(userId = 1288826), SUM(anonymous = 0)
    -> FROM Message\G
*************************** 1. row ***************************
          count(*): 4142217
 sum(groupId = 10137): 4092654
sum(userId = 1288826): 1288496
   sum(anonymous = 0): 4141934
```

It turned out that this group owned almost every row in the table, and the user had 1.3 million rows—in this case, there simply isn't an index that can help! This was because the data was migrated from another application, and all of the messages were assigned to the administrative user and group as part of the import process. The solution to this problem was to change the application code to recognize this special-case user ID and group ID, and not issue this query for that user.

The moral of this little story is that rules of thumb and heuristics can be useful, but you have to be careful not to assume that average-case performance is representative of special-case performance. Special cases can wreck performance for the whole application.

In the end, although the rule of thumb about selectivity and cardinality is interesting to explore, other factors—such as sorting, grouping, and the presence of range conditions in the query's WHERE clause—can make a much bigger difference to query performance.

Clustered Indexes

Clustered indexes[6] aren't a separate type of index. Rather, they're an approach to data storage. The exact details vary between implementations, but InnoDB's clustered indexes actually store a B-Tree index and the rows together in the same structure.

When a table has a clustered index, its rows are actually stored in the index's leaf pages. The term "clustered" refers to the fact that rows with adjacent key values are stored close to each other.[7] You can have only one clustered index per table, because you can't store the rows in two places at once. (However, *covering indexes* let you emulate multiple clustered indexes; more on this later.)

Because storage engines are responsible for implementing indexes, not all storage engines support clustered indexes. We focus on InnoDB in this section, but the principles we discuss are likely to be at least partially true for any storage engine that supports clustered indexes now or in the future.

Figure 5-3 shows how records are laid out in a clustered index. Notice that the leaf pages contain full rows but the node pages contain only the indexed columns. In this case, the indexed column contains integer values.

Some database servers let you choose which index to cluster, but none of MySQL's built-in storage engines does at the time of this writing. InnoDB clusters the data by the primary key. That means that the "indexed column" in Figure 5-3 is the primary key column.

If you don't define a primary key, InnoDB will try to use a unique nonnullable index instead. If there's no such index, InnoDB will define a hidden primary key for you and then cluster on that. InnoDB clusters records together only within a page. Pages with adjacent key values might be distant from each other.

A clustering primary key can help performance, but it can also cause serious performance problems. Thus, you should think carefully about clustering, especially when you change a table's storage engine from InnoDB to something else (or vice versa).

---

6. Oracle users will be familiar with the term "index-organized table," which means the same thing.

7. This isn't always true, as you'll see in a moment.

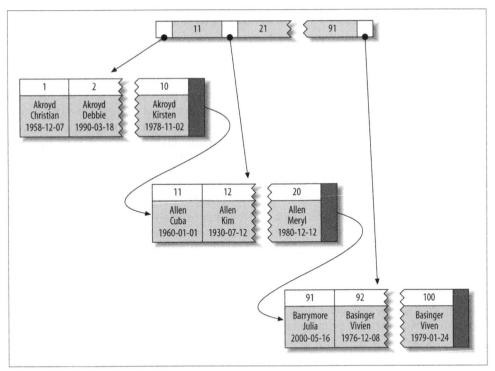

Figure 5-3. Clustered index data layout

Clustering data has some very important advantages:

- You can keep related data close together. For example, when implementing a mailbox, you can cluster by `user_id`, so you can retrieve all of a single user's messages by fetching only a few pages from disk. If you didn't use clustering, each message might require its own disk I/O.

- Data access is fast. A clustered index holds both the index and the data together in one B-Tree, so retrieving rows from a clustered index is normally faster than a comparable lookup in a nonclustered index.

- Queries that use covering indexes can use the primary key values contained at the leaf node.

These benefits can boost performance tremendously if you design your tables and queries to take advantage of them. However, clustered indexes also have disadvantages:

- Clustering gives the largest improvement for I/O-bound workloads. If the data fits in memory the order in which it's accessed doesn't really matter, so clustering doesn't give much benefit.

- Insert speeds depend heavily on insertion order. Inserting rows in primary key order is the fastest way to load data into an InnoDB table. It might be a good idea to reorganize the table with `OPTIMIZE TABLE` after loading a lot of data if you didn't load the rows in primary key order.

- Updating the clustered index columns is expensive, because it forces InnoDB to move each updated row to a new location.

- Tables built upon clustered indexes are subject to *page splits* when new rows are inserted, or when a row's primary key is updated such that the row must be moved. A page split happens when a row's key value dictates that the row must be placed into a page that is full of data. The storage engine must split the page into two to accommodate the row. Page splits can cause a table to use more space on disk.

- Clustered tables can be slower for full table scans, especially if rows are less densely packed or stored nonsequentially because of page splits.

- Secondary (nonclustered) indexes can be larger than you might expect, because their leaf nodes contain the primary key columns of the referenced rows.

- Secondary index accesses require two index lookups instead of one.

The last point can be a bit confusing. Why would a secondary index require two index lookups? The answer lies in the nature of the "row pointers" the secondary index stores. Remember, a leaf node doesn't store a pointer to the referenced row's physical location; rather, it stores the row's primary key values.

That means that to find a row from a secondary index, the storage engine first finds the leaf node in the secondary index and then uses the primary key values stored there to navigate the primary key and find the row. That's double work: two B-Tree navigations instead of one.[8] In InnoDB, the adaptive hash index can help reduce this penalty.

Comparison of InnoDB and MyISAM data layout

The differences between clustered and nonclustered data layouts, and the corresponding differences between primary and secondary indexes, can be confusing and surprising. Let's see how InnoDB and MyISAM lay out the following table:

```
CREATE TABLE layout_test (
    col1 int NOT NULL,
    col2 int NOT NULL,
    PRIMARY KEY(col1),
    KEY(col2)
);
```

Suppose the table is populated with primary key values 1 to 10,000, inserted in random order and then optimized with `OPTIMIZE TABLE`. In other words, the data is arranged optimally on disk, but the rows might be in a random order. The values for `col2` are randomly assigned between 1 and 100, so there are lots of duplicates.

---

8. Nonclustered index designs aren't always able to provide single-operation row lookups, by the way. When a row changes it might not fit in its original location anymore, so you might end up with fragmented rows or "forwarding addresses" in the table, both of which would result in more work to find the row.

MyISAM's data layout. MyISAM's data layout is simpler, so we'll illustrate that first. MyISAM stores the rows on disk in the order in which they were inserted, as shown in Figure 5-4.

We've shown the row numbers, beginning at 0, beside the rows. Because the rows are fixed-size, MyISAM can find any row by seeking the required number of bytes from the beginning of the table. (MyISAM doesn't always use "row numbers," as we've shown; it uses different strategies depending on whether the rows are fixed-size or variable-size.)

This layout makes it easy to build an index. We illustrate with a series of diagrams, abstracting away physical details such as pages and showing only "nodes" in the index. Each leaf node in the index can simply contain the row number. Figure 5-5 illustrates the table's primary key.

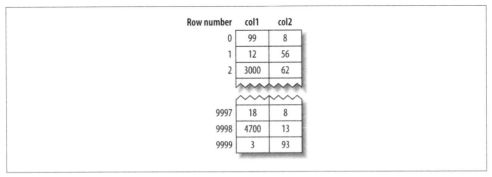

Figure 5-4. MyISAM data layout for the layout_test table

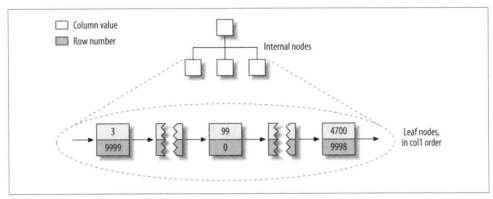

Figure 5-5. MyISAM primary key layout for the layout_test table

We've glossed over some of the details, such as how many internal B-Tree nodes descend from the one before, but that's not important to understanding the basic data layout of a nonclustered storage engine.

What about the index on col2? Is there anything special about it? As it turns out, no—it's just an index like any other. Figure 5-6 illustrates the col2 index.

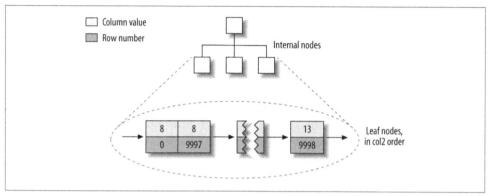

Figure 5-6. MyISAM col2 index layout for the layout_test table

In fact, in MyISAM, there is no structural difference between a primary key and any other index. A primary key is simply a unique, nonnullable index named PRIMARY.

InnoDB's data layout. InnoDB stores the same data very differently because of its clustered organization. InnoDB stores the table as shown in Figure 5-7.

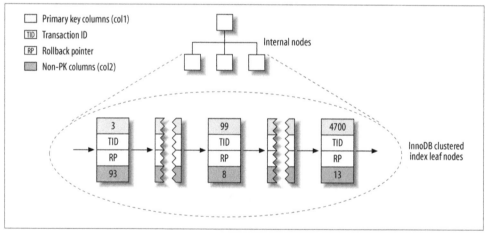

Figure 5-7. InnoDB primary key layout for the layout_test table

At first glance, that might not look very different from Figure 5-5. But look again, and notice that this illustration shows the *whole table*, not just the index. Because the clustered index "is" the table in InnoDB, there's no separate row storage as there is for MyISAM.

Each leaf node in the clustered index contains the primary key value, the transaction ID, and rollback pointer InnoDB uses for transactional and MVCC purposes, and the rest of the columns (in this case, col2). If the primary key is on a column prefix, InnoDB includes the full column value with the rest of the columns.

Also in contrast to MyISAM, secondary indexes are very different from clustered indexes in InnoDB. Instead of storing "row pointers," InnoDB's secondary index leaf nodes contain the primary key values, which serve as the "pointers" to the rows. This strategy reduces the work needed to maintain secondary indexes when rows move or when there's a data page split. Using the row's primary key values as the pointer makes the index larger, but it means InnoDB can move a row without updating pointers to it.

Figure 5-8 illustrates the col2 index for the example table. Each leaf node contains the indexed columns (in this case just col2), followed by the primary key values (col1).

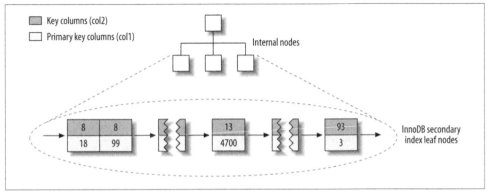

Figure 5-8. InnoDB secondary index layout for the layout_test table

These diagrams have illustrated the B-Tree leaf nodes, but we intentionally omitted details about the non-leaf nodes. InnoDB's non-leaf B-Tree nodes each contain the indexed column(s), plus a pointer to the next-deeper node (which might be either another non-leaf node or a leaf node). This applies to all indexes, clustered and secondary.

Figure 5-9 is an abstract diagram of how InnoDB and MyISAM arrange the table. This illustration makes it easier to see how differently InnoDB and MyISAM store data and indexes.

If you don't understand why and how clustered and nonclustered storage are different, and why it's so important, don't worry. It will become clearer as you learn more, especially in the rest of this chapter and in the next chapter. These concepts are complicated, and they take a while to understand fully.

Inserting rows in primary key order with InnoDB

If you're using InnoDB and don't need any particular clustering, it can be a good idea to define a *surrogate key*, which is a primary key whose value is not derived from your application's data. The easiest way to do this is usually with an AUTO_INCREMENT column. This will ensure that rows are inserted in sequential order and will offer better performance for joins using primary keys.

It is best to avoid random (nonsequential and distributed over a large set of values) clustered keys, especially for I/O-bound workloads. For example, using UUID values is a poor choice from a performance standpoint: it makes clustered index insertion random, which is a worst-case scenario, and does not give you any helpful data clustering.

To demonstrate, we benchmarked two cases. The first is inserting into a userinfo table with an integer ID, defined as follows:

```
CREATE TABLE userinfo (
    id              int unsigned NOT NULL AUTO_INCREMENT,
    name            varchar(64) NOT NULL DEFAULT '',
    email           varchar(64) NOT NULL DEFAULT '',
    password        varchar(64) NOT NULL DEFAULT '',
    dob             date DEFAULT NULL,
    address         varchar(255) NOT NULL DEFAULT '',
    city            varchar(64) NOT NULL DEFAULT '',
    state_id        tinyint unsigned NOT NULL DEFAULT '0',
    zip             varchar(8) NOT NULL DEFAULT '',
    country_id      smallint unsigned NOT NULL DEFAULT '0',
    gender          ('M','F')NOT NULL DEFAULT 'M',
    account_type    varchar(32) NOT NULL DEFAULT '',
    verified        tinyint NOT NULL DEFAULT '0',
    allow_mail      tinyint unsigned NOT NULL DEFAULT '0',
    parrent_account int unsigned NOT NULL DEFAULT '0',
    closest_airport varchar(3) NOT NULL DEFAULT '',
    PRIMARY KEY (id),
    UNIQUE  KEY email (email),
    KEY     country_id (country_id),
    KEY     state_id (state_id),
    KEY     state_id_2 (state_id,city,address)
) ENGINE=InnoDB
```

Notice the autoincrementing integer primary key.[9]

The second case is a table named userinfo_uuid. It is identical to the userinfo table, except that its primary key is a UUID instead of an integer:

```
CREATE TABLE userinfo_uuid (
    uuid varchar(36) NOT NULL,
    ...
```

We benchmarked both table designs. First, we inserted a million records into both tables on a server with enough memory to hold the indexes. Next, we inserted three million rows into the same tables, which made the indexes bigger than the server's memory. Table 5-1 compares the benchmark results.

---

9. It's worth pointing out that this is a real table, with secondary indexes and lots of columns. If we removed these and benchmarked only the primary key performance, the difference would be even larger.

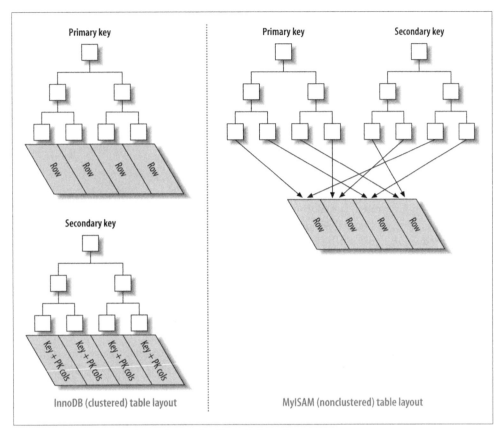

Figure 5-9. Clustered and nonclustered tables side-by-side

Table 5-1. Benchmark results for inserting rows into InnoDB tables

Table	Rows	Time (sec)	Index size (MB)
userinfo	1,000,000	137	342
userinfo_uuid	1,000,000	180	544
userinfo	3,000,000	1233	1036
userinfo_uuid	3,000,000	4525	1707

Notice that not only does it take longer to insert the rows with the UUID primary key, but the resulting indexes are quite a bit bigger. Some of that is due to the larger primary key, but some of it is undoubtedly due to page splits and resultant fragmentation as well.

To see why this is so, let's see what happened in the index when we inserted data into the first table. Figure 5-10 shows inserts filling a page and then continuing on a second page.

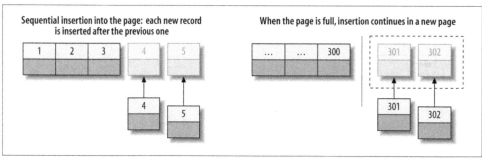

Figure 5-10. Inserting sequential index values into a clustered index

As Figure 5-10 illustrates, InnoDB stores each record immediately after the one before, because the primary key values are sequential. When the page reaches its maximum fill factor (InnoDB's initial fill factor is only 15/16 full, to leave room for modifications later), the next record goes into a new page. Once the data has been loaded in this sequential fashion, the primary key pages are packed nearly full with in-order records, which is highly desirable. (The secondary index pages are not likely to differ, however.)

Contrast that with what happened when we inserted the data into the second table with the UUID clustered index, as shown in Figure 5-11.

Because each new row doesn't necessarily have a larger primary key value than the previous one, InnoDB cannot always place the new row at the end of the index. It has to find the appropriate place for the row—on average, somewhere near the middle of the existing data—and make room for it. This causes a lot of extra work and results in a suboptimal data layout. Here's a summary of the drawbacks:

- The destination page might have been flushed to disk and removed from the caches, or might not have ever been placed into the caches, in which case InnoDB will have to find it and read it from the disk before it can insert the new row. This causes a lot of random I/O.

- When insertions are done out of order, InnoDB has to split pages frequently to make room for new rows. This requires moving around a lot of data, and modifying at least three pages instead of one.

- Pages become sparsely and irregularly filled because of splitting, so the final data is fragmented.

After loading such random values into a clustered index, you should probably do an OPTIMIZE TABLE to rebuild the table and fill the pages optimally.

The moral of the story is that you should strive to insert data in primary key order when using InnoDB, and you should try to use a clustering key that will give a monotonically increasing value for each new row.

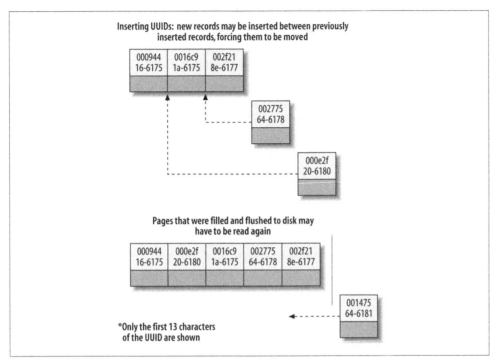

Figure 5-11. *Inserting nonsequential values into a clustered index*

When Primary Key Order Is Worse

For high-concurrency workloads, inserting in primary key order can actually create points of contention in InnoDB. The upper end of the primary key is one hot spot. Because all inserts take place there, concurrent inserts might fight over next-key locks. Another hot spot is the `AUTO_INCREMENT` locking mechanism; if you experience problems with that, you might be able to redesign your table or application, or configure `innodb_autoinc_lock_mode`. If your server version doesn't support `innodb_auto inc_lock_mode`, you can upgrade to a newer version of InnoDB that will perform better for this specific workload.

Covering Indexes

A common suggestion is to create indexes for the query's WHERE clause, but that's only part of the story. Indexes need to be designed for the whole query, not just the WHERE clause. Indexes are indeed a way to find rows efficiently, but MySQL can also use an index to retrieve a column's data, so it doesn't have to read the row at all. After all, the index's leaf nodes contain the values they index; why read the row when reading the index can give you the data you want? An index that contains (or "covers") all the data needed to satisfy a query is called a *covering index*.

Covering indexes can be a very powerful tool and can dramatically improve performance. Consider the benefits of reading only the index instead of the data:

- Index entries are usually much smaller than the full row size, so MySQL can access significantly less data if it reads only the index. This is very important for cached workloads, where much of the response time comes from copying the data. It is also helpful for I/O-bound workloads, because the indexes are smaller than the data and fit in memory better. (This is especially true for MyISAM, which can pack indexes to make them even smaller.)

- Indexes are sorted by their index values (at least within the page), so I/O-bound range accesses will need to do less I/O compared to fetching each row from a random disk location. For some storage engines, such as MyISAM and Percona XtraDB, you can even OPTIMIZE the table to get fully sorted indexes, which will let simple range queries use completely sequential index accesses.

- Some storage engines, such as MyISAM, cache only the index in MySQL's memory. Because the operating system caches the data for MyISAM, accessing it typically requires a system call. This might cause a huge performance impact, especially for cached workloads where the system call is the most expensive part of data access.

- Covering indexes are especially helpful for InnoDB tables, because of InnoDB's clustered indexes. InnoDB's secondary indexes hold the row's primary key values at their leaf nodes. Thus, a secondary index that covers a query avoids another index lookup in the primary key.

In all of these scenarios, it is typically much less expensive to satisfy a query from an index instead of looking up the rows.

A covering index can't be just any kind of index. The index must store the values from the columns it contains. Hash, spatial, and full-text indexes don't store these values, so MySQL can use only B-Tree indexes to cover queries. And again, different storage engines implement covering indexes differently, and not all storage engines support them (at the time of this writing, the Memory storage engine doesn't).

When you issue a query that is covered by an index (an *index-covered query*), you'll see "Using index" in the Extra column in EXPLAIN.[10] For example, the sakila.inventory table has a multicolumn index on (store_id, film_id). MySQL can use this index for a query that accesses only those two columns, such as the following:

```
mysql> EXPLAIN SELECT store_id, film_id FROM sakila.inventory\G
*************************** 1. row ***************************
          id: 1
```

10. It's easy to confuse "Using index" in the Extra column with "index" in the type column. However, they are completely different. The type column has nothing to do with covering indexes; it shows the query's access type, or how the query will find rows. The MySQL manual calls this the "join type."

```
    select_type: SIMPLE
         table: inventory
          type: index
 possible_keys: NULL
           key: idx_store_id_film_id
       key_len: 3
           ref: NULL
          rows: 4673
         Extra: Using index
```

Index-covered queries have subtleties that can disable this optimization. The MySQL query optimizer decides before executing a query whether an index covers it. Suppose the index covers a WHERE condition, but not the entire query. If the condition evaluates as false, MySQL 5.5 and earlier will fetch the row anyway, even though it doesn't need it and will filter it out.

Let's see why this can happen, and how to rewrite the query to work around the problem. We begin with the following query:

```
mysql> EXPLAIN SELECT * FROM products WHERE actor='SEAN CARREY'
    -> AND title like '%APOLLO%'\G
*************************** 1. row ***************************
            id: 1
    select_type: SIMPLE
         table: products
          type: ref
 possible_keys: ACTOR,IX_PROD_ACTOR
           key: ACTOR
       key_len: 52
           ref: const
          rows: 10
         Extra: Using where
```

The index can't cover this query for two reasons:

- No index covers the query, because we selected all columns from the table and no index covers all columns. There's still a shortcut MySQL could theoretically use, though: the WHERE clause mentions only columns the index covers, so MySQL could use the index to find the actor and check whether the title matches, and only then read the full row.

- MySQL can't perform the LIKE operation in the index. This is a limitation of the low-level storage engine API, which in MySQL 5.5 and earlier allows only simple comparisons (such as equality, inequality, and greater-than) in index operations. MySQL can perform prefix-match LIKE patterns in the index because it can convert them to simple comparisons, but the leading wildcard in the query makes it impossible for the storage engine to evaluate the match. Thus, the MySQL server itself will have to fetch and match on the row's values, not the index's values.

There's a way to work around both problems with a combination of clever indexing and query rewriting. We can extend the index to cover (artist, title, prod_id) and rewrite the query as follows:

```
mysql> EXPLAIN SELECT *
    -> FROM products
    ->     JOIN (
    ->         SELECT prod_id
    ->         FROM products
    ->         WHERE actor='SEAN CARREY' AND title LIKE '%APOLLO%'
    ->     ) AS t1 ON (t1.prod_id=products.prod_id)\G
*************************** 1. row ***************************
           id: 1
  select_type: PRIMARY
        table: <derived2>
               ...omitted...
*************************** 2. row ***************************
           id: 1
  select_type: PRIMARY
        table: products
               ...omitted...
*************************** 3. row ***************************
           id: 2
  select_type: DERIVED
        table: products
         type: ref
possible_keys: ACTOR,ACTOR_2,IX_PROD_ACTOR
          key: ACTOR_2
      key_len: 52
          ref:
         rows: 11
        Extra: Using where; Using index
```

We call this a "deferred join" because it defers access to the columns. MySQL uses the covering index in the first stage of the query, when it finds matching rows in the subquery in the FROM clause. It doesn't use the index to cover the whole query, but it's better than nothing.

The effectiveness of this optimization depends on how many rows the WHERE clause finds. Suppose the products table contains a million rows. Let's see how these two queries perform on three different datasets, each of which contains a million rows:

1. In the first, 30,000 products have Sean Carrey as the actor, and 20,000 of those contain "Apollo" in the title.

2. In the second, 30,000 products have Sean Carrey as the actor, and 40 of those contain "Apollo" in the title.

3. In the third, 50 products have Sean Carrey as the actor, and 10 of those contain "Apollo" in the title.

We used these three datasets to benchmark the two variations of the query and got the results shown in Table 5-2.

Table 5-2. Benchmark results for index-covered queries versus non-index-covered queries

Dataset	Original query	Optimized query
Example 1	5 queries per sec	5 queries per sec
Example 2	7 queries per sec	35 queries per sec
Example 3	2400 queries per sec	2000 queries per sec

Here's how to interpret these results:

- In example 1 the query returns a big result set, so we can't see the optimization's effect. Most of the time is spent reading and sending data.

- Example 2, where the second condition filter leaves only a small set of results after index filtering, shows how effective the proposed optimization is: performance is five times better on our data. The efficiency comes from needing to read only 40 full rows, instead of 30,000 as in the first query.

- Example 3 shows the case when the subquery is inefficient. The set of results left after index filtering is so small that the subquery is more expensive than reading all the data from the table.

In most storage engines, an index can cover only queries that access columns that are part of the index. However, InnoDB can actually take this optimization a little bit further. Recall that InnoDB's secondary indexes hold primary key values at their leaf nodes. This means InnoDB's secondary indexes effectively have "extra columns" that InnoDB can use to cover queries.

For example, the `sakila.actor` table uses InnoDB and has an index on `last_name`, so the index can cover queries that retrieve the primary key column `actor_id`, even though that column isn't technically part of the index:

```
mysql> EXPLAIN SELECT actor_id, last_name
    -> FROM sakila.actor WHERE last_name = 'HOPPER'\G
*************************** 1. row ***************************
           id: 1
  select_type: SIMPLE
        table: actor
         type: ref
possible_keys: idx_actor_last_name
          key: idx_actor_last_name
      key_len: 137
          ref: const
         rows: 2
        Extra: Using where; Using index
```

Improvements in Future MySQL Versions

Many of the particulars we've mentioned here are a result of the limited storage engine API, which doesn't allow MySQL to push filters through the API to the storage engine. If MySQL could do that, it could send the query to the data, instead of pulling the data into the server where it evaluates the query. At the time of writing, the unreleased MySQL 5.6 contains a significant improvement to the storage engine API, called *index condition pushdown*. This feature will change query execution greatly and render obsolete many of the tricks we've discussed.

Using Index Scans for Sorts

MySQL has two ways to produce ordered results: it can use a sort operation, or it can scan an index in order.[11] You can tell when MySQL plans to scan an index by looking for "index" in the type column in EXPLAIN. (Don't confuse this with "Using index" in the Extra column.)

Scanning the index itself is fast, because it simply requires moving from one index entry to the next. However, if MySQL isn't using the index to cover the query, it will have to look up each row it finds in the index. This is basically random I/O, so reading data in index order is usually much slower than a sequential table scan, especially for I/O-bound workloads.

MySQL can use the same index for both sorting and finding rows. If possible, it's a good idea to design your indexes so that they're useful for both tasks at once.

Ordering the results by the index works only when the index's order is exactly the same as the ORDER BY clause and all columns are sorted in the same direction (ascending or descending).[12] If the query joins multiple tables, it works only when all columns in the ORDER BY clause refer to the first table. The ORDER BY clause also has the same limitation as lookup queries: it needs to form a leftmost prefix of the index. In all other cases, MySQL uses a sort.

One case where the ORDER BY clause doesn't have to specify a leftmost prefix of the index is if there are constants for the leading columns. If the WHERE clause or a JOIN clause specifies constants for these columns, they can "fill the gaps" in the index.

For example, the rental table in the standard Sakila sample database has an index on (rental_date, inventory_id, customer_id):

```
CREATE TABLE rental (
   ...
   PRIMARY KEY (rental_id),
```

---

11. MySQL has two sort algorithms; you can read more about them in Chapter 7.

12. If you need to sort in different directions, a trick that sometimes helps is to store a reversed or negated value.

```
      UNIQUE KEY rental_date (rental_date,inventory_id,customer_id),
      KEY idx_fk_inventory_id (inventory_id),
      KEY idx_fk_customer_id (customer_id),
      KEY idx_fk_staff_id (staff_id),
      ...
);
```

MySQL uses the `rental_date` index to order the following query, as you can see from the lack of a filesort[13] in EXPLAIN:

```
mysql> EXPLAIN SELECT rental_id, staff_id FROM sakila.rental
    -> WHERE rental_date = '2005-05-25'
    -> ORDER BY inventory_id, customer_id\G
*************************** 1. row ***************************
          type: ref
 possible_keys: rental_date
           key: rental_date
          rows: 1
         Extra: Using where
```

This works, even though the ORDER BY clause isn't itself a leftmost prefix of the index, because we specified an equality condition for the first column in the index.

Here are some more queries that can use the index for sorting. This one works because the query provides a constant for the first column of the index and specifies an ORDER BY on the second column. Taken together, those two form a leftmost prefix on the index:

```
... WHERE rental_date = '2005-05-25' ORDER BY inventory_id DESC;
```

The following query also works, because the two columns in the ORDER BY are a leftmost prefix of the index:

```
... WHERE rental_date > '2005-05-25' ORDER BY rental_date, inventory_id;
```

Here are some queries that *cannot* use the index for sorting:

- This query uses two different sort directions, but the index's columns are all sorted ascending:

  ```
  ... WHERE rental_date = '2005-05-25' ORDER BY inventory_id DESC, customer_id ASC;
  ```

- Here, the ORDER BY refers to a column that isn't in the index:

  ```
  ... WHERE rental_date = '2005-05-25' ORDER BY inventory_id, staff_id;
  ```

- Here, the WHERE and the ORDER BY don't form a leftmost prefix of the index:

  ```
  ... WHERE rental_date = '2005-05-25' ORDER BY customer_id;
  ```

- This query has a range condition on the first column, so MySQL doesn't use the rest of the index:

  ```
  ... WHERE rental_date > '2005-05-25' ORDER BY inventory_id, customer_id;
  ```

- Here there's a multiple equality on the `inventory_id` column. For the purposes of sorting, this is basically the same as a range:

---

13. MySQL calls it a "filesort," but it doesn't necessarily use files.

```
... WHERE rental_date = '2005-05-25' AND inventory_id IN(1,2) ORDER BY customer_
id;
```

- Here's an example where MySQL could theoretically use an index to order a join, but doesn't because the optimizer places the film_actor table second in the join (the next chapter shows ways to change the join order):

```
mysql> EXPLAIN SELECT actor_id, title FROM sakila.film_actor
    -> INNER JOIN sakila.film USING(film_id) ORDER BY actor_id\G
+------------+----------------------------------------------------+
| table      | Extra                                              |
+------------+----------------------------------------------------+
| film       | Using index; Using temporary; Using filesort       |
| film_actor | Using index                                        |
+------------+----------------------------------------------------+
```

One of the most important uses for ordering by an index is a query that has both an ORDER BY and a LIMIT clause. We explore this in more detail later.

Packed (Prefix-Compressed) Indexes

MyISAM uses prefix compression to reduce index size, allowing more of the index to fit in memory and dramatically improving performance in some cases. It packs string values by default, but you can even tell it to compress integer values.

MyISAM packs each index block by storing the block's first value fully, then storing each additional value in the block by recording the number of bytes that have the same prefix, plus the actual data of the suffix that differs. For example, if the first value is "perform" and the second is "performance," the second value will be stored analogously to "7,ance". MyISAM can also prefix-compress adjacent row pointers.

Compressed blocks use less space, but they make some operations slower. Because each value's compression prefix depends on the value before it, MyISAM can't do binary searches to find a desired item in the block and must scan the block from the beginning. Sequential forward scans perform well, but reverse scans—such as ORDER BY DESC—don't work as well. Any operation that requires finding a single row in the middle of the block will require scanning, on average, half the block.

Our benchmarks have shown that packed keys make index lookups on MyISAM tables perform several times more slowly for a CPU-bound workload, because of the scans required for random lookups. Reverse scans of packed keys are even slower. The tradeoff is one of CPU and memory resources versus disk resources. Packed indexes can be about one-tenth the size on disk, and if you have an I/O-bound workload they can more than offset the cost for some queries.

You can control how a table's indexes are packed with the PACK_KEYS option to CREATE TABLE.

Redundant and Duplicate Indexes

MySQL allows you to create multiple indexes on the same column; it does not "notice" and protect you from your mistake. MySQL has to maintain each duplicate index separately, and the query optimizer will consider each of them when it optimizes queries. This can impact performance.

Duplicate indexes are indexes of the same type, created on the same set of columns in the same order. You should try to avoid creating them, and you should remove them if you find them.

Sometimes you can create duplicate indexes without knowing it. For example, look at the following code:

```
CREATE TABLE test (
    ID INT NOT NULL PRIMARY KEY,
    A  INT NOT NULL,
    B  INT NOT NULL,
    UNIQUE(ID),
    INDEX(ID)
) ENGINE=InnoDB;
```

An inexperienced user might think this identifies the column's role as a primary key, adds a UNIQUE constraint, and adds an index for queries to use. In fact, MySQL implements UNIQUE constraints and PRIMARY KEY constraints with indexes, so this actually creates three indexes on the same column! There is typically no reason to do this, unless you want to have different types of indexes on the same column to satisfy different kinds of queries.[14]

Redundant indexes are a bit different from duplicated indexes. If there is an index on (A, B), another index on (A) would be redundant because it is a prefix of the first index. That is, the index on (A, B) can also be used as an index on (A) alone. (This type of redundancy applies only to B-Tree indexes.) However, an index on (B, A) would not be redundant, and neither would an index on (B), because B is not a leftmost prefix of (A, B). Furthermore, indexes of different types (such as hash or full-text indexes) are not redundant to B-Tree indexes, no matter what columns they cover.

Redundant indexes usually appear when people add indexes to a table. For example, someone might add an index on (A, B) instead of extending an existing index on (A) to cover (A, B). Another way this could happen is by changing the index to cover (A, ID). The ID column is the primary key, so it's already included if you're using InnoDB.

In most cases you don't want redundant indexes, and to avoid them you should extend existing indexes rather than add new ones. Still, there are times when you'll need redundant indexes for performance reasons. Extending an existing index might make it much larger and reduce performance for some queries.

---

14. An index is not necessarily a duplicate if it's a different type of index; there are often good reasons to have KEY(*col*) and FULLTEXT KEY(*col*).

For example, if you have an index on an integer column and you extend it with a long VARCHAR column, it might become significantly slower. This is especially true if your queries use the index as a covering index, or if it's a MyISAM table and you perform a lot of range scans on it (because of MyISAM's prefix compression).

Consider the userinfo table, which we described previously in "Inserting rows in primary key order with InnoDB" on page 173. This table contains 1,000,000 rows, and for each state_id there are about 20,000 records. There is an index on state_id, which is useful for the following query. We refer to this query as Q1:

```
mysql> SELECT count(*) FROM userinfo WHERE state_id=5;
```

A simple benchmark shows an execution rate of almost 115 queries per second (QPS) for this query. We also have a related query that retrieves several columns instead of just counting rows. This is Q2:

```
mysql> SELECT state_id, city, address FROM userinfo WHERE state_id=5;
```

For this query, the result is less than 10 QPS.[15] The simple solution to improve its performance is to extend the index to (state_id, city, address), so the index will cover the query:

```
mysql> ALTER TABLE userinfo DROP KEY state_id,
    ->     ADD KEY state_id_2 (state_id, city, address);
```

After extending the index, Q2 runs faster, but Q1 runs more slowly. If we really care about making both queries fast, we should leave both indexes, even though the single-column index is redundant. Table 5-3 shows detailed results for both queries and indexing strategies, with MyISAM and InnoDB storage engines. Note that InnoDB's performance doesn't degrade as much for Q1 with only the state_id_2 index, because InnoDB doesn't use key compression.

Table 5-3. Benchmark results in QPS for SELECT queries with various index strategies

	state_id only	state_id_2 only	Both state_id and state_id_2
MyISAM, Q1	114.96	25.40	112.19
MyISAM, Q2	9.97	16.34	16.37
InnoDB, Q1	108.55	100.33	107.97
InnoDB, Q2	12.12	28.04	28.06

The drawback of having two indexes is the maintenance cost. Table 5-4 shows how long it takes to insert a million rows into the table.

---

15. We've used an in-memory example here. When the table is bigger and the workload becomes I/O-bound, the difference between the numbers will be much larger. It's not uncommon for COUNT() queries to become 100 or more times faster with a covering index.

Table 5-4. Speed of inserting a million rows with various index strategies

	state_id only	Both state_id and state_id_2
InnoDB, enough memory for both indexes	80 seconds	136 seconds
MyISAM, enough memory for only one index	72 seconds	470 seconds

As you can see, inserting new rows into the table with more indexes is slower. This is true in general: adding new indexes might have a performance impact for INSERT, UPDATE, and DELETE operations, especially if a new index causes you to hit memory limits.

The solution for redundant and duplicate indexes is simply to drop them, but first you need to identify them. You can write various complicated queries against the INFORMA TION_SCHEMA tables, but there are two easier techniques. You can use the views in Shlomi Noach's *common_schema*, a set of utility routines and views you can install into your server (*http://code.google.com/p/common-schema/*). This is faster and easier than writing the queries yourself. Or you can use the *pt-duplicate-key-checker* tool included with Percona Toolkit, which analyzes table structures and suggests indexes that are duplicate or redundant. The external tool is probably a better choice for very large servers; queries against the INFORMATION_SCHEMA tables can cause performance problems when there is a lot of data or a large number of tables.

Be careful when determining which indexes are candidates for dropping or extending. Recall that in InnoDB, an index on column (A) in our example table is really equivalent to an index on (A, ID) because the primary key is appended to secondary index leaf nodes. If you have a query such as WHERE A = 5 ORDER BY ID, the index will be very helpful. But if you extend the index to (A, B), then it really becomes (A, B, ID) and the query will begin to use a filesort for the ORDER BY portion of the query. It's good to validate your planned changes carefully with a tool such as *pt-upgrade* from the Percona Toolkit.

Unused Indexes

In addition to duplicate and redundant indexes, you might have some indexes that the server simply doesn't use. These are simply dead weight, and you should consider dropping them.[16] There are two tools that can help you identify unused indexes. Perhaps the easiest and most accurate is the INFORMATION_SCHEMA.INDEX_STATISTICS table in Percona Server and MariaDB. Just enable the userstats server variable (it's disabled by default) and let the server run for a while, and you'll be able to see how much each index is used.

Alternatively, you can use the *pt-index-usage* tool included in Percona Toolkit. This tool reads a log of queries and executes EXPLAIN with each one. When it completes, it

---

16. Some indexes function as unique constraints, so even if an index doesn't get used for queries, it might be used to prevent duplicate values.

prints out a report on indexes and queries. You can use this not only to find indexes that aren't used, but also to learn about the query execution plans—for example, finding similar queries that the server executes differently in some cases. This can help you identify queries that might provide poor quality of service at times, so you can optimize them to run more uniformly. The tool can also store its results into tables in MySQL, so you can run SQL queries against them.

Indexes and Locking

Indexes permit queries to lock fewer rows. If your queries never touch rows they don't need, they'll lock fewer rows, and that's better for performance for two reasons. First, even though InnoDB's row locks are very efficient and use very little memory, there's still some overhead involved in row locking. Secondly, locking more rows than needed increases lock contention and reduces concurrency.

InnoDB locks rows only when it accesses them, and an index can reduce the number of rows InnoDB accesses and therefore locks. However, this works only if InnoDB can filter out the undesired rows *at the storage engine level*. If the index doesn't permit InnoDB to do that, the MySQL server will have to apply a WHERE clause after InnoDB retrieves the rows and returns them to the server level.[17] At this point, it's too late to avoid locking the rows: InnoDB will already have locked them, and they will remain locked for some period of time. In MySQL 5.1 and newer, InnoDB can unlock rows after the server filters them out; in older versions of MySQL, InnoDB doesn't unlock the rows until the transaction commits.

This is easier to see with an example. We use the Sakila sample database again:

```
mysql> SET AUTOCOMMIT=0;
mysql> BEGIN;
mysql> SELECT actor_id FROM sakila.actor WHERE actor_id < 5
    ->    AND actor_id <> 1 FOR UPDATE;
+----------+
| actor_id |
+----------+
|        2 |
|        3 |
|        4 |
+----------+
```

This query returns only rows 2 through 4, but it actually gets exclusive locks on *rows 1 through 4*. InnoDB locked row 1 because the plan MySQL chose for this query was an index range access:

```
mysql> EXPLAIN SELECT actor_id FROM sakila.actor
    -> WHERE actor_id < 5 AND actor_id <> 1 FOR UPDATE;
+----+-------------+-------+------+---------+-------------------------+
| id | select_type | table | type | key     | Extra                   |
```

---

17. Again, MySQL 5.6 might help significantly with this problem.

```
+----+-------------+--------+-------+---------+------------------------+
|  1 | SIMPLE      | actor  | range | PRIMARY | Using where; Using index |
+----+-------------+--------+-------+---------+------------------------+
```

In other words, the low-level storage engine operation was "begin at the start of the index and fetch all rows until `actor_id < 5` is false." The server didn't tell InnoDB about the `WHERE` condition that eliminated row 1. Note the presence of "Using where" in the `Extra` column in `EXPLAIN`. This indicates that the MySQL server is applying a `WHERE` filter after the storage engine returns the rows.

Here's a second query that proves row 1 is locked, even though it didn't appear in the results from the first query. Leaving the first connection open, start a second connection and execute the following:

```
mysql> SET AUTOCOMMIT=0;
mysql> BEGIN;
mysql> SELECT actor_id FROM sakila.actor WHERE actor_id = 1 FOR UPDATE;
```

The query will hang, waiting for the first transaction to release the lock on row 1. This behavior is necessary for statement-based replication (discussed in Chapter 10) to work correctly.[18]

As this example shows, InnoDB can lock rows it doesn't really need even when it uses an index. The problem is even worse when it can't use an index to find and lock the rows: if there's no index for the query, MySQL will do a full table scan and lock every row, whether it "needs" it or not.

Here's a little-known detail about InnoDB, indexes, and locking: InnoDB can place shared (read) locks on secondary indexes, but exclusive (write) locks require access to the primary key. That eliminates the possibility of using a covering index and can make `SELECT FOR UPDATE` much slower than `LOCK IN SHARE MODE` or a nonlocking query.

An Indexing Case Study

The easiest way to understand how to apply indexing concepts is with an illustration, so we've prepared a case study in indexing.

Suppose we need to design an online dating site with user profiles that have many different columns, such as the user's country, state/region, city, sex, age, eye color, and so on. The site must support searching the profiles by various combinations of these properties. It must also let the user sort and limit results by the last time the profile's owner was online, ratings from other members, etc. How do we design indexes for such complex requirements?

---

18. Although it's possible for the server not to lock the rows in some transaction isolation levels when row-based binary logging is used, in practice it turns out to be tricky to get the desired behavior, and even in MySQL 5.6.3 with read-committed isolation and row-based logging, the example we've shown will cause blocking.

Oddly enough, the first thing to decide is whether we have to use index-based sorting, or whether post-retrieval sorting is acceptable. Index-based sorting restricts how the indexes and queries need to be built. For example, we can't use an index for a WHERE clause such as WHERE age BETWEEN 18 AND 25 if the same query uses an index to sort users by the ratings other users have given them. If MySQL uses an index for a range criterion in a query, it cannot also use another index (or a suffix of the same index) for ordering. Assuming this will be one of the most common WHERE clauses, we'll take for granted that many queries will need a sort (i.e., a filesort).

Supporting Many Kinds of Filtering

Now we need to look at which columns have many distinct values and which columns appear in WHERE clauses most often. Indexes on columns with many distinct values will be very selective. This is generally a good thing, because it lets MySQL filter out undesired rows more efficiently.

The country column might not be selective, but it'll probably be in most queries anyway. The sex column is certainly not selective, but it'll probably be in every query. With this in mind, we create a series of indexes for many different combinations of columns, prefixed with (sex,country).

The traditional wisdom is that it's useless to index columns with very low selectivity. So why would we place a nonselective column at the beginning of every index? Are we out of our minds?

We have two reasons for doing this. The first reason is that, as stated earlier, almost every query will use sex. We might even design the site such that users can choose to search for only one sex at a time. But more importantly, there's not much of a downside to adding the column, because we have a trick up our sleeves.

Here's the trick: even if a query that doesn't restrict the results by sex is issued, we can ensure that the index is usable anyway by adding AND sex IN('m', 'f') to the WHERE clause. This won't actually filter out any rows, so it's functionally the same as not including the sex column in the WHERE clause at all. However, we *need* to include this column, because it'll let MySQL use a larger prefix of the index. This trick is useful in situations like this one, but if the column had many distinct values, it wouldn't work well because the IN() list would get too large.

This case illustrates a general principle: keep all options on the table. When you're designing indexes, don't just think about the kinds of indexes you need for existing queries, but consider optimizing the queries, too. If you see the need for an index but you think some queries might suffer because of it, ask yourself whether you can change the queries. You should optimize queries and indexes together to find the best compromise; you don't have to design the perfect indexing scheme in a vacuum.

Next, we need to think about what other combinations of WHERE conditions we're likely to see and consider which of those combinations would be slow without proper indexes. An index on (sex, country, age) is an obvious choice, and we'll probably also need indexes on (sex, country, region, age) and (sex, country, region, city, age).

That's getting to be a lot of indexes. If we want to reuse indexes and it won't generate too many combinations of conditions, we can use the IN() trick and scrap the (sex, country, age) and (sex, country, region, age) indexes. If they're not specified in the search form, we can ensure the index prefix has equality constraints by specifying a list of all countries, or all regions for the country. (Combined lists of all countries, all regions, and all sexes would probably be too large.)

These indexes will satisfy the most frequently specified search queries, but how can we design indexes for less common options, such as has_pictures, eye_color, hair_color, and education? If these columns are not very selective and are not used a lot, we can simply skip them and let MySQL scan a few extra rows. Alternatively, we can add them before the age column and use the IN() technique described earlier to handle the case where they are not specified.

You might have noticed that we're keeping the age column at the end of the index. What makes this column so special, and why should it be at the end of the index? We're trying to make sure that MySQL uses as many columns of the index as possible, because it uses only the leftmost prefix, up to and including the first condition that specifies a range of values. All the other columns we've mentioned can use equality conditions in the WHERE clause, but age is almost certain to be a range (e.g., age BETWEEN 18 AND 25).

We could convert this to an IN() list, such as age IN(18, 19, 20, 21, 22, 23, 24, 25), but this won't always be possible for this type of query. The general principle we're trying to illustrate is to keep the range criterion at the end of the index, so the optimizer will use as much of the index as possible.

We've said that you can add more and more columns to the index and use IN() lists to cover cases where those columns aren't part of the WHERE clause, but you can overdo this and get into trouble. Using more than a few such lists explodes the number of combinations the optimizer has to evaluate, and this can ultimately reduce query speed. Consider the following WHERE clause:

```
WHERE eye_color   IN('brown','blue','hazel')
  AND hair_color IN('black','red','blonde','brown')
  AND sex        IN('M','F')
```

The optimizer will convert this into 4*3*2 = 24 combinations, and the WHERE clause will then have to check for each of them. Twenty-four is not an extreme number of combinations, but be careful if that number approaches thousands. Older MySQL versions had more problems with large numbers of IN() combinations: query optimization could take longer than execution and consume a lot of memory. Newer MySQL versions stop evaluating combinations if the number of combinations gets too large, but this limits how well MySQL can use the index.

Avoiding Multiple Range Conditions

Let's assume we have a `last_online` column and we want to be able to show the users who were online during the previous week:

```
WHERE  eye_color   IN('brown','blue','hazel')
  AND hair_color  IN('black','red','blonde','brown')
  AND sex         IN('M','F')
  AND last_online > DATE_SUB(NOW(), INTERVAL 7 DAY)
  AND age         BETWEEN 18 AND 25
```

What Is a Range Condition?

`EXPLAIN`'s output can sometimes make it hard to tell whether MySQL is really looking for a range of values, or for a list of values. `EXPLAIN` uses the same term, "range," to indicate both. For example, MySQL calls the following a "range" query, as you can see in the **type** column:

```
mysql> EXPLAIN SELECT actor_id FROM sakila.actor
    -> WHERE actor_id > 45\G
*********************** 1. row ***********************
          id: 1
  select_type: SIMPLE
        table: actor
        type: range
```

But what about this one?

```
mysql> EXPLAIN SELECT actor_id FROM sakila.actor
    -> WHERE actor_id IN(1, 4, 99)\G
*********************** 1. row ***********************
          id: 1
  select_type: SIMPLE
        table: actor
        type: range
```

There's no way to tell the difference by looking at `EXPLAIN`, but we draw a distinction between ranges of values and multiple equality conditions. The second query is a multiple equality condition, in our terminology.

We're not just being picky: these two kinds of index accesses perform differently. The range condition makes MySQL ignore any further columns in the index, but the multiple equality condition doesn't have that limitation.

There's a problem with this query: it has two range conditions. MySQL can use either the `last_online` criterion or the `age` criterion, but not both.

If the `last_online` restriction appears without the `age` restriction, or if `last_online` is more selective than `age`, we might wish to add another set of indexes with `last_online` at the end. But what if we can't convert the `age` to an `IN()` list, and we really need the speed boost of restricting by `last_online` and `age` simultaneously? At the moment there's no way to do this directly, but we can convert one of the ranges to an equality comparison. To do this, we add a precomputed `active` column, which we'll maintain with a periodic job. We'll set the column to 1 when the user logs in, and the job will set it back to 0 if the user doesn't log in for seven consecutive days.

This approach lets MySQL use indexes such as (active, sex, country, age). The column might not be absolutely accurate, but this kind of query might not require a high degree of accuracy. If we do need accuracy, we can leave the last_online condition in the WHERE clause, *but not index it.* This technique is similar to the one we used to simulate hash indexes for URL lookups earlier in this chapter. The condition won't use any index, but because it's unlikely to throw away many of the rows that an index would find, an index wouldn't really be beneficial anyway. Put another way, the lack of an index won't hurt the query noticeably.

By now, you can probably see the pattern: if a user wants to see both active and inactive results, we can add an IN() list. We've added a lot of these lists, but the alternative is to create separate indexes that can satisfy every combination of columns on which we need to filter. We'd have to use at least the following indexes: (active, sex, country, age), (active, country, age), (sex, country, age), and (country, age). Although such indexes might be more optimal for each specific query, the overhead of maintaining them all, combined with all the extra space they'd require, would likely make this a poor strategy overall.

This is a case where optimizer changes can really affect the optimal indexing strategy. If a future version of MySQL can do a true loose index scan, it should be able to use multiple range conditions on a single index, so we won't need the IN() lists for the kinds of queries we're considering here.

Optimizing Sorts

The last issue we want to cover in this case study is sorting. Sorting small result sets with filesorts is fast, but what if millions of rows match a query? For example, what if only sex is specified in the WHERE clause?

We can add special indexes for sorting these low-selectivity cases. For example, an index on (sex, rating) can be used for the following query:

```
mysql> SELECT <cols> FROM profiles WHERE sex='M' ORDER BY rating LIMIT 10;
```

This query has both ORDER BY and LIMIT clauses, and it would be very slow without the index.

Even with the index, the query can be slow if the user interface is paginated and someone requests a page that's not near the beginning. This case creates a bad combination of ORDER BY and LIMIT with an offset:

```
mysql> SELECT <cols> FROM profiles WHERE sex='M' ORDER BY rating LIMIT 100000, 10;
```

Such queries can be a serious problem no matter how they're indexed, because the high offset requires them to spend most of their time scanning a lot of data that they will then throw away. Denormalizing, precomputing, and caching are likely to be the only strategies that work for queries like this one. An even better strategy is to limit the number of pages you let the user view. This is unlikely to impact the user's experience, because no one really cares about the 10,000th page of search results.

Another good strategy for optimizing such queries is to use a deferred join, which again is our term for using a covering index to retrieve just the primary key columns of the rows you'll eventually retrieve. You can then join this back to the table to retrieve all desired columns. This helps minimize the amount of work MySQL must do gathering data that it will only throw away. Here's an example that requires an index on (sex, rating) to work efficiently:

```
mysql> SELECT <cols> FROM profiles INNER JOIN (
    ->     SELECT <primary key cols> FROM profiles
    ->     WHERE x.sex='M' ORDER BY rating LIMIT 100000, 10
    -> ) AS x USING(<primary key cols>);
```

Index and Table Maintenance

Once you've created tables with proper data types and added indexes, your work isn't over: you still need to maintain your tables and indexes to make sure they perform well. The three main goals of table maintenance are finding and fixing corruption, maintaining accurate index statistics, and reducing fragmentation.

Finding and Repairing Table Corruption

The worst thing that can happen to a table is corruption. With the MyISAM storage engine, this often happens due to crashes. However, all storage engines can experience index corruption due to hardware problems or internal bugs in MySQL or the operating system.

Corrupted indexes can cause queries to return incorrect results, raise duplicate-key errors when there is no duplicated value, or even cause lockups and crashes. If you experience odd behavior—such as an error that you think shouldn't be happening— run CHECK TABLE to see if the table is corrupt. (Note that some storage engines don't support this command, and others support multiple options to specify how thoroughly they check the table.) CHECK TABLE usually catches most table and index errors.

You can fix corrupt tables with the REPAIR TABLE command, but again, not all storage engines support this. In these cases you can do a "no-op" ALTER, such as altering a table to use the same storage engine it currently uses. Here's an example for an InnoDB table:

```
mysql> ALTER TABLE innodb_tbl ENGINE=INNODB;
```

Alternatively, you can either use an offline engine-specific repair utility, such as *myi-samchk*, or dump the data and reload it. However, if the corruption is in the system area, or in the table's "row data" area instead of the index, you might be unable to use any of these options. In this case, you might need to restore the table from your backups or attempt to recover data from the corrupted files.

If you experience corruption with the InnoDB storage engine, something is seriously wrong and you need to investigate it right away. InnoDB simply shouldn't corrupt. Its design makes it very resilient to corruption. Corruption is evidence of either a hardware problem such as bad memory or disks (likely), an administrator error such as manipulating the database files externally to MySQL (likely), or an InnoDB bug (unlikely). The usual causes are mistakes such as trying to make backups with *rsync*. There is no query you can execute—none—that you are supposed to avoid because it'll corrupt InnoDB's data. There is no hidden gun pointed at your foot. If you're corrupting InnoDB's data by issuing queries against it, there's a bug in InnoDB, and it's never your fault.

If you experience data corruption, the most important thing to do is try to determine why it's occurring; don't simply repair the data, or the corruption could return. You can repair the data by putting InnoDB into forced recovery mode with the `innodb_force_recovery` parameter; see the MySQL manual for details. You can also use the open source Percona InnoDB Data Recovery Toolkit (*http://www.percona.com/soft ware/mysql-innodb-data-recovery-tools/*) to extract data directly from damaged data files.

Updating Index Statistics

The MySQL query optimizer uses two API calls to ask the storage engines how index values are distributed when deciding how to use indexes. The first is the `records _in_range()` call, which accepts range end points and returns the number of records in that range. This can be exact for some storage engines such as MyISAM, but is only an estimate for InnoDB.

The second API call is `info()`, which can return various types of data, including index cardinality (approximately how many records there are for each key value).

When the storage engine provides the optimizer with inexact information about the number of rows a query might examine, or when the query plan is too complex to know exactly how many rows will be matched at various stages, the optimizer uses the index statistics to estimate the number of rows. MySQL's optimizer is cost-based, and the main cost metric is how much data the query will access. If the statistics were never generated, or if they are out of date, the optimizer can make bad decisions. The solution is to run `ANALYZE TABLE`, which regenerates the statistics.

Each storage engine implements index statistics differently, so the frequency with which you'll need to run `ANALYZE TABLE` differs, as does the cost of running the statement:

- The Memory storage engine does not store index statistics at all.
- MyISAM stores statistics on disk, and `ANALYZE TABLE` performs a full index scan to compute cardinality. The entire table is locked during this process.

- InnoDB does not store statistics on disk as of MySQL 5.5, but rather estimates them with random index dives and stores them in memory.

You can examine the cardinality of your indexes with the SHOW INDEX FROM command. For example:

```
mysql> SHOW INDEX FROM sakila.actor\G
*************************** 1. row ***************************
        Table: actor
   Non_unique: 0
     Key_name: PRIMARY
 Seq_in_index: 1
  Column_name: actor_id
    Collation: A
  Cardinality: 200
     Sub_part: NULL
       Packed: NULL
         Null:
   Index_type: BTREE
      Comment:
*************************** 2. row ***************************
        Table: actor
   Non_unique: 1
     Key_name: idx_actor_last_name
 Seq_in_index: 1
  Column_name: last_name
    Collation: A
  Cardinality: 200
     Sub_part: NULL
       Packed: NULL
         Null:
   Index_type: BTREE
      Comment:
```

This command gives quite a lot of index information, which the MySQL manual explains in detail. We do want to call your attention to the Cardinality column, though. This shows how many distinct values the storage engine estimates are in the index. You can also get this data from the INFORMATION_SCHEMA.STATISTICS table in MySQL 5.0 and newer, which can be quite handy. For example, you can write queries against the INFORMATION_SCHEMA tables to find indexes with very low selectivity. Beware, however, that on servers with a lot of data, these metadata tables can cause a lot of load on the server.

InnoDB's statistics are worth exploring more. The statistics are generated by sampling a few random pages in the index and assuming that the rest of the index looks similar. The number of pages sampled is eight in older InnoDB versions, but in more recent versions it can be controlled with the innodb_stats_sample_pages variable. Setting this to a value larger than eight can in theory help generate more representative index statistics, especially on very large tables, but your mileage may vary.

InnoDB calculates statistics for indexes when tables are first opened, when you run `ANALYZE TABLE`, and when the table's size changes significantly (a size change of 1/16th or 2 billion row insertions, whichever comes first).

InnoDB also calculates statistics for queries against some `INFORMATION_SCHEMA` tables, `SHOW TABLE STATUS` and `SHOW INDEX` queries, and when the MySQL command-line client has autocompletion enabled. This can actually become a pretty serious problem on large servers with lots of data, or when I/O is slow. Client programs or monitoring tools that cause sampling to occur can cause a lot of locking and heavy load on the server, as well as frustrating users with slow startup times. And you can't observe the index statistics without changing them, because `SHOW INDEX` will update the statistics. You can disable the `innodb_stats_on_metadata` option to avoid all of these problems.

If you're using Percona Server, which includes Percona XtraDB instead of standard InnoDB, you can configure the behavior further. The `innodb_stats_auto_update` option lets you disable auto-resampling, effectively freezing statistics unless you run `ANALYZE TABLE` manually. This can help if you're struggling with unstable query plans. We created this feature at the request of some customers with very large deployments.

For even more query plan stability, and for faster system warmups, you can use a system table to store index statistics so they are stable across server restarts and don't need to be recomputed when InnoDB opens the table for the first time after booting up. This feature is available in Percona Server 5.1 and in the development milestone releases of standard MySQL 5.6. The Percona Server feature is enabled with the `innodb_use_sys_stats_table` option, and there will also be index statistics persistence in MySQL 5.6, controlled by the `innodb_analyze_is_persistent` option.

If you configure your server not to update index statistics automatically, you need to do it manually with periodic `ANALYZE TABLE` commands, unless you know that the statistics won't change in ways that will create bad query plans.

Reducing Index and Data Fragmentation

B-Tree indexes can become fragmented, which might reduce performance. Fragmented indexes can be poorly filled and/or nonsequential on disk.

By design B-Tree indexes require random disk accesses to "dive" to the leaf pages, so random access is the rule, not the exception. However, the leaf pages can still perform better if they are physically sequential and tightly packed. If they are not, we say they are fragmented, and range scans or full index scans can be many times slower. This is especially true for index-covered queries.

The table's data storage can also become fragmented. However, data storage fragmentation is more complex than index fragmentation. There are three types of data fragmentation:

Row fragmentation

This type of fragmentation occurs when the row is stored in multiple pieces in multiple locations. Row fragmentation reduces performance even if the query needs only a single row from the index.

Intra-row fragmentation

This kind of fragmentation occurs when logically sequential pages or rows are not stored sequentially on disk. It affects operations such as full table scans and clustered index range scans, which normally benefit from a sequential data layout on disk.

Free space fragmentation

This type of fragmentation occurs when there is a lot of empty space in data pages. It causes the server to read a lot of data it doesn't need, which is wasteful.

MyISAM tables might suffer from all types of fragmentation, but InnoDB never fragments short rows; it moves them and rewrites them in a single piece.

To defragment data, you can either run OPTIMIZE TABLE or dump and reload the data. These approaches work for most storage engines. For some, such as MyISAM, they also defragment indexes by rebuilding them with a sort algorithm, which creates the indexes in sorted order. There is no way to defragment InnoDB indexes in older versions of InnoDB, but in more recent versions that include the ability to drop and build indexes "online" without rebuilding the whole table, you can drop and recreate the indexes to defragment them.

For storage engines that don't support OPTIMIZE TABLE, you can rebuild the table with a no-op ALTER TABLE. Just alter the table to have the same engine it currently uses:

```
mysql> ALTER TABLE <table> ENGINE=<engine>;
```

In Percona Server with expand_fast_index_creation enabled, rebuilding the table in this way will defragment InnoDB tables and indexes. In standard MySQL, it will defragment only the table (the clustered index). You can emulate Percona Server's functionality by dropping all indexes, rebuilding the table, and then adding the indexes back to the table.

Don't assume that you need to defragment your indexes and tables—measure them first to find out. Percona XtraBackup has a --*stats* option that makes it run in a non-backup mode. This mode prints out index and table statistics, including the amount of data and free space in pages. This is one way you can find out how fragmented your data really is. Also consider whether the data could have settled into a nice steady state that you might disrupt by packing it tightly together, causing future updates to incur a spike of page splits and reorganizations, which can impact performance until they reach the steady state again.

Summary

As you can see, indexing is a complex topic! The way MySQL and the storage engines access data, combined with the properties of indexes, make indexes a very powerful and flexible tool for influencing data access, both on disk and in memory.

Most of the time you'll use B-Tree indexes with MySQL. The other types of indexes are rather more suitable for special purposes, and it will generally be obvious when you ought to use them and how they can improve query response times. We'll say no more about them in this chapter, but it's worth wrapping up with a review of the properties and uses of B-Tree indexes.

Here are three principles to keep in mind as you choose indexes and write queries to take advantage of them:

1. Single-row access is slow, especially on spindle-based storage. (Solid-state disks are faster at random I/O, but this point remains true.) If the server reads a block of data from storage and then accesses only one row in it, it wastes a lot of work. It's much better to read in a block that contains lots of rows you need. Use indexes to create locality of reference for improved efficiency.

2. Accessing ranges of rows in order is fast, for two reasons. First, sequential I/O doesn't require disk seeks, so it is faster than random I/O, especially on spindle-based storage. Secondly, if the server can read the data in the order you need it, it doesn't need to perform any follow-up work to sort it, and GROUP BY queries don't need to sort and group rows together to compute aggregates over them.

3. Index-only access is fast. If an index contains all the columns that the query needs, the storage engine doesn't need to find the other columns by looking up rows in the table. This avoids lots of single-row access, which as we know from point 1 above is slow.

In sum, try to choose indexes and write queries so that you can avoid single-row look-ups, use the inherent ordering of the data to avoid sorting operations, and exploit index-only access. This corresponds to the three-star ranking system set out in Lahdenmaki and Leach's book, mentioned at the beginning of this chapter.

It would be great to be able to create perfect indexes for every query against your tables. Unfortunately, sometimes this would require an impractically large number of indexes, and at other times there simply is no way to create a three-star index for a given query (for example, if the query orders by two columns, one ascending and the other descending). In these cases you have to settle for the best you can do, or pursue alternative strategies, such as denormalization or summary tables.

It's very important to be able to reason through how indexes work, and to choose them based on that understanding, not on rules of thumb or heuristics such as "place the most selective columns first in multicolumn indexes" or "you should index all of the columns that appear in the WHERE clause."

How do you know whether your schema is indexed well enough? As always, we suggest that you frame the question in terms of response time. Find queries that are either taking too long or contributing too much load to the server (see Chapter 3 for more on how to measure this). Examine the schema, SQL, and index structures for the queries that need attention. Determine whether the query has to examine too many rows, perform post-retrieval sorting or use temporary tables, access data with random I/O, or look up full rows from the table to retrieve columns not included in the index.

If you find a query that doesn't benefit from all of these possible advantages of indexes, see if a better index can be created to improve performance. If not, perhaps a rewrite can transform the query so that it can use an index that either already exists or could be created. That's what the next chapter is about.

What if a query doesn't show up in the response time–based analysis explained in Chapter 3? Isn't it possible that a "bad" query could escape your notice, even though it really needs a better index for better performance? Generally, no. If profiling doesn't catch a query, it simply doesn't matter. However, the query might matter in the future, as the application, data, and workload change, so you might still wish to find queries that don't use indexes well and fix them before they become problematic. You can use the query review features in *pt-query-digest* to help you notice "new" queries, and examine their EXPLAIN plans, for this purpose.

Query Performance Optimization

In the previous chapters we explained schema optimization and indexing, which are necessary for high performance. But they aren't enough—you also need to design your queries well. If your queries are bad, even the best-designed schema and indexes will not perform well.

Query optimization, index optimization, and schema optimization go hand in hand. As you gain experience writing queries in MySQL, you will learn how to design tables and indexes to support efficient queries. Similarly, what you learn about optimal schema design will influence the kinds of queries you write. This process takes time, so we encourage you to refer back to these three chapters as you learn more.

This chapter begins with general query design considerations—the things you should consider first when a query isn't performing well. We then dig much deeper into query optimization and server internals. We show you how to find out how MySQL executes a particular query, and you'll learn how to change the query execution plan. Finally, we'll look at some places MySQL doesn't optimize queries well and explore query optimization patterns that help MySQL execute queries more efficiently.

Our goal is to help you understand deeply how MySQL really executes queries, so you can reason about what is efficient or inefficient, exploit MySQL's strengths, and avoid its weaknesses.

Why Are Queries Slow?

Before trying to write fast queries, remember that it's all about response time. Queries are tasks, but they are composed of subtasks, and those subtasks consume time. To optimize a query, you must optimize its subtasks by eliminating them, making them happen fewer times, or making them happen more quickly.[1]

---

1. Sometimes you might also need to modify a query to reduce its impact on other queries running on the system. In this case, you're trying to reduce the query's resource consumption, a topic we discussed in Chapter 3.

What are the subtasks that MySQL performs to execute a query, and which ones are slow? The full list is impossible to include here, but if you profile a query as we showed in Chapter 3, you will find out what tasks it performs. In general, you can think of a query's lifetime by mentally following the query through its sequence diagram from the client to the server, where it is parsed, planned, and executed, and then back again to the client. Execution is one of the most important stages in a query's lifetime. It involves lots of calls to the storage engine to retrieve rows, as well as post-retrieval operations such as grouping and sorting.

While accomplishing all these tasks, the query spends time on the network, in the CPU, in operations such as statistics and planning, locking (mutex waits), and most especially, calls to the storage engine to retrieve rows. These calls consume time in memory operations, CPU operations, and especially I/O operations if the data isn't in memory. Depending on the storage engine, a lot of context switching and/or system calls might also be involved.

In every case, excessive time may be consumed because the operations are performed needlessly, performed too many times, or are too slow. The goal of optimization is to avoid that, by eliminating or reducing operations, or making them faster.

Again, this isn't a complete or accurate picture of a query's life. Our goal here is to show the importance of understanding a query's lifecycle and thinking in terms of where the time is consumed. With that in mind, let's see how to optimize queries.

Slow Query Basics: Optimize Data Access

The most basic reason a query doesn't perform well is because it's working with too much data. Some queries just have to sift through a lot of data and can't be helped. That's unusual, though; most bad queries can be changed to access less data. We've found it useful to analyze a poorly performing query in two steps:

1. Find out whether your *application* is retrieving more data than you need. That usually means it's accessing too many rows, but it might also be accessing too many columns.
2. Find out whether the *MySQL server* is analyzing more rows than it needs.

Are You Asking the Database for Data You Don't Need?

Some queries ask for more data than they need and then throw some of it away. This demands extra work of the MySQL server, adds network overhead,[2] and consumes memory and CPU resources on the application server.

Here are a few typical mistakes:

---

2. Network overhead is worst if the application is on a different host from the server, but transferring data between MySQL and the application isn't free even if they're on the same server.

Fetching more rows than needed

One common mistake is assuming that MySQL provides results on demand, rather than calculating and returning the full result set. We often see this in applications designed by people familiar with other database systems. These developers are used to techniques such as issuing a SELECT statement that returns many rows, then fetching the first *N* rows and closing the result set (e.g., fetching the 100 most recent articles for a news site when they only need to show 10 of them on the front page). They think MySQL will provide them with these 10 rows and stop executing the query, but what MySQL really does is generate the complete result set. The client library then fetches all the data and discards most of it. The best solution is to add a LIMIT clause to the query.

Fetching all columns from a multitable join

If you want to retrieve all actors who appear in the film *Academy Dinosaur*, don't write the query this way:

```
mysql> SELECT * FROM sakila.actor
    -> INNER JOIN sakila.film_actor USING(actor_id)
    -> INNER JOIN sakila.film USING(film_id)
    -> WHERE sakila.film.title = 'Academy Dinosaur';
```

That returns all columns from all three tables. Instead, write the query as follows:

```
mysql> SELECT sakila.actor.* FROM sakila.actor...;
```

Fetching all columns

You should always be suspicious when you see SELECT *. Do you really need all columns? Probably not. Retrieving all columns can prevent optimizations such as covering indexes, as well as adding I/O, memory, and CPU overhead for the server.

Some DBAs ban SELECT * universally because of this fact, and to reduce the risk of problems when someone alters the table's column list.

Of course, asking for more data than you really need is not always bad. In many cases we've investigated, people tell us the wasteful approach simplifies development, because it lets the developer use the same bit of code in more than one place. That's a reasonable consideration, as long as you know what it costs in terms of performance. It might also be useful to retrieve more data than you actually need if you use some type of caching in your application, or if you have another benefit in mind. Fetching and caching full objects might be preferable to running many separate queries that retrieve only parts of the object.

Fetching the same data repeatedly

If you're not careful, it's quite easy to write application code that retrieves the same data repeatedly from the database server, executing the same query to fetch it. For example, if you want to find out a user's profile image URL to display next to a list of comments, you might request this repeatedly for each comment. Or you could cache it the first time you fetch it, and reuse it thereafter. The latter approach is much more efficient.

Is MySQL Examining Too Much Data?

Once you're sure your queries *retrieve* only the data you need, you can look for queries that *examine* too much data while generating results. In MySQL, the simplest query cost metrics are:

- Response time
- Number of rows examined
- Number of rows returned

None of these metrics is a perfect way to measure query cost, but they reflect roughly how much data MySQL must access internally to execute a query and translate approximately into how fast the query runs. All three metrics are logged in the slow query log, so looking at the slow query log is one of the best ways to find queries that examine too much data.

Response time

Beware of taking query response time at face value. Hey, isn't that the opposite of what we've been telling you? Not really. It's still true that response time is what matters, but it's a bit complicated.

Response time is the sum of two things: service time and queue time. *Service time* is how long it takes the server to actually process the query. *Queue time* is the portion of response time during which the server isn't really executing the query—it's waiting for something, such as waiting for an I/O operation to complete, waiting for a row lock, and so forth. The problem is, you can't break the response time down into these components unless you can measure them individually, which is usually hard to do. In general, the most common and important waits you'll encounter are I/O and lock waits, but you shouldn't count on that, because it varies a lot.

As a result, response time is not consistent under varying load conditions. Other factors—such as storage engine locks (table locks and row locks), high concurrency, and hardware—can also have a considerable impact on response times. Response time can also be both a symptom and a cause of problems, and it's not always obvious which is the case, unless you can use the techniques shown in "Single-Query Versus Server-Wide Problems" on page 93 to find out.

When you look at a query's response time, you should ask yourself whether the response time is reasonable for the query. We don't have space for a detailed explanation in this book, but you can actually calculate a quick upper-bound estimate (QUBE) of query response time using the techniques explained in Tapio Lahdenmaki and Mike Leach's book *Relational Database Index Design and the Optimizers* (Wiley). In a nutshell: examine the query execution plan and the indexes involved, determine how many sequential and random I/O operations might be required, and multiply these by the time it takes your hardware to perform them. Add it all up and you have a yardstick to judge whether a query is slower than it could or should be.

Rows examined and rows returned

It's useful to think about the number of rows examined when analyzing queries, because you can see how efficiently the queries are finding the data you need.

However, this is not a perfect metric for finding "bad" queries. Not all row accesses are equal. Shorter rows are faster to access, and fetching rows from memory is much faster than reading them from disk.

Ideally, the number of rows examined would be the same as the number returned, but in practice this is rarely possible. For example, when constructing rows with joins, the server must access multiple rows to generate each row in the result set. The ratio of rows examined to rows returned is usually small—say, between 1:1 and 10:1—but sometimes it can be orders of magnitude larger.

Rows examined and access types

When you're thinking about the cost of a query, consider the cost of finding a single row in a table. MySQL can use several access methods to find and return a row. Some require examining many rows, but others might be able to generate the result without examining any.

The access method(s) appear in the type column in EXPLAIN's output. The access types range from a full table scan to index scans, range scans, unique index lookups, and constants. Each of these is faster than the one before it, because it requires reading less data. You don't need to memorize the access types, but you should understand the general concepts of scanning a table, scanning an index, range accesses, and single-value accesses.

If you aren't getting a good access type, the best way to solve the problem is usually by adding an appropriate index. We discussed indexing in the previous chapter; now you can see why indexes are so important to query optimization. Indexes let MySQL find rows with a more efficient access type that examines less data.

For example, let's look at a simple query on the Sakila sample database:

```
mysql> SELECT * FROM sakila.film_actor WHERE film_id = 1;
```

This query will return 10 rows, and EXPLAIN shows that MySQL uses the ref access type on the idx_fk_film_id index to execute the query:

```
mysql> EXPLAIN SELECT * FROM sakila.film_actor WHERE film_id = 1\G
*************************** 1. row ***************************
          id: 1
 select_type: SIMPLE
       table: film_actor
        type: ref
possible_keys: idx_fk_film_id
```

```
         key: idx_fk_film_id
     key_len: 2
         ref: const
        rows: 10
       Extra:
```

EXPLAIN shows that MySQL estimated it needed to access only 10 rows. In other words, the query optimizer knew the chosen access type could satisfy the query efficiently. What would happen if there were no suitable index for the query? MySQL would have to use a less optimal access type, as we can see if we drop the index and run the query again:

```
mysql> ALTER TABLE sakila.film_actor DROP FOREIGN KEY fk_film_actor_film;
mysql> ALTER TABLE sakila.film_actor DROP KEY idx_fk_film_id;
mysql> EXPLAIN SELECT * FROM sakila.film_actor WHERE film_id = 1\G
*************************** 1. row ***************************
           id: 1
  select_type: SIMPLE
        table: film_actor
         type: ALL
possible_keys: NULL
          key: NULL
      key_len: NULL
          ref: NULL
         rows: 5073
        Extra: Using where
```

Predictably, the access type has changed to a full table scan (ALL), and MySQL now estimates it'll have to examine 5,073 rows to satisfy the query. The "Using where" in the Extra column shows that the MySQL server is using the WHERE clause to discard rows after the storage engine reads them.

In general, MySQL can apply a WHERE clause in three ways, from best to worst:

- Apply the conditions to the index lookup operation to eliminate nonmatching rows. This happens at the storage engine layer.

- Use a covering index ("Using index" in the Extra column) to avoid row accesses, and filter out nonmatching rows after retrieving each result from the index. This happens at the server layer, but it doesn't require reading rows from the table.

- Retrieve rows from the table, then filter nonmatching rows ("Using where" in the Extra column). This happens at the server layer and requires the server to read rows from the table before it can filter them.

This example illustrates how important it is to have good indexes. Good indexes help your queries get a good access type and examine only the rows they need. However, adding an index doesn't always mean that MySQL will access and return the same number of rows. For example, here's a query that uses the COUNT() aggregate function:[3]

```
mysql> SELECT actor_id, COUNT(*) FROM sakila.film_actor GROUP BY actor_id;
```

---

3. See "Optimizing COUNT() Queries" on page 241 for more on this topic.

This query returns only 200 rows, but it needs to read thousands of rows to build the result set. An index can't reduce the number of rows examined for a query like this one.

Unfortunately, MySQL does not tell you how many of the rows it accessed were used to build the result set; it tells you only the total number of rows it accessed. Many of these rows could be eliminated by a WHERE clause and end up not contributing to the result set. In the previous example, after removing the index on sakila.film_actor, the query accessed every row in the table and the WHERE clause discarded all but 10 of them. Only the remaining 10 rows were used to build the result set. Understanding how many rows the server accesses and how many it really uses requires reasoning about the query.

If you find that a huge number of rows were examined to produce relatively few rows in the result, you can try some more sophisticated fixes:

- Use covering indexes, which store data so that the storage engine doesn't have to retrieve the complete rows. (We discussed these in the previous chapter.)
- Change the schema. An example is using summary tables (discussed in Chapter 4).
- Rewrite a complicated query so the MySQL optimizer is able to execute it optimally. (We discuss this later in this chapter.)

Ways to Restructure Queries

As you optimize problematic queries, your goal should be to find alternative ways to get the result you want—but that doesn't necessarily mean getting the same result set back from MySQL. You can sometimes transform queries into equivalent forms that return the same results, and get better performance. However, you should also think about rewriting the query to retrieve *different* results, if that provides an efficiency benefit. You might be able to ultimately do the same work by changing the application code as well as the query. In this section, we explain techniques that can help you restructure a wide range of queries and show you when to use each technique.

Complex Queries Versus Many Queries

One important query design question is whether it's preferable to break up a complex query into several simpler queries. The traditional approach to database design emphasizes doing as much work as possible with as few queries as possible. This approach was historically better because of the cost of network communication and the overhead of the query parsing and optimization stages.

However, this advice doesn't apply as much to MySQL, because it was designed to handle connecting and disconnecting very efficiently and to respond to small and simple queries very quickly. Modern networks are also significantly faster than they used to be, reducing network latency. Depending on the server version, MySQL can run well over 100,000 simple queries per second on commodity server hardware and over 2,000 queries per second from a single correspondent on a gigabit network, so running multiple queries isn't necessarily such a bad thing.

Connection response is still slow compared to the number of rows MySQL can traverse per second internally, though, which is counted in millions per second for in-memory data. All else being equal, it's still a good idea to use as few queries as possible, but sometimes you can make a query more efficient by decomposing it and executing a few simple queries instead of one complex one. Don't be afraid to do this; weigh the costs, and go with the strategy that causes less work. We show some examples of this technique a little later in the chapter.

That said, using too many queries is a common mistake in application design. For example, some applications perform 10 single-row queries to retrieve data from a table when they could use a single 10-row query. We've even seen applications that retrieve each column individually, querying each row many times!

Chopping Up a Query

Another way to slice up a query is to divide and conquer, keeping it essentially the same but running it in smaller "chunks" that affect fewer rows each time.

Purging old data is a great example. Periodic purge jobs might need to remove quite a bit of data, and doing this in one massive query could lock a lot of rows for a long time, fill up transaction logs, hog resources, and block small queries that shouldn't be interrupted. Chopping up the DELETE statement and using medium-size queries can improve performance considerably, and reduce replication lag when a query is replicated. For example, instead of running this monolithic query:

```
mysql> DELETE FROM messages WHERE created < DATE_SUB(NOW(),INTERVAL 3 MONTH);
```

you could do something like the following pseudocode:

```
rows_affected = 0
do {
   rows_affected = do_query(
      "DELETE FROM messages WHERE created < DATE_SUB(NOW(),INTERVAL 3 MONTH)
      LIMIT 10000")
} while rows_affected > 0
```

Deleting 10,000 rows at a time is typically a large enough task to make each query efficient, and a short enough task to minimize the impact on the server[4] (transactional storage engines might benefit from smaller transactions). It might also be a good idea to add some sleep time between the DELETE statements to spread the load over time and reduce the amount of time locks are held.

4. Percona Toolkit's *pt-archiver* tool makes these types of jobs easy and safe.

Join Decomposition

Many high-performance applications use *join decomposition*. You can decompose a join by running multiple single-table queries instead of a multitable join, and then performing the join in the application. For example, instead of this single query:

```
mysql> SELECT * FROM tag
    ->     JOIN tag_post ON tag_post.tag_id=tag.id
    ->     JOIN post ON tag_post.post_id=post.id
    -> WHERE tag.tag='mysql';
```

You might run these queries:

```
mysql> SELECT * FROM  tag WHERE tag='mysql';
mysql> SELECT * FROM  tag_post WHERE tag_id=1234;
mysql> SELECT * FROM  post WHERE  post.id in (123,456,567,9098,8904);
```

Why on earth would you do this? It looks wasteful at first glance, because you've increased the number of queries without getting anything in return. However, such restructuring can actually give significant performance advantages:

- Caching can be more efficient. Many applications cache "objects" that map directly to tables. In this example, if the object with the tag mysql is already cached, the application can skip the first query. If you find posts with an ID of 123, 567, or 9098 in the cache, you can remove them from the IN() list. The query cache might also benefit from this strategy. If only one of the tables changes frequently, decomposing a join can reduce the number of cache invalidations.

- Executing the queries individually can sometimes reduce lock contention.

- Doing joins in the application makes it easier to scale the database by placing tables on different servers.

- The queries themselves can be more efficient. In this example, using an IN() list instead of a join lets MySQL sort row IDs and retrieve rows more optimally than might be possible with a join. We explain this in more detail later.

- You can reduce redundant row accesses. Doing a join in the application means you retrieve each row only once, whereas a join in the query is essentially a denormalization that might repeatedly access the same data. For the same reason, such restructuring might also reduce the total network traffic and memory usage.

- To some extent, you can view this technique as manually implementing a hash join instead of the nested loops algorithm MySQL uses to execute a join. A hash join might be more efficient. (We discuss MySQL's join strategy later in this chapter.)

As a result, doing joins in the application can be more efficient when you cache and reuse a lot of data from earlier queries, you distribute data across multiple servers, you replace joins with IN() lists on large tables, or a join refers to the same table multiple times.

Query Execution Basics

If you need to get high performance from your MySQL server, one of the best ways to invest your time is in learning how MySQL optimizes and executes queries. Once you understand this, much of query optimization is a matter of reasoning from principles, and query optimization becomes a very logical process.

In other words, it's time to revisit what we discussed earlier: the process MySQL follows to execute queries. Follow along with Figure 6-1 to see what happens when you send MySQL a query:

1. The client sends the SQL statement to the server.
2. The server checks the query cache. If there's a hit, it returns the stored result from the cache; otherwise, it passes the SQL statement to the next step.
3. The server parses, preprocesses, and optimizes the SQL into a query execution plan.
4. The query execution engine executes the plan by making calls to the storage engine API.
5. The server sends the result to the client.

Each of these steps has some extra complexity, which we discuss in the following sections. We also explain which states the query will be in during each step. The query optimization process is particularly complex and important to understand. There are also exceptions or special cases, such as the difference in execution path when you use prepared statements; we discuss that in the next chapter.

The MySQL Client/Server Protocol

Though you don't need to understand the inner details of MySQL's client/server protocol, you do need to understand how it works at a high level. The protocol is half-duplex, which means that at any given time the MySQL server can be either sending or receiving messages, but not both. It also means there is no way to cut a message short.

This protocol makes MySQL communication simple and fast, but it limits it in some ways too. For one thing, it means there's no flow control; once one side sends a message, the other side must fetch the entire message before responding. It's like a game of tossing a ball back and forth: only one side has the ball at any instant, and you can't toss the ball (send a message) unless you have it.

The client sends a query to the server as a single packet of data. This is why the max_allowed_packet configuration variable is important if you have large queries.[5] Once the client sends the query, it doesn't have the ball anymore; it can only wait for results.

---

5. If the query is too large, the server will refuse to receive any more data and throw an error.

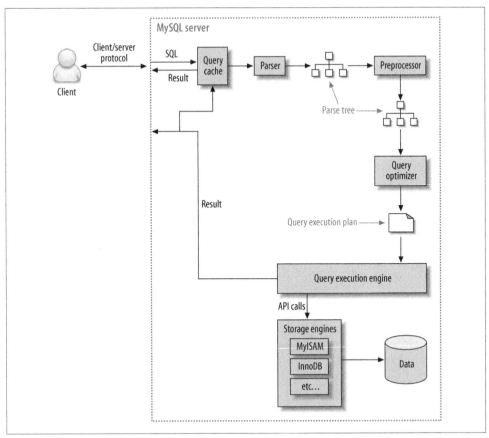

Figure 6-1. Execution path of a query

In contrast, the response from the server usually consists of many packets of data. When the server responds, the client has to receive the *entire* result set. It cannot simply fetch a few rows and then ask the server not to bother sending the rest. If the client needs only the first few rows that are returned, it either has to wait for all of the server's packets to arrive and then discard the ones it doesn't need, or disconnect ungracefully. Neither is a good idea, which is why appropriate LIMIT clauses are so important.

Here's another way to think about this: when a client fetches rows from the server, it thinks it's *pulling* them. But the truth is, the MySQL server is *pushing* the rows as it generates them. The client is only receiving the pushed rows; there is no way for it to tell the server to stop sending rows. The client is "drinking from the fire hose," so to speak. (Yes, that's a technical term.)

Most libraries that connect to MySQL let you either fetch the whole result set and buffer it in memory, or fetch each row as you need it. The default behavior is generally to fetch the whole result and buffer it in memory. This is important because until all the rows have been fetched, the MySQL server will not release the locks and other resources required by the query. The query will be in the "Sending data" state. When the client library fetches the results all at once, it reduces the amount of work the server needs to do: the server can finish and clean up the query as quickly as possible.

Most client libraries let you treat the result set as though you're fetching it from the server, although in fact you're just fetching it from the buffer in the library's memory. This works fine most of the time, but it's not a good idea for huge result sets that might take a long time to fetch and use a lot of memory. You can use less memory, and start working on the result sooner, if you instruct the library not to buffer the result. The downside is that the locks and other resources on the server will remain open while your application is interacting with the library.[6]

Let's look at an example using PHP. First, here's how you'll usually query MySQL from PHP:

```php
<?php
$link   = mysql_connect('localhost', 'user', 'p4ssword');
$result = mysql_query('SELECT * FROM HUGE_TABLE', $link);
while ( $row = mysql_fetch_array($result) ) {
    // Do something with result
}
?>
```

The code seems to indicate that you fetch rows only when you need them, in the while loop. However, the code actually fetches the entire result into a buffer with the mysql_query() function call. The while loop simply iterates through the buffer. In contrast, the following code doesn't buffer the results, because it uses mysql_unbuf fered_query() instead of mysql_query():

```php
<?php
$link   = mysql_connect('localhost', 'user', 'p4ssword');
$result = mysql_unbuffered_query('SELECT * FROM HUGE_TABLE', $link);
while ( $row = mysql_fetch_array($result) ) {
    // Do something with result
}
?>
```

Programming languages have different ways to override buffering. For example, the Perl DBD::mysql driver requires you to specify the C client library's mysql_use_result attribute (the default is mysql_buffer_result). Here's an example:

```perl
#!/usr/bin/perl
use DBI;
my $dbh = DBI->connect('DBI:mysql:;host=localhost', 'user', 'p4ssword');
my $sth = $dbh->prepare('SELECT * FROM HUGE_TABLE', { mysql_use_result => 1 });
$sth->execute();
while ( my $row = $sth->fetchrow_array() ) {
    # Do something with result
}
```

---

6. You can work around this with SQL_BUFFER_RESULT, which we'll see a bit later.

Notice that the call to prepare() specified to "use" the result instead of "buffering" it. You can also specify this when connecting, which will make every statement unbuffered:

```
my $dbh = DBI->connect('DBI:mysql:;mysql_use_result=1', 'user', 'p4ssword');
```

Query states

Each MySQL connection, or *thread*, has a state that shows what it is doing at any given time. There are several ways to view these states, but the easiest is to use the SHOW FULL PROCESSLIST command (the states appear in the Command column). As a query progresses through its lifecycle, its state changes many times, and there are dozens of states. The MySQL manual is the authoritative source of information for all the states, but we list a few here and explain what they mean:

Sleep
> The thread is waiting for a new query from the client.

Query
> The thread is either executing the query or sending the result back to the client.

Locked
> The thread is waiting for a table lock to be granted at the server level. Locks that are implemented by the storage engine, such as InnoDB's row locks, do not cause the thread to enter the Locked state. This thread state is the classic symptom of MyISAM locking, but it can occur in other storage engines that don't have row-level locking, too.

Analyzing *and* statistics
> The thread is checking storage engine statistics and optimizing the query.

Copying to tmp table [on disk]
> The thread is processing the query and copying results to a temporary table, probably for a GROUP BY, for a filesort, or to satisfy a UNION. If the state ends with "on disk," MySQL is converting an in-memory table to an on-disk table.

Sorting result
> The thread is sorting a result set.

Sending data
> This can mean several things: the thread might be sending data between stages of the query, generating the result set, or returning the result set to the client.

It's helpful to at least know the basic states, so you can get a sense of "who has the ball" for the query. On very busy servers, you might see an unusual or normally brief state, such as statistics, begin to take a significant amount of time. This usually indicates that something is wrong, and you should use the techniques shown in Chapter 3 to capture detailed diagnostic data when it happens.

The Query Cache

Before even parsing a query, MySQL checks for it in the query cache, if the cache is enabled. This operation is a case-sensitive hash lookup. If the query differs from a similar query in the cache by even a single byte, it won't match,[7] and the query processing will go to the next stage.

If MySQL does find a match in the query cache, it must check privileges before returning the cached query. This is possible without parsing the query, because MySQL stores table information with the cached query. If the privileges are OK, MySQL retrieves the stored result from the query cache and sends it to the client, bypassing every other stage in query execution. The query is never parsed, optimized, or executed.

You can learn more about the query cache in Chapter 7.

The Query Optimization Process

The next step in the query lifecycle turns a SQL query into an execution plan for the query execution engine. It has several substeps: parsing, preprocessing, and optimization. Errors (for example, syntax errors) can be raised at any point in the process. We're not trying to document the MySQL internals here, so we're going to take some liberties, such as describing steps separately even though they're often combined wholly or partially for efficiency. Our goal is simply to help you understand how MySQL executes queries so that you can write better ones.

The parser and the preprocessor

To begin, MySQL's *parser* breaks the query into tokens and builds a "parse tree" from them. The parser uses MySQL's SQL grammar to interpret and validate the query. For instance, it ensures that the tokens in the query are valid and in the proper order, and it checks for mistakes such as quoted strings that aren't terminated.

The *preprocessor* then checks the resulting parse tree for additional semantics that the parser can't resolve. For example, it checks that tables and columns exist, and it resolves names and aliases to ensure that column references aren't ambiguous.

Next, the preprocessor checks privileges. This is normally very fast unless your server has large numbers of privileges.

---

7. Percona Server has a feature that strips comments from queries before the hash lookup is performed, which can help make the query cache more effective when queries differ only in the text contained in their comments.

The query optimizer

The parse tree is now valid and ready for the *optimizer* to turn it into a query execution plan. A query can often be executed many different ways and produce the same result. The optimizer's job is to find the best option.

MySQL uses a cost-based optimizer, which means it tries to predict the cost of various execution plans and choose the least expensive. The unit of cost was originally a single random 4 KB data page read, but it has become more sophisticated and now includes factors such as the estimated cost of executing a WHERE clause comparison. You can see how expensive the optimizer estimated a query to be by running the query, then inspecting the Last_query_cost session variable:

```
mysql> SELECT SQL_NO_CACHE COUNT(*) FROM sakila.film_actor;
+----------+
| count(*) |
+----------+
|     5462 |
+----------+
mysql> SHOW STATUS LIKE 'Last_query_cost';
+-----------------+-------------+
| Variable_name   | Value       |
+-----------------+-------------+
| Last_query_cost | 1040.599000 |
+-----------------+-------------+
```

This result means that the optimizer estimated it would need to do about 1,040 random data page reads to execute the query. It bases the estimate on statistics: the number of pages per table or index, the *cardinality* (number of distinct values) of the indexes, the length of the rows and keys, and the key distribution. The optimizer does not include the effects of any type of caching in its estimates—it assumes every read will result in a disk I/O operation.

The optimizer might not always choose the best plan, for many reasons:

- The statistics could be wrong. The server relies on storage engines to provide statistics, and they can range from exactly correct to wildly inaccurate. For example, the InnoDB storage engine doesn't maintain accurate statistics about the number of rows in a table because of its MVCC architecture.

- The cost metric is not exactly equivalent to the true cost of running the query, so even when the statistics are accurate, the query might be more or less expensive than MySQL's approximation. A plan that reads more pages might actually be cheaper in some cases, such as when the reads are sequential so the disk I/O is faster, or when the pages are already cached in memory. MySQL also doesn't understand which pages are in memory and which pages are on disk, so it doesn't really know how much I/O the query will cause.

- MySQL's idea of "optimal" might not match yours. You probably want the fastest execution time, but MySQL doesn't really try to make queries fast; it tries to minimize their cost, and as we've seen, determining cost is not an exact science.

- MySQL doesn't consider other queries that are running concurrently, which can affect how quickly the query runs.
- MySQL doesn't always do cost-based optimization. Sometimes it just follows the rules, such as "if there's a full-text MATCH() clause, use a FULLTEXT index if one exists." It will do this even when it would be faster to use a different index and a non-FULLTEXT query with a WHERE clause.
- The optimizer doesn't take into account the cost of operations not under its control, such as executing stored functions or user-defined functions.
- As we'll see later, the optimizer can't always estimate every possible execution plan, so it might miss an optimal plan.

MySQL's query optimizer is a highly complex piece of software, and it uses many optimizations to transform the query into an execution plan. There are two basic types of optimizations, which we call *static* and *dynamic*. *Static optimizations* can be performed simply by inspecting the parse tree. For example, the optimizer can transform the WHERE clause into an equivalent form by applying algebraic rules. Static optimizations are independent of values, such as the value of a constant in a WHERE clause. They can be performed once and will always be valid, even when the query is reexecuted with different values. You can think of these as "compile-time optimizations."

In contrast, *dynamic optimizations* are based on context and can depend on many factors, such as which value is in a WHERE clause or how many rows are in an index. They must be reevaluated each time the query is executed. You can think of these as "runtime optimizations."

The difference is important when executing prepared statements or stored procedures. MySQL can do static optimizations once, but it must reevaluate dynamic optimizations every time it executes a query. MySQL sometimes even reoptimizes the query as it executes it.[8]

Here are some types of optimizations MySQL knows how to do:

Reordering joins
Tables don't always have to be joined in the order you specify in the query. Determining the best join order is an important optimization; we explain it in depth later in this chapter.

Converting OUTER JOINs to INNER JOINs
An OUTER JOIN doesn't necessarily have to be executed as an OUTER JOIN. Some factors, such as the WHERE clause and table schema, can actually cause an OUTER JOIN to be equivalent to an INNER JOIN. MySQL can recognize this and rewrite the join, which makes it eligible for reordering.

---

8. For example, the range check query plan reevaluates indexes for each row in a JOIN. You can see this query plan by looking for "range checked for each record" in the Extra column in EXPLAIN. This query plan also increments the Select_full_range_join server variable.

Applying algebraic equivalence rules

MySQL applies algebraic transformations to simplify and canonicalize expressions. It can also fold and reduce constants, eliminating impossible constraints and constant conditions. For example, the term (5=5 AND a>5) will reduce to just a>5. Similarly, (a<b AND b=c) AND a=5 becomes b>5 AND b=c AND a=5. These rules are very useful for writing conditional queries, which we discuss later in this chapter.

COUNT(), MIN(), *and* MAX() *optimizations*

Indexes and column nullability can often help MySQL optimize away these expressions. For example, to find the minimum value of a column that's leftmost in a B-Tree index, MySQL can just request the first row in the index. It can even do this in the query optimization stage, and treat the value as a constant for the rest of the query. Similarly, to find the maximum value in a B-Tree index, the server reads the last row. If the server uses this optimization, you'll see "Select tables optimized away" in the EXPLAIN plan. This literally means the optimizer has removed the table from the query plan and replaced it with a constant.

Likewise, COUNT(*) queries without a WHERE clause can often be optimized away on some storage engines (such as MyISAM, which keeps an exact count of rows in the table at all times).

Evaluating and reducing constant expressions

When MySQL detects that an expression can be reduced to a constant, it will do so during optimization. For example, a user-defined variable can be converted to a constant if it's not changed in the query. Arithmetic expressions are another example.

Perhaps surprisingly, even something you might consider to be a query can be reduced to a constant during the optimization phase. One example is a MIN() on an index. This can even be extended to a constant lookup on a primary key or unique index. If a WHERE clause applies a constant condition to such an index, the optimizer knows MySQL can look up the value at the beginning of the query. It will then treat the value as a constant in the rest of the query. Here's an example:

```
mysql> EXPLAIN SELECT film.film_id, film_actor.actor_id
    -> FROM sakila.film
    ->     INNER JOIN sakila.film_actor USING(film_id)
    -> WHERE film.film_id = 1;
```

id	select_type	table	type	key	ref	rows
1	SIMPLE	film	const	PRIMARY	const	1
1	SIMPLE	film_actor	ref	idx_fk_film_id	const	10

MySQL executes this query in two steps, which correspond to the two rows in the output. The first step is to find the desired row in the film table. MySQL's optimizer knows there is only one row, because there's a primary key on the film_id column, and it has already consulted the index during the query optimization stage to see how many rows it will find. Because the query optimizer has a known quantity (the value in the WHERE clause) to use in the lookup, this table's ref type is const.

In the second step, MySQL treats the film_id column from the row found in the first step as a known quantity. It can do this because the optimizer knows that by the time the query reaches the second step, it will know all the values from the first step. Notice that the film_actor table's ref type is const, just as the film table's was.

Another way you'll see constant conditions applied is by propagating a value's constant-ness from one place to another if there is a WHERE, USING, or ON clause that restricts the values to being equal. In this example, the optimizer knows that the USING clause forces film_id to have the same value everywhere in the query—it must be equal to the constant value given in the WHERE clause.

Covering indexes

MySQL can sometimes use an index to avoid reading row data, when the index contains all the columns the query needs. We discussed covering indexes at length in the previous chapter.

Subquery optimization

MySQL can convert some types of subqueries into more efficient alternative forms, reducing them to index lookups instead of separate queries.

Early termination

MySQL can stop processing a query (or a step in a query) as soon as it fulfills the query or step. The obvious case is a LIMIT clause, but there are several other kinds of early termination. For instance, if MySQL detects an impossible condition, it can abort the entire query. You can see this in the following example:

```
mysql> EXPLAIN SELECT film.film_id FROM sakila.film WHERE film_id = -1;
+----+...+-------------------------------------------------------+
| id |...| Extra                                                 |
+----+...+-------------------------------------------------------+
|  1 |...| Impossible WHERE noticed after reading const tables   |
+----+...+-------------------------------------------------------+
```

This query stopped during the optimization step, but MySQL can also terminate execution early in some other cases. The server can use this optimization when the query execution engine recognizes the need to retrieve distinct values, or to stop when a value doesn't exist. For example, the following query finds all movies without any actors:[9]

```
mysql> SELECT film.film_id
    -> FROM sakila.film
    ->    LEFT OUTER JOIN sakila.film_actor USING(film_id)
    -> WHERE film_actor.film_id IS NULL;
```

---

9. We agree, a movie without actors is strange, but the Sakila sample database lists no actors for *SLACKER LIAISONS*, which it describes as "A Fast-Paced Tale of a Shark And a Student who must Meet a Crocodile in Ancient China."

This query works by eliminating any films that have actors. Each film might have many actors, but as soon as it finds one actor, it stops processing the current film and moves to the next one because it knows the WHERE clause prohibits outputting that film. A similar "Distinct/not-exists" optimization can apply to certain kinds of DISTINCT, NOT EXISTS(), and LEFT JOIN queries.

Equality propagation

MySQL recognizes when a query holds two columns as equal—for example, in a JOIN condition—and propagates WHERE clauses across equivalent columns. For instance, in the following query:

```
mysql> SELECT film.film_id
    -> FROM sakila.film
    ->    INNER JOIN sakila.film_actor USING(film_id)
    -> WHERE film.film_id > 500;
```

MySQL knows that the WHERE clause applies not only to the film table but to the film_actor table as well, because the USING clause forces the two columns to match.

If you're used to another database server that can't do this, you might have been advised to "help the optimizer" by manually specifying the WHERE clause for both tables, like this:

```
... WHERE film.film_id > 500 AND film_actor.film_id > 500
```

This is unnecessary in MySQL. It just makes your queries harder to maintain.

IN() *list comparisons*

In many database servers, IN() is just a synonym for multiple OR clauses, because the two are logically equivalent. Not so in MySQL, which sorts the values in the IN() list and uses a fast binary search to see whether a value is in the list. This is $O(\log n)$ in the size of the list, whereas an equivalent series of OR clauses is $O(n)$ in the size of the list (i.e., much slower for large lists).

The preceding list is woefully incomplete, because MySQL performs more optimizations than we could fit into this entire chapter, but it should give you an idea of the optimizer's complexity and intelligence. If there's one thing you should take away from this discussion, it's *don't try to outsmart the optimizer*. You might end up just defeating it, or making your queries more complicated and harder to maintain for zero benefit. In general, you should let the optimizer do its work.

Of course, as smart as the optimizer is, there are times when it doesn't give the best result. Sometimes you might know something about the data that the optimizer doesn't, such as a fact that's guaranteed to be true because of application logic. Also, sometimes the optimizer doesn't have the necessary functionality, such as hash indexes; at other times, as mentioned earlier, its cost estimates might prefer a query plan that turns out to be more expensive than an alternative.

If you know the optimizer isn't giving a good result, and you know why, you can help it. Some of the options are to add a hint to the query, rewrite the query, redesign your schema, or add indexes.

Table and index statistics

Recall the various layers in the MySQL server architecture, which we illustrated in Figure 1-1. The server layer, which contains the query optimizer, doesn't store statistics on data and indexes. That's a job for the storage engines, because each storage engine might keep different kinds of statistics (or keep them in a different way). Some engines, such as Archive, don't keep statistics at all!

Because the server doesn't store statistics, the MySQL query optimizer has to ask the engines for statistics on the tables in a query. The engines provide the optimizer with statistics such as the number of pages per table or index, the cardinality of tables and indexes, the length of rows and keys, and key distribution information. The optimizer can use this information to help it decide on the best execution plan. We see how these statistics influence the optimizer's choices in later sections.

MySQL's join execution strategy

MySQL uses the term "join" more broadly than you might be used to. In sum, it considers every query a join—not just every query that matches rows from two tables, but every query, period (including subqueries, and even a SELECT against a single table). Consequently, it's very important to understand how MySQL executes joins.

Consider the example of a UNION query. MySQL executes a UNION as a series of single queries whose results are spooled into a temporary table, then read out again. Each of the individual queries is a join, in MySQL terminology—and so is the act of reading from the resulting temporary table.

At the moment, MySQL's join execution strategy is simple: it treats every join as a nested-loop join. This means MySQL runs a loop to find a row from a table, then runs a nested loop to find a matching row in the next table. It continues until it has found a matching row in each table in the join. It then builds and returns a row from the columns named in the SELECT list. It tries to build the next row by looking for more matching rows in the last table. If it doesn't find any, it backtracks one table and looks for more rows there. It keeps backtracking until it finds another row in some table, at which point it looks for a matching row in the next table, and so on.[10]

This process of finding rows, probing into the next table, and then backtracking can be written as nested loops in the execution plan—hence the name "nested-loop join." As an example, consider this simple query:

---

10. As we show later, MySQL's query execution isn't quite this simple; there are many optimizations that complicate it.

```
mysql> SELECT tbl1.col1, tbl2.col2
    -> FROM tbl1 INNER JOIN tbl2 USING(col3)
    -> WHERE tbl1.col1 IN(5,6);
```

Assuming MySQL decides to join the tables in the order shown in the query, the following pseudocode shows how MySQL might execute the query:

```
outer_iter = iterator over tbl1 where col1 IN(5,6)
outer_row  = outer_iter.next
while outer_row
    inner_iter = iterator over tbl2 where col3 = outer_row.col3
    inner_row  = inner_iter.next
    while inner_row
        output [ outer_row.col1, inner_row.col2 ]
        inner_row = inner_iter.next
    end
    outer_row = outer_iter.next
end
```

This query execution plan applies as easily to a single-table query as it does to a many-table query, which is why even a single-table query can be considered a join—the single-table join is the basic operation from which more complex joins are composed. It can support OUTER JOINs, too. For example, let's change the example query as follows:

```
mysql> SELECT tbl1.col1, tbl2.col2
    -> FROM tbl1 LEFT OUTER JOIN tbl2 USING(col3)
    -> WHERE tbl1.col1 IN(5,6);
```

Here's the corresponding pseudocode, with the changed parts in bold:

```
outer_iter = iterator over tbl1 where col1 IN(5,6)
outer_row  = outer_iter.next
while outer_row
    inner_iter = iterator over tbl2 where col3 = outer_row.col3
    inner_row  = inner_iter.next
    if inner_row
        while inner_row
            output [ outer_row.col1, inner_row.col2 ]
            inner_row = inner_iter.next
        end
    else
        output [ outer_row.col1, NULL ]
    end
    outer_row = outer_iter.next
end
```

Another way to visualize a query execution plan is to use what the optimizer folks call a "swim-lane diagram." Figure 6-2 contains a swim-lane diagram of our initial INNER JOIN query. Read it from left to right and top to bottom.

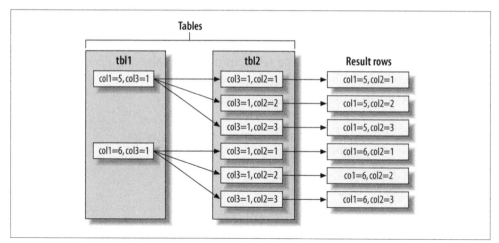

Figure 6-2. Swim-lane diagram illustrating retrieving rows using a join

MySQL executes every kind of query in essentially the same way. For example, it handles a subquery in the FROM clause by executing it first, putting the results into a temporary table,[11] and then treating that table just like an ordinary table (hence the name "derived table"). MySQL executes UNION queries with temporary tables too, and it rewrites all RIGHT OUTER JOIN queries to equivalent LEFT OUTER JOINs. In short, current versions of MySQL coerce every kind of query into this execution plan.[12]

It's not possible to execute every legal SQL query this way, however. For example, a FULL OUTER JOIN can't be executed with nested loops and backtracking as soon as a table with no matching rows is found, because it might begin with a table that has no matching rows. This explains why MySQL doesn't support FULL OUTER JOIN. Still other queries can be executed with nested loops, but perform very badly as a result. We'll look at some of those later.

The execution plan

MySQL doesn't generate byte-code to execute a query, as many other database products do. Instead, the query execution plan is actually a tree of instructions that the query execution engine follows to produce the query results. The final plan contains enough information to reconstruct the original query. If you execute EXPLAIN EXTENDED on a query, followed by SHOW WARNINGS, you'll see the reconstructed query.[13]

---

11. There are no indexes on the temporary table, which is something you should keep in mind when writing complex joins against subqueries in the FROM clause. This applies to UNION queries, too.

12. There are significant changes in MySQL 5.6 and in MariaDB, which introduce more sophisticated execution paths.

13. The server generates the output from the execution plan. It thus has the same semantics as the original query, but not necessarily the same text.

Any multitable query can conceptually be represented as a tree. For example, it might be possible to execute a four-table join as shown in Figure 6-3.

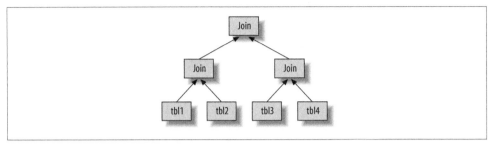

Figure 6-3. One way to join multiple tables

This is what computer scientists call a *balanced tree*. This is not how MySQL executes the query, though. As we described in the previous section, MySQL always begins with one table and finds matching rows in the next table. Thus, MySQL's query execution plans always take the form of a *left-deep tree*, as in Figure 6-4.

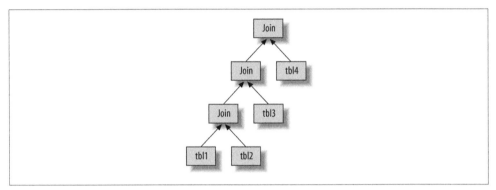

Figure 6-4. How MySQL joins multiple tables

The join optimizer

The most important part of the MySQL query optimizer is the *join optimizer*, which decides the best order of execution for multitable queries. It is often possible to join the tables in several different orders and get the same results. The join optimizer estimates the cost for various plans and tries to choose the least expensive one that gives the same result.

Here's a query whose tables can be joined in different orders without changing the results:

```
mysql> SELECT film.film_id, film.title, film.release_year, actor.actor_id,
    ->     actor.first_name, actor.last_name
    ->     FROM sakila.film
```

```
    ->    INNER JOIN sakila.film_actor USING(film_id)
    ->    INNER JOIN sakila.actor USING(actor_id);
```

You can probably think of a few different query plans. For example, MySQL could begin with the film table, use the index on film_id in the film_actor table to find actor_id values, and then look up rows in the actor table's primary key. Oracle users might phrase this as "The film table is the driver table into the film_actor table, which is the driver for the actor table." This should be efficient, right? Now let's use EXPLAIN to see how MySQL wants to execute the query:

```
*************************** 1. row ***************************
           id: 1
  select_type: SIMPLE
        table: actor
         type: ALL
possible_keys: PRIMARY
          key: NULL
      key_len: NULL
          ref: NULL
         rows: 200
        Extra:
*************************** 2. row ***************************
           id: 1
  select_type: SIMPLE
        table: film_actor
         type: ref
possible_keys: PRIMARY,idx_fk_film_id
          key: PRIMARY
      key_len: 2
          ref: sakila.actor.actor_id
         rows: 1
        Extra: Using index
*************************** 3. row ***************************
           id: 1
  select_type: SIMPLE
        table: film
         type: eq_ref
possible_keys: PRIMARY
          key: PRIMARY
      key_len: 2
          ref: sakila.film_actor.film_id
         rows: 1
        Extra:
```

This is quite a different plan from the one suggested in the previous paragraph. MySQL wants to start with the actor table (we know this because it's listed first in the EXPLAIN output) and go in the reverse order. Is this really more efficient? Let's find out. The STRAIGHT_JOIN keyword forces the join to proceed in the order specified in the query. Here's the EXPLAIN output for the revised query:

```
mysql> EXPLAIN SELECT STRAIGHT_JOIN film.film_id...\G
*************************** 1. row ***************************
           id: 1
  select_type: SIMPLE
```

```
            table: film
             type: ALL
    possible_keys: PRIMARY
              key: NULL
          key_len: NULL
              ref: NULL
             rows: 951
            Extra:
*************************** 2. row ***************************
               id: 1
      select_type: SIMPLE
            table: film_actor
             type: ref
    possible_keys: PRIMARY,idx_fk_film_id
              key: idx_fk_film_id
          key_len: 2
              ref: sakila.film.film_id
             rows: 1
            Extra: Using index
*************************** 3. row ***************************
               id: 1
      select_type: SIMPLE
            table: actor
             type: eq_ref
    possible_keys: PRIMARY
              key: PRIMARY
          key_len: 2
              ref: sakila.film_actor.actor_id
             rows: 1
            Extra:
```

This shows why MySQL wants to reverse the join order: doing so will enable it to examine fewer rows in the first table.[14] In both cases, it will be able to perform fast indexed lookups in the second and third tables. The difference is how many of these indexed lookups it will have to do:

- Placing film first will require about 951 probes into film_actor and actor, one for each row in the first table.
- If the server scans the actor table first, it will have to do only 200 index lookups into later tables.

In other words, the reversed join order will require less backtracking and rereading. To double-check the optimizer's choice, we executed the two query versions and looked at the Last_query_cost variable for each. The reordered query had an estimated cost of 241, while the estimated cost of forcing the join order was 1,154.

This is a simple example of how MySQL's join optimizer can reorder queries to make them less expensive to execute. Reordering joins is usually a very effective optimization. There are times when it won't result in an optimal plan, though, and for those times

---

14. Strictly speaking, MySQL doesn't try to reduce the number of rows it reads. Instead, it tries to optimize for fewer page reads. But a row count can often give you a rough idea of the query cost.

you can use STRAIGHT_JOIN and write the query in the order you think is best—but such times are rare. In most cases, the join optimizer will outperform a human.

The join optimizer tries to produce a query execution plan tree with the lowest achievable cost. When possible, it examines all potential combinations of subtrees, beginning with all one-table plans.

Unfortunately, a join over *n* tables will have *n*-factorial combinations of join orders to examine. This is called the *search space* of all possible query plans, and it grows very quickly—a 10-table join can be executed up to 3,628,800 different ways! When the search space grows too large, it can take far too long to optimize the query, so the server stops doing a full analysis. Instead, it resorts to shortcuts such as "greedy" searches when the number of tables exceeds the limit specified by the optimizer_search_depth variable (which you can change if necessary).

MySQL has many heuristics, accumulated through years of research and experimentation, that it uses to speed up the optimization stage. This can be beneficial, but it can also mean that MySQL might (on rare occasions) miss an optimal plan and choose a less optimal one because it's trying not to examine every possible query plan.

Sometimes queries can't be reordered, and the join optimizer can use this fact to reduce the search space by eliminating choices. A LEFT JOIN is a good example, as are correlated subqueries (more about subqueries later). This is because the results for one table depend on data retrieved from another table. These dependencies help the join optimizer reduce the search space by eliminating choices.

Sort optimizations

Sorting results can be a costly operation, so you can often improve performance by avoiding sorts or by performing them on fewer rows.

We showed you how to use indexes for sorting in Chapter 3. When MySQL can't use an index to produce a sorted result, it must sort the rows itself. It can do this in memory or on disk, but it always calls this process a *filesort*, even if it doesn't actually use a file.

If the values to be sorted will fit into the sort buffer, MySQL can perform the sort entirely in memory with a *quicksort*. If MySQL can't do the sort in memory, it performs it on disk by sorting the values in chunks. It uses a quicksort to sort each chunk and then merges the sorted chunks into the results.

There are two filesort algorithms:

Two passes (old)
> Reads row pointers and ORDER BY columns, sorts them, and then scans the sorted list and rereads the rows for output.
>
> The two-pass algorithm can be quite expensive, because it reads the rows from the table twice, and the second read causes a lot of random I/O. This is especially expensive for MyISAM, which uses a system call to fetch each row (because

MyISAM relies on the operating system's cache to hold the data). On the other hand, it stores a minimal amount of data during the sort, so if the rows to be sorted are completely in memory, it can be cheaper to store less data and reread the rows to generate the final result.

Single pass (new)

Reads all the columns needed for the query, sorts them by the ORDER BY columns, and then scans the sorted list and outputs the specified columns.

This algorithm is available only in MySQL 4.1 and newer. It can be much more efficient, especially on large I/O-bound datasets, because it avoids reading the rows from the table twice and trades random I/O for more sequential I/O. However, it has the potential to use a lot more space, because it holds all the desired columns from each row, not just the columns needed to sort the rows. This means fewer tuples will fit into the sort buffer, and the filesort will have to perform more sort merge passes.

It's tricky to say which algorithm is more efficient, and there are best and worst cases for each algorithm. MySQL uses the new algorithm if the total size of all the columns needed for the query, plus the ORDER BY columns, is no more than max_length_for_sort_data bytes, so you can use this setting to influence which algorithm is used. See "Optimizing for Filesorts" on page 377 in Chapter 8 for more on this topic.

MySQL might use much more temporary storage space for a filesort than you'd expect, because it allocates a fixed-size record for each tuple it will sort. These records are large enough to hold the largest possible tuple, including the full length of each VARCHAR column. Also, if you're using UTF-8, MySQL allocates three bytes for each character. As a result, we've seen cases where poorly optimized schemas caused the temporary space used for sorting to be many times larger than the entire table's size on disk.

When sorting a join, MySQL might perform the filesort at two stages during the query execution. If the ORDER BY clause refers only to columns from the first table in the join order, MySQL can filesort this table and then proceed with the join. If this happens, EXPLAIN shows "Using filesort" in the Extra column. In all other circumstances—such as a sort against a table that's not first in the join order, or when the ORDER BY clause contains columns from more than one table—MySQL must store the query's results into a temporary table and then filesort the temporary table after the join finishes. In this case, EXPLAIN shows "Using temporary; Using filesort" in the Extra column. If there's a LIMIT, it is applied after the filesort, so the temporary table and the filesort can be very large.

MySQL 5.6 introduces significant changes to how sorts are performed when only a subset of the rows will be needed, such as a LIMIT query. Instead of sorting the entire result set and then returning a portion of it, MySQL 5.6 can sometimes discard unwanted rows before sorting them.

The Query Execution Engine

The parsing and optimizing stage outputs a query execution plan, which MySQL's query execution engine uses to process the query. The plan is a data structure; it is not executable byte-code, which is how many other databases execute queries.

In contrast to the optimization stage, the execution stage is usually not all that complex: MySQL simply follows the instructions given in the query execution plan. Many of the operations in the plan invoke methods implemented by the storage engine interface, also known as the *handler API*. Each table in the query is represented by an instance of a handler. If a table appears three times in the query, for example, the server creates three handler instances. Though we glossed over this before, MySQL actually creates the handler instances early in the optimization stage. The optimizer uses them to get information about the tables, such as their column names and index statistics.

The storage engine interface has lots of functionality, but it needs only a dozen or so "building-block" operations to execute most queries. For example, there's an operation to read the first row in an index, and one to read the next row in an index. This is enough for a query that does an index scan. This simplistic execution method makes MySQL's storage engine architecture possible, but it also imposes some of the optimizer limitations we've discussed.

 Not everything is a handler operation. For example, the server manages table locks. The handler might implement its own lower-level locking, as InnoDB does with row-level locks, but this does not replace the server's own locking implementation. As explained in Chapter 1, anything that all storage engines share is implemented in the server, such as date and time functions, views, and triggers.

To execute the query, the server just repeats the instructions until there are no more rows to examine.

Returning Results to the Client

The final step in executing a query is to reply to the client. Even queries that don't return a result set still reply to the client connection with information about the query, such as how many rows it affected.

If the query is cacheable, MySQL will also place the results into the query cache at this stage.

The server generates and sends results incrementally. Think back to the single-sweep multijoin method we mentioned earlier. As soon as MySQL processes the last table and generates one row successfully, it can and should send that row to the client.

This has two benefits: it lets the server avoid holding the row in memory, and it means the client starts getting the results as soon as possible.[15]

Each row in the result set is sent in a separate packet in the MySQL client/server protocol, although protocol packets can be buffered and sent together at the TCP protocol layer.

Limitations of the MySQL Query Optimizer

MySQL's "everything is a nested-loop join" approach to query execution isn't ideal for optimizing every kind of query. Fortunately, there are only a limited number of cases where the MySQL query optimizer does a poor job, and it's usually possible to rewrite such queries more efficiently. Even better, when MySQL 5.6 is released it will eliminate many of MySQL's limitations and make a variety of queries execute much more quickly.

Correlated Subqueries

MySQL sometimes optimizes subqueries very badly. The worst offenders are `IN()` subqueries in the `WHERE` clause. As an example, let's find all films in the Sakila sample database's `sakila.film` table whose casts include the actress Penelope Guiness (`actor_id=1`). This feels natural to write with a subquery, as follows:

```
mysql> SELECT * FROM sakila.film
    -> WHERE film_id IN(
    ->    SELECT film_id FROM sakila.film_actor WHERE actor_id = 1);
```

It's tempting to think that MySQL will execute this query from the inside out, by finding a list of `actor_id` values and substituting them into the `IN()` list. We said an `IN()` list is generally very fast, so you might expect the query to be optimized to something like this:

```
-- SELECT GROUP_CONCAT(film_id) FROM sakila.film_actor WHERE actor_id = 1;
-- Result: 1,23,25,106,140,166,277,361,438,499,506,509,605,635,749,832,939,970,980
SELECT * FROM sakila.film
WHERE film_id
IN(1,23,25,106,140,166,277,361,438,499,506,509,605,635,749,832,939,970,980);
```

Unfortunately, exactly the opposite happens. MySQL tries to "help" the subquery by pushing a correlation into it from the outer table, which it thinks will let the subquery find rows more efficiently. It rewrites the query as follows:

```
SELECT * FROM sakila.film
WHERE EXISTS (
    SELECT * FROM sakila.film_actor WHERE actor_id = 1
    AND film_actor.film_id = film.film_id);
```

---

15. You can influence this behavior if needed—for example, with the `SQL_BUFFER_RESULT` hint. See "Query Optimizer Hints" on page 238.

Now the subquery requires the `film_id` from the outer `film` table and can't be executed first. EXPLAIN shows the result as DEPENDENT SUBQUERY (you can use EXPLAIN EXTENDED to see exactly how the query is rewritten):

```
mysql> EXPLAIN SELECT * FROM sakila.film ...;
+----+--------------------+------------+--------+-----------------------+
| id | select_type        | table      | type   | possible_keys         |
+----+--------------------+------------+--------+-----------------------+
|  1 | PRIMARY            | film       | ALL    | NULL                  |
|  2 | DEPENDENT SUBQUERY | film_actor | eq_ref | PRIMARY,idx_fk_film_id |
+----+--------------------+------------+--------+-----------------------+
```

According to the EXPLAIN output, MySQL will table-scan the `film` table and execute the subquery for each row it finds. This won't cause a noticeable performance hit on small tables, but if the outer table is very large, the performance will be extremely bad. Fortunately, it's easy to rewrite such a query as a JOIN:

```
mysql> SELECT film.* FROM sakila.film
    ->     INNER JOIN sakila.film_actor USING(film_id)
    -> WHERE actor_id = 1;
```

Another good optimization is to manually generate the IN() list by executing the subquery as a separate query with GROUP_CONCAT(). Sometimes this can be faster than a JOIN. And finally, although IN() subqueries work poorly in many cases, EXISTS() or equality subqueries sometimes work much better. Here is another way to rewrite our IN() subquery example:

```
mysql> SELECT * FROM sakila.film
    -> WHERE EXISTS(
    ->     SELECT * FROM sakila.film_actor WHERE actor_id = 1
    ->         AND film_actor.film_id = film.film_id);
```

 The optimizer limitations we'll discuss throughout this section apply to the official MySQL server from Oracle Corporation as of version 5.5. The MariaDB fork of MySQL has several related query optimizer and execution engine enhancements, such as executing correlated subqueries from the inside out.

When a correlated subquery is good

MySQL doesn't always optimize correlated subqueries badly. If you hear advice to always avoid them, don't listen! Instead, measure and make your own decision. Sometimes a correlated subquery is a perfectly reasonable, or even optimal, way to get a result. Let's look at an example:

```
mysql> EXPLAIN SELECT film_id, language_id FROM sakila.film
    -> WHERE NOT EXISTS(
    ->     SELECT * FROM sakila.film_actor
    ->     WHERE film_actor.film_id = film.film_id
    -> )\G
*************************** 1. row ***************************
         id: 1
```

```
   select_type: PRIMARY
        table: film
         type: ALL
possible_keys: NULL
          key: NULL
      key_len: NULL
          ref: NULL
         rows: 951
        Extra: Using where
*************************** 2. row ***************************
           id: 2
   select_type: DEPENDENT SUBQUERY
        table: film_actor
         type: ref
possible_keys: idx_fk_film_id
          key: idx_fk_film_id
      key_len: 2
          ref: film.film_id
         rows: 2
        Extra: Using where; Using index
```

The standard advice for this query is to write it as a LEFT OUTER JOIN instead of using a subquery. In theory, MySQL's execution plan will be essentially the same either way. Let's see:

```
mysql> EXPLAIN SELECT film.film_id, film.language_id
    -> FROM sakila.film
    ->     LEFT OUTER JOIN sakila.film_actor USING(film_id)
    -> WHERE film_actor.film_id IS NULL\G
*************************** 1. row ***************************
           id: 1
   select_type: SIMPLE
        table: film
         type: ALL
possible_keys: NULL
          key: NULL
      key_len: NULL
          ref: NULL
         rows: 951
        Extra:
*************************** 2. row ***************************
           id: 1
   select_type: SIMPLE
        table: film_actor
         type: ref
possible_keys: idx_fk_film_id
          key: idx_fk_film_id
      key_len: 2
          ref: sakila.film.film_id
         rows: 2
        Extra: Using where; Using index; **Not exists**
```

The plans are nearly identical, but there are some differences:

- The SELECT type against film_actor is DEPENDENT SUBQUERY in one query and SIM PLE in the other. This difference simply reflects the syntax, because the first query uses a subquery and the second doesn't. It doesn't make much difference in terms of handler operations.

- The second query doesn't say "Using where" in the Extra column for the film table. That doesn't matter, though: the second query's USING clause is the same thing as a WHERE clause anyway.

- The second query says "Not exists" in the film_actor table's Extra column. This is an example of the early-termination algorithm we mentioned earlier in this chapter. It means MySQL is using a not-exists optimization to avoid reading more than one row in the film_actor table's idx_fk_film_id index. This is equivalent to a NOT EXISTS() correlated subquery, because it stops processing the current row as soon as it finds a match.

So, in theory, MySQL will execute the queries almost identically. In reality, measuring is the only way to tell which approach is really faster. We benchmarked both queries on our standard setup. The results are shown in Table 6-1.

Table 6-1. NOT EXISTS versus LEFT OUTER JOIN

Query	Result in queries per second (QPS)
NOT EXISTS subquery	360 QPS
LEFT OUTER JOIN	425 QPS

Our benchmark found that the subquery is quite a bit slower!

However, this isn't always the case. Sometimes a subquery can be faster. For example, it can work well when you just want to see rows from one table that match rows in another table. Although that sounds like it describes a join perfectly, it's not always the same thing. The following join, which is designed to find every film that has an actor, will return duplicates because some films have multiple actors:

```
mysql> SELECT film.film_id FROM sakila.film
    ->    INNER JOIN sakila.film_actor USING(film_id);
```

We need to use DISTINCT or GROUP BY to eliminate the duplicates:

```
mysql> SELECT DISTINCT film.film_id FROM sakila.film
    ->    INNER JOIN sakila.film_actor USING(film_id);
```

But what are we really trying to express with this query, and is it obvious from the SQL? The EXISTS operator expresses the logical concept of "has a match" without producing duplicated rows and avoids a GROUP BY or DISTINCT operation, which might require a temporary table. Here's the query written as a subquery instead of a join:

```
mysql> SELECT film_id FROM sakila.film
    ->    WHERE EXISTS(SELECT * FROM sakila.film_actor
    ->    WHERE film.film_id = film_actor.film_id);
```

Again, we benchmarked to see which strategy was faster. The results are shown in Table 6-2.

Table 6-2. EXISTS versus INNER JOIN

Query	Result in queries per second (QPS)
INNER JOIN	185 QPS
EXISTS subquery	325 QPS

In this example, the subquery performs much faster than the join.

We showed this lengthy example to illustrate two points: you should not heed categorical advice about subqueries, and you should measure to prove your assumptions about query plans and response time. A final note on subqueries: this is one of the rare cases where we need to mention a bug in MySQL. In MySQL version 5.1.48 and earlier, the following syntax can lock a row in table2:

```
SELECT ... FROM table1 WHERE col = (SELECT ... FROM table2 WHERE ...);
```

This bug, if it affects you, can cause subqueries to behave much differently under high concurrency than if you measure their performance in a single thread. This is bug 46947, and even though it's solved, it still reinforces our point: don't assume.

UNION Limitations

MySQL sometimes can't "push down" conditions from the outside of a UNION to the inside, where they could be used to limit results or enable additional optimizations.

If you think any of the individual queries inside a UNION would benefit from a LIMIT, or if you know they'll be subject to an ORDER BY clause once combined with other queries, you need to put those clauses inside each part of the UNION. For example, if you UNION together two tables and LIMIT the result to the first 20 rows, MySQL will store both tables into a temporary table and then retrieve just 20 rows from it:

```
(SELECT first_name, last_name
 FROM sakila.actor
 ORDER BY last_name)
UNION ALL
(SELECT first_name, last_name
 FROM sakila.customer
 ORDER BY last_name)
LIMIT 20;
```

This query will store 200 rows from the actor table, and 599 from the customer table, into a temporary table and then fetch the first 20 rows from that temporary table. You can avoid this by adding LIMIT 20 redundantly to each query inside the UNION:

```
(SELECT first_name, last_name
 FROM sakila.actor
 ORDER BY last_name
 LIMIT 20)
UNION ALL
(SELECT first_name, last_name
 FROM sakila.customer
 ORDER BY last_name
 LIMIT 20)
LIMIT 20;
```

Now the temporary table will contain only 40 rows. In addition to the performance improvement, you'll probably need to correct the query: the order in which the rows are retrieved from the temporary table is undefined, so there should be an overall ORDER BY just before the final LIMIT.

Index Merge Optimizations

As discussed in the previous chapter, MySQL 5.0 and greater can access several indexes from a single table and union or intersect the results to locate rows when there are complex filtering conditions in the WHERE clause.

Equality Propagation

Equality propagation can have unexpected costs sometimes. For example, consider a huge IN() list on a column the optimizer knows will be equal to some columns on other tables, due to a WHERE, ON, or USING clause that sets the columns equal to each other.

The optimizer will "share" the list by copying it to the corresponding columns in all related tables. This is normally helpful, because it gives the query optimizer and execution engine more options for where to actually execute the IN() check. But when the list is very large, it can result in slower optimization and execution. There's no built-in workaround for this problem at the time of this writing—you'll have to change the source code if it's a problem for you. (It's not a problem for most people.)

Parallel Execution

MySQL can't execute a single query in parallel on many CPUs. This is a feature offered by some other database servers, but not MySQL. We mention it so that you won't spend a lot of time trying to figure out how to get parallel query execution on MySQL!

Hash Joins

MySQL can't do true hash joins at the time of this writing—everything is a nested-loop join. However, you can emulate hash joins using hash indexes. If you aren't using the Memory storage engine, you'll have to emulate the hash indexes, too. We showed you how to do this in "Building your own hash indexes" on page 154. MariaDB can perform true hash joins.

Loose Index Scans

MySQL has historically been unable to do loose index scans, which scan noncontiguous ranges of an index. MySQL's index scans generally require a defined start point and a defined end point in the index, even if only a few noncontiguous rows in the middle are really desired for the query. MySQL will scan the entire range of rows within these end points.

An example will help clarify this. Suppose we have a table with an index on columns (a, b), and we want to run the following query:

```
mysql> SELECT ... FROM tbl WHERE b BETWEEN 2 AND 3;
```

Because the index begins with column a, but the query's WHERE clause doesn't specify column a, MySQL will do a table scan and eliminate the nonmatching rows with a WHERE clause, as shown in Figure 6-5.

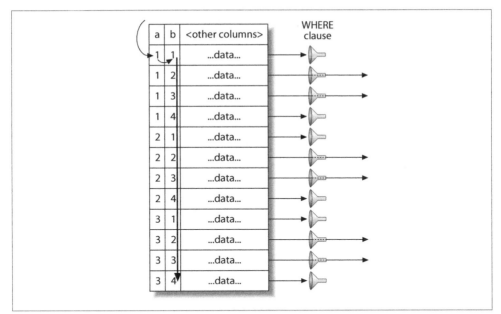

Figure 6-5. MySQL scans the entire table to find rows

It's easy to see that there's a faster way to execute this query. The index's structure (but not MySQL's storage engine API) lets you seek to the beginning of each range of values, scan until the end of the range, and then backtrack and jump ahead to the start of the next range. Figure 6-6 shows what that strategy would look like if MySQL were able to do it.

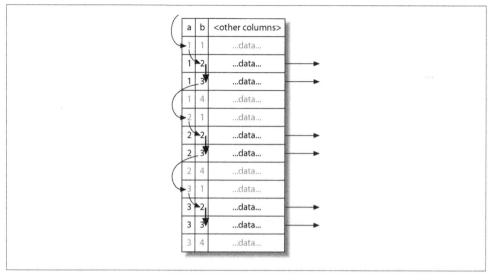

Figure 6-6. A loose index scan, which MySQL cannot currently do, would be more efficient

Notice the absence of a WHERE clause, which isn't needed because the index alone lets us skip over the unwanted rows.

This is admittedly a simplistic example, and we could easily optimize the query we've shown by adding a different index. However, there are many cases where adding another index can't solve the problem. One example is a query that has a range condition on the index's first column and an equality condition on the second column.

Beginning in MySQL 5.0, loose index scans are possible in certain limited circumstances, such as queries that find maximum and minimum values in a grouped query:

```
mysql> EXPLAIN SELECT actor_id, MAX(film_id)
    -> FROM sakila.film_actor
    -> GROUP BY actor_id\G
*************************** 1. row ***************************
           id: 1
  select_type: SIMPLE
        table: film_actor
         type: range
possible_keys: NULL
          key: PRIMARY
      key_len: 2
          ref: NULL
         rows: 396
        Extra: Using index for group-by
```

The "Using index for group-by" information in this EXPLAIN plan indicates a loose index scan. This is a good optimization for this special purpose, but it is not a general-purpose loose index scan. It might be better termed a "loose index probe."

Until MySQL supports general-purpose loose index scans, the workaround is to supply a constant or list of constants for the leading columns of the index. We showed several examples of how to get good performance with these types of queries in our indexing case study in the previous chapter.

In MySQL 5.6, some limitations on loose index scans will be fixed with an optimizer technique called "index condition pushdown."

MIN() and MAX()

MySQL doesn't optimize certain `MIN()` and `MAX()` queries very well. Here's an example:

```
mysql> SELECT MIN(actor_id) FROM sakila.actor WHERE first_name = 'PENELOPE';
```

Because there's no index on `first_name`, this query performs a table scan. If MySQL scans the primary key, it can theoretically stop after reading the first matching row, because the primary key is strictly ascending and any subsequent row will have a greater `actor_id`. However, in this case MySQL will scan the whole table, which you can verify by looking at `SHOW STATUS` counters. The workaround is to remove the `MIN()` and rewrite the query with a `LIMIT`, as follows:

```
mysql> SELECT actor_id FROM sakila.actor USE INDEX(PRIMARY)
    -> WHERE first_name = 'PENELOPE' LIMIT 1;
```

This general strategy often works well when MySQL would otherwise choose to scan more rows than necessary. If you're a purist, you might object that this query is missing the point of SQL. We're supposed to be able to tell the server *what* we want and it's supposed to figure out *how* to get that data, whereas in this case we're telling MySQL *how* to execute the query and, as a result, it's not clear from the query that *what* we're looking for is a minimal value. True, but sometimes you have to compromise your principles to get high performance.

SELECT and UPDATE on the Same Table

MySQL doesn't let you `SELECT` from a table while simultaneously running an `UPDATE` on it. This isn't really an optimizer limitation, but knowing how MySQL executes queries can help you work around it. Here's an example of a query that's disallowed, even though it is standard SQL. The query updates each row with the number of similar rows in the table:

```
mysql> UPDATE tbl AS outer_tbl
    ->    SET cnt = (
    ->        SELECT count(*) FROM tbl AS inner_tbl
    ->        WHERE inner_tbl.type = outer_tbl.type
    ->    );
ERROR 1093 (HY000): You can't specify target table 'outer_tbl' for update in FROM
clause
```

To work around this limitation, you can use a derived table, because MySQL materializes it as a temporary table. This effectively executes two queries: one SELECT inside the subquery, and one multitable UPDATE with the joined results of the table and the subquery. The subquery opens and closes the table before the outer UPDATE opens the table, so the query will now succeed:

```
mysql> UPDATE tbl
    ->    INNER JOIN(
    ->       SELECT type, count(*) AS cnt
    ->       FROM tbl
    ->       GROUP BY type
    ->    ) AS der USING(type)
    -> SET tbl.cnt = der.cnt;
```

Query Optimizer Hints

MySQL has a few optimizer hints you can use to control the query plan if you're not happy with the one MySQL's optimizer chooses. The following list identifies these hints and indicates when it's a good idea to use them. You place the appropriate hint in the query whose plan you want to modify, and it is effective for only that query. Check the MySQL manual for the exact syntax of each hint. Some of them are version-dependent. The options are:

HIGH_PRIORITY *and* LOW_PRIORITY

> These hints tell MySQL how to prioritize the statement relative to other statements that are trying to access the same tables.
>
> HIGH_PRIORITY tells MySQL to schedule a SELECT statement before other statements that might be waiting for table locks so they can modify data. In effect, it makes the SELECT go to the front of the queue instead of waiting its turn. You can also apply this modifier to INSERT, where it simply cancels the effect of a global LOW _PRIORITY server setting.
>
> LOW_PRIORITY is the reverse: it makes the statement wait at the very end of the queue if there are any other statements that want to access the tables—even if the other statements are issued after it. It's rather like an overly polite person holding the door at a restaurant: as long as there's anyone else waiting, it will starve itself! You can apply this hint to SELECT, INSERT, UPDATE, REPLACE, and DELETE statements.
>
> These hints are effective on storage engines with table-level locking, but you should never need them on InnoDB or other engines with fine-grained locking and concurrency control. Be careful when using them on MyISAM, because they can disable concurrent inserts and greatly reduce performance.
>
> The HIGH_PRIORITY and LOW_PRIORITY hints are a frequent source of confusion. They do not allocate more or fewer resources to queries to make them "work harder" or "not work as hard"; they simply affect how the server queues statements that are waiting for access to a table.

DELAYED

This hint is for use with INSERT and REPLACE. It lets the statement to which it is applied return immediately and places the inserted rows into a buffer, which will be inserted in bulk when the table is free. This is most useful for logging and similar applications where you want to insert a lot of rows without making the client wait, and without causing I/O for each statement. There are many limitations; for example, delayed inserts are not implemented in all storage engines, and LAST _INSERT_ID() doesn't work with them.

STRAIGHT_JOIN

This hint can appear either just after the SELECT keyword in a SELECT statement, or in any statement between two joined tables. The first usage forces all tables in the query to be joined in the order in which they're listed in the statement. The second usage forces a join order on the two tables between which the hint appears.

The STRAIGHT_JOIN hint is useful when MySQL doesn't choose a good join order, or when the optimizer takes a long time to decide on a join order. In the latter case, the thread will spend a lot of time in the "statistics" state, and adding this hint will reduce the search space for the optimizer.

You can use EXPLAIN to see what order the optimizer would choose, then rewrite the query in that order and add STRAIGHT_JOIN. This is a good idea as long as you don't think the fixed order will result in bad performance for some WHERE clauses. You should be careful to revisit such queries after upgrading MySQL, however, because new optimizations might appear that will be defeated by STRAIGHT_JOIN.

SQL_SMALL_RESULT *and* SQL_BIG_RESULT

These hints are for SELECT statements. They tell the optimizer how and when to use temporary tables and sort in GROUP BY or DISTINCT queries. SQL_SMALL_RESULT tells the optimizer that the result set will be small and can be put into indexed temporary tables to avoid sorting for the grouping, whereas SQL_BIG_RESULT indicates that the result will be large and that it will be better to use temporary tables on disk with sorting.

SQL_BUFFER_RESULT

This hint tells the optimizer to put the results into a temporary table and release table locks as soon as possible. This is different from the client-side buffering we described previously. Server-side buffering can be useful when you don't use buffering on the client, because it lets you avoid consuming a lot of memory on the client and still release locks quickly. The trade-off is that the server's memory is used instead of the client's.

SQL_CACHE *and* SQL_NO_CACHE

These hints instruct the server that the query either is or is not a candidate for caching in the query cache. See the next chapter for details on how to use them.

SQL_CALC_FOUND_ROWS

This hint isn't strictly an optimizer hint. It doesn't tell MySQL to plan the query differently. Instead, it provides extra functionality by changing what the query actually does. It tells MySQL to calculate a full result set when there's a LIMIT clause, even though it returns only LIMIT rows. You can retrieve the total number of rows it found via FOUND_ROWS() (but take a look at the section "Optimizing SQL_CALC_FOUND_ROWS" on page 248 for reasons why you shouldn't use this hint).

FOR UPDATE *and* LOCK IN SHARE MODE

These hints aren't really optimizer hints, either; they control locking for SELECT statements, but only for storage engines that have row-level locks. They enable you to place locks on the matched rows. These hints are not needed for INSERT ... SELECT queries, which place read locks on the source rows by default in MySQL 5.0 and newer versions. (You can disable this behavior, but it's not a good idea— we explain why in the chapters on replication and backups.)

The only built-in storage engine that supports these hints is InnoDB. Be aware that they disable some optimizations, such as covering indexes. InnoDB can't lock rows exclusively without accessing the primary key, which is where the row versioning information is stored.

Unfortunately, these hints are way overused and frequently cause severe locking problems, as we'll discuss later in this chapter. You should avoid them at pretty much all costs; there's usually a better way to do what you're trying to do.

USE INDEX, IGNORE INDEX, *and* FORCE INDEX

These hints tell the optimizer which indexes to use or ignore for finding rows in a table (for example, when deciding on a join order). In MySQL 5.0 and earlier, they don't influence which indexes the server uses for sorting and grouping; in MySQL 5.1 the syntax can take an optional FOR ORDER BY or FOR GROUP BY clause.

FORCE INDEX is the same as USE INDEX, but it tells the optimizer that a table scan is extremely expensive compared to the index, even if the index is not very useful. You can use these hints when you don't think the optimizer is choosing the right index, or when you want to take advantage of an index for some reason, such as implicit ordering without an ORDER BY. We gave an example of this previously, where we showed how to get a minimum value efficiently with LIMIT.

In MySQL 5.0 and newer, there are also some configuration variables that influence the optimizer:

optimizer_search_depth

This variable tells the optimizer how exhaustively to examine partial plans. If your queries are taking a very long time in the "Statistics" state, you might try lowering this value.

optimizer_prune_level

This variable, which is enabled by default, lets the optimizer skip certain plans based on the number of rows examined.

`optimizer_switch`

> This variable contains a set of flags that enable or disable specific optimizer features. For example, in MySQL 5.1 you can use it to disable the index merge query plan.

The first two options control optimizer shortcuts. These shortcuts are valuable for good performance on complex queries, but they can cause the server to miss optimal plans for the sake of efficiency. That's why it sometimes makes sense to change them.

Validating MySQL Upgrades

Trying to outsmart the MySQL optimizer usually is not a good idea. It generally creates more work and increases maintenance costs for very little benefit. This is especially relevant when you upgrade MySQL, because optimizer hints used in your queries might prevent new optimizer strategies from being used.

In MySQL 5.0 a number of capabilities were added to the optimizer, and the as-yet unreleased MySQL 5.6 will have the biggest changes to the optimizer in a very long time. If you are upgrading to one of these versions, you will not want to miss out on the benefits they offer.

New versions of MySQL generally improve the server by leaps and bounds, and this is especially true in the 5.5 and 5.6 versions. MySQL upgrades usually go fine, but you still need to test changes carefully. There is always a chance that you will discover an edge case that affects you. The good news is that it's really easy to prevent this with a little change management. Use the *pt-upgrade* tool from Percona Toolkit to validate that your queries run well on the new version of MySQL, and that they don't return different results.

Optimizing Specific Types of Queries

In this section, we give advice on how to optimize certain kinds of queries. We've covered most of these topics in detail elsewhere in the book, but we wanted to make a list of common optimization problems that you can refer to easily.

Most of the advice in this section is version-dependent, and it might not hold for future versions of MySQL. There's no reason why the server won't be able to do some or all of these optimizations itself someday.

Optimizing COUNT() Queries

The COUNT() aggregate function, and how to optimize queries that use it, is probably one of the top 10 most-misunderstood topics in MySQL. You can do a web search and find more misinformation on this topic than we care to think about.

Before we get into optimization, it's important that you understand what COUNT() really does.

What COUNT() does

COUNT() is a special function that works in two very different ways: it counts *values* and *rows*. A value is a non-NULL expression (NULL is the absence of a value). If you specify a column name or other expression inside the parentheses, COUNT() counts how many times that expression has a value. This is confusing for many people, in part because values and NULL are confusing. If you need to learn how this works in SQL, we suggest a good book on SQL fundamentals. (The Internet is not necessarily a good source of accurate information on this topic.)

The other form of COUNT() simply counts the number of rows in the result. This is what MySQL does when it knows the expression inside the parentheses can never be NULL. The most obvious example is COUNT(*), which is a special form of COUNT() that does not expand the * wildcard into the full list of columns in the table, as you might expect; instead, it ignores columns altogether and counts rows.

One of the most common mistakes we see is specifying column names inside the parentheses when you want to count rows. When you want to know the number of rows in the result, you should *always* use COUNT(*). This communicates your intention clearly and avoids poor performance.

Myths about MyISAM

A common misconception is that MyISAM is extremely fast for COUNT() queries. It is fast, but only for a very special case: COUNT(*) without a WHERE clause, which merely counts the number of rows in the entire table. MySQL can optimize this away because the storage engine always knows how many rows are in the table. If MySQL knows col can never be NULL, it can also optimize a COUNT(*col*) expression by converting it to COUNT(*) internally.

MyISAM does not have any magical speed optimizations for counting rows when the query has a WHERE clause, or for the more general case of counting values instead of rows. It might be faster than other storage engines for a given query, or it might not be. That depends on a lot of factors.

Simple optimizations

You can sometimes use MyISAM's COUNT(*) optimization to your advantage when you want to count all but a very small number of rows that are well indexed. The following example uses the standard world database to show how you can efficiently find the number of cities whose ID is greater than 5. You might write this query as follows:

```
mysql> SELECT COUNT(*) FROM world.City WHERE ID > 5;
```

If you examine this query with SHOW STATUS, you'll see that it scans 4,079 rows. If you negate the conditions and subtract the number of cities whose IDs are less than or equal to 5 from the total number of cities, you can reduce that to five rows:

```
mysql> SELECT (SELECT COUNT(*) FROM world.City) - COUNT(*)
    -> FROM world.City WHERE ID <= 5;
```

This version reads fewer rows because the subquery is turned into a constant during the query optimization phase, as you can see with EXPLAIN:

```
+----+-------------+-------+...+------+----------------------------+
| id | select_type | table |...| rows | Extra                      |
+----+-------------+-------+...+------+----------------------------+
|  1 | PRIMARY     | City  |...|    6 | Using where; Using index   |
|  2 | SUBQUERY    | NULL  |...| NULL | Select tables optimized away |
+----+-------------+-------+...+------+----------------------------+
```

A frequent question on mailing lists and IRC channels is how to retrieve counts for several different values in the same column with just one query, to reduce the number of queries required. For example, say you want to create a single query that counts how many items have each of several colors. You can't use an OR (e.g., SELECT COUNT(color = 'blue' OR color = 'red') FROM items;), because that won't separate the different counts for the different colors. And you can't put the colors in the WHERE clause (e.g., SELECT COUNT(*) FROM items WHERE color = 'blue' AND color = 'red';), because the colors are mutually exclusive. Here is a query that solves this problem:[16]

```
mysql> SELECT SUM(IF(color = 'blue', 1, 0)) AS blue,SUM(IF(color = 'red', 1, 0))
    -> AS red FROM items;
```

And here is another that's equivalent, but instead of using SUM() uses COUNT() and ensures that the expressions won't have values when the criteria are false:

```
mysql> SELECT COUNT(color = 'blue' OR NULL) AS blue, COUNT(color = 'red' OR NULL)
    -> AS red FROM items;
```

Using an approximation

Sometimes you don't need an accurate count, so you can just use an approximation. The optimizer's estimated rows in EXPLAIN often serves well for this. Just execute an EXPLAIN query instead of the real query.

At other times, an exact count is much less efficient than an approximation. One customer asked for help counting the number of active users on his website. The user count was cached and displayed for 30 minutes, after which it was regenerated and cached again. This was inaccurate by nature, so an approximation was acceptable. The query included several WHERE conditions to ensure that it didn't count inactive users or the "default" user, which was a special user ID in the application. Removing these conditions changed the count only slightly, but made the query much more efficient. A further optimization was to eliminate an unnecessary DISTINCT to remove a filesort. The rewritten query was much faster and returned almost exactly the same results.

---

16. You can also write the SUM() expressions as SUM(color = 'blue'), SUM(color = 'red').

More complex optimizations

In general, `COUNT()` queries are hard to optimize because they usually need to count a lot of rows (i.e., access a lot of data). Your only other option for optimizing within MySQL itself is to use a covering index. If that doesn't help enough, you need to make changes to your application architecture. Consider summary tables (covered in Chapter 4), and possibly an external caching system such as *memcached*. You'll probably find yourself faced with the familiar dilemma, "fast, accurate, and simple: pick any two."

Optimizing JOIN Queries

This topic is actually spread throughout most of the book, but we'll mention a few highlights:

- Make sure there are indexes on the columns in the `ON` or `USING` clauses. Consider the join order when adding indexes. If you're joining tables A and B on column c and the query optimizer decides to join the tables in the order B, A, you don't need to index the column on table B. Unused indexes are extra overhead. In general, you need to add indexes only on the second table in the join order, unless they're needed for some other reason.

- Try to ensure that any `GROUP BY` or `ORDER BY` expression refers only to columns from a single table, so MySQL can try to use an index for that operation.

- Be careful when upgrading MySQL, because the join syntax, operator precedence, and other behaviors have changed at various times. What used to be a normal join can sometimes become a cross product, a different kind of join that returns different results, or even invalid syntax.

Optimizing Subqueries

The most important advice we can give on subqueries is that you should usually prefer a join where possible, at least in current versions of MySQL. We covered this topic extensively earlier in this chapter. However, "prefer a join" is not future-proof advice, and if you're using MySQL 5.6 or newer versions, or MariaDB, subqueries are a whole different matter.

Optimizing GROUP BY and DISTINCT

MySQL optimizes these two kinds of queries similarly in many cases, and in fact converts between them as needed internally during the optimization process. Both types of queries benefit from indexes, as usual, and that's the single most important way to optimize them.

MySQL has two kinds of `GROUP BY` strategies when it can't use an index: it can use a temporary table or a filesort to perform the grouping. Either one can be more efficient for any given query. You can force the optimizer to choose one method or the other with the SQL_BIG_RESULT and SQL_SMALL_RESULT optimizer hints, as discussed earlier in this chapter.

If you need to group a join by a value that comes from a lookup table, it's usually more efficient to group by the lookup table's identifier than by the value. For example, the following query isn't as efficient as it could be:

```
mysql> SELECT actor.first_name, actor.last_name, COUNT(*)
    -> FROM sakila.film_actor
    ->     INNER JOIN sakila.actor USING(actor_id)
    -> GROUP BY actor.first_name, actor.last_name;
```

The query is more efficiently written as follows:

```
mysql> SELECT actor.first_name, actor.last_name, COUNT(*)
    -> FROM sakila.film_actor
    ->     INNER JOIN sakila.actor USING(actor_id)
    -> GROUP BY film_actor.actor_id;
```

Grouping by actor.actor_id could be even more efficient than grouping by film_actor.actor_id. You should test on your specific data to see.

This query takes advantage of the fact that the actor's first and last name are dependent on the actor_id, so it will return the same results, but it's not always the case that you can blithely select nongrouped columns and get the same result. You might even have the server's SQL_MODE configured to disallow it. You can use MIN() or MAX() to work around this when you know the values within the group are distinct because they depend on the grouped-by column, or if you don't care which value you get:

```
mysql> SELECT MIN(actor.first_name), MAX(actor.last_name), ...;
```

Purists will argue that you're grouping by the wrong thing, and they're right. A spurious MIN() or MAX() is a sign that the query isn't structured correctly. However, sometimes your only concern will be making MySQL execute the query as quickly as possible. The purists will be satisfied with the following way of writing the query:

```
mysql> SELECT actor.first_name, actor.last_name, c.cnt
    -> FROM sakila.actor
    ->     INNER JOIN (
    ->         SELECT actor_id, COUNT(*) AS cnt
    ->         FROM sakila.film_actor
    ->         GROUP BY actor_id
    ->     ) AS c USING(actor_id) ;
```

But the cost of creating and filling the temporary table required for the subquery may be high compared to the cost of fudging pure relational theory a little bit. Remember, the temporary table created by the subquery has no indexes.[17]

It's generally a bad idea to select nongrouped columns in a grouped query, because the results will be nondeterministic and could easily change if you change an index or the

---

17. This is another limitation that's fixed in MariaDB, by the way.

optimizer decides to use a different strategy. Most such queries we see are accidents (because the server doesn't complain), or are the result of laziness rather than being designed that way for optimization purposes. It's better to be explicit. In fact, we suggest that you set the server's SQL_MODE configuration variable to include ONLY_FULL _GROUP_BY so it produces an error instead of letting you write a bad query.

MySQL automatically orders grouped queries by the columns in the GROUP BY clause, unless you specify an ORDER BY clause explicitly. If you don't care about the order and you see this causing a filesort, you can use ORDER BY NULL to skip the automatic sort. You can also add an optional DESC or ASC keyword right after the GROUP BY clause to order the results in the desired direction by the clause's columns.

Optimizing GROUP BY WITH ROLLUP

A variation on grouped queries is to ask MySQL to do superaggregation within the results. You can do this with a WITH ROLLUP clause, but it might not be as well optimized as you need. Check the execution method with EXPLAIN, paying attention to whether the grouping is done via filesort or temporary table; try removing the WITH ROLLUP and seeing if you get the same group method. You might be able to force the grouping method with the hints we mentioned earlier in this section.

Sometimes it's more efficient to do superaggregation in your application, even if it means fetching many more rows from the server. You can also nest a subquery in the FROM clause or use a temporary table to hold intermediate results, and then query the temporary table with a UNION.

The best approach might be to move the WITH ROLLUP functionality into your application code.

Optimizing LIMIT and OFFSET

Queries with LIMITs and OFFSETs are common in systems that do pagination, nearly always in conjunction with an ORDER BY clause. It's helpful to have an index that supports the ordering; otherwise, the server has to do a lot of filesorts.

A frequent problem is having a high value for the offset. If your query looks like LIMIT 10000, 20, it is generating 10,020 rows and throwing away the first 10,000 of them, which is very expensive. Assuming all pages are accessed with equal frequency, such queries scan half the table on average. To optimize them, you can either limit how many pages are permitted in a pagination view, or try to make the high offsets more efficient.

One simple technique to improve efficiency is to do the offset on a covering index, rather than the full rows. You can then join the result to the full row and retrieve the additional columns you need. This can be much more efficient. Consider the following query:

```
mysql> SELECT film_id, description FROM sakila.film ORDER BY title LIMIT 50, 5;
```

If the table is very large, this query is better written as follows:

```
mysql> SELECT film.film_id, film.description
    -> FROM sakila.film
    ->    INNER JOIN (
    ->       SELECT film_id FROM sakila.film
    ->       ORDER BY title LIMIT 50, 5
    ->    ) AS lim USING(film_id);
```

This "deferred join" works because it lets the server examine as little data as possible in an index without accessing rows, and then, once the desired rows are found, join them against the full table to retrieve the other columns from the row. A similar technique applies to joins with LIMIT clauses.

Sometimes you can also convert the limit to a positional query, which the server can execute as an index range scan. For example, if you precalculate and index a position column, you can rewrite the query as follows:

```
mysql> SELECT film_id, description FROM sakila.film
    -> WHERE position BETWEEN 50 AND 54 ORDER BY position;
```

Ranked data poses a similar problem, but usually mixes GROUP BY into the fray. You'll almost certainly need to precompute and store ranks.

The problem with LIMIT and OFFSET is really the OFFSET, which represents rows the server is generating and throwing away. If you use a sort of bookmark to remember the position of the last row you fetched, you can generate the next set of rows by starting from that position instead of using an OFFSET. For example, if you want to paginate through rental records, starting from the newest rentals and working backward, you can rely on the fact that their primary keys are always increasing. You can fetch the first set of results like this:

```
mysql> SELECT * FROM sakila.rental
    -> ORDER BY rental_id DESC LIMIT 20;
```

This query returns rentals 16049 through 16030. The next query can continue from that point:

```
mysql> SELECT * FROM sakila.rental
    -> WHERE rental_id < 16030
    -> ORDER BY rental_id DESC LIMIT 20;
```

The nice thing about this technique is that it's very efficient no matter how far you paginate into the table.

Other alternatives include using precomputed summaries, or joining against redundant tables that contain only the primary key and the columns you need for the ORDER BY. You can also use Sphinx; see Appendix F for more information.

Optimizing SQL_CALC_FOUND_ROWS

Another common technique for paginated displays is to add the SQL_CALC_FOUND_ROWS hint to a query with a LIMIT, so you'll know how many rows would have been returned without the LIMIT. It might seem that there's some kind of "magic" happening here, whereby the server predicts how many rows it would have found. But unfortunately, the server doesn't really do that; it can't count rows it doesn't actually find. This option just tells the server to generate and throw away the rest of the result set, instead of stopping when it reaches the desired number of rows. That's very expensive.

A better design is to convert the pager to a "next" link. Assuming there are 20 results per page, the query should then use a LIMIT of 21 rows and display only 20. If the 21st row exists in the results, there's a next page, and you can render the "next" link.

Another possibility is to fetch and cache many more rows than you need—say, 1,000—and then retrieve them from the cache for successive pages. This strategy lets your application know how large the full result set is. If it's fewer than 1,000 rows, the application knows how many page links to render; if it's more, the application can just display "more than 1,000 results found." Both strategies are much more efficient than repeatedly generating an entire result and discarding most of it.

Sometimes you can also just estimate the full size of the result set by running an EXPLAIN query and looking at the rows column in the result (hey, even Google doesn't show exact result counts!). If you can't use these tactics, using a separate COUNT(*) query to find the number of rows can be much faster than SQL_CALC_FOUND_ROWS, if it can use a covering index.

Optimizing UNION

MySQL always executes UNION queries by creating a temporary table and filling it with the UNION results. MySQL can't apply as many optimizations to UNION queries as you might be used to. You might have to help the optimizer by manually "pushing down" WHERE, LIMIT, ORDER BY, and other conditions (i.e., copying them, as appropriate, from the outer query into each SELECT in the UNION).

It's important to *always* use UNION ALL, unless you need the server to eliminate duplicate rows. If you omit the ALL keyword, MySQL adds the distinct option to the temporary table, which uses the full row to determine uniqueness. This is quite expensive. Be aware that the ALL keyword doesn't eliminate the temporary table, though. MySQL always places results into a temporary table and then reads them out again, even when it's not really necessary (for example, when the results could be returned directly to the client).

Static Query Analysis

Percona Toolkit contains *pt-query-advisor*, a tool that parses a log of queries, analyzes the query patterns, and gives annoyingly detailed advice about potentially bad practices in them. It's sort of a "lint checker" for MySQL queries. It will catch many common problems such as those we've mentioned in the previous sections.

Using User-Defined Variables

It's easy to forget about MySQL's user-defined variables, but they can be a powerful technique for writing efficient queries. They work especially well for queries that benefit from a mixture of procedural and relational logic. Purely relational queries treat everything as unordered sets that the server somehow manipulates all at once. MySQL takes a more pragmatic approach. This can be a weakness, but it can be a strength if you know how to exploit it, and user-defined variables can help.

User-defined variables are temporary containers for values, which persist as long as your connection to the server lives. You define them by simply assigning to them with a SET or SELECT statement:[18]

```
mysql> SET @one       := 1;
mysql> SET @min_actor := (SELECT MIN(actor_id) FROM sakila.actor);
mysql> SET @last_week := CURRENT_DATE-INTERVAL 1 WEEK;
```

You can then use the variables in most places an expression can go:

```
mysql> SELECT ... WHERE col <= @last_week;
```

Before we get into the strengths of user-defined variables, let's take a look at some of their peculiarities and disadvantages and see what things you *can't* use them for:

- They disable the query cache.
- You can't use them where a literal or identifier is needed, such as for a table or column name, or in the LIMIT clause.
- They are connection-specific, so you can't use them for interconnection communication.
- If you're using connection pooling or persistent connections, they can cause seemingly isolated parts of your code to interact. (If so, it's because of a bug in your code or the connection pool, but it can still happen.)
- They are case sensitive in MySQL versions prior to 5.0, so beware of compatibility issues.
- You can't explicitly declare these variables' types, and the point at which types are decided for undefined variables differs across MySQL versions. The best thing to do is initially assign a value of 0 for variables you want to use for integers, 0.0 for

---

18. In some contexts you can assign with a plain = sign, but we think it's better to avoid ambiguity and always use :=.

floating-point numbers, or `''` (the empty string) for strings. A variable's type changes when it is assigned to; MySQL's user-defined variable typing is dynamic.

- The optimizer might optimize away these variables in some situations, preventing them from doing what you want.

- Order of assignment, and indeed even the time of assignment, can be nondeterministic and depend on the query plan the optimizer chose. The results can be very confusing, as you'll see later.

- The `:=` assignment operator has lower precedence than any other operator, so you have to be careful to parenthesize explicitly.

- Undefined variables do not generate a syntax error, so it's easy to make mistakes without knowing it.

Optimizing ranking queries

One of the most important features of variables is that you can assign a value to a variable and use the resulting value at the same time. In other words, an assignment is an *L-value*. Here's an example that simultaneously calculates and outputs a "row number" for a query:

```
mysql> SET @rownum := 0;
mysql> SELECT actor_id, @rownum := @rownum + 1 AS rownum
    -> FROM sakila.actor LIMIT 3;
+----------+--------+
| actor_id | rownum |
+----------+--------+
|        1 |      1 |
|        2 |      2 |
|        3 |      3 |
+----------+--------+
```

This example isn't terribly interesting, because it just shows that we can duplicate the table's primary key. Still, it has its uses—one of which is ranking. Let's write a query that returns the 10 actors who have played in the most movies, with a rank column that gives actors the same rank if they're tied. We start with a query that finds the actors and the number of movies:

```
mysql> SELECT actor_id, COUNT(*) as cnt
    -> FROM sakila.film_actor
    -> GROUP BY actor_id
    -> ORDER BY cnt DESC
    -> LIMIT 10;
+----------+-----+
| actor_id | cnt |
+----------+-----+
|      107 |  42 |
|      102 |  41 |
|      198 |  40 |
|      181 |  39 |
|       23 |  37 |
|       81 |  36 |
```

```
|      106 |  35 |
|       60 |  35 |
|       13 |  35 |
|      158 |  35 |
+----------+-----+
```

Now let's add the rank, which should be the same for all the actors who played in 35 movies. We use three variables to do this: one to keep track of the current rank, one to keep track of the previous actor's movie count, and one to keep track of the current actor's movie count. We change the rank when the movie count changes. Here's a first try:

```
mysql> SET @curr_cnt := 0, @prev_cnt := 0, @rank := 0;
mysql> SELECT actor_id,
    ->     @curr_cnt := COUNT(*) AS cnt,
    ->     @rank     := IF(@prev_cnt <> @curr_cnt, @rank + 1, @rank) AS rank,
    ->     @prev_cnt := @curr_cnt AS dummy
    -> FROM sakila.film_actor
    -> GROUP BY actor_id
    -> ORDER BY cnt DESC
    -> LIMIT 10;
+----------+-----+------+-------+
| actor_id | cnt | rank | dummy |
+----------+-----+------+-------+
|      107 |  42 |    0 |     0 |
|      102 |  41 |    0 |     0 |
...
```

Oops—the rank and count never got updated from zero. Why did this happen?

It's impossible to give a one-size-fits-all answer. The problem could be as simple as a misspelled variable name (in this example it's not), or something more involved. In this case, EXPLAIN shows there's a temporary table and filesort, so the variables are being evaluated at a different time from when we expected.

This is the type of inscrutable behavior you might experience with MySQL's user-defined variables. Debugging such problems can be tough, but it can really pay off. Ranking in SQL normally requires quadratic algorithms, such as counting the distinct number of actors who played in a greater number of movies. A user-defined variable solution can be a linear algorithm—quite an improvement.

An easy solution in this case is to add another level of temporary tables to the query, using a subquery in the FROM clause:

```
mysql> SET @curr_cnt := 0, @prev_cnt := 0, @rank := 0;
    -> SELECT actor_id,
    ->     @curr_cnt := cnt AS cnt,
    ->     @rank     := IF(@prev_cnt <> @curr_cnt, @rank + 1, @rank) AS rank,
    ->     @prev_cnt := @curr_cnt AS dummy
    -> FROM (
    ->     SELECT actor_id, COUNT(*) AS cnt
    ->     FROM sakila.film_actor
    ->     GROUP BY actor_id
    ->     ORDER BY cnt DESC
```

```
    ->     LIMIT 10
    -> ) as der;
+----------+-----+------+-------+
| actor_id | cnt | rank | dummy |
+----------+-----+------+-------+
|      107 |  42 |    1 |    42 |
|      102 |  41 |    2 |    41 |
|      198 |  40 |    3 |    40 |
|      181 |  39 |    4 |    39 |
|       23 |  37 |    5 |    37 |
|       81 |  36 |    6 |    36 |
|      106 |  35 |    7 |    35 |
|       60 |  35 |    7 |    35 |
|       13 |  35 |    7 |    35 |
|      158 |  35 |    7 |    35 |
+----------+-----+------+-------+
```

Avoiding retrieving the row just modified

What if you want to update a row, but then you want to retrieve some information about it without actually accessing the row again? Unfortunately, MySQL doesn't support anything like PostgreSQL's UPDATE RETURNING functionality, which would be useful for this purpose. But you can use variables instead. For example, one of our customers wanted a more efficient way to update a row's timestamp to the current time, and then find out what that time was. The code looked like the following:

```
UPDATE t1 SET lastUpdated = NOW() WHERE id = 1;
SELECT lastUpdated FROM t1 WHERE id = 1;
```

We rewrote those queries to use a variable instead, as follows:

```
UPDATE t1 SET lastUpdated = NOW() WHERE id = 1 AND @now := NOW();
SELECT @now;
```

There are still two queries and two network round-trips, but the second query doesn't access any tables, so it's faster. (Your mileage may vary. This might not be worthwhile for you, but it was for this customer.)

Counting UPDATEs and INSERTs

What if you're using INSERT ON DUPLICATE KEY UPDATE and you want to know how many rows were inserted without conflicting with existing rows, versus the rows that caused a conflict and updated a row? Kristian Köhntopp posted a solution to this problem on his blog.[19] The essence of the technique follows:

```
INSERT INTO t1(c1, c2) VALUES(4, 4), (2, 1), (3, 1)
ON DUPLICATE KEY UPDATE
    c1 = VALUES(c1) + ( 0 * ( @x := @x +1 ) );
```

---

19. See *http://mysqldump.azundris.com/archives/86-Down-the-dirty-road.html*.

The query increments the @x variable when there is a conflict that causes the UPDATE portion of the query to execute. It hides the variable's value inside an expression that is multiplied by zero, so the variable doesn't affect the ultimate value assigned to the column. The MySQL client protocol returns the total rows affected, so there is no need to count that with a user variable.

Making evaluation order deterministic

Most problems with user variables come from assigning to them and reading them at different stages in the query. For example, it doesn't work predictably to assign them in the SELECT statement and read from them in the WHERE clause. The following query might look like it will just return one row, but it doesn't:

```
mysql> SET @rownum := 0;
mysql> SELECT actor_id, @rownum := @rownum + 1 AS cnt
    -> FROM sakila.actor
    -> WHERE @rownum <= 1;
+----------+------+
| actor_id | cnt  |
+----------+------+
|        1 |    1 |
|        2 |    2 |
+----------+------+
```

This happens because the WHERE and SELECT are different stages in the query execution process. This is even more obvious when you add another stage to execution with an ORDER BY:

```
mysql> SET @rownum := 0;
mysql> SELECT actor_id, @rownum := @rownum + 1 AS cnt
    -> FROM sakila.actor
    -> WHERE @rownum <= 1
    -> ORDER BY first_name;
```

This query returns every row in the table, because the ORDER BY added a filesort and the WHERE is evaluated before the filesort. The solution to this problem is to assign and read in the *same* stage of query execution:

```
mysql> SET @rownum := 0;
mysql> SELECT actor_id, @rownum AS rownum
    -> FROM sakila.actor
    -> WHERE (@rownum := @rownum + 1) <= 1;
+----------+--------+
| actor_id | rownum |
+----------+--------+
|        1 | 1      |
+----------+--------+
```

Pop quiz: what will happen if you add the ORDER BY back to this query? Try it and see. If you didn't get the results you expected, why not? What about the following query, where the ORDER BY changes the variable's value and the WHERE clause evaluates it?

```
mysql> SET @rownum := 0;
mysql> SELECT actor_id, first_name, @rownum AS rownum
    -> FROM sakila.actor
    -> WHERE @rownum <= 1
    -> ORDER BY first_name, LEAST(0, @rownum := @rownum + 1);
```

The answer to most unexpected user-defined variable behavior can be found by running EXPLAIN and looking for "Using where," "Using temporary," or "Using filesort" in the Extra column.

The last example introduced another useful hack: we placed the assignment in the LEAST() function, so its value is effectively masked and won't skew the results of the ORDER BY (as we've written it, the LEAST() function will always return 0). This trick is very helpful when you want to do variable assignments solely for their side effects: it lets you hide the return value and avoid extra columns, such as the dummy column we showed in a previous example. The GREATEST(), LENGTH(), ISNULL(), NULLIF(), IF(), and COALESCE() functions are also useful for this purpose, alone and in combination, because they have special behaviors. For instance, COALESCE() stops evaluating its arguments as soon as one has a defined value.

Writing a lazy UNION

Suppose you want to write a UNION query that executes the first branch of the UNION and, if it finds any rows, skips the second branch. You might do this when you're looking for a row in a table that has "hot" rows that are accessed frequently, and another table with identical rows that happen to be accessed less often. (Partitioning hot and cold data can be a helpful way to increase cache efficiency.)

Here's a query that will look for a user in two places—the main user table, and a table of users who haven't visited in a long time and so have been archived for efficiency:[20]

```
SELECT id FROM users WHERE id = 123
UNION ALL
SELECT id FROM users_archived WHERE id = 123;
```

That query works, but it'll look for the row in the users_archived table even if it is found in the users table. We can prevent that with a lazy UNION, which lazily accesses the second table only if there are no results in the first one. We'll assign to a user variable called @found when a row is found. To make that happen, we need to place the assignment in the column list, so we'll use the GREATEST function as a container for the assignment so we don't get an extra column in the results. To make it easier to see which table the results came from, we'll add a column containing the table name. Finally, we need to reset the user variable to NULL at the end of the query, so it has no side effects and can be executed repeatedly. Here's the query:

20. Baron thinks that some social networks archive his data between his very infrequent visits. When he logs in, his account doesn't seem to exist; but then he gets an email a few minutes later welcoming him back, and *voilà*, his account has been recovered. This is a smart optimization for antisocial users, which we'll discuss further in Chapter 11.

```
SELECT GREATEST(@found := -1, id) AS id, 'users' AS which_tbl
FROM users WHERE id = 1
UNION ALL
  SELECT id, 'users_archived'
  FROM users_archived WHERE id = 1 AND @found IS NULL
UNION ALL
  SELECT 1, 'reset' FROM DUAL WHERE ( @found := NULL ) IS NOT NULL;
```

Other uses for variables

You can put variable assignments in all types of statements, not just SELECT statements. In fact, this is one of the best uses for user-defined variables. For example, you can rewrite expensive queries, such as rank calculations with subqueries, as cheap once-through UPDATE statements.

It can be a little tricky to get the desired behavior, though. Sometimes the optimizer decides to consider the variables as compile-time constants and refuses to perform assignments. Placing the assignments inside a function like LEAST() will usually help. Another tip is to check whether your variable has a defined value before executing the containing statement. Sometimes you want it to, but other times you don't.

With a little experimentation, you can do all sorts of interesting things with user-defined variables. Here are some ideas:

- Calculate running totals and averages
- Emulate FIRST() and LAST() functions for grouped queries
- Do math on extremely large numbers
- Reduce an entire table to a single MD5 hash value
- "Unwrap" a sampled value that wraps around to zero when it increases beyond a certain boundary
- Emulate read/write cursors
- Put variables in SHOW statements by embedding them into the WHERE clause

---

The C. J. Date Dilemma

C. J. Date advocates a database design approach that treats SQL databases as closely as possible to relational databases. It is enlightening to know how SQL deviates from the relational model, and frankly MySQL goes farther afield than some database management systems. However, you won't get good performance from MySQL if you try to force it to behave like a relational database with some of the techniques Mr. Date advocates in his books, such as deeply nested subqueries. It's unfortunate, but MySQL's limitations prevent a more formal approach from working well. We recommend reading his book *SQL and Relational Theory: How to Write Accurate SQL Code (http://shop.oreilly.com/product/0636920022879.do)* (O'Reilly). It'll change the way you think about SQL.

Case Studies

Sometimes it's not about query optimization, schema optimization, index optimization, or application design optimization—it's about all of these practices put together. The case studies in this section illustrate how to approach some design challenges that frequently cause problems for users. You might also be interested in Bill Karwin's book *SQL Antipatterns* (Pragmatic Bookshelf). It has recipes for solving particular problems with SQL that often trap the unwary programmer into a poor solution.

Building a Queue Table in MySQL

Building a queue in MySQL is tricky, and most designs we've seen don't work well when the system experiences high traffic and lots of concurrency. The typical pattern is to have a table that contains several types of rows: rows that haven't been processed, rows in process, and finished rows. One or more worker processes look for unprocessed rows, update them to "claim" them, and then perform the work and update them to mark them as finished. Common examples include emails that are ready to send, orders to process, comments to moderate, and so on.

There are two broad reasons why this doesn't work well. First, the table tends to grow very large, and searching for the unprocessed rows becomes slow when the table is large and the indexes are many levels deep. You can solve this by splitting the queue into two tables and moving the completed rows to the archive or history table, which helps keep the queue table small.

The second reason is that the process of finding work to do is usually implemented with polling and locking. Polling creates load on the server, and locking creates contention and serialization between worker processes. We'll see later, in Chapter 11, why that limits scalability.

Polling might actually be okay, but if it's not, you can use notifications to tell workers that there's work to do. One technique is to use the SLEEP() function with a very long timeout and an indicative comment, such as the following:

```
SELECT /* waiting on unsent_emails */ SLEEP(10000);
```

This will cause the thread to block until one of two things happens: it times out after 10,000 seconds, or another thread issues KILL QUERY and terminates it. So, after inserting a batch of queries into the table, you can look at SHOW PROCESSLIST, find threads that are running queries with the magical comment, and kill the queries. You can also implement a form of notification with the GET_LOCK() and RELEASE_LOCK() functions, or you can do it outside of the database, with a messaging service.

The final problem is how workers should claim rows so that they don't get processed multiple times. We often see this implemented with SELECT FOR UPDATE. This is usually a huge scalability bottleneck and causes a lot of pileups as transactions block on each other and wait.

In general, it's a good idea to avoid SELECT FOR UPDATE. And not just for a queue table—it's a good idea to avoid it for any purpose. There is almost always a better way to achieve your desired purpose. In the case of a queue, you can use a simple UPDATE to claim rows, and then check whether you claimed anything. Here's how. Let's start with the schema:

```
CREATE TABLE unsent_emails (
   id INT NOT NULL PRIMARY KEY AUTO_INCREMENT,
   -- columns for the message, from, to, subject, etc.
   status ENUM('unsent', 'claimed', 'sent'),
   owner  INT UNSIGNED NOT NULL DEFAULT 0,
   ts     TIMESTAMP,
   KEY    (owner, status, ts)
);
```

The owner column is used to store the connection ID of the worker process that owns the row. This is the same value returned by the CONNECTION_ID() function in MySQL. If it's 0, then the row is unclaimed.

We frequently see a technique like the following to claim 10 rows:

```
BEGIN;
SELECT id FROM unsent_emails
   WHERE owner = 0 AND status = 'unsent'
   LIMIT 10 FOR UPDATE;
-- result: 123, 456, 789
UPDATE unsent_emails
   SET status = 'claimed', owner = CONNECTION_ID()
   WHERE id IN(123, 456, 789);
COMMIT;
```

That will use the first two columns of the index, so in theory it looks rather efficient. The problem is that between the two queries, the application has some "think time," and that causes the locks on the rows to block other clients who are running the same queries. All of the queries will use the same index, so they'll begin scanning right at the front of the index and will probably block instantly.

It's much more efficient to perform the queries as follows:

```
SET AUTOCOMMIT = 1;
COMMIT;
UPDATE unsent_emails
   SET status = 'claimed', owner = CONNECTION_ID()
   WHERE owner = 0 AND status = 'unsent'
   LIMIT 10;
SET AUTOCOMMIT = 0;
SELECT id FROM unsent_emails
   WHERE owner = CONNECTION_ID() AND status = 'claimed';
-- result: 123, 456, 789
```

You don't even have to run the SELECT query to check for rows that you claimed. The client protocol will tell you how many rows were updated, so you know whether there were unsent rows to claim.

Most uses of SELECT FOR UPDATE can be rewritten to use a similar technique.

The final task is to clean up rows that were claimed but never processed because the worker quit for some reason, but that's easy. You can just run an UPDATE to reset them periodically. Execute SHOW PROCESSLIST, gather a list of all the thread IDs that are currently connected to the server, and use that in the WHERE clause to avoid stealing a row that's actually being processed. Assuming the list of thread IDs is (10, 20, 30), here's a sample query that "times out" and reclaims rows after 10 minutes:

```
UPDATE unsent_emails
    SET owner = 0, status = 'unsent'
    WHERE owner NOT IN(0, 10, 20, 30) AND status = 'claimed'
    AND ts < CURRENT_TIMESTAMP - INTERVAL 10 MINUTE;
```

By the way, notice how the index is carefully designed for the queries we're running. This is an example of the interplay between this chapter and the previous one. The query we just showed will be able to use the full width of the index, because the range condition is placed on the last column in the index. The index will also be useful for the other queries; this avoids the need for another redundant index for the two columns used by the other queries.

We've illustrated a few fundamentals in this case study:

- Stop doing things, or do them less often. Don't use polling unless you have to, because it adds load and unproductive busywork.

- Do things more quickly. Use an UPDATE instead of a SELECT FOR UPDATE followed by an UPDATE, because the faster the transaction commits, the shorter the lock duration is, and the less contention and serialization there are. Also, keep the unprocessed data separate from the processed rows, because smaller is faster.

- The overall moral of this example is that some queries can't be optimized; they must be replaced with a different query or a different strategy altogether. SELECT FOR UPDATE queries usually fall into that category.

Sometimes, the best solution is to move the queue outside of the database server entirely. Redis is good at queue operations, and occasionally you can use *memcached* for this purpose, too. Alternatively, you might evaluate the Q4M storage engine for MySQL, although we have no experience using it in production environments so we can't provide any guidance here. RabbitMQ and Gearman[21] can be very helpful for some purposes, too.

Computing the Distance Between Points

Geospatial computations crop up now and again in our work. People don't tend to use MySQL for heavy spatial computation—PostgreSQL is usually a much better choice

---

21. See *http://www.rabbitmq.com* and *http://gearman.org*.

for that—but we still see a few recurrent patterns. One is the ubiquitous query to find things within a radius of a point.

The typical use is something like finding apartments for rent within a radius of the center of a zip code, filtering "matches" on a dating site, and so on. Suppose you have the following table:

```
CREATE TABLE locations (
   id   INT NOT NULL PRIMARY KEY AUTO_INCREMENT,
   name VARCHAR(30),
   lat  FLOAT NOT NULL,
   lon  FLOAT NOT NULL
);
INSERT INTO locations(name, lat, lon)
   VALUES('Charlottesville, Virginia', 38.03, -78.48),
         ('Chicago, Illinois',        41.85, -87.65),
         ('Washington, DC',           38.89, -77.04);
```

The latitude and longitude are in degrees, and the queries usually use the great-circle (Haversine) formula to find the distance along the surface of the Earth, assuming that it is a sphere. The formula to find the distance between point A and point B, with coordinates *latA* and *lonA*, *latB*, and *lonB* in radians, can be expressed as follows:

```
ACOS(
   COS(latA) * COS(latB) * COS(lonA - lonB)
      + SIN(latA) * SIN(latB)
)
```

The result is in radians, so to find the distance in miles or kilometers, it needs to be multiplied by the Earth's radius, which is about 3,959 miles or 6,371 kilometers. Suppose we want to find all points within 100 miles of Charlottesville, where Baron lives. We need to convert the latitudes and longitudes to radians to plug them into the formula:

```
SELECT * FROM locations WHERE 3979 * ACOS(
   COS(RADIANS(lat)) * COS(RADIANS(38.03)) * COS(RADIANS(lon) - RADIANS(-78.48))
      + SIN(RADIANS(lat)) * SIN(RADIANS(38.03))
) <= 100;
+----+---------------------------+-------+--------+
| id | name                      | lat   | lon    |
+----+---------------------------+-------+--------+
|  1 | Charlottesville, Virginia | 38.03 | -78.48 |
|  3 | Washington, DC            | 38.89 | -77.04 |
+----+---------------------------+-------+--------+
```

This type of query not only can't use an index, but will also burn a ton of CPU cycles and load the server very heavily. We've seen it many times. What can we do about it?

There are several aspects of this design that can be optimized. The first is to decide whether the precision is really necessary. There's a lot of inherent imprecision:

- Locations might be within 100 miles "as the crow flies" across the surface of the Earth, but that's really not closely related to their practical distance. No matter where they are, it's pretty certain you can't get there in an absolutely straight line, and there are often a lot of obstacles in the way, such as large rivers that require long detours to cross a bridge. Distance is therefore a poor proxy for how close something actually is.

• If we've looked up someone's location from his zip code or city, we're measuring from the center of an area to the center of another area, which also adds wiggle room. Baron lives in Charlottesville, but not exactly at its center, and he's probably not interested in traveling precisely to the center of Washington.

Maybe you really do need the precision, but for most applications, it's just overkill. It's analogous to significant digits: you can't have more precision in your result than you have in the measurements. (Or, put another way, "garbage in, garbage out.")

If you don't need a lot of precision, it might be okay to pretend that the earth is flat instead of curved! This transforms the trigonometry into a much simpler computation with the Pythagorean theorem, which just uses a few sums, products, and a square root to determine whether points are within a circle on a plane.[22]

But wait, why stop there? Do we even need a circle? Why not just use a square instead? The corners of a square that's 200 miles on a side are only 141 miles from the center, which is not so far outside the desired radius of 100 miles. Let's update our query to look for a square that's 0.0253 radians (100 miles) from the center to the edges:

```
SELECT * FROM locations
WHERE lat BETWEEN  38.03 - DEGREES(0.0253) AND  38.03 + DEGREES(0.0253)
  AND lon BETWEEN -78.48 - DEGREES(0.0253) AND -78.48 + DEGREES(0.0253);
```

Now the question is how to optimize this expression with indexes. We could certainly index (lat, lon) or (lon, lat). But that won't really help the query very much. As you know, MySQL 5.5 and older versions can't take advantage of any column past the first one that is accessed with a range condition. Only one of the columns would be used effectively, because our query has two range conditions (BETWEEN is equivalent to a greater-than and a less-than-or-equal-to).

Our trusty IN() workaround comes to the rescue again. We can add two columns to store the FLOOR() of each coordinate, and then the query can use two IN() lists of integers to capture all points that fall within the desired square. Here's how to add the new columns, and an index whose purpose you'll see shortly:

```
mysql> ALTER TABLE locations
    ->     ADD lat_floor INT NOT NULL DEFAULT 0,
    ->     ADD lon_floor INT NOT NULL DEFAULT 0,
    ->     ADD KEY(lat_floor, lon_floor);
```

---

22. To help out even more, you can do the trigonometry in the application, instead of making the database server do it. Trig functions are pretty CPU-hungry. Storing radians in the table and transforming everything into radians in the application can help a lot, for example. We're trying to keep our example simple and free of magic numbers whose origin is unclear, so we don't show this additional optimization.

```
mysql> UPDATE locations
    -> SET lat_floor = FLOOR(lat), lon_floor = FLOOR(lon);
```

Now we need to search for a range of coordinates from floor to ceiling, both north and south. Here is a query that shows the range of degrees we're looking for we're using the query only for demonstration purposes; you should perform this math in the application code, not in MySQL:

```
mysql> SELECT FLOOR( 38.03 - DEGREES(0.0253)) AS lat_lb,
    ->        CEILING( 38.03 + DEGREES(0.0253)) AS lat_ub,
    ->         FLOOR(-78.48 - DEGREES(0.0253)) AS lon_lb,
    ->        CEILING(-78.48 + DEGREES(0.0253)) AS lon_ub;
+--------+--------+--------+--------+
| lat_lb | lat_ub | lon_lb | lon_ub |
+--------+--------+--------+--------+
|     36 |     40 |    -80 |    -77 |
+--------+--------+--------+--------+
```

Now we generate IN() lists with all integers between the floor and ceiling of each range. Here's the query with the extra WHERE conditions added:

```
SELECT * FROM locations
WHERE lat BETWEEN  38.03 - DEGREES(0.0253) AND  38.03 + DEGREES(0.0253)
  AND lon BETWEEN -78.48 - DEGREES(0.0253) AND -78.48 + DEGREES(0.0253)
  AND lat_floor IN(36,37,38,39,40) AND lon_floor IN(-80,-79,-78,-77);
```

Using a floor and ceiling introduces some extra slack into the computation, so the query can actually find points that lie outside the square. That's why we still need the filters on lat and lon, to discard the results that shouldn't be included. This is similar to the technique we showed in the previous chapter for simulating a hash index with a CRC32 column: create an index on a value that isn't the whole truth but nevertheless gets us close to the truth cheaply, and then post-filter to remove the few imposters.

In fact, at this point it makes sense to mention that instead of searching for a crude square and then trimming the results to fit a precise square, we could search for a square and then filter the results down with the great circle formula or the Pythagorean theorem:

```
SELECT * FROM locations
WHERE lat_floor IN(36,37,38,39,40) AND lon_floor IN(-80,-79,-78,-77)
  AND 3979 * ACOS(
    COS(RADIANS(lat)) * COS(RADIANS(38.03)) * COS(RADIANS(lon) - RADIANS(-78.48))
      + SIN(RADIANS(lat)) * SIN(RADIANS(38.03))
  ) <= 100;
```

So we're back to the beginning—a precise circle—but we're doing it better now.[23] As long as you pre-filter the result set with efficient techniques such as the auxiliary integer columns and indexes, it's usually not bad at all to post-filter with the more costly math. Just don't make the great-circle formula the first hoop the query has to jump through, or everything will be slow!

---

23. Again, though, you should use application code to compute expressions such as COS(RADIANS(38.03)).

Sphinx has some good geospatial search functions built in, which can be a lot better than using MySQL. And in case you're thinking of using MyISAM's GIS functions for the techniques shown in this section, take our word for it: they don't work much better, and MyISAM itself just doesn't work well for large, high-traffic applications, for all the usual reasons: data corruption, table-level locking, and so on.

To recap this case study, we covered the usual optimization strategies:

- Stop doing things, or do them less often. Don't run your entire dataset through the great-circle formula; trim it down first with a cheaper technique, and then run the expensive formula on a smaller set of rows.

- Do things more quickly. Make sure you design the system to be able to use indexes effectively, as discussed in the previous chapter, and use approximations (the earth is flat, and a square is an approximation of a circle) sensibly to avoid needless precision.

- Pull the work out into the application as much as you can. Get those expensive trigonometry functions out of SQL and into the application code!

Using User-Defined Functions

Our last advanced query optimization illustrates when SQL just isn't the right tool for the job. When you need raw speed, nothing beats C or C++ code. Of course, you have to be able to program in C or C++ well enough not to destroy your server. With great power comes great responsibility.

We'll show you how to write your own user-defined functions (UDFs) in the next chapter, but we thought it would be a good idea to mention a real use case for a UDF in this chapter. The project requirement from the customer was as follows: "We need to run a matching query, which is basically an XOR operation between two random 64-byte long data strings, against 35 million records in less than few seconds." A little calculation showed that this just can't be done inside MySQL with currently available hardware. How to solve this problem?

The answer was a program that Yves Trudeau wrote, which takes advantage of the SSE4.2 instruction set. It runs as a daemon on many commodity servers, and the MySQL server communicates with it over a simple network protocol via a UDF written in C. Yves benchmarked the distributed program running matches against 4 million strings in 130 milliseconds. By taking the problem out of MySQL and making MySQL talk to the distributed daemon, the customer was able to keep things simple for the application, so that it can continue acting as if MySQL is doing all the work. As they say on Twitter, #winning! This is an example of optimizing for the business, not just for the technical aspects of the problem.

Summary

Query optimization is the final piece in the interlocking puzzle of schema, index, and query design to create high-performance applications. To write good queries, you need to understand schemas and indexing, and vice versa.

Ultimately, it is still about response time, and understanding how queries execute so that you can reason about where the time is consumed. With the addition of a few things such as the parsing and optimization process, this is just the next step in understanding how MySQL accesses tables and indexes, which we discussed in the previous chapter. The extra dimension that emerges when you start studying the interplay between queries and indexes is how MySQL accesses one table or index based on the data that it finds in another one.

Optimization always requires a three-pronged approach: stop doing things, do them fewer times, and do them more quickly. We hope that the case studies we presented help to tie it all together and illustrate this approach in action.

Beyond the fundamental building blocks of queries, tables, and indexes are more advanced features in MySQL, such as partitioning, which has a similar goal to indexes but works differently. MySQL also supports features such as a query cache, which avoids the need to even execute queries (remember, "stop doing things"). We'll explore some of these features in the next chapter.

Advanced MySQL Features

MySQL 5.0 and 5.1 introduced many features, such as partitioning and triggers, which are familiar to users with a background in other database servers. The addition of these features attracted many new users to MySQL. However, their performance implications did not really become clear until people began to use them widely. In this chapter we explain what we've learned from seeing these features in the real world, beyond what the manuals and reference material have taught us.

Partitioned Tables

A partitioned table is a single logical table that's composed of multiple physical sub-tables. The partitioning code is really just a wrapper around a set of Handler objects that represent the underlying partitions, and it forwards requests to the storage engine through the Handler objects. Partitioning is a kind of black box that hides the under-lying partitions from you at the SQL layer, although you can see them quite easily by looking at the filesystem, where you'll see the component tables with a hash-delimited naming convention.

The way MySQL implements partitioning—as a wrapper over hidden tables—means that indexes are defined per-partition, rather than being created over the entire table. This is different from Oracle, for example, where indexes and tables can be partitioned in more flexible and complex ways.

MySQL decides which partition holds each row of data based on the PARTITION BY clause that you define for the table. The query optimizer can prune partitions when you execute queries, so the queries don't examine all partitions—just the ones that hold the data you are looking for.

The primary purpose of partitioning is to act as a coarse form of indexing and data clustering over the table. This can help to eliminate large parts of the table from being accessed, and to store related rows close together.

Partitioning can be very beneficial, especially in specific scenarios:

- When the table is much too big to fit in memory, or when you have "hot" rows at the end of a table that has lots of historical data.

- Partitioned data is easier to maintain than nonpartitioned data. For example, it's easier to discard old data by dropping an entire partition, which you can do quickly. You can also optimize, check, and repair individual partitions.

- Partitioned data can be distributed physically, enabling the server to use multiple hard drives more efficiently.

- You can use partitioning to avoid some bottlenecks in specific workloads, such as per-index mutexes with InnoDB or per-inode locking with the ext3 filesystem.

- If you really need to, you can back up and restore individual partitions, which is very helpful with extremely large datasets.

MySQL's implementation of partitioning is too complicated to explore in full detail here. We want to concentrate on its performance implications, so we recommend that for the basics you turn to the MySQL manual, which has a lot of material on partitioning. You should read the entire partitioning chapter, and look at the sections on `CREATE TABLE`, `SHOW CREATE TABLE`, `ALTER TABLE`, the `INFORMATION_SCHEMA.PARTITIONS` table, and `EXPLAIN`. Partitioning has made the `CREATE TABLE` and `ALTER TABLE` commands much more complex.

A few limitations apply to partitioned tables. Here are the most important ones:

- There's a limit of 1,024 partitions per table.

- In MySQL 5.1, the partitioning expression must be an integer or an expression that returns an integer. In MySQL 5.5, you can partition by columns in certain cases.

- Any primary key or unique index must include all columns in the partitioning expression.

- You can't use foreign key constraints.

How Partitioning Works

As we've mentioned, partitioned tables have multiple underlying tables, which are represented by Handler objects. You can't access the partitions directly. Each partition is managed by the storage engine in the normal fashion (all partitions must use the same storage engine), and any indexes defined over the table are actually implemented as identical indexes over each underlying partition. From the storage engine's point of view, the partitions are just tables; the storage engine doesn't really know whether a specific table it's managing is a standalone table or just part of a bigger partitioned table.

Operations on a partitioned table are implemented with the following logical operations:

SELECT *queries*

> When you query a partitioned table, the partitioning layer opens and locks all of the underlying partitions, the query optimizer determines whether any of the partitions can be ignored (pruned), and then the partitioning layer forwards the handler API calls to the storage engine that manages the partitions.

INSERT *queries*

> When you insert a row, the partitioning layer opens and locks all partitions, determines which partition should receive the row, and forwards the row to that partition.

DELETE *queries*

> When you delete a row, the partitioning layer opens and locks all partitions, determines which partition contains the row, and forwards the deletion request to that partition.

UPDATE *queries*

> When you modify a row, the partitioning layer (you guessed it) opens and locks all partitions, determines which partition contains the row, fetches the row, modifies the row and determines which partition should contain the new row, forwards the row with an insertion request to the destination partition, and forwards the deletion request to the source partition.

Some of these operations support pruning. For example, when you delete a row, the server first has to locate it. The server can prune partitions that can't contain the row if you specify a WHERE clause that matches the partitioning expression. The same applies to UPDATE queries. INSERT queries are naturally self-pruned; the server looks at the values to be inserted and finds one and only one destination partition.

Although the partitioning layer opens and locks all partitions, this doesn't mean that the partitions remain locked. A storage engine such as InnoDB, which handles its own locking at the row level, will instruct the partitioning layer to unlock the partitions. This lock-and-unlock cycle is similar to how queries against ordinary InnoDB tables are executed.

We'll show some examples a bit later that illustrate the cost and consequences of opening and locking every partition when there's any access to the table.

Types of Partitioning

MySQL supports several types of partitioning. The most common type we've seen used is range partitioning, in which each partition is defined to accept a specific range of values for some column or columns, or a function over those columns. For example, here's a simple way to place each year's worth of sales into a separate partition:

```
CREATE TABLE sales (
    order_date DATETIME NOT NULL,
    -- Other columns omitted
) ENGINE=InnoDB PARTITION BY RANGE(YEAR(order_date)) (
```

```
PARTITION p_2010 VALUES LESS THAN (2010),
PARTITION p_2011 VALUES LESS THAN (2011),
PARTITION p_2012 VALUES LESS THAN (2012),
PARTITION p_catchall VALUES LESS THAN MAXVALUE );
```

You can use many functions in the partitioning clause. The main requirement is that it must return a nonconstant, deterministic integer. We're using YEAR() here, but you can also use other functions, such as TO_DAYS(). Partitioning by intervals of time is a common way to work with date-based data, so we'll return to this example later and see how to optimize it to avoid some of the problems it can cause.

MySQL also supports key, hash, and list partitioning methods, some of which support subpartitions, which we've rarely seen used in production. In MySQL 5.5 you can use the RANGE COLUMNS partitioning type, so you can partition by date-based columns directly, without using a function to convert them to an integer. More on that later.

One use of subpartitions we've seen was to work around a per-index mutex inside InnoDB on a table designed similarly to our previous example. The partition for the most recent year was modified heavily, which caused a lot of contention on that mutex. Subpartitioning by hash helped chop the data into smaller pieces and alleviated the problem.

Other partitioning techniques we've seen include:

- You can partition by key to help reduce contention on InnoDB mutexes.
- You can partition by range using a modulo function to create a round-robin table that retains only a desired amount of data. For example, you can partition date-based data by day modulo 7, or simply by day of week, if you want to retain only the most recent days of data.
- Suppose you have a table with an autoincrementing id primary key, but you want to partition the data temporally so the "hot" recent data is clustered together. You can't partition by a timestamp column unless you include it in the primary key, but that defeats the purpose of a primary key. You can partition by an expression such as HASH(id DIV 1000000), which creates a new partition for each million rows inserted. This achieves the goal without requiring you to change the primary key. It has the added benefit that you don't need to constantly create partitions to hold new ranges of dates, as you'd need to do with range-based partitioning.

How to Use Partitioning

Imagine that you want to run queries over ranges of data from a really huge table that contains many years' worth of historical metrics in time-series order. You want to run reports on the most recent month, which is about 100 million rows. In a few years this book will be out of date, but let's pretend that you have hardware from 2012 and your table is 10 terabytes, so it's much bigger than memory, and you have traditional hard drives, not flash (most SSDs aren't big enough for this table yet). How can you query this table at all, let alone efficiently?

One thing is sure: you can't scan the whole table every time you want to query it, because it's too big. And you don't want to use an index because of the maintenance cost and space consumption. Depending on the index, you could get a lot of fragmentation and poorly clustered data, which would cause death by a thousand cuts through random I/O. You can sometimes work around this for one or two indexes, but rarely for more. Only two workable options remain: your query must be a sequential scan over a portion of the table, or the desired portion of the table and index must fit entirely in memory.

It's worth restating this: at very large sizes, B-Tree indexes don't work. Unless the index covers the query completely, the server needs to look up the full rows in the table, and that causes random I/O a row at a time over a very large space, which will just kill query response times. The cost of maintaining the index (disk space, I/O operations) is also very high. Systems such as Infobright acknowledge this and throw B-Tree indexes out entirely, opting for something coarser-grained but less costly at scale, such as per-block metadata over large blocks of data.

This is what partitioning can accomplish, too. The key is to think about partitioning as a crude form of indexing that has very low overhead and gets you in the neighborhood of the data you want. From there, you can either scan the neighborhood sequentially, or fit the neighborhood in memory and index it. Partitioning has low overhead because there is no data structure that points to rows and must be updated—partitioning doesn't identify data at the precision of rows, and has no data structure to speak of. Instead, it has an equation that says which partitions can contain which categories of rows.

Let's look at the two strategies that work at large scale:

Scan the data, don't index it
> You can create tables without indexes and use partitioning as the only mechanism to navigate to the desired kind of rows. As long as you always use a WHERE clause that prunes the query to a small number of partitions, this can be good enough. You'll need to do the math and decide whether your query response times will be acceptable, of course. The assumption here is that you're not even trying to fit the data in memory; you assume that anything you query has to be read from disk, and that that data will be replaced soon by some other query, so caching is futile. This strategy is for when you have to access a lot of the table on a regular basis. A caveat: for reasons we'll explain a bit later, you usually need to limit yourself to a couple of hundred partitions at most.

Index the data, and segregate hot data
> If your data is mostly unused except for a "hot" portion, and you can partition so that the hot data is stored in a single partition that is small enough to fit in memory along with its indexes, you can add indexes and write queries to take advantage of them, just as you would with smaller tables.

This isn't quite all you need to know, because MySQL's implementation of partitioning has a few pitfalls that can bite. Let's see what those are and how to avoid them.

What Can Go Wrong

The two partitioning strategies we just suggested are based on two key assumptions: that you can narrow the search by pruning partitions when you query, and that partitioning itself is not very costly. As it turns out, those assumptions are not always valid. Here are a few problems you might encounter:

NULLs *can defeat pruning*

Partitioning works in a funny way when the result of the partitioning function can be NULL: it treats the first partition as special. Suppose that you PARTITION BY RANGE YEAR(order_date), as in the example we gave earlier. Any row whose order_date is either NULL or not a valid date will be stored in the first partition you define.[1] Now suppose you write a query that ends as follows: WHERE order_date BETWEEN '2012-01-01' AND '2012-01-31'. MySQL will actually check two partitions, not one: it will look at the partition that stores orders from 2012, as well as the first partition in the table. It looks at the first partition because the YEAR() function can return NULL if it receives invalid input, and values that might match the range would be stored as NULL in the first partition. This affects other functions, such as TO_DAYS(), too.[2]

This can be expensive if your first partition is large, especially if you're using the "scan, don't index" strategy. Checking two partitions instead of one to find the rows is definitely undesirable. To avoid this, you can define a dummy first partition. That is, we could fix our earlier example by creating a partition such as PARTITION p_nulls VALUES LESS THAN (0). If you don't put invalid data into your table, that partition will be empty, and although it'll be checked, it'll be fast because it's empty.

This workaround is not necessary in MySQL 5.5, where you can partition by the column itself, instead of a function over the column: PARTITION BY RANGE COLUMNS(order_date). Our earlier example should use that syntax in MySQL 5.5.

Mismatched PARTITION BY *and index*

If you define an index that doesn't match the partitioning clause, queries might not be prunable. Suppose you define an index on a and partition by b. Each partition will have its own index, and a lookup on this index will open and check each index tree in *every* partition. This could be quick if the non-leaf nodes of each index are resident in memory, but it is nevertheless more costly than skipping the index lookups completely. To avoid this problem, you should try to avoid indexing on

---

1. This happens even if order_date is not nullable, because you can store a value that's not a valid date.

2. This is a bug from the user's point of view, but a feature from the server developer's point of view.

nonpartitioned columns unless your queries will also include an expression that can help prune out partitions.

This sounds simple enough to avoid, but it can catch you by surprise. For example, suppose a partitioned table ends up being the second table in a join, and the index that's used for the join isn't part of the partition clause. Each row in the join will access and search every partition in the second table.

Selecting partitions can be costly

The various types of partitioning are implemented in different ways, so of course their performance is not uniform all the time. In particular, questions such as "Where does this row belong?" or "Where can I find rows matching this query?" can be costly to answer with range partitioning, because the server scans the list of partition definitions to find the right one. This linear search isn't all that efficient, as it turns out, so the cost grows as the number of partitions grows.

The queries we've observed to suffer the worst from this type of overhead are row-by-row inserts. For every row you insert into a table that's partitioned by range, the server has to scan the list of partitions to select the destination. You can alleviate this problem by limiting how many partitions you define. In practice, a hundred or so works okay for most systems we've seen.

Other partition types, such as key and hash partitions, don't have the same limitation.

Opening and locking partitions can be costly

Opening and locking partitions when a query accesses a partitioned table is another type of per-partition overhead. Opening and locking occur before pruning, so this isn't a prunable overhead. This type of overhead is independent of the partitioning type and affects all types of statements. It adds an especially noticeable amount of overhead to short operations, such as single-row lookups by primary key. You can avoid high per-statement costs by performing operations in bulk, such as using multirow inserts or `LOAD DATA INFILE`, deleting ranges of rows instead of one at a time, and so on. And, of course, limit the number of partitions you define.

Maintenance operations can be costly

Some partition maintenance operations are very quick, such as creating or dropping partitions. (Dropping the underlying table might be slow, but that's another matter.) Other operations, such as `REORGANIZE PARTITION`, operate similarly to the way `ALTER` works: by copying rows around. For example, `REORGANIZE PARTITION` works by creating a new temporary partition, moving rows into it, and deleting the old partition when it's done.

As you can see, partitioned tables are not a "silver bullet" solution. Here is a sample of some other limitations in the current implementation:

- All partitions have to use the same storage engine.
- There are some restrictions on the functions and expressions you can use in a partitioning function.

- Some storage engines don't work with partitioning.
- For MyISAM tables, you can't use `LOAD INDEX INTO CACHE`.
- For MyISAM tables, a partitioned table requires more open file descriptors than a normal table containing the same data. Even though it looks like a single table, as you know, it's really many tables. As a result, a single table cache entry can create many file descriptors. Therefore, even if you have configured the table cache to protect your server against exceeding the operating system's per-process file-descriptor limits, partitioned tables can cause you to exceed that limit anyway.

Finally, it's worth pointing out that older server versions just aren't as good as newer ones. All software has bugs. Partitioning was introduced in MySQL 5.1, and many partitioning bugs were fixed as late as the 5.1.40s and 5.1.50s. MySQL 5.5 improved partitioning significantly in some common real-world cases. In the upcoming MySQL 5.6 release, there are more improvements, such as `ALTER TABLE EXCHANGE PARTITION`.

Optimizing Queries

Partitioning introduces new ways to optimize queries (and corresponding pitfalls). The biggest opportunity is that the optimizer can use the partitioning function to prune partitions. As you'd expect from a coarse-grained index, pruning lets queries access much less data than they'd otherwise need to (in the best case).

Thus, it's very important to specify the partitioned key in the `WHERE` clause, even if it's otherwise redundant, so the optimizer can prune unneeded partitions. If you don't do this, the query execution engine will have to access all partitions in the table, and this can be extremely slow on large tables.

You can use `EXPLAIN PARTITIONS` to see whether the optimizer is pruning partitions. Let's return to the sample data from before:

```
mysql> EXPLAIN PARTITIONS SELECT * FROM sales \G
*************************** 1. row ***************************
           id: 1
  select_type: SIMPLE
        table: sales_by_day
   partitions: p_2010,p_2011,p_2012
         type: ALL
possible_keys: NULL
          key: NULL
      key_len: NULL
          ref: NULL
         rows: 3
        Extra:
```

As you can see, the query will access all partitions. Look at the difference when we add a constraint to the `WHERE` clause:

```
mysql> EXPLAIN PARTITIONS SELECT * FROM sales_by_day WHERE day > '2011-01-01'\G
*************************** 1. row ***************************
           id: 1
```

```
      select_type: SIMPLE
            table: sales_by_day
       partitions: p_2011,p_2012
```

The optimizer is pretty good about pruning; for example, it can convert ranges into lists of discrete values and prune on each item in the list. However, it's not all-knowing. The following WHERE clause is theoretically prunable, but MySQL can't prune it:

```
mysql> EXPLAIN PARTITIONS SELECT * FROM sales_by_day WHERE YEAR(day) = 2010\G
*************************** 1. row ***************************
               id: 1
      select_type: SIMPLE
            table: sales_by_day
       partitions: p_2010,p_2011,p_2012
```

MySQL can prune only on comparisons to the partitioning function's columns. It cannot prune on the result of an expression, even if the expression is the same as the partitioning function. This is similar to the way that indexed columns must be isolated in the query to make the index usable (see Chapter 5). You can convert the query into an equivalent form, though:

```
mysql> EXPLAIN PARTITIONS SELECT * FROM sales_by_day
    -> WHERE day BETWEEN '2010-01-01' AND '2010-12-31'\G
*************************** 1. row ***************************
               id: 1
      select_type: SIMPLE
            table: sales_by_day
       partitions: p_2010
```

Because the WHERE clause now refers directly to the partitioning column, not to an expression, the optimizer can prune out other partitions. The rule of thumb is that even though you can partition by expressions, you must search by column.

The optimizer is smart enough to prune partitions during query processing, too. For example, if a partitioned table is the second table in a join, and the join condition is the partitioned key, MySQL will search for matching rows only in the relevant partitions. (EXPLAIN won't show the partition pruning, because it happens at runtime, not at query optimization time.)

Merge Tables

Merge tables are sort of an earlier, simpler kind of partitioning with different restrictions and fewer optimizations. Whereas partitioning enforces the abstraction rigorously, denying access to the underlying partitions and permitting you to reference only the partitioned table, merge tables let you access the underlying tables separately from the merge table. And whereas partitioning is more integrated with the query optimizer and is the way of the future, merge tables are quasi-deprecated and might even be removed someday.

Like partitioned tables, merge tables are wrappers around underlying MyISAM tables with the same structure. Although you can think of merge tables as an older, more limited version of partitioning, they actually provide some features you can't get with partitions.[3]

The merge table is really just a container that holds the real tables. You specify which tables to include with a special UNION syntax to CREATE TABLE. Here's an example that demonstrates many aspects of merge tables:

```
mysql> CREATE TABLE t1(a INT NOT NULL PRIMARY KEY)ENGINE=MyISAM;
mysql> CREATE TABLE t2(a INT NOT NULL PRIMARY KEY)ENGINE=MyISAM;
mysql> INSERT INTO t1(a) VALUES(1),(2);
mysql> INSERT INTO t2(a) VALUES(1),(2);
mysql> CREATE TABLE mrg(a INT NOT NULL PRIMARY KEY)
    -> ENGINE=MERGE UNION=(t1, t2) INSERT_METHOD=LAST;
mysql> SELECT a FROM mrg;
+------+
| a    |
+------+
|    1 |
|    1 |
|    2 |
|    2 |
+------+
```

Notice that the underlying tables have exactly the same number and types of columns, and that all indexes that exist on the merge table also exist on the underlying tables. These are requirements when creating a merge table. Notice also that there's a primary key on the sole column of each table, yet the resulting merge table has duplicate rows. This is one of the limitations of merge tables: each table inside the merge behaves normally, but the merge table doesn't enforce constraints over the entire set of tables.

The INSERT_METHOD=LAST instruction to the table tells MySQL to send all INSERT statements to the last table in the merge. Specifying FIRST or LAST is the only control you have over where rows inserted into the merge table are placed (you can still insert into the underlying tables directly, though). Partitioned tables give more control over where data is stored.

The results of an INSERT are visible in both the merge table and the underlying table:

```
mysql> INSERT INTO mrg(a) VALUES(3);
mysql> SELECT a FROM t2;
+---+
| a |
+---+
| 1 |
| 2 |
| 3 |
+---+
```

Merge tables have some other interesting features and limitations, such as what happens when you drop a merge table or one of its underlying tables. Dropping a merge

---

3. Some people call these features "foot-guns."

table leaves its "child" tables untouched, but dropping one of the child tables has a different effect, which is operating system–specific. On GNU/Linux, for example, the underlying table's file descriptor stays open and the table continues to exist, but only via the merge table:

```
mysql> DROP TABLE t1, t2;
mysql> SELECT a FROM mrg;
+------+
| a    |
+------+
|    1 |
|    1 |
|    2 |
|    2 |
|    3 |
+------+
```

A variety of other limitations and special behaviors exist. Here are some aspects of merge tables you should keep in mind:

- The CREATE statement that creates a merge table doesn't check that the underlying tables are compatible. If the underlying tables are defined slightly differently, MySQL might create a merge table that it can't use later. Also, if you alter one of the underlying tables after creating a valid merge table, it will stop working and you'll see this error: "ERROR 1168 (HY000): Unable to open underlying table which is differently defined or of non-MyISAM type or doesn't exist."

- REPLACE doesn't work at all on a merge table, and AUTO_INCREMENT won't work as you might expect. We'll let you read the manual for the details.

- Queries that access a merge table access every underlying table. This can make single-row key lookups relatively slow, compared to a lookup in a single table. Therefore, it's a good idea to limit the number of underlying tables in a merge table, especially if it is the second or later table in a join. The less data you access with each operation, the more important the cost of accessing each table becomes, relative to the entire operation. Here are a few things to keep in mind when planning how to use merge tables:

  — Range lookups are less affected by the overhead of accessing all the underlying tables than individual item lookups.

  — Table scans are just as fast on merge tables as they are on normal tables.

  — Unique key and primary key lookups stop as soon as they succeed. In this case, the server accesses the underlying merge tables one at a time until the lookup finds a value, and then it accesses no further tables.

  — The underlying tables are read in the order specified in the CREATE TABLE statement. If you frequently need data in a specific order, you can exploit this to make the merge-sorting operation faster.

Because merge tables don't hide the underlying MyISAM tables, they offer some features that partitions don't as of MySQL 5.5:

- A MyISAM table can be a member of many merge tables.
- You can copy underlying tables between servers by copying the *.frm, .MYI,* and *.MYD* files.
- You can add more tables to a merge collection easily; just alter the merge definition.
- You can create temporary merge tables that include only the data you want, such as data from a specific time period, which you can't do with partitions.
- You can remove a table from the merge if you want to back it up, restore it, alter it, repair it, or perform other operations on it. You can then add it back when you're done.
- You can use *myisampack* to compress some or all of the underlying tables.

In contrast, a partitioned table's partitions are hidden by the MySQL server and are accessible only through the partitioned table.

Views

Views were added in MySQL 5.0. A *view* is a virtual table that doesn't store any data itself. Instead, the data "in" the table is derived from a SQL query that MySQL runs when you access the view. MySQL treats a view exactly like a table for many purposes, and views and tables share the same namespace in MySQL; however, MySQL doesn't treat them identically. For example, you can't have triggers on views, and you can't drop a view with the DROP TABLE command.

This book does not explain how to create or use views; you can read the MySQL manual for that. We'll focus on how views are implemented and how they interact with the query optimizer, so you can understand how to get good performance from them. We use the world sample database to demonstrate how views work:

```
mysql> CREATE VIEW Oceania AS
    ->    SELECT * FROM Country WHERE Continent = 'Oceania'
    ->    WITH CHECK OPTION;
```

The easiest way for the server to implement a view is to execute its SELECT statement and place the result into a temporary table. It can then refer to the temporary table where the view's name appears in the query. To see how this would work, consider the following query:

```
mysql> SELECT Code, Name FROM Oceania WHERE Name = 'Australia';
```

Here's how the server might execute it as a temporary table. The temporary table's name is for demonstration purposes only:

```
mysql> CREATE TEMPORARY TABLE TMP_Oceania_123 AS
    ->    SELECT * FROM Country WHERE Continent = 'Oceania';
mysql> SELECT Code, Name FROM TMP_Oceania_123 WHERE Name = 'Australia';
```

There are obvious performance and query optimization problems with this approach. A better way to implement views is to rewrite a query that refers to the view, merging the view's SQL with the query's SQL. The following example shows how the query might look after MySQL has merged it into the view definition:

```
mysql> SELECT Code, Name FROM Country
    -> WHERE Continent = 'Oceania' AND Name = 'Australia';
```

MySQL can use both methods. It calls the two algorithms MERGE and TEMPTABLE,[4] and it tries to use the MERGE algorithm when possible. MySQL can even merge nested view definitions when a view is based upon another view. You can see the results of the query rewrite with EXPLAIN EXTENDED, followed by SHOW WARNINGS.

If a view uses the TEMPTABLE algorithm, EXPLAIN will usually show it as a DERIVED table. Figure 7-1 illustrates the two implementations.

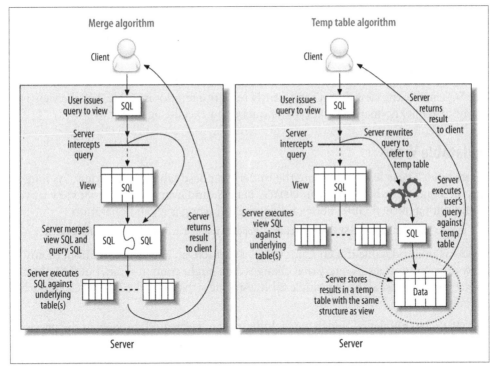

Figure 7-1. Two implementations of views

MySQL uses TEMPTABLE when the view definition contains GROUP BY, DISTINCT, aggregate functions, UNION, subqueries, or any other construct that doesn't preserve a one-to-one relationship between the rows in the underlying base tables and the rows returned from

---

4. That's "temp table," not "can be tempted." MySQL's views don't fast for 40 days and nights in the wilderness, either.

the view. This is not a complete list, and it might change in the future. If you want to know whether a view will use MERGE or TEMPTABLE, you can EXPLAIN a trivial SELECT query against the view:

```
mysql> EXPLAIN SELECT * FROM <view_name>;
+----+-------------+
| id | select_type |
+----+-------------+
|  1 | PRIMARY     |
|  2 | DERIVED     |
+----+-------------+
```

The presence of a SELECT type of DERIVED select type indicates that the view will use the TEMPTABLE algorithm. Beware, though: if the underlying derived table is expensive to produce, EXPLAIN can be quite costly and slow to execute in MySQL 5.5 and older versions, because it will actually execute and materialize the derived table.

The algorithm is a property of the view and is not influenced by the type of query that is executed against the view. For example, suppose you create a trivial view and explicitly specify the TEMPTABLE algorithm:

```
CREATE ALGORITHM=TEMPTABLE VIEW v1 AS SELECT * FROM sakila.actor;
```

The SQL inside the view doesn't inherently require a temporary table, but the view will always use one, no matter what type of query you execute against it.

Updatable Views

An *updatable view* lets you update the underlying base tables via the view. As long as specific conditions hold, you can UPDATE, DELETE, and even INSERT into a view as you would with a normal table. For example, the following is a valid operation:

```
mysql> UPDATE Oceania SET Population = Population * 1.1 WHERE Name = 'Australia';
```

A view is not updatable if it contains GROUP BY, UNION, an aggregate function, or any of a few other exceptions. A query that changes data might contain a join, but the columns to be changed must all be in a single table. Any view that uses the TEMPTABLE algorithm is not updatable.

The CHECK OPTION clause, which we included when we created the view in the previous section, ensures that any rows changed through the view continue to match the view's WHERE clause after the change. So, we can't change the Continent column, nor can we insert a row that has a different Continent. Either would cause the server to report an error:

```
mysql> UPDATE Oceania SET Continent = 'Atlantis';
ERROR 1369 (HY000): CHECK OPTION failed 'world.Oceania'
```

Some database products allow INSTEAD OF triggers on views so you can define exactly what happens when a statement tries to modify a view's data, but MySQL does not support triggers on views.

Performance Implications of Views

Most people don't think of using views to improve performance, but in some cases they can actually enhance performance in MySQL. You can also use them to aid other performance improvements. For example, refactoring a schema in stages with views can let some code continue working while you change the tables it accesses.

You can use views to implement column privileges without the overhead of actually creating those privileges:

```
CREATE VIEW public.employeeinfo AS
    SELECT firstname, lastname -- but not socialsecuritynumber
    FROM private.employeeinfo;
GRANT SELECT ON public.* TO public_user;
```

You can also sometimes use pseudotemporary views to good effect. You can't actually create a truly temporary view that persists only for your current connection, but you can create a view under a special name, perhaps in a database reserved for it, that you know you can drop later. You can then use the view in the FROM clause, much the same way you'd use a subquery in the FROM clause. The two approaches are theoretically the same, but MySQL has a different codebase for views, so performance can vary. Here's an example:

```
-- Assuming 1234 is the result of CONNECTION_ID()
CREATE VIEW temp.cost_per_day_1234 AS
    SELECT DATE(ts) AS day, sum(cost) AS cost
    FROM logs.cost
    GROUP BY day;
SELECT c.day, c.cost, s.sales
FROM temp.cost_per_day_1234 AS c
    INNER JOIN sales.sales_per_day AS s USING(day);
DROP VIEW temp.cost_per_day_1234;
```

Note that we've used the connection ID as a unique suffix to avoid name clashes. This approach can make it easier to clean up in the event that the application crashes and doesn't drop the temporary view. See "Missing Temporary Tables" on page 502 for more about this technique.

Views that use the TEMPTABLE algorithm can perform very badly (although they might still perform *better* than an equivalent query that doesn't use a view). MySQL executes them as a recursive step in optimizing the outer query, before the outer query is even fully optimized, so they don't get a lot of the optimizations you might be used to from other database products. The query that builds the temporary table doesn't get WHERE conditions pushed down from the outer query, and the temporary table does not have any indexes.[5] Here's an example, again using the temp.cost_per_day_1234 view:

---

5. This will be improved in MySQL 5.6, which is unreleased at the time of writing.

```
mysql> SELECT c.day, c.cost, s.sales
    -> FROM temp.cost_per_day_1234 AS c
    ->     INNER JOIN sales.sales_per_day AS s USING(day)
    ->     WHERE day BETWEEN '2007-01-01' AND '2007-01-31';
```

What really happens in this query is that the server executes the view and places the result into a temporary table, then joins the sales_per_day table against this temporary table. The BETWEEN restriction in the WHERE clause is not "pushed into" the view, so the view will create a result set for all dates in the table, not just the one month desired. The temporary table also lacks any indexes. In this example, this isn't a problem: the server will place the temporary table first in the join order, so the join can use the index on the sales_per_day table. However, if we were joining two such views against each other, the join would not be optimized with any indexes.

Views introduce some issues that aren't MySQL-specific. Views might trick developers into thinking they're simple, when in fact they're very complicated under the hood. A developer who doesn't understand the underlying complexity might think nothing of repeatedly querying what looks like a table but is in fact an expensive view. We've seen cases where an apparently simple query produced hundreds of lines of EXPLAIN output because one or more of the "tables" it referenced was actually a view that referred to many other tables and views.

You should always measure carefully if you're trying to use views to improve performance. Even MERGE views add overhead, and it's hard to predict how a view will impact performance. Views actually use a different execution path within the MySQL optimizer, one that isn't tested as widely and might still have bugs or problems. For that reason, views don't seem quite as mature as we'd like. For example, we've seen cases where complex views under high concurrency caused the query optimizer to spend a lot of time in the planning and statistics stages of the query, even causing server-wide stalls, which we solved by replacing the view with the equivalent SQL. This indicates that views—even those using the MERGE algorithm—don't always have an optimal implementation.

Limitations of Views

MySQL does not support the materialized views that you might be used to if you've worked with other database servers. (A *materialized view* generally stores its results in an invisible table behind the scenes, with periodic updates to refresh the invisible table from the source data.) MySQL also doesn't support indexed views. You can emulate materialized and/or indexed views by building cache and summary tables, however. You use Justin Swanhart's Flexviews tool for this purpose; see Chapter 4 for more.

MySQL's implementation of views also has a few annoyances. For example, MySQL doesn't preserve your original view SQL, so if you ever try to edit a view by executing SHOW CREATE VIEW and changing the resulting SQL, you're in for a nasty surprise. The query will be expanded to the fully canonicalized and quoted internal format, without the benefit of formatting, comments, and indenting.

If you need to edit a view and you've lost the pretty-printed query you originally used to create it, you can find it in the last line of the view's *.frm* file. If you have the FILE privilege and the *.frm* file is readable by all users, you can even load the file's contents through SQL with the LOAD_FILE() function. A little string manipulation can retrieve your original code intact, thanks to Roland Bouman's creativity:

```
mysql> SELECT
    ->     REPLACE(REPLACE(REPLACE(REPLACE(REPLACE(REPLACE(
    ->     REPLACE(REPLACE(REPLACE(REPLACE(REPLACE(
    ->       SUBSTRING_INDEX(LOAD_FILE('/var/lib/mysql/world/Oceania.frm'),
    ->       '\nsource=', -1),
    ->     '\\_','\_'), '\\%','\%'), '\\\\','\\'), '\\Z','\Z'), '\\t','\t'),
    ->     '\\r','\r'), '\\n','\n'), '\\b','\b'), '\\"','\"'), '\\\'','\''),
    ->     '\\0','\0')
    -> AS source;
+-------------------------------------------------------------------------+
| source                                                                  |
+-------------------------------------------------------------------------+
| SELECT * FROM Country WHERE continent = 'Oceania'                        |
|   WITH CHECK OPTION                                                      |
|                                                                         |
+-------------------------------------------------------------------------+
```

Foreign Key Constraints

InnoDB is currently the only bundled storage engine that supports foreign keys in MySQL, limiting your choice of storage engines if you require them (PBXT has foreign keys, too).

Foreign keys aren't free. They typically require the server to do a lookup in another table every time you change some data. Although InnoDB requires an index to make this operation faster, this doesn't eliminate the impact of these checks. It can even result in a very large index with virtually zero selectivity. For example, suppose you have a status column in a huge table and you want to constrain the status to valid values, but there are only three such values. The extra index required can add significantly to the table's total size—even if the column itself is small, and especially if the primary key is large—and is useless for anything but the foreign key checks.

Still, foreign keys can actually improve performance in some cases. If you must guarantee that two related tables have consistent data, it can be more efficient to let the server perform this check than to do it in your application. Foreign keys are also useful for cascading deletes or updates, although they do operate row by row, so they're slower than multitable deletes or batch operations.

Foreign keys cause your query to "reach into" other tables, which means acquiring locks. If you insert a row into a child table, for example, the foreign key constraint will cause InnoDB to check for a corresponding value in the parent. It must also lock the row in the parent, to ensure it doesn't get deleted before the transaction completes. This can cause unexpected lock waits and even deadlocks on tables you're not touching directly. Such problems can be very unintuitive and frustrating to debug.

You can sometimes use triggers instead of foreign keys. Foreign keys tend to outperform triggers for tasks such as cascading updates, but a foreign key that's just used as a constraint, as in our status example, can be more efficiently rewritten as a trigger with an explicit list of allowable values. (You can also just use an ENUM data type.)

Instead of using foreign keys as constraints, it's often a good idea to constrain the values in the application. Foreign keys can add significant overhead. We don't have any benchmarks to share, but we have seen many cases where server profiling revealed that foreign key constraint checks were the performance problem, and removing the foreign keys improved performance greatly.

Storing Code Inside MySQL

MySQL lets you store code inside the server in the form of triggers, stored procedures, and stored functions. In MySQL 5.1, you can also store code in periodic jobs called *events*. Stored procedures and stored functions are collectively known as "stored routines."

All four types of stored code use a special extended SQL language that contains procedural structures such as loops and conditionals.[6] The biggest difference between the types of stored code is the context in which they operate—that is, their inputs and outputs. Stored procedures and stored functions can accept parameters and return results, but triggers and events do not.

In principle, stored code is a good way to share and reuse code. Giuseppe Maxia and others have created a library of useful general-purpose stored routines at *http://mysql -sr-lib.sourceforge.net*. However, it's hard to reuse stored routines from other database systems, because most have their own language (the exception is DB2, which has a fairly similar language based on the same standard).[7]

We focus more on the performance implications of stored code than on how to write it. Guy Harrison and Steven Feuerstein's *MySQL Stored Procedure Programming* (*http: //shop.oreilly.com/product/9780596100896.do*) (O'Reilly) might be useful if you plan to write stored procedures in MySQL.

It's easy to find both advocates and opponents of stored code. Without taking sides, we'll list some of the pros and cons of using it in MySQL. First, the advantages:

---

6. The language is a subset of SQL/PSM, the Persistent Stored Modules part of the SQL standard. It is defined in ISO/IEC 9075-4:2003 (E).

7. There are also some porting utilities, such as the *tsql2mysql* project (*http://sourceforge.net/projects/ tsql2mysql*) for porting from Microsoft SQL Server.

- It runs where the data is, so you can save bandwidth and reduce latency by running tasks on the database server.
- It's a form of code reuse. It can help centralize business rules, which can enforce consistent behavior and provide more safety and peace of mind.
- It can ease release policies and maintenance.
- It can provide some security advantages and a way to control privileges more finely. A common example is a stored procedure for funds transfer at a bank: the procedure transfers the money within a transaction and logs the entire operation for auditing. You can let applications call the stored procedure without granting access to the underlying tables.
- The server caches stored procedure execution plans, which lowers the overhead of repeated calls.
- Because it's stored in the server and can be deployed, backed up, and maintained with the server, stored code is well suited for maintenance jobs. It doesn't have any external dependencies, such as Perl libraries or other software that you might not want to place on the server.
- It enables division of labor between application programmers and database programmers. It can be preferable for a database expert to write the stored procedures, as not every application programmer is good at writing efficient SQL queries.

Disadvantages include the following:

- MySQL doesn't provide good developing and debugging tools, so it's harder to write stored code in MySQL than it is in some other database servers.
- The language is slow and primitive compared to application languages. The number of functions you can use is limited, and it's hard to do complex string manipulations and write intricate logic.
- Stored code can actually add complexity to deploying your application. Instead of just application code and database schema changes, you'll need to deploy code that's stored inside the server, too.
- Because stored routines are stored with the database, they can create a security vulnerability. Having nonstandard cryptographic functions inside a stored routine, for example, will not protect your data if the database is compromised. If the cryptographic function were in the code, the attacker would have to compromise both the code and the database.
- Storing routines moves the load to the database server, which is typically harder to scale and more expensive than application or web servers.
- MySQL doesn't give you much control over the resources stored code can allocate, so a mistake can bring down the server.
- MySQL's implementation of stored code is pretty limited—execution plan caches are per-connection, cursors are materialized as temporary tables, there's very

limited ability to raise and catch errors prior to MySQL 5.5, and so on. (We mention the limitations of various features as we describe them.) In general, MySQL's stored routine language is nowhere near as capable as T-SQL or PL/SQL.

- It's hard to profile code with stored procedures in MySQL. It's difficult to analyze the slow query log when it just shows CALL XYZ('A'), because you have to go and find that procedure and look at the statements inside it. (This is configurable in Percona Server.)
- It doesn't play well with statement-based binary logging or replication. There are so many "gotchas" that you probably should not use stored code with statement-based logging unless you are very knowledgeable and strict about checking it for potential problems.

That's a long list of drawbacks—what does this all mean in the real world? Here's an example where we've seen the use of stored code backfire in real life: in one instance, using them to create an API for the application to access the database. This resulted in all access to the database—even trivial primary-key row lookups—going through CALL queries, which reduced performance by about a factor of five.

Ultimately, stored code is a way to hide complexity, which simplifies development but can be very bad for performance and add a lot of potential hazards with replication and other server features. When you're thinking about using stored code, you should ask yourself where you want your business logic to live: in application code, or in the database? Both approaches are popular. You just need to be aware that you're placing logic into the database when you use stored code.

Stored Procedures and Functions

MySQL's architecture and query optimizer place some limits on how you can use stored routines and how efficient they can be. The following restrictions apply at the time of this writing:

- The optimizer doesn't use the DETERMINISTIC modifier in stored functions to optimize away multiple calls within a single query.
- The optimizer cannot estimate how much it will cost to execute a stored function.
- Each connection has its own stored procedure execution plan cache. If many connections call the same procedure, they'll waste resources caching the same execution plan over and over. (If you use connection pooling or persistent connections, the execution plan cache can have a longer useful life.)
- Stored routines and replication are a tricky combination. You might not want to replicate the call to the routine. Instead, you might want to replicate the exact changes made to your dataset. Row-based replication, introduced in MySQL 5.1, helps alleviate this problem. If binary logging is enabled in MySQL 5.0, the server will insist that you either define all stored procedures as DETERMINISTIC or enable the elaborately named server option log_bin_trust_function_creators.

We usually prefer to keep stored routines small and simple. We like to perform complex logic outside the database in a procedural language, which is more expressive and versatile. It can also give you access to more computational resources and potentially to different forms of caching.

However, stored procedures can be much faster for certain types of operations—especially when a single stored procedure call with a loop inside it can replace many small queries. If a query is small enough, the overhead of parsing and network communication becomes a significant fraction of the overall work required to execute it. To illustrate this, we created a simple stored procedure that inserts a specified number of rows into a table. Here's the procedure's code:

```
 1  DROP PROCEDURE IF EXISTS insert_many_rows;
 2
 3  delimiter //
 4
 5  CREATE PROCEDURE insert_many_rows (IN loops INT)
 6  BEGIN
 7     DECLARE v1 INT;
 8     SET v1=loops;
 9     WHILE v1 > 0 DO
10       INSERT INTO test_table values(NULL,0,
11                 'qqqqqqqqqqwwwwwwwwwweeeeeeeeeerrrrrrrrrrtttttttttt',
12                 'qqqqqqqqqqwwwwwwwwwweeeeeeeeeerrrrrrrrrrtttttttttt');
13       SET v1 = v1 - 1;
14     END WHILE;
15  END;
16  //
17
18  delimiter ;
```

We then benchmarked how quickly this stored procedure could insert a million rows into a table, as compared to inserting one row at a time via a client application. The table structure and hardware we used doesn't really matter—what is important is the relative speed of the different approaches. Just for fun, we also measured how long the same queries took to execute when we connected through a MySQL Proxy. To keep things simple, we ran the entire benchmark on a single server, including the client application and the MySQL Proxy instance. Table 7-1 shows the results.

Table 7-1. Total time to insert one million rows one at a time

Method	Total time
Stored procedure	101 sec
Client application	279 sec
Client application with MySQL Proxy	307 sec

The stored procedure is much faster, mostly because it avoids the overhead of network communication, parsing, optimizing, and so on.

We show a typical stored procedure for maintenance jobs later in this chapter.

Triggers

Triggers let you execute code when there's an INSERT, UPDATE, or DELETE statement. You can direct MySQL to activate triggers before and/or after the triggering statement executes. They cannot return values, but they can read and/or change the data that the triggering statement changes. Thus, you can use triggers to enforce constraints or business logic that you'd otherwise need to write in client code.

Triggers can simplify application logic and improve performance, because they save round-trips between the client and the server. They can also be helpful for automatically updating denormalized and summary tables. For example, the Sakila sample database uses them to maintain the film_text table.

MySQL's trigger implementation is very limited. If you're used to relying on triggers extensively in another database product, you shouldn't assume they will work the same way in MySQL. In particular:

- You can have only one trigger per table for each event (in other words, you can't have two triggers that fire AFTER INSERT).
- MySQL supports only row-level triggers—that is, triggers always operate FOR EACH ROW rather than for the statement as a whole. This is a much less efficient way to process large datasets.

The following universal cautions about triggers apply in MySQL, too:

- They can obscure what your server is really doing, because a simple statement can make the server perform a lot of "invisible" work. For example, if a trigger updates a related table, it can double the number of rows a statement affects.
- Triggers can be hard to debug, and it's often difficult to analyze performance bottlenecks when triggers are involved.
- Triggers can cause nonobvious deadlocks and lock waits. If a trigger fails the original query will fail, and if you're not aware the trigger exists, it can be hard to decipher the error code.

In terms of performance, the most severe limitation in MySQL's trigger implementation is the FOR EACH ROW design. This sometimes makes it impractical to use triggers for maintaining summary and cache tables, because they might be too slow. The main reason to use triggers instead of a periodic bulk update is that they keep your data consistent at all times.

Triggers also might not guarantee atomicity. For example, a trigger that updates a MyISAM table cannot be rolled back if there's an error in the statement that fires it. It is possible for a trigger to cause an error, too. Suppose you attach an AFTER UPDATE trigger to a MyISAM table and use it to update another MyISAM table. If the trigger has an error that causes the second table's update to fail, the first table's update will not be rolled back.

Triggers on InnoDB tables all operate within the same transaction, so the actions they take will be atomic, together with the statement that fired them. However, if you're using a trigger with InnoDB to check another table's data when validating a constraint, be careful about MVCC, as you can get incorrect results if you're not careful. For example, suppose you want to emulate foreign keys, but you don't want to use InnoDB's foreign keys. You can write a BEFORE INSERT trigger that verifies the existence of a matching record in another table, but if you don't use SELECT FOR UPDATE in the trigger when reading from the other table, concurrent updates to that table can cause incorrect results.

We don't mean to scare you away from triggers. On the contrary, they can be useful, particularly for constraints, system maintenance tasks, and keeping denormalized data up-to-date.

You can also use triggers to log changes to rows. This can be handy for custom-built replication setups where you want to disconnect systems, make data changes, and then merge the changes back together. A simple example is a group of users who take laptops onto a job site. Their changes need to be synchronized to a master database, and then the master data needs to be copied back to the individual laptops. Accomplishing this requires two-way synchronization. Triggers are a good way to build such systems. Each laptop can use triggers to log every data modification to tables that indicate which rows have been changed. The custom synchronization tool can then apply these changes to the master database. Finally, ordinary MySQL replication can sync the laptops with the master, which will have the changes from all the laptops. However, you need to be very careful with triggers that insert rows into other tables that have autoincrementing primary keys. This doesn't play well with statement-based replication, as the autoincrement values are likely to be different on replicas.

Sometimes you can work around the FOR EACH ROW limitation. Roland Bouman found that ROW_COUNT() always reports 1 inside a trigger, except for the first row of a BEFORE trigger. You can use this to prevent a trigger's code from executing for every row affected and run it only once per statement. It's not the same as a per-statement trigger, but it is a useful technique for emulating a per-statement BEFORE trigger in some cases. This behavior might actually be a bug that will get fixed at some point, so you should use it with care and verify that it still works when you upgrade your server. Here's a sample of how to use this hack:

```
CREATE TRIGGER fake_statement_trigger
BEFORE INSERT ON sometable
FOR EACH ROW
BEGIN
    DECLARE v_row_count INT DEFAULT ROW_COUNT();
    IF v_row_count <> 1 THEN
        -- Your code here
    END IF;
END;
```

Events

Events are a new form of stored code in MySQL 5.1. They are akin to *cron* jobs but are completely internal to the MySQL server. You can create events that execute SQL code once at a specific time, or frequently at a specified interval. The usual practice is to wrap the complex SQL in a stored procedure, so the event merely needs to perform a CALL.

Events are initiated by a separate event scheduler thread, because they have nothing to do with connections. They accept no inputs and return no values—there's no connection for them to get inputs from or return values to. You can see the commands they execute in the server log, if it's enabled, but it can be hard to tell that those commands were executed from an event. You can also look in the INFORMATION_SCHEMA.EVENTS table to see an event's status, such as the last time it was executed.

Similar considerations to those that apply to stored procedures apply to events. First, you are giving the server additional work to do. The event overhead itself is minimal, but the SQL it calls can have a potentially serious impact on performance. Further, events can cause the same types of problems with statement-based replication that other stored code can cause. Good uses for events include periodic maintenance tasks, rebuilding cache and summary tables to emulate materialized views, or saving status values for monitoring and diagnostics.

The following example creates an event that will run a stored procedure for a specific database, once a week (we'll show you how to create this stored procedure later):

```
CREATE EVENT optimize_somedb ON SCHEDULE EVERY 1 WEEK
DO
CALL optimize_tables('somedb');
```

You can specify whether events should be replicated. In some cases this is appropriate, whereas in others it's not. Take the previous example, for instance: you probably want to run the OPTIMIZE TABLE operation on all replicas, but keep in mind that it could impact overall server performance (with table locks, for instance) if all replicas were to execute this operation at the same time.

Finally, if a periodic event can take a long time to complete, it might be possible for the event to fire again while its earlier execution is still running. MySQL doesn't protect against this, so you'll have to write your own mutual exclusivity code. You can use GET_LOCK() to make sure that only one event runs at a time:

```
CREATE EVENT optimize_somedb ON SCHEDULE EVERY 1 WEEK
DO
BEGIN
   DECLARE CONTINUE HANLDER FOR SQLEXCEPTION
      BEGIN END;
   IF GET_LOCK('somedb', 0) THEN
      DO CALL optimize_tables('somedb');
   END IF;
   DO RELEASE_LOCK('somedb');
END
```

The "dummy" continue handler ensures that the event will release the lock, even if the stored procedure throws an exception.

Although events are dissociated from connections, they are still associated with threads. There's a main event scheduler thread, which you must enable in your server's configuration file or with a SET command:

```
mysql> SET GLOBAL event_scheduler := 1;
```

When enabled, this thread executes events on the schedule specified in the event. You can watch the server's error log for information about event execution.

Although the event scheduler is single-threaded, events can run concurrently. The server will create a new process each time an event executes. Within the event's code, a call to CONNECTION_ID() will return a unique value, as usual—even though there is no "connection" per se. (The return value of CONNECTION_ID() is really just the thread ID.) The process and thread will live only for the duration of the event's execution. You can see it in SHOW PROCESSLIST by looking at the Command column, which will appear as "Connect".

Although the process necessarily creates a thread to actually execute, the thread is destroyed at the end of event execution, not placed into the thread cache, and the Threads_created status counter is not incremented.

Preserving Comments in Stored Code

Stored procedures, stored functions, triggers, and events can all have significant amounts of code, and it's useful to add comments. But the comments might not be stored inside the server, because the command-line client can strip them out. (This "feature" of the command-line client can be a nuisance, but *c'est la vie*.)

A useful trick for preserving comments in your stored code is to use version-specific comments, which the server sees as potentially executable code (i.e., code to be executed only if the server's version number is that high or higher). The server and client programs know these aren't ordinary comments, so they won't discard them. To prevent the "code" from being executed, you can just use a very high version number, such as 99999. Let's add some documentation to our trigger example to demystify what it does:

```
CREATE TRIGGER fake_statement_trigger
BEFORE INSERT ON sometable
FOR EACH ROW
BEGIN
   DECLARE v_row_count INT DEFAULT ROW_COUNT();
   /*!99999    ROW_COUNT() is 1 except for the first row, so this executes
      only once per statement.    */
   IF v_row_count <> 1 THEN
      -- Your code here
   END IF;
END;
```

Cursors

MySQL provides read-only, forward-only server-side cursors that you can use only from within a MySQL stored procedure or the low-level client API. MySQL's cursors are read-only because they iterate over temporary tables rather than the tables where the data originated. They let you iterate over query results row by row and fetch each row into variables for further processing. A stored procedure can have multiple cursors open at once, and you can "nest" cursors in loops.

MySQL's cursor design holds some snares for the unwary. Because they're implemented with temporary tables, they can give developers a false sense of efficiency. The most important thing to know is that *a cursor executes the entire query when you open it*. Consider the following procedure:

```
1  CREATE PROCEDURE bad_cursor()
2  BEGIN
3     DECLARE film_id INT;
4     DECLARE f CURSOR FOR SELECT film_id FROM sakila.film;
5     OPEN f;
6     FETCH f INTO film_id;
7     CLOSE f;
8  END
```

This example shows that you can close a cursor before iterating through all of its results. A developer used to Oracle or Microsoft SQL Server might see nothing wrong with this procedure, but in MySQL it causes a lot of unnecessary work. Profiling this procedure with SHOW STATUS shows that it does 1,000 index reads and 1,000 inserts. That's because there are 1,000 rows in sakila.film. All 1,000 reads and writes occur when line 5 executes, before line 6 executes.

The moral of the story is that if you close a cursor that fetches data from a large result set early, you won't actually save work. If you need only a few rows, use LIMIT.

Cursors can cause MySQL to perform extra I/O operations too, and they can be very slow. Because in-memory temporary tables do not support the BLOB and TEXT types, MySQL has to create an on-disk temporary table for cursors over results that include these types. Even when that's not the case, if the temporary table is larger than tmp_table_size, MySQL will create it on disk.

MySQL doesn't support client-side cursors, but the client API has functions that emulate client-side cursors by fetching the entire result into memory. This is really no different from putting the result in an array in your application and manipulating it there. See Chapter 6 for more on the performance implications of fetching the entire result into client-side memory.

Prepared Statements

MySQL 4.1 and newer support server-side *prepared statements* that use an enhanced binary client/server protocol to send data efficiently between the client and server. You can access the prepared statement functionality through a programming library that supports the new protocol, such as the MySQL C API. The MySQL Connector/J and MySQL Connector/NET libraries provide the same capability to Java and .NET, respectively. There's also a SQL interface to prepared statements, which we discuss later (it's confusing).

When you create a prepared statement, the client library sends the server a prototype of the actual query you want to use. The server parses and processes this "skeleton" query, stores a structure representing the partially optimized query, and returns a *statement handle* to the client. The client library can execute the query repeatedly by specifying the statement handle.

Prepared statements can have parameters, which are question-mark placeholders for values that you can specify when you execute them. For example, you might prepare the following query:

```
INSERT INTO tbl(col1, col2, col3) VALUES (?, ?, ?);
```

You could then execute this query by sending the statement handle to the server, with values for each of the question-mark placeholders. You can repeat this as many times as desired. Exactly how you send the statement handle to the server will depend on your programming language. One way is to use the MySQL connectors for Java and .NET. Many client libraries that link to the MySQL C libraries also provide some interface to the binary protocol; you should read the documentation for your chosen MySQL API.

Using prepared statements can be more efficient than executing a query repeatedly, for several reasons:

- The server has to parse the query only once.
- The server has to perform some query optimization steps only once, as it caches a partial query execution plan.
- Sending parameters via the binary protocol is more efficient than sending them as ASCII text. For example, a DATE value can be sent in just 3 bytes, instead of the 10 bytes required in ASCII. The biggest savings are for BLOB and TEXT values, which can be sent to the server in chunks rather than as a single huge piece of data. The binary protocol therefore helps save memory on the client, as well as reducing network traffic and the overhead of converting between the data's native storage format and the non-binary protocol's format.
- Only the parameters—not the entire query text—need to be sent for each execution, which reduces network traffic.

- MySQL stores the parameters directly into buffers on the server, which eliminates the need for the server to copy values around in memory.

Prepared statements can also help with security. There is no need to escape or quote values in the application, which is more convenient and reduces vulnerability to SQL injection or other attacks. (You should never trust user input, even when you're using prepared statements.)

You can use the binary protocol *only* with prepared statements. Issuing queries through the normal `mysql_query()` API function will *not* use the binary protocol. Many client libraries let you "prepare" statements with question-mark placeholders and then specify the values for each execution, but these libraries are often only emulating the prepare-execute cycle in client-side code and are actually sending each query, as text with parameters replaced by values, to the server with `mysql_query()`.

Prepared Statement Optimization

MySQL caches partial query execution plans for prepared statements, but some optimizations depend on the actual values that are bound to each parameter and therefore can't be precomputed and cached. The optimizations can be separated into three types, based on when they must be performed. The following list applies at the time of this writing:

At preparation time
> The server parses the query text, eliminates negations, and rewrites subqueries.

At first execution
> The server simplifies nested joins and converts OUTER JOINs to INNER JOINs where possible.

At every execution
> The server does the following:
> - Prunes partitions
> - Eliminates `COUNT()`, `MIN()`, and `MAX()` where possible
> - Removes constant subexpressions
> - Detects constant tables
> - Propagates equalities
> - Analyzes and optimizes `ref`, `range`, and `index_merge` access methods
> - Optimizes the join order

See Chapter 6 for more information on these optimizations. Even though some of them are theoretically possible to do only once, they are still performed as noted above.

The SQL Interface to Prepared Statements

A SQL interface to prepared statements is available in MySQL 4.1 and newer. It lets you instruct the server to create and execute prepared statements, but doesn't use the binary protocol. Here's an example of how to use a prepared statement through SQL:

```
mysql> SET @sql := 'SELECT actor_id, first_name, last_name
    -> FROM sakila.actor WHERE first_name = ?';
mysql> PREPARE stmt_fetch_actor FROM @sql;
mysql> SET @actor_name := 'Penelope';
mysql> EXECUTE stmt_fetch_actor USING @actor_name;
+----------+------------+-----------+
| actor_id | first_name | last_name |
+----------+------------+-----------+
|        1 | PENELOPE   | GUINESS   |
|       54 | PENELOPE   | PINKETT   |
|      104 | PENELOPE   | CRONYN    |
|      120 | PENELOPE   | MONROE    |
+----------+------------+-----------+
mysql> DEALLOCATE PREPARE stmt_fetch_actor;
```

When the server receives these statements, it translates them into the same operations that would have been invoked by the client library. This means that you don't have to use the special binary protocol to create and execute prepared statements.

As you can see, the syntax is a little awkward compared to just typing the SELECT statement directly. So what's the advantage of using a prepared statement this way?

The main use case is for stored procedures. In MySQL 5.0, you can use prepared statements in stored procedures, and the syntax is similar to the SQL interface. This means you can build and execute "dynamic SQL" in stored procedures by concatenating strings, which makes stored procedures much more flexible. For example, here's a sample stored procedure that can call OPTIMIZE TABLE on each table in a specified database:

```
DROP PROCEDURE IF EXISTS optimize_tables;
DELIMITER //
CREATE PROCEDURE optimize_tables(db_name VARCHAR(64))
BEGIN
   DECLARE t VARCHAR(64);
   DECLARE done INT DEFAULT 0;
   DECLARE c CURSOR FOR
      SELECT table_name FROM INFORMATION_SCHEMA.TABLES
      WHERE TABLE_SCHEMA = db_name AND TABLE_TYPE = 'BASE TABLE';
   DECLARE CONTINUE HANDLER FOR SQLSTATE '02000' SET done = 1;
   OPEN c;
   tables_loop: LOOP
      FETCH c INTO t;
      IF done THEN
         LEAVE tables_loop;
      END IF;
      SET @stmt_text := CONCAT("OPTIMIZE TABLE ", db_name, ".", t);
      PREPARE stmt FROM @stmt_text;
      EXECUTE stmt;
```

```
        DEALLOCATE PREPARE stmt;
    END LOOP;
    CLOSE c;
END//
DELIMITER ;
```

You can use this stored procedure as follows:

```
mysql> CALL optimize_tables('sakila');
```

Another way to write the loop in the procedure is as follows:

```
REPEAT
    FETCH c INTO t;
    IF NOT done THEN
        SET @stmt_text := CONCAT("OPTIMIZE TABLE ", db_name, ".", t);
        PREPARE stmt FROM @stmt_text;
        EXECUTE stmt;
        DEALLOCATE PREPARE stmt;
    END IF;
UNTIL done END REPEAT;
```

There is an important difference between the two loop constructs: REPEAT checks the loop condition twice for each loop. This probably won't cause a big performance problem in this example because we're merely checking an integer's value, but with more complex checks it could be costly.

Concatenating strings to refer to tables and databases is a good use for the SQL interface to prepared statements, because it lets you write statements that won't work with parameters. You can't parameterize database and table names because they are identifiers. Another scenario is dynamically setting a LIMIT clause, which you can't specify with a parameter either.

The SQL interface is useful for testing a prepared statement by hand, but it's otherwise not all that useful outside of stored procedures. Because the interface is through SQL, it doesn't use the binary protocol, and it doesn't really reduce network traffic because you have to issue extra queries to set the variables when there are parameters. You can benefit from using this interface in special cases, such as when preparing an enormous string of SQL that you'll execute many times without parameters.

Limitations of Prepared Statements

Prepared statements have a few limitations and caveats:

- Prepared statements are local to a connection, so another connection cannot use the same handle. For the same reason, a client that disconnects and reconnects loses the statements. (Connection pooling or persistent connections can alleviate this problem.)

- Prepared statements cannot use the query cache in MySQL versions prior to 5.1.

- It's not always more efficient to use prepared statements. If you use a prepared statement only once, you might spend more time preparing it than you would just executing it as normal SQL. Preparing a statement also requires two extra round-trips to the server (to use prepared statements properly, you should deallocate them after use).

- You cannot currently use a prepared statement inside a stored function (but you can use prepared statements inside stored procedures).
- You can accidentally "leak" a prepared statement by forgetting to deallocate it. This can consume a lot of resources on the server. Also, because there is a single global limit on the number of prepared statements, a mistake such as this can interfere with other connections' use of prepared statements.
- Some operations, such as BEGIN, cannot be performed in prepared statements.

Probably the biggest limitation of prepared statements, however, is that it's so easy to get confused about what they are and how they work. Sometimes it's very hard to explain the difference between these three kinds of prepared statements:

Client-side emulated
The client driver accepts a string with placeholders, then substitutes the parameters into the SQL and sends the resulting query to the server.

Server-side
The driver sends a string with placeholders to the server with a special binary protocol, receives back a statement identifier, then executes the statement over the binary protocol by specifying the identifier and the parameters.

SQL interface
The client sends a string with placeholders to the server as a PREPARE SQL statement, sets SQL variables to parameter values, and finally executes the statement with an EXECUTE SQL statement. All of this happens via the normal textual protocol.

User-Defined Functions

MySQL has supported *user-defined functions* (UDFs) since ancient times. Unlike stored functions, which are written in SQL, you can write UDFs in any programming language that supports C calling conventions.

UDFs must be compiled and then dynamically linked with the server, making them platform-specific and giving you a lot of power. UDFs can be very fast and can access a large range of functionality in the operating system and available libraries. SQL stored functions are good for simple operations, such as calculating the great-circle distance between two points on the globe, but if you want to send network packets, you need a UDF. Also, while you can't currently build aggregate functions in SQL stored functions, you can do this easily with a UDF.

With great power comes great responsibility. A mistake in your UDF can crash your whole server, corrupt the server's memory and/or your data, and generally wreak all the havoc that any misbehaving C code can potentially cause.

Unlike stored functions written in SQL, UDFs cannot currently read and write tables—at least, not in the same transactional context as the statement that calls them. This means they're more helpful for pure computation, or interaction with the outside world. MySQL is gaining more and more possibilities for interaction with resources outside of the server. The functions Brian Aker and Patrick Galbraith have created to communicate with *memcached* (*http://tangent.org/586/Memcached _Functions_for_MySQL.html*) are a good example of how this can be done with UDFs.

If you use UDFs, check carefully for changes between MySQL versions when you upgrade, because they might need to be recompiled or even changed to work correctly with the new MySQL server. Also make sure your UDFs are absolutely thread-safe, because they execute within the MySQL server process, which is a pure multithreaded environment.

There are good libraries of prebuilt UDFs for MySQL, and many good examples of how to implement your own. The biggest repository of UDFs is at *http://www.mysqludf.org*.

The following is the code for the NOW_USEC() UDF we'll use to measure replication speed in Chapter 10:

```
#include <my_global.h>
#include <my_sys.h>
#include <mysql.h>
#include <stdio.h>
#include <sys/time.h>
#include <time.h>
#include <unistd.h>
extern "C" {
  my_bool now_usec_init(UDF_INIT *initid, UDF_ARGS *args, char *message);
  char *now_usec(
                 UDF_INIT *initid,
                 UDF_ARGS *args,
                 char *result,
                 unsigned long *length,
                 char *is_null,
                 char *error);
}
my_bool now_usec_init(UDF_INIT *initid, UDF_ARGS *args, char *message) {
  return 0;
}
char *now_usec(UDF_INIT *initid, UDF_ARGS *args, char *result,
               unsigned long *length, char *is_null, char *error) {
  struct timeval tv;
  struct tm* ptm;
  char time_string[20]; /* e.g. "2006-04-27 17:10:52" */
  char *usec_time_string = result;
  time_t t;
  /* Obtain the time of day, and convert it to a tm struct. */
  gettimeofday (&tv, NULL);
  t = (time_t)tv.tv_sec;
```

```
    ptm = localtime (&t);
    /* Format the date and time, down to a single second. */
    strftime (time_string, sizeof (time_string), "%Y-%m-%d %H:%M:%S", ptm);
    /* Print the formatted time, in seconds, followed by a decimal point
     * and the microseconds. */
    sprintf(usec_time_string, "%s.%06ld\n", time_string, tv.tv_usec);
    *length = 26;
    return(usec_time_string);
}
```

For one example of a user-defined function at work solving a thorny problem, see the case studies in the previous chapter. We've also written UDFs that ship with the Percona Toolkit for checksumming data efficiently so you can test your replication integrity at lower cost, and one for preprocessing text before indexing it with Sphinx for searching. UDFs can be very powerful.

Plugins

In addition to UDFs, MySQL supports a variety of other plugins. They can add their own command-line options and status variables, provide INFORMATION_SCHEMA tables, run as daemons, and much more. In MySQL 5.1 and newer, the server has many more plugin APIs than it did previously, and the server can now be extended in many ways without altering its source code. Here is a short list:

Procedure plugins

Procedure plugins can post-process a result set. This is an ancient type of plugin, similar to UDFs, that most people aren't even aware of and never consider using. The built-in PROCEDURE ANALYSE is an example.

Daemon plugins

Daemon plugins run as a process within MySQL and can perform tasks such as listening on network ports or executing periodic jobs. An example is the Handler-Socket plugin included with Percona Server. It opens network ports and accepts a simple protocol that lets you access InnoDB tables through the Handler interface without using SQL, which makes it a high-performance NoSQL interface into the server.

INFORMATION_SCHEMA *plugins*

These plugins can provide arbitrary INFORMATION_SCHEMA tables.

Full-text parser plugins

These plugins provide a way to intercept the processes of reading and breaking a document into words for indexing, so you can do things such as indexing PDF documents given their filenames. You can also make it a part of the matching process during query execution.

Audit plugins

Audit plugins receive events at defined points in query execution, so they can be used (for example) as a way to log what happens in the server.

Authentication plugins

Authentication plugins can work on the client or the server side to extend the range of authentication mechanisms available to the server, including PAM and LDAP authentication, for example.

For more details, see the MySQL manual, or read the book *MySQL 5.1 Plugin Development* by Sergei Golubchik and Andrew Hutchings (Packt). If you need a plugin and don't know how to write one, many service providers have competent staff who can help you, including Monty Program, Open Query, Percona, and SkySQL.

Character Sets and Collations

A *character set* is a mapping from binary encodings to a defined set of symbols; you can think of it as how to represent a particular alphabet in bits. A *collation* is a set of sorting rules for a character set. In MySQL 4.1 and later, every character-based value can have a character set and a collation.[8] MySQL's support for character sets and collations is very full-featured, but it can add complexity, and in some cases it has a performance cost. (By the way, Drizzle discards it all and makes everything UTF-8, period.)

This section explains the settings and functionality you'll need for most situations. If you need to know the more esoteric details, you should consult the MySQL manual.

How MySQL Uses Character Sets

Character sets can have several collations, and each character set has a default collation. Collations belong to a particular character set and cannot be used with any other. You use a character set and a collation together, so we'll refer to them collectively as a character set from now on.

MySQL has a variety of options that control character sets. The options and the character sets are easy to confuse, so keep this distinction in mind: only character-based values can truly "have" a character set. Everything else is just a setting that specifies which character set to use for comparisons and other operations. A character-based value can be the value stored in a column, a literal in a query, the result of an expression, a user variable, and so on.

MySQL's settings can be divided into two classes: defaults for creating objects, and settings that control how the server and the client communicate.

Defaults for creating objects

MySQL has a default character set and collation for the server, for each database, and for each table. These form a hierarchy of defaults that influences the character set that's

---

8. MySQL 4.0 and earlier used a global setting for the entire server, and you could choose from among several 8-bit character sets.

used when you create a column. That, in turn, tells the server what character set to use for values you store in the column.

At each level in the hierarchy, you can either specify a character set explicitly or let the server use the applicable default:

- When you create a database, it inherits from the server-wide `character_set _server` setting.
- When you create a table, it inherits from the database.
- When you create a column, it inherits from the table.

Remember, columns are the only place MySQL stores values, so the higher levels in the hierarchy are only defaults. A table's default character set doesn't affect values stored in the tables; it just tells MySQL which character set to use when you create a column without specifying a character set explicitly.

Settings for client/server communication

When the server and the client communicate with each other, they might send data back and forth in different character sets. The server will translate as needed:

- The server assumes the client is sending statements in the character set specified by `character_set_client`.
- After the server receives a statement from the client, it translates it into the character set specified by `character_set_connection`. It also uses this setting to determine how to convert numbers into strings.
- When the server returns results or error messages back to the client, it translates them into `character_set_result`.

Figure 7-2 illustrates this process.

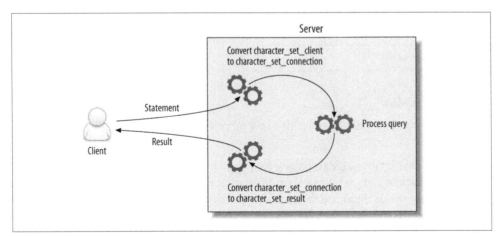

Figure 7-2. Client and server character sets

You can use the SET NAMES statement and/or the SET CHARACTER SET statement to change these three settings as needed. However, note that this command affects *only the server's settings*. The client program and the client API also need to be set correctly to avoid communication problems with the server.

Suppose you open a client connection with latin1 (the default character set, unless you've used mysql_options() to change it) and then use SET NAMES utf8 to tell the server to assume the client is sending data in UTF-8. You've created a character set mismatch, which can cause errors and even security problems. You should set the client's character set and use mysql_real_escape_string() when escaping values. In PHP, you can change the client's character set with mysql_set_charset().

How MySQL compares values

When MySQL compares two values with different character sets, it must convert them to the same character set for the comparison. If the character sets aren't compatible, this can cause an error, such as "ERROR 1267 (HY000): Illegal mix of collations." In this case, you'll generally need to use the CONVERT() function explicitly to force one of the values into a character set that's compatible with the other. MySQL 5.0 and newer often do this conversion implicitly, so this error is more common in MySQL 4.1.

MySQL also assigns a *coercibility* to values. This determines the priority of a value's character set and influences which value MySQL will convert implicitly. You can use the CHARSET(), COLLATION(), and COERCIBILITY() functions to help debug errors related to character sets and collations.

You can use *introducers* and *collate clauses* to specify the character set and/or collation for literal values in your SQL statements. For example, the following statement uses an introducer (preceded by an underscore) to specify the utf8 character set, and a collate clause to specify a binary collation:

```
mysql> SELECT _utf8 'hello world' COLLATE utf8_bin;
+--------------------------------------+
| _utf8 'hello world' COLLATE utf8_bin |
+--------------------------------------+
| hello world                          |
+--------------------------------------+
```

Special-case behaviors

MySQL's character set behavior holds a few surprises. Here are some things you should watch out for:

The magical character_set_database *setting*
> The character_set_database setting defaults to the default database's setting. As you change your default database, it will change too. If you connect to the server without a default database, it defaults to character_set_server.

LOAD DATA INFILE

LOAD DATA INFILE interprets incoming data according to the current setting of character_set_database. MySQL versions 5.0 and newer accept an optional CHAR ACTER SET clause in the LOAD DATA INFILE statement, but you shouldn't rely on this. We've found that the best way to get reliable results is to USE the desired database, execute SET NAMES to select a character set, and only then load the data. MySQL interprets all the loaded data as having the same character set, regardless of the character sets specified for the destination columns.

SELECT INTO OUTFILE

MySQL writes all data from SELECT INTO OUTFILE without converting it. There is currently no way to specify a character set for the data without wrapping each column in a CONVERT() function.

Embedded escape sequences

The MySQL server interprets escape sequences in statements according to char acter_set_client, even when there's an introducer or collate clause. This is because the parser interprets the escape sequences in literal values. The parser is not collation-aware—as far as it is concerned, an introducer isn't an instruction, it's just a token.

Choosing a Character Set and Collation

MySQL 4.1 and later support a large range of character sets and collations, including support for multibyte characters with the UTF-8 encoding of the Unicode character set (MySQL supports a three-byte subset of full UTF-8 that can store most characters in most languages). You can see the supported character sets with the SHOW CHARACTER SET and SHOW COLLATION commands.

Keep It Simple

A mixture of character sets in your database can be a real mess. Incompatible character sets tend to be terribly confusing. They might even work fine until certain characters appear in your data, at which point you'll start getting problems in all sorts of operations (such as joins between tables). You can solve the errors only by using ALTER TABLE to convert columns to compatible character sets, or casting values to the desired character set with introducers and collate clauses in your SQL statements.

For sanity's sake, it's best to choose sensible defaults on the server level, and perhaps on the database level. Then you can deal with special exceptions on a case-by-case basis, probably at the column level.

The most common choices for collations are whether letters should sort in a case-sensitive or case-insensitive manner, or according to the encoding's binary value. The collation names generally end with _cs, _ci, or _bin, so you can tell which is which easily. The difference between case-sensitive and binary collations is that binary collations sort according to the byte values of the characters, whereas case-sensitive collations might have complex sorting rules such as those regarding multiple characters in languages like German.

When you specify a character set explicitly, you don't have to name both a character set and a collation. If you omit one or both, MySQL fills in the missing pieces from the applicable default. Table 7-2 shows how MySQL decides which character set and collation to use.

Table 7-2. How MySQL determines character set and collation defaults

If you specify	Resulting character set	Resulting collation
Both character set and collation	As specified	As specified
Character set only	As specified	Character set's default collation
Collation only	Character set to which collation belongs	As specified
Neither	Applicable default	Applicable default

The following commands show how to create a database, table, and column with explicitly specified character sets and collations:

```
CREATE DATABASE d CHARSET latin1;
CREATE TABLE d.t(
   col1 CHAR(1),
   col2 CHAR(1) CHARSET utf8,
   col3 CHAR(1) COLLATE latin1_bin
) DEFAULT CHARSET=cp1251;
```

The resulting table's columns have the following collations:

```
mysql> SHOW FULL COLUMNS FROM d.t;
+------+---------+-------------------+
|Field | Type    | Collation         |
+------+---------+-------------------+
|col1  | char(1) | cp1251_general_ci |
|col2  | char(1) | utf8_general_ci   |
|col3  | char(1) | latin1_bin        |
+------+---------+-------------------+
```

How Character Sets and Collations Affect Queries

Some character sets might require more CPU operations, consume more memory and storage space, or even defeat indexing. Therefore, you should choose character sets and collations carefully.

Converting between character sets or collations can add overhead for some operations. For example, the sakila.film table has an index on the title column, which can speed up ORDER BY queries:

```
mysql> EXPLAIN SELECT title, release_year FROM sakila.film ORDER BY title\G
*************************** 1. row ***************************
           id: 1
  select_type: SIMPLE
        table: film
         type: index
possible_keys: NULL
          key: idx_title
      key_len: 767
          ref: NULL
         rows: 953
        Extra:
```

However, the server can use the index for sorting only if it's sorted by the same collation as the one the query specifies. The index is sorted by the column's collation, which in this case is utf8_general_ci. If you want the results ordered by another collation, the server will have to do a filesort:

```
mysql> EXPLAIN SELECT title, release_year
    -> FROM sakila.film ORDER BY title COLLATE utf8_bin\G
*************************** 1. row ***************************
           id: 1
  select_type: SIMPLE
        table: film
         type: ALL
possible_keys: NULL
          key: NULL
      key_len: NULL
          ref: NULL
         rows: 953
        Extra: Using filesort
```

In addition to accommodating your connection's default character set and any preferences you specify explicitly in queries, MySQL has to convert character sets so that it can compare them when they're not the same. For example, if you join two tables on character columns that don't have the same character set, MySQL has to convert one of them. This conversion can make it impossible to use an index, because it is just like a function enclosing the column. If you're not sure whether something like this is happening, you can use EXPLAIN EXTENDED followed by SHOW WARNINGS to look at the query from the server's point of view. You'll see character sets in the query and you can often tell if something is being translated between character sets.

The UTF-8 multibyte character set stores each character in a varying number of bytes (between one and three). MySQL uses fixed-size buffers internally for many string operations, so it must allocate enough space to accommodate the maximum possible length. For example, a CHAR(10) encoded with UTF-8 requires 30 bytes to store, even if the actual string contains no so-called "wide" characters. Variable-length fields (VARCHAR, TEXT) do not suffer from this on disk, but in-memory temporary tables used for processing and sorting queries will always allocate the maximum length needed.

In multibyte character sets, a character is no longer the same as a byte. Consequently, MySQL has separate LENGTH() and CHAR_LENGTH() functions, which don't return the same results on multibyte characters. When you're working with multibyte character sets, be sure to use the CHAR_LENGTH() function when you want to count characters (e.g., when you're doing SUBSTRING() operations). The same caution holds for multibyte characters in application languages.

Another possible surprise is index limitations. If you index a UTF-8 column, MySQL has to assume each character can take up to three bytes, so the usual length restrictions are suddenly shortened by a factor of three:

```
mysql> CREATE TABLE big_string(str VARCHAR(500), KEY(str)) DEFAULT CHARSET=utf8;
Query OK, 0 rows affected, 1 warning (0.06 sec)
mysql> SHOW WARNINGS;
+---------+------+------------------------------------------------------------+
| Level   | Code | Message                                                    |
+---------+------+------------------------------------------------------------+
| Warning | 1071 | Specified key was too long; max key length is 999 bytes |
+---------+------+------------------------------------------------------------+
```

Notice that MySQL shortened the index to a 333-character prefix automatically:

```
mysql> SHOW CREATE TABLE big_string\G
*************************** 1. row ***************************
       Table: big_string
Create Table: CREATE TABLE `big_string` (
  `str` varchar(500) default NULL,
  KEY `str` (`str`(333))
) ENGINE=MyISAM DEFAULT CHARSET=utf8
```

If you didn't notice the warning and check the table definition, you might not have spotted that the index was created on only a prefix of the column. This will have side effects such as disabling covering indexes.

Some people recommend that you just use UTF-8 globally to "make your life simpler." However, this is not necessarily a good idea if you care about performance. Many applications don't need to use UTF-8 at all, and depending on your data, UTF-8 can use much more storage space on disk.

When deciding on a character set, it's important to consider the kind of data you will store. For example, if you store mostly English text UTF-8 will add practically no storage penalty, because most characters in the English language fit in one byte in UTF-8. On the other hand, you might see a big difference if you store non-Latin languages such as Russian or Arabic. An application that needs to store *only* Arabic could use the cp1256 character set, which can represent all Arabic characters in one byte. But if the application needs to store many different languages and you choose UTF-8 instead, the very same Arabic characters will use more space. Likewise, if you convert a column from a national character set to UTF-8, you can increase the required storage space dramatically. If you're using InnoDB, you might increase the data size to the point that the values don't fit on the page and require external storage, which can cause a lot of wasted storage space and fragmentation.

Sometimes you don't need to use a character set at all. Character sets are mostly useful for case-insensitive comparison, sorting, and string operations that need to be character-aware, such as SUBSTRING(). If you don't need the database server to be aware of characters, you can store anything you want in BINARY columns, including UTF-8 data. If you do this, you can also add a column that tells you what character set you used to encode the data. Although this is an approach some people have used for a long time, it does require you to be more careful. It can cause hard-to-catch mistakes, such as errors with SUBSTRING() and LENGTH(), if you forget that a byte is not necessarily a character. We recommend you avoid this practice if possible.

Full-Text Searching

Most of the queries you'll write will probably have WHERE clauses that compare values for equality, filter out ranges of rows, and so on. However, you might also need to perform keyword searches, which are based on relevance instead of comparing values to each other. Full-text search systems are designed for this purpose.

Full-text searches require a special query syntax. They can work with or without indexes, but indexes can speed up the matching. The indexes used for full-text searches have a special structure to help find documents that contain the desired keywords.

You might not know it, but you're already familiar with at least one type of full-text search system: Internet search engines. Although they operate at a massive scale and don't usually have a relational database for a backend, the principles are similar.

Full-text searching lets you search character-based content (CHAR, VARCHAR, and TEXT columns), and it supports both natural-language and Boolean searching. The full-text search implementation has a number of restrictions and limitations[9] and is quite complicated, but it's still widely used because it's included with the server and is adequate for many applications. In this section, we take a general look at how to use it and how to design for performance with full-text searching.

In standard MySQL, only the MyISAM storage engine supports full-text indexing at the time of writing, though there is a lab preview of InnoDB full-text search available for the unreleased MySQL 5.6, and there are third-party storage engines for full-text search, such as Groonga.

The fact that only MyISAM supports full-text search is a serious limitation that makes it a nonstarter for most applications, because it's just too painful to deal with table-level locking, data corruption, and crash recovery. In most cases you should simply use another solution, such as Sphinx, Lucene, Solr, Groonga, Xapian, or Senna, or wait for

---

9. In MySQL 5.1, you can use full-text parser plugins to extend full-text search. Still, you might find that MySQL's full-text limitations make it impractical or impossible to use for your application. We discuss using Sphinx as an external full-text search engine in Appendix F.

MySQL 5.6 to be released and use InnoDB. Still, if using MyISAM is acceptable for your application, read on.

A MyISAM full-text index operates on a *full-text collection*, which is made up of one or more character columns from a single table. In effect, MySQL builds the index by concatenating the columns in the collection and indexing them as one long string of text.

A MyISAM full-text index is a special type of B-Tree index with two levels. The first level holds keywords. Then, for each keyword, the second level holds a list of associated *document pointers* that point to full-text collections that contain that keyword. The index doesn't contain every word in the collection. It prunes it as follows:

- A list of *stopwords* weeds out "noise" words by preventing them from being indexed. The stopword list is based on common English usage by default, but you can use the ft_stopword_file option to replace it with a list from an external file.

- The index ignores words unless they're longer than ft_min_word_len characters and shorter than ft_max_word_len characters.

Full-text indexes don't store information about which column in the collection a keyword occurs in, so if you need to search on different combinations of columns, you will need to create several indexes.

This also means you can't instruct a MATCH AGAINST clause to regard words from a particular column as more important than words from other columns. This is a common requirement when building search engines for websites. For example, you might want search results to appear first when the keywords appear in an item's title. If you need this, you'll have to write more complicated queries. (We show an example later.)

Natural-Language Full-Text Searches

A natural-language search query determines each document's relevance to the query. Relevance is based on the number of matched words and the frequency with which they occur in the document. Words that are less common in the entire index make a match more relevant. In contrast, extremely common words aren't worth searching for at all. A natural-language full-text search excludes words that exist in more than 50% of the rows in the table, even if they're not in the stopword list.[10]

The syntax of a full-text search is a little different from other types of queries. You tell MySQL to do full-text matching with MATCH AGAINST in the WHERE clause. Let's look at an example. In the standard Sakila sample database, the film_text table has a full-text index on the title and description columns:

---

10. A common mistake during testing is to put a few rows of sample data into a full-text search index, only to find that no queries match. The problem is that every word appears in more than half the rows.

```
mysql> SHOW INDEX FROM sakila.film_text;
+-----------+----------------------+-------------+------------+
| Table     | Key_name             | Column_name | Index_type |
+-----------+----------------------+-------------+------------+
| ...
| film_text | idx_title_description | title       | FULLTEXT   |
| film_text | idx_title_description | description | FULLTEXT   |
+-----------+----------------------+-------------+------------+
```

Here's an example natural-language full-text search query:

```
mysql> SELECT film_id, title, RIGHT(description, 25),
    ->     MATCH(title, description) AGAINST('factory casualties') AS relevance
    -> FROM sakila.film_text
    -> WHERE MATCH(title, description) AGAINST('factory casualties');
+---------+--------------------+---------------------------+-----------------+
| film_id | title              | RIGHT(description, 25)     | relevance       |
+---------+--------------------+---------------------------+-----------------+
|     831 | SPIRITED CASUALTIES | a Car in A Baloon Factory | 8.4692449569702 |
|     126 | CASUALTIES ENCINO  | Face a Boy in A Monastery | 5.2615661621094 |
|     193 | CROSSROADS CASUALTIES | a Composer in The Outback | 5.2072987556458 |
|     369 | GOODFELLAS SALUTE  | d Cow in A Baloon Factory | 3.1522686481476 |
|     451 | IGBY MAKER         | a Dog in A Baloon Factory | 3.1522686481476 |
+---------+--------------------+---------------------------+-----------------+
```

MySQL performed the full-text search by breaking the search string into words and matching each of them against the title and description fields, which are combined in the full-text collection upon which the index is built. Notice that only one of the results contains both words, and that the three results that contain "casualties" (there are only three in the entire table) are listed first. That's because the index sorts the results by decreasing relevance.

> Unlike with normal queries, the results of full-text searches are automatically ordered by relevance. MySQL cannot use an index for sorting when you perform a full-text search. Therefore, you shouldn't specify an ORDER BY clause if you want to avoid a filesort.

The MATCH() function actually returns the relevance as a floating-point number, as you can see from our example. You can use this to filter by relevance or to present the relevance in a user interface. There is no extra overhead from specifying the MATCH() function twice; MySQL recognizes they are the same and does the operation only once. However, if you put the MATCH() function in an ORDER BY clause, MySQL will use a filesort to order the results.

You have to specify the columns in the MATCH() clause exactly as they're specified in a full-text index, or MySQL can't use the index. This is because the index doesn't record in which column a keyword appeared.

This also means you can't use a full-text search to specify that a keyword should appear in a particular column of the index, as we mentioned previously. However, there's a workaround: you can do custom sorting with several full-text indexes on different combinations of columns to compute the desired ranking. Suppose we want the title column to be more important. We can add another index on this column, as follows:

```
mysql> ALTER TABLE film_text ADD FULLTEXT KEY(title) ;
```

Now we can make the title twice as important for purposes of ranking:

```
mysql> SELECT film_id, RIGHT(description, 25),
    -> ROUND(MATCH(title, description) AGAINST('factory casualties'), 3)
    ->    AS full_rel,
    -> ROUND(MATCH(title) AGAINST('factory casualties'), 3) AS title_rel
    -> FROM sakila.film_text
    -> WHERE MATCH(title, description) AGAINST('factory casualties')
    -> ORDER BY (2 * MATCH(title) AGAINST('factory casualties'))
    ->    + MATCH(title, description) AGAINST('factory casualties') DESC;
+---------+---------------------------+----------+-----------+
| film_id | RIGHT(description, 25)     | full_rel | title_rel |
+---------+---------------------------+----------+-----------+
|     831 | a Car in A Baloon Factory |    8.469 |     5.676 |
|     126 | Face a Boy in A Monastery |    5.262 |     5.676 |
|     299 | jack in The Sahara Desert |    3.056 |     6.751 |
|     193 | a Composer in The Outback |    5.207 |     5.676 |
|     369 | d Cow in A Baloon Factory |    3.152 |     0.000 |
|     451 | a Dog in A Baloon Factory |    3.152 |     0.000 |
|     595 | a Cat in A Baloon Factory |    3.152 |     0.000 |
|     649 | nizer in A Baloon Factory |    3.152 |     0.000 |
```

However, this is usually an inefficient approach because it causes filesorts.

Boolean Full-Text Searches

In Boolean searches, the query itself specifies the relative relevance of each word in a match. Boolean searches use the stopword list to filter out noise words, but the requirement that search terms be longer than ft_min_word_len characters and shorter than ft_max_word_len characters is disabled.[11] The results are unsorted.

When constructing a Boolean search query, you can use prefixes to modify the relative ranking of each keyword in the search string. The most commonly used modifiers are shown in Table 7-3.

Table 7-3. Common modifiers for Boolean full-text searches

Example	Meaning
dinosaur	Rows containing "dinosaur" rank higher.
~dinosaur	Rows containing "dinosaur" rank lower.
+dinosaur	Rows *must* contain "dinosaur".

11. Full-text indexes won't even contain words that are too short or too long, but that's a different matter. Here we refer to the fact that the server won't strip words from the search phrase if they're too short or too long, which it normally does as part of the query optimization process.

Example	Meaning
-dinosaur	Rows *must not* contain "dinosaur".
dino*	Rows containing words that begin with "dino" rank higher.

You can also use other operators, such as parentheses for grouping. You can construct complex searches in this way.

As an example, let's again search the `sakila.film_text` table for films that contain both "factory" and "casualties." A natural-language search returns results that match either or both of these terms, as we saw before. If we use a Boolean search, however, we can insist that both must appear:

```
mysql> SELECT film_id, title, RIGHT(description, 25)
    -> FROM sakila.film_text
    -> WHERE MATCH(title, description)
    ->     AGAINST('+factory +casualties' IN BOOLEAN MODE);
+---------+-------------------+---------------------------+
| film_id | title             | RIGHT(description, 25)    |
+---------+-------------------+---------------------------+
|     831 | SPIRITED CASUALTIES | a Car in A Baloon Factory |
+---------+-------------------+---------------------------+
```

You can also do a *phrase search* by quoting multiple words, which requires them to appear exactly as specified:

```
mysql> SELECT film_id, title, RIGHT(description, 25)
    -> FROM sakila.film_text
    -> WHERE MATCH(title, description)
    ->     AGAINST('"spirited casualties"' IN BOOLEAN MODE);
+---------+-------------------+---------------------------+
| film_id | title             | RIGHT(description, 25)    |
+---------+-------------------+---------------------------+
|     831 | SPIRITED CASUALTIES | a Car in A Baloon Factory |
+---------+-------------------+---------------------------+
```

Phrase searches tend to be quite slow. The full-text index alone can't answer a query like this one, because it doesn't record where words are located relative to each other in the original full-text collection. Consequently, the server actually has to look inside the rows to do a phrase search.

To execute such a search, the server will find all documents that contain both "spirited" and "casualties." It will then fetch the rows from which the documents were built, and check for the exact phrase in the collection. Because it uses the full-text index to find the initial list of documents that match, you might think this will be very fast—much faster than an equivalent LIKE operation. In fact, it *is* very fast, as long as the words in the phrase aren't common and not many results are returned from the full-text index to the Boolean matcher. If the words in the phrase *are* common, LIKE can actually be much faster, because it fetches rows sequentially instead of in quasirandom index order, and it doesn't need to read a full-text index.

A Boolean full-text search doesn't actually require a full-text index to work, although it does require the MyISAM storage engine. It will use a full-text index if there is one, but if there isn't, it will just scan the entire table. You can even use a Boolean full-text search on columns from multiple tables, such as the results of a join. In all of these cases, though, it will be slow.

Full-Text Changes in MySQL 5.1

MySQL 5.1 introduced quite a few changes related to full-text searching. These include performance improvements and the ability to build pluggable parsers that can enhance the built-in capabilities. For example, plugin can change the way indexing works. They can split text into words more flexibly than the defaults (you can specify that "C++" is a single word, for example), do preprocessing, index different content types (such as PDF), or do custom word stemming. The plugins can also influence the way searches work—for example, by stemming search terms.

Full-Text Tradeoffs and Workarounds

MySQL's implementation of full-text searching has several design limitations. These can be contraindications for specific purposes, but there are also many ways to work around them.

For example, there is only one form of relevance ranking in MySQL's full-text indexing: frequency. The index doesn't record the indexed word's position in the string, so proximity doesn't contribute to relevance. Although that's fine for many purposes—especially for small amounts of data—it might not be what you need, and MySQL's full-text indexing doesn't give you the flexibility to choose a different ranking algorithm. (It doesn't even store the data you'd need for proximity-based ranking.)

Size is another issue. MySQL's full-text indexing performs well when the index fits in memory, but if the index is not in memory it can be very slow, especially when the fields are large. When you're using phrase searches, the data and indexes must both fit in memory for good performance. Compared to other index types, it can be very expensive to insert, update, or delete rows in a full-text index:

- Modifying a piece of text with 100 words requires not 1 but up to 100 index operations.
- The field length doesn't usually affect other index types much, but with full-text indexing, text with 3 words and text with 10,000 words will have performance profiles that differ by orders of magnitude.
- Full-text search indexes are also much more prone to fragmentation, and you might find you need to use OPTIMIZE TABLE more frequently.

Full-text indexes affect how the server optimizes queries, too. Index choice, WHERE clauses, and ORDER BY all work differently from how you might expect:

- If there's a full-text index and the query has a `MATCH AGAINST` clause that can use it, MySQL will use the full-text index to process the query. It will not compare the full-text index to the other indexes that might be used for the query. Some of these other indexes might actually be better for the query, but MySQL will not consider them.

- The full-text search index can perform only full-text matches. Any other criteria in the query, such as `WHERE` clauses, must be applied after MySQL reads the row from the table. This is different from the behavior of other types of indexes, which can be used to check several parts of a `WHERE` clause at once.

- Full-text indexes don't store the actual text they index. Thus, you can never use a full-text index as a covering index.

- Full-text indexes cannot be used for any type of sorting, other than sorting by relevance in natural-language mode. If you need to sort by something other than relevance, MySQL will use a filesort.

Let's see how these constraints affect queries. Suppose you have a million documents, with an ordinary index on the document's author and a full-text index on the content. You want to do a full-text search on the document content, but only for author 123. You might write the query as follows:

```
... WHERE MATCH(content) AGAINST ('High Performance MySQL')
    AND author = 123;
```

However, this query will be very inefficient. MySQL will search all one million documents first, because it prefers the full-text index. It will then apply the `WHERE` clause to restrict the results to the given author, but this filtering operation won't be able to use the index on the author.

One workaround is to include the author IDs in the full-text index. You can choose a prefix that's very unlikely to appear in the text, then append the author's ID to it, and include this "word" in a `filters` column that's maintained separately (perhaps by a trigger).

You can then extend the full-text index to include the `filters` column and rewrite the query as follows:

```
... WHERE MATCH(content, filters)
    AGAINST ('High Performance MySQL +author_id_123' IN BOOLEAN MODE);
```

This might be more efficient if the author ID is very selective, because MySQL will be able to narrow the list of documents very quickly by searching the full-text index for "author_id_123". If it's not selective, though, the performance might be worse. Be careful with this approach.

Sometimes you can use full-text indexes for bounding-box searches. For instance, if you want to restrict searches to a range of coordinates (for geographically constrained searches), you can encode the coordinates into the full-text collection. Suppose the coordinates for a given row are X=123 and Y=456. You can interleave the coordinates with the most significant digits first, as in XY142536, and place them in a column that is included in the full-text index. Now if you want to limit searches to, for example, a rectangle bounded by X between 100 and 199 and Y between 400 and 499, you can add "+XY14*" to the search query. This can be faster than filtering with a WHERE clause.

A technique that sometimes works well with full-text indexes, especially for paginated displays, is to select a list of primary keys by a full-text query and cache the results. When the application is ready to render some results, it can issue another query that fetches the desired rows by their IDs. This second query can include more complicated criteria or joins that need to use other indexes to work well.

Even though only MyISAM supports full-text indexes, if you need to use InnoDB or another storage engine instead, you can replicate your tables to a server that uses the MyISAM storage engine, then use the replica to serve full-text queries. If you don't want to serve some queries from a different server, you can partition a table vertically by breaking it into two, keeping textual columns separate from the rest of the data.

You can also duplicate some columns into a table that's full-text indexed. You can see this strategy in action in the `sakila.film_text` table, which is maintained with triggers. Yet another alternative is to use an external full-text engine, such as Lucene or Sphinx. You can read more about Sphinx in Appendix F.

GROUP BY queries with full-text searches can be performance killers, again because the full-text query typically finds a lot of matches; these cause random disk I/O, followed by a temporary table or filesort for the grouping. Because such queries are often just looking for the top items per group, a good optimization is to sample the results instead of trying for complete accuracy. For example, select the first 1,000 rows into a temporary table, then return the top result per group from that.

Full-Text Configuration and Optimization

Regular maintenance of your full-text indexes is one of the most important things you can do to enhance performance. The double-B-Tree structure of full-text indexes, combined with the large number of keywords in typical documents, means they suffer from fragmentation much more than normal indexes. You might need to use OPTIMIZE TABLE frequently to defragment the indexes. If your server is I/O-bound, it might be much faster to just drop and recreate the full-text indexes periodically.

A server that must perform well for full-text searches needs key buffers that are large enough to hold the full-text indexes, because they work much better when they're in memory. You can use dedicated key buffers to make sure other indexes don't flush your full-text indexes from the key buffer. See Chapter 8 for more details on MyISAM key buffers.

It's also important to provide a good stopword list. The defaults will work well for English prose, but they might not be good for other languages or for specialized texts, such as technical documents. For example, if you're indexing a document about

MySQL, you might want "mysql" to be a stopword, because it's too common to be helpful.

You can often improve performance by skipping short words. The length is configurable with the ft_min_word_len parameter. Increasing the default value will skip more words, making your index smaller and faster, but less accurate. Also bear in mind that for special purposes, you might need very short words. For example, a full-text search of consumer electronics products for the query "cd player" is likely to produce lots of irrelevant results unless short words are allowed in the index. A user searching for "cd player" won't want to see MP3 and DVD players in the results, but if the minimum word length is the default four characters, the search will actually be for just "player," so all types of players will be returned.

The stopword list and the minimum word length can improve search speeds by keeping some words out of the index, but the search quality can suffer as a result. The right balance is application-dependent. If you need good performance and good-quality results, you'll have to customize both parameters for your application. It's a good idea to build in some logging and then investigate common searches, uncommon searches, searches that don't return results, and searches that return a lot of results. You can gain insight about your users and your searchable content this way, and then use that insight to improve performance and the quality of your search results.

 Be aware that if you change the minimum word length, you'll have to rebuild the index with OPTIMIZE TABLE for the change to take effect. A related parameter is ft_max_word_len, which is mainly a safeguard to avoid indexing very long keywords.

If you're importing a lot of data into a server and you want full-text indexing on some columns, disable the full-text indexes before the import with DISABLE KEYS and enable them afterward with ENABLE KEYS. This is usually much faster because of the high cost of updating the index for each row inserted, and you'll get a defragmented index as a bonus.

For large datasets, you might need to manually partition the data across many nodes and search them in parallel. This is a difficult task, and you might be better off using an external full-text search engine, such as Lucene or Sphinx. Our experience shows they can have orders of magnitude better performance.

Distributed (XA) Transactions

Whereas storage engine (see "Transactions" on page 6) transactions give ACID properties inside the storage engine, a distributed (XA) transaction is a higher-level transaction that can extend some ACID properties outside the storage engine—and even outside the database—with a two-phase commit. MySQL 5.0 and newer have partial support for XA transactions.

An XA transaction requires a transaction coordinator, which asks all participants to prepare to commit (phase one). When the coordinator receives a "ready" from all participants, it tells them all to go ahead and commit. This is phase two. MySQL can act as a participant in XA transactions, but not as a coordinator.

There are actually two kinds of XA transactions in MySQL. The MySQL server can participate in an externally managed distributed transaction, but it also uses XA internally to coordinate storage engines and binary logging.

Internal XA Transactions

The reason for MySQL's internal use of XA transactions is the architectural separation between the server and the storage engines. Storage engines are completely independent from and unaware of each other, so any cross-engine transaction is distributed by nature and requires a third party to coordinate it. That third party is the MySQL server. Were it not for XA transactions, for example, a cross-engine transaction commit would require sequentially asking each engine involved to commit. That would introduce the possibility of a crash after one engine had committed but before another did, which would break the rules of transactions (recall that transactions are supposed to be all-or-nothing operations).

If you consider the binary log to be a "storage engine" for log events, you can see why XA transactions are necessary even when only a single transactional engine is involved. Synchronizing a storage engine commit with "committing" an event to the binary log is a distributed transaction, because the server—not the storage engine—handles the binary log.

XA currently creates a performance dilemma. It has broken InnoDB's support for *group commit* (a technique that can commit several transactions with a single I/O operation) since MySQL 5.0, so it causes many more `fsync()` calls than it should.[12] It also causes each transaction to require a binary log sync if binary logs are enabled and requires two InnoDB transaction log flushes per commit instead of one. In other words, if you want the binary log to be safely synchronized with your transactions, each transaction will require a total of at least three `fsync()` calls. The only way to prevent this is to disable the binary log and set `innodb_support_xa` to 0.[13]

---

12. At the time of writing, a lot of work has gone into fixing the group commit problem, and there are at least three competing implementations. It remains to be seen which one ends up in the official MySQL source code that most people will use, or which version it will be fixed in. The version available in MariaDB and Percona Server appears to be a good solution.

13. A common misconception is that `innodb_support_xa` is only needed if you use XA transactions. This is incorrect: it controls the internal XA transactions between the storage engine and the binary log, and if you value your data, you need this setting to be enabled.

These settings are unsafe and incompatible with replication. Replication requires binary logging and XA support, and in addition—to be as safe as possible—you need sync_binlog set to 1, so the storage engine and the binary log are synchronized. (The XA support is worthless otherwise, because the binary log might not be "committed" to disk.) This is one of the reasons we strongly recommend using a RAID controller with a battery-backed write cache: the cache can speed up the extra fsync() calls and restore performance.

The next chapter goes into more detail on how to configure transaction logging and binary logging.

External XA Transactions

MySQL can participate in, but not manage, external distributed transactions. It doesn't support the full XA specification. For example, the XA specification allows connections to be joined in a single transaction, but that's not possible in MySQL at this time.

External XA transactions are even more expensive than internal ones, due to the added latency and the greater likelihood of a participant failing. Using XA over a WAN, or even over the Internet, is a common trap because of unpredictable network performance. It's generally best to avoid XA transactions when there's an unpredictable component, such as a slow network or a user who might not click the "Save" button for a long time. Anything that delays the commit has a heavy cost, because it's causing delays not just on one system, but potentially on many.

You can design high-performance distributed transactions in other ways, though. For instance, you can insert and queue data locally, then distribute it atomically in a much smaller, faster transaction. You can also use MySQL replication to ship data from one place to another. We've found that some applications that use distributed transactions really don't need to use them at all.

That said, XA transactions can be a useful way to synchronize data between servers. This method works well when you can't use replication for some reason, or when the updates are not performance-critical.

The MySQL Query Cache

Many database products can cache query execution plans, so the server can skip the SQL parsing and optimization stages for repeated queries. MySQL can do this in some circumstances, but it also has a different type of cache (known as the *query cache*) that stores *complete result sets* for SELECT statements. This section focuses on that cache.

The MySQL query cache holds the exact bits that a completed query returned to the client. When a query cache hit occurs, the server can simply return the stored results immediately, skipping the parsing, optimization, and execution steps.

The query cache keeps track of which tables a query uses, and if any of those tables changes, it invalidates the cache entry. This coarse invalidation policy might seem inefficient, because the changes made to the tables might not affect the results stored in the cache, but it's a simple approach with low overhead, which is important on a busy system.

The query cache is designed to be completely transparent to the application. The application does not need to know whether MySQL returned data from the cache or actually executed the query. The result should be the same either way. In other words, the query cache doesn't change semantics; the server appears to behave the same way with it enabled or disabled.[14]

As servers have gotten larger and more powerful, the query cache has unfortunately proven not to be a very scalable part of MySQL. It is effectively a single point of contention for the whole server, and it can cause severe stalls on multicore servers. Although we'll go into quite a bit of detail about how to configure it, we think that the best approach is actually to disable it by default, and configure a small query cache (no more than a few dozen megabytes) only if it's very beneficial. We'll explain later how to determine if the query cache is likely to be beneficial for your workload.

How MySQL Checks for a Cache Hit

The way MySQL checks for a cache hit is simple: the cache is a lookup table. The lookup key is a hash of the query text itself, the current database, the client protocol version, and a handful of other things that might affect the actual bytes in the query's result.

MySQL does not parse, "normalize," or parameterize a statement when it checks for a cache hit; it uses the statement and other bits of data exactly as the client sends them. Any difference in character case, spacing, or comments—any difference at all—will prevent a query from matching a previously cached version.[15] This is something to keep in mind while writing queries. Using consistent formatting and style is a good habit anyway, but in this case it can even make your system faster.

Another caching consideration is that the query cache will not store a result unless the query that generated it was deterministic. Thus, any query that contains a nondeterministic function, such as NOW() or CURRENT_DATE(), will not be cached. Similarly, functions such as CURRENT_USER() or CONNECTION_ID() might vary when executed by different users, thereby preventing a cache hit. In fact, the query cache does not work for queries

---

14. The query cache actually does change semantics in one subtle way: by default, a query can still be served from the cache when one of the tables to which it refers is locked with LOCK TABLES. You can disable this with the query_cache_wlock_invalidate variable.

15. Percona Server is an exception to this rule; it can strip comments from queries before comparing them to the query cache. This feature is needed because it's a common, and good, practice to insert comments into queries with additional information about the process that invoked them. The PHP instrumentation software that we discussed in Chapter 3 relies on this, for example.

---

that refer to user-defined functions, stored functions, user variables, temporary tables, tables in the `mysql` database, or any table that has a column-level privilege. (For a list of everything that makes a query uncacheable, see the MySQL manual.)

We've heard statements such as "MySQL doesn't check the cache if the query contains a nondeterministic function." This is incorrect. MySQL cannot know whether a query contains a nondeterministic function unless it parses the query, and the cache lookup happens *before* parsing. The server performs a case-insensitive check to verify that the query begins with the letters `SEL`, but that's all.

However, it is correct to say "The server will find no results in the cache if the query contains a function such as `NOW()`," because even if the server executed the same query earlier, it will not have cached the results. MySQL marks a query as uncacheable as soon as it notices a construct that forbids caching, and the results generated by such a query are not stored.

A useful technique to enable the caching of queries that refer to the current date is to include the date as a literal value, instead of using a function. For example:

```
... DATE_SUB(CURRENT_DATE, INTERVAL 1 DAY) -- Not cacheable!
... DATE_SUB('2007-07-14', INTERVAL 1 DAY) -- Cacheable
```

Because the query cache works at the level of a complete `SELECT` statement when the server first receives it from the client connection, identical queries made inside a subquery or view cannot use the query cache, and neither can queries in stored procedures. Prepared statements also cannot use the query cache in versions prior to MySQL 5.1.

MySQL's query cache can sometimes improve performance, but there are a few issues you should be aware of when using it. First, enabling the query cache adds some overhead for both reads and writes:

- Read queries must check the cache before beginning.
- If the query is cacheable and isn't in the cache yet, there's some overhead due to storing the result after generating it.
- There's overhead for write queries, which must invalidate the cache entries for queries that use tables they change. Invalidation can be very costly if the cache is fragmented and/or large (has many cached queries, or is configured to use a large amount of memory).

The query cache can still be a net gain. However, as we explain later, the extra overhead can add up, especially in combination with contention caused by queries trying to lock the cache to perform operations on it.

For InnoDB users, another problem is that transactions limit the query cache's usefulness. When a statement inside a transaction modifies a table, the server invalidates any cached queries that refer to the table, even though InnoDB's multiversioning might hide the transaction's changes from other statements. The table is also globally uncacheable until the transaction commits, so no further queries against that table—

whether inside or outside the transaction—can be cached until the transaction commits. Long-running transactions can, therefore, increase the number of query cache misses.

Invalidation can become a very serious problem with a large query cache. If there are many queries in the cache, the invalidation can take a long time and cause the entire system to stall while it works. This is because there's a single global lock on the query cache, which will block all queries that need to access it. Accessing happens both when checking for a hit and when checking whether there are any queries to invalidate. Chapter 3 includes a real case study that shows excessive query cache invalidation overhead.

How the Cache Uses Memory

MySQL stores the query cache completely in memory, so you need to understand how it uses memory before you can configure it correctly. The cache stores more than just query results in its memory. It's a lot like a filesystem in some ways: it keeps structures that help it figure out which memory in its pool is free, mappings between tables and query results, query text, and the query results.

Aside from some basic housekeeping structures, which require about 40 KB, the query cache's memory pool is available to be used in variable-sized *blocks*. Every block knows what type it is, how large it is, and how much data it contains, and it holds pointers to the next and previous logical and physical blocks. Blocks can be of several types: they can store cache results, lists of tables used by a query, query text, and so on. However, the different types of blocks are treated in much the same way, so there's no need to distinguish among them for purposes of configuring the query cache.

When the server starts, it initializes the memory for the query cache. The memory pool is initially a single free block. This block is as large as the entire amount of memory the cache is configured to use, minus the housekeeping structures.

When the server caches a query's results, it reserves a block from its memory pool to store those results. This block must be a minimum of query_cache_min_res_unit bytes, though it might be larger if the server knows it is storing a larger result. Unfortunately, the server cannot choose a block of precisely the right size, because it makes its initial choice before the result set is complete. The server does not build the entire result set in memory and then send it—it's much more efficient to send each row as it's generated. Consequently, when it begins caching the result set, the server has no way of knowing how large it will eventually be.

Assigning blocks is a relatively slow process, because it requires the server to look at its lists of free blocks to find one that's big enough. Therefore, the server tries to minimize the number of times it performs this task. When it needs to cache a result set, it chooses a block of at least the minimum size (possibly larger, for reasons too complex to explain) and begins placing the results in that block. If the block becomes full while there is still data left to store, the server reserves a new block—again of at least the minimum size—and continues storing the data in that block. When the result is finished, if there is space left in the last block the server trims it to size and merges the leftover space into the adjacent free block. Figure 7-3 illustrates this process.[16]

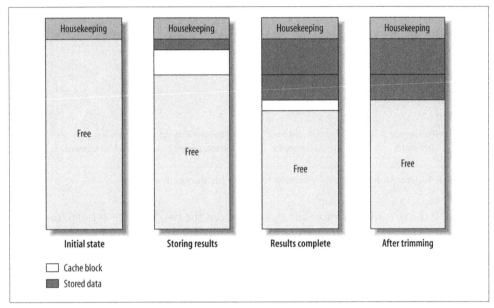

Figure 7-3. How the query cache allocates blocks to store a result

When we say the server "reserves a block," we don't mean it is asking the operating system to allocate memory with malloc() or a similar call. It does that only once, when it creates the query cache. What we mean is that the server is examining its list of blocks and either choosing the best place to put a new block or, if necessary, removing the oldest cached query to make room. In other words, the MySQL server manages its own memory; it does not rely on the operating system to do it.

So far, this is all pretty straightforward. However, the picture can become quite a bit more complicated than it appeared in Figure 7-3. Let's suppose the average result is quite small, and the server is sending results to two client connections simultaneously. Trimming the results can leave a free block that's smaller than query_cache _min_res_unit and cannot be used for storing future cache results. The block allocation might end up looking something like Figure 7-4.

---

16. We've simplified the diagrams in this section for the purposes of illustration. The server really reserves query cache blocks in a more complicated fashion than we've shown here. If you're interested in how it works, the comments at the top of *sql/sql_cache.cc* in the server's source code explain it very clearly.

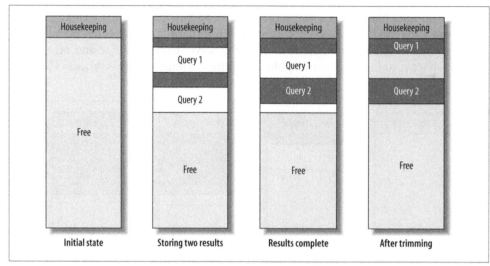

Housekeeping	Housekeeping	Housekeeping	Housekeeping
Free	Query 1	Query 1	Query 1
	Query 2	Query 2	Query 2
	Free	Free	Free
Initial state	Storing two results	Results complete	After trimming

Figure 7-4. Fragmentation caused by storing results in the query cache

Trimming the first result to size left a gap between the two results—a block too small to use for storing a different query result. The appearance of such gaps is called *fragmentation*, and it's a classic problem in memory and filesystem allocation. Fragmentation can happen for a number of reasons, including cache invalidations, which can leave blocks that are too small to reuse later.

When the Query Cache Is Helpful

Caching queries isn't automatically more efficient than not caching them. Caching takes work, and the query cache results in a net gain only if the savings are greater than the overhead. This will depend on your server's workload.

In theory, you can tell whether the cache is helpful by comparing the amount of work the server has to do with the cache enabled and disabled. With the cache disabled, each read query has to execute and return its results, and each write query has to execute. With the cache enabled, each read query has to first check the cache and then either return the stored result or, if there isn't one, execute, generate the result, store it, and return it. Each write query has to execute and then check whether there are any cached queries that must be invalidated.

Although this might sound straightforward, it's not—it's hard to calculate or predict the query cache's benefit. You must also take into account external factors. For example, the query cache can reduce the amount of time required to produce a query's result, but not the time it takes to send the result to the client program, which might be the dominating factor.

In addition, MySQL provides no good way to determine how beneficial the query cache is for individual queries,[17] because the counters in SHOW STATUS are aggregated over the whole workload. But the average behavior usually isn't really interesting. For example, you might have one slow query that becomes much faster with the help of the query cache, even though it makes everything else a little bit slower or even makes the server slower on average. Is this what you want? It might actually be the right thing to do, if the queries that get faster are ones to which users are very sensitive and the others aren't so important. This would be a good candidate for selective use of the cache with the SQL_CACHE directive.

The type of query that benefits most from caching is one whose result is expensive to generate but doesn't take up much space in the cache, so it's cheap to store, return to the client, and invalidate. Aggregate queries, such as small COUNT() results from large tables, fit into this category. However, some other types of queries might be worth caching, too. As a rule of thumb, you can consider the query cache if your workload is dominated by complex SELECT queries, such as multitable joins with ORDER BY and LIMIT clauses, which produce small result sets. You should have very few UPDATE, DELETE, and INSERT queries in comparison to these complex SELECT queries.

One of the ways to tell if you are benefiting from the query cache is to examine the query cache hit rate. This is the number of queries that are served from the cache instead of being executed by the server. When the server receives a SELECT statement, it increments either the Qcache_hits or the Com_select status variable, depending on whether the query was cached. Thus, the query cache hit rate is given by the formula Qcache_hits / (Qcache_hits+Com_select).

Unfortunately, the cache hit rate isn't easy to interpret. What's a good cache hit rate? It depends. Even a 30% hit rate can be very helpful, because the work saved by not executing queries could be much more (per query) than the overhead of invalidating entries and storing results in the cache. It is also important to know which queries are cached. If the cache hits represent the most expensive queries, even a low hit rate could save work for the server. So there is no simple rule that tells you whether the query cache hit rate is good or not.

Any SELECT query that MySQL doesn't serve from the cache is a *cache miss*. A cache miss can occur for any of the following reasons:

- The query is not cacheable, either because it contains a nondeterministic construct (such as CURRENT_DATE) or because its result set is too large to store. Both types of uncacheable queries increment the Qcache_not_cached status variable.
- The server has never seen the query before, so it never had a chance to cache its result.

---

17. The enhanced "slow query log" in Percona Server and MariaDB reveals whether individual queries were cache hits.

- The query's result was previously cached, but the server removed it. This can happen because there wasn't enough memory to keep it, because someone instructed the server to remove it, or because it was invalidated (more on invalidations in a moment).

If your server has a lot of cache misses but very few uncacheable queries, one of the following must be true:

- The query cache is not warmed up yet. That is, the server hasn't had a chance to fill the cache with result sets.
- The server is seeing queries it hasn't seen before. If you don't have a lot of repeated queries, this can happen even after the cache is warmed up.
- There are a lot of cache invalidations.

Cache invalidations can happen because of fragmentation, insufficient memory, or data modifications. If you have allocated enough memory to the cache and configured the query_cache_min_res_unit value properly, most cache invalidations should be due to data modifications. You can see how many queries have modified data by examining the Com_* status variables (Com_update, Com_delete, and so forth), and you can check the Qcache_lowmem_prunes variable to see how many queries have been invalidated due to low memory.

It's a good idea to consider the overhead of invalidation separately from the hit rate. As an extreme example, suppose you have one table that gets all the reads and has a 100% query cache hit rate, and another table that gets only updates. If you simply calculate the hit rate from the status variables, you will see a 100% hit rate. However, the query cache can still be inefficient, because it will slow down the update queries. All update queries will have to check whether any of the queries in the query cache need to be invalidated as a result of their modifications, but since the answer will always be "no," this is wasted work. You might not spot a problem such as this unless you check the number of uncacheable queries as well as the hit rate.

A server that handles a balanced blend of writes and cacheable reads on the same tables also might not benefit much from the query cache. The writes will constantly invalidate cached results, while at the same time the cacheable reads will constantly insert new results into the cache. These will be beneficial only if they are subsequently served from the cache.

If a cached result is invalidated before the server receives the same SELECT statement again, storing it was a waste of time and memory. Examine the relative sizes of Com_select and Qcache_inserts to see whether this is happening. If nearly every SELECT is a cache miss (thus incrementing Com_select) and subsequently stores its result into the cache, Qcache_inserts will be nearly as large as Com_select. Thus, you'd like Qcache_inserts to be much smaller than Com_select, at least when the cache is properly warmed up. However, this is still a hard-to-interpret ratio because of the subtleties of what's happening inside the cache and the server.

As you've seen, the hit rate and the insert-to-select rate are not good guides. It's really best to measure and calculate how much the cache could help your workload. But if you want, you can look at a different ratio, the hit-to-insert ratio. That indicates the size of Qcache_hits relative to Qcache_inserts. As a rough rule of thumb, a hit-to-insert ratio of 3:1 or better might be worth considering for average quick queries, but it's much better to have 10:1 or higher. If you aren't achieving this level of benefit from your query cache, it's probably better to disable it, unless you have done the math and determined that two things are true for your server: hits are way cheaper than misses, and query cache contention isn't a problem.

Every application has a finite *potential cache size*, even if there are no write queries. The potential cache size is the amount of memory required to store every possible cacheable query the application will ever issue. In theory, this is an extremely large number for most applications. In practice, many applications have a much smaller usable cache size than you might expect, because of the number of invalidations. Even if you make the query cache very large, it will never fill up more than the potential cache size.

You should monitor how much of the query cache your server actually uses. If it doesn't use as much memory as you've given it, make it smaller. If memory restrictions are causing excessive invalidations you can try making it bigger, but as mentioned previously, it can be dangerous to exceed a few dozen megabytes. (This depends on your hardware and workload.)

You also have to balance the query cache with the other server caches, such as the InnoDB buffer pool or the MyISAM key cache. It's not possible to just give a ratio or a simple formula for this, because the right balance depends on the application.

The best way to know how beneficial the query cache really is is to measure how long queries take to execute with and without the cache, if possible. Percona Server's extended slow query log can report whether a query was a cache hit or not. If the query cache isn't saving you a significant amount of time, it's probably best to try disabling it.

How to Configure and Maintain the Query Cache

Once you understand how the query cache works, it's easy to configure. It has only a few moving parts:

query_cache_type
: Whether the query cache is enabled. Possible values are OFF, ON, or DEMAND, where the latter means that only queries containing the SQL_CACHE modifier are eligible for caching. This is both a session-level and a global variable. (See Chapter 8 for details on session and global variables.)

`query_cache_size`

> The total memory to allocate to the query cache, in bytes. This must be a multiple of 1,024 bytes, so MySQL might use a slightly different value than the one you specify.

`query_cache_min_res_unit`

> The minimum size when allocating a block. We explained this setting previously; it's discussed further in the next section.

`query_cache_limit`

> The largest result set that MySQL will cache. Queries whose results are larger than this setting will not be cached. Remember that the server caches results as it generates them, so it doesn't know in advance when a result will be too large to cache.
>
> If the result exceeds the specified limit, MySQL will increment the `Qcache_not_cached` status variable and discard the results cached so far. If you know this happens a lot, you can add the `SQL_NO_CACHE` hint to queries you don't want to incur this overhead.

`query_cache_wlock_invalidate`

> Whether to serve cached results that refer to tables other connections have locked. The default value is `OFF`, which makes the query cache change the server's semantics because it lets you read cached data from a table another connection has locked, which you wouldn't normally be able to do. Changing it to `ON` will keep you from reading this data, but it might increase lock waits. This really doesn't matter for most applications, so the default is generally fine.

In principle, configuring the cache is pretty simple, but understanding the effects of your changes is more complicated. In the following sections, we'll try to help you make good decisions.

Reducing fragmentation

There's no way to avoid all fragmentation, but choosing your `query_cache_min_res_unit` value carefully can help you avoid wasting a lot of memory in the query cache. The trick is to balance the size of each new block against the number of allocations the server has to do while storing results. If you make this value too small, the server will waste less memory, but it will have to allocate blocks more frequently, which is more work for the server. If you make it too large, you'll get too much fragmentation. The trade-off is wasting memory versus using more CPU cycles during allocation.

The best setting varies with the size of your typical query result. You can see the average size of the queries in the cache by dividing the memory used (approximately `query_cache_size - Qcache_free_memory`) by the `Qcache_queries_in_cache` status variable. If you have a mixture of large and small results, you might not be able to choose a size that avoids fragmentation while also avoiding too many allocations. However, you might have reason to believe that it's not beneficial to cache the larger results (this is frequently true). You can keep large results from being cached by lowering the value of the `query_cache_limit` variable, which can sometimes help achieve a better balance between fragmentation and the overhead of storing results in the cache.

You can detect query cache fragmentation by examining the `Qcache_free_blocks` status variable, which shows you how many blocks in the query cache are of type FREE. In the final configuration shown in Figure 7-4, there are two free blocks. The worst possible fragmentation is when there's a slightly-too-small free block between every pair of blocks used to store data, so every other block is a free block. Thus, if `Qcache_free_blocks` approaches `Qcache_total_blocks / 2`, your query cache is severely fragmented. If the `Qcache_lowmem_prunes` status variable is increasing and you have a lot of free blocks, fragmentation is causing queries to be deleted from the cache prematurely.

You can defragment the query cache with FLUSH QUERY CACHE. This command compacts the query cache by moving all blocks "upward" and removing the free space between them, leaving a single free block at the bottom. Contrary to its name, it does not remove queries from the cache; that's what RESET QUERY CACHE does. FLUSH QUERY CACHE blocks access to the query cache while it runs, which effectively locks the whole server, so be very careful with it. One rule of thumb for query cache sizing is to keep it small enough that the stalls caused by FLUSH QUERY CACHE are acceptably short.

Improving query cache usage

If your query cache isn't fragmented but you're still not getting a good hit rate, you might have given it too little memory. If the server can't find any free blocks that are large enough to use for a new block, it must "prune" some queries from the cache.

When the server prunes cache entries, it increments the `Qcache_lowmem_prunes` status variable. If this value increases rapidly, there are two possible causes:

- If there are many free blocks, fragmentation is the likely culprit (see the previous section).
- If there are few free blocks, it might mean that your workload can use a larger cache size than you're giving it. You can see the amount of unused memory in the cache by examining `Qcache_free_memory`.

If there are many free blocks, fragmentation is low, there are few prunes due to low memory, and the hit rate is *still* low, your workload probably won't benefit much from the query cache. Something is keeping it from being used. If you have a lot of updates, that's probably the culprit; it's also possible that your queries are not cacheable.

If you've measured the cache hit ratio and you're still not sure whether the server is benefiting from the query cache, you can disable it and monitor performance, then reenable it and see how performance changes. To disable the query cache, set `query_cache_size` to 0. (Changing `query_cache_type` globally won't affect connections that are already open, and it won't return the memory to the server.) You can also benchmark, but it's sometimes tricky to get a realistic combination of cached queries, uncached queries, and updates.

Figure 7-5 shows a flowchart with a basic example of the process you can use to analyze and configure your server's query cache.

InnoDB and the Query Cache

InnoDB interacts with the query cache in a more complex way than other storage engines, because of its implementation of MVCC. In MySQL 4.0 the query cache is disabled entirely within transactions, but in MySQL 4.1 and newer InnoDB indicates to the server, on a per-table basis, whether a transaction can access the query cache. It controls access to the query cache for both reads (retrieving results from the cache) and writes (saving results to the cache).

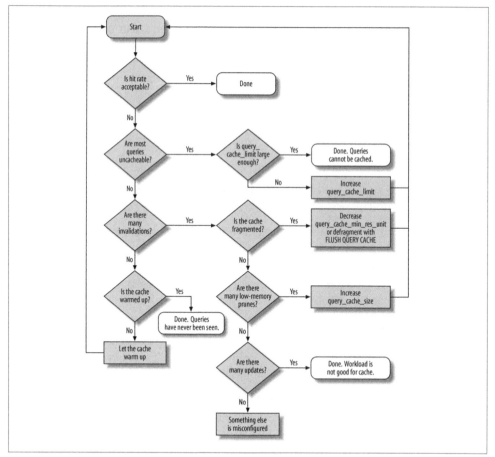

Figure 7-5. How to analyze and configure the query cache

The factors that determine access are the transaction ID and whether there are any locks on the table. Each table in InnoDB's in-memory data dictionary has an associated transaction ID counter. Transactions whose IDs are less than the counter value are forbidden to read from or write to the query cache for queries that involve that table.

Any locks on a table also make queries that access it uncacheable. For example, if a transaction performs a SELECT FOR UPDATE query on a table, no other transactions will be able to read from or write to the query cache for queries involving that table until the locks are released.

When a transaction commits, InnoDB updates the counters for the tables upon which the transaction has locks. A lock is a rough heuristic for determining whether the transaction has modified a table; it is possible for a transaction to lock rows in a table and not update them, but it is not possible for it to modify the table's contents without acquiring any locks. InnoDB sets each table's counter to the system's transaction ID, which is the maximum transaction ID in existence.

This has the following consequences:

- The table's counter is an absolute lower bound on which transactions can use the query cache. If the system's transaction ID is 5 and a transaction acquires locks on rows in a table and then commits, transactions 1 through 4 can never read from or write to the query cache for queries involving that table again.

- The table's counter is updated not to the transaction ID of the transaction that locked rows in it, but to the system's transaction ID. As a result, transactions that lock rows in tables might find themselves blocked from reading from or writing to the query cache for queries involving that table in the future.

Query cache storage, retrieval, and invalidation are handled at the server level, and InnoDB cannot bypass or delay this. However, InnoDB can tell the server explicitly to invalidate queries that involve specific tables. This is necessary when a foreign key constraint, such as ON DELETE CASCADE, alters the contents of a table that isn't mentioned in a query.

In principle, InnoDB's MVCC architecture could let queries be served from the cache when modifications to a table don't affect the consistent read view other transactions see. However, implementing this would be complex. InnoDB's algorithm takes some shortcuts for simplicity, at the cost of locking transactions out of the query cache when this might not really be necessary.

General Query Cache Optimizations

Many schema, query, and application design decisions affect the query cache. In addition to what we discussed in the previous sections, here are some points to keep in mind:

- Having multiple smaller tables instead of one huge one can help the query cache. This design effectively makes the invalidation strategy work at a finer level of granularity. Don't let this unduly influence your schema design, though, as other factors can easily outweigh the benefit.

- It's more efficient to batch writes than to do them singly, because this method invalidates cached cache entries only once. (Be careful not to delay and batch so much that the invalidations caused by the writes will stall the server for too long, however.)

- We've noticed that the server can stall for a long time while invalidating entries in or pruning a very large query cache. A possible solution is to not make query_cache_size very large, but in some cases you simply have to disable it altogether, because nothing is small enough.

- You cannot control the query cache on a per-database or per-table basis, but you can include or exclude individual queries with the SQL_CACHE and SQL_NO_CACHE modifiers in the SELECT statement. You can also enable or disable the query cache on a per-connection basis by setting the session-level query_cache_type server variable to the appropriate value.

- For a write-heavy application, disabling the query cache completely might improve performance. Doing so eliminates the overhead of caching queries that would be invalidated soon anyway. Remember to set query_cache_size to 0 when you disable it, so it doesn't consume any memory.

- Disabling the query cache might be beneficial for a read-heavy application, too, because of contention on the single query cache mutex. If you need good performance at high concurrency, be sure to validate it with high-concurrency tests, because enabling the query cache and testing at low concurrency can be very misleading.

If you want to avoid the query cache for most queries, but you know that some will benefit significantly from caching, you can set the global query_cache_type to DEMAND and then add the SQL_CACHE hint to those queries you want to cache. Although this requires you to do more work, it gives you very fine-grained control over the cache. Conversely, if you want to cache most queries and exclude just a few, you can add SQL_NO_CACHE to them.

Alternatives to the Query Cache

The MySQL query cache works on the principle that the fastest query is the one you don't have to execute, but you still have to issue the query, and the server still needs to do a little bit of work. What if you really didn't have to talk to the database server at all for particular queries? Client-side caching can help ease the workload on your MySQL server even more. We explain caching more in Chapter 14.

Summary

This chapter has been more of a potpourri of different topics than some of the previous chapters were. We'll wrap up by revisiting some of the most important points from each topic:

Partitioned tables

Partitioning is a kind of cheap, coarse indexing that works at large scale. For best results, either forget about indexing and plan to full-scan selected partitions, or make sure that only one partition is hot and it fits in memory, including its indexes. Stick to about 150 or fewer partitions per table, watch out for subtleties that defeat pruning, and monitor the per-row and per-query overhead of partitioning.

Views

Views can be useful for abstracting underlying tables and complex queries. Beware of views that use temporary tables, though, because they don't push your WHERE clauses down to the underlying queries; nor do they have indexes themselves, so you can't query them efficiently in a join. Using views as conveniences is probably the best approach.

Foreign keys

Foreign key constraints push constraints into the server, where they can be more efficient. However, they can also add complexity, extra indexing overhead, and interactions between tables that cause more locking and contention. We think foreign keys are a nice-to-have feature for ensuring system integrity, but they're a luxury for applications that need extremely high performance; most people don't use them when performance is a concern, preferring instead to trust the application code.

Stored routines

MySQL's implementation of stored procedures, triggers, stored functions, and events is quite frankly pretty unimpressive. There are also a lot of problems with statement-based replication. Use these features when they can save you a lot of network round-trips—in such cases, you can get much better performance by cutting out costly latency. You can also use them for the usual reasons (centralizing business logic, enforcing privileges, and so on), but this just doesn't work as well in MySQL as it does in the bigger, more complex and mature database servers.

Prepared statements

Prepared statements are useful when a large portion of the cost of executing statements is from transferring statements across the network, parsing the SQL, and optimizing the SQL. If you'll repeat the same statement many times, you can save on these costs by using prepared statements because they're parsed once, there is some execution plan caching, and the binary protocol is more efficient than the ordinary text-based protocol.

Plugins

Plugins are written in C or C++ and let you extend the functionality of the server in many ways. They're very powerful, and we've written many UDFs and plugins for various purposes when the problem is best solved inside the server in native code.

Character sets

A character set is a mapping between byte values and characters, and a collation is the sort order of the characters. Most people use either the `latin1` (the default, suitable for English and some European languages) or UTF-8 character sets. If you use UTF-8, beware of temporary tables and buffers: the server allocates three bytes per character, so you can use a lot of disk and memory space if you're not careful. Be very careful to make character sets and character set configuration options match, from the client-side connections all the way through, or you'll cause conversions that defeat indexing.

Full-text searching

Only MyISAM supports full-text indexes at the time of writing, though it looks like InnoDB will offer this capability when MySQL 5.6 is released. MyISAM is basically unusable for large-scale full-text searching due to locking and lack of crash resilience, and we generally help people set up and use Sphinx instead.

XA transactions

Most people don't use XA transactions with MySQL. However, *don't disable* `innodb_support_xa` *unless you know what you are doing*. It is *not*, as many people think, unnecessary if you don't do explicit XA transactions. It is used for coordinating InnoDB and the binary log so crash recovery will work correctly.

The query cache

The query cache prevents queries from being reexecuted if the stored result of an exactly identical query is already cached. Our experience with the query cache in high-load environments has been peppered with server lockups and stalls. If you use the query cache, don't make it very large, and use it only if you know it's highly beneficial. How can you know that? The best way is to use Percona Server's extended query logging facilities and a little math. Barring that, you can look at the cache hit ratio (not always helpful), the select-to-insert ratio (also hard to interpret), or the hit-to-insert ratio (a bit more meaningful). In the final analysis, the query cache is convenient because it's transparent and doesn't require any additional coding on your part, but if you need a highly efficient cache for high performance, you're better off looking at *memcached* or another external solution. More on this in Chapter 14.

Optimizing Server Settings

In this chapter, we'll explain a process by which you can create a good configuration file for your MySQL server. It is a roundabout trip, with many points of interest and side trips to scenic overlooks. These are necessary, because determining the shortest path to a good configuration doesn't start with studying configuration options and asking which ones you should set or how you should change them, nor does it start with examining server behavior and asking whether any configuration options can improve it. It's best to begin with an understanding of MySQL's internals and behavior. You can then use that knowledge as a guide for how MySQL should be configured. Finally, you can compare the desired configuration to the current configuration and correct any differences that are important and worthwhile.

People often ask, "What's the optimal configuration file for my server with 32 GB of RAM and 12 CPU cores?" Unfortunately, it's not that simple. The server should be configured for the workload, data, and application requirements, not just the hardware. MySQL has scores of settings that you can change—but you shouldn't. It's usually better to configure the basic settings correctly (and there are only a few that really matter in most cases) and spend more time on schema optimization, indexes, and query design. After you've set MySQL's basic configuration options correctly, the potential gains from further changes are usually small.

On the other hand, the potential downside of fiddling with the configuration can be great. We've seen more than one "highly tuned" server that was crashing constantly, stalling, or performing slowly due to unwise settings. We'll spend a bit of time on why that can happen and what not to do.

So what *should* you do? Make sure the basics such as the InnoDB buffer pool and log file size are appropriate, set a few safety and sanity options if you wish to prevent bad behavior (but note that these usually won't improve performance—they'll only avoid problems), and then leave the rest of the settings alone. If you begin to experience a problem, diagnose it carefully with the techniques shown in Chapter 3. If the problem is caused by a part of the server whose behavior can be corrected with a configuration option, then you might need to change it.

Sometimes you might also need to set specific configuration options that can have a significant performance impact in special cases. However, these should not be part of a basic server configuration file. You should set them only when you find the specific performance problems they address. That's why we don't suggest that you approach configuration options by looking for bad things to improve. If something needs to be improved, it should show up in query response times. It's best to start your search with queries and their response times, not with configuration options. This could save you a lot of time and prevent many problems.

Another good way to save time and trouble is to use the defaults unless you know you shouldn't. There is safety in numbers, and a lot of people are running with default settings. That makes them the most thoroughly tested settings. Unexpected bugs can arise when you change things needlessly.

How MySQL's Configuration Works

We'll begin by explaining MySQL's configuration mechanisms, before covering what you should configure in MySQL. MySQL is generally pretty forgiving about its configuration, but following these suggestions might save you a lot of work and time.

The first thing to know is where MySQL gets configuration information: from command-line arguments and settings in its configuration file. On Unix-like systems, the configuration file is typically located at */etc/my.cnf* or */etc/mysql/my.cnf*. If you use your operating system's startup scripts, this is typically the only place you'll specify configuration settings. If you start MySQL manually, which you might do when you're running a test installation, you can also specify settings on the command line. The server actually reads the contents of the configuration file, removes any comment lines and newlines, and then processes it together with the command-line options.

 A note on terminology: because many of MySQL's command-line options correspond to server variables, we sometimes use the terms *option* and *variable* interchangeably. Most variables have the same names as their corresponding command-line options, but there are a few exceptions. For example, *--memlock* sets the locked_in_memory variable.

Any settings you decide to use permanently should go into the global configuration file, instead of being specified at the command line. Otherwise, you risk accidentally starting the server without them. It's also a good idea to keep all of your configuration files in a single place so that you can inspect them easily.

Be sure you know where your server's configuration file is located! We've seen people try unsuccessfully to configure a server with a file it doesn't read, such as */etc/my.cnf* on Debian servers, which look in */etc/mysql/my.cnf* for their configuration. Sometimes there are files in several places, perhaps because a previous system administrator was confused as well. If you don't know which files your server reads, you can ask it:

```
$ which mysqld
/usr/sbin/mysqld
$ /usr/sbin/mysqld --verbose --help | grep -A 1 'Default options'
Default options are read from the following files in the given order:
/etc/mysql/my.cnf ~/.my.cnf /usr/etc/my.cnf
```

This applies to typical installations, where there's a single server on a host. You can design more complicated configurations, but there's no standard way to do this. The MySQL server distribution used to include a now-deprecated program called *mysql-manager*, which can run multiple instances from a single configuration with separate sections. (This was a replacement for the even older *mysqld_multi* script.) However, many operating system distributions don't include or use this program in their startup scripts. In fact, many don't use the MySQL-provided startup script at all.

The configuration file is divided into sections, each of which begins with a line that contains the section name in square brackets. A MySQL program will generally read the section that has the same name as that program, and many client programs also read the client section, which gives you a place to put common settings. The server usually reads the mysqld section. Be sure you place your settings in the correct section in the file, or they will have no effect.

Syntax, Scope, and Dynamism

Configuration settings are written in all lowercase, with words separated by underscores or dashes. The following are equivalent, and you might see both forms in command lines and configuration files:

```
/usr/sbin/mysqld --auto-increment-offset=5
/usr/sbin/mysqld --auto_increment_offset=5
```

We suggest that you pick a style and use it consistently. This makes it easier to search for settings in your files.

Configuration settings can have several scopes. Some settings are server-wide (global scope); others are different for each connection (session scope); and others are per-object. Many session-scoped variables have global equivalents, which you can think of as defaults. If you change the session-scoped variable, it affects only the connection from which you changed it, and the changes are lost when the connection closes. Here are some examples of the variety of behaviors of which you should be aware:

- The query_cache_size variable is globally scoped.
- The sort_buffer_size variable has a global default, but you can set it per-session as well.

- The `join_buffer_size` variable has a global default and can be set per-session, but a single query that joins several tables can allocate one join buffer *per join*, so there might be several join buffers per query.

In addition to setting variables in the configuration files, you can also change many (but not all) of them while the server is running. MySQL refers to these as *dynamic* configuration variables. The following statements show different ways to change the session and global values of `sort_buffer_size` dynamically:

```
SET             sort_buffer_size  = <value>;
SET GLOBAL      sort_buffer_size  = <value>;
SET            @@sort_buffer_size := <value>;
SET @@session.sort_buffer_size := <value>;
SET  @@global.sort_buffer_size := <value>;
```

If you set variables dynamically, be aware that those settings will be lost when MySQL shuts down. If you want to keep the settings, you'll have to update your configuration file as well.

If you set a variable's global value while the server is running, the values for the current session and any other existing sessions are not affected. This is because the session values are initialized from the global value when the connections are created. You should inspect the output of SHOW GLOBAL VARIABLES after each change to make sure it's had the desired effect.

Variables use different kinds of units, and you have to know the correct unit for each variable. For example, the `table_cache` variable specifies the number of tables that can be cached, not the size of the table cache in bytes. The `key_buffer_size` is specified in bytes, whereas still other variables are specified in number of pages or other units, such as percentages.

Many variables can be specified with a suffix, such as 1M for one megabyte. However, this works only in the configuration file or as a command-line argument. When you use the SQL SET command, you must use the literal value 1048576, or an expression such as 1024 * 1024. You can't use expressions in configuration files.

There is also a special value you can assign to variables with the SET command: the keyword DEFAULT. Assigning this value to a session-scoped variable sets that variable to the corresponding globally scoped variable's value; assigning it to a globally scoped variable sets the variable to the compiled-in default (not the value specified in the configuration file). This is useful for resetting session-scoped variables back to the values they had when you opened the connection. We advise you not to use it for global variables, because it probably won't do what you want—that is, it doesn't set the values back to what they were when you started the server.

Side Effects of Setting Variables

Setting variables dynamically can have unexpected side effects, such as flushing dirty blocks from buffers. Be careful which settings you change online, because this can cause the server to do a lot of work.

Sometimes you can infer a variable's behavior from its name. For example, max_heap_table_size does what it sounds like: it specifies the *maximum* size to which implicit in-memory temporary tables are allowed to grow. However, the naming conventions aren't completely consistent, so you can't always guess what a variable will do by looking at its name.

Let's take a look at some commonly used variables and the effects of changing them dynamically:

key_buffer_size
> Setting this variable allocates the designated amount of space for the key buffer (or key cache) all at once. However, the operating system doesn't actually commit memory to it until it is used. Setting the key buffer size to one gigabyte, for example, doesn't mean you've instantly caused the server to actually commit a gigabyte of memory to it. (We discuss how to watch the server's memory usage in the next chapter.)
>
> MySQL lets you create multiple key caches, as we explain later in this chapter. If you set this variable to 0 for a nondefault key cache, MySQL discards any indexes cached in the specified cache, begins to cache them in the default cache, and deletes the specified cache when nothing is using it anymore. Setting this variable for a nonexistent cache creates it. Setting the variable to a nonzero value for an existing cache will flush the specified cache's memory. This blocks all operations that try to access the cache until the flush is finished.

table_cache_size
> Setting this variable has no immediate effect—the effect is delayed until the next time a thread opens a table. When this happens, MySQL checks the variable's value. If the value is larger than the number of tables in the cache, the thread can insert the newly opened table into the cache. If the value is smaller than the number of tables in the cache, MySQL deletes unused tables from the cache.

thread_cache_size
> Setting this variable has no immediate effect—the effect is delayed until the next time a connection is closed. At that time, MySQL checks whether there is space in the cache to store the thread. If so, it caches the thread for future reuse by another connection. If not, it kills the thread instead of caching it. In this case, the number of threads in the cache, and hence the amount of memory the thread cache uses, does not immediately decrease; it decreases only when a new connection removes a thread from the cache to use it. (MySQL adds threads to the cache only when connections close and removes them from the cache only when new connections are created.)

query_cache_size

> MySQL allocates and initializes the specified amount of memory for the query cache all at once when the server starts. If you update this variable (even if you set it to its current value), MySQL immediately deletes all cached queries, resizes the cache to the specified size, and reinitializes the cache's memory. This can take a long time and stalls the server until it completes, because MySQL deletes all of the cached queries one by one, not instantaneously.

read_buffer_size

> MySQL doesn't allocate any memory for this buffer until a query needs it, but then it immediately allocates the entire chunk of memory specified here.

read_rnd_buffer_size

> MySQL doesn't allocate any memory for this buffer until a query needs it, and then it allocates only as much memory as needed. (The name max_read_rnd _buffer_size would describe this variable more accurately.)

sort_buffer_size

> MySQL doesn't allocate any memory for this buffer until a query needs to do a sort. However, when there's a sort, MySQL allocates the entire chunk of memory immediately, whether the full size is required or not.

We explain what these variables do in more detail elsewhere, and this isn't an exhaustive list. Our goal here is simply to show you what behavior to expect when you change a few common variables.

You should *not* raise the value of a per-connection setting globally unless you know it's the right thing to do. Some buffers are allocated all at once, even if they're not needed, so a large global setting can be a huge waste. Instead, you can raise the value when a query needs it.

The most common example of a variable that you should probably keep small and raise only for certain queries is sort_buffer_size, which controls how large the sort buffer should be for filesorts. MySQL performs some work to initialize the sort buffer after allocating it.

In addition, the sort buffer is allocated to its full size even for very small sorts, so if you make it much larger than the average sort requires, you'll be wasting memory and adding allocation cost. This can be surprising to those readers who think of memory allocation as an inexpensive operation. Without digging into all of the technical details, it's enough to say that memory allocation includes setting up the address space, which can be relatively expensive; in Linux in particular, memory allocation uses a couple of strategies with varying cost depending on the size.

In summary, a large sort buffer can be very expensive, so don't increase its size unless you know it's needed.

When you find a query that needs a larger sort buffer to perform well, you can raise the sort_buffer_size value just before the query and then restore it to DEFAULT afterward. Here's an example of how to do this:

```
SET @@session.sort_buffer_size := <value>;
-- Execute the query...
SET @@session.sort_buffer_size := DEFAULT;
```

Wrapper functions can be handy for this type of code. Other variables you might set on a per-connection basis are read_buffer_size, read_rnd_buffer_size, tmp_table _size, and myisam_sort_buffer_size (if you're repairing tables).

If you need to save and restore a possibly customized value, you can do something like the following:

```
SET @saved_<unique_variable_name> := @@session.sort_buffer_size;
SET @@session.sort_buffer_size := <value>;
-- Execute the query...
SET @@session.sort_buffer_size := @saved_<unique_variable_name>;
```

 The sort buffer size is one of the settings that is the focus of far too much "tuning." Some people seem to have the idea that bigger is better, and we've even seen servers with this variable set to 1 GB. Perhaps not surprisingly, this can cause the server to try to allocate too much memory and crash, or simply to burn a lot of CPU time when initializing the sort buffer for a query; see MySQL bug 37359 for more on this.

Don't assign too much importance to the sort buffer size. Do you really need your queries to allocate 128 MB of memory to sort 10 rows and return them to the client? Think about what kinds of sorting your queries are doing, and how much, and try to avoid them with proper indexing and query design (see Chapter 5 and Chapter 6) rather than trying to make the sorting operation itself faster. And you should definitely profile your queries to see whether sorting is where you should focus your attention anyway; see Chapter 3 for an example of a query that performs a sort but doesn't spend much of its time sorting.

Getting Started

Be careful when setting variables. More is not always better, and if you set the values too high, you can easily cause problems: you might run out of memory, causing your server to swap, or run out of address space.[1]

---

1. A common mistake we've seen is to set up a server with twice as much memory as your existing server, and—using the old server's configuration as a baseline—create the new server's configuration by multiplying everything by two. This doesn't work.

You should always have a monitoring system in place to measure whether a change improves or hurts your server's overall performance in real life. Benchmarks aren't enough, because they're not real. If you don't measure your server's actual performance, you might hurt performance without knowing it. We've seen many cases where someone changed a server's configuration and thought it improved performance, when in fact the server's performance worsened overall because of a different workload at a different time of day or day of the week.

If you take notes, perhaps with comments in the configuration file, you might save yourself (and your colleagues) a lot of work. An even better idea is to place your configuration file under version control. This is a good practice anyway, because it lets you undo changes. To reduce the complexity of managing many configuration files, simply create a symbolic link from the configuration file to a central version control repository.

Before you start changing your configuration, you should optimize your queries and your schema, addressing at least the obvious things such as adding indexes. If you get deep into tweaking the configuration and then change your queries or schema, you might need to reevaluate the configuration. Keep in mind that unless your hardware, workload, and data are completely static, chances are you'll need to revisit your configuration later. And in fact, most people's servers don't even have a steady workload throughout the day—meaning that the "perfect" configuration for the middle of the morning is not right for midafternoon! Obviously, chasing the mythical "perfect" configuration is completely impractical. Thus, you don't need to squeeze every last ounce of performance out of your server; in fact, the return for such an investment of time will probably be very small. We suggest that you stop at "good enough," unless you have reason to believe you're forgoing a significant performance improvement.

Iterative Optimization by Benchmarking

You might be expected (or believe that you're expected) to set up a benchmark suite and "tune" your server by changing its configuration iteratively in search of optimal settings. This usually is not something we advise most people to do. It requires so much work and research, and the potential payoff is so small in most cases, that it can be a huge waste of time. You are probably better off spending that time on other things such as checking your backups, monitoring changes in query plans, and so on.

It's also very hard to know what side effects your changes might have over the long run. If you change an option and it appears to improve your benchmark, but your benchmark doesn't measure everything that's important, or you don't run it long enough to detect changes in the system's long-term steady-state behavior, you might cause problems such as periodic server stalls or sporadic slow queries. These can be difficult to detect.

We do sometimes run sets of benchmarks to examine or stress particular parts of the server so we can understand their behavior better. A good example is the many benchmarks we've run over the years to understand InnoDB's flushing behavior, in our quest to develop better flushing algorithms for various workloads and types of hardware. It often happens that we benchmark extensively with different settings to understand their effects and how to optimize them. But this is not a small undertaking—it can take many days or weeks—and it is also not beneficial for most people to do, because such tunnel vision about a specific part of the server often obscures other concerns. For example, sometimes we find that specific combinations of settings enable better performance in edge cases, but the configuration options are not really practical for production usage, due to factors such as wasting a huge amount of memory or optimizing for throughput while ignoring the impact on crash recovery altogether.

If you must do this, we suggest that you develop a custom benchmark suite before you begin configuring your server. You need something that represents your overall workload and includes edge cases such as very large and complex queries. Replaying your actual workload against your actual data is usually a good approach. If you have identified a particular problem spot—such as a single query that runs slowly—you can also try to optimize for that case, but you risk impacting other queries negatively without knowing it.

The best way to proceed is to change one or two variables, a little at a time, and run the benchmarks after each change, being sure to run them long enough to observe the steady-state behavior. Sometimes the results will surprise you; you might increase a variable a little and see an improvement, then increase it a little more and see a sharp drop in performance. If performance suffers after a change, you might be asking for too much of some resource, such as too much memory for a buffer that's frequently allocated and deallocated. You might also have created a mismatch between MySQL and your operating system or hardware. For example, we've found that the optimal sort_buffer_size might be affected by how the CPU cache works, and the read_buffer_size needs to be matched to the server's read-ahead and general I/O subsystem configuration. Larger is not always better, and can be much worse. Some variables are also dependent on others, which is something you learn with experience and by understanding the system's architecture.

When Benchmarking Is Good

There are exceptions to our advice not to benchmark. We sometimes do advise people to run some iterative benchmarks, although usually in a different context than "server tuning." Here are some examples:

- If you're approaching a large investment, such as purchasing a number of new servers, you can run benchmarks to understand your hardware needs. (The context here is capacity planning, not server tuning.) In particular, we like to run benchmarks with different amounts of memory allocated to the InnoDB buffer pool, which helps us draw a "memory curve" that shows how much memory is really needed and how it impacts the demands on the storage systems.

- If you want to understand how long it will take InnoDB to recover from a crash, you can repeatedly set up a replica, crash it intentionally, and "benchmark" how long InnoDB takes to recover after restarting. The context here is for high availability planning.

- For read-mostly applications, it can be a great idea to capture all queries with the slow query log (or from TCP traffic with *pt-query-digest*), use *pt-log-player* to replay it against the server with full slow query logging enabled, and then analyze the resulting log with *pt-query-digest*. This lets you see how various types of queries perform with different hardware, software, and server settings. For example, we once helped a customer assess the performance changes of a migration to a server with much more memory, but with slower hard drives. Most queries became faster, but some analytical queries slowed down because they remained I/O-bound. The context of this exercise was workload comparison.

What Not to Do

Before we get started with server configuration, we want to encourage you to avoid a few common practices that we've found to be risky or harmful. Warning: rants ahead!

First, you should not "tune by ratio." The classic "tuning ratio" is the rule of thumb that your key cache hit ratio should be higher than some percentage, and you should increase the cache size if the hit rate is too low. This is very wrong advice. Regardless of what anyone tells you, *the cache hit ratio has nothing to do with whether the cache is too large or too small*. To begin with, the hit ratio depends on the workload—some workloads simply aren't cacheable no matter how big the cache is—and secondly, cache hits are meaningless, for reasons we'll explain later. It sometimes happens that when the cache is too small, the hit rate is low, and increasing the cache size increases the hit rate. However, this is an accidental correlation and does not indicate anything about performance or proper sizing of the cache.

The problem with correlations that sometimes appear to be true is that people begin to believe they will always be true. Oracle DBAs abandoned ratio-based tuning years ago, and we wish MySQL DBAs would follow their lead.[2] We wish even more fervently that people wouldn't write "tuning scripts" that codify these dangerous practices and teach them to thousands of people. This leads to our second suggestion of what not to do: don't use tuning scripts! There are several very popular ones that you can find on the Internet. It's probably best to ignore them.[3]

We also suggest that you avoid the word "tuning," which we've used liberally in the past few paragraphs. We favor "configuration" or "optimization" instead (as long as that's what you're actually doing; see Chapter 3). The word "tuning" conjures up images of an undisciplined novice who tweaks the server and sees what happens. We suggested in the previous section that this practice is best left to those who are researching server internals. "Tuning" your server can be a stunning waste of time.

On a related topic, searching the Internet for configuration advice is not always a great idea. You can find a lot of bad advice in blogs, forums, and so on.[4] Although many experts contribute what they know online, it is not always easy to tell who is qualified. We can't give unbiased recommendations about where to find real experts, of course. But we can say that the credible, reputable MySQL service providers are a safer bet in general than what a simple Internet search turns up, because people who have happy customers are probably doing something right. Even their advice, however, can be dangerous to apply without testing and understanding, because it might have been directed at a situation that differed from yours in a way you don't understand.

Finally, don't believe the popular memory consumption formula—yes, the very one that MySQL itself prints out when it crashes. (We won't repeat it here.) This formula is from an ancient time. It is not a reliable or even useful way to understand how much memory MySQL can use in the worst case. You might see some variations on this formula on the Internet, too. These are similarly flawed, even though they add in more factors that the original formula doesn't have. The truth is that you can't put an upper bound on MySQL's memory consumption. It is not a tightly regulated database server that controls memory allocation. You can prove that very simply by logging into the server and running a number of queries that consume a lot of memory:

```
mysql> SET @crash_me_1 := REPEAT('a', @@max_allowed_packet);
mysql> SET @crash_me_2 := REPEAT('a', @@max_allowed_packet);
```

---

2. If you are not convinced that "tuning by ratio" is bad, please read *Optimizing Oracle Performance* by Cary Millsap (O'Reilly). He even devotes an appendix to the topic, with a tool that can artificially generate any cache hit ratio you wish, no matter how badly your system is performing! Of course, it's all for the purpose of illustrating how useless the ratio is.

3. An exception: we maintain a (good) free online configuration tool at *http://tools.percona.com*. Yes, we're biased.

4. Q: How is query formed? A: They need to do way instain DBAs who kill thier querys, becuse these querys cant frigth back?

```
                # ... run a lot of these ...
                mysql> SET @crash_me_1000000 := REPEAT('a', @@max_allowed_packet);
```

Run that in a loop, creating new variables each time, and you'll eventually run the server out of memory and crash it! And it requires no privileges to execute.

The points we've tried to illustrate in this section have sometimes made us unpopular with people who perceive us as arrogant, think that we're trying to discredit others and set ourselves up as the sole authority, or feel that we're trying to promote our services. It is not our intention to be self-serving. We have simply seen so much bad advice that appears legitimate if you are not experienced enough to know better, and helped clean up the wreckage so many times, that we think it is important to debunk a few myths and warn our readers to be careful whose expertise they trust. We'll try to avoid ranting from here on.

Creating a MySQL Configuration File

As we mentioned at the beginning of this chapter, we don't have a one-size-fits-all "best configuration file" for, say, a 4-CPU server with 16 GB of memory and 12 hard drives. You really do need to develop your own configurations, because even a good starting point will vary widely depending on how you're using the server.

MySQL's compiled-in default settings aren't all great, although most of them are fine. They are designed not to use a lot of resources, because MySQL is intended to be very versatile, and it does not assume it is the only thing running on the server on which it is installed. By default, MySQL uses just enough resources to start and run simple queries with a little bit of data. You'll certainly need to customize it if you have more than a few megabytes of data.

You can start with one of the sample configuration files included with the MySQL server distribution, but they have their own problems. For example, they have a lot of commented-out settings that might tempt you to think that you should choose values and uncomment them (it's a bit reminiscent of an Apache configuration file). And they have a lot of prose comments that explain the options, but these explanations are not always well-balanced, complete, or even correct. Some of the options don't even apply to popular operating systems at all! Finally, the samples are perpetually out of date for modern hardware and workloads.

MySQL experts have had many conversations about how to fix these problems over the years, but the issues remain. Here's our suggestion: don't use those files as a starting point, and don't use the samples that ship with your operating system's packages either. It's better to start from scratch.

That's what we'll do in this chapter. It's actually a weakness that MySQL is so configurable, because it makes it seem as though you should spend a lot of time on configuration, when in fact most things are fine at their defaults, and you are often better off setting and forgetting. That's why we've created a sane minimal sample configuration file for this book, which you can use as a good starting point for your own servers. You must choose values for a few of the settings; we'll explain those later in this chapter. Our base file looks like this:

```
[mysqld]
# GENERAL
datadir                      = /var/lib/mysql
socket                       = /var/lib/mysql/mysql.sock
pid_file                     = /var/lib/mysql/mysql.pid
user                         = mysql
port                         = 3306
storage_engine               = InnoDB
# INNODB
innodb_buffer_pool_size      = <value>
innodb_log_file_size         = <value>
innodb_file_per_table        = 1
innodb_flush_method          = O_DIRECT
# MyISAM
key_buffer_size              = <value>
# LOGGING
log_error                    = /var/lib/mysql/mysql-error.log
log_slow_queries             = /var/lib/mysql/mysql-slow.log
# OTHER
tmp_table_size               = 32M
max_heap_table_size          = 32M
query_cache_type             = 0
query_cache_size             = 0
max_connections              = <value>
thread_cache_size            = <value>
table_cache_size             = <value>
open_files_limit             = 65535
[client]
socket                       = /var/lib/mysql/mysql.sock
port                         = 3306
```

This might seem *too* minimal in comparison to what you're used to seeing,[5] but it's actually more than many people need. There are a few other types of configuration options that you are likely to use as well, such as binary logging; we'll cover those later in this and other chapters.

The first thing we configured is the location of the data. We chose */var/lib/mysql* for this, because it's a popular location on many Unix variants. There is nothing wrong with choosing another location; you decide. We've put the PID file into the same location, but many operating systems will want to place it in */var/run* instead. That's fine, too. We simply needed to have something configured for these settings. By the way, don't let the socket and PID file be located according to the server's compiled-in defaults; there are some bugs in various MySQL versions that can cause problems with this. It's best to set these locations explicitly. (We're not advising you to choose different

---

5. Question: where are the settings for the sort buffer size and read buffer size? Answer: they're off minding their own business. Leave them at their defaults unless you can prove the defaults are not good enough.

locations; we're just advising you to make sure the *my.cnf* file mentions those locations explicitly, so they won't change and break things if you upgrade the server.)

We also specified that *mysqld* should run as the *mysql* user account on the operating system. You'll need to make sure this account exists, and that it owns the data directory. The port is set to the default of 3306, but sometimes that is something you'll want to change.

We've chosen the default storage engine to be InnoDB, and this is worth explaining. We think InnoDB is the best choice in most situations, but that's not always the case. Some third-party software, for example, might assume the default is MyISAM, and will create tables without specifying the engine. This might cause the software to malfunction if, for example, it assumes that it can create full-text indexes. And the default storage engine is used for explicitly created temporary tables, too, which can cause quite a bit of unexpected work for the server. If you want your permanent tables to use InnoDB but any temporary tables to use MyISAM, you should be sure to specify the engine explicitly in the CREATE TABLE statement.

In general, if you decide to use a storage engine as your default, it's best to configure it as the default. Many users think they use only a specific storage engine, but then discover another engine has crept into use because of the configured default.

We'll illustrate the basics of configuration with InnoDB. All InnoDB really needs to run well in most cases is a proper buffer pool size and log file size. The defaults are far too small. All of the other settings for InnoDB are optional, although we've enabled innodb_file_per_table for manageability and flexibility reasons. Setting the InnoDB log file size is a topic that we'll discuss later in this chapter, as is the setting of innodb _flush_method, which is Unix-specific.

There's a popular rule of thumb that says you should set the buffer pool size to around 75% or 80% of your server's memory. This is another accidental ratio that seems to work okay sometimes, but isn't always correct. It's a better idea to set the buffer pool roughly as follows:

1. Begin with the amount of memory in the server.
2. Subtract out a bit for the operating system and perhaps for other programs, if MySQL isn't the only thing running on the server.
3. Subtract some more for MySQL's memory needs; it uses various buffers for per-query operations, for example.
4. Subtract enough for the InnoDB log files, so the operating system has enough memory to cache them, or at least the recently accessed portion thereof. (This advice applies to standard MySQL; in Percona Server, you can configure the log files to be opened with O_DIRECT, bypassing the operating system caches.) It might also be a good idea to leave some memory free for caching at least the tail of the binary logs, especially if you have replicas that are delayed, because they can sometimes read old binary log files on the master, causing some pressure on its memory.

5. Subtract enough for any other buffers and caches that you configure inside MySQL, such as the MyISAM key cache or the query cache.

6. Divide by 105%, which is an approximation of the overhead InnoDB adds on to manage the buffer pool itself.

7. Round the result down to a sensible number. Rounding down won't change things much, but overallocating can be a bad thing.

We were a bit blasé about some of the amounts of memory involved here—what exactly is "a bit for the operating system," anyway? That varies, and we'll discuss it in some depth later in this chapter and the rest of this book. You need to understand your system and estimate how much memory you think it'll need to run well. This is why one-size-fits-all configuration files are not possible. Experience and sometimes a bit of math will be your guide.

Here's an example. Suppose you have a server with 192 GB of memory, and you want to dedicate it to MySQL and to use only InnoDB, with no query cache and not very many connections to the server. If your log files are 4 GB in total, you might proceed as follows: "I think that 2 GB or 5% of overall memory, whichever is larger, should be enough for the OS and for MySQL's other memory needs; subtract 4 GB for the log files; use everything else for InnoDB." The result is about 177 GB, but it's probably a good idea to round that down a bit. You might configure the server with 168 GB or so of buffer pool. If the server tends to run with a fair amount of unallocated memory in practice, you might set the buffer pool larger when there is an opportunity to restart it for some other purpose.

The result would be very different if you had a number of MyISAM tables and needed to cache their indexes, naturally. It would also be quite different on Windows, which has trouble using large amounts of memory in most MySQL versions (although it's improved in MySQL 5.5), or if you chose not to use O_DIRECT for some reason.

As you can see, it's not crucial to get this setting precisely right from the beginning. It's better to start with a safe value that's larger than the default but not as large as it could be, run the server for a while, and see how much memory it really uses. These things can be hard to anticipate, because MySQL's memory usage isn't always predictable: it can depend on factors such as the query complexity and concurrency. With a simple workload, MySQL's memory needs are pretty minimal—around 256 KB per connection. But complex queries that use temporary tables, sorting, stored procedures, and so forth can use a lot more RAM.

That's why we chose a pretty safe starting point. You can see that even the conservative setting for InnoDB's buffer pool is actually 87.5% of the server's installed RAM—more than 75%, which is why we said that simple ratios aren't the right approach.

We suggest that when it comes to configuring the memory buffers, you err on the side of caution, rather than making them too large. If you make the buffer pool 20% smaller than it could be, you'll likely impact performance only a small amount—maybe a few percent. If you set it 20% too large, you'll probably cause much more severe problems: swapping, thrashing the disks, or even running out of memory and crashing hard.

This InnoDB configuration example illustrates our preferred approach to configuring the server: understand what it does internally and how that interacts with the settings, and then decide.

Time Changes Everything

The need to configure MySQL's memory buffers precisely has become less important over time. When a powerful server had 4 GB of memory, we worked hard to balance its resources so it could run a thousand connections. This typically required us to reserve a gigabyte or so for MySQL's needs, which was a quarter of the server's total memory and greatly influenced how we sized the buffer pool.

Nowadays a comparable server has 144 GB of memory, but we typically see about the same number of connections in most applications, and the per-connection buffers haven't really changed much either. As a result, we might generously reserve 4 GB of memory for MySQL, which is a drop in the bucket. It doesn't impact how we size the buffer pool very much.

Most of the other settings in our sample file are pretty self-explanatory, and many of them are a matter of judgment. We'll explore several of them in the rest of this chapter. You can see that we've enabled logging, disabled the query cache, and so on. We'll also discuss some safety and sanity settings later in this chapter, which can be very helpful for making your server more robust and helping prevent bad data and other problems. We don't show those settings here.

One setting to explain here is the `open_files_limit` option. We've set this as large as possible on a typical Linux system. Open filehandles are very cheap on modern operating systems. If this setting isn't large enough, you'll see error 24, "too many open files."

Skipping all the way to the end, the last section in the configuration file is for client programs such as *mysql* and *mysqladmin*, and simply lets them know how to connect to the server. You should set the values for client programs to match those you chose for the server.

Inspecting MySQL Server Status Variables

Sometimes you can use the output from SHOW GLOBAL STATUS as input to your configuration to help customize the settings better for your workload. For the best results, look both at absolute values and at how the values change over time, preferably with several snapshots at peak and off-peak times. You can use the following command to see incremental changes to status variables every 60 seconds:

```
$ mysqladmin extended-status -ri60
```

We will frequently refer to changes in status variables over time as we explain various configuration settings. We will usually expect you to be examining the output of a command such as the one we just showed. Other helpful tools that can provide a compact display of status counter changes are Percona Toolkit's *pt-mext* or *pt-mysql-summary*.

Now that we've shown you the preliminaries, we'll take you on a guided tour of some server internals, interleaved with advice on configuration. This will give you the background you'll need to choose appropriate values for configuration options when we return to the sample configuration file later.

Configuring Memory Usage

Configuring MySQL to use memory correctly is vital to good performance. You'll almost certainly need to customize MySQL's memory usage for your needs. You can think of MySQL's memory consumption as falling into two categories: the memory you can control, and the memory you can't. You can't control how much memory MySQL uses merely to run the server, parse queries, and manage its internals, but you have a lot of control over how much memory it uses for specific purposes. Making good use of the memory you can control is not hard, but it does require you to know what you're configuring.

As shown previously, you can approach memory configuration in steps:

1. Determine the absolute upper limit of memory MySQL can possibly use.
2. Determine how much memory MySQL will use for per-connection needs, such as sort buffers and temporary tables.
3. Determine how much memory the operating system needs to run well. Include memory for other programs that run on the same machine, such as periodic jobs.
4. Assuming that it makes sense to do so, use the rest of the memory for MySQL's caches, such as the InnoDB buffer pool.

We go over each of these steps in the following sections, and then we take a more detailed look at the various MySQL caches' requirements.

How Much Memory Can MySQL Use?

There is a hard upper limit on the amount of memory that can possibly be available to MySQL on any given system. The starting point is the amount of physically installed memory. If your server doesn't have it, MySQL can't use it.

You also need to think about operating system or architecture limits, such as restrictions 32-bit operating systems place on how much memory a given process can address. Because MySQL runs in a single process with multiple threads, the amount of memory it can use overall might be severely limited by such restrictions—for example,

32-bit Linux kernels limit the amount of memory any one process can address to a value that is typically between 2.5 and 2.7 GB. Running out of address space is very dangerous and can cause MySQL to crash. This is pretty rare to see these days, but it used to be common.

There are many other operating system–specific parameters and oddities that must be taken into account, including not just the per-process limits, but also stack sizes and other settings. The system's *glibc* libraries can also impose limits per single allocation. For example, you might not be able to set innodb_buffer_pool larger than 2 GB if that's all your *glibc* libraries support in a single allocation.

Even on 64-bit servers, some limitations still apply. For example, many of the buffers we discuss, such as the key buffer, are limited to 4 GB on a 64-bit server in 5.0 and older MySQL versions. Some of these restrictions are lifted in MySQL 5.1, and the MySQL manual documents each variable's maximum value.

Per-Connection Memory Needs

MySQL needs a small amount of memory just to hold a connection (thread) open. It also requires a base amount of memory to execute any given query. You'll need to set aside enough memory for MySQL to execute queries during peak load times. Otherwise, your queries will be starved for memory, and they will run poorly or fail.

It's useful to know how much memory MySQL will consume during peak usage, but some usage patterns can unexpectedly consume a lot of memory, which makes this hard to predict. Prepared statements are one example, because you can have many of them open at once. Another example is the InnoDB data dictionary (more about this later).

You don't need to assume a worst-case scenario when trying to predict peak memory consumption. For example, if you configure MySQL to allow a maximum of 100 connections, it theoretically might be possible to simultaneously run large queries on all 100 connections, but in reality this probably won't happen. For example, if you set myisam_sort_buffer_size to 256M, your worst-case usage is at least 25 GB, but this level of consumption is highly unlikely to actually occur. Queries that use many large temporary tables, or complex stored procedures, are the most likely causes of high per-connection memory consumption.

Rather than calculating worst cases, a better approach is to watch your server under a real workload and see how much memory it uses, which you can see by watching the process's virtual memory size. In many Unix-like systems, this is reported in the VIRT column in *top*, or VSZ in *ps*. The next chapter has more information on how to monitor memory usage.

Reserving Memory for the Operating System

Just as with queries, you need to reserve enough memory for the operating system to do its work. The best indication that the operating system has enough memory is that it's not actively swapping (paging) virtual memory to disk. (See the next chapter for more on this topic.)

You should reserve at least a gigabyte or two for the operating system—more for machines with a lot of memory. We suggest starting with 2 GB or 5% of total memory as the baseline, whichever is greater. Add in some extra for safety, and add in some more if you'll be running periodic memory-intensive jobs on the machine (such as backups). Don't add any memory for the operating system's caches, because they can be very large. The operating system will generally use any leftover memory for these caches, and we consider them separately from the operating system's own needs in the following sections.

Allocating Memory for Caches

If the server is dedicated to MySQL, any memory you don't reserve for the operating system or for query processing is available for caches.

MySQL needs more memory for caches than anything else. It uses caches to avoid disk access, which is orders of magnitude slower than accessing data in memory. The operating system might cache some data on MySQL's behalf (especially for MyISAM), but MySQL needs lots of memory for itself, too.

The following are the most important caches to consider for most installations:

- The InnoDB buffer pool
- The operating system caches for InnoDB log files and MyISAM data
- MyISAM key caches
- The query cache
- Caches you can't really configure, such as the operating system's caches of binary logs and table definition files

There are other caches, but they generally don't use much memory. We discussed the query cache in detail in the previous chapter, so the following sections concentrate on the caches InnoDB and MyISAM need to work well.

It is much easier to configure a server if you're using only one storage engine. If you're using only MyISAM tables, you can disable InnoDB completely, and if you're using only InnoDB, you need to allocate only minimal resources for MyISAM (MySQL uses MyISAM tables internally for some operations). But if you're using a mixture of storage engines, it can be very hard to figure out the right balance between them. The best approach we've found is to make an educated guess and then observe the server in operation.

The InnoDB Buffer Pool

If you use mostly InnoDB tables, the InnoDB buffer pool probably needs more memory than anything else. The InnoDB buffer pool doesn't just cache indexes: it also holds row data, the adaptive hash index, the insert buffer, locks, and other internal structures. InnoDB also uses the buffer pool to help it delay writes, so it can merge many writes together and perform them sequentially. In short, InnoDB relies *heavily* on the buffer pool, and you should be sure to allocate enough memory to it, typically with a process such as that shown earlier in this chapter. You can use variables from SHOW commands or tools such as *innotop* to monitor your InnoDB buffer pool's memory usage.

If you don't have much data, and you know that your data won't grow quickly, you don't need to overallocate memory to the buffer pool. It's not really beneficial to make it much larger than the size of the tables and indexes that it will hold. There's nothing wrong with planning ahead for a rapidly growing database, of course, but sometimes we see huge buffer pools with a tiny amount of data. This isn't necessary.

Large buffer pools come with some challenges, such as long shutdown and warmup times. If there are a lot of dirty (modified) pages in the buffer pool InnoDB can take a long time to shut down, because it writes the dirty pages to the data files upon shutdown. You can force it to shut down quickly, but then it just has to do more recovery when it restarts, so you can't actually speed up the shutdown and restart cycle time. If you know in advance when you need to shut down, you can change the innodb_max_dirty_pages_pct variable at runtime to a lower value, wait for the flush thread to clean up the buffer pool, and then shut down once the number of dirty pages becomes small. You can monitor the number of dirty pages by watching the Innodb_buffer_pool_pages_dirty server status variable or using *innotop* to monitor SHOW INNODB STATUS.

Lowering the value of the innodb_max_dirty_pages_pct variable doesn't actually guarantee that InnoDB will keep fewer dirty pages in the buffer pool. Instead, it controls the threshold at which InnoDB stops being "lazy." InnoDB's default behavior is to flush dirty pages with a background thread, merging writes together and performing them sequentially for efficiency. This behavior is called "lazy" because it lets InnoDB delay flushing dirty pages in the buffer pool, unless it needs to use the space for some other data. When the percentage of dirty pages exceeds the threshold, InnoDB will flush pages as quickly as it can to try to keep the dirty page count lower. InnoDB will also go into "furious flushing" mode when there isn't enough space left in the transaction logs, which is one reason that large logs can improve performance.

When you have a large buffer pool, especially in combination with slow disks, the server might take a long time (many hours or even days) to warm up after a restart. In such cases, you might benefit from using Percona Server's feature to reload the pages after restart. This can reduce warmup times to a few minutes. MySQL 5.6 will introduce a similar feature. This is especially beneficial on replicas, which pay an extra warmup penalty due to the single-threaded nature of replication.

If you can't use Percona Server's fast warmup feature, some people issue full-table scans or index scans immediately after a restart to load indexes into the buffer pool. This is crude, but can sometimes be better than nothing. You can use the `init_file` setting to accomplish this. You can place SQL into a file that's executed when MySQL starts up. The filename must be specified in the `init_file` option, and the file can include multiple SQL commands, each on a single line (no comments are allowed).

The MyISAM Key Caches

The MyISAM key caches are also referred to as *key buffers*; there is one by default, but you can create more. Unlike InnoDB and some other storage engines, MyISAM itself caches only indexes, not data (it lets the operating system cache the data). If you use mostly MyISAM, you should allocate a lot of memory to the key caches.

The most important option is the `key_buffer_size`. Any memory not allocated to it will be available for the operating system caches, which the operating system will usually fill with data from MyISAM's *.MYD* files. MySQL 5.0 has a hard upper limit of 4 GB for this variable, no matter what architecture you're running. MySQL 5.1 allows larger sizes. Check the current documentation for your version of the server.

When you're deciding how much memory to allocate to the key caches, it might help to know how much space your MyISAM indexes are actually using on disk. You don't need to make the key buffers larger than the data they will cache. You can query the `INFORMATION_SCHEMA` tables and sum up the `INDEX_LENGTH` column to find out the size of the files storing the indexes:

```
SELECT SUM(INDEX_LENGTH) FROM INFORMATION_SCHEMA.TABLES WHERE ENGINE='MYISAM';
```

If you have a Unix-like system, you can also use a command like the following:

```
$ du -sch `find /path/to/mysql/data/directory/ -name "*.MYI"`
```

How big should you set the key caches? No bigger than the total index size or 25% to 50% of the amount of memory you reserved for operating system caches, whichever is smaller.

By default, MyISAM caches all indexes in the default key buffer, but you can create multiple named key buffers. This lets you keep more than 4 GB of indexes in memory at once. To create key buffers named `key_buffer_1` and `key_buffer_2`, each sized at 1 GB, place the following in the configuration file:

```
key_buffer_1.key_buffer_size = 1G
key_buffer_2.key_buffer_size = 1G
```

Now there are three key buffers: the two explicitly created by those lines and the default buffer. You can use the `CACHE INDEX` command to map tables to caches. You can tell MySQL to use `key_buffer_1` for the indexes from tables t1 and t2 with the following SQL statement:

```
mysql> CACHE INDEX t1, t2 IN key_buffer_1;
```

Now when MySQL reads blocks from the indexes on these tables, it will cache the blocks in the specified buffer. You can also preload the tables' indexes into the cache with the init_file option and the LOAD INDEX command:

```
mysql> LOAD INDEX INTO CACHE t1, t2;
```

Any indexes you don't explicitly map to a key buffer will be assigned to the default buffer the first time MySQL needs to access the *.MYI* file.

You can monitor key buffer usage with information from SHOW STATUS and SHOW VARI ABLES. You can calculate the percentage of the buffer in use with this equation:

```
100 - ( (Key_blocks_unused * key_cache_block_size) * 100 / key_buffer_size )
```

If the server doesn't use all of its key buffer after it's been running for a long time, you can consider making the buffer smaller.

What about the key buffer hit ratio? As we explained previously, this number is useless. For example, the difference between 99% and 99.9% looks small, but it really represents a tenfold increase. The cache hit ratio is also application-dependent: some applications might work fine at 95%, whereas others might be I/O-bound at 99.9%. You might even be able to get a 99.99% hit ratio with properly sized caches.

The number of cache *misses* per second is much more empirically useful. Suppose you have a single hard drive that can do 100 random reads per second. Five misses per second will not cause your workload to be I/O-bound, but 80 per second will likely cause problems. You can use the following equation to calculate this value:

```
Key_reads / Uptime
```

Calculate the number of misses incrementally over intervals of 10 to 100 seconds, so you can get an idea of the current performance. The following command will show the incremental values every 10 seconds:

```
$ mysqladmin extended-status -r -i 10 | grep Key_reads
```

Remember that MyISAM uses the operating system cache for the data files, which are often larger than the indexes. Therefore, it often makes sense to leave more memory for the operating system cache than for the key caches. Even if you have enough memory to cache all the indexes, and the key cache miss rate is very low, cache misses when MyISAM tries to read from the data files (not the index files!) happen at the operating system level, which is completely invisible to MySQL. Thus, you can have a lot of data file cache misses independently of your index cache miss rate.

Finally, even if you don't have any MyISAM tables, bear in mind that you still need to set key_buffer_size to a small amount of memory, such as 32M. The MySQL server sometimes uses MyISAM tables for internal purposes, such as temporary tables for GROUP BY queries.

The MyISAM key block size

The key block size is important (especially for write-intensive workloads) because of the way it causes MyISAM, the operating system cache, and the filesystem to interact. If the key block size is too small, you might encounter *read-around writes*, which are writes that the operating system cannot perform without first reading some data from the disk. Here's how a read-around write happens, assuming the operating system's page size is 4 KB (typically true on the x86 architecture) and the key block size is 1 KB:

1. MyISAM requests a 1 KB key block from disk.
2. The operating system reads 4 KB of data from the disk and caches it, then passes the desired 1 KB of data to MyISAM.
3. The operating system discards the cached data in favor of some other data.
4. MyISAM modifies the 1 KB key block and asks the operating system to write it back to disk.
5. The operating system reads the same 4 KB of data from the disk into the operating system cache, modifies the 1 KB that MyISAM changed, and writes the entire 4 KB back to disk.

The read-around write happened in step 5, when MyISAM asked the operating system to write only part of a 4 KB page. If MyISAM's block size had matched the operating system's, the disk read in step 5 could have been avoided.[6]

Unfortunately, in MySQL 5.0 and earlier there's no way to configure the key block size. However, in MySQL 5.1 and later you can avoid read-around writes by making MyISAM's key block size the same as the operating system's. The `myisam_block_size` variable controls the key block size. You can also specify the size for each key with the `KEY_BLOCK_SIZE` option in a `CREATE TABLE` or `CREATE INDEX` statement, but because all keys are stored in the same file, you really need all of them to have blocks as large as or larger than the operating system's to avoid alignment issues that could still cause read-around writes. (For example, if one key has 1 KB blocks and another has 4 KB blocks, the 4 KB block boundaries might not match the operating system's page boundaries.)

The Thread Cache

The thread cache holds threads that aren't currently associated with a connection but are ready to serve new connections. When there's a thread in the cache and a new connection is created, MySQL removes the thread from the cache and gives it to the new connection. When the connection is closed, MySQL places the thread back into

---

6. Theoretically, if you could ensure that the original 4 KB of data was still in the operating system's cache, the read wouldn't be needed. However, you have no control over which blocks the operating system decides to keep in its cache. You can find out which blocks are in the cache with the *fincore* tool, available at *http://net.doit.wisc.edu/~plonka/fincore/*.

the cache, if there's room. If there isn't room, MySQL destroys the thread. As long as MySQL has a free thread in the cache it can respond rapidly to connection requests, because it doesn't have to create a new thread for each connection.

The thread_cache_size variable specifies the number of threads MySQL can keep in the cache. You probably won't need to configure this value unless your server gets many connection requests. To check whether the thread cache is large enough, watch the Threads_created status variable. We generally try to keep the thread cache large enough that we see fewer than 10 new threads created each second, but it's often pretty easy to get this number lower than 1 per second.

A good approach is to watch the Threads_connected variable and try to set thread _cache_size large enough to handle the typical fluctuation in your workload. For example, if Threads_connected usually stays between 100 and 120, you can set the cache size to 20. If it stays between 500 and 700, a thread cache of 200 should be large enough. Think of it this way: at 700 connections, there are probably no threads in the cache; at 500 connections, there are 200 cached threads ready to be used if the load increases to 700 again.

Making the thread cache very large is probably not necessary for most uses, but keeping it small doesn't save much memory, so there's little benefit in doing so. Each thread that's in the thread cache or sleeping typically uses around 256 KB of memory. This is not very much compared to the amount of memory a thread can use when a connection is actively processing a query. In general, you should keep your thread cache large enough that Threads_created doesn't increase very often. If this is a very large number, however (e.g., many thousand threads), you might want to set it lower because some operating systems don't handle very large numbers of threads well, even when most of them are sleeping.

The Table Cache

The table cache is similar in concept to the thread cache, but it stores objects that represent tables. Each object in the cache contains the associated table's parsed .frm file, plus other data. Exactly what else is in the object depends on the table's storage engine. For example, for MyISAM, it holds the table data and/or index file descriptors. For merge tables it might hold many file descriptors, because merge tables can have many underlying tables.

The table cache can help you reuse resources. For instance, when a query requests access to a MyISAM table, MySQL might be able to give it a file descriptor from the cached object. Although this does avoid the cost of opening a file descriptor, that's not as expensive as you might think. Opening and closing file descriptors is very fast on local storage; the server should be able to do it a million times a second easily (it's different on network-attached storage, though). The real benefit of the table cache is for MyISAM tables, where it lets the server avoid modifying the MyISAM file headers to mark a table as "in use."[7]

The table cache's design is one of the areas where the separation between the server and the storage engines is not completely clean, for historical reasons. The table cache is a little less important for InnoDB, because InnoDB doesn't rely on it for as many purposes (such as holding file descriptors; it has its own version of a table cache for this purpose). However, even InnoDB benefits from caching the parsed *.frm* files.

In MySQL 5.1, the table cache is separated into two parts: a cache of open tables and a table definition cache (configured via the `table_open_cache` and `table_definition _cache` variables). Thus, the table definitions (the parsed *.frm* files) are separated from the other resources, such as file descriptors. Opened tables are still per-thread, per-table-used, but the table definitions are global and can be shared among all connections efficiently. You can generally set `table_definition_cache` high enough to cache all your table definitions. Unless you have tens of thousands of tables, this is likely to be the easiest approach.

If the `Opened_tables` status variable is large or increasing, the table cache might not be large enough, and you can consider increasing the `table_cache` system variable (or `table_open_cache`, in MySQL 5.1). However, note that this counter increases when you create and drop temporary tables, so if you do that a lot, you'll never get the counter to stop increasing.

One downside to making the table cache very large is that it might cause longer shutdown times when your server has a lot of MyISAM tables, because the key blocks have to be flushed and the tables have to be marked as no longer open. It can also make `FLUSH TABLES WITH READ LOCK` take a long time to complete, for the same reason.

More seriously, the algorithms that check the table cache aren't very efficient; more on this later.

If you get errors indicating that MySQL can't open any more files (use the *perror* utility to check what the error number means), you might need to increase the number of files MySQL is allowed to keep open. You can do this with the `open_files_limit` server variable in your *my.cnf* file.

The thread and table caches don't really use much memory, and they can be beneficial when they conserve resources. Although creating a new thread and opening a new table aren't really expensive compared to other things MySQL might do, the overhead can add up. Caching threads and tables can sometimes improve efficiency.

---

7. The concept of an "opened table" can be a little confusing. MySQL counts a table as opened many times when different queries are accessing it simultaneously, or even when a single query refers to the same table more than once, as in a subquery or a self-join. MyISAM's index files contain a counter that MyISAM increments when the table is opened and decrements when it is closed. This lets MyISAM see when the table wasn't closed cleanly: if it opens a table for the first time and the counter is not zero, the table wasn't closed cleanly.

The InnoDB Data Dictionary

InnoDB has its own per-table cache, variously called a *table definition cache* or *data dictionary*, which you cannot configure in current versions of MySQL. When InnoDB opens a table, it adds a corresponding object to the data dictionary. Each table can take up 4 KB or more of memory (although much less space is required in MySQL 5.1). Tables are not removed from the data dictionary when they are closed.

As a result, the server can appear to leak memory over time, due to an ever-increasing number of entries in the dictionary cache. It isn't truly leaking memory; it just isn't implementing any kind of cache expiration. This is normally a problem only when you have many (thousands or tens of thousands) large tables. If this is a problem for you, you can use Percona Server, which has an option to limit the data dictionary's size by removing tables that are unused. There is a similar feature in the yet-to-be-released MySQL 5.6.

The other performance issue is computing statistics for the tables when opening them for the first time, which is expensive because it requires a lot of I/O. In contrast to MyISAM, InnoDB doesn't store statistics in the tables permanently; it recomputes them each time it starts, and thereafter when various intervals expire or events occur (changes to the table's contents, queries against the INFORMATION_SCHEMA, and so on). If you have a lot of tables, your server can take hours to start and fully warm up, during which time it might not be doing much other than waiting for one I/O operation after another. You can enable the innodb_use_sys_stats_table option in Percona Server (also in MySQL 5.6, but called innodb_analyze_is_persistent) to store the statistics persistently on disk and solve this problem.

Even after startup, InnoDB statistics operations can have an impact on the server and on individual queries. You can turn off the innodb_stats_on_metadata option to avoid time-consuming refreshes of table statistics. This can make a big difference when tools such as IDEs are querying the INFORMATION_SCHEMA tables.

If you use InnoDB's innodb_file_per_table option (described later), there's a separate limit on the number of *.ibd* files InnoDB can keep open at any time. This is handled by the InnoDB storage engine, not the MySQL server, and is controlled by innodb_open_files. InnoDB doesn't open files the same way MyISAM does: whereas MyISAM uses the table cache to hold file descriptors for open tables, in InnoDB there is no direct relationship between open tables and open files. InnoDB uses a single, global file descriptor for each *.ibd* file. If you can afford it, it's best to set innodb_open_files large enough that the server can keep all *.ibd* files open simultaneously.

Configuring MySQL's I/O Behavior

A few configuration options affect how MySQL synchronizes data to disk and performs recovery. These can affect performance dramatically, because they involve expensive I/O operations. They also represent a trade-off between performance and data safety.

In general, it's expensive to ensure that your data is written to disk immediately and consistently. If you're willing to risk the danger that a disk write won't really make it to permanent storage, you can increase concurrency and/or reduce I/O waits, but you'll have to decide for yourself how much risk you can tolerate.

InnoDB I/O Configuration

InnoDB permits you to control not only how it recovers, but also how it opens and flushes its data, which greatly affects recovery and overall performance. InnoDB's recovery process is automatic and always runs when InnoDB starts, though you can influence what actions it takes. Leaving aside recovery and assuming nothing ever crashes or goes wrong, there's still a lot to configure for InnoDB. It has a complex chain of buffers and files designed to increase performance and guarantee ACID properties, and each piece of the chain is configurable. Figure 8-1 illustrates these files and buffers.

A few of the most important things to change for normal usage are the InnoDB log file size, how InnoDB flushes its log buffer, and how InnoDB performs I/O.

The InnoDB transaction log

InnoDB uses its log to reduce the cost of committing transactions. Instead of flushing the buffer pool to disk when each transaction commits, it logs the transactions. The changes transactions make to data and indexes often map to random locations in the tablespace, so flushing these changes to disk would require random I/O. InnoDB assumes it's using conventional disks, where random I/O is much more expensive than sequential I/O because of the time it takes to seek to the correct location on disk and wait for the desired part of the disk to rotate under the head.

InnoDB uses its log to convert this random disk I/O into sequential I/O. Once the log is safely on disk, the transactions are permanent, even though the changes haven't been written to the data files yet. If something bad happens (such as a power failure), InnoDB can replay the log and recover the committed transactions.

Of course, InnoDB does ultimately have to write the changes to the data files, because the log has a fixed size. It writes to the log in a circular fashion: when it reaches the end of the log, it wraps around to the beginning. It can't overwrite a log record if the changes contained there haven't been applied to the data files, because this would erase the only permanent record of the committed transaction.

InnoDB uses a background thread to flush the changes to the data files intelligently. This thread can group writes together and make the data writes sequential, for improved efficiency. In effect, the transaction log converts random data file I/O into mostly sequential log file and data file I/O. Moving flushes into the background makes queries complete more quickly and helps cushion the I/O system from spikes in the query load.

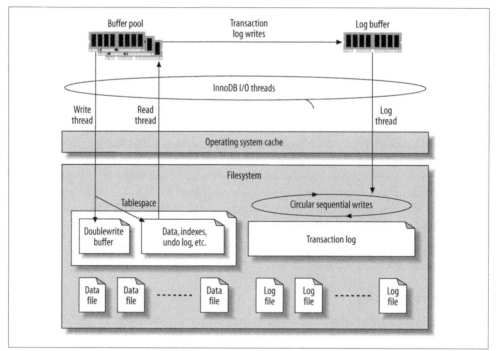

Figure 8-1. InnoDB's buffers and files

The overall log file size is controlled by `innodb_log_file_size` and `innodb_log_files_in_group`, and it's very important for write performance. The total size is the sum of each file's size. By default there are two 5 MB files, for a total of 10 MB. This is much too small for a high-performance workload. You need hundreds of megabytes, or even gigabytes, of log files.

InnoDB uses multiple files as a single circular log. You usually don't need to change the default number of logs, just the size of each log file. To change the log file size, shut down MySQL cleanly, move the old logs away, reconfigure, and restart. Be sure MySQL shuts down cleanly, or the log files will actually have entries that need to be applied to the data files! Watch the MySQL error log when you restart the server. After you've restarted successfully, you can delete the old log files.

Log file size and the log buffer. To determine the ideal size for your log files, you'll have to weigh the overhead of routine data changes against the recovery time required in the event of a crash. If the log is too small, InnoDB will have to do more checkpoints, causing more log writes. In extreme cases, write queries might stall and have to wait for changes to be applied to the data files before there is room to write into the log. On the other hand, if the log is too large, InnoDB might have to do a lot of work when it recovers. This can greatly increase recovery time, although this process is much more efficient in newer MySQL versions.

Your data size and access patterns will influence the recovery time, too. Suppose you have a terabyte of data and 16 GB of buffer pool, and your total log size is 128 MB. If you have a lot of dirty pages (i.e., pages whose changes have not yet been flushed to the data files) in the buffer pool and they are uniformly spread across your terabyte of data, recovery after a crash might take a long time. InnoDB will have to scan through the log, examine the data files, and apply changes to the data files as needed. That's a lot of reading and writing! On the other hand, if the changes are localized—say, if only a few hundred megabytes of data are updated frequently—recovery might be fast, even when your data and log files are huge. Recovery time also depends on the size of a typical modification, which is related to your average row length. Short rows let more modifications fit in the log, so InnoDB might need to replay more modifications on recovery.[8]

When InnoDB changes any data, it writes a record of the change into its *log buffer*, which it keeps in memory. InnoDB flushes the buffer to the log files on disk when the buffer gets full, when a transaction commits, or once per second—whichever comes first. Increasing the buffer size, which is 1 MB by default, can help reduce I/O if you have large transactions. The variable that controls the buffer size is called `innodb_log_buffer_size`.

You usually don't need to make the buffer very large. The recommended range is 1 to 8 MB, and this usually will be enough unless you write a lot of huge `BLOB` records. The log entries are very compact compared to InnoDB's normal data. They are not page-based, so they don't waste space storing whole pages at a time. InnoDB also makes log entries as short as possible. They are sometimes even stored as the function number and parameters of a C function!

There's an additional circumstance where a larger value might be beneficial: when it can reduce contention during allocation of space in the buffer. When we're configuring servers with a large amount of memory, we'll sometimes allocate 32 to 128 MB of log buffer simply because spending such a relatively small amount of extra memory is not detrimental and it can help avoid pressure on a bottleneck. The bottleneck shows up as contention on the log buffer mutex when it's a problem.

You can monitor InnoDB's log and log buffer I/O performance by inspecting the LOG section of the output of SHOW INNODB STATUS, and by watching the `Innodb_os_log_written` status variable to see how much data InnoDB writes to the log files. A good rule of thumb is to watch it over intervals of 10 to 100 seconds and note the peak value. You can use this to judge whether your log buffer is sized right. For example, if you see a peak of 100 KB written to the log per second, a 1 MB log buffer is probably plenty.

You can also use this metric to decide on a good size for your log files. If the peak is 100 KB per second, a 256 MB log file is enough to store at least 2,560 seconds of log

---

8. For the curious, Percona Server's `innodb_recovery_stats` option can help you understand your server's workload from the standpoint of performing crash recovery.

entries, which is likely to be enough. As a rule of thumb, you can make your total log file size large enough to hold an hour's worth of server activity.

How InnoDB flushes the log buffer. When InnoDB flushes the log buffer to the log files on disk, it locks the buffer with a mutex, flushes it up to the desired point, and then moves any remaining entries to the front of the buffer. It is possible that more than one transaction will be ready to flush its log entries when the mutex is released. InnoDB has a group commit feature that can commit all of them to the log in a single I/O operation, but this is broken in MySQL 5.0 when the binary log is enabled. We wrote about group commit in the previous chapter.

The log buffer *must* be flushed to durable storage to ensure that committed transactions are fully durable. If you care more about performance than durability, you can change `innodb_flush_log_at_trx_commit` to control where and how often the log buffer is flushed. Possible settings are as follows:

0

> Write the log buffer to the log file and flush the log file every second, but do nothing at transaction commit.

1

> Write the log buffer to the log file and flush it to durable storage every time a transaction commits. This is the default (and safest) setting; it guarantees that you won't lose any committed transactions, unless the disk or operating system "fakes" the flush operation.

2

> Write the log buffer to the log file at every commit, but don't flush it. InnoDB schedules a flush once every second. The most important difference from the 0 setting (and what makes 2 the preferable setting) is that 2 won't lose any transactions if the MySQL process crashes. If the entire server crashes or loses power, however, you can still lose transactions.

It's important to know the difference between *writing* the log buffer to the log file and *flushing* the log to durable storage. In most operating systems, writing the buffer to the log simply moves the data from InnoDB's memory buffer to the operating system's cache, which is also in memory. It doesn't actually write the data to durable storage. Thus, settings 0 and 2 *usually* result in at most one second of lost data if there's a crash or a power outage, because the data might exist only in the operating system's cache. We say "usually" because InnoDB tries to flush the log file to disk about once per second no matter what, but it is possible to lose more than a second of transactions in some cases, such as when a flush gets stalled.

In contrast, flushing the log to durable storage means InnoDB asks the operating system to actually flush the data out of the cache and ensure it is *written to the disk*. This is a blocking I/O call that doesn't complete until the data is completely written. Because writing data to a disk is slow, this can dramatically reduce the number of transactions InnoDB can commit per second when `innodb_flush_log_at_trx_commit` is set to 1. Today's high-speed drives[9] can perform only a couple of hundred real disk transactions per second, simply because of the limitations of drive rotation speed and seek time.

Sometimes the hard disk controller or operating system fakes a flush by putting the data into yet *another* cache, such as the hard disk's own cache. This is faster but very dangerous, because the data might still be lost if the drive loses power. This is even worse than setting innodb_flush_log_at_trx_commit to something other than 1, because it can cause data corruption, not just lost transactions.

Setting innodb_flush_log_at_trx_commit to anything other than 1 can cause you to lose transactions. However, you might find the other settings useful if you don't care about durability (the D in ACID). Maybe you just want some of InnoDB's other features, such as clustered indexes, resistance to data corruption, and row-level locking. This is not uncommon when using InnoDB to replace MyISAM solely for performance reasons.

The best configuration for high-performance transactional needs is to leave innodb_flush_log_at_trx_commit set to 1 and place the log files on a RAID volume with a battery-backed write cache. This is both safe and very fast. In fact, we dare say that any production database server that's expected to handle a serious workload needs to have this kind of hardware.

Percona Server extends innodb_flush_log_at_trx_commit to make it a per-session variable, instead of global for the whole server. This allows applications with varying performance and durability needs to use the same database, and avoids the one-size-fits-all solution offered by standard MySQL.

How InnoDB opens and flushes log and data files

The innodb_flush_method option lets you configure how InnoDB actually interacts with the filesystem. Despite its name, it can affect how InnoDB reads data, not just how it writes it. The Windows and non-Windows values for this option are mutually exclusive: you can use async_unbuffered, unbuffered, and normal only on Windows, and you cannot use any other values on Windows. The default value is unbuffered on Windows and fdatasync on all other systems. (If SHOW GLOBAL VARIABLES shows the variable with an empty value, that means it's set to the default.)

 Changing how InnoDB performs I/O operations can impact performance greatly, so be sure you understand what you're doing before you change anything!

This is a slightly confusing option, because it affects both the log files and the data files, and it sometimes does different things to each kind of file. It would be nice to have one

---

9. We're talking about spindle-based disk drives with rotating platters, not solid-state hard drives, which have completely different performance characteristics.

configuration option for the logs and another for the data files, but they're combined. Here are the possible values:

fdatasync

> The default value on non-Windows systems: InnoDB uses `fsync()` to flush both data and log files.

> InnoDB generally uses `fsync()` instead of `fdatasync()`, even though this value seems to indicate the contrary. `fdatasync()` is like `fsync()`, except it flushes only the file's data, not its metadata (last modified time, etc.). Therefore, `fsync()` can cause more I/O. However, the InnoDB developers are very conservative, and they found that `fdatasync()` caused corruption in some cases. InnoDB determines which methods can be used safely; some options are set at compile time and some are discovered at runtime. It uses the fastest safe method it can.

> The disadvantage of using `fsync()` is that the operating system buffers at least some of the data in its own cache. In theory, this is wasteful double buffering, because InnoDB manages its own buffers more intelligently than the operating system can. However, the ultimate effect is very system- and filesystem-dependent. The double buffering might not be a bad thing if it lets the filesystem do smarter I/O scheduling and batching. Some filesystems and operating systems can accumulate writes and execute them together, reorder them for efficiency, or write to multiple devices in parallel. They might also do read-ahead optimizations, such as instructing the disk to preread the next sequential block if several have been requested in sequence.

> Sometimes these optimizations help, and sometimes they don't. You can read your system's manpage for `fsync(2)` if you're curious about exactly what your version of `fsync()` does.

> `innodb_file_per_table` causes each file to be `fsync()`ed separately, which means writes to multiple tables can't be combined into a single I/O operation. This might require InnoDB to perform a higher total number of `fsync()` operations.

O_DIRECT

> InnoDB uses the `O_DIRECT` flag, or `directio()`, depending on the system, on the data files. This option does not affect the log files and is not necessarily available on all Unix-like operating systems. At least GNU/Linux, FreeBSD, and Solaris (late 5.0 and newer) support it. Unlike the `O_DSYNC` flag, it affects both reads and writes.

> This setting still uses `fsync()` to flush the files to disk, but it instructs the operating system not to cache the data and not to use read-ahead. This disables the operating system's caches completely and makes all reads and writes go directly to the storage device, avoiding double buffering.

> On most systems, this is implemented with a call to `fcntl()` to set the `O_DIRECT` flag on the file descriptor, so you can read the `fcntl(2)` manpage for your system's details. On Solaris, this option uses `directio()`.

> If your RAID card does read-ahead, this setting will not disable that. It disables only the operating system's and/or filesystem's read-ahead capabilities.

You generally need a RAID card with a write cache set to a write-back policy if you use O_DIRECT, because that's typically the only thing that keeps performance good. Using O_DIRECT when there is no buffer between InnoDB and the actual storage device, such as when you have no write cache on your RAID card, can cause performance to degrade greatly. This is a bit less of a problem nowadays with multiple write threads (and native asynchronous I/O introduced in MySQL 5.5), but it's still the case in general.

This setting can cause the server's warmup time to increase significantly, especially if the operating system's cache is very large. It can also make a small buffer pool (e.g., a buffer pool of the default size) much slower than buffered I/O would. This is because the operating system won't "help out" by keeping more of the data in its own cache. If the desired data isn't in the buffer pool, InnoDB will have to read it directly from disk.

This setting does not impose any extra penalty on the use of innodb_file_per_table. However, the reverse can be true: if you do not use innodb_file_per_table, you can suffer from some serialization of I/O when you use O_DIRECT. This happens because some filesystems (including all of Linux's *ext* filesystems) have a per-inode mutex. When you use O_DIRECT with such filesystems, you really need innodb_file_per_table to be enabled. We delve more into filesystems in the next chapter.

ALL_O_DIRECT

This option is available in Percona Server and MariaDB. It lets the server open the log files, not just the data files, in the same way that standard MySQL opens the data files.

O_DSYNC

This option sets the O_SYNC flag on the open() call for the log files. It makes all writes synchronous—in other words, writes do not return until the data is written to disk. This option does not affect the data files.

The difference between the O_SYNC flag and the O_DIRECT flag is that O_SYNC doesn't disable caching at the operating system level. Therefore, it doesn't avoid double buffering, and it doesn't make writes go directly to disk. With O_SYNC, writes modify the data in the cache, and then it is sent to the disk.

While synchronous writes with O_SYNC might sound very similar to what fsync() does, the two can be implemented very differently on both the operating system and the hardware level. When the O_SYNC flag is used, the operating system might pass a "use synchronous I/O" flag down to the hardware level, telling the device not to use caches. On the other hand, fsync() tells the operating system to flush modified buffers to the device, followed by an instruction for the device to flush its own caches, if applicable, so it is certain that the data has been recorded on the physical media. Another difference is that with O_SYNC, every write() or pwrite() operation syncs data to disk before it finishes, blocking the calling process. In contrast, writing without the O_SYNC flag and then calling fsync() allows writes to accumulate in the cache (which makes each write fast), and then flushes them all at once.

Again, despite its name, this option sets the O_SYNC flag, not the O_DSYNC flag, because the InnoDB developers found bugs with O_DSYNC. O_SYNC and O_DSYNC are similar to fysnc() and fdatasync(): O_SYNC syncs both data and metadata, whereas O_DSYNC syncs data only.

async_unbuffered

This is the default value on Windows. This option causes InnoDB to use unbuffered I/O for most writes; the exception is that it uses buffered I/O to the log files when innodb_flush_log_at_trx_commit is set to 2.

This setting causes InnoDB to use the operating system's native asynchronous (overlapped) I/O for both reads and writes on Windows 2000, XP, and newer. On older Windows versions, InnoDB uses its own asynchronous I/O, which is implemented with threads.

unbuffered

Windows-only. This option is similar to async_unbuffered but does not use native asynchronous I/O.

normal

Windows-only. This option causes InnoDB not to use native asynchronous I/O or unbuffered I/O.

nosync *and* littlesync

For development use only. These options are undocumented and unsafe for production; they should *not* be used.

If that all seemed like a lot of explanation with no advice, here's the advice: if you use a Unix-like operating system and your RAID controller has a battery-backed write cache, we recommend that you use O_DIRECT. If not, either the default or O_DIRECT will probably be the best choice, depending on your application.

The InnoDB tablespace

InnoDB keeps its data in a *tablespace*, which is essentially a virtual filesystem spanning one or many files on disk. InnoDB uses the tablespace for many purposes, not just for storing tables and indexes. It keeps its undo log (old row versions), insert buffer, doublewrite buffer (described in an upcoming section), and other internal structures in the tablespace.

Configuring the tablespace. You specify the tablespace files with the innodb_data_file _path configuration option. The files are all contained in the directory given by innodb_data_home_dir. Here's an example:

```
innodb_data_home_dir  = /var/lib/mysql/
innodb_data_file_path = ibdata1:1G;ibdata2:1G;ibdata3:1G
```

That creates a 3 GB tablespace in three files. Sometimes people wonder whether they can use multiple files to spread load across drives, like this:

```
innodb_data_file_path = /disk1/ibdata1:1G;/disk2/ibdata2:1G;...
```

While that does indeed place the files in different directories, which represent different drives in this example, InnoDB concatenates the files end-to-end. Thus, you usually don't gain much this way. InnoDB will fill the first file, then the second when the first is full, and so on; the load isn't really spread in the fashion you need for higher performance. A RAID controller is a smarter way to spread load.

To allow the tablespace to grow if it runs out of space, you can make the last file autoextend as follows:

```
...ibdata3:1G:autoextend
```

The default behavior is to create a single 10 MB autoextending file. If you make the file autoextend, it's a good idea to place an upper limit on the tablespace's size to keep it from growing very large, because once it grows, it doesn't shrink. For example, the following example limits the autoextending file to 2 GB:

```
...ibdata3:1G:autoextend:max:2G
```

Managing a single tablespace can be a hassle, especially if it autoextends and you want to reclaim the space (for this reason, we recommend disabling the autoextend feature, or at least setting a reasonable cap on the space). The only way to reclaim space is to dump your data, shut down MySQL, delete all the files, change the configuration, restart, let InnoDB create new empty files, and restore your data. InnoDB is completely unforgiving about its tablespace—you cannot simply remove files or change their sizes. It will refuse to start if you corrupt its tablespace. It is likewise very strict about its log files. If you're used to casually moving files around with MyISAM, take heed!

The innodb_file_per_table option lets you configure InnoDB to use one file per table in MySQL 4.1 and later. It stores the data in the database directory as *tablename.ibd* files. This makes it easier to reclaim space when you drop a table, and it can be useful for spreading tables across multiple disks. However, placing the data in multiple files can actually result in more wasted space overall, because it trades internal fragmentation in the single InnoDB tablespace for wasted space in the *.ibd* files. This is more of an issue for very small tables, because InnoDB's page size is 16 KB. Even if your table has only 1 KB of data, it will still require at least 16 KB on disk.

Even if you enable the innodb_file_per_table option, you'll still need the main tablespace for the undo logs and other system data. It will be smaller if you're not storing all the data in it, but it's still a good idea to disable autoextend, because you can't shrink the file without reloading all your data.

Some people like to use innodb_file_per_table just because of the extra manageability and visibility it gives you. For example, it's much faster to find a table's size by examining a single file than it is to use SHOW TABLE STATUS, which has to perform more complex work to determine how many pages are allocated to a table.

There is a dark side to `innodb_file_per_table`: slow `DROP TABLE` performance. This can be severe enough to cause a noticeable server-wide stall, for two reasons:

- Dropping the table unlinks (deletes) the file at the filesystem level, which can be very slow on some filesystems (ext3, we're looking at you). You can shorten the duration of this with tricks on the filesystem: link the *.ibd* file to a zero-sized file, then delete the file manually, instead of waiting for MySQL to do it.

- When you enable this option, each table gets its own tablespace inside InnoDB. It turns out that removing the tablespace actually requires InnoDB to lock and scan the buffer pool while it looks for pages belonging to this tablespace, which is very slow on a server with a large buffer pool. If you're going to be dropping a lot of InnoDB tables (including temporary tables) and you use `innodb_file_per_table`, you might benefit from the fix included with Percona Server, which lets the server lazily invalidate the pages belonging to the dropped tables. You just need to set the `innodb_lazy_drop_table` option.

What's the final recommendation? We suggest that you use `innodb_file_per_table` and cap the size of your shared tablespace to make your life easier. If you run into any circumstances that make this painful, as noted above, consider one of the fixes we suggested.

We should also note that you don't actually have to store your InnoDB files in a traditional filesystem. Like many traditional database servers, InnoDB offers the option of using a raw device—i.e., an unformatted partition—for its storage. However, today's filesystems can handle sufficiently large files that you shouldn't need to use this option. Using raw devices might improve performance by a few percentage points, but we don't think this small increase justifies the disadvantages of not being able to manipulate the data as files. When you store your data on a raw partition, you can't use *mv*, *cp*, or any other tools on it. Ultimately, the tiny performance gains you get from using raw devices aren't worth the extra hassle.

Old row versions and the tablespace. InnoDB's tablespace can grow very large in a write-heavy environment. If transactions stay open for a long time (even if they're not doing any work) and they're using the default `REPEATABLE READ` transaction isolation level, InnoDB won't be able to remove old row versions, because the uncommitted transactions will still need to be able to see them. InnoDB stores the old versions in the tablespace, so it continues to grow as more data is updated. Sometimes the problem isn't uncommitted transactions, but just the workload: the purge process is only a single thread until recent versions of MySQL, and it might not be able to keep up with the number of old row versions that need to be purged.

In either case, the output of `SHOW INNODB STATUS` can help you pinpoint the problem. Look at the history list length; it shows the size of the undo log, in units of pages.

You can corroborate this by examining the first and second lines of the `TRANSACTIONS` section, which show the current transaction number and the point to which the purge has completed. If the difference is large, you might have a lot of unpurged transactions. Here's an example:

```
------------
TRANSACTIONS
------------
Trx id counter 0 80157601
Purge done for trx's n:o <0 80154573 undo n:o <0 0
```

The transaction identifier is a 64-bit number composed of two 32-bit numbers (it's a hexadecimal number in newer versions of InnoDB), so you might have to do a little math to compute the difference. In this case it's easy, because the high bits are just zeros: there are 80,157,601 − 80,154,573 = 3,028 potentially unpurged transactions (*innotop* can do this math for you). We said "potentially" because a large difference doesn't necessarily mean there are a lot of unpurged rows. Only transactions that change data will create old row versions, and there might be many transactions that haven't changed any data (conversely, a single transaction could have changed many rows).

If you have a large undo log and your tablespace is growing because of it, you can force MySQL to slow down enough for InnoDB's purge thread to keep up. This might not sound attractive, but there's no alternative. Otherwise, InnoDB will keep writing data and filling up your disk until the disk runs out of space or the tablespace reaches the limits you've defined.

To throttle the writes, set the innodb_max_purge_lag variable to a value other than 0. This value indicates the maximum number of transactions that can be waiting to be purged before InnoDB starts to delay further queries that update data. You'll have to know your workload to decide on a good value. As an example, if your average transaction affects 1 KB of rows and you can tolerate 100 MB of unpurged rows in your tablespace, you could set the value to 100000.

Bear in mind that unpurged row versions impact all queries, because they effectively make your tables and indexes larger. If the purge thread simply can't keep up, performance can decrease dramatically. Setting the innodb_max_purge_lag variable will slow down performance too, but it's the lesser of the two evils.[10]

In newer versions of MySQL, and even in older versions of Percona Server and MariaDB, the purging process is significantly improved and separated from other internal housekeeping tasks. You can even create multiple dedicated purge threads to do this background work more quickly. This is a better option than throttling the server, if you can take advantage of it.

---

10. Note that the way this ought to be implemented is a topic of some debate; see MySQL bug 60776 for the details.

The doublewrite buffer

InnoDB uses a *doublewrite buffer* to avoid data corruption in case of partial page writes. A partial page write occurs when a disk write doesn't complete fully, and only a portion of a 16 KB page is written to disk. There are a variety of reasons (crashes, bugs, and so on) that a page might be partially written to disk. The doublewrite buffer guards against data corruption if this happens.

The doublewrite buffer is a special reserved area of the tablespace, large enough to hold 100 pages in a contiguous block. It is essentially a backup copy of recently written pages. When InnoDB flushes pages from the buffer pool to the disk, it writes (and flushes) them first to the doublewrite buffer, then to the main data area where they really belong. This ensures that every page write is atomic and durable.

Doesn't this mean that every page is written twice? Yes, it does, but because InnoDB writes several pages to the doublewrite buffer sequentially and only then calls fsync() to sync them to disk, the performance impact is relatively small—generally a few percentage points, not double, although the overhead is more noticeable on solid-state drives, as we'll discuss in the next chapter. More importantly, this strategy allows the log files to be much more efficient. Because the doublewrite buffer gives InnoDB a very strong guarantee that the data pages are not corrupt, InnoDB's log records don't have to contain full pages; they are more like binary deltas to pages.

If there's a partial page write to the doublewrite buffer itself, the original page will still be on disk in its real location. When InnoDB recovers, it will use the original page instead of the corrupted copy in the doublewrite buffer. However, if the doublewrite buffer succeeds and the write to the page's real location fails, InnoDB will use the copy in the doublewrite buffer during recovery. InnoDB knows when a page is corrupt because each page has a checksum at the end; the checksum is the last thing to be written, so if the page's contents don't match the checksum, the page is corrupt. Upon recovery, therefore, InnoDB just reads each page in the doublewrite buffer and verifies the checksums. If a page's checksum is incorrect, it reads the page from its original location.

In some cases, the doublewrite buffer really isn't necessary—for example, you might want to disable it on replicas. Also, some filesystems (such as ZFS) do the same thing themselves, so it is redundant for InnoDB to do it. You can disable the doublewrite buffer by setting innodb_doublewrite to 0. In Percona Server, you can configure the doublewrite buffer to be stored in its own file, so you can separate this workload from the rest of the server's work by placing it on separate disk drives.

Other I/O configuration options

The sync_binlog option controls how MySQL flushes the binary log to disk. Its default value is 0, which means MySQL does no flushing and it's up to the operating system to decide when to flush its cache to durable storage. If the value is greater than 0, it specifies how many binary log writes happen between flushes to disk (each write is a single statement if `autocommit` is set, and otherwise a transaction). It's rare to set this option to anything other than 0 or 1.

If you don't set `sync_binlog` to 1, it's likely that a crash will cause your binary log to be out of sync with your transactional data. This can easily break replication and make point-in-time recovery impossible. However, the safety provided by setting this option to 1 comes at high price. Synchronizing the binary log and the transaction log requires MySQL to flush two files in two distinct locations. This might require a disk seek, which is relatively slow.

As with the InnoDB log file, placing the binary log on a RAID volume with a battery-backed write cache can give a huge performance boost. In fact, writing and flushing the binary logs is actually more expensive than writing and flushing the InnoDB transaction logs, because unlike the InnoDB transaction logs, every write to the binary logs increases their size. That requires a metadata update at the filesystem level for every write. Thus, setting `sync_binlog=1` can be much more detrimental to performance than setting `innodb_flush_log_at_trx_commit=1`, especially on network filesystems such as NFS.

A non-performance-related note on the binary logs: if you want to use the `expire_logs_days` option to remove old binary logs automatically, don't remove them with *rm*. The server will get confused and refuse to remove them automatically, and `PURGE MASTER LOGS` will stop working. The solution, should you find yourself entangled in this situation, is to manually resync the *hostname-bin.index* file with the list of files that still exist on disk.

We cover RAID in more depth in the next chapter, but it's worth repeating here that good-quality RAID controllers, with battery-backed write caches set to use the write-back policy, can handle *thousands* of writes per second and still give you durable storage. The data gets written to a fast cache with a battery, so it will survive even if the system loses power. When the power comes back, the RAID controller will write the data from the cache to the disk before making the disk available for use. Thus, a good RAID controller with a large enough battery-backed write cache can improve performance dramatically and is a very good investment. Of course, solid-state storage is another option; we also cover that in the next chapter.

MyISAM I/O Configuration

Let's begin by considering how MyISAM performs I/O for its indexes. MyISAM normally flushes index changes to disk after every write. If you're going to make many modifications to a table, however, it might be faster to batch these writes together.

One way to do this is with `LOCK TABLES`, which defers writes until you unlock the tables. This can be a valuable technique for improving performance, because it lets you control exactly which writes are deferred and when the writes are flushed to disk. You can defer writes for precisely the statements you want.

You can also defer index writes by using the `delay_key_write` variable. If you do this, modified key buffer blocks are not flushed until the table is closed.[11] The possible settings are as follows:

OFF
> MyISAM flushes modified blocks in the key buffer (key cache) to disk after every write, unless the table is locked with `LOCK TABLES`.

ON
> Delayed key writes are enabled, but only for tables created with the `DELAY_KEY_WRITE` option.

ALL
> All MyISAM tables use delayed key writes.

Delaying key writes can be helpful in some cases, but it doesn't usually create a big performance boost. It's most useful with smaller data sizes, when the key cache's read hit ratio is good but the write hit ratio is bad. It also has quite a few drawbacks:

- If the server crashes and the blocks haven't been flushed to disk, the index will be corrupt.

- If many writes are delayed, it'll take longer for MySQL to close a table, because it will have to wait for the buffers to be flushed to disk. This can cause long table cache locks in MySQL 5.0.

- `FLUSH TABLES` can take a long time, for the reason just mentioned. This in turn can increase the time it takes to run `FLUSH TABLES WITH READ LOCK` for a logical volume manager (LVM) snapshot or other backup operation.

- Unflushed dirty blocks in the key buffer might not leave any room in the buffer for new blocks to be read from disk. Therefore, queries might stall while waiting for MyISAM to free up some space in the key buffer.

In addition to configuring MyISAM's index I/O, you can configure how MyISAM tries to recover from corruption. The `myisam_recover` option controls how MyISAM looks for and repairs errors. You have to set this option in the configuration file or at the command line. You can view, but not change, the option's value with this SQL statement (this is not a typo—the system variable has a different name from the corresponding command-line option):

```
mysql> SHOW VARIABLES LIKE 'myisam_recover_options';
```

Enabling this option instructs MySQL to check MyISAM tables for corruption when it opens them, and to repair them if problems are found. You can set the following values:

---

11. The table can be closed for several reasons. For example, the server might close the table because there's not enough room in the table cache, or someone might execute `FLUSH TABLES`.

DEFAULT *(or no setting)*
> Instructs MySQL to try to repair any table that is marked as having crashed or not marked as having been closed cleanly. The default setting performs no other actions upon recovery. In contrast to how most variables work, this DEFAULT value is not an instruction to reset the variable to its compiled-in value; it essentially means "no setting."

BACKUP
> Makes MySQL write a backup of the data file into a *.BAK* file, which you can examine afterward.

FORCE
> Makes recovery continue even if more than one row will be lost from the *.MYD* file.

QUICK
> Skips recovery unless there are delete blocks. These are blocks of deleted rows that are still occupying space and can be reused for future INSERT statements. This can be useful because MyISAM recovery can take a very long time on large tables.

You can use multiple settings, separated by commas. For example, BACKUP,FORCE will force recovery and create a backup. This is what we used in our sample configuration file earlier in this chapter.

We recommend that you enable this option, especially if you have just a few small MyISAM tables. Running a server with corrupted MyISAM tables is dangerous, because they can sometimes cause more data corruption and even server crashes. However, if you have large tables, automatic recovery might be impractical: it causes the server to check and repair all MyISAM tables when they're opened, which is inefficient. During this time, MySQL tends to block connections from performing any work. If you have a lot of MyISAM tables, it might be a good idea to use a less intrusive process that runs CHECK TABLES and REPAIR TABLES after startup.[12] Either way, it is very important to check and repair the tables.

Enabling memory-mapped access to data files is another useful MyISAM option. Memory mapping lets MyISAM access the *.MYD* files directly via the operating system's page cache, avoiding costly system calls. In MySQL 5.1 and newer, you can enable memory mapping with the myisam_use_mmap option. Older versions of MySQL use memory mapping for compressed MyISAM tables only.

Configuring MySQL Concurrency

When you're running MySQL in a high-concurrency workload, you might run into bottlenecks you wouldn't otherwise experience. This section explains how to detect

---

12. Some Debian systems do this automatically, which is a swing of the pendulum too far in the other direction. It's not a good idea to just configure this behavior by default as Debian does; the DBA should decide.

these problems when they happen, and how to get the best performance possible under these workloads for MyISAM and InnoDB.

InnoDB Concurrency Configuration

InnoDB is designed for high concurrency, and it has improved dramatically in the last few years, but it's still not perfect. The InnoDB architecture still shows some roots in limited-memory, single-CPU, single-disk systems. Some aspects of InnoDB's performance can degrade in high-concurrency situations, and your only recourse is to limit concurrency. You can use the techniques shown in Chapter 3 to diagnose concurrency problems.

If you have problems with InnoDB concurrency, the solution is usually to upgrade the server. In comparison with current versions, older versions such as MySQL 5.0 and early MySQL 5.1 were an unmitigated disaster under high concurrency. Everything queued on global mutexes such as the buffer pool mutex, and the server practically ground to a halt. If you upgrade to one of the newer versions of MySQL, you don't need to limit concurrency in most cases.

If you do, here's how it works. InnoDB has its own "thread scheduler" that controls how threads enter its kernel to access data, and what they can do once they're inside the kernel. The most basic way to limit concurrency is with the innodb_thread_concurrency variable, which limits how many threads can be in the kernel at once. A value of 0 means there is no limit on the number of threads. If you are having InnoDB concurrency problems in older MySQL versions, this variable is the most important one to configure.[13]

It's impossible to name a good value for any given architecture and workload. In theory, the following formula gives a good value:

```
concurrency = Number of CPUs * Number of Disks * 2
```

But in practice, it can be better to use a much smaller value. You will have to experiment to find the best value for your system.

If more than the allowed number of threads are already in the kernel, a thread can't enter the kernel. InnoDB uses a two-phase process to try to let threads enter as efficiently as possible. The two-phase policy reduces the overhead of context switches caused by the operating system scheduler. The thread first sleeps for innodb_thread_sleep_delay microseconds, and then tries again. If it still can't enter, it goes into a queue of waiting threads and yields to the operating system.

The default sleep time in the first phase is 10,000 microseconds. Changing this value can help in high-concurrency environments, when the CPU is underused with a lot of

---

13. In fact, in some workloads, the system that implements the concurrency limits itself can become a bottleneck, so sometimes it needs to be enabled, and at other times it needs to be disabled. Profiling will show you which to do.

threads in the "sleeping before entering queue" status. The default value can also be much too large if you have a lot of small queries, because it adds 10 milliseconds to query latency.

Once a thread is inside the kernel, it has a certain number of "tickets" that let it back into the kernel for "free," without any concurrency checks. This limits how much work it can do before it has to get back in line with other waiting threads. The `innodb_con currency_tickets` option controls the number of tickets. It rarely needs to be changed unless you have a lot of extremely long-running queries. Tickets are granted per-query, not per-transaction. Once a query finishes, its unused tickets are discarded.

In addition to the bottlenecks in the buffer pool and other structures, there's another concurrency bottleneck at the commit stage, which is largely I/O-bound because of flush operations. The `innodb_commit_concurrency` variable governs how many threads can commit at the same time. Configuring this option might help if there's a lot of thread thrashing even when `innodb_thread_concurrency` is set to a low value.

Finally, there's a new solution that might be worth considering: using a thread pool to limit concurrency. The original thread pool implementation was in the abandoned MySQL 6.0 source tree, and had serious flaws. But it's been reimplemented in MariaDB, and Oracle has recently released a commercial plugin to provide a thread pool for MySQL 5.5. We don't have enough experience with either of these to guide you, so we'll confuse you further by pointing out that neither implementation seemed to satisfy Facebook, which has met its unique needs with so-called "admission control" features in its own private branch of MySQL. Hopefully by the fourth edition of this book we'll have some more knowledge to share on thread pools and when they work or don't work.

MyISAM Concurrency Configuration

MyISAM allows concurrent inserts and reads under some conditions, and it lets you "schedule" some operations to try to block as little as possible.

Before we look at MyISAM's concurrency settings, it's important to understand how MyISAM deletes and inserts rows. Delete operations don't rearrange the entire table; they just mark rows as deleted, leaving "holes" in the table. MyISAM prefers to fill the holes if it can, reusing the spaces for inserted rows. If there are no holes, it appends new rows to the end of the table.

Even though MyISAM has table-level locks, it can append new rows concurrently with reads. It does this by stopping the reads at the last row that existed when they began. This avoids inconsistent reads.

However, it is much more difficult to provide consistent reads when something is changing the middle of the table. MVCC is the most popular way to solve this problem: it lets readers read old versions of data while writers create new versions. However,

MyISAM doesn't support MVCC as InnoDB does, so it doesn't support concurrent inserts unless they go at the end of the table.

You can configure MyISAM's concurrent insert behavior with the `concurrent_insert` variable, which can have the following values:

0

MyISAM allows no concurrent inserts; every insert locks the table exclusively.

1

This is the default value. MyISAM allows concurrent inserts, as long as there are no holes in the table.

2

This value is available in MySQL 5.0 and newer. It forces concurrent inserts to append to the end of the table, even when there are holes. If there are no threads reading from the table, MySQL will place the new rows in the holes. The table can become more fragmented than usual with this setting.

You can also configure MySQL to delay some operations to a later time, when they can be combined for greater efficiency. For instance, you can delay index writes with the `delay_key_write` variable, which we mentioned earlier in this chapter. This involves the familiar trade-off: write the index right away (safe but expensive), or wait and hope the power doesn't fail before the write happens (faster, but likely to cause massive index corruption in the event of a crash because the index file will be very out of date).

You can also give `INSERT`, `REPLACE`, `DELETE`, and `UPDATE` queries lower priority than `SELECT` queries with the `low_priority_updates` option. This is equivalent to globally applying the `LOW_PRIORITY` modifier to `UPDATE` queries. It's actually a very important option when you use MyISAM; it lets you get decent concurrency for `SELECT` queries that would otherwise starve in the presence of a very small number of queries getting top priority for write locks.

Finally, even though InnoDB's scalability issues are more often talked about, MyISAM has also had problems with mutexes for a long time. In MySQL 4.0 and earlier, a global mutex protected any I/O to the key buffer, which caused scalability problems with multiple CPUs and multiple disks. MySQL 4.1's key buffer code is improved and doesn't have this problem anymore, but it still holds a mutex on each key buffer. This is an issue when a thread copies key blocks from the key buffer into its local storage, rather than reading from the disk. The disk bottleneck is gone, but there's still a bottleneck when accessing data in the key buffer. You can sometimes work around this problem with multiple key buffers, but this approach isn't always successful. For example, there's no way to solve the problem when it involves only a single index. As a result, concurrent `SELECT` queries can perform significantly worse on multi-CPU machines than on a single-CPU machine, even when these are the only queries running. MariaDB offers segmented (partitioned) key buffers, which can help significantly when you experience this problem.

Workload-Based Configuration

One goal of configuring your server is to customize it for your specific workload. This requires intimate knowledge of the number, type, and frequency of all kinds of server activities—not just queries, but other activities too, such as connecting to the server and flushing tables.

The first thing you should do, if you haven't done it already, is become familiar with your server. Know what kinds of queries run on it. Monitor it with tools such as *inno-top*, and use *pt-query-digest* to create a query report. It's helpful to know not only what your server is doing overall, but what each MySQL query spends a lot of time doing. Chapter 3 explains how to find this out.

Try to log all queries when your server is running at full capacity, because that's the best way to see what kinds of queries suffer most. At the same time, capture snapshots of the process list and aggregate them by their state or command (*innotop* can do this for you, or you can use the scripts shown in Chapter 3). For example, are there a lot of queries copying results to temporary tables, or sorting results? If so, you might need to optimize the queries, and potentially look at the configuration settings for temporary tables and sort buffers.

Optimizing for BLOB and TEXT Workloads

BLOB and TEXT columns are a special type of workload for MySQL. (We'll refer to all of the BLOB and TEXT types as BLOB here for simplicity, because they belong to the same class of data types.) There are several restrictions on BLOB values that make the server treat them differently from other types. One of the most important considerations is that the server cannot use in-memory temporary tables for BLOB values.[14] Thus, if a query involving BLOB values requires a temporary table—no matter how small—it will go to disk immediately. This is very inefficient, especially for otherwise small and fast queries. The temporary table could be most of the query's cost.

There are two ways to ease this penalty: convert the values to VARCHAR with the SUB STRING() function (see Chapter 4 for more on this), or make temporary tables faster.

The best way to make temporary tables faster is to place them on a memory-based filesystem (*tmpfs* on GNU/Linux). This removes some overhead, although it's still much slower than using in-memory tables. Using a memory-based filesystem is helpful because the operating system tries to avoid writing data to disk.[15] Normal filesystems are cached in memory too, but the operating system might flush normal filesystem data every few seconds. A *tmpfs* filesystem never gets flushed. The *tmpfs* filesystem is also

---

14. Recent versions of Percona Server lift this restriction in some cases.

15. Data can still go to disk if the operating system swaps it.

designed for low overhead and simplicity. For example, there's no need for the filesystem to make any provisions for recovery. That makes it faster.

The server setting that controls where temporary tables are placed is `tmpdir`. Monitor how full the filesystem gets to ensure you have enough space for temporary tables. If necessary, you can even specify several temporary table locations, which MySQL will use in a round-robin fashion.

If your `BLOB` columns are very large and you use InnoDB, you might also want to increase InnoDB's log buffer size. We wrote more about this earlier in this chapter.

For long variable-length columns (e.g., `BLOB`, `TEXT`, and long character columns), InnoDB stores a 768-byte prefix in-page with the rest of the row.[16] If the column's value is longer than this prefix length, InnoDB might allocate external storage space outside the row to store the rest of the value. It allocates this space in whole 16 KB pages, just like all other InnoDB pages, and each column gets its own page (columns do not share external storage space). InnoDB allocates external storage space to a column a page at a time until 32 pages are used; then it allocates 64 pages at a time.

Note that we said InnoDB *might* allocate external storage. If the total length of the row, including the full value of the long column, is shorter than InnoDB's maximum row length (a little less than 8 KB), InnoDB will not allocate external storage even if the long column's value exceeds the prefix length.

Finally, when InnoDB updates a long column that is placed in external storage, it doesn't update it in place. Instead, it writes the new value to a new location in external storage and deletes the old value.

All of this has the following consequences:

- Long columns can waste a lot of space in InnoDB. For example, if you store a column value that is one byte too long to fit in the row, it will use an entire page to store the remaining byte, wasting most of the page. Likewise, if you have a value that is slightly more than 32 pages long, it *might* actually use 96 pages on disk.

- External storage disables the adaptive hash index, which needs to compare the full length of columns to verify that it has found the right data. (The hash helps InnoDB find "guesses" very quickly, but it must check that its "guess" is correct.) Because the adaptive hash index is completely in-memory and is built directly "on top of" frequently accessed pages in the buffer pool, it doesn't work with external storage.

- Long values can make any query with a `WHERE` clause that doesn't use an index run slowly. MySQL reads all columns before it applies the `WHERE` clause, so it might ask InnoDB to read a lot of external storage, then check the `WHERE` clause and throw away all the data it read. It's never a good idea to select columns you don't need,

---

16. This is long enough to create a 255-character index on a column, even if it's `utf8`, which might require up to three bytes per character. This prefix is specific to the Antelope InnoDB file format; it doesn't apply to the Barracuda format, which is available in MySQL 5.1 and newer (though not enabled by default).

but this is a special case where it's even more important to avoid doing so. If you find your queries are suffering from this limitation, you can try to use covering indexes to help.

- If you have many long columns in a single table, it might be better to combine the data they store into a single column, perhaps as an XML document. That lets all the values share external storage, rather than using their own pages.

- You can sometimes gain significant space and performance benefits by storing long columns in a BLOB and compressing them with COMPRESS(), or compressing them in the application before sending them to MySQL.

Optimizing for Filesorts

Recall from Chapter 6 that MySQL has two filesort algorithms. It uses the two-pass algorithm if the total size of all the columns needed for the query, plus the ORDER BY columns, exceeds max_length_for_sort_data bytes. It also uses this algorithm when any of the required columns—even those not used for the ORDER BY—is a BLOB or TEXT column. (You can use SUBSTRING() to convert such columns to types that can work with the single-pass algorithm.)

MySQL has two variables that can help you control how it performs filesorts. You can influence MySQL's choice of algorithm by changing the value of the max_length_for_sort_data variable.[17] Because the single-pass algorithm creates a fixed-size buffer for each row it will sort, the maximum length of VARCHAR columns is what counts toward max_length_for_sort_data, not the actual size of the stored data. This is one of the reasons why we recommend you make these columns only as large as necessary.

When MySQL has to sort on BLOB or TEXT columns, it uses only a prefix and ignores the remainder of the values. This is because it has to allocate a fixed-size structure to hold the values and copy the prefix from external storage into that structure. You can specify how large this prefix should be with the max_sort_length variable.

Unfortunately, MySQL doesn't really give you any visibility into which sort algorithm it uses. If you increase the max_length_for_sort_data variable and your disk usage goes up, your CPU usage goes down, and the Sort_merge_passes status variable begins to grow more quickly than it did before the change, you've probably forced more sorts to use the single-pass algorithm.

---

17. MySQL 5.6 will introduce changes to the way the sort buffer is used in queries with a LIMIT clause and will fix a problem that caused a large sort buffer to perform an expensive setup routine, so when you upgrade to MySQL 5.6 you should carefully check any customizations you've made to these settings.

Completing the Basic Configuration

We're done with the tour of server internals—hope you enjoyed the trip! Now let's return to our sample configuration file and see how to choose values for the settings that remain.

We've already discussed how to choose values for the general settings such as the data directory, the InnoDB and MyISAM caches, logs, and a few other things. Let's go over what remains:

`tmp_table_size` *and* `max_heap_table_size`

These settings control how large an in-memory temporary table using the Memory storage engine can grow. If an implicit temporary table's size exceeds either of these settings, it will be converted to an on-disk MyISAM table so it can keep growing. (An implicit temporary table is one that you don't create yourself; the server creates it for you to hold an intermediate result while executing a query.)

You should simply set both of these variables to the same value. We've chosen the value `32M` for our sample configuration file. This might not be enough, but beware of setting this variable too large. It's good for temporary tables to live in memory, but if they're simply going to be huge, it's actually best for them to just use on-disk tables, or you could run the server out of memory.

Assuming that your queries aren't creating enormous temporary tables (which you can often avoid with proper indexing and query design), it's a good idea to set these variables large enough that you don't have to go through the process of converting an in-memory table to an on-disk table. This procedure will show up in the process list.

You can look at how the server's `SHOW STATUS` counters change over time to understand how often you create temporary tables and whether they go to disk. You can't tell whether a table was created in memory and then converted to on-disk or just created on-disk to begin with (perhaps because of a `BLOB` column), but you can at least see how often the tables go to disk. Examine the `Created_tmp_disk_tables` and `Created_tmp_tables` variables.

`max_connections`

This setting acts like an emergency brake to keep your server from being overwhelmed by a surge of connections from the application. If the application misbehaves, or the server encounters a problem such as a stall, a lot of new connections can be opened. But opening a connection does no good if it can't execute queries, so being denied with a "too many connections" error is a way to fail fast and fail cheaply.

Set `max_connections` high enough to accommodate the usual load that you think you'll experience, as well as a safety margin to permit logging in and administering the server. For example, if you think you'll have 300 or so connections in normal operations, you might set this to 500 or so. If you don't know how many connections you'll get, 500 is not an unreasonable starting point anyway. The default is 100, but that's not enough for a lot of applications.

Beware also of surprises that might make you hit the limit of connections. For example, if you restart an application server, it might not close its connections cleanly, and MySQL might not realize they've been closed. When the application server comes back up and tries to open connections to the database, it might be refused due to the dead connections that haven't timed out yet.

Watch the Max_used_connections status variable over time. It is a high-water mark that shows you if the server has had a spike in connections at some point. If it reaches max_connections, chances are a client has been denied at least once, and you should probably use the techniques shown in Chapter 3 to capture server activity when that occurs.

thread_cache_size
You can compute a reasonable value for this variable by observing the server's behavior over time. Watch the Threads_connected status variable and find its typical maximum and minimum. You might want to set the thread cache large enough to hold the difference between the peak and off-peak usage, and go ahead and be generous, because if you set it a bit too high it's not a big problem. You might set it two or three times as large as needed to hold the fluctuations in usage. For example, if the Threads_connected status variable seems to vary between 150 and 175, you could set the thread cache to 75. But you probably shouldn't set it very large, because it isn't really useful to keep around a huge amount of spare threads waiting for connections; a ceiling of 250 is a nice round number (or 256, if you prefer a power of two).

You can also watch the change over time in the Threads_created status variable. If this value is large or increasing, it's another clue that you might need to increase the thread_cache_size variable. Check Threads_cached to see how many threads are in the cache already.

A related status variable is Slow_launch_threads. A large value for this status variable means that something is delaying new threads upon connection. This is a clue that something is wrong with your server, but it doesn't really indicate what. It usually means there's a system overload, causing the operating system not to schedule any CPU time for newly created threads. It doesn't necessarily indicate that you need to increase the size of the thread cache. You should diagnose the problem and fix it rather than masking it with a cache, because it might be affecting other things, too.

table_cache_size
This cache (or the two caches into which it was split in MySQL 5.1) should be set large enough to keep from reopening and reparsing table definitions all the time. You can check this by inspecting the value of Open_tables and the change over time in the value of Opened_tables. If you see many Opened_tables per second, your table_cache value might not be large enough. Explicit temporary tables can also

cause a growing number of opened tables even when the table cache isn't fully used, though, so it might be nothing to worry about. Your clue would be that `Opened_tables` grows constantly even though `Open_tables` isn't as large as `table_cache_size`.

Even if the table cache is useful, you should not set this variable too large. It turns out that the table cache can be counterproductive in two circumstances.

First, MySQL doesn't use a very efficient algorithm to check the cache, so if it's really big, it can get really slow. You probably shouldn't set it higher than 10,000 in most cases, or 10,240 if you like those powers of two.[18]

The second reason to avoid setting this very large is that some workloads simply aren't cacheable. If the workload isn't cacheable, and everything is going to be a cache miss no matter how large you make the cache, forget the cache and set it to zero! This helps you avoid making the situation worse; a cache miss is better than an expensive cache check followed by a cache miss. What kinds of workloads aren't cacheable? If you have tens or hundreds of thousands of tables and you use them all pretty uniformly, you probably can't cache them all, and you're better off setting this variable small. This is sometimes appropriate on systems that have a very large number of collocated applications, none of which is very busy.

A reasonable starting value for this setting is 10 times as big as `max_connections`, but again, keep it under 10,000 or so in most cases.

There are several other kinds of settings that you will frequently include in your configuration file, including binary logging and replication settings. Binary logging is useful for enabling point-in-time recovery and for replication, and replication has a few settings of its own. We'll cover the important settings in the chapters on replication and backups, later in this book.

Safety and Sanity Settings

After your basic configuration settings are in place, you might wish to enable a number of settings that make the server safer and more reliable. Some of them influence performance, because safety and reliability are often more costly to guarantee. Some are just sensible, however: they prevent silly mistakes such as inserting nonsensical data into the server. And some don't make a difference in day-to-day operation, but prevent bad things from happening in edge cases.

Let's look at a collection of useful options for general server behavior first:

---

18. Have you heard the joke about powers of two? There are 10 types of people in the world: those who understand binary, and those who don't. There are also another 10 types of people: those who think binary/decimal jokes are funny, and those who have sex. We won't say whether or not we think that's hilarious.

expire_logs_days

If you enable binary logging, you should enable this option, which causes the server to purge old binary logs after the specified number of days. If you don't enable it, you will eventually run the server out of disk space, and it will freeze or crash. We suggest setting this option large enough that you can recover from at least two backups ago (in case the most recent backup fails). Even if you take backups every day, still leave yourself at least 7 to 14 days' worth of binary logs. Our experience shows that you'll be grateful for a week or two of binary logs when you have some unusual problem, such as rebuilding a replica and then trying to get it caught up again with the master. You want to keep enough binary logs around to give yourself some breathing room for operations such as these.

max_allowed_packet

This setting prevents the server from sending too large a packet, and also controls how large a packet it will accept. The default is probably too small, but it can also be set dangerously large. If it's set too small, sometimes problems can occur in replication, typically when the replica can't retrieve data from the master that it needs for replication. You might increase the setting from its default to 16 MB or so.

It's not documented, but this option also controls the maximum size of a user-defined variable, so if you need very large variables, be careful—they can be truncated or set to NULL if they exceed the size of this variable.

max_connect_errors

If something goes wrong with your networking for a moment, there is an application or configuration error, or there is another problem such as privileges that prevent connections from completing successfully for a brief period of time, clients can get blacklisted and will be unable to connect again until you flush the host cache. The default setting for this option is so small that this problem can happen too easily. You might want to increase it, and in fact, if you know that the server is adequately secured against brute-force attacks, you can just make it very large to effectively disable host blacklisting.

skip_name_resolve

This setting disables another networking- and authentication-related trap: DNS lookups. DNS is one of the weak points in MySQL's connection process. When you connect to the server, by default it tries to determine the hostname from which you're connecting and uses that as part of the authentication credentials. (That is, your credentials are your username, hostname, and password—not just your username and password.) But to verify your hostname, the server needs to perform both a reverse and a forward DNS lookup. This is all fine until DNS starts to have problems, which is pretty much a certainty at some point in time. When that happens, everything piles up and eventually the connection times out. To prevent this, we strongly recommend that you set this option, which disables DNS lookups during authentication. However, if you do this you will need to convert all of your hostname-based grants to use IP addresses, wildcards, or the special hostname "localhost," because hostname-based accounts will be disabled.

sql_mode

This setting can accept a variety of options that modify server behavior. We don't recommend changing these just for the fun of it; it's better to let MySQL be MySQL in most ways and not try to make it behave like other database servers. (Many client and GUI tools expect MySQL to have its own flavor of SQL, for example, so if you change it to speak more ANSI-compliant SQL some things might break.) However, several of the settings are very useful, and some might be worth considering in your specific cases. You might want to look at the documentation for the following options and consider using them: STRICT_TRANS_TABLES, ERROR_FOR_DIVISION_BY _ZERO, NO_AUTO_CREATE_USER, NO_AUTO_VALUE_ON_ZERO, NO_ENGINE_SUBSTITUTION, NO_ZERO_DATE, NO_ZERO_IN_DATE, and ONLY_FULL_GROUP_BY.

However, be aware that it might not be a good idea to change these settings for existing applications, because doing so might make the server incompatible with the application's expectations. It's pretty common for people to unwittingly write queries that refer to columns not in the GROUP BY clause or use aggregate functions, for example, so if you want to enable the ONLY_FULL_GROUP_BY option it's a good idea to do it in a development or staging server first, and only deploy it in production once you're sure everything is working.

sysdate_is_now

This is another setting that might be backward-incompatible with applications' expectations. But if you don't explicitly desire the SYSDATE() function to have non-deterministic behavior, which can break replication and make point-in-time recovery from backups unreliable, you might want to enable this option and make its behavior deterministic.

A few options control replication behavior and are very helpful for preventing problems on replicas:

read_only

This option prevents unprivileged users from making changes on replicas, which should be receiving changes only from the master, not from the application. We strongly recommend setting replicas to read-only mode.

skip_slave_start

This option prevents MySQL from taking the bit between its teeth and attempting to start replication automatically. You want to disable automatic starting because it is unsafe after a crash or other problem; a human needs to examine the server manually and determine that it is safe to start replication.

slave_net_timeout

This option controls how long it'll be before a replica notices that its connection to its master has failed and needs to be reconnected. The default option, one hour, is way too long. Set it to a minute or less.

sync_master_info, sync_relay_log, *and* sync_relay_log_info

These options, available in MySQL 5.5 and newer, correct longstanding problems with replicas: they don't sync their status files to disk, so if the server crashes it can be anyone's guess what the replica's position relative to the master actually was, and there can be corruption in the relay logs. These options make replicas much more likely to be recoverable after a crash. They are not enabled by default, because they cause extra fsync() operations on replicas, which can slow them down. We suggest enabling these options if you have decent hardware, and disabling them if there is a problem with replication that you can trace to latency caused by fsync().

There's a less intrusive way to do this in Percona Server, enabled with the innodb_overwrite_relay_log_info option. This makes InnoDB store the replication position in the InnoDB transaction logs, which is fully transactional and doesn't require any extra fsync() operations. During crash recovery, InnoDB will check the replication metadata files and update them to have the correct position if they're out of date.

Advanced InnoDB Settings

Recall our discussion of InnoDB's history in Chapter 1: it was first built in, then available in two versions, and now the newer version of the engine is once again built into the server. The newer InnoDB code has more features and is much more scalable. If you're using MySQL 5.1, you should configure MySQL explicitly to ignore the old version of InnoDB and use the newer version. It will improve server performance greatly. You'll need to enable the ignore_builtin_innodb option, and then configure the plugin_load option to enable InnoDB as a plugin. Consult the InnoDB manual for the exact syntax for your platform.[19]

Several options are available in the newer version of InnoDB, once you've enabled it. Some of these are quite important for server performance, and there are also a couple of safety and sanity options:

innodb

This rather innocuous-looking option is actually very important. If you set its value to FORCE, the server will not be able to start unless InnoDB can start. If you use InnoDB as your default storage engine, this is definitely what you want. You do not want the server to start when InnoDB fails because of some error such as a misconfiguration, because a badly behaved application could then connect to the server and cause who knows what harm and confusion. It's much better for the server to fail as a whole, which will force you to look at the error log instead of believing that the server started okay.

---

19. In Percona Server, there's only one version of InnoDB and it's built in, so you don't need to disable one version and load another one to replace it.

`innodb_autoinc_lock_mode`

This option controls how InnoDB generates autoincrementing primary key values, which can be a bottleneck in some cases, such as high-concurrency inserts. If you have many transactions waiting on the autoincrement lock (you can see this in `SHOW ENGINE INNODB STATUS`), you should investigate this setting. We won't repeat the manual's explanation of the options and their behaviors.

`innodb_buffer_pool_instances`

This setting divides the buffer pool into multiple segments in MySQL 5.5 and newer, and is probably one of the most important ways to improve MySQL's scalability on multicore machines with a highly concurrent workload. Multiple buffer pools partition the workload so that some of the global mutexes are not such hot contention points.

It is not yet clear what kind of guidelines we should develop for choosing the number of buffer pool instances. We have run most of our benchmarks with eight instances, but we probably won't understand some of the subtleties of multiple buffer pool instances until MySQL 5.5 has been deployed more widely for a longer time.

We don't mean that to imply that MySQL 5.5 isn't deployed widely in production. It's just that the most extreme cases of mutex contention we've helped solve have been for very large, very conservative users, for whom an upgrade can require many months to plan, validate, and execute. These users are sometimes running a highly customized version of MySQL, which makes it doubly important for them to be careful with upgrades. When more of these folks upgrade to MySQL 5.5 and stress it in their own unique ways, we'll probably learn some interesting things about multiple buffer pools that we haven't seen yet. Until then, we can say that it appears to be very beneficial to run with eight buffer pool instances.

It's worth noting that Percona Server takes a different approach to solving InnoDB's mutex contention issues. Instead of partitioning the buffer pool—an admittedly tried-and-true approach in many systems like InnoDB—we opted to divide some of the global mutexes into smaller, more special-purpose mutexes. Our benchmarks show that the best improvement of all comes from a combination of the two approaches, which is available in Percona Server version 5.5: multiple buffer pools and more fine-grained mutexes.

`innodb_io_capacity`

InnoDB used to be hardcoded to assume that it ran on a single hard disk capable of 100 I/O operations per second. This was a bad default. Now you can inform InnoDB how much I/O capacity is available to it. InnoDB sometimes needs this set quite high (tens of thousands on extremely fast storage such as PCI-E flash devices) to flush dirty pages in a steady fashion, for reasons that are quite complex to explain.

innodb_read_io_threads *and* innodb_write_io_threads

These options control how many background threads are available for I/O operations. The default in recent versions of MySQL is to have four read threads and four write threads, which is enough for a lot of servers, especially with the native asynchronous I/O available in MySQL 5.5. If you have many hard drives and a high-concurrency workload, and you see that the threads are having a hard time keeping up, you can increase the number of threads, or you can simply set them to the number of physical spindles you have for I/O (even if they're behind a RAID controller).

innodb_strict_mode

This setting makes InnoDB throw errors instead of warnings for some conditions, especially invalid or possibly dangerous CREATE TABLE options. If you enable this option, be certain to check all of your CREATE TABLE options, because it might not let you create some tables that used to be fine. Sometimes it's a bit pessimistic and overly restrictive. You wouldn't want to find this out when you were trying to restore a backup.

innodb_old_blocks_time

InnoDB has a two-part buffer pool least recently used (LRU) list, which is designed to prevent ad hoc queries from evicting pages that are used many times over the long term. A one-off query such as those issued by *mysqldump* will typically bring a page into the buffer pool LRU list, read the rows from it, and move on to the next page. In theory, the two-part LRU list will prevent this page from displacing pages that will be needed for a long time by placing it into the "young" sublist and only moving it to the "old" sublist after it has been accessed multiple times. But InnoDB is not configured to prevent this by default, because the page has multiple rows, and thus the multiple accesses to read rows from the page will cause it to be moved to the "old" sublist immediately, placing pressure on pages that need a long lifetime. This variable specifies the number of milliseconds that must elapse before a page can move from the "young" part of the LRU list to the "old" part. It's set to 0 by default, and setting it to a small value such as 1000 (one second) has proven very effective in our benchmarks.

Summary

After you've worked through this chapter, you should have a server configuration that is much better than the defaults. Your server should be fast and stable, and you should not need to tweak the configuration unless you run into an unusual circumstance.

To review, we suggest that you begin with our sample configuration file, set the basic options for your server and workload, add safety and sanity options as desired, and, if appropriate, configure the new options available in the InnoDB plugin and in MySQL 5.5. That's really all you need to do.

The most important options are these two, assuming that you use InnoDB, which most people should:

- `innodb_buffer_pool_size`
- `innodb_log_file_size`

Congratulations—you just solved the vast majority of real-world configuration problems we've seen! If you use our configuration tool at *http://tools.percona.com*, you will get good suggestions for a starting point on these and other configuration options.

We've also made a lot of suggestions about what not to do. The most important of these are not to "tune" your server; not to use ratios, formulas, or "tuning scripts" as a basis for setting the configuration variables; not to trust advice from unknown people on the Internet; and not to go hunting in SHOW STATUS counters for things that look bad. If something is actually wrong, it'll show up in your server profiling.

There are a few significant settings we didn't discuss in this chapter, which are important for specific types of hardware and workloads. We delayed discussion of these settings because we believe that any advice on settings needs to be paired with an explanation of the internal processes at work. This brings us to the next chapter, which will show you how to optimize your hardware and operating system for MySQL, and vice versa.

Operating System and Hardware Optimization

Your MySQL server can perform only as well as its weakest link, and the operating system and the hardware on which it runs are often limiting factors. The disk size, the available memory and CPU resources, the network, and the components that link them all limit the system's ultimate capacity. Thus, you need to choose your hardware carefully, and configure the hardware and operating system appropriately. For example, if your workload is I/O-bound, one approach is to design your application to minimize MySQL's I/O workload. However, it's often smarter to upgrade the I/O subsystem, install more memory, or reconfigure existing disks.

Hardware changes very rapidly, so anything we write about particular products or components in this chapter will become outdated quickly. As usual, our goal is to help improve your understanding so that you can apply your knowledge in situations we don't cover directly. However, we will use currently available hardware to illustrate our points.

What Limits MySQL's Performance?

Many different hardware components can affect MySQL's performance, but the two most frequent bottlenecks we see are CPU and I/O saturation. CPU saturation happens when MySQL works with data that either fits in memory or can be read from disk as fast as needed. A lot of datasets fit completely in memory with the large amounts of RAM available these days.

I/O saturation, on the other hand, generally happens when you need to work with much more data than you can fit in memory. If your application is distributed across a network, or if you have a huge number of queries and/or low latency requirements, the bottleneck might shift to the network instead.

The techniques shown in Chapter 3 will help you find your system's limiting factor, but look beyond the obvious when you think you've found a bottleneck. A weakness in one area often puts pressure on another subsystem, which then appears to be the problem. For example, if you don't have enough memory, MySQL might have to flush caches to make room for data it needs—and then, an instant later, read back the data it just flushed (this is true for both read and write operations). The memory scarcity can thus appear to be a lack of I/O capacity. When you find a component that's limiting the system, ask yourself, "Is the component itself the problem, or is the system placing unreasonable demands on this component?" We explored this question in our diagnostics case study in Chapter 3.

Here's another example: a saturated memory bus can appear to be a CPU problem. In fact, when we say that an application has a "CPU bottleneck" or is "CPU-bound," what we really mean is that there is a computational bottleneck. We delve into this issue next.

How to Select CPUs for MySQL

You should consider whether your workload is CPU-bound when upgrading current hardware or purchasing new hardware.

You can identify a CPU-bound workload by checking the CPU utilization, but instead of looking only at how heavily your CPUs are loaded overall, look at the balance of CPU usage and I/O for your most important queries, and notice whether the CPUs are loaded evenly. You can use the tools discussed later in this chapter to figure out what limits your server's performance.

Which Is Better: Fast CPUs or Many CPUs?

When you have a CPU-bound workload, MySQL generally benefits most from *faster* CPUs (as opposed to more CPUs).

This isn't always true, because it depends on the workload and the number of CPUs. Older versions of MySQL had scaling issues with multiple CPUs, and even new versions cannot run a single query in parallel across many CPUs. As a result, the CPU speed limits the response time for each individual CPU-bound query.

When we discuss CPUs, we're a bit casual with the terminology, to help keep the text easy to read. Modern commodity servers usually have multiple sockets, each with several CPU cores (which have independent execution units), and each core might have multiple "hardware threads." These complex architectures require a bit of patience to understand, and we won't always draw clear distinctions among them. In general, though, when we talk about CPU speed we're really talking about the speed of the execution unit, and when we mention the number of CPUs we're referring to the number that the operating system sees, even though that might be a multiple of the number of independent execution units.

Modern CPUs are much improved over those available a few years ago. For example, today's Intel CPUs are much faster than previous generations, due to advances such as directly attached memory and improved interconnects to devices such as PCIe cards. This is especially good for very fast storage devices, such as Fusion-io and Virident PCIe flash drives.

Hyperthreading also works much better now than it used to, and operating systems know how to use hyperthreading quite well these days. It used to be that operating systems weren't aware when two virtual CPUs really resided on the same die and would schedule tasks on two virtual processors on the same physical execution unit, believing them to be independent. Of course, a single execution unit can't really run two processes at the same time, so they'd conflict and fight over resources. Meanwhile, the operating system would leave other CPUs idle, thus wasting power. The operating system needs to be hyperthreading-aware because it has to know when the execution unit is actually idle, and switch tasks accordingly. A common cause of such problems used to be waits on the memory bus, which can take up to a hundred CPU cycles and is analogous to an I/O wait at a very small scale. That's all much improved in newer operating systems. Hyperthreading now works fine; we used to advise people to disable it sometimes, but we don't do that anymore.

All this is to say that you can get lots of fast CPUs now—many more than you could when we published the second edition of this book. So which is best, many or fast? Usually, you want both. Broadly speaking, you might have two goals for your server:

Low latency (fast response time)
  To achieve this you need fast CPUs, because each query will use only a single CPU.

High throughput
  If you can run many queries at the same time, you might benefit from multiple CPUs to service the queries. However, whether this works in practice depends on your situation. Because MySQL doesn't scale perfectly on multiple CPUs, there is a limit to how many CPUs you can use anyway. In older versions of the server (up to late releases of MySQL 5.1, give or take) that was a serious limitation. In newer versions, you can confidently scale to 16 or 24 CPUs and perhaps beyond, depending on which version you're using (Percona Server tends to have a slight edge here).

If you have multiple CPUs and you're not running queries concurrently, MySQL can still use the extra CPUs for background tasks such as purging InnoDB buffers, network operations, and so on. However, these jobs are usually minor compared to executing queries.

MySQL replication (discussed in the next chapter) also works best with fast CPUs, not many CPUs. If your workload is CPU-bound, a parallel workload on the master can easily serialize into a workload the replica can't keep up with, even if the replica is more powerful than the master. That said, the I/O subsystem, not the CPU, is usually the bottleneck on a replica.

If you have a CPU-bound workload, another way to approach the question of whether you need fast CPUs or many CPUs is to consider what your queries are really doing. At the hardware level, a query can either be executing or waiting. The most common causes of waiting are waiting in the run queue (when the process is runnable, but all the CPUs are busy), waiting for latches or locks, and waiting for the disk or network. What do you expect your queries to be waiting for? If they'll be waiting for latches or locks, you generally need faster CPUs; if they're waiting in the run queue, then either more or faster CPUs will help. (There might be exceptions, such as a query waiting for the InnoDB log buffer mutex, which doesn't become free until the I/O completes—this might indicate that you actually need more I/O capacity.)

That said, MySQL can use many CPUs effectively on some workloads. For example, suppose you have many connections querying distinct tables (and thus not contending for table locks, which can be a problem with MyISAM and Memory tables), and the server's total throughput is more important than any individual query's response time. Throughput can be very high in this scenario because the threads can all run concurrently without contending with each other.

Again, this might work better in theory than in practice: InnoDB has global shared data structures regardless of whether queries are reading from distinct tables or not, and MyISAM has global locks on each key buffer. It's not just the storage engines, either; InnoDB used to get all the blame, but some of the improvements it's received lately have exposed other bottlenecks at higher levels in the server. The infamous LOCK_open mutex can be a real problem on MySQL 5.1 and older versions; ditto for some of the other server-level mutexes (the query cache, for example).

You can usually diagnose these types of contention with stack traces. See the *pt-pmp* tool in Percona Toolkit, for example. If you encounter such problems, you might have to change the server's configuration to disable or alter the offending component, partition (shard) your data, or change how you're doing things in some way. There are too many possible problems and corresponding solutions for us to list them all, but fortunately, the answer is usually obvious once you have a firm diagnosis. Also fortunately, most of the problems are edge cases you're unlikely to encounter; the most common cases are being fixed in the server itself as time passes.

CPU Architecture

Probably upwards of 99% of MySQL server instances (excluding embedded usage) run on the x86 architecture, on either Intel or AMD chips. This is what we focus on in this book, for the most part.

Sixty-four-bit architectures are now the default, and it's hard to even buy a 32-bit CPU these days. MySQL works fine on 64-bit architectures, though some things didn't become 64-bit capable for a while, so if you're using an older version of the server, you might need to take care. For example, in early MySQL 5.0 releases, each MyISAM key buffer was limited to 4 GB, the size addressable by a 32-bit integer. (You can create multiple key buffers to work around this, though.)

Make sure you use a 64-bit operating system on your 64-bit hardware! It's less common these days than it used to be, but for a while most hosting providers would install 32-bit operating systems on servers even when the servers had 64-bit CPUs. This meant that you couldn't use a lot of memory: even though some 32-bit systems can support large amounts of memory, they can't use it as efficiently as a 64-bit system, and no single process can address more than 4 GB of memory on a 32-bit system.

Scaling to Many CPUs and Cores

One place where multiple CPUs can be quite helpful is an online transaction processing (OLTP) system. These systems generally do many small operations, which can run on multiple CPUs because they're coming from multiple connections. In this environment, concurrency can become a bottleneck. Most web applications fall into this category.

OLTP servers generally use InnoDB, which has some unresolved concurrency issues with many CPUs. However, it's not just InnoDB that can become a bottleneck: any shared resource is a potential point of contention. InnoDB gets a lot of attention because it's the most common storage engine for high-concurrency environments, but MyISAM is no better when you really stress it, even when you're not changing any data. Many of the concurrency bottlenecks, such as InnoDB's row-level locks and MyISAM's table locks, can't be optimized away internally—there's no solution except to do the work as fast as possible, so the locks can be granted to whatever is waiting for them. It doesn't matter how many CPUs you have if a single lock is causing them all to wait. Thus, even some high-concurrency workloads benefit from faster CPUs.

There are actually two types of concurrency problems in databases, and you need different approaches to solve them:

Logical concurrency issues
> Contention for resources that are visible to the application, such as table or row locks. These problems usually require tactics such as changing your application, using a different storage engine, changing the server configuration, or using different locking hints or transaction isolation levels.

Internal concurrency issues
> Contention for resources such as semaphores, access to pages in the InnoDB buffer pool, and so on. You can try to work around these problems by changing server settings, changing your operating system, or using different hardware, but you might just have to live with them. In some cases, using a different storage engine or a patch to a storage engine can help ease these problems.

The number of CPUs MySQL can use effectively and how it scales under increasing load—its "scaling pattern"—depend on both the workload and the system architecture. By "system architecture," we mean the operating system and hardware, not the application that uses MySQL. The CPU architecture (RISC, CISC, depth of pipeline, etc.), CPU model, and operating system all affect MySQL's scaling pattern. This is why benchmarking is so important: some systems might continue to perform very well under increasing concurrency, while others perform much worse.

Some systems can even give lower total performance with more processors. This used to be quite common; we know of many people who tried to upgrade to systems with more CPUs, only to be forced to revert to the older systems (or bind the MySQL process to only some of the cores) because of lower performance. In the MySQL 5.0 days, before the advent of the Google patches and then Percona Server, the magic number was 4 cores, but these days we're seeing people running on servers with up to 80 "CPUs" reported to the operating system. If you're planning a big upgrade, you'll have to consider your hardware, server version, and workload.

Some MySQL scalability bottlenecks are in the server, whereas others are in the storage engine layer. How the storage engine is designed is crucial, and you can sometimes switch to a different storage engine and get more from multiple CPUs.

The processor speed wars we saw around the turn of the century have subsided to some extent, and CPU vendors are now focusing more on multicore CPUs and variations such as multithreading. The future of CPU design might well be hundreds of processor cores; quad-core and hex-core CPUs are common today. Internal architectures vary so widely across vendors that it's impossible to generalize about the interaction between threads, CPUs, and cores. How the memory and bus are designed is also very important. In the final analysis, whether it's better to have multiple cores or multiple physical CPUs is also architecture-specific.

Two other complexities of modern CPUs deserve mention. Frequency scaling is the first. This is a power management technique that changes the CPU clock speed dynamically, depending on the demand placed on the CPU. The problem is that it sometimes doesn't cope well with query traffic that's composed of bursts of short queries, because the operating system might take a little while to decide that the CPUs should be clocked back up. As a result, queries might run for a while at a lower speed, and experience increased response time. Frequency scaling can make performance slow on intermittent workloads, but perhaps more importantly, it can create inconsistent performance.

The second is turbo boost technology, which is a paradigm shift in how we think about CPUs. We are used to thinking that our four-core 2 GHz CPU has four equally powerful cores, whether some of them are idle or not. A perfectly scalable system could therefore be expected to get four times as much work done when it uses all four cores. But that's not really true anymore, because when the system uses only one core, the processor might run at a higher clock speed, such as 3 GHz. This throws a wrench into a lot of capacity planning and scalability modeling, because the system doesn't behave linearly. It also means that an "idle CPU" doesn't represent a wasted resource to the same extent; if you have a server that just runs replication and you think it's single-threaded and there are three other idle CPUs you can use for other tasks without impacting replication, you might be wrong.

Balancing Memory and Disk Resources

The biggest reason to have a lot of memory isn't so you can hold a lot of data in memory: it's ultimately so you can avoid disk I/O, which is orders of magnitude slower than accessing data in memory. The trick is to balance the memory and disk size, speed, cost, and other qualities so you get good performance for your workload. Before we look at how to do that, let's go back to the basics for a moment.

Computers contain a pyramid of smaller, faster, more expensive caches, one upon the other, as depicted in Figure 9-1.

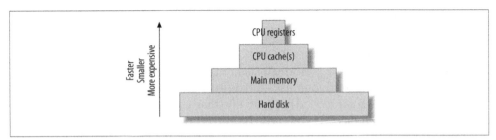

Figure 9-1. The cache hierarchy

Every level in this cache hierarchy is best used to cache "hot" data so it can be accessed more quickly, usually using heuristics such as "recently used data is likely to be used again soon" and "data that's near recently used data is likely to be used soon." These heuristics work because of spatial and temporal *locality of reference*.

From the programmer's point of view, CPU registers and caches are transparent and architecture-specific. It is the compiler's and CPU's job to manage these. However, programmers are very conscious of the difference between main memory and the hard disk, and programs usually treat these very differently.[1]

This is especially true of database servers, whose behavior often goes against the predictions made by the heuristics we just mentioned. A well-designed database cache (such as the InnoDB buffer pool) is usually more efficient than an operating system's cache, which is tuned for general-purpose tasks. The database cache has much more knowledge about its data needs, and it has special-purpose logic (write ordering, for example) that helps meet those needs. Also, a system call is not required to access the data in the database cache.

---

1. However, programs might rely on the operating system to cache in memory a lot of data that's conceptually "on disk." This is what MyISAM does, for example. It treats the data files as disk-resident, and lets the operating system take care of caching the disk's data to make it faster.

These special-purpose cache requirements are why you'll have to balance your cache hierarchy to suit the particular access patterns of a database server. Because the registers and on-chip caches are not user-configurable, memory and the storage are the only things you can change.

Random Versus Sequential I/O

Database servers use both sequential and random I/O, and random I/O benefits the most from caching. You can convince yourself of this by thinking about a typical mixed workload, with some balance of single-row lookups and multirow range scans. The typical pattern is for the "hot" data to be randomly distributed; caching this data will therefore help avoid expensive disk seeks. In contrast, sequential reads generally go through the data only once, so it's useless to cache it unless it fits completely in memory.

Another reason sequential reads don't benefit much from caching is because they are faster than random reads. There are two reasons for this:

Sequential I/O is faster than random I/O.
Sequential operations are performed faster than random operations, both in memory and on disk. Suppose your disks can do 100 random I/O operations per second and can read 50 MB per second sequentially (that's roughly what a consumer-grade disk can achieve today). If you have 100-byte rows, that's 100 rows per second randomly, versus 500,000 rows per second sequentially—a difference of 5,000 times, or several orders of magnitude. Thus, the random I/O benefits more from caching in this scenario.

Accessing in-memory rows sequentially is also faster than accessing in-memory rows randomly. Today's memory chips can typically access about 250,000 100-byte rows per second randomly, and 5 million per second sequentially. Note that random accesses are some 2,500 times faster in memory than on disk, while sequential accesses are only 10 times faster in memory.

Storage engines can perform sequential reads faster than random reads.
A random read generally means that the storage engine must perform index operations. (There are exceptions to this rule, but it's true for InnoDB and MyISAM.) That usually requires navigating a B-Tree data structure and comparing values to other values. In contrast, sequential reads generally require traversing a simpler data structure, such as a linked list. That's a lot less work, so again, sequential reads are faster.

Finally, random reads are typically executed to find individual rows, but the read isn't just one row—it is a whole page of data, most of which isn't needed. That's a lot of wasted work. A sequential read, on the other hand, typically happens when you want all of the rows on the page, so it's much more cost-effective.

As a result, you can save work by caching sequential reads, but you can save much more work by caching random reads instead. In other words, *adding memory is the best solution for random-read I/O problems* if you can afford it.

Caching, Reads, and Writes

If you have enough memory, you can insulate the disk from read requests completely. If all your data fits in memory, every read will be a cache hit once the server's caches are warmed up. There will still be *logical reads*, but no *physical reads*. Writes are a different matter, though. A write can be performed in memory just as a read can, but sooner or later it has to be written to the disk so it's permanent. In other words, a cache can delay writes, but caching cannot eliminate writes as it can reads.

In fact, in addition to allowing writes to be delayed, caching can permit them to be grouped together in two important ways:

Many writes, one flush
> A single piece of data can be changed many times in memory without all of the new values being written to disk. When the data is eventually flushed to disk, all the modifications that happened since the last physical write are made permanent. For example, many statements could update an in-memory counter. If the counter is incremented 100 times and then written to disk, 100 modifications have been grouped into one write.

I/O merging
> Many different pieces of data can be modified in memory and the modifications can be collected together, so the physical writes can be performed as a single disk operation.

This is why many transactional systems use a *write-ahead logging* strategy. Write-ahead logging lets them make changes to the pages in memory without flushing the changes to disk, which usually involves random I/O and is very slow. Instead, they write a record of the changes to a sequential log file, which is much faster. A background thread can flush the modified pages to disk later; when it does, it can optimize the writes.

Writes benefit greatly from buffering, because it converts random I/O into more sequential I/O. Asynchronous (buffered) writes are typically handled by the operating system and are batched so they can be flushed to disk more optimally. Synchronous (unbuffered) writes have to be written to disk before they finish. That's why they benefit from buffering in a RAID controller's battery-backed write-back cache (we discuss RAID a bit later).

What's Your Working Set?

Every application has a "working set" of data—that is, the data that it really needs to do its work. A lot of databases also have plenty of data that's not in the working set.

You can imagine the database as a desk with filing drawers. The working set consists of the papers you need to have on the desktop to get your work done. The desktop is main memory in this analogy, while the filing drawers are the hard disks.

Just as you don't need to have *every* piece of paper on the desktop to get your work done, you don't need the whole database to fit in memory for optimal performance— just the working set.

The working set's size varies greatly depending on the application. For some applications the working set might be 1% of the total data size, while for others it could be close to 100%. When the working set doesn't fit in memory, the database server will have to shuffle data between the disk and memory to get its work done. This is why a memory shortage might look like an I/O problem. Sometimes there's no way you can fit your entire working set in memory, and sometimes you don't actually want to (for example, if your application needs a lot of sequential I/O). Your application architecture can change a lot depending on whether you can fit the working set in memory.

The working set can be defined as a time-based percentile. For example, the 95th percentile one-hour working set is the set of pages that the database uses during one hour, except for the 5% of pages that are least frequently used. A percentile is the most useful way to think about this, because you might need to access only 1% of your data every hour, but over a 24-hour period that might add up to around 20% of the distinct pages in the whole database. It might be more intuitive to think of the working set in terms of how much data you need to have cached, so your workload is mostly CPU-bound. If you can't cache enough data, your working set doesn't fit in memory.

You should think about the working set in terms of the most frequently *used* set of pages, not the most frequently read or written set of pages. This means that determining the working set requires instrumentation inside the application; you cannot just look at external usage such as I/O accesses, because I/O to the pages is not the same thing as logical access to the pages. MySQL might read a page into memory and then access it millions of times, but you'll see only one I/O operation if you're looking at *strace*, for example. The lack of instrumentation needed for determining the working set is probably the biggest reason that there isn't a lot of research into this topic.

The working set consists of both data and indexes, and you should count it in *cache units*. A cache unit is the smallest unit of data that the storage engine works with.

The size of the cache unit varies between storage engines, and therefore so does the size of the working set. For example, InnoDB works in pages of 16 KB by default. If you do a single-row lookup and InnoDB has to go to disk to get it, it'll read the entire page containing that row into the buffer pool and cache it there. This can be wasteful. Suppose you have 100-byte rows that you access randomly. InnoDB will use a lot of extra memory in the buffer pool for these rows, because it will have to read and cache a complete 16 KB page for each row. Because the working set includes indexes too, InnoDB will also read and cache the parts of the index tree it needed to find the row. InnoDB's index pages are also 16 KB in size, which means it might have to store a total of 32 KB (or more, depending on how deep the index tree is) to access a single 100-byte row. The cache unit is, therefore, another reason why well-chosen clustered indexes are so important in InnoDB. Clustered indexes not only let you optimize disk accesses but also help you keep related data on the same pages, so you can fit more of your working set in your cache.

Finding an Effective Memory-to-Disk Ratio

A good memory-to-disk ratio is best discovered by experimentation and/or benchmarking. If you can fit everything into memory, you're done—there's no need to think about it further. But most of the time you can't, so you have to benchmark with a subset of your data and see what happens. What you're aiming for is an acceptable *cache miss rate*. A cache miss is when your queries request some data that's not cached in main memory, and the server has to get it from disk.

The cache miss rate really governs how much of your CPU is used, so the best way to assess your cache miss rate is to look at your CPU usage. For example, if your CPU is used 99% of the time and waiting for I/O 1% of the time, your cache miss rate is good.

Let's consider how your working set influences your cache miss rate. It's important to realize that your working set isn't just a single number: it's a statistical distribution, and your cache miss rate is nonlinear with regard to the distribution. For example, if you have 10 GB of memory and you're getting a 10% cache miss rate, you might think you just need to add 11% more memory[2] to reduce the cache miss rate to zero. But in reality, inefficiencies such as the size of the cache unit might mean you'd theoretically need 50 GB of memory just to get a 1% miss rate. And even with a perfect cache unit match, the theoretical prediction can be wrong: factors such as data access patterns can complicate things even more. A 1% cache miss rate might require 500 GB of memory, depending on your workload!

It's easy to get sidetracked focusing on optimizing something that might not give you much benefit. For example, a 10% miss rate might result in 80% CPU usage, which is already pretty good. Suppose you add memory and are able to get the cache miss rate down to 5%. As a gross oversimplification, you'll be delivering approximately another 6% data to the CPUs. Making another gross oversimplification, we could say that you've increased your CPU usage to 84.8%. However, this isn't a very big win, considering how much memory you might have purchased to get that result. And in reality, because of the differences between the speed of memory and disk accesses, what the CPU is really doing with the data, and many other factors, lowering the cache miss rate by 5% might not change your CPU usage much at all.

---

2. The right number is 11%, not 10%. A 10% miss rate is a 90% hit rate, so you need to divide 10 GB by 90%, which is 11.111 GB.

This is why we said you should strive for an *acceptable* cache miss rate, not a zero cache miss rate. There's no single number you should target, because what's considered "acceptable" will depend on your application and your workload. Some applications might do very well with a 1% cache miss rate, while others really need a rate as low as 0.01% to perform well. (A "good cache miss rate" is a fuzzy concept, and the fact that there are many ways to count the miss rate further complicates matters.)

The best memory-to-disk ratio also depends on other components in your system. Suppose you have a system with 16 GB of memory, 20 GB of data, and lots of unused disk space. The system is performing nicely at 80% CPU usage. If you wish to place twice as much data on this system and maintain the same level of performance, you might think you can just double the number of CPUs and the amount of memory. However, even if every component in the system scaled perfectly with the increased load (an unrealistic assumption), this probably wouldn't work. The system with 20 GB of data is likely to be using more than 50% of some component's capacity—for example, it might already be performing 80% of its maximum number of I/O operations per second. And queueing inside the system is nonlinear, too. The server won't be able to handle twice as much load. Thus, the best memory-to-disk ratio depends on the system's weakest component.

Choosing Hard Disks

If you can't fit enough data in memory—for example, if you estimate you would need 500 GB of memory to fully load your CPUs with your current I/O system—you should consider a more powerful I/O subsystem, sometimes even at the expense of memory. And you should design your application to handle I/O wait.

This might seem counterintuitive. After all, we just said that more memory can ease the pressure on your I/O subsystem and reduce I/O waits. Why would you want to beef up the I/O subsystem if adding memory could solve the problem? The answer lies in the balance between the factors involved, such as the number of reads versus writes, the size of each I/O operation, and how many such operations happen every second. For example, if you need fast log writes, you can't shield the disk from these writes by increasing the amount of available memory. In this case, it might be a better idea to invest in a high-performance I/O system with a battery-backed write cache, or solid-state storage.

As a brief refresher, reading data from a conventional hard disk is a three-step process:

1. Move the read head to the right position on the disk's surface.
2. Wait for the disk to rotate, so the desired data is under the read head.
3. Wait for the disk to rotate all the desired data past the read head.

How quickly the disk can perform these operations can be condensed to two numbers: *access time* (steps 1 and 2 combined) and *transfer speed*. These two numbers also determine *latency* and *throughput*. Whether you need fast access times or fast transfer speeds—or a mixture of the two—depends on the kinds of queries you're running. In terms of total time needed to complete a disk read, small random lookups are dominated by steps 1 and 2, while big sequential reads are dominated by step 3.

Several other factors can also influence the choice of disk, and which are important will depend on your application. Let's imagine you're choosing disks for an online application such as a popular news site, which does a lot of small, random reads. You might consider the following factors:

Storage capacity
This is rarely an issue for online applications, because today's disks are usually more than big enough. If they're not, combining smaller disks with RAID is standard practice.[3]

Transfer speed
Modern disks can usually transfer data very quickly, as we saw earlier. Exactly how quickly depends mostly on the spindle rotation speed and how densely the data is stored on the disk's surface, plus the limitations of the interface with the host system (many modern disks can read data faster than the interface can transfer it). Regardless, transfer speed is usually not a limiting factor for online applications, because they generally do a lot of small, random lookups.

Access time
This is usually the dominating factor in how fast your random lookups will perform, so you should look for fast access time.

Spindle rotation speed
Common rotation speeds today are 7,200 RPM, 10,000 RPM, and 15,000 RPM. The rotation speed contributes quite a bit to the speed of both random lookups and sequential scans.

Physical size
All other things being equal, the physical size of the disk makes a difference, too: the smaller the disk is, the less time it takes to move the read head. Server-grade 2.5-inch disks are often faster than their larger cousins. They also use less power, and you can usually fit more of them into the chassis.

Just as with CPUs, how MySQL scales to multiple disks depends on the storage engine and the workload. InnoDB scales well to many hard drives. However, MyISAM's table locks limit its write scalability, so a write-heavy workload on MyISAM probably won't benefit much from having many drives. Operating system buffering and parallel background writes help somewhat, but MyISAM's write scalability is inherently more limited than InnoDB's.

---

3. Interestingly, some people deliberately buy larger-capacity disks, then use only 20–30% of their capacity. This increases the data locality and decreases the seek time, which can sometimes justify the higher price.

As with CPUs, more disks is not always better. Some applications that demand low latency need faster drives, not more drives. For example, replication usually performs better with faster drives, because updates on a replica are single-threaded.

Solid-State Storage

Solid-state (flash) storage is actually a 30-year-old technology, but it's become a hot new thing as a new generation of devices have evolved over the last few years. Solid-state storage has now become sufficiently cheap and mature that it is in widespread use, and it will probably replace traditional hard drives for many purposes in the near future.

Solid-state storage devices use nonvolatile flash memory chips composed of cells, instead of magnetic platters. They're also called NVRAM, or *nonvolatile random access memory*. They have no moving parts, which makes them behave very differently from hard drives. We will explore the differences in detail.

The current technologies of interest to MySQL users can be divided into two major categories: SSDs (solid-state drives) and PCIe cards. SSDs emulate standard hard drives by implementing the SATA (Serial Advanced Technology Attachment) interface, so they are drop-in replacements for the hard drive that's in your server now and can fit into the existing slots in the chassis. PCIe cards use special operating system drivers that present the storage as a block device. PCIe and SSD devices are sometimes casually referred to as simply SSDs.

Here's a quick summary of flash performance. High-quality flash devices have:

- Much better random read and write performance compared to hard drives. Flash devices are usually slightly better at reads than writes.

- Better sequential read and write performance than hard drives. However, it's not as dramatic an improvement as that of random I/O, because hard drives are much slower at random I/O than they are at sequential I/O. Entry-level SSDs can actually be slower than conventional drives here.

- Much better support for concurrency than hard drives. Flash devices can support many more concurrent operations, and in fact, they don't really achieve their top throughput until you have lots of concurrency.

The most important things are the improvements in random I/O and concurrency. Flash memory gives you very good random I/O performance at high concurrency, which is exactly what properly normalized databases need. One of the most common reasons for denormalizing a schema is to avoid random I/O and make it possible for sequential I/O to serve the queries.

As a result, we believe that solid-state storage is going to change RDBMS technology fundamentally in the future. The current generation of RDBMS technology has undergone decades of optimizations for spindle-based storage. The same maturity and depth of research and engineering don't quite exist yet for solid-state storage.[4]

An Overview of Flash Memory

Hard drives with spinning platters and oscillating heads have inherent limitations and characteristics that are consequences of the physics involved. The same is true of solid-state storage, which is built on top of flash memory. Don't get the idea that solid-state storage is simple. It's actually more complex than a hard drive in some ways. The limitations of the flash memory are actually pretty severe and hard to overcome, so the typical solid-state device has an intricate architecture with lots of abstractions, caching, and proprietary "magic."

The most important characteristic of flash memory is that it can be read many times rapidly, and in small units, but writes are much more challenging. You can't rewrite a cell[5] without a special erase operation, and you can erase only in large blocks—for example, 512 KB. The erase cycle is slow, and eventually wears out the block. The number of erase cycles a block can tolerate depends on the underlying technology it uses; more about this later.

The limitations on writes are the reason for the complexity of solid-state storage. This is why some devices provide stable, consistent performance and others don't. The magic is all in the proprietary firmware, drivers, and other bits and pieces that make a solid-state device run. To make writes perform well and avoid wearing out the blocks of flash memory prematurely, the device must be able to relocate pages and perform garbage collection and so-called *wear leveling*. The term *write amplification* is used to describe the additional writes caused by moving data from place to place, writing data and metadata multiple times due to partial block writes. If you're interested, Wikipedia's article on write amplification is a good place to learn more.

Garbage collection is important to understand. In order to keep some blocks fresh and ready for new writes, the device reclaims blocks. This requires some free space on the device. Either the device will have some reserved space internally that you can't see, or you will need to reserve space yourself by not filling it up all the way—this varies from device to device. Either way, as the device fills up, the garbage collector has to work harder to keep some blocks clean, so the write amplification factor increases.

As a result, many devices get slower as they fill up. How much slower is different for every vendor and model, and depends on the device's architecture. Some devices are designed for high performance even when they are pretty full, but in general, a 100 GB file will perform differently on a 160 GB SSD than on a 320 GB SSD. The slowdown is caused by having to wait for erases to complete when there are no free blocks. A write

---

4. Some companies claim that they're starting with a clean slate, free of the fetters of the spindle-based past. Mild skepticism is warranted; solving RDBMS challenges is not easy.

5. This is a simplification, but the details are not important here. You can read more on Wikipedia if you like.

to a free block takes a couple of hundred microseconds, but an erase is much slower—typically a few milliseconds.

Flash Technologies

There are two major types of flash devices, and when you're considering a flash storage purchase, it's important to understand the differences. The two types are *single-level cell* (SLC) and *multi-level cell* (MLC).

SLC stores a single bit of data per cell: it can be either a 0 or a 1. SLC is relatively expensive, but it is very fast and durable, with a lifetime of up to 100,000 write cycles depending on the vendor and model. This might not sound like much, but in reality a good SLC device ought to last about 20 years or so, and is said to be more durable and reliable than the controller on which the card is mounted. On the downside, the storage density is relatively low, so you can't get as much storage space per device.

MLC stores two bits per cell, and three-bit devices are entering the market. This makes it possible to get much higher storage density (larger capacities) with MLC devices. The cost is lower, but so is the speed and durability. A good MLC device might be rated for around 10,000 write cycles.

You can purchase both types of flash devices on the mass market, and there is active development and competition between them. At present, SLC still holds the reputation for being the "enterprise" server-grade storage solution, and MLC is usually regarded as consumer-grade, for use in laptops and cameras and so on. However, this is changing, and there is an emerging category of so-called *enterprise MLC* (eMLC) storage.

The development of MLC technology is interesting and bears close watching if you're considering purchasing flash storage. MLC is very complex, with a lot of important factors that contribute to a device's quality and performance. Any given chip by itself is not durable, with a relatively short lifetime and a high probability of errors that must be corrected. As the market moves to even smaller, higher-density chips where the cells can store three bits, the individual chips become even less reliable and more error-prone.

However, this isn't an insurmountable engineering problem. Vendors are building devices with lots and lots of spare capacity that's hidden from you, so there is internal redundancy. There are rumors that some devices might have up to twice as much storage as their rated size, although flash vendors guard their trade secrets very closely. Another way to make MLC chips more durable is through the firmware logic. The algorithms for wear leveling and remapping are very important.

Longevity therefore depends on the true capacity, the firmware logic, and so on—it is ultimately vendor-specific. We've heard reports of devices being destroyed in a couple of weeks of intensive use!

As a result, the most critical aspects of an MLC device are the algorithms and intelligence built into it. It's much harder to build a good MLC device than an SLC device, but it is possible. With great engineering and increases in capacity and density, some of the best vendors are offering devices that are worthy of the eMLC label. This is definitely an area where you'll want to keep track of progress over time; this book's advice on MLC versus SLC is likely to become outdated pretty quickly.

How Long Will Your Device Last?

Virident guarantees that its FlashMax 1.4 TB MLC device will last for 15 PB (petabytes) of writes, but that's at the flash level, and user-visible writes are amplified. We ran a little experiment to discover the write amplification factor for a specific workload.

We created a 500 GB dataset and ran the *tpcc-mysql* benchmark on it for an hour. During this hour /proc/diskstats reported 984 GB of writes, and the Virident configuration utility showed 1,125GB of writes at the flash level, for a write amplification factor of 1.14. Remember, this will be higher if more space is consumed on the device, and it varies based on whether the writes are sequential or random.

At this rate, if we ran the benchmark continuously for a year and a half, we'd wear out the device. Of course, most real workloads are nowhere close to this write-intensive, so the card should last many years in practical usage. The point of this sidebar is not to say that the device will wear out quickly—it is to say that the write amplification factor is hard to predict, and you need to check your device under your workload to see how it behaves.

Size also matters a lot for longevity, as we've mentioned. Bigger devices should last significantly longer, which is why MLC is getting more popular—we're seeing large enough capacities these days for the longevity to be reasonable.

Benchmarking Flash Storage

Benchmarking flash storage is complicated and difficult. There are many ways to do it wrong, and it requires device-specific knowledge, as well as great care and patience, to do it right.

Flash devices have a three-stage pattern that we call the A-B-C performance characteristics. They start out running fast (stage A), and then the garbage collector starts to work. This causes a period during which the device is transitioning to a steady state (stage B), and finally the device enters a steady state (stage C). All of the devices we've tested have this characteristic pattern.

Of course, what you're interested in is the performance in stage C, so your benchmarks need to measure only that portion of the run. This means that the benchmark needs to be more than just a benchmark: it needs to be a warmup workload followed by a benchmark. Defining where the warmup ends and the benchmark begins can be tricky, though.

Devices, filesystems, and operating systems vary in their support for the TRIM command, which marks space as ready to reuse. Sometimes the device will TRIM when you delete all of the files. If that happens between runs of the benchmark, the device will reset to stage A, and you'll have to cycle it through stages A and B between runs. Another factor is the differing performance when the device is more or less filled up. A repeatable benchmark has to account for all of these factors.

As a result of the above complexities, vendor benchmarks and specifications are a minefield for the unwary, even when they're reported faithfully and with good intentions. You typically get four numbers from vendors. Here's an example of a device's specifications:

1. The device can read up to 520 MB/s.
2. The device can write up to 480 MB/s.
3. The device can perform sustained writes up to 420 MB/s.
4. The device can perform 70,000 random 4 KB writes per second.

If you cross-check those numbers, you will notice that the peak IOPS (input/output operations per second) of 70,000 random 4 KB writes per second is only about 274 MB/s, which is a lot less than the peak write bandwidths listed in points 2 and 3. This is because the peak write bandwidth is achieved with large block sizes such as 64 KB or 128 KB, and the peak IOPS is achieved with small block sizes.

Most applications don't write in such large blocks. InnoDB typically writes a combination of 16 KB blocks and 512-byte blocks. As a result, you should really expect only 274 MB/s of write bandwidth from this device—and that's in stage A, before the garbage collector kicks in and the device reaches its steady-state long-term performance levels!

You can find current benchmarks of MySQL and raw file I/O workloads on solid-state devices at our blogs, *http://www.ssdperformanceblog.com* and *http://www.mysqlperformanceblog.com*.

Solid-State Drives (SSDs)

SSDs emulate SATA hard drives. This is a compatibility feature: a replacement for a SATA drive doesn't require any special drivers or interconnects.

Intel X-25E drives are probably the most common SSDs we see used in servers today, but there are lots of other options. The X-25E is sold for the "enterprise" market, but there is also the X-25M, which has MLC storage and is intended for the mass market of laptop users and so forth. Intel also sells the 320 series, which a lot of people are using as well. Again, this is just one vendor—there are many, and by the time this book goes to print, some of what we've written about SSDs will likely already be outdated.

The good thing about SSDs is that they are readily available in lots of brands and models, they're relatively cheap, and they're a lot faster than hard drives. The biggest downside is that they're not always as reliable as hard drives, depending on the brand and model. Until recently, most devices didn't have an onboard battery, but most devices do have a write cache to buffer writes. This write cache isn't durable without a battery to back it, but it can't be disabled without greatly increasing the write load on the underlying flash storage. So, if you disable your drive's cache to get really durable storage, you will wear the device out faster, and in some cases this will void the warranty.

Some manufacturers don't exactly rush to inform people about this characteristic of the SSDs they sell, and they guard details such as the internal architecture of the devices pretty jealously. Whether there is a battery or capacitor to keep the write cache's data safe in case of a power failure is usually an open question. In some cases the drive will accept a command to disable the cache, but ignore it. So you really won't know whether your drive is durable unless you do crash testing. We crash-tested some drives and found varying results. These days some drives ship with a capacitor to protect the cache, making it durable, but in general, *if your drive doesn't brag that it has a battery or capacitor, then it doesn't*. This means it isn't durable in case of power outages, so you'll get data corruption, possibly without knowing it. A capacitor or battery is a feature you should definitely look for in SSDs.

You generally get what you pay for with SSDs. The challenges of the underlying technology aren't easy to solve. Lots of manufacturers make drives that fail shockingly quickly under load, or don't provide consistent performance. Some low-end manufacturers have a habit of releasing a new generation of drives every time you turn around, and claiming that they've solved all the problems of the older generation. This tends to be untrue, of course. The "enterprise-grade" devices are usually worth the price if you care about reliability and consistently high performance.

Using RAID with SSDs

We recommend that you use RAID (Redundant Array of Inexpensive Disks) with SATA SSDs. They are simply not reliable enough to trust a single drive with your data.

Many older RAID controllers weren't SSD-ready. They assumed that they were managing spindle-based hard drives, and they did things like buffering and reordering writes, assuming that it would be more efficient. This was just wasted work and added latency, because the logical locations that the SSD exposes are mapped to arbitrary locations in the underlying flash memory. The situation is a bit better today. Some RAID controllers have a letter at the end of their model numbers, indicating that they are SSD-ready. For example, the Adaptec controllers use a Z for this purpose.

Even flash-ready controllers are not *really* flash-ready, however. For example, Vadim benchmarked an Adaptec 5805Z controller with a variety of drives in RAID 10, using a 500 GB file and a concurrency of 16. The results were terrible: the 95th percentile latency for random writes was in the double-digit milliseconds, and in the worst case, it was over a second.[6] (You should expect sub-millisecond writes.)

This specific comparison was for a customer who wanted to see whether Micron SSDs would be better than 64 GB Intel SSDs, which they already used in the same configuration. When we benchmarked the Intel drives, we found the same performance characteristics. So we tried some other configurations of drives, with and without a SAS expander, to see what would happen. Table 9-1 shows the results.

Table 9-1. Benchmarks with SSDs on an Adaptec RAID controller

Drives	Brand	Size	SAS expander	Random read	Random write
34	Intel	64 GB	Yes	310 MB/s	130 MB/s
14	Intel	64 GB	Yes	305 MB/s	145 MB/s
24	Micron	50 GB	No	350 MB/s	120 MB/s
34	Intel	50 GB	No	350 MB/s	180 MB/s

None of these results approached what we should expect from so many drives. In general, the RAID controller was giving us the performance we'd expect from six or eight drives, not dozens. The RAID controller was simply saturated. The point of this story is that you should benchmark carefully before investing heavily in hardware—the results might be quite different from your expectations.

PCIe Storage Devices

In contrast to SATA SSDs, PCIe devices don't try to emulate hard drives. This is a good thing: the interface between the server and the hard drives isn't capable of handling the full performance of flash. The SAS/SATA interconnect has lower bandwidth than PCIe, so PCIe is a better choice for high performance. PCIe devices also have much lower latency, because they are physically closer to the CPUs.

Nothing matches the performance you can get from PCIe devices. The downside is that they're relatively expensive.

All of the models we're familiar with require a special driver to create a block device that the operating system sees as a hard drive. They use a mixture of strategies for their wear leveling and other logic; some of them use the host system's CPU and memory, and some have onboard logic controllers and RAM. In many cases the host system has plentiful CPU and RAM resources, so using them is actually a more cost-effective strategy than buying a card that has its own.

We don't recommend RAID with PCIe devices. They're too expensive to use with RAID, and most devices have their own onboard RAID anyway. We don't really know

---

6. But that's not all. We checked the drives after the benchmark and found two dead SSDs and one with inconsistencies.

how likely the controller is to fail, but the vendors say that their controllers should be as good as network cards or RAID controllers in general, and this seems likely to be true. In other words, the mean time between failures (MTBF) for these devices is likely to be similar to the motherboard, so using RAID with the devices would just add a lot of cost without much benefit.

There are several vendors making PCIe flash cards. The most popular brands among MySQL users are Fusion-io and Virident, but vendors such as Texas Memory Systems, STEC, and OCZ also have offerings. Both SLC and MLC cards are available.

Other Types of Solid-State Storage

In addition to SSDs and PCIe devices, there are other options from companies such as Violin Memory, SandForce, and Texas Memory Systems. These companies provide large boxes full of flash memory that are essentially flash SANs, with tens of terabytes of storage. They're used mostly for large-scale data center storage consolidation. They're very expensive and very high-performance. We know of some people who use them, and we have measured their performance in some cases. They provide very decent latency despite the network round-trip time—for example, less than four milliseconds of latency over NFS.

These aren't really a good fit for the general MySQL market, though. They're more targeted towards other databases, such as Oracle, which can use them for shared-storage clustering. MySQL can't take advantage of such powerful storage at such a large scale, in general, as it doesn't typically run well with databases in the tens of terabytes—MySQL's answer to such a large database is to shard and scale out horizontally in a shared-nothing architecture.

Specialized solutions might be able to use these large storage devices, though—Infobright might be a candidate, for example. ScaleDB can be deployed in a shared-storage architecture, but we haven't seen it in production, so we don't know how well it might work.

When Should You Use Flash?

The most obvious use case for solid-state storage is any workload that has a lot of random I/O. Random I/O is usually caused by the data being larger than the server's memory. With standard hard drives, you're limited by rotation speed and seek latency. Flash devices can ease the pain significantly.

Of course, sometimes you can simply buy more RAM so the random workload will fit into memory, and the I/O goes away. But when you can't buy enough RAM, flash can help. Another problem that you can't always solve with RAM is that of a high-throughput write workload. Adding memory will help reduce the write workload that reaches the disks, because more memory creates more opportunities to buffer and combine writes. This allows you to convert a random write workload into a more sequential one.

However, this doesn't work infinitely, and some transactional or insert-heavy workloads don't benefit from this approach anyway. Flash storage can help here, too.

Single-threaded workloads are another characteristic scenario where flash can potentially help. When a workload is single-threaded it is very sensitive to latency, and the lower latency of solid-state storage makes a big difference. In contrast, multi-threaded workloads can often simply be parallelized more heavily to get more throughput. MySQL replication is the obvious example of a single-threaded workload that benefits a lot from reduced latency. Using flash storage on replicas can often improve their performance significantly when they are having trouble keeping up with the master.

Flash is also great for server consolidation, especially in the PCIe form factor. We've seen opportunities to consolidate many server instances onto a single physical server—sometimes up to a 10- or 15-fold consolidation is possible. See Chapter 11 for more on this topic.

Flash isn't always the answer, though. A good example is for sequential write workloads such as the InnoDB log files. Flash doesn't offer much of a cost-to-performance advantage in this scenario, because it's not much faster at sequential writes than standard hard drives are. Such workloads are also high-throughput, which will wear out the device faster. It's often a better idea to store your log files on standard hard drives, with a RAID controller that has a battery-backed write cache.

And sometimes the answer lies in the memory-to-disk ratio, not just in the disk. If you can buy enough RAM to cache your workload, you may find this cheaper and more effective than purchasing a flash storage device.

Using Flashcache

Although there are many opportunities to make tradeoffs between flash storage, hard disks, and RAM, these don't have to be treated as single-component tiers in the storage hierarchy. Sometimes it makes sense to use a combination of disk and memory technologies, and that's what Flashcache does.

Flashcache is one implementation of a technique you can find used in many systems, such as Oracle Database, the ZFS filesystem, and even many modern hard drives and RAID controllers. Much of the following discussion applies broadly, but to keep things concrete we'll focus only on Flashcache, because it is vendor-and filesystem-agnostic.

Flashcache is a Linux kernel module that uses the Linux device mapper. It creates an intermediate layer in the memory hierarchy, between RAM and the disk. It is one of the open source technologies created by Facebook and is used to help optimize Facebook's hardware for its database workload.

Flashcache creates a block device, which can be partitioned and used to create a filesystem like any other. The trick is that this block device is backed by both flash and disk storage. The flash device is used as an intelligent cache for both reads and writes.

The virtual block device is much larger than the flash device, but that's okay, because the disk is considered to be the ultimate repository for the data. The flash device is just there to buffer writes and to effectively extend the server's memory size for caching reads.

How good is performance? Flashcache seems to have relatively high kernel overhead. (The device mapper doesn't seem to be as efficient as it should be, but we haven't probed deeply to find out why.) However, even though it seems that Flashcache could theoretically be more efficient, and the ultimate performance is not as good as the performance of the underlying flash storage, it's still a lot faster than disks. So it might be worthwhile to consider.

We evaluated Flashcache's performance in a series of hundreds of benchmarks, and we found that it's rather difficult to test meaningfully on an artificial workload. We concluded that it's not clear how beneficial Flashcache is for write workloads in general, but for read workloads it can be very helpful. This matches the use case for which it was designed: servers that are heavily I/O-bound on reads, with a much larger working set than the memory size.

In addition to lab testing, we have some experience with Flashcache in production workloads. One case of a four-terabyte database comes to mind. This database suffered greatly from replication lag. We modified the system by adding a Virident PCIe card with half a terabyte of storage. Then we installed Flashcache and used the PCIe card as the flash portion of the device. This doubled replication speed.

The Flashcache use case is most economical when the flash card is pretty full, so it's important to have a card whose performance doesn't degrade much when it fills up. That's why we chose the Virident card.

Flashcache really is a cache, so it has to warm up just like any other cache. This warmup period can be extremely long, though. For example, in the case we just mentioned, Flashcache required a week to warm up and really help accelerate the workload.

Should you use Flashcache? Your mileage will vary, so we think it's a good idea to get expert advice on this point if you feel uncertain. It's complex to understand the mechanics of Flashcache, and how they impact your database's working set size and the (at least) three layers of storage underneath the database:

- First there's the InnoDB buffer pool, whose size relative to the working set size determines one cache miss rate. Hits from this cache are very fast, and the response time is very uniform.
- Misses from the buffer pool propagate down to the Flashcache device, which has a complex distribution of response times. Flashcache's cache miss rate is determined by the working set size and the size of the flash device that backs it. Hits from this cache are a lot faster than disk retrievals.
- Misses from Flashcache's cache propagate down to the disks, which have a fairly uniform distribution of response times.

There might be more layers beyond that: your SAN or your RAID controller cache, for example.

Here's a thought experiment that illustrates how these layers interact. It's clear that the response times from a Flashcache device will not be as stable or fast as they would be from the flash device alone. But imagine that you have a terabyte of data, and 100 GB of this data receives 99% of the I/O operations over a long period of time. That is, the long-term 99th percentile working set size is 100 GB.

Now suppose that we have the following storage devices: a large RAID volume that can perform 1,000 IOPS, and a much smaller flash device that can perform 100,000 IOPS. The flash device is not big enough to store all of the data—let's pretend it is 128 GB— so using flash alone isn't an option. If we use the flash device for Flashcache, we can expect cache hits to be much faster than disk retrievals, but slower than the responses from flash device itself. Let's stick with round numbers and say that 90% of the requests to the Flashcache device can be served at a rate equivalent to 50,000 IOPS.

What is the outcome of this thought experiment? There are two major points:

1. Our system provides a lot better performance with Flashcache than without it, because most of the page accesses that are cache misses in the buffer pool are served from the flash card at a very high speed relative to disk accesses. (The 99th percentile working set fits entirely into the flash card.)

2. The 90% hit rate at the Flashcache device means there is a 10% miss rate. Because the underlying disks can serve only 1,000 IOPS, the most we can expect to push to the Flashcache device is 10,000 IOPS. To understand why this is true, imagine what would happen if we requested more than that: with 10% of the I/O operations missing the cache and falling through to the RAID volume, we'd be requesting more than 1,000 IOPS of the RAID volume, and we know it can't handle that. As a result, even though Flashcache is slower than the flash card, the system as a whole is still limited by the RAID volume, not the flash card or Flashcache.

In the final analysis, whether Flashcache is right for you is a complex decision that will involve lots of factors. In general, it seems best suited to heavily I/O-bound read-mostly workloads whose working set size is much too large to be optimized economically with memory.

Optimizing MySQL for Solid-State Storage

If you're running MySQL on flash, there are some configuration parameters that can provide better performance. The default configuration of InnoDB, in particular, is tailored to hard drives, not solid-state drives. Not all versions of InnoDB provide the same level of configurability. In particular, many of the improvements designed for flash have appeared first in Percona Server, although many of these have either already been re-implemented in Oracle's version of InnoDB, or appear to be planned for future versions. Improvements include:

Increasing InnoDB's I/O capacity

Flash supports much higher concurrency than conventional hard drives, so you can increase the number of read and write I/O threads to as high as 10 or 15 with good results. You can also increase the `innodb_io_capacity` option to between 2000 and 20000, depending on the IOPS your device can actually perform. This is especially necessary with the official InnoDB from Oracle, which has more internal algorithms that depend on this setting.

Making the InnoDB log files larger

Even with the improved recovery algorithms in recent versions of InnoDB, you don't want your log files to be too large on hard drives, because the random I/O required for crash recovery is slow and can cause recovery to take a long time. Flash storage makes this much faster, so you can have larger InnoDB log files, which can help improve and stabilize performance. This is especially necessary with the official InnoDB from Oracle, which has trouble maintaining a consistent dirty page flush rate unless the log files are fairly large—4 GB or larger seems to be a good range on typical servers at the time of writing. Percona Server and MySQL 5.6 support log files larger than 4 GB.

Moving some files from flash to RAID

In addition to making the InnoDB log files larger, it can be a good idea to store the log files separately from the data files, placing them on a RAID controller with a battery-backed write cache instead of on the solid-state device. There are several reasons for this. One is that the type of I/O the log files receive isn't much faster on flash devices than it is on such a RAID setup. InnoDB writes the log files sequentially in 512-byte units and never reads them except during crash recovery, when it reads them sequentially. It's kind of wasteful to use your flash storage for this. It's also a good idea to move these small writes to the RAID volume because very small writes increase the write amplification factor on flash devices, which can be a problem for some devices' longevity. A mixture of large and small writes can also cause increased latency for some devices.

It's also sometimes beneficial to move your binary log files to the RAID volume, for similar reasons; and you might consider moving your *ibdata1* file, too. The *ibdata1* file contains the doublewrite buffer and the insert buffer. The doublewrite buffer, in particular, gets a lot of repeated writes. In Percona Server, you can remove the doublewrite buffer from the *ibdata1* file and store it in a separate file, which you can place on the RAID volume.

There's another option, too: you can take advantage of Percona Server's ability to write the transaction logs in 4-kilobyte blocks instead of 512-byte blocks. This can be more efficient for flash storage as well as for the server itself.

All of the above advice is rather hardware-specific, and your mileage may vary, so be sure you understand the factors involved—and test appropriately—before you make such a large change to your storage layout.

Disabling read-ahead

Readahead optimizes device access by noticing and predicting read patterns, and requesting data from the device when it believes that it will be needed in the future. There are actually two types of read-ahead in InnoDB, and in various circumstances we've found that performance problems can actually be caused by read-ahead and the way it works internally. The overhead is greater than the benefit in many cases, especially on flash storage, but we don't have hard evidence or guidelines as to exactly how much you can improve performance by disabling read-ahead.

Oracle disabled so-called "random read-ahead" in the InnoDB plugin in MySQL 5.1, then reenabled it in MySQL 5.5 with a parameter to configure it. Percona Server lets you configure both random and linear read-ahead in older server versions as well.

Configuring the InnoDB flushing algorithm

The way that InnoDB decides when, how many, and which pages to flush is a highly complex topic to explore, and we don't have room to discuss it in great detail here. This is also a subject of active research, and in fact several algorithms are available in various versions of InnoDB and MySQL.

The standard InnoDB's algorithms don't offer much configurability that is beneficial on flash storage, but if you're using Percona XtraDB (included in Percona Server and MariaDB), we recommend setting the `innodb_adaptive_checkpoint` option to `keep_average`, instead of the default value of `estimate`. This will help ensure more consistent performance and avoid server stalls, because the `estimate` algorithm can stall on flash storage. We developed `keep_average` specifically for flash storage, because we realized that it's possible to push as much I/O to the device as we want without causing a bottleneck and an ensuing stall.

In addition, we recommend setting `innodb_flush_neighbor_pages` to 0 on flash storage. This will prevent InnoDB from trying to find nearby dirty pages to flush together. The algorithm that performs this operation can cause large spikes of writes, high latency, and internal contention. It's not necessary or beneficial on flash storage, because the neighboring pages can be flushed individually without impacting performance.

Potentially disabling the doublewrite buffer

Instead of moving the doublewrite buffer off the flash device, you can consider disabling it altogether. Some vendors claim that their devices support atomic 16 KB writes, which makes the doublewrite buffer redundant. You need to ensure that the entire storage system is configured to support atomic 16 KB writes, which generally requires O_DIRECT and the XFS filesystem.

We don't have conclusive evidence that the claim of atomicity is true, but because of how flash storage works, we believe that the chance of partial page writes to the data files is greatly decreased. And the gains are much greater on flash devices than they are on conventional hard drives. Disabling the doublewrite buffer can improve

MySQL's overall performance on flash storage by a factor of 50% or so, so although we don't know that it's 100% safe, it's something you can consider doing.

Restricting the insert buffer size

The insert buffer (or change buffer, in newer versions of InnoDB) is designed to reduce random I/O to nonunique secondary index pages that aren't in memory when rows are updated. On hard drives, it can make a huge difference in reducing random I/O. For some workloads, the difference may reach nearly two orders of magnitude when the working set is much larger than memory. Letting the insert buffer grow large is very helpful in such cases.

However, this isn't as necessary on flash storage. Random I/O is much faster on flash devices, so even if you disable the insert buffer completely, it doesn't hurt as badly. You probably don't want to disable it, though. It's better to leave it enabled, because the I/O is only one part of the cost of updating index pages that aren't in memory. The main thing to configure on flash devices is the maximum permitted size. You can restrict it to a relatively small size, instead of letting it grow huge; this can avoid consuming a lot of space on your device and help prevent the *ibdata1* file from growing very large. At the time of writing you can't configure the maximum size in standard InnoDB, but you can in Percona XtraDB, which is included in Percona Server and MariaDB. MySQL 5.6 will add a similar option, too.

In addition to the aforementioned configuration suggestions, some other optimizations have been proposed or discussed for flash storage. However, these are not all as clear-cut, so we will mention them but leave you to research their benefit for your specific case. The first is the InnoDB page size. We've found mixed results, so we don't have a definite recommendation yet. The good news is that the page size is configurable without recompiling the server in Percona Server, and this will also be possible in MySQL 5.6. Previous versions of MySQL required you to recompile the server to use a different page size, so the general public has by far the most experience running with standard 16 KB pages. When the page size becomes easier for more people to experiment with, we expect a lot more testing with nonstandard sizes, and it's likely that we'll learn a great deal from this.

Another proposed optimization is alternative algorithms for InnoDB's page checksums. When the storage system responds very quickly, the checksum computation can actually start to take a significant amount of time relative to the I/O operation, and for some people this has become the bottleneck instead of the I/O being the bottleneck. Our benchmarks haven't shown repeatable results that are applicable to a broad spectrum of use cases, so your mileage may vary. Percona XtraDB permits you to change the checksum algorithm, and MySQL 5.6 will also have this capability.

You might have noticed that we've referred a lot to features and optimizations that aren't available yet in standard InnoDB. We hope and believe that many of the improvements we've built into Percona Server and XtraDB will eventually become available to a wider audience. In the meantime, if you're using the official MySQL distribution from Oracle, there are still steps you can take to optimize your server for flash storage. You should use `innodb_file_per_table`, and place the data directory on your flash device. Then move the *ibdata1* and log files, and all other log files (binary logs, relay logs, etc.), to a RAID volume as discussed previously. This will concentrate the random I/O workload on your flash device and move as many of the write-heavy, sequentially written files off this device as possible, so you can save space on your flash device and reduce wear.

In addition, for all versions of the server, you should ensure that hyperthreading is enabled. It helps a lot when you use flash storage, because the disk is generally no longer the bottleneck, and tasks become more CPU-bound instead of being I/O-bound.

Choosing Hardware for a Replica

Choosing hardware for a replica is generally similar to choosing hardware for a master, though there are some differences. If you're planning to use a replica for failover, it usually needs to be at least as powerful as the master. And regardless of whether the replica is acting as a standby to replace the master, it must be powerful enough to perform all the writes that occur on the master, with the extra handicap that it must perform them serially. (There's more information about this in the next chapter.)

The main consideration for a replica's hardware is cost: do you need to spend as much on your replica's hardware as you do on the master? Can you configure the replica differently, so you can get more performance from it? Will the replica have a different workload from the master, and potentially benefit from very different hardware?

It all depends. If the replica is a standby, you probably want the master and replica to have the same hardware and configuration. But if you're using replication solely as a cheap way to get more overall read capacity from your system, you can take a variety of shortcuts on a replica. You might want to use a different storage engine on the replica, for example, and some people use cheaper hardware or use RAID 0 instead of RAID 5 or RAID 10. You can also disable some consistency and durability guarantees to let the replica do less work.

These measures can be cost-efficient on a large scale, but they might just make things more complex on a small scale. In practice, most people seem to use one of two strategies for replicas: they use identical hardware everywhere, or they buy new hardware for the master and use the master's old hardware for a replica.

Using solid-state drives on a replica can make a lot of sense when the replica is having a hard time keeping up with the master. The fast random I/O helps ease the single-threaded replication thread's handicap.

RAID Performance Optimization

Storage engines often keep their data and/or indexes in single large files, which means RAID (Redundant Array of Inexpensive Disks) is usually the most feasible option for storing a lot of data.[7] RAID can help with redundancy, storage size, caching, and speed. But as with the other optimizations we've been looking at, there are many variations on RAID configurations, and it's important to choose one that's appropriate for your needs.

We won't cover every RAID level here, or go into the specifics of exactly how the different RAID levels store data. Good material on this topic is widely available in books and online.[8] Instead, we focus on how RAID configurations satisfy a database server's needs. The most important RAID levels are:

RAID 0

> RAID 0 is the cheapest and highest-performance RAID configuration, at least when you measure cost and performance simplistically (if you include data recovery, for example, it starts to look more expensive). Because it offers no redundancy, we recommend RAID 0 only for servers you don't care about, such as replicas or servers that are "disposable" for some reason. The typical scenario is a replica server that can easily be cloned from another replica.
>
> Again, note that *RAID 0 does not provide any redundancy*, even though "redundant" is the R in the RAID acronym. In fact, the probability of a RAID 0 array failing is actually *higher* than the probability of any single disk failing, not lower!

RAID 1

> RAID 1 offers good read performance for many scenarios, and it duplicates your data across disks, so there's good redundancy. RAID 1 is a little bit faster than RAID 0 for reads. It's good for servers that handle logging and similar workloads, because sequential writes rarely need many underlying disks to perform well (as opposed to random writes, which can benefit from parallelization). It is also a typical choice for low-end servers that need redundancy but have only two hard drives.
>
> RAID 0 and RAID 1 are very simple, and they can often be implemented well in software. Most operating systems will let you create software RAID 0 and RAID 1 volumes easily.

---

7. Partitioning (see Chapter 7) is another good practice, because it usually splits the file into many files, which you can place on different devices. However, even compared to partitioning, RAID is a simple solution for very large data volumes. It doesn't require you to balance the load manually or intervene when the load distribution changes, and it gives redundancy, which you won't get by assigning partitions to different disks.

8. Two good learning resources are the Wikipedia article on RAID (*http://en.wikipedia.org/wiki/RAID*) and the AC&NC tutorial at *http://www.acnc.com/04_00.html*.

RAID 5

RAID 5 is a little scary, but it's the inevitable choice for some applications because of price constraints and/or constraints on the number of disks that can physically fit in the server. It spreads the data across many disks, with distributed parity blocks so that if any one disk fails the data can be rebuilt from the parity blocks. If two disks fail, the entire volume fails unrecoverably. In terms of cost per unit of storage, it's the most economical redundant configuration, because you lose only one disk's worth of storage space across the entire array.

Random writes are expensive in RAID 5, because each write to the volume requires two reads and two writes to the underlying disks to compute and store the parity bits. Writes can perform a little better if they are sequential, or if there are many physical disks. On the other hand, both random and sequential reads perform decently. RAID 5 is an acceptable choice for data volumes, or data and logs, for many read-mostly workloads, where the cost of the extra I/O operations for writes isn't a big deal.

The biggest performance cost with RAID 5 occurs if a disk fails, because the data has to be reconstructed by reading all the other disks. This affects performance severely, and it's even worse if you have lots of disks. If you're trying to keep the server online during the rebuild, don't expect either the rebuild or the array's performance to be good. If you use RAID 5, it's best to have some mechanism to fail over and take a machine out of service when there's a problem. Either way, it's a good idea to benchmark your system with a failed drive and during recovery, so you know what to expect. The disk performance might degrade by a factor of two or more with a failed drive and by a factor of five or more when rebuilding is in progress, and a server with storage that's two to five times slower might be disproportionately affected overall.

Other performance costs include limited scalability because of the parity blocks—RAID 5 doesn't scale well past 10 disks or so—and caching issues. Good RAID 5 performance depends heavily on the RAID controller's cache, which can conflict with the database server's needs. We discuss caching a bit later.

One of the mitigating factors for RAID 5 is that it's so popular. As a result, RAID controllers are often highly optimized for RAID 5, and despite the theoretical limits, smart controllers that use caches well can sometimes perform nearly as well as RAID 10 controllers for some workloads. This might actually reflect that the RAID 10 controllers are less highly optimized, but regardless of the reason, this is what we've seen.

RAID 10

RAID 10 is a very good choice for data storage. It consists of mirrored pairs that are striped, so it scales both reads and writes well. It is fast and easy to rebuild, in comparison to RAID 5. It can also be implemented in software fairly well.

The performance loss when one hard drive goes out can still be significant, because that stripe can become a bottleneck. Performance can degrade by up to 50%, depending on the workload. One thing to watch out for is RAID controllers that use a "concatenated mirror" implementation for RAID 10. This is suboptimal because of the absence of striping: your most frequently accessed data might be placed on only one pair of spindles, instead of being spread across many, so you'll get poor performance.

RAID 50

RAID 50 consists of RAID 5 arrays that are striped, and it can be a good compromise between the economy of RAID 5 and the performance of RAID 10, if you have many disks. This is mainly useful for very large datasets, such as data warehouses or extremely large OLTP systems.

Table 9-2 summarizes various RAID configurations.

Table 9-2. Comparison of RAID levels

Level	Synopsis	Redundancy	Disks required	Faster reads	Faster writes
RAID 0	Cheap, fast, dangerous	No	N	Yes	Yes
RAID 1	Fast reads, simple, safe	Yes	2 (usually)	Yes	No
RAID 5	A safety, speed, and cost compromise cost	Yes	N + 1	Yes	Depends
RAID 10	Expensive, fast, safe	Yes	2N	Yes	Yes
RAID 50	For very large data stores	Yes	2(N + 1)	Yes	Yes

RAID Failure, Recovery, and Monitoring

RAID configurations (with the exception of RAID 0) offer redundancy. This is important, but it's easy to underestimate the likelihood of concurrent disk failures. You shouldn't think of RAID as a strong guarantee of data safety.

RAID doesn't eliminate—or even reduce—the need for backups. When there is a problem, the recovery time will depend on your controller, the RAID level, the array size, the disk speed, and whether you need to keep the server online while you rebuild the array.

There is a chance of disks failing at exactly the same time. For example, a power spike or overheating can easily kill two or more disks. What's more common, however, is two disk failures happening close together. Many such issues can go unnoticed. A common case is corruption on the physical media holding data that's seldom accessed. This might go undetected for months, until either you try to read the data, or another drive fails and the RAID controller tries to use the corrupted data to rebuild the array. The larger the hard drive is, the more likely this is.

That's why it's important to monitor your RAID arrays. Most controllers offer some software to report on the array's status, and you need to keep track of this because you might otherwise be totally ignorant of a drive failure. You might miss your opportunity to recover the data and discover the problem only when a second drive fails, when it's too late. You should configure a monitoring system to alert you when a drive or volume changes to a degraded or failed status.

You can mitigate the risk of latent corruption by actively checking your arrays for consistency at regular intervals. Background Patrol Read, a feature of some controllers that checks for damaged media and fixes it while all the drives are online, can also help avert such problems. As with recovery, extremely large arrays can be slow to check, so make sure you plan accordingly when you create large arrays.

You can also add a hot spare drive, which is unused and configured as a standby for the controller to automatically use for recovery. This is a good idea if you depend on every server. It's expensive with servers that have only a few hard drives, because the cost of having an idle disk is proportionately higher, but if you have many disks, it's almost foolish not to have a hot spare. Remember that the probability of a drive failure increases rapidly with more disks.

In addition to monitoring your drives for failures, you should monitor the RAID controller's battery backup unit and write cache policy. If the battery fails, by default most controllers will disable write caching by changing the cache policy to WriteThrough instead of WriteBack. This can cause a severe drop in performance. Many controllers will also periodically cycle the battery through a learning process, during which time the cache is also disabled. Your RAID controller's management utility should let you view and configure when the learning cycle is scheduled, so that it doesn't catch you off guard.

You might also want to benchmark your system with the cache policy set to Write-Through so you'll know what to expect. You might need to schedule your battery learn cycles at night or on the weekend, reconfigure your servers by changing the innodb_flush_log_at_trx_commit and sync_binlog variables, or simply fail over to another server and let the battery learn cycles happen one server at a time.

Balancing Hardware RAID and Software RAID

The interaction between the operating system, the filesystem, and the number of drives the operating system sees can be complicated. Bugs or limitations—or just misconfigurations—can reduce performance well below what is theoretically possible.

If you have 10 hard disks, ideally they should be able to serve 10 requests in parallel, but sometimes the filesystem, the operating system, or the RAID controller will serialize requests. One possible solution to this problem is to try different RAID configurations. For example, if you have 10 disks and you want to use mirroring for redundancy and performance, you could configure them in several ways:

- Configure a single RAID 10 volume consisting of five mirrored pairs. The operating system will see a single large disk volume, and the RAID controller will hide the 10 underlying disks.

- Configure five RAID 1 mirrored pairs in the RAID controller, and let the operating system address five volumes instead of one.

- Configure five RAID 1 mirrored pairs in the RAID controller, and then use software RAID 0 to make the five volumes appear as one logical volume, effectively implementing RAID 10 partially in hardware and partially in software.

Which option is best? It depends on how all the components in your system interact. The configurations might perform identically, or they might not.

We've noticed serialization in various configurations. For example, the ext3 filesystem has a single mutex per inode, so when InnoDB is configured with `innodb_flush_method=O_DIRECT` (the usual configuration) there will be inode-level locking in the filesystem. This makes it impossible to have concurrent I/O to the files, and the system performs well below its theoretical ability.

In another case we saw, requests to each *device* were serialized with a 10-disk RAID 10 volume, the ReiserFS filesystem, and InnoDB with `innodb_file_per_table` enabled. Switching to software RAID 0 on top of hardware RAID 1 gave five times more throughput, because the storage system began to behave like five spindles instead of one. This situation was caused by a bug that has since been fixed, but it's a good illustration of the sort of thing that can happen.

Serialization can happen on any layer in the software or hardware stack. If you see this problem occurring, you might need to change the filesystem, upgrade your kernel, expose more devices to the operating system, or use a different mixture of software or hardware RAID. You should check your device's concurrency and make sure it really is doing concurrent I/O (more on this topic later in the chapter).

Finally, don't forget to benchmark when you set up a new server! This will help you verify that you're getting the performance you expect. For example, if one hard drive can do 200 random reads per second, a RAID 10 volume with eight hard drives should do close to 1,600 random reads per second. If you're observing a much lower number, such as 500 random reads per second, you should research the problem. Make sure your benchmarks exercise the I/O subsystem in the same way MySQL will—for example, use the `O_DIRECT` flag and test I/O performance to a single file if you're using InnoDB without `innodb_file_per_table` enabled. We usually use *sysbench* for validating that new hardware is set up correctly.

RAID Configuration and Caching

You can usually configure the RAID controller itself by entering its setup utility during the machine's boot sequence, or by running it from the command prompt. Although most controllers offer a lot of options, the two we focus on are the *chunk size* for striped arrays, and the *on-controller cache* (also known as the *RAID cache*; we use the terms interchangeably).

The RAID stripe chunk size

The optimal stripe chunk size is workload- and hardware-specific. In theory, it's good to have a large chunk size for random I/O, because it means more reads can be satisfied from a single drive.

To see why this is so, consider the size of a typical random I/O operation for your workload. If the chunk size is at least that large, and the data doesn't span the border between chunks, only a single drive needs to participate in the read. But if the chunk size is smaller than the amount of data to be read, there's no way to avoid involving more than one drive in the read.

So much for theory. In practice, many RAID controllers don't work well with large chunks. For example, the controller might use the chunk size as the cache unit in its cache, which could be wasteful. The controller might also match the chunk size, cache size, and read-unit size (the amount of data it reads in a single operation). If the read unit is too large, its cache might be less effective, and it might end up reading a lot more data than it really needs, even for tiny requests.

Also, in practice it's hard to know whether any given piece of data will span multiple drives. Even if the chunk size is 16 KB, which matches InnoDB's page size, you can't be certain all of the reads will be aligned on 16 KB boundaries. The filesystem might fragment the file, and it will typically align the fragments on the filesystem block size, which is often 4 KB. Some filesystems might be smarter, but you shouldn't count on it.

You can configure the system so that blocks are aligned all the way from the application down to the underlying storage: InnoDB's blocks, the filesystem's blocks, LVM, the partition offset, the RAID stripe, and disk sectors. Our benchmarks showed that when everything is aligned, there can be a performance improvement on the order of 15% to 23% for random reads and random writes, respectively. The exact techniques for aligning everything are too specific to cover here, but there's a lot of good information on it elsewhere, including our blog, *http://www.mysqlperformanceblog.com*.

The RAID cache

The RAID cache is a (relatively) small amount of memory that is physically installed on the RAID controller. It can be used to buffer data as it travels between the disks and the host system. Here are some of the reasons a RAID card might use the cache:

Caching reads

> After the controller reads some data from the disks and sends it to the host system, it can store the data; this will enable it to satisfy future requests for the same data without having to go to disk again.
>
> This is usually a very poor use of the RAID cache. Why? Because the operating system and the database server have their own, much larger, caches. If there's a cache hit in one of these caches, the data in the RAID cache won't be used. Conversely, if there's a miss in one of the higher-level caches, the chance that there'll

be a hit in the RAID cache is vanishingly small. Because the RAID cache is so much smaller, it will almost certainly have been flushed and filled with other data, too. Either way you look at it, it's a waste of memory to cache reads in the RAID cache.

Caching read-ahead data

If the RAID controller notices sequential requests for data, it might decide to do a read-ahead read—that is, to prefetch data it predicts will be needed soon. It has to have somewhere to put the data until it's requested, though. It can use the RAID cache for this. The performance impact of this can vary widely, and you should check to ensure it's actually helping. Read-ahead operations might not help if the database server is doing its own smart read-ahead (as InnoDB does), and it might interfere with the all-important buffering of synchronous writes.

Caching writes

The RAID controller can buffer writes in its cache and schedule them for a later time. The advantage to doing this is twofold: first, it can return "success" to the host system much more quickly than it would be able to if it had to actually perform the writes on the physical disks, and second, it can accumulate writes and do them more efficiently.

Internal operations

Some RAID operations are very complex—especially RAID 5 writes, which have to calculate parity bits that can be used to rebuild data in the event of a failure. The controller needs to use some memory for this type of internal operation.

This is one reason why RAID 5 can perform poorly on some controllers: it needs to read a lot of data into the cache for good performance. Some controllers can't balance caching writes with caching for the RAID 5 parity operations.

In general, the RAID controller's memory is a scarce resource that you should try to use wisely. Using it for reads is usually a waste, but using it for writes is an important way to speed up your I/O performance. Many controllers let you choose how to allocate the memory. For example, you can choose how much of it to use for caching writes and how much for reads. For RAID 0, RAID 1, and RAID 10, you should probably allocate 100% of the controller's memory for caching writes. For RAID 5, you should reserve some of the controller's memory for its internal operations. This is generally good advice, but it doesn't always apply—different RAID cards require different configurations.

When you're using the RAID cache for write caching, many controllers let you configure how long it's acceptable to delay the writes (one second, five seconds, and so on). A longer delay means more writes can be grouped together and flushed to the disks optimally. The downside is that your writes will be more "bursty." That's not a bad thing, unless your application happens to make a bunch of write requests just as the controller's cache fills up, when it's about to be flushed to disk. If there's not enough room for your application's write requests, it'll have to wait. Keeping the delay shorter means you'll have more write operations and they'll be less efficient, but it smoothes out the spikiness and helps keep more of the cache free to handle bursts from the application. (We're simplifying here—controllers often have complex, vendor-specific balancing algorithms, so we're just trying to cover the basic principles.)

The write cache is very helpful for synchronous writes, such as issuing `fsync()` calls on the transaction logs and creating binary logs with `sync_binlog` enabled, but you shouldn't enable it unless your controller has a battery backup unit (BBU) or other non-volatile storage.[9] Caching writes without a BBU is likely to corrupt your database, and even your transactional filesystem, in the event of power loss. If you have a BBU, however, enabling the write cache can increase performance by a factor of 20 or more for workloads that do a lot of log flushes, such as flushing the transaction log when a transaction commits.

A final consideration is that many hard drives have write caches of their own, which can "fake" `fsync()` operations by lying to the controller that the data has been written to physical media. Hard drives that are attached directly (as opposed to being attached to a RAID controller) can sometimes let their caches be managed by the operating system, but this doesn't always work either. These caches are typically flushed for an `fsync()` and bypassed for synchronous I/O, but again, the hard drive can lie. You should either ensure that these caches are flushed on `fsync()` or disable them, because they are not battery-backed. Hard drives that aren't managed properly by the operating system or RAID firmware have caused many instances of data loss.

For this and other reasons, it's always a good idea to do genuine crash testing (literally pulling the power plug out of the wall) when you install new hardware. This is often the only way to find subtle misconfigurations or sneaky hard drive behaviors. A handy script for this can be found at *http://brad.livejournal.com/2116715.html*.

To test whether you can really rely on your RAID controller's BBU, make sure you leave the power cord unplugged for a realistic amount of time. Some units don't last as long without power as they're supposed to. Here again, one bad link can render your whole chain of storage components useless.

Storage Area Networks and Network-Attached Storage

Storage area networks (SANs) and *network-attached storage* (NAS) are two related ways to attach external file storage devices to a server. The difference is really in the way you access the storage. You access a SAN through a block-level interface that a server sees as being directly attached, but you use a NAS device through a file-based protocol such as NFS or SMB. A SAN is usually connected to the server via the Fibre Channel Protocol (FCP) or iSCSI, while a NAS device is connected via a standard network connection. Some devices, such as the NetApp Filer storage systems, can be accessed both ways.

---

9. There are several techniques, including capacitors and flash storage, but we'll lump it all under BBU here.

In the discussion that follows, we'll lump both types of storage into one acronym—SAN—and you should keep that in mind as you read. The primary difference is whether you access your storage as files or as blocks.

A SAN permits a server to access a very large number of hard drives—often 50 or more—and typically has large, intelligent caches to buffer writes. The block-level interface appears to the server as logical unit numbers (LUNs), or virtual volumes (unless you're using NFS). Many SANs also allow multiple nodes to be "clustered" to get better performance or to increase storage capacity.

The current generation of SANs are different from those available a few years ago. Many new SANs have hybrid flash and hard drive storage, not just hard drives. They often have flash caches as large as a terabyte or more, unlike older SANs, which had relatively small caches. Also, the older SANs couldn't help "enlarge the buffer pool" with a larger cache tier, as new SANs can sometimes do. The newer SANs can thus provide better performance than older ones in some types of comparisons.

SAN Benchmarks

We have benchmarked a variety of products from many SAN vendors. Table 9-3 shows a selection of typical results at low concurrency.

Table 9-3. Synchronous single-threaded 16 KB operations per second on a 4 GB file

Device	Sequential write	Sequential read	Random write	Random read
SAN1 with RAID 5	2428	5794	629	258
SAN1 with RAID 10	1765	3427	1725	213
SAN2 over NFS	1768	3154	2056	166
10k RPM hard drives, RAID 1	7027	4773	2302	310
Intel SSD	3045	6266	2427	4397

The exact SAN vendors and configurations shall remain a secret, although we can reveal that these are not low-budget SANs. We ran these benchmarks with synchronous 16 KB operations, which emulates the way that InnoDB operates when configured in O_DIRECT mode.

What conclusions can we draw from Table 9-3? The systems we tested aren't all directly comparable, so it's not a good idea to pore over the finer points. However, the results are a good illustration of the general performance you can expect from these types of devices. SANs are able to absorb lots of sequential writes because they can buffer and combine them. They can serve sequential reads without trouble, because they can predict the reads, prefetch them, and serve them from the cache. They slow down a bit on random writes because the writes can't be combined as much. And they are quite poor at random reads, because the reads are usually cache misses, so they must wait for the hard drives to respond. On top of that, there is transport latency between the server and the SAN. This is why the SAN that's connected over NFS can't even serve as many random reads per second as you'd expect from a single locally attached hard drive.

We've benchmarked with larger file sizes, but we didn't have results at those sizes for all of the above systems. The outcome, however, is always predictable: no matter how large and powerful the SAN, you can't get good response times or throughput for small, random operations. There's just too much latency due to the distance between the server and the SAN.

Our benchmarks show throughput in operations per second, and they don't tell the full story. There are at least three other important metrics: throughput in bytes per second, concurrency, and response time. In general, compared to directly attached storage, a SAN will provide good sequential throughput in bytes per second for both reads and writes. Most SANs can support lots of concurrency, and we benchmarked only a single thread to illustrate the worst case. But when the working set doesn't fit well into the SAN's caches, random reads will be very poor in terms of throughput and latency, and even when it does, latency will be higher than with directly attached storage.

Using a SAN over NFS or SMB

Some SANs, such as NetApp filers, are commonly accessed over NFS instead of via Fibre Channel or iSCSI. This used to be something you'd want to avoid, but NFS works a lot better these days than it used to. You can get decent performance over NFS, although the network needs to be configured specifically for it. The SAN vendors provide best practice guides that should help you with configuration.

The main consideration is how the NFS protocol itself affects performance. Many file metadata operations, which are typically performed in memory on a local filesystem or a non-NFS SAN, can require a network round trip with NFS. For example, we've noticed a severe performance penalty from storing binary logs on NFS, even with sync_bin log disabled. This is because appending to the binary log increases its size, which requires a metadata operation that causes an extra round trip.

You can also access a SAN or NAS over the SMB protocol, and similar considerations apply: there can be a lot more latency-sensitive network round trips. These don't matter much for the typical desktop user who's storing some spreadsheets or other documents on a drive he's mounted, or even for operations such as copying backups to another server, but it can be a serious mismatch for the way MySQL reads and writes its files.

MySQL Performance on a SAN

The I/O benchmarks are one way to look at things, but what about MySQL performance on a SAN? In many cases, MySQL works just fine, and you can avoid many of the situations where the SAN would cause some degradation in performance. Careful logical and physical design, including indexing, and appropriate server hardware (lots of memory!) can avoid many random I/O operations, or transform them into sequential ones. However, you should be aware that such a system can reach a slightly delicate balance over a period of time—one that's easy to perturb with the introduction of a new query, a schema change, or an infrequent operation.

For example, one SAN user we know was quite happy with its day-to-day performance until he wanted to purge a lot of rows from an old table that had grown very large. This resulted in a long-running DELETE statement that was deleting only a couple of hundred rows per second, because each row required random I/O that the SAN couldn't perform quickly. There was no way to accelerate the operation; it was simply going to take a very long time to complete. Another surprise for the same user came when an ALTER on a large table slowed down to a similar pace.

Those are typical examples of what doesn't work well on a SAN: single-threaded tasks that perform lots of random I/O. Replication is another single-threaded task in current versions of MySQL; as a result, replicas whose data is stored on a SAN might be more likely to lag behind the master. Batch jobs might also run more slowly. You might be able to perform one-off latency-sensitive operations at off-peak hours or on the weekend, but always-on parts of the server such as replication, binary logs, and InnoDB's transaction logs need good performance on small and/or random I/O operations at all times.

Should You Use a SAN?

Ah, that's the perennial question—in some cases, the million-dollar question. There are many factors to consider, and we'll list a few of them:

Backups

Centralized storage can make backups easier to manage. When everything is stored in one place, you can just back up the SAN, and you know that you've accounted for all of your data. This simplifies questions such as "Are you sure we're backing up all of our data?" In addition, some devices have features such as continuous data protection (CDP), and powerful snapshot capabilities that make backups much easier and more flexible.

Simplified capacity planning

Not sure how much capacity you need? A SAN gives you the ability to buy storage in bulk, share it, and resize and redistribute it on demand.

Storage consolidation versus server consolidation

Some CIOs take stock of what's running in their data centers and conclude that there is a lot of wasted I/O capacity, in terms of storage space as well as I/O operations. No arguments there—but if you centralize your storage to make sure it's better utilized, how will that impact the systems that use the storage? The difference in performance for typical database operations can literally be orders of magnitude, and as a result you might find that you need to run 10 times as many servers (or more) to handle your workload. And although the data center's I/O capacity might be much better utilized in a SAN, that can come at the cost of many other systems being underutilized (the database server spends a lot of time waiting for I/O, the application server spends a lot of time waiting for the database, and so on). We've seen many real-world opportunities to consolidate servers and cut costs by *decentralizing* storage.

High availability

Sometimes people think of a SAN as a high-availability solution. We'll suggest in Chapter 12 that this could be due to disagreement over what high availability really means.

In our experience, SANs are pretty frequently implicated in failures and downtime. This is not because they are unreliable—which they aren't—but because people are reluctant to believe such a miracle of engineering can actually fail. In addition, a SAN is sometimes a complex, mystifying black box that nobody knows how to troubleshoot when something goes wrong, and it can be expensive and difficult to build the expertise needed to manage a SAN well. The lack of visibility into most SANs is why you should never simply trust the SAN administrator, support staff, or management console. We've seen cases where all three are wrong, and the SAN turned out to have a problem such as a failed hard drive that was causing degraded performance.[10] This is another reason to get comfortable with *sysbench*: so you can dash off an I/O benchmark to prove or disprove the SAN's culpability.

Interaction between servers

Shared storage can cause seemingly independent systems to affect each other, sometimes very badly. For example, one SAN user we know had a rather rude awakening when an I/O-intensive operation on a development server caused his database server to grind nearly to a halt. Batch jobs, ALTER TABLE, backups—anything that causes a lot of I/O on one system can cause starvation on other systems. Sometimes the impact is much worse than your intuition would suggest; a seemingly trivial workload can cause a surprisingly severe degradation of performance.

Cost

Cost of what? Cost of management and administration? Cost per I/O operation per second (IOPS)? Sticker price?

There are good reasons to use SANs, but regardless of what the salespeople say, performance—at least, performance of the type that MySQL needs—just isn't a valid reason. (Pick a SAN vendor and call a salesperson, and you're likely to hear them agree in general, but then tell you that their product is an exception to the rule.) If you consider performance and price together, it becomes even clearer, because if it's a good price-to-performance ratio you want, flash storage or

---

10. The web-based SAN management console insisted that all hard drives were healthy—until we asked the administrator to press Shift-F5 to disable his browser cache and force the console to refresh!

old-fashioned hard drives with a good RAID controller and a battery-backed write cache offer much better performance at a much lower price.

On this topic, don't forget to ask the salesperson to quote you a price for two SANs. You need at least two, or you just have a single expensive point of failure.

We could relate many war stories and cautionary tales, but we're not trying to scare you away from using a SAN. Most of the SAN users we know absolutely love them! If you're trying to decide whether to use a SAN, the most important thing is to be very clear on what problems you want to solve. A SAN can do lots of things, but solving a performance problem is rarely one of them. In contrast, a SAN can be great when you don't demand a lot of high-performance random I/O, but you are interested in features such as snapshots, storage consolidation, data deduplication, and virtualization.

As a result, most web applications don't use SANs for databases, but they're very popular for so-called enterprise applications. Enterprises are usually less constrained by budget, so they can afford "luxury items" such as SANs. (Sometimes a SAN is even seen as a status symbol!)

Using Multiple Disk Volumes

Sooner or later, the question of where to place files will come up. MySQL creates a variety of files:

- Data and index files
- Transaction log files
- Binary log files
- General log files (e.g., for the error log, query log, and slow query log)
- Temporary files and tables

MySQL doesn't have many features for complex tablespace management. By default, it simply places all files for each database (schema) into a single directory. You have a few options to control where the data goes. For example, you can specify an index location for MyISAM tables, and you can use MySQL 5.1's partitioned tables.

If you're using InnoDB's default configuration, all data and indexes go in a single set of files, and only the table definition files are placed in the database directory. As a result, most people place all data and indexes on a single volume.

Sometimes, however, using multiple volumes can help you manage a heavy I/O load. For example, a batch job that writes data to a massive table can benefit from being on a separate volume, so it doesn't starve other queries for I/O. Ideally, you should analyze the I/O access to the different parts of your data so you can place the data appropriately, but this is hard to do unless you already have the data on different volumes.

You've probably heard the standard advice to place your transaction logs and data files on different volumes, so the sequential I/O of the logs doesn't interfere with the random

I/O of the data. But unless you have many hard drives (20 or so), or flash storage, you should think carefully before doing this.

The real advantage of separating the binary log and data files is the reduced likelihood of losing both your data and your log files in the event of a crash. Separating them is good practice if you don't have a battery-backed write cache on your RAID controller. But if you have a battery backup unit, a separate volume isn't needed as often as you might think. Performance is rarely a determining factor. This is because even though there are lots of writes to transaction logs, most of them are small. As a result, the RAID cache will usually merge the requests together, and you'll typically get just a couple of sequential physical write requests per second. This usually won't interfere with the random I/O to your data files, unless you're really saturating the RAID controller overall. The general logs, which have sequential asynchronous writes and low load, can also share a volume with the data comfortably.

There's another way to look at it, though, which a lot of people don't consider. Does placing logs on separate volumes improve performance? Typically, yes—but is it worth it? The answer is frequently no.

Here's why: it's *expensive* to dedicate hard drives to transaction logs. Suppose you have six hard drives. The obvious choices are to place all six into one RAID volume, or split them into four for the data and two for the transaction logs. If you do this, though, you've reduced the number of drives available for the data files by a third, which is a significant decrease; also, you're dedicating two drives to a possibly trivial workload (assuming that your RAID controller has a battery-backed write cache).

On the other hand, if you have many hard drives, dedicating some to the transaction logs is proportionately less expensive and can be beneficial. If you have a total of 30 hard drives, for example, you can ensure that the log writes are as fast as possible by dedicating 2 drives (configured as a RAID 1 volume) to the logs. For extra performance, you might also dedicate some write cache space for this RAID volume in the RAID controller.

Cost effectiveness isn't the only consideration. Another reason why you might want to keep InnoDB data and transaction logs on the same volume is that this strategy lets you use LVM snapshots for lock-free backups. Some filesystems allow consistent multivolume snapshots, and for those filesystems it might not be a big deal, but it's something to keep in mind for ext3. (You can also use Percona XtraBackup for lock-free backups; see Chapter 15 for more on this topic.)

If you have enabled sync_binlog, binary logs are similar to transaction logs in terms of performance. However, it's actually a *good* idea to store binary logs on a different volume from your data—it's safer to have them stored separately, so they can survive even if the data is lost. That way, you can use them for point-in-time recovery. This consideration doesn't apply to the InnoDB transaction logs, because they're useless without the data files; you can't apply transaction logs to last night's backup. (This distinction between transaction logs and binary logs might seem artificial to DBAs used to other databases, where they are one and the same.)

The only other common scenario for separating out files is the temporary directory, which MySQL uses for filesorts and on-disk temporary tables. If these won't be too big to fit, it's probably best to put them in a temporary memory-only filesystem such as *tmpfs*. This will be the fastest choice. If that isn't feasible on your system, put them on the same device as the operating system.

A typical disk layout is to have the operating system, swap partition, and binary logs on a RAID 1 volume, and a separate RAID 5 or RAID 10 volume that holds everything else.

Network Configuration

Just as latency and throughput are limiting factors for a hard drive, latency and bandwidth (which really means the same thing as throughput) are limiting factors for a network connection. The biggest problem for most applications is latency; a typical application does a lot of small network transfers, and the slight delay for each transfer adds up.

A network that's not operating correctly is a major performance bottleneck, too. Packet loss is a common problem. Even 1% loss is enough to cause significant performance degradation, because various layers in the protocol stack will try to fix the problems with strategies such as waiting a while and then resending packets, which adds extra time. Another common problem is broken or slow Domain Name System (DNS) resolution.

DNS is enough of an Achilles heel that enabling `skip_name_resolve` is a good idea for production servers. Broken or slow DNS resolution is a problem for lots of applications, but it's particularly severe for MySQL. When MySQL receives a connection request, it does both a forward and a reverse DNS lookup. There are lots of reasons that this could go wrong. When it does, it will cause connections to be denied, slow down the process of connecting to the server, and generally wreak havoc, up to and including denial-of-service attacks. If you enable the `skip_name_resolve` option, MySQL won't do any DNS lookups at all. However, this also means that your user accounts must have only IP addresses, "localhost," or IP address wildcards in the `host` column. Any user account that has a hostname in the `host` column will not be able to log in.

Another common source of problems in typical web applications is the TCP backlog, which you can configure through MySQL's `back_log` option. This option controls the size of MySQL's queue for incoming TCP connections. In environments where a lot of connections are created and destroyed every second, the default value of 50 is not enough. The symptom is that the client will see a sporadic "connection refused" error, paired with three-second timeouts. This option should usually be increased on busy systems. There doesn't seem to be any harm in increasing it to hundreds or even thousands, in fact—but if you go that far, you'll probably also need to configure your operating system's TCP networking settings. On GNU/Linux systems, you need to increase the `somaxconn` limit from its default of `128`, and check the `tcp_max_syn_back log` settings in *sysctl* (there's an example a bit later in this section).

You need to design your network for good performance, rather than just accepting whatever you get by default. To begin, analyze how many hops are between the nodes, and map the physical network layout. For instance, suppose you have 10 web servers connected to a "Web" switch via gigabit Ethernet (1 GigE), and this switch is connected to the "Database" switch via 1 GigE as well. If you don't take the time to trace the connections, you might never realize that your total bandwidth from all database servers to all web servers is limited to a gigabit! Each hop adds latency, too.

It's a good idea to monitor network performance and errors on all network ports. Monitor every port on servers, on routers, and on switches. The Multi Router Traffic Grapher, or MRTG (*http://oss.oetiker.ch/mrtg/*), is the tried-and-true open source solution for device monitoring. Other common tools for monitoring network performance (as opposed to devices) are Smokeping (*http://oss.oetiker.ch/smokeping/*) and Cacti (*http://www.cacti.net*).

Physical separation matters a lot in networking. Inter-city networks will have much worse latency than your data center's LAN, even if the bandwidth is technically the same. If the nodes are really widely separated, the speed of light actually matters. For example, if you have data centers on the west and east coasts of the US, they'll be separated by about 3,000 miles. The speed of light is 186,000 mps, so a one-way trip cannot be any faster than 16 ms, and a round-trip takes at least 32 ms. The physical distance is not the only performance consideration, either: there are devices in between as well. Repeaters, routers, and switches all degrade performance somewhat. Again, the more widely separated the network nodes are, the more unpredictable and unreliable the links will be.

It's a good idea to try to avoid real-time cross-data center operations as much as possible.[11] If this isn't possible, you should make sure your application handles network failures gracefully. For example, you don't want your web servers to fork too many Apache processes because they are all stalled trying to connect to a remote data center over a link that has significant packet loss.

At the local level, use at least 1 GigE if you're not already. You might need to use a 10 GigE connection for the backbone between switches. If you need more bandwidth than that, you can use *network trunking*: connecting multiple network interface cards (NICs) to get more bandwidth. Trunking is essentially parallelization of networking, and it can be very helpful as part of a high-availability strategy.

---

11. Replication doesn't count as a real-time cross-data center operation. It's not real-time, and it's often a good idea to replicate your data to a remote location for safety. We cover this more in the next chapter.

When you need very high throughput, you might be able to improve performance by changing your operating system's networking configuration. If you don't have many connections but you have large queries or result sets, you can increase the TCP buffer size. How you do this varies from system to system, but in most GNU/Linux systems you can change the values in */etc/sysctl.conf* and execute *sysctl -p*, or use the */proc* filesystem by echoing new values into the files found at */proc/sys/net/*. You can find good tutorials on this topic online with a search for "TCP tuning guide."

It's usually more important, though, to adjust your settings to deal efficiently with a lot of connections and small queries. One of the more common tweaks is to change your local port range. Here's a system that is configured to default values:

```
[root@server ~]# cat /proc/sys/net/ipv4/ip_local_port_range
32768    61000
```

Sometimes you might need to change these values to a larger range. For example:

```
[root@server ~]# echo 1024 65535 > /proc/sys/net/ipv4/ip_local_port_range
```

You can allow more connections to queue up as follows:

```
[root@server ~]# echo 4096 > /proc/sys/net/ipv4/tcp_max_syn_backlog
```

For database servers that are used only locally, you can shorten the timeout that comes after closing a socket in the event that the peer is broken and doesn't close its side of the connection. The default is one minute on most systems, which is rather long:

```
[root@server ~]# echo <value> > /proc/sys/net/ipv4/tcp_fin_timeout
```

Most of the time these settings can be left at their defaults. You'll typically need to change them only when something unusual is happening, such as extremely poor network performance or very large numbers of connections. An Internet search for "TCP variables" will turn up lots of good reading about these and many more variables.

Choosing an Operating System

GNU/Linux is the most common operating system for high-performance MySQL installations today, but MySQL will run on many operating systems.

Solaris is the leader on SPARC hardware, and it runs on x86 hardware too. It's frequently used in applications that demand high reliability. Solaris has a reputation for being more difficult to work with than GNU/Linux in some ways, but it's a solid operating system with many advanced features. In particular, Solaris 10 added the ZFS filesystem, a lot of advanced troubleshooting tools (such as DTrace), good threading performance, and a virtualization technology called Solaris Zones that helps with resource management.

FreeBSD is another option. It has historically had a number of problems with MySQL, mostly related to threading support, but newer versions are much better. Today, it's not uncommon to see MySQL deployed at a large scale on FreeBSD. ZFS is also available on FreeBSD.

Windows is typically used for development and when MySQL is used with desktop applications. There are enterprise MySQL deployments on Windows, but Unix-like operating systems are more commonly used for these purposes. While we don't want to start any debates about operating systems, we will point out that there are no problems using a heterogeneous environment with MySQL. It's perfectly reasonable to run your MySQL server on a Unix-like operating system and run Windows on your web servers, connecting them via the high-quality .NET connector (which is freely available from MySQL). It's just as easy to connect from Unix to a MySQL server hosted on Windows as it is to connect to another Unix server.

When you choose an operating system, make sure you install the 64-bit version if you're using a 64-bit architecture (see "CPU Architecture" on page 390).

When it comes to GNU/Linux distributions, personal preference is often the deciding factor. We think the best policy is to use a distribution explicitly designed for server applications, as opposed to a desktop distribution. Consider the distribution's lifecycle, release, and update policies, and check whether vendor support is available. Red Hat Enterprise Linux is a good-quality, stable distribution; CentOS is a popular (and free) binary-compatible alternative, but has gained a reputation for lagging behind; Oracle distributes Oracle Enterprise Linux; and Ubuntu and Debian are popular, too.

Choosing a Filesystem

Your filesystem choices are pretty dependent on your operating system. In many systems, such as Windows, you really have only one or two choices, and only one (NTFS) is really viable. GNU/Linux, on the other hand, supports many filesystems.

Many people want to know which filesystems will give the best performance for MySQL on GNU/Linux, or, even more specifically, which of the choices is best for InnoDB and which for MyISAM. The benchmarks actually show that most of them are very close in most respects, but looking to the filesystem for performance is really a distraction. The filesystem's performance is very workload-specific, and no filesystem is a magic bullet. Most of the time, a given filesystem won't perform significantly better or worse than any other filesystem. The exception is if you run into some filesystem limit, such as how it deals with concurrency, working with many files, fragmentation, and so on.

It's more important to consider crash recovery time and whether you'll run into specific limits, such as slow performance on directories with many files (a notorious problem with ext2 and older versions of ext3, but solved in modern versions of ext3 and ext4 with the dir_index option). The filesystem you choose is very important in ensuring your data's safety, so we strongly recommend you don't experiment on production systems.

When possible, it's best to use a journaling filesystem, such as ext3, ext4, XFS, ZFS, or JFS. If you don't, a filesystem check after a crash can take a long time. If the system is not very important, nonjournaling filesystems might perform better than transactional ones. For example, ext2 might perform better than ext3, or you can use *tunefs* to disable the journaling feature on ext3. Mount time is also a factor for some filesystems. ReiserFS, for instance, can take a long time to mount and perform journal recovery on large partitions.

If you use ext3 or its successor ext4, you have three options for how the data is journaled, which you can place in the */etc/fstab* mount options:

data=writeback

This option means only metadata writes are journaled. Writes to the metadata are not synchronized with the data writes. This is the fastest configuration, and it's *usually* safe to use with InnoDB because it has its own transaction log. The exception is that a crash at just the right time could cause corruption in a *.frm* file.

Here's an example of how this configuration could cause problems. Say a program decides to extend a file to make it larger. The metadata (the file's size) will be logged and written before the data is actually written to the (now larger) file. The result is that the file's tail—the newly extended area—contains garbage.

data=ordered

This option also journals only the metadata, but it provides some consistency by writing the data before the metadata so that they stay consistent. It's only slightly slower than the `writeback` option, and it's much safer when there's a crash.

In this configuration, if we suppose again that a program wants to extend a file, the file's metadata won't reflect the file's new size until the data that resides in the newly extended area has been written.

data=journal

This option provides atomic journaled behavior, writing the data to the journal before it's written to the final location. It is usually unnecessary and has much higher overhead than the other two options. However, in some cases it can improve performance because the journaling lets the filesystem delay the writes to the data's final location.

Regardless of the filesystem, there are some specific options that it's best to disable, because they don't provide any benefit and can add quite a bit of overhead. The most famous is recording access time, which requires a write even when you're reading a file or directory. To disable this option, add the `noatime,nodiratime` mount options to your */etc/fstab*; this can sometimes boost performance by as much as 5–10%, depending on the workload and the filesystem (although it might not make much difference in other cases). Here's a sample */etc/fstab* line for the ext3 options we mentioned:

```
/dev/sda2 /usr/lib/mysql ext3 noatime,nodiratime,data=writeback 0 1
```

You can also tune the filesystem's read-ahead behavior, because it might be redundant. For example, InnoDB does its own read-ahead prediction. Disabling or limiting read-ahead is especially beneficial on Solaris's UFS. Using O_DIRECT automatically disables read-ahead.

Some filesystems don't support features you might need. For example, support for direct I/O might be important if you're using the O_DIRECT flush method for InnoDB. Also, some filesystems handle a large number of underlying drives better than others; XFS is often much better at this than ext3, for instance. Finally, if you plan to use LVM snapshots for initializing replicas or taking backups, you should verify that your chosen filesystem and LVM version work well together.

Table 9-4 summarizes the characteristics of some common filesystems.

Table 9-4. Common filesystem characteristics

Filesystem	Operating system	Journaling	Large directories
ext2	GNU/Linux	No	No
ext3	GNU/Linux	Optional	Optional/partial
ext4	GNU/Linux	Yes	Yes
HFS Plus	Mac OS	Optional	Yes
JFS	GNU/Linux	Yes	No
NTFS	Windows	Yes	Yes
ReiserFS	GNU/Linux	Yes	Yes
UFS (Solaris)	Solaris	Yes	Tunable
UFS (FreeBSD)	FreeBSD	No	Optional/partial
UFS2	FreeBSD	No	Optional/partial
XFS	GNU/Linux	Yes	Yes
ZFS	Solaris, FreeBSD	Yes	Yes

We usually recommend that our customers use the XFS filesystem. The ext3 filesystem just has too many serious limitations, such as its single mutex per inode, and bad behavior such as flushing all dirty blocks in the whole filesystem on fsync() instead of just one file's dirty blocks. The ext4 filesystem is too new for many people to feel comfortable running it in production, although it seems to be gaining popularity gradually.

Choosing a Disk Queue Scheduler

On GNU/Linux, the queue scheduler determines the order in which requests to a block device are actually sent to the underlying device. The default is Completely Fair Queueing, or cfq. It's okay for casual use on laptops and desktops, where it helps prevent I/O starvation, but it's terrible for servers. It causes very poor response times under the types of workload that MySQL generates, because it stalls some requests in the queue needlessly.

You can see which schedulers are available, and which one is active, with the following command:

```
$ cat /sys/block/sda/queue/scheduler
noop deadline [cfq]
```

You should replace *sda* with the device name of the disk you're interested in. In our example, the square brackets indicate which scheduler is in use for this device. The other two choices are suitable for server-class hardware, and in most cases they work about equally well. The `noop` scheduler is appropriate for devices that do their own scheduling behind the scenes, such as hardware RAID controllers and SANs, and `deadline` is fine both for RAID controllers and disks that are directly attached. Our benchmarks show very little difference between these two. The main thing is to use anything but `cfq`, which can cause severe performance problems.

Take this advice with a grain of salt, though, because the disk schedulers actually come in many variations in different kernels, and there is no indication of that in their names.

Threading

MySQL uses one thread per connection, plus housekeeping threads, special-purpose threads, and any threads the storage engine creates. In MySQL 5.5, a thread pool plugin is available from Oracle, but it's not yet clear how beneficial this is in the real world.

Either way, MySQL requires efficient support for a large number of threads. It really needs support for kernel-level threads, as opposed to userland threads, so it can use multiple CPUs efficiently. It also needs efficient synchronization primitives, such as mutexes. The operating system's threading libraries must provide all of these.

GNU/Linux offers two thread libraries: LinuxThreads and the newer Native POSIX Threads Library (NPTL). LinuxThreads is still used in some cases, but modern distributions have made the switch to NPTL, and most don't ship LinuxThreads at all anymore. NPTL is lighter and more efficient, and it doesn't suffer from a lot of the problems LinuxThreads had.

FreeBSD also ships a number of threading libraries. Historically it had weak support for threading, but it has gotten a lot better, and in some tests it even outperforms GNU/Linux on SMP systems. In FreeBSD 6 and newer, the recommended threading library is *libthr*; earlier versions should use *linuxthreads*, which is a FreeBSD port of GNU/Linux's LinuxThreads.

In general, threading problems are a thing of the past, now that GNU/Linux and FreeBSD have gotten good libraries.

Solaris and Windows have always had very good support for threads. One note, though: MyISAM didn't use threads well on Windows until the 5.5 release, where it was significantly improved.

Swapping

Swapping occurs when the operating system writes some virtual memory to disk because it doesn't have enough physical memory to hold it.[12] Swapping is transparent to processes running on the operating system. Only the operating system knows whether a particular virtual memory address is in physical memory or on disk.

Swapping is very bad for MySQL's performance. It defeats the purpose of caching in memory, and it results in *lower* efficiency than using too little memory for the caches. MySQL and its storage engines have many algorithms that treat in-memory data differently from data on disk, because they assume that in-memory data is cheap to access. Because swapping is invisible to user processes, MySQL (or the storage engine) won't know when data it thinks is in memory is actually moved onto the disk.

The result can be very poor performance. For example, if the storage engine thinks the data is still in memory, it might decide it's OK to lock a global mutex (such as the InnoDB buffer pool mutex) for a "short" memory operation. If this operation actually causes disk I/O, it can stall everything until the I/O completes. This means swapping is much worse than simply doing I/O as needed.

On GNU/Linux, you can monitor swapping with *vmstat* (we show some examples in the next section). You need to look at the swap I/O activity, reported in the si and so columns, rather than the swap usage, which is reported in the swpd column. The swpd column can show processes that have been loaded but aren't being used, which are not really problematic. We like the si and so column values to be 0, and they should definitely be less than 10 blocks per second.

In extreme cases, too much swapping can cause the operating system to run out of swap space. If this happens, the resulting lack of virtual memory can crash MySQL. But even if it doesn't run out of swap space, very active swapping can cause the entire operating system to become unresponsive, to the point that you can't even log in and kill the MySQL process. Sometimes the Linux kernel can even hang completely when it runs out of swap space.

Never let your system run out of virtual memory! Monitor and alert on swap space usage. If you don't know how much swap space you need, allocate lots of it on disk; it doesn't impact performance, it only consumes disk space. Some large organizations know exactly what their memory consumption will be and have swapping under very tight control, but that's usually impractical in an environment with only a few

---

12. Swapping is sometimes called *paging*. Technically, they are different things, but people often use them as synonyms.

multipurpose MySQL instances that serve variable workloads. If the latter describes you, be sure to give your server some breathing room by setting aside enough swap space.

Another thing that frequently happens under extreme virtual memory pressure is that the out-of-memory (OOM) killer process will kick in and kill something. This is frequently MySQL, but it can also be another process such as SSH, which can leave you with a system that's not accessible from the network. You can prevent this by setting the SSH process's `oom_adj` or `oom_score_adj` value.

You can solve most swapping problems by configuring your MySQL buffers correctly, but sometimes the operating system's virtual memory system decides to swap MySQL anyway. This usually happens when the operating system sees a lot of I/O from MySQL, so it tries to increase the file cache to hold more data. If there's not enough memory, something must be swapped out, and that something might be MySQL itself. Some older Linux kernel versions also have counterproductive priorities that swap things when they shouldn't, but this has been alleviated a bit in more recent kernels.

Some people advocate disabling the swap file entirely. Although this sometimes works in extreme cases where the kernel just refuses to behave, it can degrade the operating system's performance. (It shouldn't in theory, but in practice it can.) It's also dangerous, because disabling swapping places an inflexible limit on virtual memory. If MySQL has a temporary spike in memory requirements, or if there are memory-hungry processes running on the same machine (nightly batch jobs, for example), MySQL can run out of memory, crash, or be killed by the operating system.

Operating systems usually allow some control over virtual memory and I/O. We mention a few ways to control them on GNU/Linux. The most basic is to change the value of */proc/sys/vm/swappiness* to a low value, such as 0 or 1. This tells the kernel not to swap unless the need for virtual memory is extreme. For example, here's how to check the current value:

```
$ cat /proc/sys/vm/swappiness
60
```

The value shown, 60, is the default swappiness setting (the range is from 0 to 100). This is a very bad default for servers. It's only appropriate for laptops. Servers should be set to 0:

```
$ echo 0 > /proc/sys/vm/swappiness
```

Another option is to change how the storage engines read and write data. For example, using `innodb_flush_method=O_DIRECT` relieves I/O pressure. Direct I/O is not cached, so the operating system doesn't see it as a reason to increase the size of the file cache. This parameter works only for InnoDB. You can also use large pages, which are not swappable. This works for MyISAM and InnoDB.

Another option is to use MySQL's `memlock` configuration option, which locks MySQL in memory. This will avoid swapping, but it can be dangerous: if there's not enough lockable memory left, MySQL can crash when it tries to allocate more memory. Problems can also be caused if too much memory is locked and there's not enough left for the operating system.

Many of the tricks are specific to a kernel version, so be careful, especially when you upgrade. In some workloads, it's hard to make the operating system behave sensibly, and your only recourse might be to lower the buffer sizes to suboptimal values.

Operating System Status

Your operating system provides tools to help you find out what the operating system and hardware are doing. In this section we'll show you examples of how to use two widely available tools, *iostat* and *vmstat*. If your system doesn't provide either of these tools, chances are it will provide something similar. Thus, our goal isn't to make you an expert at using *iostat* or *vmstat*, but simply to show you what to look for when you're trying to diagnose problems with tools such as these.

In addition to these tools, your operating system might provide others, such as *mpstat* or *sar*. If you're interested in other parts of your system, such as the network, you might want to instead use tools such as *ifconfig* (which shows how many network errors have occurred, among other things) or *netstat*.

By default, *vmstat* and *iostat* produce just one report showing the average values of various counters since the server was started, which is not very useful. However, you can give both tools an interval argument. This makes them generate incremental reports showing what the server is doing right now, which is much more relevant. (The first line shows the statistics since the system was started; you can just ignore this line.)

How to Read vmstat Output

Let's look at an example of *vmstat* first. To make it print out a new report every five seconds, use the following command:

```
$ vmstat 5
procs -----------memory---------- ---swap-- -----io---- -system-- ----cpu----
 r  b   swpd   free   buff  cache   si   so    bi    bo   in   cs us sy id wa
 0  0   2632  25728  23176 740244    0    0   527   521   11    3 10  1 86  3
 0  0   2632  27808  23180 738248    0    0     2   430  222   66  2  0 97  0
```

You can stop *vmstat* with Ctrl-C. The output you see depends on your operating system, so you might need to read the manual page to figure it out.

As stated earlier, even though we asked for incremental output, the first line of values shows the averages since the server was booted. The second line shows what's happening right now, and subsequent lines will show what's happening at five-second intervals. The columns are grouped by headers:

procs

The r column shows how many processes are waiting for CPU time. The b column shows how many are in uninterruptible sleep, which generally means they're waiting for I/O (disk, network, user input, and so on).

memory

The swpd column shows how many blocks are swapped out to disk (paged). The remaining three columns show how many blocks are free (unused), how many are being used for buffers, and how many are being used for the operating system's cache.

swap

These columns show swap activity: how many blocks per second the operating system is swapping in (from disk) and out (to disk). They are much more important to monitor than the swpd column.

We like to see si and so at 0 most of the time, and we definitely don't like to see more than 10 blocks per second. Bursts are also bad.

io

These columns show how many blocks per second are read in from (bi) and written out to (bo) block devices. This usually reflects disk I/O.

system

These columns show the number of interrupts per second (in) and the number of context switches per second (cs).

cpu

These columns show the percentages of total CPU time spent running user (non-kernel) code, running system (kernel) code, idle, and waiting for I/O. A possible fifth column (st) shows the percent "stolen" from a virtual machine if you're using virtualization. This refers to the time during which something was runnable on the virtual machine, but the hypervisor chose to run something else instead. If the virtual machine doesn't want to run anything and the hypervisor runs something else, that doesn't count as stolen time.

The *vmstat* output is system-dependent, so you should read your system's vmstat(8) manpage if yours looks different from the sample we've shown. One important note: the memory, swap, and I/O statistics are in blocks, not in bytes. In GNU/Linux, blocks are usually 1,024 bytes.

How to Read iostat Output

Now let's move on to *iostat*.[13] By default, it shows some of the same CPU usage information as *vmstat*. We're usually interested in just the I/O statistics, though, so we use the following command to show only extended device statistics:

```
$ iostat -dx 5
Device:   rrqm/s wrqm/s r/s w/s rsec/s wsec/s avgrq-sz avgqu-sz await svctm %util
  sda        1.6    2.8 2.5 1.8  138.8   36.9     40.7      0.1  23.2   6.0   2.6
```

As with *vmstat*, the first report shows averages since the server was booted (we generally omit it to save space), and the subsequent reports show incremental averages. There's one line per device.

There are various options that show or hide columns. The official documentation is a bit confusing, and we had to dig into the source code to figure out what was really being shown. The columns we've shown are the following:

rrqm/s *and* wrqm/s
> The number of merged read and write requests queued per second. "Merged" means the operating system took multiple logical requests from the queue and grouped them into a single request to the actual device.

r/s *and* w/s
> The number of read and write requests sent to the device per second.

rsec/s *and* wsec/s
> The number of sectors read and written per second. Some systems also output rkB/s and wkB/s, the number of kilobytes read and written per second. We omit those for brevity.

avgrq-sz
> The request size in sectors.

avgqu-sz
> The number of requests waiting in the device's queue.

await
> The number of milliseconds spent in the disk queue. Unfortunately, *iostat* doesn't show separate statistics for read and write requests, which are so different that they really shouldn't be averaged together. This is often very important when you're trying to diagnose a performance issue.

svctm
> The number of milliseconds spent servicing requests, excluding queue time.

---

13. The *iostat* examples we show in this book have been slightly reformatted for printing: we've reduced the number of decimal places in the values to avoid line wrapping. Also, we're showing examples on GNU/Linux; other operating systems will give completely different output.

`%util`

The percentage of time during which at least one request was active. This is very confusingly named. It is *not* the device's utilization, if you're familiar with the standard definition of utilization in queueing theory. A device with more than one hard drive (such as a RAID controller) should be able to support a higher concurrency than 1, but `%util` will never exceed 100% unless there's a rounding error in the math used to compute it. As a result, it is *not* a good indication of device saturation, contrary to what the documentation says, except in the special case where you're looking at a single physical hard drive.

You can use the output to deduce some facts about a machine's I/O subsystem. One important metric is the number of requests served concurrently. Because the reads and writes are per second and the service time's unit is thousandths of a second, you can use Little's Law to derive the following formula for the number of concurrent requests the device is serving:[14]

```
concurrency = (r/s + w/s) * (svctm/1000)
```

Here's a sample of *iostat* output:

```
Device: rrqm/s wrqm/s r/s w/s rsec/s wsec/s avgrq-sz avgqu-sz await svctm %util
 sda        105    311 298 820   3236   9052       10      127   113     9    96
```

Plugging the numbers into the concurrency formula gives a concurrency of about 9.6.[15] This means that on average, the device was serving 9.6 requests at a time during the sampling interval. The sample is from a 10-disk RAID 10 volume, so the operating system is parallelizing requests to this device quite well. On the other hand, here's a device that appears to be serializing requests instead:

```
Device: rrqm/s wrqm/s r/s w/s rsec/s wsec/s avgrq-sz avgqu-sz await svctm %util
 sdc         81      0 280   0   3164      0       11        2     7     3    99
```

The concurrency formula shows that this device is handling just one request per second. Both devices are close to fully utilized, but they're giving very different performances. If your device is busy nearly all the time, as these samples show, you should check the concurrency and note whether it is close to the number of physical spindles included in the device. A lower number can indicate problems such as filesystem serialization, which we discussed earlier.

Other Helpful Tools

We've shown *vmstat* and *iostat* because they're widely available, and *vmstat* is usually installed by default on many Unix-like operating systems. However, each of these tools

---

14. Another way to calculate concurrency is by the average queue size, service time, and average wait: (avuqu_sz * svctm) / await.

15. If you do the math, you'll get about 10, because we've rounded the *iostat* output for formatting purposes. Trust us, it's really 9.6.

has its limitations, such as confusing units of measurement, sampling at intervals that don't correspond to when the operating system updates the statistics, and the inability to see all of the metrics at once. If these tools don't meet your needs, you might be interested in *dstat* (*http://dag.wieers.com/home-made/dstat/*) or *collectl* (*http://collectl.sourceforge.net*).

We also like to use *mpstat* to watch CPU statistics; it provides a much better idea of how the CPUs are behaving individually, instead of grouping them all together. Sometimes this is very important when you're diagnosing a problem. You might find *blktrace* to be helpful when you're examining disk I/O usage, too.

We wrote our own replacement for *iostat*, called *pt-diskstats*. It's part of Percona Toolkit. It addresses some of our complaints about *iostat*, such as the way that it presents reads and writes in aggregate, and the lack of visibility into concurrency. It is also interactive and keystroke-driven, so you can zoom in and out, change the aggregation, filter out devices, and show and hide columns. It is a great way to slice and dice a sample of disk statistics, which you can gather with a simple shell script even if you don't have the tool installed. You can capture samples of disk activity and email or save them for later analysis. In fact, the *pt-stalk*, *pt-collect*, and *pt-sift* trio of tools that we introduced in Chapter 3 are designed to work well with *pt-diskstats*.

A CPU-Bound Machine

The *vmstat* output for a CPU-bound server usually shows a high value in the us column, which reports time spent running non-kernel code. There can also be a high value in the sy column, which is the system CPU usage; a value over 20% here is worrisome. In most cases, there will also be several processes queued up for CPU time (reported in the r column). Here's a sample:

```
$ vmstat 5
procs -----------memory---------- ---swap-- -----io---- --system-- ----cpu----
 r  b   swpd   free   buff  cache   si   so    bi    bo   in    cs us sy id wa
10  2 740880  19256  46068 13719952   0    0  2788 11047 1423 14508 89  4  4  3
11  0 740880  19692  46144 13702944   0    0  2907 14073 1504 23045 90  5  2  3
 7  1 740880  20460  46264 13683852   0    0  3554 15567 1513 24182 88  5  3  3
10  2 740880  22292  46324 13670396   0    0  2640 16351 1520 17436 88  4  4  3
```

Notice that there are also a reasonable number of context switches (the cs column), although we won't worry much about this unless there are 100,000 or more per second. A *context switch* is when the operating system stops one process from running and replaces it with another.

For example, a query that performs a noncovering index scan on a MyISAM table will read an entry from the index, then read the row from a page on disk. If the page isn't in the operating system cache, there will be a physical read to the disk, which will cause a context switch to suspend the process until the I/O completes. Such a query can cause lots of context switches.

If we take a look at the *iostat* output for the same machine (again omitting the first sample, which shows averages since boot), you can see that disk utilization is less than 50%:

```
$ iostat -dx 5
Device: rrqm/s wrqm/s r/s w/s rsec/s wsec/s avgrq-sz avgqu-sz await svctm %util
sda        0   3859  54  458   2063  34546       71        3     6     1    47
dm-0       0      0  54 4316   2063  34532        8       18     4     0    47
Device: rrqm/s wrqm/s r/s w/s rsec/s wsec/s avgrq-sz avgqu-sz await svctm %util
sda        0   2898  52  363   1767  26090       67        3     7     1    45
dm-0       0      0  52 3261   1767  26090        8       15     5     0    45
```

This machine is not I/O-bound, but it's still doing a fair amount of I/O, which is not unusual for a database server. On the other hand, a typical web server will consume a lot of CPU resources but do very little I/O, so a web server's output will not usually look like this sample.

An I/O-Bound Machine

In an I/O-bound workload, the CPUs spend a lot of time waiting for I/O requests to complete. That means *vmstat* will show many processes in uninterruptible sleep (the b column), and a high value in the wa column. Here's an example:

```
$ vmstat 5
procs -----------memory---------- ---swap-- -----io---- --system-- ----cpu----
 r  b   swpd   free   buff  cache    si   so    bi    bo    in    cs us sy id wa
 5  7 740632  22684  43212 13466436   0    0  6738 17222  1738 16648 19  3 15 63
 5  7 740632  22748  43396 13465436   0    0  6150 17025  1731 16713 18  4 21 58
 1  8 740632  22380  43416 13464192   0    0  4582 21820  1693 15211 16  4 24 56
 5  6 740632  22116  43512 13463484   0    0  5955 21158  1732 16187 17  4 23 56
```

This machine's *iostat* output shows that the disks are always busy:[16]

```
$ iostat -dx 5
Device: rrqm/s wrqm/s r/s w/s rsec/s wsec/s avgrq-sz avgqu-sz await svctm %util
sda        0   5396 202  626   7319  48187       66       12    14     1   101
dm-0       0      0 202 6016   7319  48130        8       57     9     0   101
Device: rrqm/s wrqm/s r/s w/s rsec/s wsec/s avgrq-sz avgqu-sz await svctm %util
sda        0   5810 184  665   6441  51825       68       11    13     1   102
dm-0       0      0 183 6477   6441  51817        8       54     7     0   102
```

The %util value can be greater than 100% because of rounding errors.

What does it mean for a machine to be I/O-bound? If there's enough buffer capacity to serve write requests, it generally—but not always—means the disks can't keep up with *read* requests, even if the machine is doing a lot of writes. That might seem counterintuitive until you think about the nature of reads and writes:

---

16. In the second edition of this book, we conflated "always busy" with "completely saturated." Disks that are always doing something aren't necessarily maxed out, because they might be able to support some concurrency, too.

- Write requests can be either buffered or synchronous. They can be buffered at any of the levels we've discussed elsewhere in this book: the operating system, the RAID controller, and so on.

- Read requests are synchronous by nature. It's possible for a program to predict that it'll need some data and issue an asynchronous *prefetch* (read-ahead) request for it. However, it's more common for programs to discover they need data before they can continue working. That forces the request to be synchronous: the program must block until the request completes.

Think of it this way: you can issue a write request that goes into a buffer somewhere and completes at a later time. You can even issue many of these per second. If the buffer is working correctly and has enough space, each request can complete very quickly, and the actual writes to the physical disk can be batched and reordered for efficiency.

However, there's no way to do that with a read—no matter how few or how small the requests are, it's impossible for the disk to respond with "Here's your data, I'll do the read later." That's why reads are usually responsible for I/O wait.

A Swapping Machine

A machine that's swapping might or might not show a high value in the swpd column. However, you'll see high values in the si and so columns, which you don't want. Here's what the *vmstat* output looks like on a machine that's swapping heavily:

```
$ vmstat 5
procs -----------memory------------- ---swap---- -----io---- --system-- ----cpu----
 r  b   swpd    free   buff    cache    si    so    bi    bo   in    cs us sy id wa
 0 10 3794292  24436  27076 14412764 19853  9781 57874  9833 4084  8339  6 14 58 22
 4 11 3797936  21268  27068 14519324 15913 30870 40513 30924 3600  7191  6 11 36 47
 0 37 3847364  20764  27112 14547112   171 38815 22358 39146 2417  4640  6  8  9 77
```

An Idle Machine

For the sake of completeness, here's the *vmstat* output on an idle machine. Notice that there are no runnable or blocked processes, and the idle column shows that the CPUs are 100% idle. This sample comes from a machine running Red Hat Enterprise Linux 5, and it shows the st column, which is time "stolen" from a virtual machine:

```
$ vmstat 5
procs -----------memory---------- ---swap-- -----io---- --system-- -----cpu------
 r  b   swpd   free   buff  cache    si    so    bi    bo   in   cs us sy  id wa st
 0  0   108 492556  6768 360092     0     0   345   209    2   65  2  0  97  1  0
 0  0   108 492556  6772 360088     0     0     0    14  357   19  0  0 100  0  0
 0  0   108 492556  6776 360084     0     0     0     6  355   16  0  0 100  0  0
```

Summary

Choosing and configuring hardware for MySQL, and configuring MySQL for the hardware, is not a mystical art. In general, you need the same skills and knowledge that you need for most other purposes. However, there are some MySQL-specific things you should know.

What we commonly suggest for most people is to find a good balance between performance and cost. First, we like to use commodity servers, for many reasons. For example, if you're having trouble with a server and you need to take it out of service while you try to diagnose it, or if you simply want to try swapping it with another server as a form of diagnosis, this is a lot easier to do with a $5,000 server than one that costs $50,000 or more. MySQL is also typically a better fit—both in terms of the software itself and in terms of the typical workloads it runs—for commodity hardware.

The four fundamental resources MySQL needs are CPU, memory, disk, and network resources. The network doesn't tend to show up as a serious bottleneck very often, but CPUs, memory, and disks certainly do. You generally want many fast CPUs for MySQL, although if you must choose between many and fast, choose fast instead of many (all other things being equal).

The relationship between CPUs, memory, and disks is intricate, with problems in one area often showing up elsewhere. Before you throw resources at a problem, ask yourself whether you should be throwing resources at a different problem instead. If you're disk-bound, do you need more I/O capacity, or just more memory? The answer hinges on the working set size, which is the set of data that's needed most frequently over a given duration.

At the time of writing, we think it makes sense to proceed as follows. First, it's generally good not to exceed two sockets. Even a two-socket system can offer a lot of CPU cores and hardware threads, and the CPUs available for four sockets are dramatically more expensive. In addition, they are less widely used (and thus less tested and less reliable), and they come with lower clock frequencies. Finally, four-socket systems appear to suffer from the increased cost of cross-socket synchronization. On the memory front, we like to fill our servers with economically priced server-class memory. Many commodity servers currently have 18 DIMM slots, and 8 GB DIMMs are a good size—their price is the same per gigabyte as smaller DIMMs, but much less than 16 GB DIMMs. That's why we see a lot of servers with 144 GB of memory these days. This equation will change over time—the sweet spot will eventually be 16 GB DIMMs, and there might be a different number of slots in common server form factors—but the general principle will probably remain.

Your choices for durable storage essentially boil down to three options, in increasing order of performance: SANs, conventional disks, and solid-state devices. In a nutshell:

- SANs are nice when you need their features and sheer capacity. They perform well for many workloads, but they're costly and they have high latency for small, random I/O operations, especially when you use a slower interconnect such as NFS or when the working set is too larger to fit in the SAN's internal cache. Beware of performance surprises with SANs, and plan carefully for disaster scenarios.

- Conventional disks are big, cheap, and slow at random reads. For most scenarios, the best choice is a RAID 10 volume of server-grade disks. You should usually use a hardware RAID controller with a battery backup unit and the write cache set to the WriteBack policy. Such a configuration should perform very well for most workloads you throw at it.

- Solid-state drives are relatively small and expensive, but they're very fast at random I/O. There are two classes: SSDs and PCIe devices. To paint these with a broad brush, SSDs are cheaper, slower, and less reliable. You need to RAID them for durability, but most hardware RAID controllers aren't up to the task. PCIe devices are expensive and have limited capacity, but they're extremely fast and reliable, and they don't need RAID.

Solid-state devices are great for improving server performance overall, and sometimes an inexpensive SSD is just the ticket for helping out a particular workload that suffers a lot on conventional disks, such as replication. If you really need horsepower, you need a PCIe device. Adding fast I/O to the server tends to shift the bottleneck to the CPU, and sometimes to the network.

MySQL and InnoDB aren't fully capable of taking advantage of the performance available from high-end solid-state storage, and in some cases the operating systems aren't either. But this is improving pretty rapidly. Percona Server has a lot of improvements for solid-state storage, and many of these are finding their way into mainstream MySQL in the upcoming 5.6 release.

In terms of the operating system, there are just a few Big Things that you need to get right, mostly related to storage, networking, and virtual memory management. If you use GNU/Linux, as most MySQL users do, we suggest using the XFS filesystem and setting the swappiness and disk queue scheduler to values that are appropriate for a server. There are some network parameters that you might need to change, and you might wish to tweak a number of other things (such as disabling SELinux), but those changes are a matter of preference.

Replication

MySQL's built-in replication is the foundation for building large, high-performance applications on top of MySQL, using the so-called "scale-out" architecture. Replication lets you configure one or more servers as replicas[1] of another server, keeping their data synchronized with the master copy. This is not just useful for high-performance applications—it is also the cornerstone of many strategies for high availability, scalability, disaster recovery, backups, analysis, data warehousing, and many other tasks. In fact, scalability and high availability are related topics, and we'll be weaving these themes through this chapter and the next two.

In this chapter, we examine all aspects of replication. We begin with an overview of how it works, then look at basic server setup, designing more advanced replication configurations, and managing and optimizing your replicated servers. Although we generally focus a lot on performance in this book, we are equally concerned with correctness and reliability when it comes to replication, so'll we show you how replication can fail and how to make it work well.

Replication Overview

The basic problem replication solves is keeping one server's data synchronized with another's. Many replicas can connect to a single master and stay in sync with it, and a replica can, in turn, act as a master. You can arrange masters and replicas in many different ways.

MySQL supports two kinds of replication: *statement-based replication* and *row-based replication*. Statement-based (or "logical") replication has been available since MySQL 3.23. Row-based replication was added in MySQL 5.1. Both kinds work by recording changes in the master's binary log[2] and replaying the log on the replica, and both are

---

1. You might see replicas referred to as "slaves." We avoid this term wherever possible.

2. If you're new to the binary log, you can find more information in Chapter 8, the rest of this chapter, and Chapter 15.

asynchronous—that is, the replica's copy of the data isn't guaranteed to be up-to-date at any given instant. There are no guarantees as to how large the latency on the replica might be. Large queries can make the replica fall seconds, minutes, or even hours behind the master.

MySQL's replication is mostly backward-compatible. That is, a newer server can usually be a replica of an older server without trouble. However, older versions of the server are often unable to serve as replicas of newer versions: they might not understand new features or SQL syntax the newer server uses, and there might be differences in the file formats replication uses. For example, you can't replicate from a MySQL 5.1 master to a MySQL 4.0 replica. It's a good idea to test your replication setup before upgrading from one major or minor version to another, such as from 4.1 to 5.0, or 5.1 to 5.5. Upgrades within a minor version, such as from 5.1.51 to 5.1.58, are usually compatible—read the changelog to find out exactly what changed from version to version.

Replication generally doesn't add much overhead on the master. It requires binary logging to be enabled on the master, which can have significant overhead, but you need that for proper backups and point-in-time recovery anyway. Aside from binary logging, each attached replica also adds a little load (mostly network I/O) on the master during normal operation. If replicas are reading old binary logs from the master, rather than just following along with the newest events, the overhead can be a lot higher due to the I/O required to read the old logs. This process can also cause some mutex contention that hinders transaction commits. Finally, if you are replicating a very high-throughput workload (say, 5,000 or more transactions per second) to many replicas, the overhead of waking up all the replica threads to send them the events can add up.

Replication is relatively good for scaling reads, which you can direct to a replica, but it's not a good way to scale writes unless you design it right. Attaching many replicas to a master simply causes the writes to be done many times, once on each replica. The entire system is limited to the number of writes the weakest part can perform.

Replication is also wasteful with more than a few replicas, because it essentially duplicates a lot of data needlessly. For example, a single master with 10 replicas has 11 copies of the same data and duplicates most of the same data in 11 different caches. This is analogous to 11-way RAID 1 at the server level. This is not an economical use of hardware, yet it's surprisingly common to see this type of replication setup. We discuss ways to alleviate this problem throughout the chapter.

Problems Solved by Replication

Here are some of the more common uses for replication:

Data distribution
> MySQL's replication is usually not very bandwidth-intensive, although, as we'll see later, the row-based replication introduced in MySQL 5.1 can use much more

bandwidth than the more traditional statement-based replication. You can also stop and start it at will. Thus, it's useful for maintaining a copy of your data in a geographically distant location, such as a different data center. The distant replica can even work with a connection that's intermittent (intentionally or otherwise). However, if you want your replicas to have very low replication lag, you'll need a stable, low-latency link.

Load balancing

MySQL replication can help you distribute read queries across several servers, which works very well for read-intensive applications. You can do basic load balancing with a few simple code changes. On a small scale, you can use simplistic approaches such as hardcoded hostnames or round-robin DNS (which points a single hostname to multiple IP addresses). You can also take more sophisticated approaches. Standard load-balancing solutions, such as network load-balancing products, can work well for distributing load among MySQL servers. The Linux Virtual Server (LVS) project also works well. We cover load balancing in Chapter 11.

Backups

Replication is a valuable technique for helping with backups. However, a replica is neither a backup nor a substitute for backups.

High availability and failover

Replication can help avoid making MySQL a single point of failure in your application. A good failover system involving replication can help reduce downtime significantly. We cover failover in Chapter 12.

Testing MySQL upgrades

It's common practice to set up a replica with an upgraded MySQL version and use it to ensure that your queries work as expected, before upgrading every instance.

How Replication Works

Before we get into the details of setting up replication, let's look at how MySQL actually replicates data. At a high level, replication is a simple three-part process:

1. The master records changes to its data in its binary log. (These records are called *binary log events*.)
2. The replica copies the master's binary log events to its relay log.
3. The replica replays the events in the relay log, applying the changes to its own data.

That's just the overview—each of those steps is quite complex. Figure 10-1 illustrates replication in more detail.

The first part of the process is binary logging on the master (we'll show you how to set this up a bit later). Just before each transaction that updates data completes on the master, the master records the changes in its binary log. MySQL writes transactions

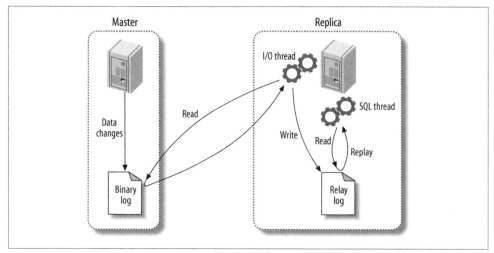

Figure 10-1. How MySQL replication works

serially in the binary log, even if the statements in the transactions were interleaved during execution. After writing the events to the binary log, the master tells the storage engine(s) to commit the transactions.

The next step is for the replica to copy the master's binary log to its own hard drive, into the so-called *relay log*. To begin, it starts a worker thread, called the *I/O slave thread*. The I/O thread opens an ordinary client connection to the master, then starts a special *binlog dump* process (there is no corresponding SQL command). The binlog dump process reads events from the master's binary log. It doesn't poll for events. If it catches up to the master, it goes to sleep and waits for the master to signal it when there are new events. The I/O thread writes the events to the replica's relay log.

 Prior to MySQL 4.0, replication worked quite differently in many ways. For example, MySQL's first replication functionality didn't use a relay log, so replication used only two threads, not three. Most people are running more recent versions of the server, so we won't mention any further details about very old versions of MySQL in this chapter.

The *SQL slave thread* handles the last part of the process. This thread reads and replays events from the relay log, thus updating the replica's data to match the master's. As long as this thread keeps up with the I/O thread, the relay log usually stays in the operating system's cache, so relay logs have very low overhead. The events the SQL thread executes can optionally go into the replica's own binary log, which is useful for scenarios we mention later in this chapter.

Figure 10-1 showed only the two replication threads that run on the replica, but there's also a thread on the master: like any connection to a MySQL server, the connection that the replica opens to the master starts a thread on the master.

This replication architecture decouples the processes of fetching and replaying events on the replica, which allows them to be asynchronous. That is, the I/O thread can work independently of the SQL thread. It also places constraints on the replication process, the most important of which is that *replication is serialized on the replica*. This means updates that might have run in parallel (in different threads) on the master cannot be parallelized on the replica, because they're executed in a single thread. As we'll see later, this is a performance bottleneck for many workloads. There are some solutions to this, but most users are still subject to the single-threaded constraint.

Setting Up Replication

Setting up replication is a fairly simple process in MySQL, but there are many variations on the basic steps, depending on the scenario. The most basic scenario is a freshly installed master and replica. At a high level, the process is as follows:

1. Set up replication accounts on each[3] server.
2. Configure the master and replica.
3. Instruct the replica to connect to and replicate from the master.

This assumes that many default settings will suffice, which is true if you've just installed the master and replica and they have the same data (the default `mysql` database). We show you here how to do each step in turn, assuming your servers are called `server1` (IP address 192.168.0.1) and `server2` (IP address 192.168.0.2). We then explain how to initialize a replica from a server that's already up and running and explore the recommended replication configuration.

Creating Replication Accounts

MySQL has a few special privileges that let the replication processes run. The slave I/O thread, which runs on the replica, makes a TCP/IP connection to the master. This means you must create a user account on the master and give it the proper privileges, so the I/O thread can connect as that user and read the master's binary log. Here's how to create that user account, which we'll call *repl*:

```
mysql> GRANT REPLICATION SLAVE, REPLICATION CLIENT ON *.*
    -> TO repl@'192.168.0.%' IDENTIFIED BY 'p4ssword',;
```

We create this user account on both the master and the replica. Note that we restricted the user to the local network, because the replication account has the ability to read all changes to the server, which makes it a privileged account. (Even though it has no ability to SELECT or change data, it can still see some of the data in the binary logs.)

---

3. This isn't strictly necessary, but it's something we recommend; we'll explain later.

The replication user actually needs only the REPLICATION SLAVE privilege on the master and doesn't really need the REPLICATION CLIENT privilege on either server. So why did we grant these privileges on both servers? We're keeping things simple, actually. There are two reasons:

- The account you use to monitor and manage replication will need the REPLICATION CLIENT privilege, and it's easier to use the same account for both purposes (rather than creating a separate user account for this purpose).
- If you set up the account on the master and then clone the replica from it, the replica will be set up correctly to act as a master, in case you want the replica and master to switch roles.

Configuring the Master and Replica

The next step is to enable a few settings on the master, which we assume is named server1. You need to enable binary logging and specify a server ID. Enter (or verify the presence of) the following lines in the master's *my.cnf* file:

```
log_bin    = mysql-bin
server_id  = 10
```

The exact values are up to you. We're taking the simplest route here, but you can do something more elaborate.

You must explicitly specify a unique server ID. We chose to use 10 instead of 1, because 1 is the default value a server will typically choose when no value is specified. (This is version-dependent; some MySQL versions just won't work at all.) Therefore, using 1 can easily cause confusion and conflicts with servers that have no explicit server IDs. A common practice is to use the final octet of the server's IP address, assuming it doesn't change and is unique (i.e., the servers belong to only one subnet). You should choose some convention that makes sense to you and follow it.

If binary logging wasn't already specified in the master's configuration file, you'll need to restart MySQL. To verify that the binary log file is created on the master, run SHOW MASTER STATUS and check that you get output similar to the following. MySQL will append some digits to the filename, so you won't see a file with the exact name you specified:

```
mysql> SHOW MASTER STATUS;
+------------------+----------+--------------+------------------+
| File             | Position | Binlog_Do_DB | Binlog_Ignore_DB |
+------------------+----------+--------------+------------------+
| mysql-bin.000001 |       98 |              |                  |
+------------------+----------+--------------+------------------+
1 row in set (0.00 sec)
```

The replica requires a configuration in its *my.cnf* file similar to the master, and you'll also need to restart MySQL on the replica:

```
log_bin            = mysql-bin
server_id          = 2
relay_log          = /var/lib/mysql/mysql-relay-bin
log_slave_updates  = 1
read_only          = 1
```

Several of these options are not technically necessary, and for some we're just making defaults explicit. In reality, only the `server_id` parameter is required on a replica, but we enabled `log_bin` too, and we gave the binary log file an explicit name. By default it is named after the server's hostname, but that can cause problems if the hostname changes. We are using the same name for the master and replicas to keep things simple, but you can choose differently if you like.

We also added two other optional configuration parameters: `relay_log` (to specify the location and name of the relay log) and `log_slave_updates` (to make the replica log the replicated events to its own binary log). The latter option causes extra work for the replicas, but as you'll see later, we have good reasons for adding these optional settings on every replica.

Some people enable just the binary log and not `log_slave_updates`, so they can see whether anything, such as a misconfigured application, is modifying data on the replica. If possible, it's better to use the `read_only` configuration setting, which prevents anything but specially privileged threads from changing data. (Don't grant your users more privileges than they need!) However, `read_only` is often not practical, especially for applications that need to be able to create tables on replicas.

 Don't place replication configuration options such as `master_host` and `master_port` in the replica's *my.cnf* file. This is an old, deprecated way to configure a replica. It can cause problems and has no benefits.

Starting the Replica

The next step is to tell the replica how to connect to the master and begin replaying its binary logs. You should not use the *my.cnf* file for this; instead, use the CHANGE MASTER TO statement. This statement replaces the corresponding *my.cnf* settings completely. It also lets you point the replica at a different master in the future, without stopping the server. Here's the basic statement you'll need to run on the replica to start replication:

```
mysql> CHANGE MASTER TO MASTER_HOST='server1',
    -> MASTER_USER='repl',
    -> MASTER_PASSWORD='p4ssword',
    -> MASTER_LOG_FILE='mysql-bin.000001',
    -> MASTER_LOG_POS=0;
```

The MASTER_LOG_POS parameter is set to 0 because this is the beginning of the log. After you run this, you should be able to inspect the output of SHOW SLAVE STATUS and see that the replica's settings are correct:

```
mysql> SHOW SLAVE STATUS\G
*************************** 1. row ***************************
             Slave_IO_State:
                Master_Host: server1
                Master_User: repl
                Master_Port: 3306
              Connect_Retry: 60
            Master_Log_File: mysql-bin.000001
        Read_Master_Log_Pos: 4
             Relay_Log_File: mysql-relay-bin.000001
              Relay_Log_Pos: 4
      Relay_Master_Log_File: mysql-bin.000001
           Slave_IO_Running: No
          Slave_SQL_Running: No
                          ...omitted...
      Seconds_Behind_Master: NULL
```

The Slave_IO_State, Slave_IO_Running, and Slave_SQL_Running columns show that the replication processes are not running. Astute readers will also notice that the log position is 4 instead of 0. That's because 0 isn't really a log position; it just means "at the start of the log file." MySQL knows that the first event is really at position 4.[4]

To start replication, run the following command:

```
mysql> START SLAVE;
```

This command should produce no errors or output. Now inspect SHOW SLAVE STATUS again:

```
mysql> SHOW SLAVE STATUS\G
*************************** 1. row ***************************
             Slave_IO_State: Waiting for master to send event
                Master_Host: server1
                Master_User: repl
                Master_Port: 3306
              Connect_Retry: 60
            Master_Log_File: mysql-bin.000001
        Read_Master_Log_Pos: 164
             Relay_Log_File: mysql-relay-bin.000001
              Relay_Log_Pos: 164
      Relay_Master_Log_File: mysql-bin.000001
           Slave_IO_Running: Yes
          Slave_SQL_Running: Yes
                          ...omitted...
      Seconds_Behind_Master: 0
```

Notice that the slave I/O and SQL threads are both running, and Seconds_Behind_Master is no longer NULL (we'll examine what Seconds_Behind_Master means later). The I/O thread is waiting for an event from the master, which means it has fetched all of the master's binary logs. The log positions have incremented, which means some

---

4. Actually, as you can see in the earlier output from SHOW MASTER STATUS, it's really at position 98. The master and s/slave/replica/ will work that out together once the s/slave/replica/ connects to the master, which hasn't yet happened.

events have been fetched and executed (your results will vary). If you make a change on the master, you should see the various file and position settings increment on the replica. You should also see the changes in the databases on the replica!

You will also be able to see the replication threads in the process list on both the master and the replica. On the master, you should see a connection created by the replica's I/O thread:

```
mysql> SHOW PROCESSLIST\G
*************************** 1. row ***************************
     Id: 55
   User: repl
   Host: replica1.webcluster_1:54813
     db: NULL
Command: Binlog Dump
   Time: 610237
  State: Has sent all binlog to slave; waiting for binlog to be updated
   Info: NULL
```

On the replica, you should see two threads. One is the I/O thread, and the other is the SQL thread:

```
mysql> SHOW PROCESSLIST\G
*************************** 1. row ***************************
     Id: 1
   User: system user
   Host:
     db: NULL
Command: Connect
   Time: 611116
  State: Waiting for master to send event
   Info: NULL
*************************** 2. row ***************************
     Id: 2
   User: system user
   Host:
     db: NULL
Command: Connect
   Time: 33
  State: Has read all relay log; waiting for the slave I/O thread to update it
   Info: NULL
```

The sample output we've shown comes from servers that have been running for a long time, which is why the I/O thread's Time column on the master and the replica has a large value. The SQL thread has been idle for 33 seconds on the replica, which means no events have been replayed for 33 seconds.

These processes will always run under the "system user" user account, but the other column values might vary. For example, when the SQL thread is replaying an event on the replica, the Info column will show the query it is executing.

If you just want to experiment with MySQL replication, Giuseppe Maxia's MySQL Sandbox script (*http://mysqlsandbox.net*) can quickly start a throwaway installation from a freshly downloaded MySQL tarball. It takes just a few keystrokes and about 15 seconds to get a running master and two running replicas:

```
$ ./set_replication.pl /path/to/mysql-tarball.tar.gz
```

Initializing a Replica from Another Server

The previous setup instructions assumed that you started the master and replica with the default initial data after a fresh installation, so you implicitly had the same data on both servers and you knew the master's binary log coordinates. This is not typically the case. You'll usually have a master that has been up and running for some time, and you'll want to synchronize a freshly installed replica with the master, even though it doesn't have the master's data.

There are several ways to initialize, or "clone," a replica from another server. These include copying data from the master, cloning a replica from another replica, and starting a replica from a recent backup. You need three things to synchronize a replica with a master:

- A snapshot of the master's data at some point in time.
- The master's current log file, and the byte offset within that log at the exact point in time you took the snapshot. We refer to these two values as the *log file coordinates*, because together they identify a binary log position. You can find the master's log file coordinates with the SHOW MASTER STATUS command.
- The master's binary log files from that time to the present.

Here are some ways to clone a replica from another server:

With a cold copy
> One of the most basic ways to start a replica is to shut down the master-to-be and copy its files to the replica (see Appendix C for more on how to copy files efficiently). You can then start the master again, which begins a new binary log, and use CHANGE MASTER TO to start the replica at the beginning of that binary log. The disadvantage of this technique is obvious: you need to shut down the master while you make the copy.

With a warm copy
> If you use only MyISAM tables, you can use *mysqlhotcopy* or *rsync* to copy files while the server is still running. See Chapter 15 for details.

Using mysqldump
> If you use only InnoDB tables, you can use the following command to dump everything from the master, load it all into the replica, and change the replica's coordinates to the corresponding position in the master's binary log:

```
$ mysqldump --single-transaction --all-databases --master-data=1--host=server1 \
  | mysql --host=server2
```

The *--single-transaction* option causes the dump to read the data as it existed at the beginning of the transaction. If you're not using transactional tables, you can use the *--lock-all-tables* option to get a consistent dump of all tables.

With a snapshot or backup

As long as you know the corresponding binary log coordinates, you can use a snapshot from the master or a backup to initialize the replica (if you use a backup, this method requires that you've kept all of the master's binary logs since the time of the backup). Just restore the backup or snapshot onto the replica, then use the appropriate binary log coordinates in CHANGE MASTER TO. There's more detail about this in Chapter 15. You can use LVM snapshots, SAN snapshots, EBS snapshots—any snapshot will do.

With Percona XtraBackup

Percona XtraBackup is an open source hot backup tool we introduced several years ago. It can make backups without blocking the server's operation, which makes it the cat's meow for setting up replicas. You can create replicas by cloning the master, or by cloning an existing replica.

We show more details about how to use Percona XtraBackup in Chapter 15, but we'll mention the relevant bits of functionality here. Just create the backup (either from the master, or from an existing replica), and restore it to the target machine. Then look in the backup for the correct position to start replication:

- If you took the backup from the new replica's master, you can start replication from the position mentioned in the xtrabackup_binlog_pos_innodb file.
- If you took the backup from another replica, you can start replication from the position mentioned in the xtrabackup_slave_info file.

Using InnoDB Hot Backup or MySQL Enterprise Backup, both covered in Chapter 15, is another good way to initialize a replica.

From another replica

You can use any of the snapshot or copy techniques just mentioned to clone one replica from another. However, if you use *mysqldump*, the *--master-data* option doesn't work.

Also, instead of using SHOW MASTER STATUS to get the master's binary log coordinates, you'll need to use SHOW SLAVE STATUS to find the position at which the replica was executing on the master when you snapshotted it.

The biggest disadvantage of cloning one replica from another is that if your replica has become out of sync with the master, you'll be cloning bad data.

 Don't use LOAD DATA FROM MASTER or LOAD TABLE FROM MASTER! They are obsolete, slow, and very dangerous. They also work only with MyISAM.

No matter what technique you choose, get comfortable with it, and document or script it. You will probably be doing it more than once, and you need to be able to do it in a pinch if something goes wrong.

Recommended Replication Configuration

There are many replication parameters, and most of them have at least some effect on data safety and performance. We explain later which rules to break and when. In this section, we show a recommended, "safe" replication configuration that minimizes the opportunities for problems.

The most important setting for binary logging on the master is `sync_binlog`:

```
sync_binlog=1
```

This makes MySQL synchronize the binary log's contents to disk each time it commits a transaction, so you don't lose log events if there's a crash. If you disable this option, the server will do a little less work, but binary log entries could be corrupted or missing after a server crash. On a replica that doesn't need to act as a master, this option creates unnecessary overhead. It applies only to the binary log, not to the relay log.

We also recommend using InnoDB if you can't tolerate corrupt tables after a crash. MyISAM is fine if table corruption isn't a big deal, but MyISAM tables are likely to be in an inconsistent state after a replica server crashes. Chances are good that a statement will have been incompletely applied to one or more tables, and the data will be inconsistent even after you've repaired the tables.

If you use InnoDB, we strongly recommend setting the following options on the master:

```
innodb_flush_logs_at_trx_commit=1 # Flush every log write
innodb_support_xa=1               # MySQL 5.0 and newer only
innodb_safe_binlog                # MySQL 4.1 only, roughly equivalent to
                                  # innodb_support_xa
```

These are the default settings in MySQL 5.0 and newer. We also recommend specifying a binary log base name explicitly, to create uniform binary log names on all servers and prevent changes in binary log names if the server's hostname changes. You might not think that it's a problem to have binary logs named after the server's hostname automatically, but our experience is that it causes a lot of trouble when moving data between servers, cloning new replicas, and restoring backups, and in lots of other ways you wouldn't expect. To avoid this, specify an argument to the `log_bin` option, optionally with an absolute path, but certainly with the base name (as shown earlier in this chapter):

```
log_bin=/var/lib/mysql/mysql-bin  # Good; specifies a path and base name
#log_bin                          # Bad; base name will be server's hostname
```

On the replica, we also recommend enabling the following configuration options. We also recommend using an absolute path for the relay log location:

```
relay_log=/path/to/logs/relay-bin
skip_slave_start
read_only
```

The `relay_log` option prevents hostname-based relay log file names, which avoids the same problems we mentioned earlier that can happen on the master, and giving the absolute path to the logs avoids bugs in various versions of MySQL that can cause the relay logs to be created in an unexpected location. The `skip_slave_start` option will prevent the replica from starting automatically after a crash, which can give you a chance to repair a server if it has problems. If the replica starts automatically after a crash and is in an inconsistent state, it might cause so much additional corruption that you'll have to throw away its data and start fresh.

The `read_only` option prevents most users from changing non-temporary tables. The exceptions are the replication SQL thread and threads with the SUPER privilege. This is one of the many reasons you should try to avoid giving your normal accounts the SUPER privilege.

Even if you've enabled all the options we've suggested, a replica can easily break after a crash, because the relay logs and *master.info* file aren't crash-safe. They're not even flushed to disk by default, and there's no configuration option to control that behavior until MySQL 5.5. You should enable those options if you're using MySQL 5.5 and if you don't mind the performance overhead of the extra `fsync()` calls:

```
sync_master_info    = 1
sync_relay_log      = 1
sync_relay_log_info = 1
```

If a replica is very far behind its master, the slave I/O thread can write many relay logs. The replication SQL thread will remove them as soon as it finishes replaying them (you can change this with the `relay_log_purge` option), but if it is running far behind, the I/O thread could actually fill up the disk. The solution to this problem is the `relay_log_space_limit` configuration variable. If the total size of all the relay logs grows larger than this variable's size, the I/O thread will stop and wait for the SQL thread to free up some more disk space.

Although this sounds nice, it can actually be a hidden problem. If the replica hasn't fetched all the relay logs from the master, those logs might be lost forever if the master crashes. And this option has had some bugs in the past, and seems to be uncommonly used, so the risk of bugs is higher when you use it. Unless you're worried about disk space, it's probably a good idea to let the replica use as much space as it needs for relay logs. That's why we haven't included the `relay_log_space_limit` setting in our recommended configuration.

Replication Under the Hood

Now that we've explained some replication basics, let's dive deeper into it. Let's take a look at how replication really works, see what strengths and weaknesses it has as a result, and examine some more advanced replication configuration options.

Statement-Based Replication

MySQL 5.0 and earlier support only *statement-based replication* (also called *logical replication*). This is unusual in the database world. Statement-based replication works by recording the query that changed the data on the master. When the replica reads the event from the relay log and executes it, it is reexecuting the actual SQL query that the master executed. This arrangement has both benefits and drawbacks.

The most obvious benefit is that it's fairly simple to implement. Simply logging and replaying any statement that changes data will, in theory, keep the replica in sync with the master. Another benefit of statement-based replication is that the binary log events tend to be reasonably compact. So, relatively speaking, statement-based replication doesn't use a lot of bandwidth—a query that updates gigabytes of data might use only a few dozen bytes in the binary log. Also, the *mysqlbinlog* tool, which we mention throughout the chapter, is most convenient to use with statement-based logging.

In practice, however, statement-based replication is not as simple as it might seem, because many changes on the master can depend on factors besides just the query text. For example, the statements will execute at slightly—or possibly greatly—different times on the master and replica. As a result, MySQL's binary log format includes more than just the query text; it also transmits several bits of metadata, such as the current timestamp. Even so, there are some statements that MySQL can't replicate correctly, such as queries that use the CURRENT_USER() function. Stored routines and triggers are also problematic with statement-based replication.

Another issue with statement-based replication is that the modifications must be serializable. This requires more locking—sometimes significantly more. Not all storage engines work with statement-based replication, although those provided with the official MySQL server distribution up to and including MySQL 5.5 do.

You can find a complete list of statement-based replication's limitations in the MySQL manual's chapter on replication.

Row-Based Replication

MySQL 5.1 added support for *row-based replication*, which records the actual data changes in the binary log and is more similar to how most other database products implement replication. This scheme has several advantages and drawbacks of its own. The biggest advantages are that MySQL can replicate every statement correctly, and some statements can be replicated much more efficiently.

Row-based logging is not backward-compatible. The *mysqlbinlog* utility distributed with MySQL 5.1 can read binary logs that contain events logged in row-based format (they are not human-readable, but the MySQL server can interpret them). However, versions of *mysqlbinlog* from earlier MySQL distributions will fail to recognize such log events and will exit with an error upon encountering them.

MySQL can replicate some changes more efficiently using row-based replication, because the replica doesn't have to replay the queries that changed the rows on the master. Replaying some queries can be very expensive. For example, here's a query that summarizes data from a very large table into a smaller table:

```
mysql> INSERT INTO summary_table(col1, col2, sum_col3)
    -> SELECT col1, col2, sum(col3)
    -> FROM enormous_table
    -> GROUP BY col1, col2;
```

Imagine that there are only three unique combinations of col1 and col2 in the enormous_table table. This query will scan many rows in the source table but will result in only three rows in the destination table. Replicating this event as a statement will make the replica repeat all that work just to generate a few rows, but replicating it with row-based replication will be trivially cheap on the replica. In this case, row-based replication is much more efficient.

On the other hand, the following event is much cheaper to replicate with statement-based replication:

```
mysql> UPDATE enormous_table SET col1 = 0;
```

Using row-based replication for this query would be very expensive because it changes every row: every row would have to be written to the binary log, making the binary log event extremely large. This would place more load on the master during both logging and replication, and the slower logging might reduce concurrency.

Because neither format is perfect for every situation, MySQL can switch between statement-based and row-based replication dynamically. By default, it uses statement-based replication, but when it detects an event that cannot be replicated correctly with a statement, it switches to row-based replication. You can also control the format as needed by setting the binlog_format session variable.

It's harder to do point-in-time recovery with a binary log that has events in row-based format, but not impossible. A log server can be helpful—more on that later.

Statement-Based or Row-Based: Which Is Better?

We've mentioned advantages and disadvantages for both replication formats. Which is better in practice?

In theory, row-based replication is probably better all-around, and in practice it generally works fine for most people. But its implementation is new enough that it hasn't had years of little special-case behaviors baked in to support all the operational needs of MySQL administrators, and as a result it's still a nonstarter for some people. Here's a more complete discussion of the benefits and drawbacks of each format to help you decide which is more suitable for your needs:

Statement-based replication advantages

Logical replication works in more cases when the schema is different on the master and the replica. For example, it can be made to work in more cases where the tables have different but compatible data types, different column orders, and so on. This makes it easier to perform schema changes on a replica and then promote it to master, reducing downtime. Statement-based replication generally permits more operational flexibility.

The replication-applying process in statement-based replication is normal SQL execution, by and large. This means that all changes on the server are taking place through a well-understood mechanism, and it's easy to inspect and determine what is happening if something isn't working as expected.

Statement-based replication disadvantages

The list of things that can't be replicated correctly through statement-based logging is so large that any given installation is likely to run into at least one of them. In particular, there were tons of bugs affecting replication of stored procedures, triggers, and so on in the 5.0 and 5.1 series of the server—so many that the way these are replicated was actually changed around a couple of times in attempts to make it work better. Bottom line: if you're using triggers or stored procedures, don't use statement-based replication unless you're watching like a hawk to make sure you don't run into problems.

There are also lots of problems with temporary tables, mixtures of storage engines, specific SQL constructs, nondeterministic statements, and so on. These range from annoying to show-stopping.

Row-based replication advantages

There are a lot fewer cases that don't work in row-based replication. It works correctly with all SQL constructs, with triggers, with stored procedures, and so on. It generally only fails when you're trying to do something clever such as schema changes on the replica.

It also creates opportunities for reduced locking, because it doesn't require such strong serialization to be repeatable.

Row-based replication works by logging the data that's changed, so the binary log is a record of what has actually changed on the master. You don't have to look at a statement and guess whether it changed any data. Thus, in some ways you actually know more about what's changed in your server, and you have a better record of the changes. Also, in some cases the row-based binary logs record what the data used to be, so they can potentially be more useful for some kinds of data recovery efforts.

Row-based replication can be less CPU-intensive in many cases, due to the lack of a need to plan and execute queries in the same way that statement-based replication does.

Finally, row-based replication can help you find and solve data inconsistencies more quickly in some cases. For example, statement-based replication won't fail if you update a row on the master and it doesn't exist on the replica, but row-based replication will throw an error and stop.

Row-based replication disadvantages

The statement isn't included in the log event, so it can be tough to figure out what SQL was executed. This is important in many cases, in addition to knowing the row changes. (This will probably be fixed in a future version of MySQL.)

Replication changes are applied on replicas in a completely different manner—it isn't SQL being executed. In fact, the process of applying row-based changes is pretty much a black box with no visibility into what the server is doing, and it's not well documented or explained, so when things don't work right, it can be tough to troubleshoot. As an example, if the replica chooses an inefficient way to find rows to change, you can't observe that.

If you have multiple levels of replication servers, and all are configured for row-based logging, a statement that you execute while your session-level `@@binlog_format` variable is set to `STATEMENT` will be logged as a statement on the server where it originates, but then the first-level replicas might relay the event in row-based format to further replicas in the chain. That is, your desired statement-based logging will get switched back to row-based logging as it propagates through the replication topology.

Row-based logging can't handle some things that statement-based logging can, such as schema changes on replicas.

Replication will sometimes halt in cases where statement-based replication would continue, such as when the replica is missing a row that's supposed to be changed. This could be regarded as a good thing. In any case, it is configurable with the `slave_exec_mode` option.

Many of these disadvantages are being lifted as time passes, but at the time of writing, they are still true in most production deployments.

Replication Files

Let's take a look at some of the files replication uses. You already know about the binary log and the relay log, but there are several other files, too. Where MySQL places them depends mostly on your configuration settings. Different MySQL versions place them in different directories by default. You can probably find them either in the data directory or in the directory that contains the server's *.pid* file (possibly */var/run/ mysqld/* on Unix-like systems). Here they are:

mysql-bin.index

> A server that has binary logging enabled will also have a file named the same as the binary logs, but with a *.index* suffix. This file keeps track of the binary log files that exist on disk. It is not an index in the sense of a table's index; rather, each line in the file contains the filename of a binary log file.

> You might be tempted to think that this file is redundant and can be deleted (after all, MySQL could just look at the disk to find its files), but don't. MySQL relies on this index file, and it will not recognize a binary log file unless it's mentioned here.

mysql-relay-bin.index

> This file serves the same purpose for the relay logs as the binary log index file does for the binary logs.

master.info

> This file contains the information a replica needs to connect to its master. The format is plain text (one value per line) and varies between MySQL versions. Don't delete it, or your replica will not know how to connect to its master after it restarts. This file contains the replication user's password, in plain text, so you might want to restrict its permissions.

relay-log.info

> This file contains the replica's current binary log and relay log coordinates (i.e., the replica's position on the master). Don't delete this either, or the replica will forget where it was replicating from after a restart and might try to replay statements it has already executed.

These files are a rather crude way of recording MySQL's replication and logging state. Unfortunately, they are not written synchronously, so if your server loses power and the files haven't yet been flushed to disk, they can be inaccurate when the server restarts. This is improved in MySQL 5.5, as mentioned previously.

The *.index* files interact with another setting, expire_logs_days, which specifies how MySQL should purge expired binary logs. If the *mysql-bin.index* files mention files that don't exist on disk, automatic purging will not work in some MySQL versions; in fact, even the PURGE MASTER LOGS statement won't work. The solution to this problem is generally to use the MySQL server to manage the binary logs, so it doesn't get confused. (That is, you shouldn't use *rm* to purge files yourself.)

You need to implement some sort of log purging strategy explicitly, either with expire_logs_days or another means, or MySQL will fill up the disk with binary logs. You should consider your backup policy when you do this.

Sending Replication Events to Other Replicas

The `log_slave_updates` option lets you use a replica as a master of other replicas. It instructs MySQL to write the events the replication SQL thread executes into its own binary log, which its own replicas can then retrieve and execute. Figure 10-2 illustrates this.

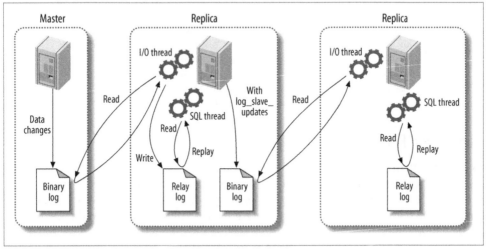

Figure 10-2. Passing on a replication event to further replicas

In this scenario, a change on the master causes an event to be written to its binary log. The first replica then fetches and executes the event. At this point, the event's life would normally be over, but because `log_slave_updates` is enabled, the replica writes it to its binary log instead. Now the second replica can retrieve the event into its own relay log and execute it. This configuration means that changes on the original master can propagate to replicas that are not attached to it directly. We prefer setting `log_slave_updates` by default because it lets you connect a replica without having to restart the server.

When the first replica writes a binary log event from the master into its own binary log, that event will almost certainly be at a different position in the log from its position on the master—that is, it could be in a different log file or at a different numerical position within the log file. This means you can't assume all servers that are at the same logical point in replication will have the same log coordinates. As we'll see later, this makes it quite complicated to do some tasks, such as changing replicas to a different master or promoting a replica to be the master.

Unless you've taken care to give each server a unique server ID, configuring a replica in this manner can cause subtle errors and might even cause replication to complain and stop. One of the more common questions about replication configuration is why one needs to specify the server ID. Shouldn't MySQL be able to replicate statements without knowing where they originated? Why does MySQL care whether the server ID is globally unique? The answer to this question lies in how MySQL prevents an infinite loop in replication. When the replication SQL thread reads the relay log, it discards any event whose server ID matches its own. This breaks infinite loops in replication. Preventing infinite loops is important for some of the more useful replication topologies, such as master-master replication.[5]

 If you're having trouble getting replication set up, the server ID is one of the things you should check. It's not enough to just inspect the @@server_id variable. It has a default value, but replication won't work unless it's explicitly set, either in *my.cnf* or via a SET command. If you use a SET command, be sure you update the configuration file too, or your settings won't survive a server restart.

Replication Filters

Replication filtering options let you replicate just part of a server's data, which is much less of a good thing than you might think. There are two kinds of replication filters: those that filter events out of the binary log on the master, and those that filter events coming from the relay log on the replica. Figure 10-3 illustrates the two types.

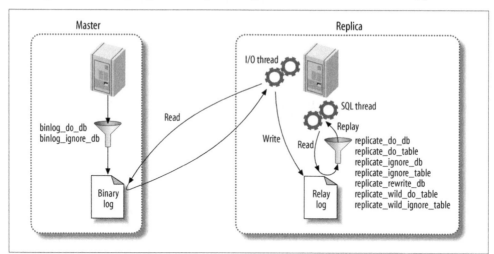

Figure 10-3. Replication filtering options

The options that control binary log filtering are binlog_do_db and binlog_ignore_db. You should *not* enable these, as we'll explain in a moment, unless you think you'll enjoy explaining to your boss why the data is gone permanently and can't be recovered.

---

5. Statements running around in infinite loops are also one of the many joys of multi-server ring replication topologies, which we'll show later. Avoid ring replication like the plague.

On the replica, the `replicate_*` options filter events as the replication SQL thread reads them from the relay log. You can replicate or ignore one or more databases, rewrite one database to another database, and replicate or ignore tables based on `LIKE` pattern matching syntax.

The most important thing to understand about these options is that the `*_do_db` and `*_ignore_db` options, both on the master and on the replica, do not work as you might expect. You might think they filter on the object's database name, but they actually filter *on the current default database.*[6] That is, if you execute the following statements on the master:

```
mysql> USE test;
mysql> DELETE FROM sakila.film;
```

the `*_do_db` and `*_ignore_db` parameters will filter the `DELETE` statement on `test`, not on `sakila`. This is not usually what you want, and it can cause the wrong statements to be replicated or ignored. The `*_do_db` and `*_ignore_db` parameters have uses, but they're limited and rare, and you should be very careful with them. If you use these parameters, it's very easy to for replication to get out of sync or fail.

 The `binlog_do_db` and `binlog_ignore_db` options don't just have the potential to break replication; they also make it impossible to do point-in-time recovery from a backup. For most situations, *you should never use them.* They can cause endless grief. We show some alternative ways to filter replication with Blackhole tables later in this chapter.

In general, replication filters are a problem waiting to happen. For example, suppose you want to prevent privilege changes from propagating to replicas, a fairly common goal. (The desire to do this should probably tip you off that you're doing something wrong; there are probably other ways to accomplish your real goal.) Replication filters on the system tables will certainly prevent `GRANT` statements from replicating, but they will prevent events and routines from replicating, too. Such unforeseen consequences are a reason to be careful with filters. It might be a better idea to prevent specific statements from being replicated, usually with `SET SQL_LOG_BIN=0`, though that practice has its own hazards. In general, you should use replication filters very carefully, and only if you really need them, because they make it so easy to break replication and cause problems that will manifest when it's least convenient, such as during disaster recovery.

The filtering options are well documented in the MySQL manual, so we won't repeat the details here.

---

6. If you're using statement-based replication, that is. If you're using row-based replication, they don't behave quite the same (another good reason to stay away from them).

Replication Topologies

You can set up MySQL replication for almost any configuration of masters and replicas, with the limitation that a given MySQL replica instance can have only one master. Many complex topologies are possible, but even the simple ones can be very flexible. A single topology can have many different uses. The variety of ways you can use replication could easily fill its own book.

We've already seen how to set up a master with a single replica. In this section, we look at some other common topologies and discuss their strengths and limitations. As we go, remember these basic rules:

- A MySQL replica instance can have only one master.
- Every replica must have a unique server ID.
- A master can have many replicas (or, correspondingly, a replica can have many siblings).
- A replica can propagate changes from its master, and be the master of other replicas, if you enable `log_slave_updates`.

Master and Multiple Replicas

Aside from the basic two-server master-replica setup we've already mentioned, this is the simplest replication topology. In fact, it's just as simple as the basic setup, because the replicas don't interact with each other;[7] they each connect only to the master. Figure 10-4 shows this arrangement.

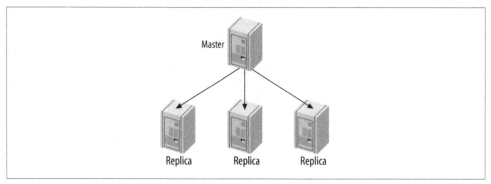

Figure 10-4. A master with multiple replicas

---

7. This isn't technically true. If they have duplicate server IDs, they'll get into a catfight and kick each other off the master repeatedly.

This configuration is most useful when you have few writes and many reads. You can spread reads across any number of replicas, up to the point where the replicas put too much load on the master or network bandwidth from the master to the replicas becomes a problem. You can set up many replicas at once, or add replicas as you need them, using the same steps we showed earlier in this chapter.

Although this is a very simple topology, it is flexible enough to fill many needs. Here are just a few ideas:

- Use different replicas for different roles (for example, add different indexes or use different storage engines).
- Set up one of the replicas as a standby master, with no traffic other than replication.
- Put one of the replicas in a remote data center for disaster recovery.
- Time-delay one or more of the replicas for disaster recovery.
- Use one of the replicas for backups, for training, or as a development or staging server.

One of the reasons this topology is popular is that it avoids many of the complexities that come with other configurations. Here's an example: it's easy to compare one replica to another in terms of binary log positions on the master, because they'll all be the same. In other words, if you stop all the replicas at the same logical point in replication, they'll all be reading from the same physical position in the master's logs. This is a nice property that simplifies many administrative tasks, such as promoting a replica to be the master.

This property holds only among "sibling" replicas. It's more complicated to compare log positions between servers that aren't in a direct master-replica or sibling relationship. Many of the topologies we mention later, such as tree replication or distribution masters, make it harder to figure out where in the logical sequence of events a replica is really replicating.

Master-Master in Active-Active Mode

Master-master replication (also known as dual-master or bidirectional replication) involves two servers, each configured as both a master and a replica of the other—in other words, a pair of co-masters. Figure 10-5 shows the setup.

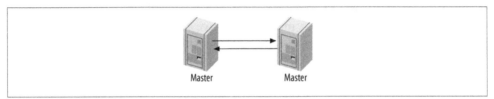

Figure 10-5. Master-master replication

MySQL Does Not Support Multisource Replication

We use the term *multisource replication* very specifically to describe the scenario where there is a replica with more than one master. Regardless of what you might have been told, MySQL (unlike some other database servers) does not support the configuration illustrated in Figure 10-6 at present. However, we show you some ways to emulate multisource replication later in this chapter.

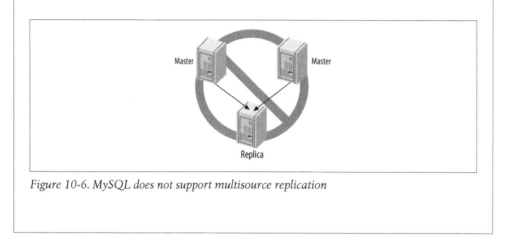

Figure 10-6. MySQL does not support multisource replication

Master-master replication in active-active mode has uses, but they're generally special-purpose. One possible use is for geographically separated offices, where each office needs its own locally writable copy of data.

The biggest problem with such a configuration is how to handle conflicting changes. The list of possible problems caused by having two writable co-masters is very long. Problems usually show up when a query changes the same row simultaneously on both servers or inserts into a table with an AUTO_INCREMENT column at the same time on both servers.[8]

MySQL 5.0 added some replication features that make this type of replication setup slightly less of a foot-gun: the auto_increment_increment and auto_increment_offset settings. These settings let servers autogenerate nonconflicting values for INSERT queries. However, allowing writes to both masters is still extremely dangerous. Updates that happen in a different order on the two machines can still cause the data to silently become out of sync. For example, imagine you have a single-column, single-row table containing the value 1. Now suppose these two statements execute simultaneously:

---

8. Actually, these problems usually show up at 3am on a weekend, and we've seen them take months to resolve.

- On the first co-master:

  ```
  mysql> UPDATE tbl SET col=col + 1;
  ```

- On the second:

  ```
  mysql> UPDATE tbl SET col=col * 2;
  ```

The result? One server has the value 4, and the other has the value 3. And yet, there are no replication errors at all.

Data getting out of sync is only the beginning. What if normal replication stops with an error, but applications keep writing to both servers? You can't just clone one of the servers from the other, because each of them will have changes that you need to copy to the other. Solving this problem is likely to be very hard. Consider yourself warned!

If you set up a master-master active-active configuration carefully, perhaps with well-partitioned data and privileges, and if you *really* know what you're doing, you can avoid some of these problems.[9] However, it's hard to do well, and there's almost always a better way to achieve what you need.

In general, allowing writes on both servers causes way more trouble than it's worth. However, an active-passive configuration is very useful indeed, as you'll see in the next section.

Master-Master in Active-Passive Mode

There's a variation on master-master replication that avoids the pitfalls we just discussed and is, in fact, a very powerful way to design fault-tolerant and highly available systems. The main difference is that one of the servers is a read-only "passive" server, as shown in Figure 10-7.

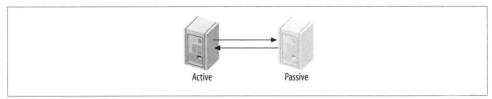

Active   Passive

Figure 10-7. Master-master replication in active-passive mode

This configuration lets you swap the active and passive server roles back and forth very easily, because the servers' configurations are symmetrical. This makes failover and failback easy. It also lets you perform maintenance, optimize tables, upgrade your operating system (or application, or hardware), and do other tasks without any downtime.

---

9. Some, but not all—we can play devil's advocate and show you flaws in just about any setup you can imagine.

For example, running an ALTER TABLE statement locks the entire table, blocking reads and writes to it. This can take a long time and disrupt service. However, the master-master configuration lets you stop the replication threads on the active server (so it doesn't process any updates from the passive server), alter the table on the passive server, switch the roles, and restart replication on the formerly active server.[10] That server then reads its relay log and executes the same ALTER TABLE statement. Again, this might take a long time, but it doesn't matter because the server isn't serving any live queries.

The active-passive master-master topology lets you sidestep many other problems and limitations in MySQL. There are some toolsets to help with this type of operational task, too.

Let's see how to configure a master-master pair. Perform these steps on *both* servers, so they end up with symmetrical configurations:

1. Ensure that the servers have exactly the same data.
2. Enable binary logging, choose unique server IDs, and add replication accounts.
3. Enable logging replica updates. This is crucial for failover and failback, as we'll see later.
4. Optionally configure the passive server to be read-only to prevent changes that might conflict with changes on the active server.
5. Start each server's MySQL instance.
6. Configure each server as a replica of the other, beginning with the newly created binary log.

Now let's trace what happens when there's a change to the active server. The change gets written to its binary log and flows through replication to the passive server's relay log. The passive server executes the query and writes the event to its own binary log, because you enabled log_slave_updates. The active server then ignores the event, because the server ID in the event matches its own. See the section "Changing Masters" on page 489 to learn how to switch roles.

Setting up an active-passive master-master topology is a little like creating a hot spare in some ways, except that you can use the "spare" to boost performance. You can use it for read queries, backups, "offline" maintenance, upgrades, and so on—things you can't do with a true hot spare. However, you cannot use it to gain better write performance than you can get with a single server (more about that later).

As we discuss more scenarios and uses for replication, we'll come back to this configuration. It is a very important and common replication topology.

---

10. You can also disable binary logging temporarily with SET SQL_LOG_BIN=0, instead of stopping replication. Some commands, such as OPTIMIZE TABLE, also support a LOCAL or NO_WRITE_TO_BINLOG option that prevents logging. This can allow you to choose your timing more precisely, rather than just letting the ALTER happen when it occurs in the replication stream.

Master-Master with Replicas

A related configuration is to add one or more replicas to each co-master, as shown in Figure 10-8.

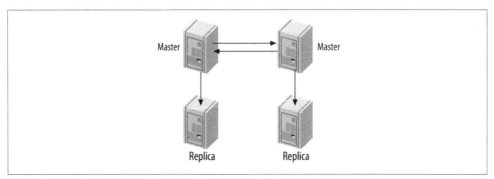

Figure 10-8. Master-master topology with replicas

The advantage of this configuration is extra redundancy. In a geographically distributed replication topology, it removes the single point of failure at each site. You can also offload read-intensive queries to the replicas, as usual.

If you're using a master-master topology locally for fast failover, this configuration is still useful. Promoting one of the replicas to replace a failed master is possible, although it's a little more complex. The same is true of moving one of the replicas to point to a different master. The added complexity is an important consideration.

Ring Replication

The dual-master configuration is really just a special case[11] of the ring replication configuration, shown in Figure 10-9. A ring has three or more masters. Each server is a replica of the server before it in the ring, and a master of the server after it. This topology is also called *circular replication*.

Rings don't have some of the key benefits of a master-master setup, such as symmetrical configuration and easy failover. They also depend completely on every node in the ring being available, which greatly increases the probability of the entire system failing. And if you remove one of the nodes from the ring, any replication events that originated at that node can go into an infinite loop: they'll cycle forever through the chain of servers, because the only server that will filter out an event based on its server ID is the server that created it. In general, rings are brittle and best avoided, no matter how clever you are.

---

11. A slightly more sane special case, we might add.

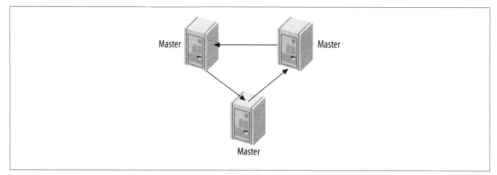

Figure 10-9. A replication ring topology

You can mitigate some of the risk of a ring replication setup by adding replicas to provide redundancy at each site, as shown in Figure 10-10. This merely protects against the risk of a server failing, though. A loss of power or any other problem that affects any connection between the sites will still break the entire ring.

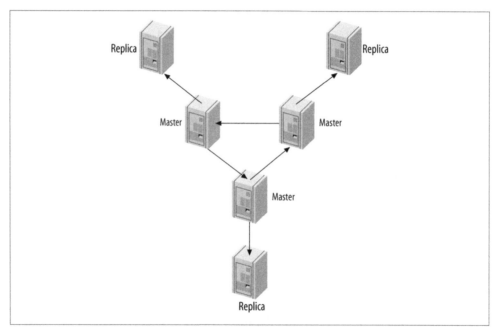

Figure 10-10. A replication ring with additional replicas at each site

Master, Distribution Master, and Replicas

We've mentioned that replicas can place quite a load on the master if there are enough of them. Each replica creates a new thread on the master, which executes the special *binlog dump* command. This command reads the data from the binary log and sends it to the replica. The work is repeated for each replica; they don't share the resources required for a binlog dump.

If there are many replicas and there's a particularly large binary log event, such as a huge LOAD DATA INFILE, the master's load can go up significantly. The master might even run out of memory and crash because of all the replicas requesting the same huge event at the same time. On the other hand, if the replicas are all requesting *different* binlog events that aren't in the filesystem cache anymore, that can cause a lot of disk seeks, which might also interfere with the master's performance and cause mutex contention.

For this reason, if you need many replicas, it's often a good idea to remove the load from the master and use a *distribution master*. A distribution master is a replica whose only purpose is to read and serve the binary logs from the master. Many replicas can connect to the distribution master, which insulates the original master from the load. To remove the work of actually executing the queries on the distribution master, you can change its tables to the Blackhole storage engine, as shown in Figure 10-11.

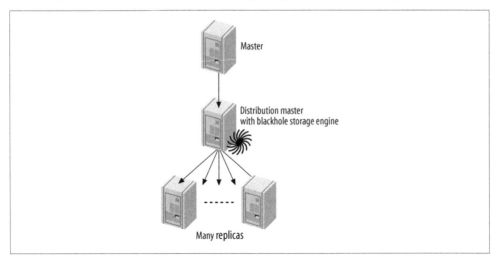

Figure 10-11. A master, a distribution master, and many replicas

It's hard to say exactly how many replicas a master can handle before it needs a distribution master. As a very rough rule of thumb, if your master is running near its full capacity, you might not want to put more than about 10 replicas on it. If there's very little write activity, or you're replicating only a fraction of the tables, the master can probably serve many more replicas. Additionally, you don't have to limit yourself to just one distribution master. You can use several if you need to replicate to a really large number of replicas, or you can even use a pyramid of distribution masters. In some cases it also helps to set slave_compressed_protocol, to save some bandwidth on the master. This is most helpful for cross–data center replication.

You can also use the distribution master for other purposes, such as applying filters and rewrite rules to the binary log events. This is much more efficient than repeating the logging, rewriting, and filtering on each replica.

If you use Blackhole tables on the distribution master, it will be able to serve more replicas than it could otherwise. The distribution master will execute the queries, but the queries will be extremely cheap, because the Blackhole tables will not have any data. The drawback of Blackhole tables is that they have bugs, such as forgetting to put autoincrementing IDs into their binary logs in some circumstances, so be very careful with Blackhole tables if you use them.[12]

A common question is how to ensure that all tables on the distribution master use the Blackhole storage engine. What if someone creates a new table on the master and specifies a different storage engine? Indeed, the same issue arises whenever you want to use a different storage engine on a replica. The usual solution is to set the server's `storage_engine` option:

```
storage_engine = blackhole
```

This will affect only `CREATE TABLE` statements that don't specify a storage engine explicitly. If you have an existing application that you can't control, this topology might be fragile. You can disable InnoDB and make tables fall back to MyISAM with the `skip_innodb` option, but you can't disable the MyISAM or Memory engines.

The other major drawback is the difficulty of replacing the master with one of the (ultimate) replicas. It's hard to promote one of the replicas into its place, because the intermediate master ensures that they will almost always have different binary log coordinates than the original master does.[13]

Tree or Pyramid

If you're replicating a master to a very large number of replicas—whether you're distributing data geographically or just trying to build in more read capacity—it can be more manageable to use a pyramid design, as illustrated in Figure 10-12.

The advantage of this design is that it eases the load on the master, just as the distribution master did in the previous section. The disadvantage is that any failure in an intermediate level will affect multiple servers, which wouldn't happen if the replicas were each attached to the master directly. Also, the more intermediate levels you have, the harder and more complicated it is to handle failures.

---

12. See MySQL bugs 35178 and 62829 for starters. In general, anytime you use a nonstandard storage engine or feature, it can be a good idea to look for open and closed bugs affecting it.

13. You can use Percona Toolkit's *pt-heartbeat* to create a crude global transaction ID to help with this. It makes it much easier to find binary log positions on various servers, because the heartbeat table itself has the approximate binary log positions in it.

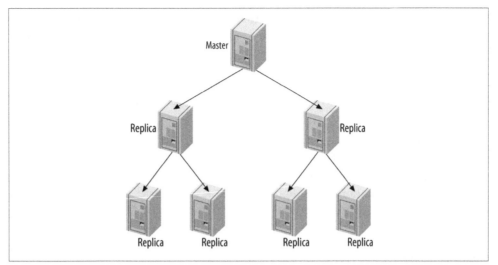

Figure 10-12. A pyramid replication topology

Custom Replication Solutions

MySQL replication is flexible enough that you can often design a custom solution for your application's needs. You'll typically use some combination of filtering, distribution, and replicating to different storage engines. You can also use "hacks," such as replicating to and from servers that use the Blackhole storage engine (as discussed earlier in this chapter). Your design can be as elaborate as you want. The biggest limitations are what you can monitor and administer reasonably and what resource constraints you have (network bandwidth, CPU power, etc.).

Selective replication

To take advantage of locality of reference and keep your working set in memory for reads, you can replicate a small amount of data to each of many replicas. If each replica has a fraction of the master's data and you direct reads to the replicas, you can make much better use of the memory on each replica. Each replica will also have only a fraction of the master's write load, so the master can become more powerful without making the replicas fall behind.

This scenario is similar in some respects to the horizontal data partitioning we'll talk more about in the next chapter, but it has the advantage that one server still hosts *all* the data—the master. This means you never have to look on more than one server for the data needed for a write query, and if you have read queries that need data that doesn't all exist on any single replica server, you have the option of doing those reads on the master instead. Even if you can't do all reads on the replicas, you should be able to move many of them off the master.

The simplest way to do this is to partition the data into different databases on the master, and then replicate each database to a different replica server. For example, if you want to replicate data for each department in your company to a different replica, you can create databases called `sales`, `marketing`, `procurement`, and so on. Each replica should then have a `replicate_wild_do_table` configuration option that limits its data to the given database. Here's the configuration option for the `sales` database:

```
replicate_wild_do_table = sales.%
```

Filtering with a distribution master is also useful. For example, if you want to replicate just part of a heavily loaded server across a slow or very expensive network, you can use a local distribution master with Blackhole tables and filtering rules. The distribution master can have replication filters that remove undesired entries from its logs. This can help avoid dangerous logging settings on the master, and it doesn't require you to transfer all the logs across the network to the remote replicas.

Separating functions

Many applications have a mixture of online transaction processing (OLTP) and online analytical processing (OLAP) queries. OLTP queries tend to be short and transactional. OLAP queries are usually large and slow and don't require absolutely up-to-date data. The two types of queries also place very different stresses on the server. Thus, they perform best on servers that are configured differently and perhaps even use different storage engines and hardware.

A common solution to this problem is to replicate the OLTP server's data to replicas specifically designed for the OLAP workload. These replicas can have different hardware, configurations, indexes, and/or storage engines. If you dedicate a replica to OLAP queries, you might also be able to tolerate more replication lag or otherwise degraded quality of service on that replica. That might mean you can use it for tasks that would result in unacceptable performance on a nondedicated replica, such as executing very long-running queries.

No special replication setup is required, although you might choose to omit some of the data from the master if you'll achieve significant savings by not having it on the replica. Filtering out even a small amount of data with replication filters on the relay log might help reduce I/O and cache activity.

Data archiving

You can archive data on a replica server—that is, keep it on the replica but remove it from the master—by running delete queries on the master and ensuring that those queries don't execute on the replica. There are two common ways to do this: one is to selectively disable binary logging on the master, and the other is to use `replicate_ignore_db` rules on the replica. (Yes, both are dangerous.)

The first method requires executing SET SQL_LOG_BIN=0 in the process that purges the data on the master, then purging the data. This has the advantage of not requiring any special replication configuration on the replica, and because the statements aren't even logged to the master's binary log, it's slightly more efficient there too. The main disadvantage is that you won't be able to use the binary log on the master for auditing or point-in-time recovery anymore, because it won't contain every modification made to the master's data. It also requires the SUPER privilege.

The second technique is to USE a certain database on the master before executing the statements that purge the data. For example, you can create a database named purge, and then specify replicate_ignore_db=purge in the replica's *my.cnf* file and restart the server. The replica will ignore statements that USE this database. This approach doesn't have the first technique's weaknesses, but it has the (minor) drawback of making the replica fetch binary log events it doesn't need. There's also a potential for someone to mistakenly execute non-purge queries in the purge database, thus causing the replica not to replay events you want it to.

Percona Toolkit's *pt-archiver* tool supports both methods.

 A third option is to use binlog_ignore_db to filter out replication events, but as we stated earlier, we consider this too dangerous.

Using replicas for full-text searches

Many applications require a combination of transactions and full-text searches. However, at the time of writing only MyISAM tables offer built-in full-text search capabilities, and MyISAM doesn't support transactions. (There's a laboratory preview of InnoDB full-text search in MySQL 5.6, but it isn't GA yet.) A common workaround is to configure a replica for full-text searches by changing the storage engine for certain tables to MyISAM on the replica. You can then add full-text indexes and perform full-text search queries on the replica. This avoids potential replication problems with transactional and nontransactional storage engines in the same query on the master, and it relieves the master of the extra work of maintaining the full-text indexes.

Read-only replicas

Many organizations prefer replicas to be read-only, so unintended changes don't break replication. You can achieve this with the read_only configuration variable. It disables most writes: the exceptions are the replica processes, users who have the SUPER privilege, and temporary tables. This is perfect as long as you don't give the SUPER privilege to ordinary users, which you shouldn't do anyway.

Emulating multisource replication

MySQL does not currently support multisource replication (i.e., a replica with more than one master). However, you can emulate this topology by changing a replica to point at different masters in turn. For example, you can point the replica at master A and let it run for a while, then point it at master B for a while, and then switch it back to master A again. How well this will work depends on your data and how much work the two masters will cause the single replica to do. If your masters are relatively lightly loaded and their updates won't conflict at all, it might work very well.

You'll need to do a little work to keep track of the binary log coordinates for each master. You also might want to ensure that the replica's I/O thread doesn't fetch more data than you intend it to execute on each cycle; otherwise, you could increase the network traffic and load on the master significantly by fetching and throwing away a lot of data on each cycle.

You can also emulate multisource replication using master-master (or ring) replication and the Blackhole storage engine with a replica, as depicted in Figure 10-13.

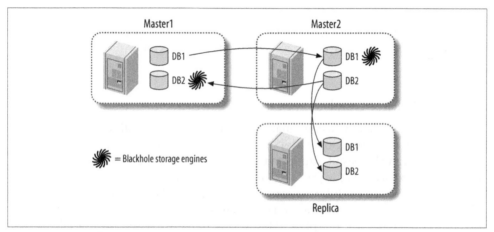

Figure 10-13. Emulating multisource replication with dual masters and the Blackhole storage engine

In this configuration, the two masters each contain their own data. They each also contain the tables from the other master, but use the Blackhole storage engine to avoid actually storing the data in those tables. A replica is attached to one of the co-masters—it doesn't matter which one. This replica does not use the Blackhole storage engine at all, so it is effectively a replica of both masters.

In fact, it's not really necessary to use a master-master topology to achieve this. You can simply replicate from server1 to server2 to the replica. If server2 uses the Blackhole storage engine for tables replicated from server1, it will not contain any data from server1, as shown in Figure 10-14.

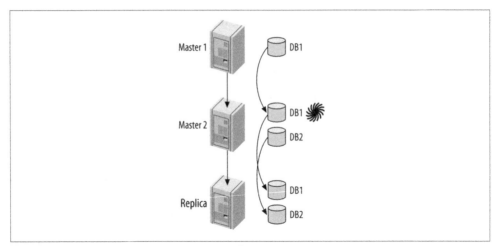

Figure 10-14. Another way to emulate multisource replication

Either of these configurations can suffer from the usual problems, such as conflicting updates and CREATE TABLE statements that explicitly specify a storage engine.

Another option is to use Continuent's Tungsten Replicator, which we'll discuss later in this chapter.

Creating a log server

One of the things you can do with MySQL replication is create a "log server" with no data, whose only purpose is to make it easy to replay and/or filter binary log events. As you'll see later in this chapter, this is very useful for restarting replication after crashes. It's also useful for point-in-time recovery, which we discuss in Chapter 15.

Imagine you have a set of binary logs or relay logs—perhaps from a backup, perhaps from a server that crashed—and you want to replay the events in them. You could use *mysqlbinlog* to extract the events, but it's more convenient and efficient to just set up a MySQL instance without any data and let it think the binary logs are its own. You can use the MySQL Sandbox script available at *http://mysqlsandbox.net* to create the log server if you'll need it only temporarily. The log server *does not need any data* because it won't be executing the logs—it will only be serving the logs to other servers. (It does need to have a replication user, however.)

Let's take a look at how this technique works (we show some applications for it later). Suppose the logs are called *somelog-bin.000001*, *somelog-bin.000002*, and so on. Place these files into your log server's binary log directory. We'll assume it's */var/log/mysql*. Then, before you start the log server, edit its *my.cnf* file as follows:

```
log_bin       = /var/log/mysql/somelog-bin
log_bin_index = /var/log/mysql/somelog-bin.index
```

The server doesn't automatically discover log files, so you'll also need to update the server's log index file. The following command will accomplish this on Unix-like systems:[14]

```
# /bin/ls -1 /var/log/mysql/somelog-bin.[0-9]* > /var/log/mysql/somelog-bin.index
```

Make sure the user account under which MySQL runs can read and write the log index file. Now you can start your log server and verify that it sees the log files with SHOW MASTER LOGS.

Why is a log server better than using *mysqlbinlog* for recovery? For several reasons:

- Replication is a means of applying binary logs that's been tested by millions of users and is known to work. The *mysqlbinlog* tool isn't guaranteed to work in the same way as replication and might not reproduce the changes from the binary log faithfully.
- It's faster because it eliminates the need to extract statements from the log and pipe them into *mysql*.
- You can see the progress easily.
- You can work with errors easily. For example, you can skip statements that fail to replicate.
- You can filter replication events easily.
- Sometimes *mysqlbinlog* might not be able to read the binary log, because of changes to the logging format.

Replication and Capacity Planning

Writes are usually the replication bottleneck, and it's hard to scale writes with replication. You need to make sure you do the math right when you plan how much capacity replicas will add to your system overall. It's easy to make mistakes where replication is concerned.

For example, imagine your workload is 20% writes and 80% reads. To make the math easy, let's grossly oversimplify and assume the following are true:

- Read and write queries involve an identical amount of work.
- All servers are exactly equal and have a capacity of exactly 1,000 queries per second.
- Replicas and masters have the same performance characteristics.
- You can move all read queries to the replicas.

If you currently have one server handling 1,000 queries per second, how many replicas will you need to add so that you can handle twice your current load and move all read queries to the replicas?

---

14. We use */bin/ls* explicitly to avoid invoking common aliases that add terminal escape codes for coloring.

It might seem that you could add two replicas and split the 1,600 reads between them. However, don't forget that your write workload has also increased to 400 queries per second, and this cannot be divided between the master and replicas. Each replica must perform 400 writes per second. That means each replica is 40% busy with writes and can serve only 600 reads per second. Thus, you'll need not two but *three* replicas to handle twice the traffic.

What if your traffic doubles again? There will be 800 writes per second, so the master will still be able to keep up. But the replicas will each be 80% busy with writes too, so you'll need 16 replicas to handle the 3,200 reads per second. And if the traffic increases just a little more, it will be too much for the master.

This is far from linear scalability: you need 17 times as many servers to handle 4 times as many queries. This illustrates that you quickly reach a point of diminishing returns when adding replicas to a single master. And this is even with our unrealistic assumptions, which ignore, for example, the fact that single-threaded statement-based replication usually causes replicas to have lower capacity than the master. A real replication setup is likely to perform even worse than our theoretical one.

Why Replication Doesn't Help Scale Writes

The fundamental problem with the poor server-to-capacity ratio we just discussed is that you cannot distribute the writes equally among the machines, as you can with the reads. Another way to say this is that replication scales reads, but it doesn't scale writes.

You might wonder whether there's a way to add write capacity with replication. The answer is no—not even a little. Partitioning your data, which we cover in the next chapter, is the only way you can scale writes.

Some readers might have thought about using a master-master topology (see "Master-Master in Active-Active Mode" on page 469) and writing to both masters. This configuration can handle slightly more writes as compared to a master-replicas topology, because you can share the serialization penalty equally between the two servers. If you do 50% of the writes on each server, only the 50% that execute via replication from the other server must be serialized. In theory, that's better than doing 100% of the writes in parallel on one machine (the master) and 100% of the writes serially on the other machine (the replica).

This might seem attractive. However, such a configuration still can't handle as many writes as a single server. A server whose write workload is 50% serialized is slower than a single server that can do all its writes in parallel.

That's why this tactic does not scale writes. It's only a way to share the serialized-write disadvantage over two servers, so the "weakest link in the chain" isn't quite so weak. It provides only a relatively small improvement over an active-passive setup, adding a lot of risk for a small gain—and it generally won't benefit you anyway, as we explain in the next section.

When Will Replicas Begin to Lag?

A common question about replicas is how to predict when they won't be able to keep up with the changes coming from the master. It can be hard to tell the difference between a replica that's at 5% of its capacity and one that's at 95%. However, it's possible to get at least a little advance warning of impending saturation and estimate replication capacity.

The first thing you should do is watch for spikes of lag. If you have graphs of replication lag, you should notice little bumps in the graphs as the replica begins to encounter short periods where there's more work and it can't keep up. As the workload gets closer to consuming the replica's capacity, you'll see these bumps get higher and wider. The front side of the bump will generally have a consistent angle, but the back side, when the replica is catching up after lagging behind, will become a gentler and gentler slope. The presence of these bumps, and growth in them, is a warning sign that you're approaching your limits.

To predict what's going to happen at some point in the future, deliberately delay a replica, and then see how fast it can catch up. The goal is to explicitly see how steep the back side of that slope is. If you stop a replica for an hour, then start it and it catches up in one hour, it is running at half of its capacity. That is, if you stop it at noon and restart it at 1:00, and it's caught up again at 2:00, it has applied all of the changes from 12:00 to 2:00 in an hour, so it went at double speed.

Finally, in Percona Server and MariaDB you can measure the replication utilization directly. Enable the `userstat` server variable, and then you'll be able to do the following:

```
mysql> SELECT * FROM INFORMATION_SCHEMA.USER_STATISTICS
    -> WHERE USER='#mysql_system#'\G
*************************** 1. row ***************************
                  USER: #mysql_system#
     TOTAL_CONNECTIONS: 1
CONCURRENT_CONNECTIONS: 2
        CONNECTED_TIME: 46188
             BUSY_TIME: 719
          ROWS_FETCHED: 0
          ROWS_UPDATED: 1882292
       SELECT_COMMANDS: 0
       UPDATE_COMMANDS: 580431
        OTHER_COMMANDS: 338857
   COMMIT_TRANSACTIONS: 1016571
 ROLLBACK_TRANSACTIONS: 0
```

You can compare the BUSY_TIME to one-half of the CONNECTED_TIME (because there are two replication threads on the replica) to see how much of the time the replication thread was actively processing statements.[15] In our example, the replica is using around

---

15. If the replication threads are always running, you can just use the server's uptime instead of half the CONNECTED_TIME.

3% of its capacity. This doesn't mean it won't have occasional spikes of lag—if the master executes a change that takes 10 minutes to complete, it's likely that the replica will lag by about the same amount of time while applying the change—but it's a good indication that the replica will be able to recover from any spikes it experiences.

Plan to Underutilize

Intentionally underutilizing your servers can be a smart and cost-effective way to build a large application, especially when you use replication. Servers that have spare capacity can tolerate surges better, have more power to handle slow queries and maintenance jobs (such as OPTIMIZE TABLE operations), and will be better able to keep up in replication.

Trying to reduce the replication penalty a little by writing to both nodes in a master-master topology is typically a false economy. You should usually load the master-master pair less than 50% with reads, because if you add more load, there won't be enough capacity if one of the servers fails. If both servers can handle the load by themselves, you probably won't need to worry much about the single-threaded replication penalty.

Building in excess capacity is also one of the best ways to achieve high availability, although there are other ways, such as running your application in "degraded" mode when there's a failure. Chapter 12 covers this in more detail.

Replication Administration and Maintenance

Setting up replication probably isn't something you'll do constantly, unless you have many servers. But once it's in place, monitoring and administering your replication topology will be a regular job, no matter how many servers you have.

You should try to automate this work as much as possible. You might not need to write your own tools for this purpose, though: in Chapter 16, we discuss several productivity tools for MySQL, many of which have built-in replication monitoring capabilities or plugins.

Monitoring Replication

Replication increases the complexity of MySQL monitoring. Although replication actually happens on both the master and the replica, most of the work is done on the replica, and that is where the most common problems occur. Are all the replicas working? Has any replica had errors? How far behind is the slowest replica? MySQL provides most of the information you need to answer these questions, but automating the monitoring process and making replication robust is left up to you.

On the master, you can use the SHOW MASTER STATUS command to see the master's current binary log position and configuration (see the section "Configuring the Master and Replica" on page 452). You can also ask the master which binary logs exist on disk:

```
mysql> SHOW MASTER LOGS;
+------------------+-----------+
| Log_name         | File_size |
+------------------+-----------+
| mysql-bin.000220 |    425605 |
| mysql-bin.000221 |   1134128 |
| mysql-bin.000222 |     13653 |
| mysql-bin.000223 |     13634 |
+------------------+-----------+
```

This information is useful in determining what parameters to give the PURGE MASTER LOGS command. You can also view replication events in the binary log with the SHOW BINLOG EVENTS command. For example, after running the previous command, we created a table on an otherwise unused server. Because we knew this was the only statement that changed any data, we knew the statement's offset in the binary log was 13634, so we were able to view it as follows:

```
mysql> SHOW BINLOG EVENTS IN 'mysql-bin.000223' FROM 13634\G
*************************** 1. row ***************************
   Log_name: mysql-bin.000223
        Pos: 13634
 Event_type: Query
  Server_id: 1
End_log_pos: 13723
       Info: use `test`; CREATE TABLE test.t(a int)
```

Measuring Replication Lag

One of the most common things you'll need to monitor is how far behind the master a replica is running. Although the Seconds_behind_master column in SHOW SLAVE STATUS theoretically shows the replica's lag, in fact it's not always accurate, for a variety of reasons:

- The replica calculates Seconds_behind_master by comparing the server's current timestamp to the timestamp recorded in the binary log event, so the replica can't even report its lag unless it is processing a query.
- The replica will usually report NULL if the replication processes aren't running.
- Some errors (for example, mismatched max_allowed_packet settings between the master and replica, or an unstable network) can break replication and/or stop the replication threads, but Seconds_behind_master will report 0 rather than indicating an error.
- The replica sometimes can't calculate the lag even if the replication processes *are* running. If this happens, the replica might report either 0 or NULL.

- A very long transaction can cause the reported lag to fluctuate. For example, if you have a transaction that updates data, stays open for an hour, and then commits, the update will go into the binary log an hour after it actually happened. When the replica processes the statement, it will temporarily report that it is an hour behind the master, and then it will jump back to zero seconds behind.

- If a distribution master is falling behind and has replicas of its own that are caught up with it, the replicas will report that they are zero seconds behind, even if there is lag relative to the ultimate master.

The solution to these problems is to ignore Seconds_behind_master and monitor replica lag with something you can observe and measure directly. The best solution is a *heartbeat record*, which is a timestamp that you update once per second on the master. To calculate the lag, you can simply subtract the heartbeat from the current timestamp on the replica. This method is immune to all the problems we just mentioned, and it has the added benefit of creating a handy timestamp that shows to what point in time the replica's data is current. The *pt-heartbeat* script, included in Percona Toolkit, is the most popular implementation of a replication heartbeat.

A heartbeat has other benefits, too. The replication heartbeat records in the binary log are useful for many purposes, such as disaster recovery in otherwise hard-to-solve scenarios.

None of the lag metrics we just mentioned gives a sense of how long it will take for a replica to actually catch up to the master. This depends upon many factors, such as how powerful the replica is and how many write queries the master continues to process. See the section "When Will Replicas Begin to Lag?" on page 484 for more on that topic.

Determining Whether Replicas Are Consistent with the Master

In a perfect world, a replica would always be an exact copy of its master. But in the real world, errors in replication can cause the replica's data to "drift" out of sync with the master's. Even if there are apparently no errors, replicas can still get out of sync because of MySQL features that don't replicate correctly, bugs in MySQL, network corruption, crashes, ungraceful shutdowns, or other failures.[16]

Our experience is that this is the rule, not the exception, which means checking your replicas for consistency with their masters should probably be a routine task. This is especially important if you use replication for backups, because you don't want to take backups from a corrupted replica.

MySQL has no built-in method of determining whether one server has the same data as another server. It does provide some building blocks for checksumming tables and

---

16. If you're using a nontransactional storage engine, shutting down the server without first running STOP SLAVE is ungraceful.

data, such as CHECKSUM TABLE. However, it's nontrivial to compare a replica to its master while replication is working.

Percona Toolkit has a tool called *pt-table-checksum* that solves this and several other problems. The tool's main feature is that it can verify that a replica's data is in sync with its master's data. It works by running INSERT ... SELECT queries on the master.

These queries checksum the data and insert the results into a table. The statements flow through replication and execute again on the replica. You can then compare the results on the master to the results on the replica and see whether the data differs. Because this process works through replication, it gives consistent results without the need to lock tables on both servers simultaneously.

A typical way to use the tool is to run it on the master, with parameters similar to the following:

```
$ pt-table-checksum --replicate=test.checksum <master_host>
```

This command checksums all tables and inserts the results into the test.checksum table. After the queries have executed on the replicas, a simple query can check each replica for differences from the master. *pt-table-checksum* can discover the server's replicas, run the query on each replica, and output the results automatically. At the time of this writing, *pt-table-checksum* is the only tool that can reliably compare a replica's data to its master's.

Resyncing a Replica from the Master

You'll probably have to deal with an out-of-sync replica more than once in your career. Perhaps you used the checksum technique and found differences; perhaps you know that the replica skipped a query or that someone changed the data on the replica.

The traditional advice for fixing an out-of-sync replica is to stop it and reclone it from the master. If an inconsistent replica is a critical problem, you should probably stop it and remove it from production as soon as you find it. You can then reclone the replica or restore it from a backup.

The drawback to this approach is the inconvenience factor, especially if you have a lot of data. If you can find out which data is different, you can probably do it more efficiently than by recloning the entire server. And if the inconsistency you discovered isn't critical, you might be able to leave the replica online and resync only the affected data.

The simplest fix is to dump and reload only the affected data with *mysqldump*. This can work very well if your data isn't changing while you do it. You can simply lock the table on the master, dump the table, wait for the replica to catch up to the master, and then import the table on the replica. (You need to wait for the replica to catch up so you don't introduce more inconsistencies in other tables, such as those that might be updated in joins against the out-of-sync table.)

Although this works acceptably for many scenarios, it's often impossible to do on a busy server. It also has the disadvantage of changing the replica's data outside of replication. Changing a replica's data through replication (by making changes on the master) is usually the safest technique, because it avoids nasty race conditions and other surprises. If the table is very large or network bandwidth is limited, dumping and reloading is also prohibitively expensive. What if only every thousandth row in a million-row table is different? Dumping and reloading the whole table is wasteful in this case.

pt-table-sync is another tool from Percona Toolkit that solves some of these problems. It can find and resolve differences between tables efficiently. It can also operate through replication, resynchronizing the replica by executing queries on the master, so there are no race conditions. It integrates with the checksum table created by *pt-table-check-sum*, so it can operate only on chunks of tables that are known to differ. It doesn't work in all scenarios, though: it requires that replication is running in order to sync a master and replica correctly, so it won't work when there's a replication error. *pt-table-sync* is designed to be efficient, but it still might be impractical for extremely large data sizes. Comparing a terabyte of data on the master and the replica inevitably causes extra work for both servers. Still, for those cases where it works, it can save you a great deal of time and effort.

Changing Masters

Sooner or later, you'll need to point a replica at a new master. Maybe you're rotating servers for an upgrade, maybe there was a failure and you need to promote a replica to be the master, or maybe you're just reallocating capacity. Regardless of the reason, you have to inform the replica about its new master.

When the process is planned, it's easy (or at least easier than it is in a crisis). You simply need to issue the CHANGE MASTER TO command on the replica, using the appropriate values. Most of the values are optional; you can specify just the ones you're changing. The replica will discard its current configuration and relay logs and begin replicating from the new master. It will also update the *master.info* file with the new parameters, so the change will persist across a replica restart.

The hardest part of this process is figuring out the desired position on the new master, so the replica begins at the same logical position at which it stopped on the old master.

Promoting a replica to a master is a little harder. There are two basic scenarios for replacing a master with one of its replicas. The first is when it's a planned promotion; the second is when it's unplanned.

Planned promotions

Promoting a replica to a master is conceptually simple. Briefly, here are the steps involved:

1. Stop writes to the old master.
2. Optionally let its replicas catch up in replication (this makes the subsequent steps simpler).
3. Configure a replica to be the new master.
4. Point replicas and write traffic to the new master, then enable writes on it.

The devil is in the details, however. Several scenarios are possible, depending on your replication topology. For example, the steps are slightly different in a master-master topology than in a master-replica setup.

In more depth, here are the steps you'll probably need to take for most setups:

1. Stop all writes on the current master. If possible, you might even want to force all client programs (not replication connections) to quit. It helps if you've built your client programs with a "do not run" flag you can set. If you use virtual IP addresses, you can simply shut off the virtual IP and then kill all client connections to close their open transactions.
2. Optionally stop all write activity on the master with FLUSH TABLES WITH READ LOCK. You can also set the master to be read-only with the read_only option. From this point on, you should forbid any writes to the soon-to-be-replaced master, because once it's no longer a master, writing to it means losing data! Note, however, that setting read_only doesn't prevent existing transactions from committing. For a stronger guarantee, kill all open transactions; this will really stop all writes.
3. Choose one of the replicas to be the new master, and ensure it is completely caught up in replication (i.e., let it finish executing all the relay logs it has fetched from the old master).
4. Optionally verify that the new master contains the same data as the old master.
5. Execute STOP SLAVE on the new master.
6. Execute CHANGE MASTER TO MASTER_HOST='' followed by RESET SLAVE on the new master, to make it disconnect from the old master and discard the connection information in its *master.info* file. (This will not work correctly if connection information is specified in *my.cnf*, which is one reason we recommend you don't put it there.)
7. Note the new master's binary log coordinates with SHOW MASTER STATUS.
8. Make sure all other replicas are caught up.
9. Shut down the old master.
10. In MySQL 5.1 and newer, activate events on the new master if necessary.
11. Let clients connect to the new master.

---

12. Issue a `CHANGE MASTER TO` command on each replica, pointing it to the new master. Use the binary log coordinates you gathered from `SHOW MASTER STATUS`.

> When you promote a replica to a master, be sure to remove from it any replica-specific databases, tables, and privileges. You also need to change any replica-specific configuration parameters, such as a relaxed `innodb_flush_log_at_trx_commit` option. Likewise, if you demote a master to a replica, be sure to reconfigure it as needed.
>
> If you configure your masters and replicas identically, you won't need to change anything.

Unplanned promotions

If the master crashes and you have to promote a replica to replace it, the process might not be as easy. If there's only one replica, you just use the replica. But if there's more than one, you'll have to do a few extra steps to promote a replica to be the new master.

There's also the added problem of potentially lost replication events. It's possible that some updates that have happened on the master will not yet have been replicated to any of its replicas. It's even possible that a statement was executed and then rolled back on the master, but not rolled back on the replica—so the replica could actually be *ahead* of the master's logical replication position.[17] If you can recover the master's data at some point, you might be able to retrieve the lost statements and apply them manually.

In all of the following steps, be sure to use the `Master_Log_File` and `Read_Master_Log_Pos` values in your calculations. Here is the procedure to promote a replica in a master-and-replicas topology:

1. Determine which replica has the most up-to-date data. Check the output of `SHOW SLAVE STATUS` on each replica and choose the one whose `Master_Log_File`/`Read_Master_Log_Pos` coordinates are newest.

2. Let all replicas finish executing the relay logs they fetched from the old master before it crashed. If you change a replica's master before it's done executing the relay log, it will throw away the remaining log events and you won't know where it stopped.

3. Perform steps 5–7 from the list in the preceding section.

4. Compare every replica's `Master_Log_File`/`Read_Master_Log_Pos` coordinates to those of the new master.

5. Perform steps 10–12 from the list in the preceding section.

---

17. This really is possible, even though MySQL doesn't log any events until the transaction commits. See "Mixing Transactional and Nontransactional Tables" on page 498 for the details. Another scenario where this can happen is when the master crashes and recovers, but it didn't have `innodb_flush_log_at_trx_commit` set to 1, so it loses some changes.

We're assuming you have `log_bin` and `log_slave_updates` enabled on all your replicas, as we advised you to do in the beginning of this chapter. Enabling this logging lets you recover all replicas to a consistent point in time, which you can't reliably do otherwise.

Locating the desired log positions

If any replica isn't at the same position as the new master, you'll have to find the position in the new master's binary logs corresponding to the last event that replica executed, and use it for `CHANGE MASTER TO`. You can use the *mysqlbinlog* tool to examine the last query the replica executed and find that same query in the new master's binary log. A little math can often help, too.

To illustrate this, let's assume that log events have increasing ID numbers and that the most up-to-date replica—the new master—had just retrieved event 100 when the old master crashed. Now let's assume that there are two more replicas, `replica2` and `replica3`; `replica2` had retrieved event 99, and `replica3` had retrieved event 98. If you point both replicas at the new master's current binary log position, they will begin replicating event 101, so they'll be out of sync. However, as long as the new master's binary log was enabled with `log_slave_updates`, you can find events 99 and 100 in the new master's binary log, so you can bring the replicas back to a consistent state.

Because of server restarts, different configurations, log rotations, or `FLUSH LOGS` commands, the same events can exist at different byte offsets in different servers. Finding the events can be slow and tedious, but it's usually not hard. Just examine the last event executed on each replica by running *mysqlbinlog* on the replica's binary log or relay log. Then find the same query in the new master's binary log, also with *mysqlbinlog*; it will print the byte offset of the query, and you can use this offset in the `CHANGE MASTER TO` query.[18]

You can make the process faster by subtracting the byte offsets at which the new master and the replica stopped, which tells you the difference in their byte positions. If you then subtract this value from the new master's current binary log position, chances are the desired query will be at that position. You just need to verify that it is, and you've found the position at which you need to start the replica.

Let's look at a concrete example. Suppose `server1` is the master of `server2` and `server3`, and it crashes. According to `Master_Log_File`/`Read_Master_Log_Pos` in `SHOW SLAVE STATUS`, `server2` has managed to replicate all the events that were in `server1`'s binary log, but `server3` isn't as up-to-date. Figure 10-15 illustrates this scenario (the log events and byte offsets are for demonstration purposes only).

As Figure 10-15 illustrates, we can be sure that `server2` has replicated all the events in the master's binary log because its `Master_Log_File` and `Read_Master_Log_Pos` match

---

18. As mentioned earlier, heartbeat records from *pt-heartbeat* can be a great help in figuring out approximately where in a binary log you should be looking for your event.

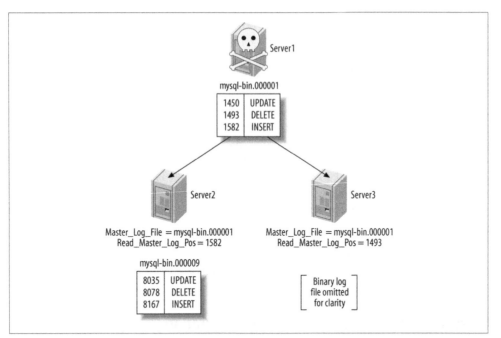

Figure 10-15. When server1 crashed, server2 was caught up, but server3 was behind in replication

the last positions on server1. Therefore, we can promote server2 to be the new master and make server3 a replica of it.

But what parameters should we use in the CHANGE MASTER TO command on server3? This is where we need to do a little math and investigation. server3 stopped at offset 1493, which is 89 bytes behind offset 1582, the last command server2 executed. server2 is currently writing to position 8167 in its binary log. 8167 − 89 = 8078, so in theory we need to point server3 at that offset in server2's logs. It's a good idea to investigate the log events around this position and verify that server2 really has the right events at that offset in its logs, though. It might have something else there because of a data update that happened only on server2, for example.

Assuming that the events are the same upon inspection, the following command will switch server3 to be a replica of server2:

```
server2> CHANGE MASTER TO MASTER_HOST="server2", MASTER_LOG_FILE="mysql-bin.000009",
         MASTER_LOG_POS=8078;
```

What if server1 had actually finished executing and logging one more event, beyond offset 1582, when it crashed? Because server2 had read and executed only up to offset 1582, you might have lost one event forever. However, if the old master's disk isn't damaged, you can still recover the missing event from its binary log with *mysqlbinlog* or with a log server.

If you need to recover missing events from the old master, we recommend that you do so *after* you promote the new master, but *before* you let clients connect to it. This way, you won't have to execute the missing events on every replica; replication will take care of that for you. If the failed master is totally unavailable, however, you might have to wait and do this work later.

A variation on this procedure is to use a reliable way to store the master's binary log files, such as a SAN or a distributed replicated block device (DRBD). Even if the master has a complete failure, you'll still have its binary log files. You can set up a log server, point the replicas to it, and then let them all catch up to the point at which the master failed. This makes it trivial to promote one of the replicas to be a new master—it's essentially the same process we showed for a planned promotion. We discuss these storage options further in the next chapter.

 When you promote a replica to master, don't change its server ID to match the old master's. If you do, you won't be able to use a log server to replay events from the old master. This is one of many reasons it's a good idea to treat server IDs as fixed.

Switching Roles in a Master-Master Configuration

One of the advantages of master-master replication is that you can switch the active and passive roles easily, because of the symmetrical configuration. In this section, we show you how to accomplish the switch.

When switching the roles in a master-master configuration, the most important thing is to ensure that only one of the co-masters is written to at any time. If writes from one master are interleaved with writes from the other, the writes can conflict. In other words, the passive server must not receive any binary log events from the active server after the roles are switched. You can guarantee this doesn't happen by ensuring that the passive server's replication SQL thread is caught up to the active server before you make it writable.

The following steps switch the roles without danger of conflicting updates:

1. Stop all writes on the active server.
2. Execute SET GLOBAL read_only = 1 on the active server, and set the read_only option in its configuration file for safety in case of a restart. Remember, this won't stop users with the SUPER privilege from making changes. If you want to prevent changes from all users, use FLUSH TABLES WITH READ LOCK. If you don't do this, you must kill all client connections to make sure there are no long-running statements or uncommitted transactions.
3. Execute SHOW MASTER STATUS on the active server and note the binary log coordinates.

4. Execute `SELECT MASTER_POS_WAIT()` on the passive server with the active server's binary log coordinates. This command will block until the replication processes catch up to the active server.

5. Execute `SET GLOBAL read_only = 0` on the passive server, thus making it the active server.

6. Reconfigure your applications to write to the newly active server.

Depending on your application's configuration, you might need to do other tasks as well, including changing the IP addresses on the two servers. We discuss this in the following chapters.

Replication Problems and Solutions

Breaking MySQL's replication isn't hard. The simple implementation that makes it easy to set up also means there are many ways to stop, confuse, and otherwise disrupt it. This section shows common problems, how they manifest themselves, and how you can solve or even prevent them.

Errors Caused by Data Corruption or Loss

For a variety of reasons, MySQL replication is not very resilient to crashes, power outages, and corruption caused by disk, memory, or network errors. You'll almost certainly have to restart replication at some point due to one of these problems.

Most of the problems you'll have with replication after an unexpected shutdown stem from one of the servers not flushing something to disk. Here are the issues you might encounter in the event of an unexpected shutdown:

Unexpected master shutdown
> If the master isn't configured with `sync_binlog`, it might not have flushed its last several binary log events to disk before crashing. The replication I/O thread may, therefore, have been in the middle of reading from an event that never made it to disk. When the master restarts, the replica will reconnect and try to read that event again, but the master will respond by telling it that there's no such binlog offset. The binlog dump process is typically almost instantaneous, so this is not uncommon.
>
> The solution to this problem is to instruct the replica to begin reading from the beginning of the next binary log. However, some log events will have been lost permanently, so you will need to use Percona Toolkit's *pt-table-checksum* tool to check the server for inconsistencies so you can fix them. This loss of data could have been prevented by configuring the master with `sync_binlog`.
>
> Even if you've configured `sync_binlog`, MyISAM data can still get corrupted when there's a crash, and InnoDB transactions can be lost (but data won't be corrupted) if `innodb_flush_logs_at_trx_commit` is not set to 1.

Unexpected replica shutdown

When the replica restarts after an unplanned shutdown, it reads its *master.info* file to determine where it stopped replicating. Unfortunately, this file is not synchronized to disk, so the information it contains is likely to be wrong. The replica will probably try to reexecute a few binary log events, which could cause some unique index violations. Unless you can determine where the replica really stopped, which is unlikely, you'll have no choice but to skip the errors that result. The *pt-slave-restart* tool, part of Percona Toolkit, can help you with this.

If you use all InnoDB tables, you can look at the MySQL error log after restarting the replica. The InnoDB recovery process prints the binary log coordinates up to the point where it recovered, and you can use them to determine where to point the replica on the master. Percona Server offers a feature to automatically extract this information during the recovery process and update the *master.info* file for you, essentially making the replication coordinates transactional on the replica. MySQL 5.5 also offers options to control how the *master.info* and other files are synced to disk, helping reduce these problems.

In addition to data losses resulting from MySQL being shut down uncleanly, it's not uncommon for binary logs or relay logs to be corrupted on disk. The following are some of the more common scenarios:

Binary logs corrupted on the master

If the binary log is corrupted on the master, you'll have no choice but to try to skip the corrupted portion. You can run `FLUSH LOGS` on the master so it starts a new log file and point the replica at the beginning of the new log, or you can try to find the end of the bad region. Sometimes you can use `SET GLOBAL SQL_SLAVE_SKIP_COUNTER = 1` to skip a single corrupt event. If there is more than one corrupt event, just repeat the process until they've all been skipped. If there's a lot of corruption, though, you might not be able to do that; corrupt event headers can prevent the server from being able to find the next event. In that case you might have to do some manual work to find the next good event.

Relay logs corrupted on the replica

If the master's binary logs are intact, you can use `CHANGE MASTER TO` to discard and refetch the corrupt relay logs. Just point the replica at the same position from which it's currently replicating (`Relay_Master_Log_File/Exec_Master_Log_Pos`). This will cause it to throw away any relay logs on disk. MySQL 5.5 has some improvements in this regard: it can refetch relay logs automatically after a crash.

Binary log out of sync with the InnoDB transaction log

If the master crashes, InnoDB might record a transaction as committed even if it didn't get written to the binary log on disk. There's no way to recover the missing transaction, unless it's in a replica's relay log. You can prevent this with the `sync_binlog` parameter in MySQL 5.0, or the `sync_binlog` and `safe_binlog` parameters in MySQL 4.1.

When a binary log is corrupt, how much data you can recover depends on the type of corruption. There are several common types:

Bytes changed, but the event is still valid SQL
> Unfortunately, MySQL cannot even detect this type of corruption. This is why it can be a good idea to routinely check that your replicas have the right data. This might be fixed in a future version of MySQL.

Bytes changed and the event is invalid SQL
> You might be able to extract the event with *mysqlbinlog* and see garbled data, such as the following:

```
UPDATE tbl SET col?????????????????
```

> Try to find the beginning of the next event, which you can do by adding the offset and length, and print it. You might be able to skip just this event.

Bytes omitted and/or the event's length is wrong
> In this case, *mysqlbinlog* will sometimes exit with an error or crash because it can't read the event and can't find the beginning of the next event.

Several events corrupted or were overwritten, or offsets have shifted and the next event starts at the wrong offset
> Again, *mysqlbinlog* will not be much use.

When the corruption is bad enough that *mysqlbinlog* can't read the log events, you'll have to resort to some hex editing or other tedious techniques to find the boundaries between log events. This usually isn't hard to do, because recognizable markers separate the events.

Here's an example. First, let's look at log event offsets for a sample log, as reported by *mysqlbinlog*:

```
$ mysqlbinlog mysql-bin.000113 | egrep '^# at '
# at 4
# at 98
# at 185
# at 277
# at 369
# at 447
```

A simple way to find offsets in the log is to compare the offsets to the output of the following *strings* command:

```
$ strings -n 2 -t d mysql-bin.000113
      1 binpC'G
     25 5.0.38-Ubuntu_0ubuntu1.1-log
     99 C'G
    146 std
    156 test
    161 create table test(a int)
    186 C'G
    233 std
    243 test
```

```
248 insert into test(a) values(1)
278 C'G
325 std
335 test
340 insert into test(a) values(2)
370 C'G
417 std
427 test
432 drop table test
448 D'G
474 mysql-bin.000114
```

There's a pretty recognizable pattern that should allow you to locate the beginnings of events. Notice that the strings that end with 'G are located one byte after the beginning of the log event. They are part of the fixed-length log event header.

The exact value will vary from server to server, so your results will vary depending on the server whose log you're examining. With a little sleuthing, though, you should be able to find the pattern in your binary log and determine the next intact log event's offset. You can then try to skip past the bad event(s) with the *--start-position* argument to *mysqlbinlog*, or use the MASTER_LOG_POS parameter to CHANGE MASTER TO.

Using Nontransactional Tables

If all goes well, statement-based replication usually works fine with nontransactional tables. However, if there's an error in an update to a nontransactional table, such as the statement being killed before it is complete, the master and replica will end up with different data.

For example, suppose you're updating a MyISAM table with 100 rows. If the statement updates 50 of the rows and then someone kills it, what happens? Half of the rows will have been changed, but not the other half. Replication is bound to get out of sync as a result, because the statement will replay on the replica and change all 100 rows. (MySQL will then notice that the statement caused an error on the master but not the replica, and replication will stop with an error.)

If you're using MyISAM tables, be sure to run STOP SLAVE before stopping the MySQL server, or the shutdown will kill any running queries (including any incomplete update statements). Transactional storage engines don't have this problem. If you're using transactional tables, the failed update will be rolled back on the master and not logged to the binary log.

Mixing Transactional and Nontransactional Tables

When you use a transactional storage engine, MySQL doesn't log the statements you execute to the binary log until the transactions commit. Thus, if a transaction is rolled back, MySQL won't log the statements, so they won't get replayed on the replica.

However, if you mix transactional and nontransactional tables and there's a rollback, MySQL will be able to roll back the changes to the transactional tables, but the non-transactional ones will be changed permanently. As long as there are no errors, such as an update being killed partway through execution, this is not a problem: instead of just not logging the statements, MySQL logs the statements and then logs a ROLLBACK statement to the binary log. The result is that the same statements execute on the replica, and all is well. It's a little less efficient, because the replica must do some work and then throw it away, but the replica will theoretically still be in sync with the master.

So far, so good. The problem is when the replica has a deadlock that didn't happen on the master. The tables that use a transactional storage engine will roll back on the replica, but the replica won't be able to roll back the nontransactional tables. As a result, the replica's data will be different from the master's.

The only way to prevent this problem is to avoid mixing transactional and nontransactional tables. If you do encounter the problem, the only way to fix it is to skip the error on the replica and resync the involved tables.

Row-based replication does not suffer from this problem. Row-based replication logs changes to rows, not SQL statements. If a statement changes some rows in a MyISAM table and an InnoDB table and then deadlocks on the master and rolls back the InnoDB table, the changes to the MyISAM table will still be logged to the binary log and replayed on the replica.

Nondeterministic Statements

Any statement that changes data in a nondeterministic way can cause a replica's data to become different from its master's when using statement-based replication. For example, an UPDATE with a LIMIT relies on the order in which the statement finds rows in the table. Unless the order is guaranteed to be the same on the master and the replica—for example, if the rows are ordered by primary key—the statement might change different rows on the two servers. Such problems can be subtle and difficult to notice, so some people make a policy of never using LIMIT with any statement that changes data. Another surprising source of nondeterministic behavior is a REPLACE or INSERT IGNORE on a table with more than one unique index—the server might choose a different "winner" on the master than on the replica.

Watch out for statements that involve INFORMATION_SCHEMA tables, too. These can easily differ between the master and the replica, so the results might vary as well. Finally, be aware that most server variables, such as @@server_id and @@hostname, will not replicate correctly before MySQL 5.1.

Row-based replication does not have these limitations.

Different Storage Engines on the Master and Replica

It's often handy to have different storage engines on a replica, as we've mentioned throughout this chapter. However, in some circumstances, statement-based replication might produce different results on a replica with different storage engines than the master. For example, nondeterministic statements (such as the ones mentioned in the previous section) are more likely to cause problems if the storage engines on the master and the replica differ.

If you find that your replica's data is falling out of sync with the master in specific tables, you should examine the storage engines used on both servers, as well as the queries that update those tables.

Data Changes on the Replica

Statement-based replication relies upon the replica having the same data as the master, so you should not make or allow any changes on the replica (using the read_only configuration variable accomplishes this nicely). Consider the following statement:

```
mysql> INSERT INTO table1 SELECT * FROM table2;
```

If table2 contains different data on the replica, table1 will end up with different data, too. In other words, data differences tend to propagate from table to table. This happens with all types of queries, not just INSERT ... SELECT queries. There are two possible outcomes: you'll get an error such as a duplicate index violation on the replica, or you won't get any error at all. Getting an error is a blessing, because at least it alerts you that your data isn't the same on the replica. Invisibly different data can silently wreak all kinds of havoc.

The only solution to this problem is to resync the data from the master.

Nonunique Server IDs

This is one of the more elusive problems you might encounter with replication. If you accidentally configure two replicas with the same server ID, they might seem to work just fine if you're not watching closely. But if you watch their error logs, or watch the master with *innotop*, you'll notice something very odd.

On the master, you'll see only one of the two replicas connected at any time. (Usually, all replicas are connected and replicating all the time.) On the replica, you'll see frequent disconnect and reconnect error messages in the error log, but no mention of a misconfigured server ID.

Depending on the MySQL version, the replicas might replicate correctly but slowly, or they might not actually replicate correctly—any given replica might miss binary log events, or even repeat them, causing duplicate key errors (or silent data corruption). You can also cause problems on the master because of the increased load from the replicas fighting amongst themselves. And if replicas are fighting each other badly enough, the error logs can grow enormous in a very short time.

The only solution to this problem is to be careful when setting up your replicas. You might find it helpful to create a master list of replica-to–server ID mappings so that you don't lose track of which ID belongs to each replica.[19] If your replicas live entirely within one network subnet, you can choose unique IDs by using the last octet of each machine's IP address.

Undefined Server IDs

If you don't define the server ID in the *my.cnf* file, MySQL will appear to set up replication with CHANGE MASTER TO but will not let you start the replica:

```
mysql> START SLAVE;
ERROR 1200 (HY000): The server is not configured as slave; fix in config file or with
CHANGE MASTER TO
```

This error is especially confusing if you've just used CHANGE MASTER TO and verified your settings with SHOW SLAVE STATUS. You might get a value from SELECT @@server_id, but it's just a default. You have to set the value explicitly.

Dependencies on Nonreplicated Data

If you have databases or tables on the master that don't exist on the replica, or vice versa, it's quite easy to accidentally break replication. Suppose there's a scratch database on the master that doesn't exist on the replica. If any data updates on the master refer to a table in this database, replication will break when the replica tries to replay the updates. Similarly, if you create a table on the master and it already exists on the replica, replication will break.

There's no way around this problem. The only way to prevent it is to avoid creating tables on the master that don't exist on the replica.

How does such a table get created? There are many possible ways, and some are harder to prevent than others. For example, suppose you originally created a scratch database on the replica that didn't exist on the master, and then you switched the master and replica for some reason. When you did this, you might have forgotten to remove the scratch database and its privileges. Now someone might connect to the new master and run a query in that database, or a periodic job might discover the tables and run OPTIMIZE TABLE on each of them.

This is one of the things to keep in mind when promoting a replica to master, or when deciding how to configure replicas. Anything that makes replicas different from masters, or vice versa, is a potential future problem.

---

19. Perhaps you'd like to store it in a database table? We're only half joking... you can add a unique index on the ID column.

Missing Temporary Tables

Temporary tables are handy for some uses, but unfortunately they're incompatible with statement-based replication. If a replica crashes, or if you shut it down, any temporary tables the replica thread was using disappear. When you restart the replica, any further statements that refer to the missing temporary tables will fail.

There's no safe way to use temporary tables on the master with statement-based replication. Many people love temporary tables dearly, so it can be hard to convince them of this, but it's true.[20] No matter how briefly they exist, temporary tables make it difficult to stop and start replicas and to recover from crashes. This is true even if you use them only within a single transaction. (It's slightly less problematic to use temporary tables on a replica, where they can be convenient, but if the replica is itself a master, the problem still exists.)

If replication stops because the replica can't find a temporary table after a restart, there are really only a couple of things to do: you can skip the errors that occur, or you can manually create a table that has the same name and structure as the now-vanished temporary table. Either way, your data will likely become different on the replica if any write queries refer to the temporary table.

It's not as hard as it seems to eliminate temporary tables. The two most useful properties of temporary tables are as follows:

- They're visible only to the connection that created them, so they don't conflict with other connections' temporary tables of the same names.
- They go away when the connection closes, so you don't have to remove them explicitly.

You can emulate these properties easily by reserving a database exclusively for pseudotemporary tables, where you'll create permanent tables instead. You just have to choose unique names for them. Fortunately, that's pretty easy to do: simply append the connection ID to the table name. For example, where you used to execute CREATE TEMPORARY TABLE top_users(...), now you can execute CREATE TABLE temp .top_users_1234(...), where 1234 is the value returned by CONNECTION_ID(). After your application is done with the pseudotemporary table, you can either drop it or let a cleanup process remove it instead. Having the connection ID in the table name makes it easy to determine which tables are not in use anymore—you can get a list of active connections from SHOW PROCESSLIST and compare it to the connection IDs in the table names.[21]

---

20. We've had people stubbornly try all sorts of ways to work around this, but there is no way to make temporary tables safe for statement-based replication. Period. No matter what you're thinking of, we've proven it won't work.

21. *pt-find*—yet another tool in the Percona Toolkit—can remove pseudotemporary tables easily with the *--connection-id* and *--server-id* options.

Using real tables instead of temporary tables has other benefits, too. For example, it makes it easier to debug your applications, because you can see the data the applications are manipulating from another connection. If you used a temporary table, you wouldn't be able to do that as easily.

Real tables do have some overhead temporary tables don't, however: it's slower to create them because the *.frm* files associated with these tables must be synced to disk. You can disable the sync_frm option to speed this up, but it's more dangerous.

If you do use temporary tables, you should ensure that the Slave_open_temp_tables status variable is 0 before shutting down a replica. If it's not 0, you're likely to have problems restarting the replica. The proper procedure is to run STOP SLAVE, examine the variable, and only then shut down the replica. If you examine the variable before stopping the replica processes, you're risking a race condition.

Not Replicating All Updates

If you misuse SET SQL_LOG_BIN=0 or don't understand the replication filtering rules, your replica might not execute some updates that have taken place on the master. Sometimes you want this for archiving purposes, but it's usually accidental and has bad consequences.

For example, suppose you have a replicate_do_db rule to replicate only the sakila database to one of your replicas. If you execute the following commands on the master, the replica's data will become different from the data on the master:

```
mysql> USE test;
mysql> UPDATE sakila.actor ...
```

Other types of statements can even cause replication to fail with an error because of nonreplicated dependencies.

Lock Contention Caused by InnoDB Locking Selects

InnoDB's SELECT statements are normally nonlocking, but in certain cases they do acquire locks. In particular, INSERT ... SELECT locks all the rows it reads from the source table by default when using statement-based replication. MySQL needs the locks to ensure that the statement produces the same result on the replica when it executes there. In effect, the locks serialize the statement on the master, which matches how the replica will execute it.

You might encounter lock contention, blocking, and lock wait timeouts because of this design. One way to alleviate the problems is not to hold a transaction open longer than needed, so the locks cause less blocking. You can release the locks by committing the transaction as soon as possible on the master.

It can also help to keep your statements short, by breaking up large statements into several smaller ones. This is a very effective way to reduce lock contention, and even when it's hard to do, it's often worth it. (It's quite simple with the *pt-archiver* tool in Percona Toolkit.)

Another workaround is to replace `INSERT ... SELECT` statements with a combination of `SELECT INTO OUTFILE` followed by `LOAD DATA INFILE` on the master. This is fast and doesn't require locking. It is admittedly a hack, but it's sometimes useful anyway. The biggest issues are choosing a unique name for the output file, which must not already exist, and cleaning up the output file when you're done with it. You can use the `CONNECTION_ID()` technique we just discussed to ensure that the filename is unique, and you can use a periodic job (*crontab* on Unix, scheduled tasks on Windows) to purge unused output files after the connections that created them are finished with them.

You might be tempted to try to disable the locks instead of using these workarounds. There is a way to do so, but it's not a good idea for most scenarios, because it makes it possible for your replica to fall silently out of sync with the master. It also makes the binary log useless for recovering a server. If, however, you decide that the risks are worth the benefits, the configuration change that accomplishes this is as follows:

```
# THIS IS NOT SAFE!
innodb_locks_unsafe_for_binlog = 1
```

This allows a statement's results to depend on data it doesn't lock. If a second statement modifies that data and then commits before the first statement, the two statements might not produce the same results when you replay the binary log. This is true both for replication and for point-in-time recovery.

To see how locking reads prevent chaos, imagine you have two tables: one without rows, and one whose single row has the value 99. Two transactions update the data. Transaction 1 inserts the second table's contents into the first table, and transaction 2 updates the second (source) table, as depicted in Figure 10-16.

Step 2 in this sequence of events is very important. In it, transaction 2 tries to update the source table, which requires it to place an exclusive (write) lock on the rows it wants to update. An exclusive lock is incompatible with any other lock, including the shared lock transaction 1 has placed on that row, so transaction 2 is forced to wait until transaction 1 commits. The transactions are serialized in the binary log in the order they committed, so replaying these transactions in binary log (commit) order will give the same results.

On the other hand, if transaction 1 doesn't place a shared lock on the rows it reads for the `INSERT`, no such guarantee exists. Study Figure 10-17, which shows a possible sequence of events without the lock.

The absence of locks allows the transactions to be written to the binary log in an order that will produce different results when that log is replayed, as you can see in the illustration. MySQL logs transaction 2 first, so it will affect transaction 1's results on the replica. This didn't happen on the master. As a result, the replica will contain different data than the master.

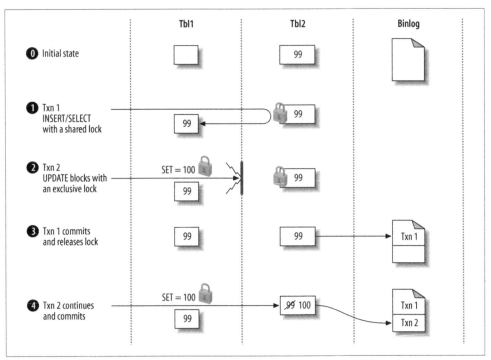

Figure 10-16. Two transactions update data, with shared locks to serialize the updates

We strongly suggest that you leave the `innodb_locks_unsafe_for_binlog` configuration variable set to 0 in most situations. Row-based replication avoids this whole scenario, of course, by logging actual data changes instead of statements.

Writing to Both Masters in Master-Master Replication

Writing to both masters is a terrible idea. If you're trying to make it safe to write to both masters at the same time, some of the problems have solutions, but not all. It takes an expert with a lot of battle scars to know the difference.

In MySQL 5.0, two server configuration variables help address the problem of conflicting AUTO_INCREMENT primary keys. The variables are `auto_increment_increment` and `auto_increment_offset`. You can use them to "stagger" the numbers the servers generate, so they interleave rather than collide.

However, this doesn't solve all the problems you'll have with two writable masters; it solves only the autoincrement problem, which probably accounts for just a small subset of the conflicting writes you're likely to have. In fact, it actually adds several new problems:

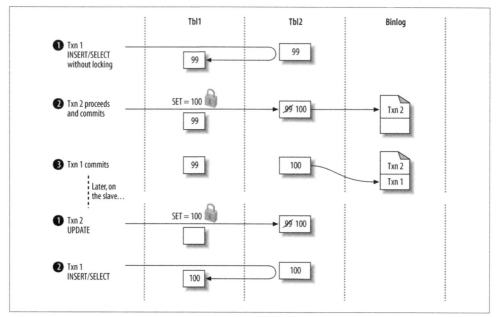

Figure 10-17. Two transactions update data, but without a shared lock to serialize the updates

- It makes it harder to move servers around in the replication topology.
- It wastes key space by potentially introducing gaps between numbers.
- It doesn't help unless all your tables have AUTO_INCREMENT primary keys, and it's not always a good idea to use AUTO_INCREMENT primary keys universally.

You can generate your own nonconflicting primary key values. One way is to create a multicolumn primary key and use the server ID for the first column. This works well, but it makes your primary keys larger, which has a compound effect on secondary keys in InnoDB.

You can also use a single-column primary key, and use the "high bits" of the integer to store the server ID. A simple left-shift (or multiplication) and addition can accomplish this. For example, if you're using the 8 most significant bits of an unsigned BIGINT (64-bit) column to hold the server ID, you can insert the value 11 on server 15 as follows:

```
mysql> INSERT INTO test(pk_col, ...) VALUES( (15 << 56) + 11, ...);
```

If you convert the result to base 2 and pad it out to 64 bits wide, the effect is easier to see:

```
mysql> SELECT LPAD(CONV(pk_col, 10, 2), 64, '0') FROM test;
+------------------------------------------------------------------+
| LPAD(CONV(pk_col, 10, 2), 64, '0')                               |
+------------------------------------------------------------------+
| 0000111100000000000000000000000000000000000000000000000000001011 |
+------------------------------------------------------------------+
```

The problem with this method is that you need an external way to generate key values, because `AUTO_INCREMENT` can't do it for you. Don't use `@@server_id` in place of the constant value `15` in the `INSERT`, because you'll get a different result on the replica.

You can also turn to pseudorandom values using a function such as `MD5()` or `UUID()`, but these can be bad for performance—they're big, and they're essentially random, which is bad for InnoDB in particular. (Don't use `UUID()` unless you generate the values in the application, because `UUID()` doesn't replicate correctly with statement-based replication.)

It's a hard problem to solve, and we usually recommend redesigning your application so that you have only one writable master instead. Who'd have guessed it?

Excessive Replication Lag

Replication lag is a frequent problem. No matter what, it's a good idea to design your applications to tolerate some lag on the replicas. If the system can't function with lagging replicas, replication might not be the correct architecture for your application. However, there are some steps you can take to help replicas keep up with the master.

The single-threaded nature of MySQL replication means it's relatively inefficient on the replica. Even a fast replica with lots of disks, CPUs, and memory can easily fall behind a master, because the replica's single thread usually uses only one CPU and disk efficiently. In fact, each replica typically needs to be at least as powerful as the master.

Locking on the replicas is also a problem. Other queries running on a replica might acquire locks that block the replication thread. Because replication is single-threaded, the replication thread won't be able to do other work while it waits.

Replication tends to fall behind in two ways: spikes of lag followed by catching up, or staying steadily behind. The former pattern is usually caused by single queries that run for a long time, but the latter can crop up even when there are no long queries.

Unfortunately, at present it's not as easy as we'd like to find out whether a replica is close to its capacity, as discussed earlier in this chapter. If your load were perfectly uniform at all times, your replicas would perform nearly as well at 99% capacity as at 10% capacity and when they reached 100% capacity they'd abruptly begin to fall behind. In reality, the load is unlikely to be steady, so when a replica is close to its write capacity you'll probably see increased replication lag during times of peak load.

Logging queries on a replica and using a log analysis tool to see what's really slow is one of the best things to do when replicas can't keep up. Don't rely on your instincts about what's slow, and don't base your opinion on how queries perform on the master, because replicas and masters have very different performance profiles. The best way to do this analysis is to enable the slow query log on a replica for a while, and then analyze it with *pt-query-digest* as discussed in Chapter 3. The standard MySQL slow query log can log queries the replication thread executes in MySQL 5.1 and newer, if you enable the `log_slow_slave_statements` option, so you can see which queries are slow when they're replicated. Percona Server and MariaDB let you enable and disable this without restarting the server.

There's not much you can tweak or tune on a replica that can't keep up, aside from buying faster disks and CPUs (solid-state drives can help tremendously; see Chapter 9 for details). Most of the options involve disabling some things that cause extra work on the replica to try to reduce its load. One easy change is to configure InnoDB to flush changes to disk less frequently, so transactions commit more quickly. You can accomplish this by setting `innodb_flush_log_at_trx_commit` to 2. You can also disable binary logging on the replica, set `innodb_locks_unsafe_for_binlog` to 1, and set `delay_key_write` to ALL for MyISAM. These settings trade safety for speed, though. If you promote a replica to be a master, make sure to reset these settings to safe values.

Don't duplicate the expensive part of writes

Rearchitecting your application and/or optimizing your queries is often the best way to help the replicas keep up. Try to minimize the amount of work that has to be duplicated through your system. Any write that's expensive on the master will be replayed on every replica. If you can move the work off the master onto a replica, only one of the replicas will have to do the work. You can then push the write results back up to the master, for example, with `LOAD DATA INFILE`.

Here's an example. Suppose you have a very large table that you summarize into a smaller table for frequent processing:

```
mysql> REPLACE INTO main_db.summary_table (col1, col2, ...)
    -> SELECT col1, sum(col2, ...)
    -> FROM main_db.enormous_table GROUP BY col1;
```

If you perform that operation on the master, every replica will have to repeat the enormous `GROUP BY` query. If you do enough of this, the replicas will not be able to keep up. Moving the number crunching to one of the replicas can help. On the replica, perhaps in a special database reserved for the purpose of avoiding conflicts with the data being replicated from the master, you can run the following:

```
mysql> REPLACE INTO summary_db.summary_table (col1, col2, ...)
    -> SELECT col1, sum(col2, ...)
    -> FROM main_db.enormous_table GROUP BY col1;
```

Now you can use `SELECT INTO OUTFILE`, followed by `LOAD DATA INFILE` on the master, to move the results back up to the master. *Voilà*—the duplicated work is reduced to a simple `LOAD DATA INFILE`. If you have N replicas, you have just saved $N - 1$ enormous `GROUP BY` queries.

The problem with this strategy is dealing with stale data. Sometimes it's hard to get consistent results by reading on the replica and writing on the master (a problem we address in detail in the following chapters). If it's hard to do the read on the replica, you can simplify and still save your replicas a lot of work. If you separate the `REPLACE` and SELECT parts of the query, you can fetch the results into your application and then insert them back into the master. First, perform the following query on the master:

```
mysql> SELECT col1, sum(col2, ...) FROM main_db.enormous_table GROUP BY col1;
```

You can then insert the results back into the summary table by repeating the following query for every row in the result set:

```
mysql> REPLACE INTO main_db.summary_table (col1, col2, ...)  VALUES (?, ?, ...);
```

Again, you've spared the replicas from the large GROUP BY portion of the query; separating the SELECT from the REPLACE means that the SELECT part of the query isn't replayed on every replica.

This general strategy—saving the replicas from the expensive portion of a write—can help in many cases where you have queries whose results are expensive to calculate but cheap to handle once they've been calculated.

Do writes in parallel outside of replication

Another tactic for avoiding excessive lag on the replicas is to circumvent replication. Any writes you do on the master must be serialized on the replica, so it makes sense to think of "serialized writes" as a scarce resource. Do all your writes need to flow from the master to the replica? How can you reserve your replica's limited serialized write capacity for the writes that really need to be done via replication?

Thinking of it in this light might help you prioritize writes. In particular, if you can identify some writes that are easy to do outside of replication, you can parallelize writes that would otherwise claim precious write capacity on the replica.

One great example is data archiving, which we discussed earlier in this chapter. OLTP archiving queries are often simple single-row operations. If you're just moving unneeded rows from one table to another, there might be no reason these writes have to be replicated to replicas. Instead, you can disable binary logging for the archiving statements, and then run separate but identical archiving processes on the master and replicas.

It might sound crazy to copy the data to another server yourself instead of letting replication do it, but it can actually make sense for some applications. This is especially true if an application is the only source of updates to a certain set of tables. Replication bottlenecks often center around a small set of tables, and if you can handle just those tables outside of replication, you might be able to speed it up significantly.

Prime the cache for the replication thread

If you have the right kind of workload, you might benefit from parallelizing I/O on replicas by prefetching data into memory. This technique is not well known, for good reason. Most people should not use it, because it won't work unless you have the right workload characteristics and hardware configuration. The other types of changes we've just been discussing are usually far better options, and there are lots more ways to apply them than you might think. However, we know of a small handful of large applications that benefit from prefetching data from disk.

There are two workable implementations for this. One idea is to use a program that reads slightly ahead of the replica's SQL thread in the relay logs and executes the queries as SELECT statements. This causes the server to fetch some of the data from the disk into memory, so when the replica's SQL thread executes the statement from the relay log, it doesn't need to wait for data to be fetched from disk. In effect, the SELECT parallelizes I/O that the replica SQL thread must normally do serially. While one statement is changing data, the next statement's data is being fetched from disk into memory.

The following conditions might indicate that prefetching will work:

- The replication SQL thread is I/O-bound, but the replica server isn't I/O-bound overall. A completely I/O-bound server won't benefit from prefetching, because it won't have any idle hard drives to do the work.
- The replica has a lot of disk drives—perhaps eight or more drives per replica.
- You use the InnoDB storage engine, and the working set is much too large to fit in memory.

An example workload that benefits from prefetching is one with a lot of widely scattered single-row UPDATE statements, which are typically high-concurrency on the master. DELETE statements might also benefit from this approach, but INSERT statements are less likely to—especially when rows are inserted sequentially—because the end of the index will already be "hot" from previous inserts.

If a table has many indexes, it might not be possible to prefetch all the data the statement will modify. The UPDATE statement might modify every index, but the SELECT will typically read only the primary key and one secondary index, in the best case. The UPDATE will still need to fetch other indexes for modification. That decreases how effective this tactic can be on tables with many indexes.

This technique is not a silver bullet. There are many reasons why it might not work for you or might even cause more problems. You should attempt it only if you know your hardware and operating system well. We know some people for whom this approach increased replication speed by 300% to 400%, but we've tried it ourselves many times and found it usually doesn't work. Getting the parameters right is important, but there isn't always a right combination of parameters.

The *mk-slave-prefetch* tool, which is part of Maatkit, is one implementation of the ideas we've described in this section. It has a lot of sophisticated features to try to work in as many cases as possible, but the drawback is that it has a lot of complexity and requires a lot of expertise to use. Another is Anders Karlsson's *slavereadahead* tool, available from *http://sourceforge.net/projects/slavereadahead/*.

Another technique entirely, which is under development at the time of writing, is internal to InnoDB. It puts transactions into a special mode that causes InnoDB to "fake" updates, so a process can execute these fake updates and then the replication thread can do the real updates quickly. This is something we're developing in Percona Server specifically for a very popular Internet-scale web application. Check on the status of this, because it's bound to have changed by the time this book is published.

If you're considering this technique, we think you would be well advised to get qualified advice from an expert who's familiar with when it works and what other options are available. This is best reserved as a last-resort measure for when all else fails.

Oversized Packets from the Master

Another hard-to-trace problem in replication can occur when the master's max_ allowed_packet size doesn't match the replica's. In this case, the master can log a packet the replica considers oversized, and when the replica retrieves that binary log event, it might suffer from a variety of problems. These include an endless loop of errors and retries, or corruption in the relay log.

Limited Replication Bandwidth

If you're replicating over limited bandwidth, you can enable the slave_compressed _protocol option on the replica (available in MySQL 4.0 and newer). When the replica connects to the master, it will request a compressed connection—the same compression any MySQL client connection can use. The compression engine used is *zlib*, and our tests show it can compress some textual data to roughly a third of its original size. The trade-off is that extra CPU time is required to compress the data on the master and decompress it on the replica.

If you have a slow link with a master on one side and many replicas on the other side, you might want to colocate a distribution master with the replicas. That way only one server connects to the master over the slow link, reducing the bandwidth load on the link and the CPU load on the master.

No Disk Space

Replication can indeed fill up your disks with binary logs, relay logs, or temporary files, especially if you do a lot of LOAD DATA INFILE queries on the master and have log _slave_updates enabled on the replica. The more a replica falls behind, the more disk space it is likely to use for relay logs that have been retrieved from the master but not yet executed. You can prevent these errors by monitoring disk usage and setting the relay_log_space configuration variable.

Replication Limitations

MySQL replication can fail or get out of sync, with or without errors, just because of its inherent limitations. A fairly large list of SQL functions and programming practices simply won't replicate reliably (we've mentioned many of them in this chapter). It's hard to ensure that none of these finds a way into your production code, especially if your application or team is large.[22]

Another issue is bugs in the server. We don't want to sound negative, but many major versions of the MySQL server have historically had bugs in replication, especially in the first releases of the major version. New features, such as stored procedures, have usually caused more problems.

For most users, this is not a reason to avoid new features. It's just a reason to test carefully, especially when you upgrade your application or MySQL. Monitoring is also important; you need to know when something causes a problem.

MySQL replication is complicated, and the more complicated your application is, the more careful you need to be. However, if you learn how to work with it, it works quite well.

How Fast Is Replication?

A common question about replication is "How fast is it?" The short answer is that it runs as quickly as MySQL can copy the events from the master and replay them, with very little overhead. If you have a slow network and very large binary log events, the delay between binary logging and execution on the replica might be perceptible. If your queries take a long time to run and you have a fast network, you can generally expect the query time on the replica to contribute more to the time it takes to replicate an event.

A more complete answer requires measuring every step of the process and deciding which steps will take the most time in your application. Some readers might care only that there's usually very little delay between logging events on the master and copying them to the replica's relay log. For those who would like more details, we did a quick experiment.

We elaborated on the process described in the first edition of this book, and methods used by Giuseppe Maxia,[23] to measure replication speed with high precision. We built a nondeterministic UDF that returns the system time to microsecond precision (see "User-Defined Functions" on page 295 for the source code):

---

22. Alas, MySQL doesn't have a `forbid_operations_unsafe_for_replication` option. In recent versions, however, it does warn pretty vigorously about some unsafe things, and even refuses certain ones.

23. See *http://datacharmer.blogspot.com/2006/04/measuring-replication-speed.html*.

```
mysql> SELECT NOW_USEC()
+----------------------------+
| NOW_USEC()                 |
+----------------------------+
| 2007-10-23 10:41:10.743917 |
+----------------------------+
```

This lets us measure replication speed by inserting the value of NOW_USEC() into a table on the master, then comparing it to the value on the replica.

We measured the delay by setting up two instances of MySQL on the same server to avoid inaccuracies caused by the clock. We configured one instance as a replica of the other, then ran the following queries on the master instance:

```
mysql> CREATE TABLE test.lag_test(
    ->    id INT NOT NULL AUTO_INCREMENT PRIMARY KEY,
    ->    now_usec VARCHAR(26) NOT NULL
    -> );
mysql> INSERT INTO test.lag_test(now_usec) VALUES( NOW_USEC() );
```

We used a VARCHAR column because MySQL's built-in time types can't store times with subsecond resolution (although some of its time functions can do subsecond calculations). All that remained was to compare the difference between the replica and the master. We decided to use a Federated table to help.[24] On the replica, we ran:

```
mysql> CREATE TABLE test.master_val (
    ->    id INT NOT NULL AUTO_INCREMENT PRIMARY KEY,
    ->    now_usec VARCHAR(26) NOT NULL
    -> ) ENGINE=FEDERATED
    ->    CONNECTION='mysql://user:pass@127.0.0.1/test/lag_test',;
```

A simple join and the TIMESTAMPDIFF() function show the microseconds of lag between the time the query executed on the master and on the replica:

```
mysql> SELECT m.id, TIMESTAMPDIFF(FRAC_SECOND, m.now_usec, s.now_usec) AS usec_lag
    -> FROM test.lag_test as s
    ->    INNER JOIN test.master_val AS m USING(id);
+----+----------+
| id | usec_lag |
+----+----------+
|  1 |      476 |
+----+----------+
```

We inserted 1,000 rows into the master with a Perl script, with a 10-millisecond delay between row insertions to prevent the master and replica instances from fighting each other for CPU time. We then built a temporary table containing the lag of each event:

```
mysql> CREATE TABLE test.lag AS
    >  SELECT TIMESTAMPDIFF(FRAC_SECOND, m.now_usec, s.now_usec) AS lag
    -> FROM test.master_val AS m
    ->    INNER JOIN test.lag_test as s USING(id);
```

Next, we grouped the results by lag time to see what the most frequent lag times were:

---

24. By the way, this is the only time that some of the authors have used the Federated engine.

```
mysql> SELECT ROUND(lag / 1000000.0, 4) * 1000 AS msec_lag, COUNT(*)
    -> FROM lag
    -> GROUP BY msec_lag
    -> ORDER BY msec_lag;
+----------+----------+
| msec_lag | COUNT(*) |
+----------+----------+
|   0.1000 |      392 |
|   0.2000 |      468 |
|   0.3000 |       75 |
|   0.4000 |       32 |
|   0.5000 |       15 |
|   0.6000 |        9 |
|   0.7000 |        2 |
|   1.3000 |        2 |
|   1.4000 |        1 |
|   1.8000 |        1 |
|   4.6000 |        1 |
|   6.6000 |        1 |
|  24.3000 |        1 |
+----------+----------+
```

The results show that most small queries take less than 0.3 milliseconds to replicate, from execution time on the master to execution time on the replica.

The part of replication this *doesn't* measure is how soon an event arrives at the replica after being logged to the binary log on the master. It would be nice to know this, because the sooner the replica receives the log event, the better. If the replica has received the event, it can provide a copy if the master crashes.

Although our measurements don't show exactly how long this part of the process takes, in theory it should be extremely fast (i.e., bounded only by the network speed). The MySQL binlog dump process does *not* poll the master for events, which would be inefficient and slow. Instead, the master notifies the replica of events. Reading a binary log event from the master is a blocking network call that begins sending data practically instantaneously after the master logs the event. Thus, it's probably safe to say the event will reach the replica as quickly as the replication thread can wake up and the network can transfer the data.

Advanced Features in MySQL Replication

Oracle released significant enhancements to replication in MySQL 5.5, and many more are in development milestone releases, to be included in MySQL 5.6. Some of these make replication more robust, others add multithreaded (parallel) replication apply to alleviate the current single-threaded bottleneck, and still others add advanced features for more flexibility and control. We won't speculate much on functionality that isn't in a GA release, but there are a few things we want to mention about MySQL 5.5's enhancements.

The first is semisynchronous replication. Based on work that Google did several years ago, this is probably the biggest change to replication since MySQL 5.1 introduced row-based replication. It helps you ensure that your replicas actually have a copy of the master's data, so there is less potential for data loss in the event of a complete loss of the master server.

Semisynchronous replication adds a delay to the commit process: when you commit a transaction, the binary log events must be transmitted to at least one connected replica before the client connection receives notification that the query has completed. This delay is added *after* the master commits the transaction to its disks. As such, it really just adds latency to the clients so that they can't push a bunch of transactions into the master faster than it can send them to replicas.

There are some common misconceptions about semisynchronous replication. Here's what it doesn't do:

- It does not block the commit on the master until the replicas have acknowledged receipt. The commit completes on the master, and only the client's notification of the commit is delayed.
- It does not block the client until the replicas have applied the transaction. They acknowledge after receiving the transaction, not after applying it.
- It isn't bulletproof. If replicas don't acknowledge receipt, it'll time out and revert to "normal" asynchronous replication mode.

Still, it is a very useful tool to help ensure that replicas really do provide greater redundancy and durability.

In terms of performance, semisynchronous replication adds a bit of latency to commits from the client's point of view. There is a slight delay due to the network transfer time, the time needed to write and sync data to the replica's disk (if so configured), and the network time for the acknowledgment. It sounds like this might add up, but in tests it has proven to be barely measurable, probably because the latency is hidden by other causes of latency. Giuseppe Maxia found about a 200-microsecond performance penalty per commit.[25] The overhead will be more noticeable with extremely small transactions, as you might expect.

In fact, semisynchronous replication can actually give you enough flexibility to improve performance in some cases, by making it safer to relax `sync_binlog` on the master. Writing to remote memory (a replica's acknowledgment) is faster than writing to the local disk (syncing on commit). Henrik Ingo ran some benchmarks that showed about a twofold performance improvement when he used semisynchronous replication instead of insisting on strong durability on the master.[26] There's no such thing as absolute durability in any system—just higher and higher levels of it—and it looks like

25. See *http://datacharmer.blogspot.com/2011/05/price-of-safe-data-benchmarking-semi.html*.

26. See *http://openlife.cc/blogs/2011/may/drbd-and-semi-sync-shootout-large-server*.

semisynchronous replication could be a lower-cost way to raise a system's data durability than some of the alternatives.

In addition to semisynchronous replication, MySQL 5.5 also sports replication heartbeats, which help replicas stay in touch with the master and avoid silent disconnections. If there's a dropped network connection, the replica will notice the lack of a heartbeat. There's an improved ability to deal with differing data types between master and replica when row-based replication is used, and there are several options to configure how replication metadata files are actually synced to disk and how relay logs are treated after a crash, reducing some of the opportunities for problems after a replica crashes and recovers.

That said, we haven't yet seen wide production deployment of any of MySQL 5.5's improvements to replication, so there is certainly more to learn.

Aside from the above, here's a quick rundown of improvements in the works, either in MySQL or in third-party branches such as Percona Server and MariaDB:

- Oracle has many improvements in MySQL 5.6 lab builds and development milestone releases:
  - Transactional replication state—no more metadata files to get out of sync on a crash. (Percona Server and MariaDB have had this for a while in a different form.)
  - Binary log event checksums to help detect corrupted events in a relay log.
  - Time-delayed replication to replace Percona Toolkit's *pt-slave-delay* tool.
  - Row-based binary log events can contain the original SQL executed on the master.
  - Multi-threaded replication apply (parallelized replication).
- MySQL 5.6, Percona Server, Facebook's patches, and MariaDB have three different fixes for the group commit problems introduced in MySQL 5.0.

Other Replication Technologies

Built-in replication isn't the only way to replicate your data from one server to another, although it probably is the best for most purposes. (In contrast to PostgreSQL, MySQL doesn't have a wide variety of add-on replication options, probably because built-in replication was added early in the product's life.)

We've brushed elbows with a few of the add-on technologies for MySQL replication, such as Oracle GoldenGate, but we're really not familiar enough with most of them to write much about them. There are two that we want to mention, however. The first is Percona XtraDB Cluster's synchronous replication, which we'll discuss in Chapter 12 because it fits better into a chapter on high availability. The second is Continuent's Tungsten Replicator (*http://code.google.com/p/tungsten-replicator/*).

Tungsten is an open source middleware replication product written in Java. It has similarities to Oracle GoldenGate and seems poised to gain a lot of sophisticated features in future releases. At the time of writing, it already offers features such as replicating data between servers, sharding data automatically, applying changes in parallel on replicas (multithreaded replication), promoting a replica if a master fails, cross-platform replication, and multisource replication (many sources replicating to a single destination). It is the open source version of the Tungsten Enterprise database clustering suite, which is commercial software from Continuent.

Tungsten also implements multimaster clusters, where writes can be directed to any server in the cluster. A generic implementation of this architecture requires conflict detection and/or resolution. This is very hard, and it isn't always what is needed. Instead, Tungsten provides a slightly limited implementation wherein not all data is writable on all nodes; instead, each node is tagged as the system of record for specific bits of data. This means that, for example,the Seattle office can own and write to its data, which is replicated to Houston and Baltimore. In Houston and Baltimore, the data is available locally for low-latency reads, but Tungsten prevents it from being written to, so conflicting updates are not possible. Houston and Baltimore can update their own data, of course, which is also replicated to each of the other locations. This "system of record" approach solves a need that people frequently try to satisfy with MySQL's built-in replication in a ring, which, as we've discussed, is far from safe or robust.

Tungsten Replicator doesn't just plug into or manage MySQL replication; it replaces it. It captures data changes on servers by reading their binary logs, but that's where the built-in MySQL functionality stops and Tungsten Replicator takes over. It reads the binary logs and extracts the transactions, then executes them on the replicas.

This process has a richer feature set than MySQL replication does. In particular, Tungsten Replicator was the first to offer parallel replication apply for MySQL. We haven't seen it in production yet, but it's claimed to offer up to a threefold improvement in replication speed, depending on the workload characteristics. This seems credible to us, based on the architecture and what we know of the product.

Here are some things we like about Tungsten Replicator:

- It provides built-in data consistency checking. Enough said.
- It offers a plugin capability so you can write your own custom functionality. MySQL's replication source code is very hard to understand and harder to modify. Even very talented programmers have introduced bugs into the server when've they tried to modify the replication code. It's nice to have an option to change replication without changing the MySQL replication code.
- There are global transaction IDs, which enable you to figure out the state of servers relative to each other without trying to match up binary log names and offsets.

- It's a good high-availability solution, with the ability to promote a replica to be the master quickly.

- It supports heterogeneous replication (between MySQL and PostgreSQL or MySQL and Oracle, for example).

- It supports replication between MySQL versions in cases where MySQL's replication isn't backward-compatible. This is very nice for certain upgrade scenarios, where you might not otherwise be able to create a workable rollback scenario in case the upgrade doesn't go well, or you'd have to upgrade servers in an order you'd prefer not to.

- The parallel replication design is a good match for sharded or multitenant applications.

- Java applications can transparently write to masters and read from replicas.

- It's a lot simpler and easier to set up and administer than it used to be, thanks in large part to Giuseppe Maxia's diligent work as QA Director.

And here are some drawbacks:

- It's arguably more complex than built-in MySQL replication, with more moving parts to set up and administer. It is middleware, after all.

- It's one more thing to learn and understand in your application stack.

- It's not as lightweight as built-in MySQL replication and doesn't have as good performance. Single-threaded replication is slower than MySQL's single-threaded replication.

- It's not as widely tested and deployed as MySQL replication, so the risk of bugs and problems is higher.

All in all, we're happy that Tungsten Replicator is available and is under active development, with new features and functionality being released steadily. It's nice to have an alternative to built-in replication, making MySQL suitable for more use cases and flexible enough to satisfy requirements that MySQL replication will probably never meet.

Summary

MySQL replication is the Swiss Army Knife of MySQL's built-in capabilities, and it increases MySQL's range of functionality and usefulness dramatically. It is probably one of the key reasons why MySQL became so popular so quickly, in fact.

Although replication has many limitations and caveats, it turns out that most of them are relatively unimportant or easy for most users to avoid. Many of the drawbacks are simply special-case behaviors of advanced features that most people won't use, but which are very helpful for the minority of users who need them.

Because replication offers such important and complex functionality, the server itself doesn't offer every bell and whistle that you'll need to configure, monitor, administer, and optimize it. Third-party tools can be a tremendous help. We're biased, but we think the most notable tools for improving your life with replication are bound to be Percona Toolkit and Percona XtraBackup. Before you use any other tools, we advise you to inspect their test suites. If they don't have formal, automated test suites, think hard before trusting them with your data.

When it comes to replication, your motto should be K.I.S.S.[27] Don't do anything fancy, such as using replication rings, Blackhole tables, or replication filters, unless you really need to. Use replication simply to mirror an entire copy of your data, including all privileges. Keeping your replicas identical to the master in every way will help you avoid many problems.

Speaking of keeping replicas identical to the master, here's a short list of important things to do when you use replication:

- Use Percona Toolkit's *pt-table-checksum* to verify that replicas are true copies of the master.
- Monitor replication to ensure that it's running and isn't lagging behind the master.
- Understand the asynchronous nature of replication, and design your application to avoid or tolerate reading stale data from replicas.
- Don't write to more than one server in a replication topology. Configure replicas as read-only, and lock down privileges to prevent changes to data.
- Enable sanity and safety settings as described in this chapter.

As we'll discuss in Chapter 12, replication failure is one of the most common reasons for MySQL downtime. To avoid problems with replication, read that chapter, and try to put its suggestions into practice. You should also read the replication section of the MySQL manual thoroughly, and learn how replication works and how to administer it. If you like reading, the book *MySQL High Availability* (*http://shop.oreilly.com/prod uct/9780596807290.do*) by Charles Bell et al. (O'Reilly) also has useful information about replication internals. But you still need to read the manual!

---

27. Keep It Simple, Schwartz! Some of us think that's what K.I.S.S. means, anyway.

Scaling MySQL

This chapter shows you how to build MySQL-based applications that can grow very large while remaining fast, efficient, and economical.

Which scalability advice is relevant to applications that can fit on a single server or a handful of servers? Most people will never maintain systems at an extremely large scale, and the tactics used at very large and popular companies shouldn't always be emulated. We'll try to cover a range of strategies in this chapter. We've built or helped build many applications, ranging from those that use a single server or a handful of servers to those that use thousands. Choosing the appropriate strategy for your application is often the key to saving money and time that can be invested elsewhere.

MySQL has been criticized for being hard to scale, and sometimes that's true, but usually you can make MySQL scale well if you choose the right architecture and implement it well. Scalability is not always a well-understood topic, however, so we'll begin by clearing up the confusion.

What Is Scalability?

People often use terms such as "scalability," "high availability," and "performance" as synonyms in casual conversation, but they're completely different. As we explained in Chapter 3, we define performance as response time. Scalability can be defined precisely too; we'll explore that more fully in a moment, but in a nutshell it's the system's ability to deliver equal bang for the buck as you add resources to perform more work. Poorly scalable systems reach a point of diminishing returns and can't grow further.

Capacity is a related concept. The system's capacity is the amount of work it can perform in a given amount of time.[1] However, capacity must be qualified. The system's maximum throughput is not the same as its capacity. Most benchmarks measure a

---

1. In the physical sciences, work per unit of time is called power, but in computing "power" is such an overloaded term that it's ambiguous and we avoid it. However, a precise definition of capacity is the system's maximum power output.

system's maximum throughput, but you can't push real systems that hard. If you do, performance will degrade and response times will become unacceptably large and variable. We define the system's actual capacity as the throughput it can achieve while still delivering acceptable performance. This is why benchmark results usually shouldn't be reduced to a single number.

Capacity and scalability are independent of performance. To make an analogy with cars on a highway:

- Performance is how fast the car is.
- Capacity is the number of lanes times the maximum safe speed.
- Scalability is the degree to which you can add more cars and more lanes without slowing traffic.

In this analogy, scalability depends on factors such as how well the interchanges are designed, how many cars have accidents or break down, and whether the cars drive at different speeds or change lanes a lot—but generally *not* on how powerful the cars' engines are. This is not to say that performance doesn't matter, because it does. We're just pointing out that systems can be scalable even if they aren't high-performance.

From the 50,000-foot view, *scalability is the ability to add capacity by adding resources.*

Even if your MySQL architecture is scalable, your application might not be. If it's hard to increase capacity for any reason, your application isn't scalable overall. We defined capacity in terms of throughput a moment ago, but it's worth looking at capacity from the same 50,000-foot view. From this vantage point, capacity simply means the ability to handle load, and it's useful to think of load from several different angles:

Quantity of data

The sheer volume of data your application can accumulate is one of the most common scaling challenges. This is particularly an issue for many of today's web applications, which never delete any data. Social networking sites, for example, typically never delete old messages or comments.

Number of users

Even if each user has only a small amount of data, if you have a lot of users it adds up—and the data size can grow disproportionately faster than the number of users. Many users generally means more transactions too, and the number of transactions might not be proportional to the number of users. Finally, many users (and more data) can mean increasingly complex queries, especially if queries depend on the number of relationships among users. (The number of relationships is bounded by $(N * (N{-}1)) / 2$, where N is the number of users.)

User activity

Not all user activity is equal, and user activity is not constant. If your users suddenly become more active, for example because of a new feature they like, your load can increase significantly. User activity isn't just a matter of the number of page views, either—the same number of page views can cause more work if part of the site that requires a lot of work to generate becomes more popular. Some users are much more active than others, too: they might have many more friends, messages, or photos than the average user.

Size of related datasets

If there are relationships among users, the application might need to run queries and computations on entire groups of related users. This is more complex than just working with individual users and their data. Social networking sites often face challenges due to popular groups or users who have many friends.[2]

A Formal Definition

It's worth exploring a mathematical definition of scalability, as it will enable you to think clearly about the higher-level concepts. If you don't have that grounding, you might not understand or be able to communicate scalability precisely. Don't worry, this won't involve advanced mathematics—you'll be able to understand it intuitively even if you're not a math whiz.

The key is the phrase we used earlier: "equal bang for the buck." Another way to say this is that scalability is the degree to which the system provides an equal return on investment (ROI) as you add resources to handle the load and increase capacity. Let's suppose that we have a system with one server, and we can measure its maximum capacity. Figure 11-1 illustrates this scenario.

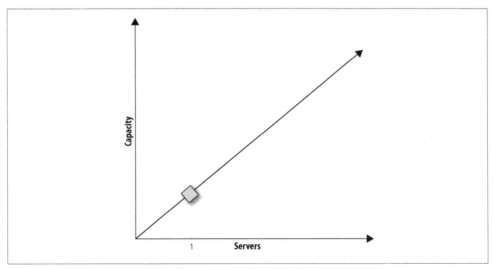

Figure 11-1. A system with one server

2. Justin Bieber, we still love you!

Now suppose that we add one more server, and the system's capacity doubles, as shown in Figure 11-2.

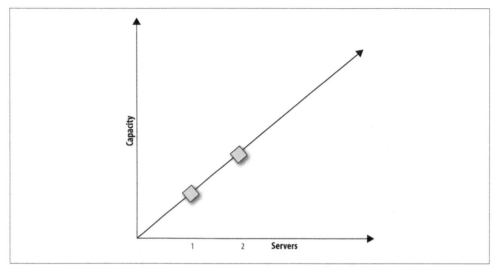

Figure 11-2. A linearly scalable system with two servers has twice the capacity

This is linear scalability. We doubled the number of servers, and as a result, we doubled the system's capacity. Most systems aren't linearly scalable; they often scale a bit like Figure 11-3 instead.

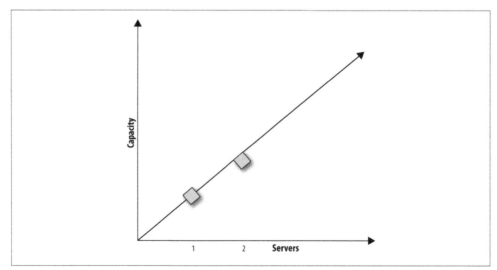

Figure 11-3. A system that doesn't scale linearly

Most systems provide slightly less than linear scalability at small scaling factors, and the deviation from linearity becomes more obvious at higher scaling factors. In fact, most systems eventually reach a point of maximum throughput, beyond which additional investment provides a *negative* return—add more workload and you'll actually reduce the system's throughput![3]

How is this possible? Many models of scalability have been created over the years, with varying degrees of success and realism. The scalability model that we refer to here is based on some of the underlying mechanisms that influence systems as they scale. It is Dr. Neil J. Gunther's Universal Scalability Law (USL). Dr. Gunther has written about it at length in his books, including *Guerrilla Capacity Planning* (Springer). We will not go deeply into the mathematics here, but if you are interested, his book and the training courses offered by his company, Performance Dynamics, might be good resources for you.[4]

The short introduction to the USL is that the deviation from linear scalability can be modeled by two factors: a portion of the work cannot be done in parallel, and a portion of the work requires crosstalk. Modeling the first factor results in the well-known Amdahl's Law, which causes throughput to level off. When part of the task can't be parallelized, no matter how much you divide and conquer, the task takes at least as long as the serial portion.

Adding the second factor—intra-node or intra-process communication—to Amdahl's Law results in the USL. The cost of this communication depends on the number of communication channels, which grows quadratically with respect to the number of workers in the system. Thus, the cost eventually grows faster than the benefit, and that's what is responsible for retrograde scalability. Figure 11-4 illustrates the three concepts we've talked about so far: linear scaling, Amdahl scaling, and USL scaling. Most real systems look like the USL curve.

The USL can be applied both to hardware and to software. In the hardware case, the x-axis represents units of hardware, such as servers or CPUs; the workload, data size, and query complexity per unit of hardware must be held constant.[5] In the software case, the x-axis on the plot represents units of concurrency, such as users or threads; the workload per unit of concurrency must be held constant.

---

3. In fact, the term "return on investment" can also be considered in light of your financial investment. Upgrading a component to double its capacity often costs more than twice as much as the initial investment. Although we often consider this in the real world, we'll omit it from our discussion here to avoid complicating an already confusing topic.

4. You can also read our white paper, *Forecasting MySQL Scalability with the Universal Scalability Law*, which gives a condensed summary of the mathematics and principles at work in the USL. It is available at *http://www.percona.com*.

5. In the real world, it is very difficult to define hardware scalability precisely, because it's hard to actually hold all those variables constant as you vary the number of servers in the system.

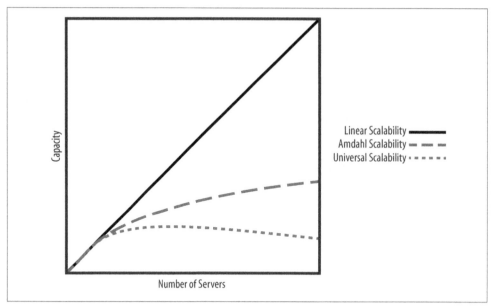

Figure 11-4. Comparison of linear scalability, Amdahl scalability, and the Universal Scalability Law

It is important to understand that the USL won't describe any real system perfectly, because it is a simplified model. However, it is a good framework for understanding why systems fail to provide equal bang for the buck as they grow. It also reveals an important principle for building highly scalable systems: try to avoid serialization and crosstalk within the system.

It is possible to measure a system and use regression to determine the amount of seriality and crosstalk it exhibits. You can use this as a best-case upper bound for capacity planning and performance forecasting estimates. You can also examine how the system deviates from the USL model, using it as a worst-case lower bound to point out areas where your system isn't performing as well as it should. In both cases, the USL gives you a reference to discuss scalability. Without it, you'd look at the system and not know what expectations you should have. A full exploration of this topic deserves its own book, and Dr. Gunther already wrote that, so we won't go into this further.

Another framework for understanding scalability problems is the theory of constraints, which explains how to improve a system's throughput and efficiency by reducing dependent events and statistical variations. It is explored in Eliyahu M. Goldratt's book *The Goal* (North River), which is an extended parable about a manager at a manufacturing facility. Although it might seem far removed from the realm of a database server, the principles involved are the same as those in queueing theory and other aspects of operational research.

Scaling MySQL

Placing all of your application's data in a single MySQL instance simply will not scale well. Sooner or later you'll hit performance bottlenecks. The traditional solution in many types of applications is to buy more powerful servers. This is what's known as "scaling vertically" or "scaling up." The opposite approach is to divide your work across many computers, which is usually called "scaling horizontally" or "scaling out." We'll discuss how to combine scale-out and scale-up solutions with consolidation, and how to scale with clustering solutions. Finally, most applications also have some data that's rarely or never needed and that can be purged or archived. We call this approach "scaling back," just to give it a name that matches the other strategies.

Planning for Scalability

People usually start to think about scalability when the server has difficulty keeping up with increased load. This usually shows up as a shift in workload from CPU-bound to

I/O-bound, contention among concurrent queries, and increasing latency. Common culprits are increased query complexity, or a portion of the data or index that used to fit into memory but no longer does. You might see a change in certain types of queries and not others. For example, long or complex queries often show the strain before smaller queries.

If your application is highly scalable, you can simply plug in more servers to handle the load, and the performance problems will disappear. If it's not scalable, you might find yourself fighting fires endlessly. You can avoid this by planning for scalability.

The hardest part of scalability planning is estimating how much load you'll need to handle. You don't need to get it exactly right, but you need to be within an order of magnitude. If you overestimate, you'll waste resources on development, but if you underestimate, you'll be unprepared for the load.

You also need to estimate your schedule approximately right—that is, you need to know where the "horizon" is. For some applications, a simple prototype could work fine for a few months, giving you a chance to raise capital and build a more scalable architecture. For other applications, you might need your current architecture to provide enough capacity for two years.

Here are some questions you can ask yourself to help plan for scalability:

- How complete is your application's functionality? A lot of the scaling solutions we suggest can make it harder to implement certain features. If you haven't yet implemented some of your application's core features, it might be hard to see how you can build them in a scaled application. Likewise, it could be hard to decide on a scaling solution before you've seen how these features will really work.

- What is your expected peak load? Your application should work even at this load. What would happen if your site made the front page of Yahoo! News or Slashdot? Even if your application isn't a popular website, you can still have peak loads. For example, if you're an online retailer, the holiday season—especially the infamous online shopping days in the few weeks before Christmas—is often a time of peak load. In the US, Valentine's Day and the weekend before Mother's Day are also a peak times for online florists.

- If you rely on every part of your system to handle the load, what will happen if part of it fails? For example, if you rely on replicas to distribute the read load, can you still keep up if one of them fails? Will you need to disable some functionality to do so? You can build in some spare capacity to help alleviate these concerns.

Buying Time Before Scaling

In a perfect world, you would be able to plan ahead for any eventuality, would always have enough developers, would never run into budget limitations, and so on. In the real world, things are usually more complicated, and you'll need to make some compromises as you scale your application. In particular, you might need to put off big application changes for a while. Before we get deep into the details of scaling MySQL, here are some things you might be able to do now, before you make major scaling efforts:

Optimize performance

You can often get significant performance improvements from relatively simple changes, such as indexing tables correctly or switching from MyISAM to the InnoDB storage engine. If you're facing performance limitations now, one of the first things you should do is enable and analyze the slow query log. See Chapter 3 for more on this topic.

There is a point of diminishing returns. After you've fixed most of the major problems, it gets harder and harder to improve performance. Each new optimization makes less of a difference and requires more effort, and they often make your application much more complicated.

Buy more powerful hardware

Upgrading your servers, or adding more of them, can sometimes work well. Especially for an application that's early in its lifecycle, it's often a good idea to buy a few more servers or get some more memory. The alternative might be to try to keep the application running on a single server. It can be more practical just to buy some more hardware than to change your application's design, especially if time is critical and developers are scarce.

Buying more hardware works well if your application is either small or designed so it can use more hardware well. This is common for new applications, which are usually very small or reasonably well designed. For larger, older applications, buying more hardware might not work, or might be too expensive. For example, going from 1 to 3 servers isn't a big deal, but going from 100 to 300 is a different story—it's very expensive. At that point, it's worth putting in a lot of time and effort to get as much performance as possible out of your existing systems.

Scaling Up

Scaling up means buying more powerful hardware, and for many applications this is all you need to do. There are many advantages to this strategy. A single server is so much easier to maintain and develop against than multiple servers that it offers significant cost savings, for example. Backing up and restoring your application on a single server is also simpler because there's never any question about consistency or which dataset is the authoritative one. The reasons go on. Cost is complexity, and scaling up is simpler than scaling out.

You can scale up quite far. Commodity servers are readily available today with half a terabyte of memory, 32 or more CPU cores, and more I/O power than you can even use for MySQL (flash storage on PCIe cards, for example). With intelligent application and database design, and good performance optimization skills, you can build very large applications with MySQL on such servers.

How large can MySQL scale on modern hardware? Although it's possible to run it on very powerful servers, it turns out that like most database servers, MySQL doesn't scale perfectly (surprise!) as you add hardware resources. To run MySQL on big-iron boxes, you will definitely need a recent version of the server. The MySQL 5.0 and 5.1 series will choke badly on such large hardware, due to internal scalability issues. You will need either MySQL 5.5 or newer, or Percona Server 5.1 or newer. Even so, the currently reasonable "point of diminishing returns" is probably somewhere around 256 GB of RAM, 32 cores, and a PCIe flash drive. MySQL will continue to provide improved performance on bigger hardware than that, but the price-to-performance ratio will not be as good, and in fact even on these systems you can often get much better performance by running several smaller instances of MySQL instead of one big instance that uses all of the server's resources. This is a rapidly moving target, so this advice will probably be out of date pretty soon.

Scaling up can work for a while, and many applications will not outgrow this strategy, but if your application grows extremely large[6] it ultimately won't work. The first reason is money. Regardless of what software you're running on the server, at some point scaling up will become a bad financial decision. Outside the range of hardware that offers the best price-to-performance ratio, the hardware tends to become more proprietary and unusual, and correspondingly more expensive. This means there's a practical limit on how far up you can afford to scale. If you use replication and upgrade your master to high-end hardware, there's also little chance that you'll be able to build a replica server that's powerful enough to keep up. A heavily loaded master can easily do more work than a replica server with the same hardware can handle, because the replication thread can't use multiple CPUs and disks efficiently.

Finally, you can't scale up indefinitely, because even the most powerful computers have limits. Single-server applications usually run into read limits first, especially if they run complicated read queries. Such queries are single-threaded inside MySQL, so they'll use only one CPU, and money can't buy them much more performance. The fastest server-grade CPUs you can buy are only a couple of times faster than commodity CPUs. Adding many CPUs or CPU cores won't help the slow queries run faster. The server will also begin to run into memory limits as your data becomes too large to cache effectively. This will usually show up as heavy disk usage, and disks are the slowest parts of modern computers.

The most obvious place where you can't scale up is in the cloud. You generally can't get very powerful servers in most public clouds, so scaling up is not an option if your application must grow very large. We'll discuss this topic further in Chapter 13.

---

6. We're avoiding the phrase "web scale," because it has become utterly meaningless. See *http://www .xtranormal.com/watch/6995033/*.

As a result, we recommend that you don't plan to scale up indefinitely if the prospect of a hitting a scalability ceiling is real and would be a serious business problem. If you know your application will grow very large, it's fine to buy a more powerful server for the short term while you work on another solution. However, in general you'll ultimately have to scale out, which brings us to our next topic.

Scaling Out

We can lump scale-out tactics into three broad groups: replication, partitioning, and sharding.

The simplest and most common way to scale out is to distribute your data across several servers with replication, and then use the replicas for read queries. This technique can work well for a read-heavy application. It has drawbacks, such as cache duplication, but even that might not be a severe problem if the data size is limited. We wrote quite a bit about these issues in the previous chapter, and we'll return to them later in this one.

The other common way to scale out is to *partition* your workload across multiple "nodes." Exactly how you partition the workload is an intricate decision. Most large MySQL applications don't automate the partitioning, at least not completely. In this section, we take a look at some of the possibilities for partitioning and explore their strengths and drawbacks.

A *node* is the functional unit in your MySQL architecture. If you're not planning for redundancy and high availability, a node might be one server. If you're designing a redundant system with failover, a node is generally one of the following:

- A master-master replication pair, with an active server and a passive replica
- A master and many replicas
- An active server that uses a distributed replicated block device (DRBD) for a standby
- A SAN-based "cluster"

In most cases, all servers within a node should have the same data. We like the master-master replication architecture for two-server active-passive nodes.

Functional partitioning

Functional partitioning, or division of duties, means dedicating different nodes to different tasks. We've mentioned some similar approaches before; for example, we wrote about how to design different servers for OLTP and OLAP workloads in the previous chapter. Functional partitioning usually takes that strategy even further by dedicating individual servers or nodes to different applications, so each contains only the data its particular application needs.

We're using the word "application" a bit broadly here. We don't mean a single computer program, but a set of related programs that's easily separated from other, unrelated programs. For example, if you have a website with distinct sections that don't need to share data, you can partition by functional area on the website. It's common to see portals that tie the different areas together; from the portal, you can browse to the news section of the site, the forums, the support area and knowledge base, and so on. The data for each of these functional areas could be on a dedicated MySQL server. Figure 11-5 depicts this arrangement.

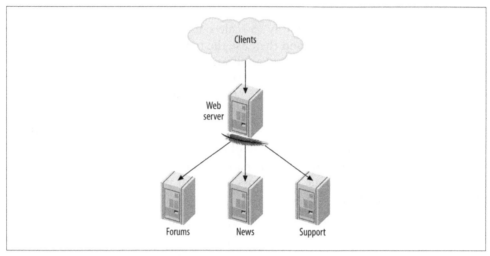

Figure 11-5. A portal and nodes dedicated to functional areas

If the application is huge, each functional area can also have its own dedicated web server, but that's less common.

Another possible functional partitioning approach is to split a single application's data by determining sets of tables that you never join to each other. If it becomes necessary, you can usually perform a few such joins in the application if they're not performance-critical. There are a few variations on this approach, but they have the common property that each type of data can be found on only a single node. This is not a common way to partition data, because it's very difficult to do effectively and it doesn't offer any advantages over other methods.

In the final analysis, you still can't scale functional partitioning indefinitely, because each functional area must scale vertically if it is tied to a single MySQL node. One of the applications or functional areas is likely to eventually grow too large, forcing you to find a different strategy. And if you take functional partitioning too far, it can be harder to change to a more scalable design later.

Data sharding

Data sharding[7] is the most common and successful approach for scaling today's very large MySQL applications. You shard the data by splitting it into smaller pieces, or shards, and storing them on different nodes.

Sharding works well when combined with some type of functional partitioning. Most sharded systems also have some "global" data that isn't sharded at all (say, lists of cities, or login data). This global data is usually stored on a single node, often behind a cache such as *memcached*.

In fact, most applications shard only the data that needs sharding—typically, the parts of the dataset that will grow very large. Suppose you're building a blogging service. If you expect 10 million users, you might not need to shard the user registration information because you might be able to fit all of the users (or the active subset of them) entirely in memory. If you expect 500 million users, on the other hand, you should probably shard this data. The user-generated content, such as posts and comments, will almost certainly require sharding in either case, because these records are much larger and there are many more of them.

Large applications might have several logical datasets that you can shard differently. You can store them on different sets of servers, but you don't have to. You can also shard the same data multiple ways, depending on how you access it. We show an example of this approach later.

Sharding is dramatically different from the way most applications are designed initially, and it can be difficult to change an application from a monolithic data store to a sharded architecture. That's why it's much easier to build an application with a sharded data store from the start if you anticipate that it will eventually need one.

Most applications that don't build in sharding from the beginning go through stages as they get larger. For example, you can use replication to scale read queries on your blogging service until it doesn't work any more. Then you can split the service into three parts: users, posts, and comments. You can place these on different servers (functional partitioning), perhaps with a service-oriented architecture, and perform the joins in the application. Figure 11-6 shows the evolution from a single server to functional partitioning.

Finally, you can shard the posts and comments by the user ID, and keep the user information on a single node. If you keep a master-replica configuration for the global node and use master-master pairs for the sharded nodes, the final data store might look like Figure 11-7.

---

7. Sharding is also called "splintering" and "partitioning," but we use the term "sharding" to avoid confusion. Google calls it sharding, and if it's good enough for Google, it's good enough for us.

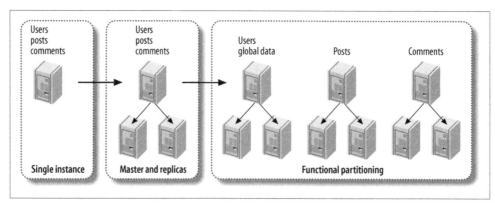

Figure 11-6. From a single instance to a functionally partitioned data store

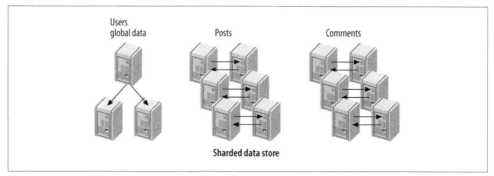

Figure 11-7. A data store with one global node and six master-master nodes

If you know in advance that you'll need to scale very large, and you know the limitations of functional partitioning, you might choose to skip the steps in the middle and go straight from a single node to a sharded data store. In fact, foresight can often help you avoid ugly sharding schemes that might arise from meeting each challenge as it comes.

Sharded applications often have a database abstraction library that eases the communication between the application and the sharded data store. Such libraries usually don't hide the sharding completely, because the application usually knows something about a query that the data store doesn't. Too much abstraction can cause inefficiencies, such as querying all nodes for data that lives on a single node.

A sharded data store might feel like an elegant solution, but it's hard to build. So why choose this architecture? The answer is simple: if you want to scale your write capacity, you *must* partition your data. You cannot scale write capacity if you have only a single master, no matter how many replicas you have. Sharding, for all its drawbacks, is our preferred solution to this problem.

To Shard or Not to Shard?

That is the question, isn't it? Here's the simple answer: don't shard unless you need to. See if you can delay it via performance optimization or a better application or database design. If you can put off sharding long enough, you might be able to just buy a bigger server, upgrade MySQL to a new higher-performance version, and keep on chugging with a single server, plus or minus replication.

In a nutshell, sharding is inevitable when either the data size or the write workload becomes too much for a single server. You'd be surprised how far systems can be scaled without sharding, using intelligent application design. Some very popular applications you'd probably assume were sharded from day one in fact grew to multi-billion-dollar valuations and insane amounts of traffic without sharding. It's not the only game in town, and it's a tough way to build an application if it's not needed.

Choosing a partitioning key

The most important challenge with sharding is finding and retrieving data. How you find data depends on how you shard it. There are many ways to do this, and some are better than others.

The goal is to make your most important and frequent queries touch as few shards as possible (remember, one of the scalability principles is to avoid crosstalk between nodes). The most important part of that process is choosing a *partitioning key* (or keys) for your data. The partitioning key determines which rows should go onto each shard. If you know an object's partitioning key, you can answer two questions:

- Where should I store this data?
- Where can I find the data I need to fetch?

We'll show you a variety of ways to choose and use a partitioning key later. For now, let's look at an example. Suppose we do as MySQL's NDB Cluster does, and use a hash of each table's primary key to partition the data across all the shards. This is a very simple approach, but it doesn't scale well because it frequently requires you to check all the shards for the data you want. For example, if you want user 3's blog posts, where can you find them? They are probably scattered evenly across all the shards, because they're partitioned by the primary key, not by the user. Using a primary key hash makes it simple to know where to store the data, but it might make it harder to fetch it, depending on which data you need and whether you know the primary key.

Cross-shard queries are worse than single-shard queries, but as long as you don't touch too many shards, they might not be too bad. The worst case is when you have no idea where the desired data is stored, and you need to scan every shard to find it.

A good partitioning key is usually the primary key of a very important entity in the database. These keys determine the *unit of sharding*. For example, if you partition your data by a user ID or a client ID, the unit of sharding is the user or client.

A good way to start is to diagram your data model with an entity-relationship diagram, or an equivalent tool that shows all the entities and their relationships. Try to lay out the diagram so that the related entities are close together. You can often inspect such a diagram visually and find candidates for partitioning keys that you'd otherwise miss. Don't just look at the diagram, though; consider your application's queries as well. Even if two entities are related in some way, if you seldom or never join on the relationship, you can break the relationship to implement the sharding.

Some data models are easier to shard than others, depending on the degree of connectivity in the entity-relationship graph. Figure 11-8 depicts an easily sharded data model on the left, and one that's difficult to shard on the right.

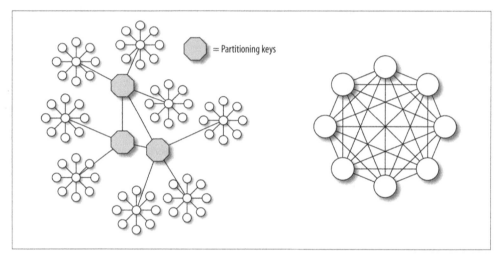

Figure 11-8. Two data models, one easy to shard and the other difficult

The data model on the left is easy to shard because it has many connected subgraphs consisting mostly of nodes with just one connection, and you can "cut" the connections between the subgraphs relatively easily. The model on the right is hard to shard, because there are no such subgraphs. Most data models, luckily, look more like the lefthand diagram than the righthand one.

When choosing a partitioning key, try to pick something that lets you avoid cross-shard queries as much as possible, but also makes shards small enough that you won't have problems with disproportionately large chunks of data. You want the shards to end up uniformly small, if possible, and if not, at least small enough that they're easy to balance by grouping different numbers of shards together. For example, if your application is US-only and you want to divide your dataset into 20 shards, you probably shouldn't shard by state, because California has such a huge population. But you could shard by county or telephone area code, because even though these won't be uniformly populated, there are enough of them that you can still choose 20 sets that will be roughly equally populated in total, and you can choose them with an affinity that helps avoid cross-shard queries.

Multiple partitioning keys

Complicated data models make data sharding more difficult. Many applications have more than one partitioning key, especially if there are two or more important "dimensions" in the data. In other words, the application might need to see an efficient, coherent view of the data from different angles. This means you might need to store at least some data twice within the system.

For example, you might need to shard your blogging application's data by both the user ID and the post ID, because these are two common ways the application looks at the data. Think of it this way: you frequently want to see all posts for a user, and all comments for a post. But sharding by user doesn't help you find comments for a post, and sharding by post doesn't help you find posts for a user. If you need both types of queries to touch only a single shard, you'll have to shard both ways.

Just because you need multiple partitioning keys doesn't mean you'll need to design two completely redundant data stores. Let's look at another example: a social networking book club website, where the site's users can comment on books. The website can display all comments for a all book, as well as all books a user has read and commented on.

You might build one sharded data store for the user data and another for the book data. Comments have both a user ID and a post ID, so they cross the boundaries between shards. Instead of completely duplicating comments, you can store the comments with the user data. Then you can store just a comment's headline and ID with the book data. This might be enough to render *most* views of a book's comments without accessing both data stores, and if you need to display the complete comment text, you can retrieve it from the user data store.

Querying across shards

Most sharded applications have at least some queries that need to aggregate or join data from multiple shards. For example, if the book club site shows the most popular or active users, it must by definition access every shard. Making such queries work well is the most difficult part of implementing data sharding, because what the application sees as a single query needs to be split up and executed in parallel as many queries, one per shard. A good database abstraction layer can help ease the pain, but even then such queries are so much slower and more expensive than in-shard queries that aggressive caching is usually necessary as well.

Some languages, such as PHP, don't have good support for executing multiple queries in parallel. A common way to work around this is to build a helper application, often in C or Java, to execute the queries and aggregate the results. The PHP application then queries the helper application, which is often a web service or a worker service such as Gearman.

Cross-shard queries can also benefit from summary tables. You can build them by traversing all the shards and storing the results redundantly on each shard when they're complete. If duplicating the data on each shard would be too wasteful, you can consolidate the summary tables onto another data store, so they're stored only once.

Nonsharded data often lives in the global node, with heavy caching to shield it from the load.

Some applications use essentially random sharding when perfectly even data distribution is important, or when there is no good partitioning key. A distributed search application is a good example. In this case, cross-shard queries and aggregation are the norm, not the exception.

Querying across shards isn't the only thing that's harder with sharding. Maintaining data consistency is also difficult. Foreign keys won't work across shards, so the normal solution is to check referential integrity as needed in the application, or use foreign keys within a shard, because internal consistency within a shard might be the most important thing. It's possible to use XA transactions, but this is uncommon in practice because of the overhead.

You can also design cleanup processes that run intermittently. For example, if a user's book club account expires, you don't have to remove it immediately. You can write a periodic job to remove the user's comments from the per-book shard, and you can build a checker script that runs periodically and makes sure the data is consistent across the shards.

Allocating data, shards, and nodes

Shards and nodes don't have to have a one-to-one relationship. It's often a good idea to make a shard's size much smaller than a node's capacity, so you can store multiple shards on a single node.

Keeping each shard small helps keep the data manageable. It makes it easier to do database backups and recovery, and if the tables are small, it can ease jobs such as schema changes. For example, suppose you have a 100 GB table that you can either store as it is or split into 100 shards of 1 GB tables, which you would store on a single node. Now suppose you want to add an index to the table(s). This would take much longer on a 100 GB shard than it would on all the 1 GB shards combined, because the 1 GB shards fit completely in memory. You also might need to make the data unavailable while ALTER TABLE is running, and blocking 1 GB of data is much better than blocking 100 GB.

Smaller shards are easier to move around, too. This makes it easier to reallocate capacity and rebalance the shards among the nodes. Moving a shard is generally not an efficient process. You typically need to put the affected shard into read-only mode (a feature you'll need to build into your application), extract the data, and move it to another node. This usually involves using *mysqldump* to export the data and *mysql* to reload it. If you're using Percona Server, you can use XtraBackup to move the files between servers, which is much more efficient than dumping and reloading.

In addition to moving shards between nodes, you might need to think about moving data between shards, preferably without interrupting service for the whole application. If your shards are large, it will be harder to balance capacity by moving entire shards around, so you'll probably need a way to move the individual bits of data (for example, a single user) between shards. Moving data between shards is usually a lot more complicated than just moving shards, so it's best not to do it if possible. That's one reason we recommend keeping the shard size manageable.

The relative size of your shards depends on the application's needs. As a rough guide, a "manageable size" for us is one that keeps tables small enough that we can perform regular maintenance jobs, such as `ALTER TABLE`, `CHECK TABLE`, or `OPTIMIZE TABLE`, within 5 or 10 minutes.

If you make your shards too small, you might end up with too many tables, which can cause problems with the filesystem or MySQL's internal structures. Small shards might also increase the number of cross-shard queries you need to make.

Arranging shards on nodes

You'll need to decide how you want to arrange the shards on a node. Here are some common methods:

- Use a single database per shard, and use the same name for each shard's database. This method is typical when you want each shard to mirror the original application's structure. It can work well when you're making many application instances, each of which is aware of only one shard.

- Place tables from several shards into one database, and include the shard number in each table's name (e.g., `bookclub.comments_23`). A single database can hold multiple shards in this configuration.

- Use a single database per shard, and include all the application's tables in the database. Include the shard number in the database name but not the table name (e.g., the tables might be named `bookclub_23.comments`, `bookclub_23.users`, and so on). This is common when an application connects to a single database and doesn't specify the database name in any of its queries. The advantage is that you don't need to customize the queries per shard, and it can ease the transition to sharding for an application that uses only one database.

- Use a single database per shard, and include the shard number in both the database and table names (e.g., the table name would become `bookclub_23.comments_23`).
- Run multiple MySQL instances per node, each with one or more shards, arranged in any sensible combination of the ways we've just mentioned.

If you include the shard number in the table name, you'll need some way to insert the shard number into templated queries. Typical practices include special "magic" placeholder values in queries, `sprintf()`-style formatting specifications such as `%s`, and string interpolation with variables. Here is one way you can create templated queries in PHP:

```
$sql = "SELECT book_id, book_title FROM bookclub_%d.comments_%d... ";
$res = mysql_query(sprintf($sql, $shardno, $shardno), $conn);
```

You could also just use string interpolation:

```
$sql = "SELECT book_id, book_title FROM bookclub_$shardno.comments_$shardno ...";
$res = mysql_query($sql, $conn);
```

This is easy to build into a new application, but it might be harder for existing applications. When we're building new applications and query templating isn't an issue, we like to use a single database per shard, with the shard number in both the database and the table name. It adds some complexity for jobs such as scripting `ALTER TABLE`, but it has advantages, too:

- You can move a shard easily if it's completely contained in a single database.
- Because a database is a directory in the filesystem, you can manage a shard's files easily.
- It's easy to find out how large the shard is if it isn't mixed up with other shards.
- The globally unique table names help avoid mistakes. If table names are the same everywhere, it's easy to accidentally query the wrong shard because you connected to the wrong node, or import one shard's data into another shard's tables.

You might want to consider whether your application's data has any *shard affinity*. You might benefit from placing certain shards "near" each other (on the same server, on the same subnet, in the same data center, or on the same switch) to exploit some similarity in the data access patterns. For example, you can shard by user and then place users from the same country into shards on the same nodes.

Adding sharding support to an existing application often results in one shard per node. This simplification helps limit how much you need to change the application's queries. Sharding is usually a pretty disruptive change for an application, so it makes sense to simplify where possible. If you shard so each node looks like a miniature copy of the whole application's data, you might not have to change most of the queries or worry about routing queries to the desired node.

Fixed allocation

There are two main ways to allocate data to shards: the *fixed* and *dynamic* allocation strategies. Both require a partitioning function that takes a row's partitioning key as input and returns the shard that holds the row.[9]

Fixed allocation uses a partitioning function that depends only on the partitioning key's value. Hash functions and modulus are good examples. These functions map each value of the partitioning key into a limited number of "buckets" that can hold the data.

Suppose you want 100 buckets, and you want to find out where to put user 111. If you're using a modulus, the answer is easy: 111 modulus 100 is 11, so you should place the user into shard 11.

If, on the other hand, you're using the CRC32() function for hashing, the answer is 81:

```
mysql> SELECT CRC32(111) % 100;
+------------------+
| CRC32(111) % 100 |
+------------------+
|               81 |
+------------------+
```

The primary advantages of a fixed strategy are simplicity and low overhead. You can also hardcode it into the application.

However, a fixed allocation strategy has disadvantages, too:

- If the shards are large and there are few of them, it can be hard to balance the load across shards.
- Fixed allocation doesn't let you decide where to store each piece of data, which is important for applications that don't have a very uniform load on the unit of sharding. Some pieces of data will likely be much more active than others, and if many of those happen to fall into the same shard, a fixed allocation strategy doesn't let you ease the strain by moving some of them to another shard. (This is not as much of a problem when you have many small pieces of data in each shard, because the law of large numbers will help even things out.)
- It's usually harder to change the sharding, because it requires reallocating existing data. For example, if you've sharded by a hash function modulus 10, you'll have 10 shards. If the application grows and the shards get too large, you might want to increase the number of shards to 20. That will require rehashing everything, updating a lot of data, and moving data between shards.

Because of these limitations, we usually prefer dynamic allocation for new applications. But if you're sharding an existing application, you might find it easier to build a fixed

---

9. We're using "function" in its mathematical sense here to refer to a mapping from the input (domain) to the output (range). As you'll see, you can create such a function in many ways, including using a lookup table in your database.

allocation strategy instead of a dynamic one, because it's simpler. That said, most applications that use fixed allocation end up with a dynamic allocation strategy sooner or later.

Dynamic allocation

The alternative to fixed allocation is a dynamic allocation strategy that you store separately, mapping each unit of data to a shard. An example is a two-column table of user IDs and shard IDs:

```
CREATE TABLE user_to_shard (
   user_id INT NOT NULL,
   shard_id INT NOT NULL,
   PRIMARY KEY (user_id)
);
```

The table itself is the partitioning function. Given a value for the partitioning key (the user ID), you can find the shard ID. If the row doesn't exist, you can pick the desired shard and add it to the table. You can also change it later—that's what makes this a dynamic allocation strategy.

Dynamic allocation adds overhead to the partitioning function because it requires a call to an external resource, such as a *directory server* (a data storage node that stores the mapping). Such an architecture often needs more layers for efficiency. For example, you can use a distributed caching system to store the directory server's data in memory, because in practice it doesn't change all that much. Or—perhaps more commonly—you can just add a shard_id column to the users table and store it there.

The biggest advantage of dynamic allocation is fine-grained control over where the data is stored. This makes it easier to allocate data to the shards evenly and gives you a lot of flexibility to accommodate changes you don't foresee.

A dynamic mapping also lets you build multiple levels of sharding strategies on top of the simple key-to-shard mapping. For example, you can build a dual mapping that assigns each unit of sharding to a group (e.g., a group of users in the book club), and then keeps the groups together on a shard where possible. This lets you take advantage of shard affinities, so you can avoid cross-shard queries.

If you use a dynamic allocation strategy, you can have imbalanced shards. This can be useful when your servers aren't all equally powerful, or when you want to use some of them for different purposes, such as archived data. If you also have the ability to rebalance shards at any time, you can maintain a one-to-one mapping of shards to nodes without wasting capacity. Some people prefer the simplicity of one shard per node. (But remember, there are advantages to keeping shards small.)

Dynamic allocation and smart use of shard affinities can prevent your cross-shard queries from growing as you scale. Imagine a cross-shard query in a data store with four nodes. In a fixed allocation, any given query might require touching all shards, but a dynamic allocation strategy might let you run the same query on only three of the nodes. This might not seem like a big difference, but consider what will happen when your data store grows to 400 shards: the fixed allocation will require querying all 400 shards, while the dynamic allocation might still require querying only 3.

Dynamic allocation lets you make your sharding strategy as complex as you wish. Fixed allocation doesn't give you as many choices.

Mixing dynamic and fixed allocation

You can use a mixture of fixed and dynamic allocation, which is often helpful and sometimes required. Dynamic allocation works well when the directory mapping isn't too large. If there are many units of sharding, it might not work so well.

An example is a system that's designed to store links between websites. Such a site needs to store tens of billions of rows, and the partitioning key is the combination of source and target URLs. (Just one of the two URLs might have hundreds of millions of links, so neither URL is selective enough by itself.) However, it's not feasible to store all of the source and target URL combinations in the mapping table, because there are many of them, and each URL requires a lot of storage space.

One solution is to concatenate the URLs and hash them into a fixed number of buckets, which you can then map dynamically to shards. If you make the number of buckets large enough—say, a million—you'll be able to fit quite a few of them into each shard. The result is that you get most of the benefits of dynamic sharding, without having a huge mapping table.

Explicit allocation

A third allocation strategy is to let the application choose each row's desired shard explicitly when it creates the row. This is harder to do with existing data, so it's not very common when adding sharding to an application. However, it can be helpful sometimes.

The idea is to encode the shard number into the ID, similar to the technique we showed for avoiding duplicate key values in master-master replication. (See "Writing to Both Masters in Master-Master Replication" on page 505 for more details.)

For example, suppose your application wants to create user 3 and assign it to shard 11, and you've reserved the eight most significant bits of a BIGINT column for the shard number. The resulting ID value is (11 << 56) + 3, or 792633534417207299. The application can easily extract the user ID and the shard ID later. Here's an example:

```
mysql> SELECT (792633534417207299 >> 56) AS shard_id,
    -> 792633534417207299 & ~(11 << 56) AS user_id;
+----------+---------+
| shard_id | user_id |
+----------+---------+
|       11 |       3 |
+----------+---------+
```

Now suppose you want to create a comment for this user and store it in the same shard. The application can assign the comment ID 5 for the user, and combine the value 5 with the shard ID 11 in the same way.

The benefit of this approach is that each object's ID carries its partitioning key along with it, whereas other approaches usually require a join or another lookup to find the partitioning key. If you want to retrieve a certain comment from the database, you don't need to know which user owns it; the object's ID tells you where to find it. If the object were sharded dynamically by user ID, you'd have to find the comment's user, then ask the directory server which shard to look on.

Another solution is to store the partitioning key together with the object in separate columns. For example, you'd never refer just to comment 5, but to comment 5 belonging to user 3. This approach will probably make some people happier, because it doesn't violate first normal form; however, the extra column causes more overhead, coding, and inconvenience. (This is one case where we feel there's an advantage to storing two values in a single column.)

The drawback of explicit allocation is that the sharding is fixed, and it's harder to balance shards. On the other hand, this approach works well with the combination of fixed and dynamic allocation. Instead of hashing to a fixed number of buckets and mapping these to nodes, you encode the bucket as part of each object. This gives the application control over where the data is located, so it can place related data together on the same shard.

BoardReader (*http://boardreader.com*) uses a variation of this technique: it encodes the partitioning key in the Sphinx document ID. This makes it easy to find each search result's related data in the sharded data store. See Appendix F for more on Sphinx.

We've described mixed allocation because we've seen cases where it's useful, but normally we don't recommend it. We like to use dynamic allocation when possible, and avoid explicit allocation.

Rebalancing shards

If necessary, you can move data to different shards to rebalance the load. For example, many readers have probably heard developers from large photo-sharing sites or popular social networking sites mention their tools for moving users to different shards.

The ability to move data between shards has its benefits. For example, it can help you upgrade your hardware by enabling you to move users off the old shard onto the new one without taking the whole shard down or making it read-only.

However, we like to avoid rebalancing shards if possible, because it can disrupt service to your users. Moving data between shards also makes it harder to add features to the application, because new features might have to include an upgrade to the rebalance script. If you keep your shards small enough, you might not need to do this; you can often rebalance the load by moving entire shards, which is easier than moving part of a shard (and more efficient, in terms of cost per row of data).

One strategy that works well is to use a dynamic sharding strategy and assign new data to shards randomly. When a shard gets full enough, you can set a flag that tells the application not to give it any new data. You can then flip the flag back if you want more data on that shard in the future.

Suppose you install a new MySQL node and place 100 shards on it. To begin, you set their flags to 1, so the application knows they're ready for new data. Once they each have enough data (10,000 users each, for example), you set their flags to 0. Then, if the node becomes underloaded after a while because of abandoned accounts, you can re-open some of the shards and add new users to them.

If you upgrade the application and add features that make each shard's query load higher, or if you just miscalculated the load, you can move some of the shards to new nodes to ease the load. The drawback is that an entire shard might be read-only or offline while you do this. It's up to you and your users to decide whether that's acceptable.

Another tactic we use a lot is to set up two replicas of a shard, each with a complete copy of the shard's data. We then make each replica responsible for half of the data, and stop sending queries to the master completely. Each replica contains some data it doesn't use; we set up a background job with a tool such as Percona Toolkit's *pt-archiver* to remove the unwanted data. This is simple and requires practically zero downtime.

Generating globally unique IDs

When you convert a system to use a sharded data store, you frequently need to generate globally unique IDs on many machines. A monolithic data store often uses AUTO_INCREMENT columns for this purpose, but that doesn't tend to work well across many servers. There are several ways to solve this problem:

Use auto_increment_increment *and* auto_increment_offset
These two server settings instruct MySQL to increment AUTO_INCREMENT columns by a desired value and to begin numbering from a desired offset. For example, in the simplest case with two servers, you can configure the servers to increment by two, set one server's offset to one, and set the other's to two (you can't set either value to zero). Now one server's columns will always contain even numbers, and the other's will always contain odd numbers. The setting applies to all tables in the server.

Because of its simplicity and lack of dependency on a central node, this is a popular way to generate values, but it requires you to be careful with your server configurations. It's easy to accidentally configure servers so that they generate duplicate numbers, especially if you move them into different roles as you add more servers, or when you recover from failures.

Create a table in the global node

You can create a table with an AUTO_INCREMENT column in your global database node, and applications can use this to generate unique numbers.

Use memcached

There's an incr() function in the *memcached* API that can increment a number atomically and return the result. You can use Redis, too.

Allocate numbers in batches

The application can request a batch of numbers from a global node, use all the numbers, and then request more.

Use a combination of values

You can use a combination of values, such as the shard ID and an incrementing number, to make each server's values unique. See the discussion of this technique in the previous section.

Use GUID values

You can generate globally unique values with the UUID() function. Beware, though: this function does not replicate correctly with statement-based replication, although it works fine if your application selects the value into its own memory and then uses it as a literal in statements. GUID values are large and nonsequential, so they don't make good primary keys for InnoDB tables. See "Inserting rows in primary key order with InnoDB" on page 173 for more on this. There's also a UUID_SHORT() function in MySQL 5.1 and newer versions, which has some nice properties such as being sequential and only 64 bits instead of 128.

If you use a global allocator to generate values, be careful that the single point of contention doesn't create a bottleneck for your application.

Although the *memcached* approach can be very fast (tens of thousands of values per second), it isn't persistent. Each time you restart the *memcached* service, you'll need to initialize the value in the cache. This could require you to find the maximum value that's in use across all shards, which might be very slow and difficult to do atomically.

Tools for sharding

One of the first things you'll have to do when designing a sharded application is write code for querying multiple data sources.

It's generally a poor design to expose the multiple data sources to the application without any abstraction, because it can add a lot of code complexity. It's better to hide the data sources behind an abstraction layer. This layer might handle the following tasks:

- Connecting to the correct shard and querying it
- Distributed consistency checks

- Aggregating results across shards
- Cross-shard joins
- Locking and transaction management
- Creating shards (or at least discovering new shards on the fly) and rebalancing shards if you have time to implement this

You might not have to build your own sharding infrastructure from scratch. There are several tools and systems that either provide some of the necessary functionality or are specifically designed to implement a sharded architecture.

One database abstraction layer with sharding support is Hibernate Shards (*http://shards .hibernate.org*), Google's extension to the open source Java-based Hibernate object-relational mapping (ORM) library. It provides shard-aware implementations of the Hibernate Core interfaces, so applications don't necessarily have to be redesigned to use a sharded data store; in fact, they might not even have to be aware that they're using one. Hibernate Shards uses a fixed allocation strategy to allocate data to the shards. Another Java sharding system is HiveDB (*http://www.hivedb.org*).

In PHP, you can use Justin Swanhart's Shard-Query system (*http://code.google.com/p/ shard-query/*), which automatically decomposes queries, executes them in parallel, and combines the results. Commercial systems targeted at similar use cases are ScaleBase (*http://www.scalebase.com*), ScalArc (*http://www.scalarc.com*), and dbShards (*http:// www.dbshards.com*).

Sphinx is a full-text search engine, not a sharded data storage and retrieval system, but it is still useful for some types of queries across sharded data stores. It can query remote systems in parallel and aggregate the results. Sphinx is discussed further in Appendix F.

Scaling by Consolidation

A heavily sharded architecture creates an opportunity to get more out of your hardware. Our research and experience have shown that MySQL can't use the full power of modern hardware. As you scale beyond about 24 CPU cores, MySQL's efficiency starts to level off. A similar thing happens beyond 128 MB of memory, and MySQL can't even come close to using the full I/O power of high-end PCIe flash devices such as Virident and Fusion-io cards.

Instead of using a single server instance on a powerful machine, there's another option. You can make your shards small enough that you can fit several per machine (a practice we've been advocating anyway), and run several instances per server, carving up the server's physical resources to give each instance a portion.

This actually works, although we wish it weren't necessary. It's a combination of the scale-up and scale-out approaches. You can do it in other ways—you don't have to use sharding—but sharding is a natural fit for consolidation on large servers.

Some people like to achieve consolidation with virtualization, which has its benefits. But virtualization also has a pretty hefty performance cost itself in many cases. It depends on the technology, but it's usually noticeable, and the overhead is especially exaggerated when I/O is very fast. As an alternative, you can run multiple MySQL instances, each listening on different network ports or binding to different IP addresses.

We've been able to achieve a consolidation factor of up to 10x or 15x on powerful hardware. You'll have to balance the cost of the administrative complexity with the benefit of better performance to determine what's best for you.

At this point, the network is likely to become the bottleneck—a problem most MySQL users don't run into very often. You can address the problem by using multiple NICs and bonding them. The Linux kernel isn't ideal for this, depending on the version, because older kernels can use only one CPU for network interrupts per bonded device. As a result, you shouldn't bond too many cables into too few virtual devices, or you'll run into a different network bottleneck inside the kernel. Newer kernels should help with this, so check your distribution to find out what your options are.

Another way you can get more out of this strategy is to bind each MySQL instance to specific cores. This helps for two reasons: first because MySQL gets more performance per core at lower core counts due to its internal scalability limitations, and second when an instance is running threads on many cores, there's less overhead due to synchronizing shared data between the cores. This helps avoid the scalability limitations of the hardware itself. Limiting MySQL to only some cores can reduce the crosstalk between CPU cores. Notice the recurring theme? Pin the process to cores that are on the same physical socket for the best results.

Scaling by Clustering

The dream scenario for scaling is a single logical database that can hold as much data, serve as many queries, and grow as large as you need it to. Many people's first thought is to create a "cluster" or "grid" that handles this seamlessly, so the application doesn't need to do any dirty work or know that the data really lives in many servers instead of just one. With the rise of the cloud, autoscaling—dynamically adding servers to or removing them from the cluster in response to changes in workload or data size—is also becoming interesting.

In the second edition of this book, we expressed our regret that the available technology wasn't really up to the task. Since then, a lot of the buzz has centered around so-called *NoSQL* technologies. Many *NoSQL* proponents made strange and unsubstantiated claims such as "the relational model can't scale," or "SQL can't scale." New concepts emerged, and new catchphrases were on everyone's lips. Who hasn't heard of eventual consistency, BASE, vector clocks, or the CAP theorem these days?

But as time has passed, sanity has been at least partially restored. Experience is beginning to reveal that many of the NoSQL databases are primitive in their own ways and aren't really up to a lot of tasks themselves.[10] In the meantime, a variety of SQL-based technologies have arisen—what Matt Aslett of the 451 Group calls *NewSQL* databases. What's the difference between SQL and NewSQL? The NewSQL databases are setting out to prove that SQL and relational technology aren't the problem. Rather, the scalability problems in relational databases are implementation problems, and new implementations are showing better results.

Is everything old new again? Yes and no. A lot of the high-performance implementations of clustered relational databases are built on low-level building blocks that look remarkably like NoSQL databases, especially key-value stores. For example, NDB Cluster isn't a SQL database; it's a scalable database that can be accessed through its native API, which is very much NoSQL, but it can also talk SQL when you put a MySQL storage engine in front of it. It is a fully distributed, shared-nothing, high-performance, auto-sharded, transactional database server with no single point of failure. It's a very advanced database that has no equal for particular uses. And it has become much more powerful, sophisticated, and general-purpose in the last few years. At the same time, the NoSQL databases are gradually starting to look more like relational databases, and some are even developing query languages that resemble SQL. The typical clustered database of the future will probably look a bit like a blend of SQL and NoSQL, with multiple access mechanisms to suit different use cases. So we're learning from NoSQL, but SQL is here to stay in clustered databases, too.

At the time of writing, the current breed of clustered or distributed database technologies that rub shoulders with the MySQL world roughly include the following: NDB Cluster, Clustrix, Percona XtraDB Cluster, Galera, Schooner Active Cluster, Continuent Tungsten, ScaleBase, ScaleArc, dbShards, Xeround, Akiban, VoltDB, and GenieDB. These are all more or less built on, accessible through, or related to MySQL. We cover some of them elsewhere in the book—for example, we'll look at Xeround in Chapter 13, and we discussed Continuent Tungsten and several other technologies back in Chapter 10—but we'll devote a little space to a couple of them here as well.

Before we start, we need to point out again that scalability, high availability, transactionality, and so on are really orthogonal properties of database systems. Some people get confused and treat them as the same thing, but they're not. In this chapter we're focusing on scalability. However, in real life a scalable database isn't much good unless it's also high-performance, and who wants to scale without high availability, and so on. Some combination of all these nice properties is the holy grail of databases, and it happens to be very hard to achieve, but that's out of scope for this chapter.

Finally, most of the clustered NewSQL products are relatively new on the scene, with the exception of NDB Cluster. We haven't seen enough production deployment to know their strengths and limitations thoroughly. And although they might speak the MySQL wire protocol or otherwise be related to MySQL, they aren't MySQL, so they're

---

10. Yeah, yeah, we know, choose the right tool for the job. Insert other self-obvious but insightful-sounding quote here.

really out of scope for this whole book. As a result, we'll just mention them and leave it to you to judge their suitability.

MySQL Cluster (NDB Cluster)

MySQL Cluster is a combination of two technologies: the NDB database, and a MySQL storage engine as a SQL frontend. NDB is a distributed, fault-tolerant, shared-nothing database that offers synchronous replication and automatic data partitioning across the nodes. The NDB Cluster storage engine translates SQL into NDB API calls, and performs operations inside the MySQL server when they can't be pushed to NDB for execution. (NDB is a key-value data store, and it can't do complex operations such as joins and aggregation.)

NDB is a sophisticated database that has very little in common with MySQL. You don't even need MySQL to use NDB: you can run it as a standalone key-value database server. Its strong points include extremely high throughput for writes and lookups by key. NDB automatically decides which node should hold a given value, based on a hash of the key. When you access NDB through MySQL, the row's primary key is the key, and the rest of the row is the value.

Because it's based on a whole new set of technologies, and because the cluster is fault-tolerant and distributed, NDB is specialized and nontrivial to administer correctly. There are a lot of moving parts, and operations such as upgrading the cluster or adding a node must be performed in exactly the right way to avoid problems. NDB is open source technology, but you can purchase commercial support from Oracle. Part of that subscription is the proprietary Cluster Manager product, which helps automate many tedious and tricky tasks. (Severalnines also offers a cluster management product; see *http://www.severalnines.com*)

MySQL Cluster has been rapidly gaining more features and capabilities. In recent versions, for example, it supports more types of changes to the cluster without downtime, and it can execute some kinds of queries on the nodes, where the data is stored, to reduce the need to pull data across the wire and execute the queries inside MySQL. (This feature has been renamed from *push-down joins* to *adaptive query localization*.)

NDB used to have a completely different performance profile from other MySQL storage engines, but recent versions are more general-purpose. It's becoming a better solution for an increasing variety of applications, including games and mobile applications. We should emphasize that NDB is serious technology that powers some of the world's largest mission-critical applications under extremely high loads, with demanding latency and uptime requirements. Practically every phone call placed on a cellular network anywhere in the world uses NDB, for example, and not just in a casual way— it's the central and vital database for many cellular providers.

NDB needs a fast and reliable network to connect the nodes, and it's better to have special high-speed interconnects for the best performance. It also operates mostly in memory, so it requires a lot of memory across the servers.

What isn't it good at? It's not great at complex queries yet, such as those with lots of joins or aggregation. Don't count on using it for data warehousing, for example. It is a transactional system, but it does not have MVCC support, and reads are locking. It also does not do any deadlock detection. If there's a deadlock, NDB resolves it with a time-out. There are many other fine points and caveats you should know about, which deserve a dedicated book. (There are books on MySQL Cluster, but most are outdated. Your best bet is the manual.)

Clustrix

Clustrix (*http://www.clustrix.com*) is a distributed database that understands the MySQL protocol, so it is a drop-in replacement for MySQL. Beyond understanding the protocol, it is completely new technology and isn't built on MySQL at all. It is a fully ACID, transactional SQL database with MVCC, targeted at OLTP workloads. Clustrix partitions the data across nodes for fault tolerance and distributes queries to the data to execute in parallel on the nodes, rather than fetching the data from the storage nodes to a centralized execution node. The cluster is expandable online by adding more nodes to handle more data or more load. Clustrix is similar to MySQL Cluster in some ways; key differences are its fully distributed execution and its lack of a top-level "proxy" or query coordinator in front of the cluster. Clustrix understands the MySQL protocol natively, so it doesn't need MySQL to translate between the MySQL protocol and its own. In contrast, MySQL cluster is really assembled from three components: MySQL, the NDBCLUSTER storage engine, and NDB.

Our laboratory evaluations and benchmarks confirm that Clustrix offers high performance and scalability. Clustrix looks like a very promising technology, and we are continually watching and evaluating it.

ScaleBase

ScaleBase (*http://www.scalebase.com*) is a software proxy that sits between your application and a number of backend MySQL servers. It splits incoming queries into pieces, distributes them for simultaneous execution on the backend servers, and assembles the results for delivery back to the application. At the time of writing we have no experience with it in production, however. Competing technologies include ScaleArc (*http://www.scalearc.com*) and dbShards (*http://www.dbshards.com*).

GenieDB

GenieDB (*http://www.geniedb.com*) was born as a NoSQL document store for geographically distributed deployment. It now also has a SQL layer, which is accessible through a MySQL storage engine. It is built on a collection of technologies including a local in-memory cache, a messaging layer, and a persistent disk data store. These work together to provide the application with the choice of executing queries quickly against local data with relaxed eventual consistency guarantees, or against the distributed cluster (with added network latency) to guarantee the latest view of the data.

The MySQL compatibility layer through the storage engine doesn't offer 100% of MySQL's features, but it is rich enough to support applications such as Joomla!, WordPress, and Drupal out of the box. The use case for the MySQL storage engine is to make GenieDB available alongside an ACID storage engine such as InnoDB. GenieDB is not an ACID database.

We have not worked with GenieDB ourselves, nor have we seen any production deployments.

Akiban

Akiban (*http://www.akiban.com*) is probably best described as a query accelerator. It stores data physically to match query patterns, making it possible to perform joins across tables with much lower cost. Although similar to denormalization, the data layout is not redundant, so it is not the same thing as precomputing joins and storing the results. Instead, tuples from the joined tables are interleaved with one another, so they can be scanned in join order sequentially. This requires the administrator to identify the query patterns that would benefit from the so-called "table grouping" technique and design table groups optimized for the queries. The currently suggested system architecture is to configure Akiban to replicate from your MySQL master, and use it to serve queries that would otherwise be slow to execute. The speedup factor is claimed to be one to two orders of magnitude. However, we have neither seen production deployments nor conducted laboratory evaluations.[11]

Scaling Back

One of the simpler ways to deal with an increasing data size and workload is to archive and purge unneeded data. Depending on your workload and data characteristics, you might be able to realize significant gains from archiving and purging data you don't need. This doesn't replace other scaling strategies, but it can be part of a short-term strategy to buy time and should probably be part of a long-term plan to cope with large data volumes.

Here are some things to think about when designing archiving and purging strategies:

Impact on the application
> A well-designed archiving strategy can move data away from a heavily loaded OLTP server without impacting transaction processing noticeably. The key is to make it efficient to find the rows to remove, and to remove them in small chunks. You'll usually need to balance the number of rows you archive at once with the size of a transaction to find a good compromise between lock contention and transactional overhead. You should design your archive jobs to yield to transactional processing jobs when necessary.

---

11. We might be cheating a bit by including Akiban in the list of clustered databases, because it's not really clustered. However, it's similar to some of the other NewSQL databases in some ways.

Which rows to archive

You can purge or archive data once you know you'll never refer to it again, but you can also design your application to archive seldom-accessed data. You can store the archived data adjacent to the core tables and access it through views, or even move it to another server entirely.

Maintaining data consistency

Data relationships make archiving and purging more complex. A well-designed archiving job keeps the data logically consistent, or at least as consistent as the application needs, without involving multiple tables in huge transactions.

Deciding which tables to archive first is always a challenge when there are relationships among the tables. You'll have to consider the impact of "orphaned" or "widowed" rows while archiving. The main choice is usually whether to violate foreign keys (you can disable InnoDB foreign key constraints with SET FOREIGN _KEY_CHECKS=0) or to leave "dangling pointer" records temporarily. Which is preferable depends on how your application views the data. If the application views a particular set of related tables from the top down, you should probably archive them in the same order. For example, if your application always examines orders before invoices, archive the orders first; your application shouldn't see the orphaned invoices, and you can archive them next.

Avoiding data loss

If you're archiving between servers, you probably shouldn't do distributed transactions, and you might be archiving into MyISAM or another nontransactional storage engine anyway. Therefore, to avoid data loss, you should insert into the destination before deleting from the source. It might also be a good idea to write archived data to a file along the way. You should design your archive jobs so you can kill and restart them at will, without causing inconsistencies or index-violation errors.

Unarchiving

You can often trim a lot more data by archiving with an unarchiving strategy. This helps because it lets you archive data you're not sure you'll need, with the option of bringing it back later. If you can identify a few points of entry where your system can check whether it needs to retrieve some archived data, it might be fairly easy to implement such a strategy. For example, if you archive possibly inactive users, the entry point might be the login process. If a login fails because there's no such user, you can check the archive to see whether the user exists there, and if so, retrieve the user from the archive and process the login.

 Percona Toolkit contains *pt-archiver*, a tool that can help you archive and/or purge MySQL tables efficiently. It does not offer any support for unarchiving, however.

Keeping active data separate

Even if you don't actually move stale data away to another server, many applications can benefit from separating active and inactive datasets. This helps keep caches efficient, and enables you to use different kinds of hardware or application architectures for the active and inactive data. Here are some ways to accomplish this:

Splitting tables into parts

It's often smart to split tables, especially if the entire table won't fit in memory. For example, you can split the users table into active_users and inactive_users. You might think this isn't necessary because the database will cache only the "hot" data anyway, but that depends on your storage engine. If you use InnoDB, caching works a page at a time. If you can fit 100 users on a page and only 10% of your users are active, that probably makes every page "hot" from InnoDB's point of view—yet 90% of each "hot" page will be wasted space. Splitting the table in two could improve your memory usage dramatically.

MySQL partitioning

MySQL 5.1 offers natively partitioned tables, which can help keep the most recent data in memory. See Chapter 7 for more about partitioning.

Time-based data partitioning

If your application continually gets new data, it's likely that the newest data will be far more active than the older data. For example, we know of one blog service whose traffic is mostly from posts and comments created in the last seven days. Most of its updates are to the same set of data. As a result, this data is kept entirely in memory, with replication to ensure there is a recoverable copy on disk if there's a failure. The rest of the data lives forever in another location.

We've also seen designs that store each user's data in shards on two nodes. New data goes to the "active" node, which has a lot of memory and fast disks. This data is optimized for very fast access. The other node stores older data, with very large (but slower) disks. The application assumes that it's not likely to need the older data. This is a good assumption for a lot of applications, which might be able to satisfy 90% or more of requests from only the most recent 10% of the data.

You can implement this sharding policy easily with dynamic sharding. For example, your sharding directory's table definition might look something like the following:

```
CREATE TABLE users (
    user_id            int unsigned not null,
    shard_new          int unsigned not null,
    shard_archive      int unsigned not null,
    archive_timestamp  timestamp,
    PRIMARY KEY (user_id)
);
```

An archive script can move older data from the active node to the archive node, updating the archive_timestamp column when it moves a user's data to the archive node. The `shard_new` and `shard_archive` columns tell you which shard numbers hold the data.

Load Balancing

The basic idea behind load balancing is simple: to share the workload among a collection of servers. The usual way to do this is to place a load balancer (often a specialized piece of hardware) in front of the servers. The load balancer then routes incoming connections to the least busy available server. Figure 11-9 shows a typical load-balancing setup for a large website, with one load balancer for the HTTP traffic and another for MySQL traffic.

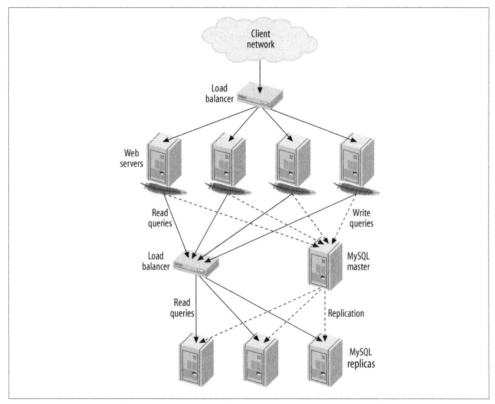

Figure 11-9. Typical load-balancing architecture for a read-intensive website

Load balancing has five common goals:

Scalability

    Load balancing can help with certain kinds of scalability strategies, such as read-write splitting to read from replicas.

Efficiency

Load balancing helps you use resources more efficiently because you have control over how requests are routed. This is particularly important if your servers aren't all equally powerful: you can direct more work to the more powerful machines.

Availability

A smart load-balancing solution uses the servers that are available at each moment.

Transparency

Clients don't need to know about the load-balancing setup. They don't have to care about how many machines are behind the load balancer, or what their names are; the load balancer lets the clients see a single virtual server.

Consistency

If your application is stateful (database transactions, website sessions, etc.), the load balancer should direct related requests to a single server so that the state isn't lost between requests. This relieves the application of having to keep track of which server it's connected to.

In the MySQL world, load-balancing architectures are often tightly coupled with sharding and replication. You can mix and match load-balancing and high-availability solutions and place them at whatever level is appropriate within your application. For example, you can load balance across multiple SQL nodes in a MySQL Cluster installation. You can also load balance across data centers, and within each data center you might have a sharded architecture, each node of which is actually part of a master-master replication pair with many replicas that are load balanced yet again. The same is true of high-availability strategies; you can have multiple levels of failover in an architecture.

Load balancing has many nuances. For example, one of the challenges is managing read/write policies. Some load-balancing technologies do this themselves, whereas others require the application to be aware of which nodes are readable and writable.

You should consider these factors when you decide how to implement load balancing. A wide variety of load-balancing solutions are available, ranging from peer-based implementations such as Wackamole (*http://www.backhand.org/wackamole/*) to DNS, LVS (Linux Virtual Server; *http://www.linuxvirtualserver.org*), hardware load balancers, TCP proxies, MySQL Proxy, and managing the load balancing in the application.

Among our customers, perhaps the most common tactic is to use hardware load balancers. Many of them use HAProxy (*http://haproxy.1wt.eu*), which seems to be very popular and work quite well. Some people use another TCP proxy, such as Pen (*http://siag.nu/pen/*). We don't see MySQL Proxy used very often.

Connecting Directly

Some people automatically associate load balancing with a central system that's inserted between the application and the MySQL servers. This isn't the only way to load balance, though. You can load balance and yet still connect directly from the application to the MySQL servers. In fact, centralized load-balancing systems usually work well only when there's a pool of servers the application can treat as interchangeable. If the application needs to make a decision such as whether it's safe to perform a read from a replica server, it usually needs to connect directly to the server.

Besides making special-case logic possible, handling the load-balancing decisions in the application can actually be very efficient. For example, if you have two identical replicas, you can choose to use one of them for all queries that touch certain shards and the other for queries that touch other shards. This makes good use of the replicas' memory, because each of them caches only a portion of the data from its disks in memory. And if one of the replicas fails, the other still has all the data required to serve queries to both shards.

The following sections discuss some common ways to connect directly from the application, and some of the things you should consider as you evaluate each option.

Splitting reads and writes in replication

MySQL replication gives you multiple copies of your data and lets you choose whether to run a query on the master or a replica. The primary difficulty is how to handle stale data on the replica, because replication is asynchronous. You should also treat replicas as read-only, but the master can handle both read and write queries.

You usually have to modify your application so that it's aware of these concerns. The application can then use the master for writes and split the reads between the master and the replicas; it can use the replicas when possibly stale data doesn't matter and use the master for data that has to be up-to-date. We call this *read/write splitting*.

If you use a master-master pair with an active and a passive master, the same considerations hold. In this configuration, though, only the active server should receive writes. Reads can go to the passive server if it's OK to read potentially stale data.

The biggest problem is how to avoid artifacts caused by reading stale data. The classic artifact is when a user makes some change, such as adding a comment to a blog post, then reloads the page but doesn't see the change because the application read stale data from a replica.

Some of the most common methods of splitting reads and writes are as follows:

Query-based split
> The simplest split is to direct all writes and any reads that can never tolerate stale data to the active or master server. All other reads go to the replica or passive server. This strategy is easy to implement, but in practice it won't use the replica as often as it could, because very few read queries can always tolerate stale data.

Stale-data split
> This is a minor enhancement of the query-based split strategy. Relatively little extra work is required to make the application check the replica's lag and decide whether

or not its data is too stale to read. Many reporting applications can use this strategy: as long as the nightly data load has finished replicating to the replica, they don't care whether it is 100% caught up with the master.

Session-based split

A slightly more sophisticated way to decide whether a read can go to a replica is to note whether the user has changed any data. The user doesn't have to see the most up-to-date data from other users but should see her own changes. You can implement this at the session level by flagging the session as having made a change and directing the user's read queries to the master for a certain period of time after that. This is the strategy we usually suggest to clients, because it's a good compromise between simplicity and effectiveness.

If you want to get fancy, you can combine session-based splitting with replication lag monitoring. If the user changed some data 10 seconds ago and no replica is more than 5 seconds behind, it's safe to read from a replica. It's a very good idea to select one of the replicas and use it for the whole session, though, or the user might see strange effects caused by some of the replicas being farther behind than others.

Version-based split

This is similar to session-based splitting: you can track version numbers and/or timestamps for objects, and read the object's version or timestamp from the replica to determine whether its data is fresh enough to use. If the replica's data is too old, you can read the fresh data from the master. You can also increment the top-level item's version number even when the object itself doesn't change, which simplifies staleness checks (you need to look in only one place—at the top-level item). For example, you can update the user's version if he posts a new blog entry. This will cause reads to go to the master.

Reading the object's version from the replica adds overhead, which you can reduce with caching. We discuss caching and object versioning further in later chapters.

Global version/session split

This is a variation on version- and session-based splitting. When the application performs a write, it runs SHOW MASTER STATUS after the transaction commits. It stores the master's log coordinates in the cache as the modified object's and/or session's version number. Then, when the application connects to the replica, it runs SHOW SLAVE STATUS and compares the replica's coordinates to the stored version. If the replica has advanced to at least the point at which the master committed the transaction, the replica is safe to use for the read.

Most read/write splitting solutions require you to monitor replication lag and use it to decide where to direct reads, either in the application or through a load balancer or another man-in-the-middle system. If you do this, be aware that the Seconds_behind _master column from SHOW SLAVE STATUS is not a reliable way to monitor lag. (See Chapter 10 for details.) The *pt-heartbeat* tool from Percona Toolkit can help you monitor replication delay, and help maintain metadata such as binary log positions, which can ease the problems with some of the strategies we just discussed.

If you don't care how much hardware it takes to serve your load, you can keep things simpler and not use replication for scaling reads. That might let you avoid the complexity of splitting reads between the master and replicas. Some people think this makes sense; others think it wastes hardware. This division reflects differing goals: do you want scalability only, or both scalability and efficiency? If you want efficiency too, and thus want to use the replicas for something other than just keeping a copy of the data, you'll probably have to deal with some added complexity.

Changing the application configuration

One way you can distribute load is to reconfigure your application. For example, you can configure several machines to share the load of generating large reports. Each machine's configuration can instruct it to connect to a different MySQL replica and generate reports for every *N*th customer or site.

This system is generally very simple to implement, but if it requires any code changes—including changes to configuration files—it becomes brittle and unwieldy. Anything hardcoded that you have to change on every server, or change in a central location and "publish" via file copies or source-control update commands, is inherently limited. If you store the configuration in the database and/or a cache, you can avoid the need to publish code changes.

Changing DNS names

A crude load-balancing technique, but one that works acceptably for some simple applications, is to create DNS names for various purposes. You can then point the names at different servers as appropriate. The simplest implementation is to have one DNS name for the read-only servers and one for the writable server. If the replicas are keeping up with the master, you can change the read-only DNS name to point to the replicas; when they fall behind, you can point it back to the master.

The DNS technique is very easy to implement, but it has many drawbacks. The biggest problem is that DNS is not completely under your control:

- DNS changes are not instantaneous or atomic. It can take a long time for DNS changes to propagate throughout a network or between networks.
- DNS data is cached in various places, and expiry times are advisory, not mandatory.
- DNS changes might require an application or server restart to take effect fully.
- It's not a good idea to use multiple IP addresses for a DNS name and rely on round-robin behavior to balance requests. The round-robin behavior isn't always predictable.
- The DBA might not always have direct access to DNS.

Unless the application is very simple, it's dangerous to rely on a system that's not controllable. You can improve your control a little by making changes to */etc/hosts* instead of DNS. When you publish a change to this file, you know the change has taken effect. This is better than waiting for a cached DNS entry to expire, but it is still not ideal.

We usually advise people to build for zero reliance on DNS. It's a good idea to avoid it even for simple applications, because you never know how large your application will grow.

Moving IP addresses

Some load-balancing solutions rely on moving virtual IP addresses[12] between servers, which can work very well. This might sound similar to making DNS changes, but it's not the same thing. Servers don't listen for network traffic to a DNS name; they listen for traffic to a specific IP address, so moving IP addresses allows DNS names to remain static. You can force IP address changes to be noticed very quickly and atomically via Address Resolution Protocol (ARP) commands.

The most common technology we see used for this is Pacemaker, the successor to the Linux-HA project's Heartbeat tool. For example, you can have a single IP address associated with a role such as "read-only," and it takes care of moving the IP address between machines as needed. Other tools for this purpose include LVS and Wackamole.

One handy technique is to assign a fixed IP address to each physical server. This IP address defines the server itself and never changes. You can then use a virtual IP address for each logical "service." These can move between servers easily, which makes it easy to move services and application instances around without reconfiguring the application. This is a nice feature, even if you don't move IP addresses a lot.

Introducing a Middleman

So far, the techniques we've discussed all assume your application is communicating directly with MySQL servers. However, many load-balancing solutions introduce a middleman whose job is to act as a proxy for the network traffic. The middleman accepts all traffic on one side and directs it to the desired server on the other, then routes the responses back to the originating machine. Sometimes the middleman is a piece of hardware, and sometimes it's software.[13] Figure 11-10 illustrates this architecture. Such solutions generally work well, although unless you make the load balancer itself redundant, they add a single point of failure. We've seen a variety of load balancers

---

12. Virtual IP addresses aren't connected to any specific computer or network interfaces; they "float" between computers.

13. You can configure some solutions such as LVS so they are involved only when an application needs to create a new connection, and don't act as a middleman after that.

---

used with success, from open source software such as HAProxy to pretty much any commercial system you can name.

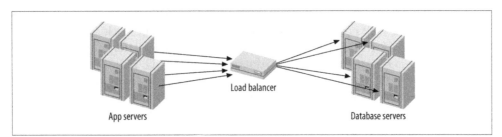

Figure 11-10. A load balancer that acts as a middleman

Load balancers

There is a wide variety of load-balancing hardware and software on the market, but few of the offerings are designed specifically for balancing load to MySQL servers.[14] Web servers need load balancing much more often, so many general-purpose load-balancing devices have special features for HTTP and only a few basic features for everything else. MySQL connections are just normal TCP/IP connections, so you can use general-purpose load balancers for MySQL. However, the lack of MySQL-specific features does add some limitations:

- Unless the load balancer is aware of MySQL's true load, it's unlikely to *balance load* so much as *distribute requests*. Not all queries are equal, but general-purpose load balancers usually treat all requests as equal.

- Most load balancers know how to inspect an HTTP request and "stick a session" to a server to preserve session state on one web server. MySQL connections are stateful too, but the load balancer is unlikely to know how to "stick" all connection requests from a single HTTP session to a single MySQL server. This results in a loss of efficiency (if a single session's requests all go to the same MySQL server, the server's cache will be more efficient).

- Connection pooling and persistent connections can interfere with a load balancer's ability to distribute connection requests. For example, suppose a connection pool opens its configured number of connections, and the load balancer distributes them among the existing four MySQL servers. Now say you add two more MySQL servers. Because the connection pool isn't requesting any new connections, they'll sit idle. The connections in the pool also might end up being unfairly distributed among the servers, so some are overloaded and others are underloaded. You can work around these problems by expiring the connections in the pool at various

---

14. MySQL Proxy is an exception, but it hasn't proved to work all that well in the field, due to problems such as added latency and scalability bottlenecks.

levels, but that's complicated and difficult to do. Connection pooling solutions work best when they do their own load balancing.

- Most general-purpose load balancers know how to do health and load checks only for HTTP servers. A simple load balancer can verify that the server accepts connections on a TCP port, which is the bare minimum. A better load balancer can make an HTTP request and check the response code to determine whether the web server is running well. MySQL doesn't accept HTTP requests to port 3306, though, so you'll have to build a custom health check. You can install HTTP server software on the MySQL server and point the load balancer at a custom script that actually checks the MySQL server's status and returns an appropriate status code.[15] The most important things to check are the operating system load (generally by looking at /proc/loadavg), the replication status, and the number of MySQL connections.

Load-balancing algorithms

There are many different algorithms to determine which server should receive the next connection. Each vendor uses different terminology, but this list should provide an idea of what's available:

Random
> The load balancer directs each request to a server selected at random from the pool of available servers.

Round-robin
> The load balancer sends requests to servers in a repeating sequence: A, B, C, A, B, C, etc.

Fewest connections
> The next connection goes to the server with the fewest active connections.

Fastest response
> The server that has been handling requests the fastest receives the next connection. This can work well when the pool contains a mix of fast and slow machines. However, it's very tricky with SQL when the query complexity varies widely. Even the same query can perform very differently under different circumstances, such as when it's served from the query cache or when the server's caches already contain the needed data.

Hashed
> The load balancer hashes the connection's source IP address, which maps it to one of the servers in the pool. Each time a connection request comes from the same IP address, the load balancer sends it to the same server. The bindings change only when the number of machines in the pool does.

---

15. Actually, if your coding kung fu is up to the task of writing a program to listen on port 80, or if you configure *xinetd* to invoke your program, you don't even need to install a web server.

Weighted

The load balancer can combine and weight several of the other algorithms. For example, you might have single- and dual-CPU machines. The dual-CPU machines are roughly twice as powerful, so you can tell the load balancer to send them an average of twice as many requests.

The best algorithm for MySQL depends on your workload. The least-connections algorithm, for example, might flood new servers when you add them to the pool of available servers—before when their caches are warmed up. The authors of this book's first edition experienced that problem firsthand.

You'll need to experiment to find the best performance for your workload. Be sure to consider what happens in extraordinary circumstances as well as in the day-to-day norm. It is in those extraordinary circumstances—e.g., during times of high load, when you're doing schema changes, or when an unusual number of servers go offline—that you can least afford something going terribly wrong.

We've described only instant-provisioning algorithms here, which don't queue connection requests. Sometimes algorithms that use queuing can be more efficient. For example, an algorithm might maintain a given concurrency on the database server, such as allowing no more than *N* active transactions at the same time. If there are too many active transactions, the algorithm can put a new request in a queue and serve it from the first server that becomes "available" according to the criteria. Some connection pools support queuing algorithms.

Adding and removing servers in the pool

Adding a new server to the pool is usually not as simple as plugging it in and notifying the load balancer of its existence. You might think it'll be OK as long as it doesn't get flooded with connections, but that's not always true. Sometimes you can add load to a server slowly, but some servers whose caches are cold might be so slow that they shouldn't get *any* user queries for a while. If it takes 30 seconds to return the data a user needs to see for a page view, the server is unusable even for a small amount of traffic. You can avoid this problem by mirroring SELECT traffic from an active server for a while before you notify the load balancer about the new server. You can do this by reading and replaying the active server's log files on the newly started server, or by capturing the production server's network traffic and replaying a portion of its queries. The *pt-query-digest* tool from Percona Toolkit can help with this. Another tactic that can work well is to use the fast warmup features in Percona Server or MySQL 5.6.

You should configure the servers in the connection pool so that there is enough unused capacity to let you take servers out for maintenance, or to handle the load when servers fail. You need more than just "enough" capacity on each server.

Make sure your configuration limits are high enough to work when servers are out of the pool. For example, if you find that each MySQL server typically has 100 connections, you should set max_connections to 200 on each server in the pool. Then, even if half the servers fail, the pool should be able to handle the same number of connections as a whole.

Load Balancing with a Master and Multiple Replicas

The most common replication topology is a single master with multiple replicas. It can be difficult to move away from this architecture. Many applications assume there's a single destination for all writes, or that all data will always be available on a single server. Though this is not the most scalable architecture, there are ways you can use it to good effect with load balancing. This section examines some of those techniques:

Functional partitioning
> You can stretch capacity quite a bit by configuring replicas or groups of replicas for particular purposes, as discussed previously. Common functions you might consider separating are reporting and analytics, data warehousing, and full-text searching. You can find more ideas in Chapter 10.

Filtering and data partitioning
> You can partition data among otherwise similar replicas with replication filters (see Chapter 10). This strategy can work well as long as your data is already separated into different databases or tables on the master. Unfortunately, there's no built-in way to filter replication at the level of individual rows. You'd have to do something creative (read: hackish) to accomplish this, perhaps with triggers and a bunch of different tables.

> Even if you don't partition the data amongst the replicas, you can improve cache efficiency by partitioning reads instead of distributing them randomly. For instance, you might direct all reads for users whose names begin with the letters A–M to a given replica, and all reads for users whose names begin with N–Z to another replica. This helps use each machine's cache more fully, because repeated reads are more likely to find the relevant data in the cache. In the best case, where there are no writes, this strategy effectively gives you a total cache size the same as the two machines' cache sizes combined. In comparison, if you distribute the reads randomly among the replicas, every machine's cache essentially duplicates the data, and your total effective cache size is only as big as a single replica's cache, no matter how many replicas you have.

Moving parts of writes to a replica
> The master doesn't always have to do all the work involved in writes. You can save a significant amount of redundant work for the master *and* the replicas by decomposing write queries and running parts of them on replicas. See Chapter 10 for more on this topic.

Guaranteeing a replica is caught up
> If you want to run a certain process on the replica, and it needs to know that its data is current as of a certain point in time—even if it has to wait a while for that to happen—you can use the MASTER_POS_WAIT() function to block until the replica

catches up to the desired point on the master. Alternatively, you can use a repli-cation heartbeat to check for up-to-dateness; see Chapter 10 for more on this.

Write synchronization

You can also use `MASTER_POS_WAIT()` to make sure your writes actually reach one or more replicas. If your application needs to emulate synchronous replication to guarantee data safety, it can cycle between each replica, running `MASTER_POS_WAIT()` on each. This creates a "synchronization barrier" that can take a long time to pass if any of the replicas is far behind in replication, so it's a good idea to use it only when absolutely necessary. (You can also wait until just one replica receives the event if your goal is only to ensure that some replica has the event. MySQL 5.5 adds semisynchronous replication, which supports this technique natively.)

Summary

Scaling MySQL correctly is a bit less glamorous than it often seems. The right way to scale isn't to build the next Facebook architecture from day one. A better strategy is to do what's clearly needed for your application, and plan ahead so that if you do grow very rapidly, your success will finance whatever steps are necessary to meet the demand.

It is valuable to have a mathematical definition of scalability, just as it's useful to have a precise concept of performance, and the Universal Scalability Law can provide a helpful framework. Knowing that systems fail to scale linearly because of costs such as serialization and crosstalk can help you avoid building those problems into your application. At the same time, many scalability problems aren't mathematical; they may be due to problems within the organization, such as lack of teamwork or other less concrete issues. Dr. Neil J. Gunther's book *Guerrilla Capacity Planning* and Eliyahu M. Goldratt's book *The Goal* are good reading for anyone interested in understanding more about why systems don't scale.

In terms of MySQL scalability strategies, the typical application that grows very large usually moves from a single server, to a scale-out architecture with read replicas, to sharding and/or functional partitioning. We disagree with those who advocate a "shard early, shard often" approach for every application. It's complicated and expensive, and many applications will never need it. It is perfectly legitimate to bide your time and see what happens with new hardware, new versions of MySQL, or new developments in MySQL Cluster, and even to evaluate a proprietary system such as Clustrix. Sharding is a hand-built clustering system, after all, and it's a good idea not to reinvent the wheel if you don't need to.

Where there are multiple servers, there are problems with consistency and atomicity. The most common problems we see are lack of session consistency (posting a comment on a website, refreshing the page, and not seeing the comment you just posted) and failures when telling the application which servers are readable and writable. The latter are much more serious, because if you direct writes to more than one place in your application you'll inevitably end up with data problems, which can be amazingly difficult and time-consuming to solve. Load balancers can help with this, but load balancers can also create problems of their own, sometimes even aggravating the problems they're intended to help solve. This is why our next chapter is on high availability.

High Availability

This chapter covers the third of our little trio of topics: replication, scalability, and high availability. At the end of the day, high availability really means "less downtime." Unfortunately, high availability is frequently conflated with related concepts such as redundancy, protection against data loss, and load balancing. We hope that the preceding two chapters have set the stage for a clear understanding of high availability. However, this chapter can't be singularly focused; like the others in the trio, it must synthesize a few related topics.

What Is High Availability?

High availability is actually a bit of a mythical beast. It's usually expressed as a percentage, which is a hint in itself: there is no absolute *high* availability, only relatively *higher* availability. 100% availability is simply impossible. The "nines" rule of availability is the most common way to express an availability goal. As you probably know, "five nines" means 99.999% uptime, which is just over five minutes of downtime per year. That's pretty impressive for most applications, although some achieve even more nines than that.

Applications have vastly different availability needs. Before you set your heart on a certain uptime goal, ask yourself what you really need to achieve. Each increment of availability usually costs far more than the previous one; the ratio of availability to effort and cost is nonlinear. How much uptime you need usually depends on how much you can afford. The trick with high availability is to balance the cost of downtime against the cost of reducing downtime. Put another way, if you have to spend a lot of money to achieve better uptime, but the increased uptime earns you only a little more money, it might not be worth it. In general, making an application highly available is difficult and expensive past a certain point, so we advise setting realistic goals and avoiding overengineering. Fortunately, the effort required to build two or three nines of uptime might not be that high, depending on the application.

Sometimes people define availability as the portion of time that a service is running. We think the definition should also include whether the application is serving requests with good performance. There are many ways that a server can be running but not really available. A common case is just after a MySQL server is restarted. It could take many hours for a big server to warm up enough to serve queries with acceptable response times, even if the server receives only a small portion of its normal traffic.

A related consideration is whether you'll lose any data, even if your application doesn't go offline. If a server has a truly catastrophic failure, you might lose at least some data, such as the last few transactions that were written to the (now lost) binary log and didn't make it to a replica's relay log. Can you tolerate this? Most applications can; the alternatives are usually expensive, complex, or have some performance overhead. For example, you can use synchronous replication, or place the binary log on a device that's replicated by DRBD so you won't lose it even if the server fails completely. (You can still lose power to the whole data center, though.)

A smart application architecture can often reduce your availability needs, at least for part of the system, and thus make high availability easier to achieve. Separating critical and noncritical parts of your application can save you a lot of work and money, because it's much easier to improve availability for a smaller system. You can identify high-priority risks by calculating your "risk exposure," which is the probability of failure multiplied by the cost of failure. A simple spreadsheet of risks—with columns for the probability, the cost, and the exposure—can help you prioritize your efforts.

In the previous chapter we examined how to achieve better scalability by avoiding the causes of poor scalability. We'll take a similar approach here, because we believe that availability is best understood by studying its opposite: downtime. Let's begin by discussing why downtime happens.

What Causes Downtime?

We've heard it said that the main cause of downtime in database servers is badly written SQL queries, but is that really true? In 2009 we decided to analyze our database of customer incidents and determine what really causes downtime, and how to prevent it.[1] Although the results affirmed some of what we already believed, they contradicted other beliefs, and we learned a lot.

We first categorized the downtime incidents by the way they manifested, rather than by cause. Broadly speaking, what we call the "operating environment" was the leading place that downtime appeared, with about 35% of incidents landing in this category. The operating environment is the set of systems and resources that support the database

---

1. We wrote a lengthy white paper with the full analysis of our customers' downtime-causing incidents, and followed it with another on how to prevent downtime, including detailed checklists of activities you can schedule periodically. There wasn't room to include all the details in this book, but you can find both white papers on Percona's website (*http://www.percona.com*).

server, such as the operating system, disks, and network. Performance problems were a close runner-up, with about another 35% of the downtime-causing incidents. Replication followed that, accounting for 20% of the incidents; and the last 10% were down to various types of data loss or corruption, plus a few miscellaneous problems.

After we categorized the incidents by type, we identified the causes of the incidents. Here are a few highlights:

- Within the operating environment, the most prevalent problem by a large margin was running out of disk space.
- The biggest cause of downtime in the performance problem category was indeed bad SQL execution, although badly written queries were not always to blame; many problems were caused by server bugs or misbehavior, for example.
- Bad schema and indexing design were the next most common performance problems.
- Replication problems were usually caused by differences in data between the master and replica.
- Data loss issues were usually caused by `DROP TABLE`, and were always combined with a lack of usable backups.

Notice that replication—one of the tactics people use to try to improve uptime—often causes downtime. That's usually because it's used incorrectly, but even so, it illustrates a common theme: many high-availability tactics can and do backfire. We'll see this again later.

Now that we know the broad categories of downtime and where to point the finger of blame, we'll get into specifics of how to achieve high availability.

Achieving High Availability

High availability is achieved by two practices, which should go hand-in-hand. First, try to reduce downtime by preventing the causes of downtime. Many of them are easily preventable with steps such as proper configuration, monitoring, and policies or safeguards to avoid human error. Second, try to ensure that when downtime happens, you can recover quickly. The usual tactic is building redundancy and failover capability into systems. These two dimensions of high availability can be measured by two corresponding metrics: mean time between failures (MTBF) and mean time to recovery (MTTR). Some organizations track these metrics carefully.

The second activity—quick recovery through redundancy—is unfortunately what seems to get the most attention, but the return on investment from prevention efforts can be quite high. Let's explore prevention a bit.

Improving Mean Time Between Failures

You can avoid a lot of downtime with a little due diligence. When we categorized downtime incidents and attributed them to root causes, we also identified ways they could have been prevented. We found that most downtime incidents can be averted through an overall common-sense approach to managing systems. The following suggestions are selected from the guidelines in the white paper we wrote detailing the results of our analysis:

- Test your recovery tools and procedures, including restores from backups.
- Follow the principle of least privilege.
- Keep your systems clean and neat.
- Use good naming and organization conventions to avoid confusion, such as whether servers are for development or production use.
- Upgrade your database server on a prudent schedule to keep it current.
- Test carefully with a tool such as *pt-upgrade* from Percona Toolkit before upgrading.
- Use InnoDB, configure it properly, and ensure that it is set as the default storage engine and the server cannot start if it is disabled.
- Make sure the basic server settings are configured properly.
- Disable DNS with `skip_name_resolve`.
- Disable the query cache unless it has proven beneficial.
- Avoid complexity, such as replication filters and triggers, unless absolutely needed.
- Monitor important components and functions, especially critical items such as disk space and RAID volume status, but avoid false positives by alerting only on conditions that reliably indicate problems.
- Record as many historical metrics as possible about server status and performance, and keep them forever if you can.
- Test replication integrity on a regular basis.
- Make replicas read-only, and don't let replication start automatically.
- Perform regular query reviews.
- Archive and purge unneeded data.
- Reserve some space in filesystems. In GNU/Linux, you can use the *–m* option to reserve space in the filesystem itself. You can also leave space free in your LVM volume group. Or, perhaps simplest of all, just create a large dummy file that you can delete if the filesystem becomes completely full.[2]

---

2. It's 100% cross-platform-compatible!

- Make a habit of reviewing and managing system changes and status and performance information.

We found that lapses in system change management were the most important overall reason for downtime incidents. Typical mistakes include careless upgrades, failing to upgrade at all and encountering bugs, pushing schema or query changes to production without testing them, and failing to plan for things such as reaching the limits of disk capacity. Another leading cause of problems is lack of due diligence, such as neglecting to verify that backups are restorable. Finally, people generally monitor the wrong things about MySQL. Alerts on metrics such as cache hit ratios, which don't indicate a real problem and create lots of false positives, cause the monitoring system to be regarded as unhelpful, so people ignore alerts. Sometimes the monitoring system fails and nobody even notices, leading to tough questions from the boss later on, such as "Why didn't Nagios alert us about the disk being full?"

Improving Mean Time to Recovery

As we mentioned, it can be tempting to focus exclusively on reducing recovery time to achieve high availability. In fact, sometimes people go even further and focus on only one aspect of reducing recovery time: preventing complete system failure by building redundancy into systems and avoiding single points of failure.

It is very important to invest in quick recovery time, and a good system architecture that provides redundancy and failover capabilities is a key part of that, but achieving high availability is not solely a technical problem. There is a large human and organizational component. Organizations and individuals vary in their level of maturity and capability to avoid and recover from downtime incidents.

Your people are your most important high-availability asset, so good procedures for recovery are vital. Skilled, adaptable, and well-trained staff members, supported by well-documented and well-tested procedures for dealing with emergencies, can contribute greatly to quick recovery from downtime. Trusting solely to tools and systems is usually a mistake, because they don't understand nuanced situations, and they sometimes do what would usually be the right thing, but is utterly catastrophic in your case.

Reviewing downtime incidents can be very helpful in improving organizational learning, to help avoid similar incidents in the future. Beware, however, of overvaluing practices such as "after-action reviews" or "post-mortems." Hindsight is badly distorted, and the desire to find a single root cause tends to impair judgment.[3] Many popular approaches, such as the "Five Whys" approach, can be applied badly, causing people to focus their attention on finding a single scapegoat. It's difficult to look back at a

---

3. Two refutations of common wisdom for further reading: Richard Cook's paper entitled "How Complex Systems Fail" (*http://www.ctlab.org/documents/How%20Complex%20Systems%20Fail.pdf*) and Malcolm Gladwell's essay on the Challenger space shuttle disaster, in his book *What the Dog Saw* (Little, Brown).

situation we've resolved and understand the real causes, and there are always multiple causes. As a result, while after-action reviews can be beneficial, you should take the conclusions with a grain of salt. Even our own recommendations, based as they are on lengthy studies of the causes and preventions of downtime, are just opinions.

This bears repeating: *all downtime incidents are caused by multiple failures in combination*, and thus they could have been averted by the proper functioning of a single safeguard. The entire chain must be broken, not merely a single link. For example, people who ask us for help with data recovery are usually suffering both from a loss of data (storage failure, DBA mistake, etc.) and a lack of usable backups.

With that said, most people and organizations are not guilty of overdoing it when it comes to investigating and trying to prevent or hasten recovery from failures. Instead, they can be prone to focusing on technical measures—especially the cool ones, such as clustered systems and redundant architectures. There is a place for this, but keep in mind that systems are fallible, too. In fact, one of the tools we mentioned in the second edition of this book, the MMM replication manager, has fallen out of our favor because it turns out that it might cause even more downtime than it prevents. You probably aren't surprised that a set of Perl scripts can go haywire, but even extremely expensive and elaborate systems fail in catastrophic ways—yes, even the SAN that cost you a king's ransom. We've seen a lot of SAN failures.

Avoiding Single Points of Failure

Finding and eliminating single points of failure in your system, combined with a mechanism to switch to using a spare component, is one way of improving availability by reducing recovery time (MTTR). If you're clever, you can sometimes reduce the recovery time to effectively zero, though this is rather difficult in the general case. (Even very impressive technologies such as expensive load balancers cause some delay while they notice problems and respond to them.)

Think through your application and try to identify any single points of failure. Is it a hard drive, a server, a switch or router, or the power for one rack? Are your machines all in one data center, or are your "redundant" data centers provided by the same company? Any point in your system that isn't redundant is a single point of failure. Other common single points of failure, depending on your point of view, are reliance on services such as DNS, a single network provider,[4] a single cloud "availability zone," and a single power grid.

You can't always eliminate single points of failure. Making a component redundant might not be possible because of some limitation you can't work around, such as a geographic, budgetary, or timing constraint. Try to understand all of the components

---

4. Feeling paranoid? Check that your redundant network connections are really connected to different Internet backbones, and make sure they aren't physically cabled on the same street or strung on the same poles, so they won't get cut by the same backhoe or hit by the same car.

that affect availability, take a balanced view of the risks, and work on the biggest ones first. Some people work hard to build software that can handle any kind of hardware failure, but bugs in this kind of software can cause more downtime than it saves. Some people build "unsinkable" systems with all kinds of redundancy, but they forget that the data center can lose power or connectivity. Or maybe they completely forget about the possibility of malicious attackers or programmer mistakes that delete or corrupt data—a careless DROP TABLE can cause downtime, too.

Adding redundancy to your system can take two forms: adding spare capacity and duplicating components. It's actually quite easy to add spare capacity—you can use any of the techniques we mention throughout this chapter or the previous one. One way to increase availability is to create a cluster or pool of servers and add a load-balancing solution. If one server fails, the other servers take over its load. Some people underutilize components intentionally, because it leaves much more "headroom" to handle performance problems caused either by increased load or by component failures.

For many purposes, you will need to duplicate components and have a standby ready to take over if the main component fails. A duplicated component can be as simple as a spare network card, router, or hard drive—whatever you think is most likely to fail. Duplicating entire MySQL servers is a little harder, because a server is useless without its data. That means you must ensure that your standby servers have access to the primary server's data. Shared or replicated storage is one popular way to accomplish this. But is it really a high-availability architecture? Let's dig in and see.

Shared Storage or Replicated Disk

Shared storage is a way to decouple your database server and its storage, usually with a SAN. With shared storage, the server mounts the filesystem and operates normally. If the server dies, a standby server can mount the same filesystem, perform any necessary recovery operations, and start MySQL on the failed server's data. This process is logically no different from fixing the failed server, except that it's faster because the standby server is already booted and ready to go. Filesystem checks, InnoDB recovery, and warmup[5] are the biggest delays you're likely to encounter once failover is initiated, but failure detection itself can take quite a long time in many setups, too.

Shared storage has two advantages: it helps avoid data loss from the failure of any component other than the storage, and it makes it possible to build redundancy in the non-storage components. As a result, it's a strategy for helping to reduce availability requirements in some parts of the system, making it easier to achieve high availability by concentrating your efforts on a smaller set of components. But *the shared storage*

---

5. Percona Server offers a feature to restore the buffer pool to its saved state after a restart, and this works fine with shared storage. This can reduce warmup time by hours or days. MySQL 5.6 will have a similar feature.

itself is still a single point of failure. If it goes down, the whole system goes down, and although SANs are generally very well engineered, they can and do fail, sometimes spectacularly. Even SANs that are themselves redundant can fail.

What About Active-Active Access to Shared Storage?

What about running many servers in active-active mode on a SAN, NAS, or clustered filesystem? MySQL can't do that. It is not designed to synchronize its access to data with other MySQL instances, so you can't fire up multiple instances of MySQL working on the same data. (Technically you could, if you used MyISAM on read-only static data, but we've never seen a real use for that.)

A storage engine for MySQL called ScaleDB operates through an API with a shared-storage architecture underneath, but we have neither evaluated it nor seen it in production use. It's in beta at the time of writing.

Shared storage has its risks. If a failure such as a MySQL crash corrupts your data files, that might prevent the standby server from recovering. We highly recommend using InnoDB or another robust ACID storage engine with shared storage. A crash will almost certainly corrupt MyISAM tables, and repairing them can take a long time and result in lost rows. We also strongly recommend a journaling filesystem with shared storage. We've seen cases of severe, unrecoverable corruption with a nonjournaling filesystem and a SAN. (It was the filesystem's fault, not the SAN's.)

A replicated disk is another way to achieve the same ends as a SAN. The type of disk replication most commonly used for MySQL is DRBD (*http://www.drbd.org*), in combination with tools from the Linux-HA project (more on this later).

DRBD is synchronous, block-level replication implemented as a Linux kernel module. It copies every block from a primary device over a network card to another server's block device (the secondary device), and writes it there before committing the block on the primary device.[6] Because writes must complete on the secondary DRBD device before the writes on the primary are considered complete, the secondary device must perform at least as well as the primary, or it will limit write performance on the primary. Also, if you're using DRBD disk replication to have an interchangeable standby in the event that the primary fails, the standby server's hardware should match the primary server's. And a good RAID controller with a battery-backed write cache is all but mandatory with DRBD; performance will be very poor without it.

If the active server fails, you can promote the secondary device to be the primary. Because DRBD replicates the disk at the block layer, however, the filesystem can become inconsistent. This means it's essential to use a journaling filesystem for fast recovery.

---

6. You can actually adjust the level of synchronization for DRDB. You can set it to be asynchronous, to wait until the remote device receives the data, or to block until the remote device writes the data to disk. Also, it is strongly recommended that you dedicate a network card to DRBD.

Once recovery is complete, MySQL will need to run its own recovery as well. If the first server recovers, it resyncs its device with the new primary device and assumes the secondary role.

In terms of how you actually implement failover, DRBD is similar to a SAN: you have a hot standby machine, and you begin serving from the same data as the failed machine. The biggest difference is that it is replicated storage—not shared storage—so with DRBD you're serving a replicated copy of the data, while with a SAN you're serving the same data from the same physical device as the failed machine. In other words, replicated disks create data redundancy, so neither the storage nor the data itself is a single point of failure. In both cases, the MySQL server's caches will be empty when you start it on the standby machine. In contrast, a replica's caches are likely to be at least partially warmed up.

DRBD has some nice features and capabilities that can prevent problems common to clustering software. An example is *split-brain syndrome*, which occurs when two nodes promote themselves to primary simultaneously. You can configure DRBD so it won't let this happen. However, DRBD isn't a perfect solution for every need. Let's take a look at its drawbacks:

- DRBD's failover is not subsecond. It will generally require at least a few seconds to promote the secondary device to primary, not including any necessary filesystem and MySQL recovery.

- It's expensive, because you must run it in active-passive mode. The hot standby server's replicated device is not usable for any other tasks while it's in passive mode. Whether this is really a shortcoming depends on your point of view. If you want truly high availability and can't tolerate degraded service when there's a failure, you can't place more than one machine's worth of load on any two machines, because if you did, you wouldn't be able to handle the load if one of them failed. You can use the standby server for something else, such as a replica, but you'll still waste some resources.

- It's practically unusable for MyISAM tables, because they take too long to check and repair. MyISAM is not a good choice for any installation that requires high availability; use InnoDB or another storage engine that allows quick, reliable recovery instead.

- It does not replace backups. If your data becomes corrupt on disk due to malicious interference, mistakes, bugs, or hardware failures, DRBD will not help: the replicated data will be a perfect copy of the corrupted original. You need backups (or time-delayed MySQL replication) to protect against these problems.

- It introduces some overhead for writes. How much overhead? It's popular to cite a percentage, but that's not a good metric. Instead you need to understand that writes suffer added latency due to the network round-trip and the remote server's storage, and this is relatively larger for small writes. Although the added network latency might only be about 0.3 ms, which seems small relative to the 4 ms–10 ms latency of an actual I/O on local disk, it's about three or four times the latency you should expect from a good RAID controller's write cache. The most common reason for the server to become slower with DRBD is that MySQL with InnoDB in full durability mode does a lot of short writes and fsync() calls that will be slowed greatly by DRBD.[7]

Our favorite way to use DRBD is to replicate only the device that holds the binary logs. If the active node fails, you can start a log server on the passive node and use the recovered binary logs to bring all of the failed master's replicas up to the latest binary log position. You can then choose one of the replicas and promote it to master, replacing the failed system.

In the final analysis, shared storage and replicated disks aren't as much of a high-availability (low-downtime) solution as they are a way to keep your data safe. As long as you have your data, you can recover from failures, with a lower MTTR than not being able to recover. (Even a long recovery time is still faster than no recovery at all.) However, as compared to architectures that permit the standby server to be up and running all the time, most shared storage or replicated disk architectures will *increase* the MTTR. There are two ways to have standbys up and running: standard MySQL replication, which we discussed in Chapter 10, and synchronous replication, which is the topic of our next section.

Synchronous MySQL Replication

In synchronous replication, a transaction cannot complete on the master until it commits on one or more replica servers. This accomplishes two goals: no committed transactions are lost if a server crashes, and there is at least one other server with a "live" copy of the data. Most synchronous replication architectures run in active-active mode. That means every server is a candidate for failover at any time, making high availability through redundancy much simpler.

MySQL itself does not offer synchronous replication at the time of this writing,[8] but there are two MySQL-based clustering solutions that do support it. You should also review Chapter 10, Chapter 11, and Chapter 13 for discussions of other products, such as Continuent Tungsten and Clustrix, that might be of interest.

MySQL Cluster

The first place to look for synchronous replication in MySQL is MySQL Cluster (NDB Cluster). It has synchronous active-active replication between all nodes. That means you can write to any node; they're all equally capable of serving reads and writes. Every

---

7. On the other hand, large sequential writes are a different story. The added *latency* introduced by DRBD practically vanishes, but *throughput* limitations will come into play. A decent RAID array should give you 200 to 500 MB/second of sequential write throughput, well above what a GigE network can achieve.

8. There is support for semisynchronous replication in MySQL 5.5; see Chapter 10.

---

row is stored redundantly, so you can lose a node without losing data, and the cluster remains functional. Although MySQL Cluster still isn't a complete solution for every type of application, as we mentioned in the previous chapter, it has been improved rapidly in recent releases and now has a huge list of new features and characteristics: disk storage for nonindexed data, online scaling by adding data nodes, ndbinfo tables for managing the cluster, scripts for provisioning and managing the cluster, multi-threaded operation, push-down joins (now called adaptive query localization), the ability to handle BLOBs and tables with many columns, centralized user management, and NoSQL access through the NDB API as well as the *memcached* protocol. Upcoming releases will include the ability to run in eventual-consistency mode, with per-transaction conflict detection and resolution across a WAN, for active-active replication between datacenters. In short, MySQL Cluster is an impressive piece of technology.

There are also at least two providers of add-on products to simplify cluster deployment and management: Oracle support contracts for MySQL Cluster include its MySQL Cluster Manager product, and Severalnines offers a Cluster Control product (*http://www.severalnines.com*). This product is also capable of helping deploy and manage replication clusters.

Percona XtraDB Cluster

Percona XtraDB Cluster is a relatively new technology that adds synchronous replication and clustering capabilities to the XtraDB (InnoDB) storage engine itself, rather than through a new storage engine or an external server. It is built on Galera,[9] a library that replicates writes across nodes in a cluster. Like MySQL Cluster, Percona XtraDB Cluster offers synchronous multi-master replication,[10] with true write-anywhere capabilities. Also like MySQL Cluster, it can provide high availability as well as guarantee zero data loss (durability, the D in ACID) when a node fails, and of course nodes can fail without causing the whole cluster to fail.

The underlying technology, Galera, uses a technique called *write-set replication*. Write sets are actually encoded as row-based binary log events for the purpose of transmitting them between nodes and updating the other nodes in the cluster, though the binary log is not required to be enabled.

Percona XtraDB Cluster is very fast. Cross-node replication can actually be faster than not clustering, because writing to remote RAM is faster than writing to the local disk in full durability mode. You have the option of relaxing durability on each node for performance, if you wish, and relying on the presence of multiple nodes with copies of

---

9. The Galera technology is developed by Codership Oy (*http://www.codership.com*) and is available as a patch for standard MySQL and InnoDB. Percona XtraDB Cluster includes a modified version of that patchset, as well as other features and functionality. Percona XtraDB Cluster is a Galera-based solution that's ready to use out of the box.

10. You can also use it in a master-replica configuration by writing to just one node, but there's no difference in the cluster configuration for this mode of operation.

the data for durability. NDB operates on the same principle. The cluster's durability as a whole is not reduced; only the local durability is reduced. In addition, it supports parallel (multithreaded) replication at the row level, so multiple CPU cores can be used to apply write sets. These characteristics combine to make Percona XtraDB Cluster attractive in cloud computing environments, where disks and CPUs are usually slower than normal.

The cluster implements autoincrementing keys with `auto_increment_offset` and `auto_increment_increment` so that nodes won't generate conflicting values. Locking is generally the same as it is in standard InnoDB. It uses optimistic concurrency control. Changes are serialized and transmitted between nodes at transaction commit, with a certification process so that if there is a conflicting update, someone has to lose. As a result, if many nodes are changing the same rows simultaneously, there can be lots of deadlocks and rollbacks.

Percona XtraDB Cluster provides high availability by keeping the nodes online as long as they form a quorum. If nodes discover that they are not part of a quorum, they are ejected from the cluster, and they must resync before joining the cluster again. As a result, the cluster can't handle split-brain scenarios; it will stop if that happens. When a node fails in a two-node cluster, the remaining node isn't a quorum and will stop functioning, so in practice you need at least three nodes to have a high-availability cluster.

Percona XtraDB Cluster has lots of benefits:

- It provides transparent clustering based on InnoDB, so there's no need to move to another technology such as NDB, which is a whole different beast to learn and administer.

- It provides real high availability, with all nodes equal and ready for reads and writes at all times. In contrast, MySQL's built-in asynchronous or semisynchronous replication must have one master, can't guarantee that your data is replicated, and can't guarantee that replicas are up-to-date and ready for reads or to be promoted to master.

- It protects you against data loss when a node fails. In fact, because all nodes have all the data, you can lose every node but one and still not lose the data (even if the cluster has a split brain and stops working). This is different from NDB, where the data is partitioned across node groups and some data can be lost if all servers in a node group are lost.

- Replicas cannot fall behind, because write sets are propagated to and certified on every node in the cluster before the transaction commits.

- Because it uses row-based log events to apply changes to replicas, applying write sets can be less expensive than generating them, just as with normal row-based replication. This, combined with multithreaded application of write sets, can make its replication more scalable than MySQL replication.

Of course, we need to mention its drawbacks, too:

- It's new. There isn't a huge body of experience with its strengths, weaknesses, and appropriate use cases.
- The whole cluster performs writes as slowly as the weakest node. Thus, all nodes need similar hardware, and if one node slows down (e.g., because the RAID card does a battery-learn cycle), all of them slow down. If one node has probability P of being slow to accept writes, a three-node cluster has probability $3P$ of being slow.
- It isn't as space-efficient as NDB, because every node has all the data, not just a portion. On the other hand, it is based on Percona XtraDB (which is an enhanced version of InnoDB), so it doesn't have NDB's limitations regarding on-disk data.
- It currently disallows some operational tricks that are possible with asynchronous replication, such as making schema changes offline on a replica and promoting it to be master so you can repeat the changes on other nodes offline. The current alternative is to use a technique such as Percona Toolkit's online schema change tool. Rolling schema upgrades are nearly ready for release at the time of writing, however.
- Adding a new node to a cluster requires copying data to it, plus the ability to keep up with ongoing writes, so a big cluster with lots of writes could be hard to grow. This will put a practical limit on the cluster's data size. We aren't sure how large this is, but a pessimistic estimate is that it could be as low as 100 GB or so. It could be much larger; time and experience will tell.
- The replication protocol seems to be somewhat sensitive to network hiccups at the time of writing, and that can cause nodes to stop themselves and drop out of the cluster, so we recommend a high-performance network with good redundancy. If you don't have a reliable network, you might end up adding nodes back to the cluster too often. This requires a resynchronization of the data. At the time of writing, incremental state transfer to avoid a full copy of the dataset is almost ready to use, so this should not be as much of a problem in the future. It's also possible to configure Galera to be more tolerant of network timeouts (at the cost of delayed failure detection), and more reliable algorithms are planned for future releases.
- If you aren't watching carefully, your cluster could grow too big to restart nodes that fail, just as backups can get too big to restore in a reasonable amount of time if you don't practice it routinely. We need more practical experience to know how this will work in reality.
- Because of the cross-node communication required at transaction commit, writes will get slower, and deadlocks and rollbacks will get more frequent, as you add nodes to the cluster. (See the previous chapter for more on why this happens.)

Both Percona XtraDB Cluster and Galera are still early in their lifecycles and are changing and improving rapidly. At the time of writing, we can point to recent or forthcoming improvements to quorum behavior, security, synchronicity, memory management, state transfer, and a host of other things. You will also be able to take nodes offline for operations such as rolling schema changes in the future.

Replication-Based Redundancy

Replication managers are tools that attempt to use standard MySQL replication as a building block for redundancy.[11] Although it is possible to improve availability with replication, there is a "glass ceiling" that blocks MySQL's current asynchronous and semisynchronous replication from achieving what can be done with true synchronous replication. You can't guarantee instantaneous failover and zero data loss, nor can you treat all nodes as identical.

Replication managers typically monitor and manage three things: the communication between the application and MySQL, the health of the MySQL servers, and replication relationships between MySQL servers. They either alter the configuration of load balancing or move virtual IP addresses as necessary to make the application connect to the proper servers, and they manipulate replication to elect a server as the writable node in the pseudo-cluster. In principle, it's not complicated: just make sure that writes are never directed to a server that's not ready for writes, and make sure to get replication coordinates right when promoting a replica to master status.

This sounds workable in theory, but our experience has been that it doesn't always work so well in practice. It's too bad, really, because it would sometimes be nice to have a lightweight set of tools to help recover from common failures and get a little bit higher availability on the cheap. Unfortunately, we don't know of any good toolset that accomplishes this reliably at the time of writing. We'll mention two replication managers in a moment,[12] but one is new and the other has a lot of issues.

We've also seen many people try to write their own replication managers. They usually fall into the same traps that have snared others before them. It's not a great idea to roll your own. Coaxing good behavior from asynchronous components with oodles of failure modes you've never personally experienced, many of which simply cannot be understood and handled appropriately by a program, is very hard, and it's riddled with opportunities to lose data. In fact, a machine can begin with a situation that could be fixed by a skilled human, and make it much worse by doing the wrong thing.

The first replication manager we want to mention is MMM (*http://mysql-mmm.org*). The authors of this book don't all agree on how suitable this toolkit is for production deployment (although the original author of the toolkit has opined that it's not trustworthy). Some of us think it can be helpful in some cases in manual-failover mode, and others would rather never use it in any mode. It is certain, however, that many of our

---

11. We're being careful to avoid confusion in this section. Redundancy is not the same thing as high availability.

12. We're also working on a solution that's based on Pacemaker and the Linux-HA stack, but it's not ready to mention in this book. This footnote will self-destruct in 10..9..8..

customers who use it in automatic-failover mode have a lot of serious issues with it. It can take healthy servers offline, send writes to the wrong place, and move replicas to the wrong coordinates. Chaos sometimes ensues.

The other tool, which is rather new, is Yoshinori Matsunobu's MHA toolkit (*http://code.google.com/p/mysql-master-ha/*). It is similar to MMM in that it is a set of scripts to build a pseudo-cluster with some of the same general techniques, but it is not a complete replacement; it doesn't attempt to do as many things, and it relies on Pacemaker to move virtual IP addresses. One major difference is that it has a test suite, which should prevent some of the problems MMM has encountered. Other than this, we don't have a strong opinion on the toolkit yet. We haven't talked with anyone other than Yoshinori who is using it in production, and we haven't used it ourselves.

Replication-based redundancy is ultimately a mixed blessing. The candidate use case is when availability is much more important than consistency or zero-data-loss guarantees. For example, some people don't really make any money from their site's functionality, only from its availability. Who cares if there's a failure and the site loses a few comments on a photo or something? As long as the ad revenue keeps rolling in, the cost of truly high availability might not be worth it. But sticking with the "best effort" high availability you can build with replication carries the potential for serious downtime that can be extremely laborious to fix. It's a pretty big gamble, and one that's probably too risky for all but the most blasé (or expert) of users.

The problem is, many users don't know how to self-qualify and assess whether Replication Roulette is suitable for them. There are two reasons for this. First, they don't see the glass ceiling, and they mistakenly believe that a set of virtual IP addresses, replication, and management scripts can deliver "real" high availability. Second, they underestimate the complexity of the technology, and therefore the severity of the failures that can happen and the difficulty of recovering from them. As a result, sometimes people think they can live with replication-based redundancy, but they might later wish that they'd chosen a simpler system with stronger guarantees.

Other types of replication, such as DRBD or a SAN, have their flaws, too—please don't think we are promoting them as bulletproof and saying that MySQL replication is a mess, because that's not our intention. You can write poor-quality failover scripts for DRBD just easily as you can for MySQL replication. The main difference is that MySQL replication is a lot more complex, with a lot more nuances, and it doesn't prevent you from doing bad things.

Failover and Failback

Redundancy is great, but it actually doesn't buy you anything except the opportunity to recover from a failure. (Heck, you can get that with backups.) Redundancy doesn't increase availability or reduce downtime one whit. High availability is built on top of redundancy, through the process of *failover*. When a component fails and there is redundancy, you can stop using the failed piece and start using its redundant standby instead. The combination of redundancy and failover can enable you to recover more quickly, and as you know, reducing MTTR reduces downtime and improves availability.

Before we continue, we should talk about a few terms. We use "failover" consistently; some people use "fallback" as a synonym. Sometimes people also say "switchover" to denote a switch that's planned instead of a response to a failure. Po-tay-toe, po-tah-toe. We also use the term "failback" to indicate the reverse of failover. If you have failback capability, failover can be a two-way process: when server A fails and server B replaces it, you can repair server A and fail back to it.

Failover is good for more than just recovery from failures. You can also do planned failovers to reduce downtime (improve availability) for events such as upgrades, schema changes, application modifications, or scheduled maintenance.

You need to identify how fast failover needs to be, but you also need to know how quickly you have to replace the failed component after a failover. Until you restore the system's depleted standby capacity, you have less redundancy and you're exposed to extra risk. Thus, having a standby doesn't eliminate the need for timely replacement of failed components. How quickly can you build a new standby server, install its operating system, and give it a fresh copy of your data? Do you have enough standby machines? You might need more than one.

Failover comes in many flavors. We've already discussed several of them, because load balancing and failover are similar in many ways, and the line between them is a bit fuzzy. In general, we think a full failover solution, at a minimum, needs to be able to monitor and automatically replace a component. This should ideally be transparent to the application. Load balancing need not provide this capability.

In the Unix world, failover is often accomplished with the tools provided by the High Availability Linux project (*http://linux-ha.org*), which run on many Unix-like operating systems, not just Linux. The Linux-HA stack has become significantly more featureful in the last few years. Today most people think of Pacemaker as the main component in the stack. Pacemaker replaces the older heartbeat tool. Various other tools accomplish IP takeover and load-balancing functionality. You can combine them with DRBD and/or LVS.

The most important part of failover is failback. If you can't switch back and forth between servers at will, failover is a dead end and only postpones downtime. This is why we like symmetrical replication topologies, such as the dual-master configuration, and we dislike ring replication with three or more co-masters. If the configuration is symmetrical, failover and failback are the same operation in opposite directions. (It's worth mentioning that DRBD has built-in failback capabilities.)

In some applications, it's critical that failover and failback be as fast and atomic as possible. Even when it's not critical, it's still a good idea not to rely on things that are out of your control, such as DNS changes or application configuration files. Some of the worst problems don't show up until a system becomes larger, when issues such as forced application restarts and the need for atomicity rear their heads.

Because load balancing and failover are closely related, and the same piece of hardware or software often serves both purposes, we suggest that any load-balancing technique you choose should provide failover capabilities as well. This is the real reason we suggested you avoid DNS or code changes for load balancing. If you use these strategies for load balancing, you'll create extra work: you'll have to rewrite the affected code later when you need high availability.

The following sections discuss some common failover techniques. You can perform these manually, or use tools to accomplish them.

Promoting a Replica or Switching Roles

Promoting a replica to master, or switching the active and passive roles in a master-master replication setup, is an important part of many failover strategies for MySQL. See Chapter 10 for detailed explanations of how to accomplish this manually. As mentioned earlier in this chapter, we aren't aware of any automated tools that always do the right thing in all situations—or at least, none that we'll put our reputations behind.

Depending on your workload, you shouldn't assume that you can fail over to a passive replica instantly. Replicas replay the master's writes, but if you're not also using them for reads, they will not be warmed up to serve the production workload. If you want a replica to be ready for read traffic, you have to continuously "train" it, either by letting it participate in the production workload or by mirroring production read queries onto it. We've sometimes done this by sniffing TCP traffic, filtering out everything but SELECT queries, and replaying those against the replica. Percona Toolkit has tools that can help with this.

Virtual IP Addresses or IP Takeover

You can assign a logical IP address to a MySQL instance that you expect to perform certain services. If the MySQL instance fails, you can move the IP address to a different MySQL server. This is essentially the same approach we wrote about in the previous chapter, except that now we're using it for failover instead of load balancing.

The benefit of this approach is its transparency for the application. It will abort existing connections, but it doesn't require you to change your application's configuration. It is also sometimes possible to move the IP address atomically, so all applications see the change at the same time. This can be especially important when a server is "flapping" between available and unavailable states.

The downsides are as follows:

- You need to either define all IP addresses on the same network segment, or use network bridging.

- Changing the IP address requires root access to the system.

- Sometimes you need to update address resolution protocol (ARP) caches. Some network devices might cache ARP entries for too long, and might not instantly switch an IP address to a different MAC address. We've seen lots of cases where network hardware or other components decide not to cooperate, and thus the various parts of the system don't agree on where the IP address really lives.

- You need to make sure the network hardware supports fast IP takeover. Some hardware requires MAC address cloning for this to work properly.

- It's possible for a server to keep its IP address even though it's not fully functional, so you might need to physically shut it down or disconnect it from the network. This is known by the lovely acronym of STONITH: "shoot the other node in the head." It's also called "fencing," which is a more delicate and official-sounding name.

Floating IP addresses and IP takeover can work well for failover between machines that are local to each other—that is, on the same subnet. In the end, however, you need to be aware that this isn't always a bulletproof strategy, depending on your network hardware and so on.

Waiting for Changes to Propagate

Often, when you define redundancy on one layer, you have to wait for a lower layer to actually carry out a change. Earlier in this chapter, we pointed out that changing servers through DNS is a weak solution because DNS is slow to propagate changes. Changing IP addresses gives you more control, but IP addresses on a LAN also depend on a lower layer—ARP—to propagate changes.

Middleman Solutions

You can use proxies, port forwarding, network address translation (NAT), and hardware load balancers for failover and failback. They're nice because unlike other solutions that tend to introduce uncertainty (do all of the system components really agree on which one is the master database? can it be changed instantaneously and atomically?), they're a central authority that controls connections between the application and the database. However, they do introduce a single point of failure themselves, and you'll need to make them redundant to avoid that problem.

One of the nice things you can do with such a solution is make a remote data center appear to be on the same network as your application. This lets you use techniques such as floating IP addresses to make your application begin communicating with an entirely different data center. You can configure each application server in each data center to connect through its own middleman, each of which routes traffic to the machines in the active data center. Figure 12-1 illustrates this configuration.

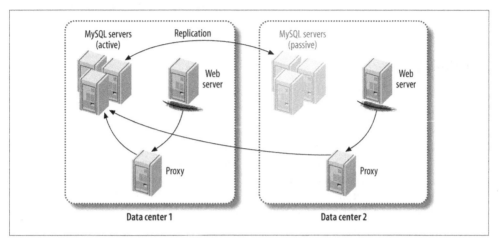

Figure 12-1. Using a middleman to route MySQL connections across data centers

If the active data center's MySQL installation fails entirely, the middleman can route the traffic to the pool of servers in the other data center, and the application never needs to know the difference.

The major disadvantage of this configuration is the high latency between the Apache server in one data center and the MySQL servers in the other data center. To alleviate this problem, you can run the web server in redirect mode. This will redirect traffic to the data center that houses the pool of active MySQL servers. You can also achieve this with an HTTP proxy.

Figure 12-1 shows a proxy as the means of connecting to the MySQL servers, but you can combine this approach with many middleman architectures, such as LVS and hardware load balancers.

Handling Failover in the Application

Sometimes it's easier or more flexible to let the application handle failover. For example, if the application experiences an error that isn't normally detected by an outside observer, such as an error message indicating database corruption, it can handle the failover process itself.

Although integrating the failover process into the application might seem attractive, it tends not to work as well as you might think it will. Most applications have many components, such as *cron* jobs, configuration files, and scripts written in different programming languages. Integrating failover into the application can therefore become unwieldy, especially as the application grows and becomes more complicated.

However, it's a good idea to build monitoring into your application and let it *initiate* the failover process if it needs to. The application should also be able to manage the user experience, by degrading functionality and showing appropriate messages to the user.

Summary

You can achieve high availability by reducing downtime, which you should attack from two directions: increasing time between failures (MTBF), and reducing time to recover from failures (MTTR).

To increase time between failures, try to prevent them. Sadly, when you're preventing failures it can feel like you're not doing very much, so preventive efforts are often neglected. We mentioned the highlights of how to prevent downtime on MySQL systems; for the long-winded details, see our white papers, available on *http://www.percona .com*. And do try to learn from your downtime, but beware of placing root cause analysis and post-mortems on a pedestal.

Shortening recovery time can get complex and expensive. On the simple and easy side, you can monitor so that you notice problems more quickly, and record lots of metrics to help diagnose the problems. As a bonus, these can sometimes be used to spot problems before they become downtime. Monitor and alert selectively to avoid noise, but record status and performance metrics eagerly.

Another tactic for shortening recovery time is to build redundancy into the system, and make the system capable of failover so you can switch between redundant components when one fails. Unfortunately, redundancy makes systems really complicated. Now things are no longer centralized; they're distributed, and that means coordination and synchronization and CAP theorems and Byzantine Generals and all that messy stuff. This is why systems like NDB Cluster are both hard to build and hard to make general-purpose enough to serve everyone's workloads. But the situation is improving, and maybe by the fourth edition we'll be able to sing the praises of one or more clustered databases.

This chapter and the previous two have covered topics that are often lumped together: replication, scalability, and high availability. We've attempted to consider them as separately as possible, because it is helpful to be clear on the differences between these topics. So how are these three chapters related?

People generally want three things from their databases as their applications grow:

- They want to be able to add capacity to serve increasing load without sacrificing performance.
- They want protection against losing a committed transaction.
- They want the applications to remain online and servicing transactions so they keep making money.

To accomplish this combination of goals, people usually start by adding redundancy. That, combined with a failover mechanism, provides high availability through minimizing MTTR. The redundancy also adds spare capacity to serve more load.

Of course, you have to duplicate the data too, not just the resources. This can help prevent losing the data when you lose a server, which adds durability. The only way to duplicate data is to replicate it somehow. Unfortunately, data duplication introduces the possibility of inconsistency. Dealing with that requires coordination and communication between nodes. This adds extra overhead to the system; that's why systems are more or less scalable.

Duplication also requires more resources (more hard drives, more RAM, etc.), which adds cost. One way to reduce both the resource consumption and the overhead of maintaining consistency is to partition (shard) the data and distribute each shard only to certain systems. This reduces the number of times the data is duplicated and decouples data redundancy from resource redundancy.

So, although one thing leads to the next, again we're really talking about a group of related concepts and practices to address a set of goals. They're not just different ways of talking about the same thing.

In the end, you need to choose a strategy that makes sense for you and your application. Deciding on a full end-to-end high-availability strategy is not something you should tackle with simple rules of thumb, but perhaps we can help by giving broad-brush guidelines.

To achieve very short downtimes, you need redundant servers that are ready to take over the application's workload instantly. They must be online and processing queries all the time, not just standing by, so they are "warmed up" and ready to go. If you want strong guarantees, you need a clustering product such as MySQL Cluster, Percona XtraDB Cluster, or Clustrix. If you can tolerate a bit more slack in the failover process, standard replication can be quite a good alternative. Be cautious about using automatic failover mechanisms; they can wreck your data if they don't get it right.

If you don't care as much about the failover time but you want to avoid data loss, you need some kind of strongly guaranteed data redundancy—i.e., synchronous replication. At the storage layer, you can do it on the cheap with DRBD, or on the other end of the cost spectrum you can get two SANs that have synchronous replication between them. Alternatively, you can replicate the data at the database layer instead, with a technology such as MySQL Cluster, Percona XtraDB Cluster, or Clustrix. You can also use middleware such as Tungsten Replicator. If you don't need strong protection and you want to keep things as simple as possible, normal asynchronous or semisynchronous replication might be a good option at a reasonable cost.

Or you could just put your application into the cloud. Why not? Won't that instantly make it highly available and infinitely scalable? Let's find out.

MySQL in the Cloud

It should be no surprise that many people are running MySQL in the cloud, sometimes at a very large scale. In our experience, most of them are using the Amazon Web Services (AWS) platform: specifically Amazon's Elastic Compute Cloud (EC2), Elastic Block Store (EBS) volumes, and, to a lesser extent, the Relational Database Service (RDS).

One way to frame the discussion about MySQL in the cloud is to divide it into two rough categories:

IaaS (Infrastructure as a Service)
> IaaS is cloud infrastructure for hosting your own MySQL server. You can purchase a virtual server resource in the cloud and use it to install and run your MySQL instance. You can configure MySQL and the operating system as you wish, but you have no access or insight into the underlying physical hardware.

DBaaS (Database as a Service)
> MySQL itself is the cloud-managed resource. You receive access credentials to a MySQL server. You can configure some of MySQL's settings, but you have no access or insight into the underlying operating system or virtual server instance. An example is Amazon RDS running MySQL. Some of these services aren't really stock MySQL, but they are compatible with the MySQL protocol and query language.

We focus most on the first category: cloud hosting on platforms such as AWS, Rackspace Cloud, and Joyent.[1] There are many good resources for learning how to deploy and manage MySQL and the resources needed to run it, and there are too many platforms for us to cover them all, so we don't show code samples or discuss operational techniques. Instead, this chapter focuses on the key differences between running MySQL in the cloud versus traditional server deployment, and on the resulting economic and performance characteristics. We assume that you're familiar with cloud computing. This is not an introduction to the topic; our goal is just to help you avoid some pitfalls you might encounter if you're not a MySQL-in-the-cloud expert.

---

1. OK, OK, we admit it. Amazon Web Services *is* the cloud. This chapter is mostly about AWS.

In general, MySQL runs fine in the cloud. Running MySQL in the cloud isn't dramatically different from running MySQL on any other platform, but there are several very important distinctions. You need to be aware of them and design your application and architecture accordingly to get good results. In some circumstances hosting MySQL in the cloud is not a great fit, and sometimes it's the best thing since sliced bread, but in most cases it's just another deployment platform.

It is important to understand that the cloud is a deployment platform, not an architecture. Your architecture is influenced by the platform, but the platform and the architecture are distinct. If you confuse the two, you might be more likely to make poor choices that can cause problems in the future. That's why we'll spend so much time discussing which differences matter for MySQL in the cloud.

Benefits, Drawbacks, and Myths of the Cloud

Cloud computing has many benefits, few of which are specific to using it with MySQL. There are books written on this topic,[2] and we don't want to spend too much time on it. But we'll list a few big items for your consideration, because we're going to discuss drawbacks in a moment, and we don't want you to think we're overly critical of the cloud:

- The cloud is a way of outsourcing some of your infrastructure so you don't have to manage it. You don't have to purchase hardware and develop supply-chain relationships, you don't have to replace failed hard drives, and so on.
- The cloud is generally priced pay-as-you-go, converting upfront capital expenses into ongoing operational expenses.
- The cloud offers increasing value over time as providers deliver new services and lower costs. You don't have to do anything yourself (such as upgrading your servers) to take advantage of these improvements; you simply have more and better options available to you at a lower cost as time passes.
- The cloud lets you provision servers and other resources easily, and shut them down when you're done, without having to dispose of them or reclaim costs by reselling them.
- The cloud represents a different way of thinking about infrastructure—as resources that are defined by and controlled through APIs—and this allows a lot more automation. You can also get these benefits in a "private cloud."

Of course, not everything about the cloud is good. Here are some drawbacks that can pose challenges (we'll list some MySQL-specific drawbacks later in this chapter):

- Resources are shared and unpredictable, and you can actually get more than you're paying for. This might sound good, but it can make it difficult to do capacity

2. See George Reese's *Cloud Application Architectures* (O'Reilly).

planning. If you're getting more than your share of computing resources and you don't know it there's a risk that someone else will claim their fair share of resources, bumping your performance back to what it's supposed to be. In general, it can be difficult to know for certain what you're supposed to be getting, and most cloud hosting providers don't provide concrete answers about such questions.

- There are no guarantees about capacity or availability. You may assume that you can provision new instances, but what if the provider becomes oversubscribed? This happens with many shared resources, and it could happen in the cloud, too.

- Virtualized and shared resources can be harder to troubleshoot, especially because you don't have access to the underlying physical hardware to inspect and measure what's happening. For example, we've seen systems where *iostat* claimed that the I/O was fine or *vmstat* showed that the CPU was fine, and yet when we actually measured the time elapsed to complete tasks, the resources were clearly overloaded by something else on the system. If you run into performance problems on a cloud platform, it is even more important than usual to measure carefully. If you're not good at this, you might not be able to identify whether the underlying system is just performing badly, or whether you've done something that's causing the application to make unreasonable demands on the system.

We can summarize the above points by saying that there is reduced transparency and control over performance, availability, and capacity in the cloud. Finally, here are a few cloud myths to keep in mind:

The cloud is inherently more scalable

Applications, their architectures, and the organizations that manage them are scalable (or not). The cloud isn't inherently scalable just because it's a cloud, and choosing a scalable platform doesn't automatically make your application scalable. It's true that if the cloud hosting provider isn't oversubscribed, there are resources that you can purchase on demand, but availability of resources when you need them is only one aspect of scalability.

The cloud automatically improves or even guarantees uptime

Individual cloud-hosted servers are actually more likely to fail or have outages, in general, than well-designed dedicated infrastructure. Many people don't realize this, however. For example, one person wrote "we are upgrading our infrastructure to a cloud-based system to give us 100% uptime and scalability." This was just after AWS had suffered two huge outages that affected large portions of its user base. A good architect can design reliable systems with unreliable components, but in general a more reliable infrastructure contributes to higher availability. (There's no such thing as 100% uptime, of course.)

On the other hand, by subscribing to a cloud computing service, you're buying a platform that was built by experts. They have taken care of a lot of low-level things for you, and that means you can focus on higher-level tasks. If you build your own platform and you're not an expert on all those minutiae, you're likely to make some beginner's mistakes, which will probably cause some downtime sooner or later. In this way, cloud computing can help you improve your uptime.

The cloud is the only thing that provides [insert benefit here]

Actually, many of the benefits of the cloud are inherited from the technologies used to build cloud platforms and can be obtained with or without the cloud.[3] With properly managed virtualization and capacity planning, for example, you can spin up a new machine as easily and quickly as you can in any cloud. You don't need the cloud for this.

The cloud is a silver bullet

It might seem absurd that anyone would actually say this, but some do. There is no such thing.

Cloud computing provides unique benefits, to be sure, and over time we will develop a greater shared understanding of what those are and when they're useful. One thing is certain: this is all new, and any predictions we make now are unlikely to age well. We'll take the safe course in this book and leave the rest of this topic to in-person discussions.

The Economics of MySQL in the Cloud

Cloud hosting can certainly be more economical than traditional server deployment in some cases. In our experience, cloud hosting is a great match for a lot of prototype-phase businesses, or businesses who are perpetually spinning out new concepts and essentially running them through a feasibility trial-by-fire. Mobile app developers and game developers come to mind immediately. The market for these technologies is exploding with the spread of mobile computing, and it's a fast-paced world. In many cases, success comes through factors that are out of the developer's control, such as word-of-mouth referrals or timing that coincides with important world events.

We have helped many companies build mobile, social networking, and gaming applications in the cloud. One strategy many of them use is to develop and release applications as quickly and cheaply as possible. If an application happens to catch on, the company will invest resources into making it work at a larger scale; otherwise, they'll terminate it quickly. Some companies build and release such applications in lifecycles as short as a few weeks. In such an environment, cloud hosting is a no-brainer.

If you're a small-scale company, you probably can't afford your own data center with enough hardware to meet the scaling curve of a virally popular Facebook application. We've also helped scale some of the largest Facebook applications ever built, and it can be astonishing how fast they can grow—sometimes, it seems, faster than some managed hosting companies can rack servers. But even worse, the growth of these apps

---

3. We're not saying it would be easy or cheap. We're just saying that the cloud isn't the only place you can get these benefits.

is completely unpredictable; they could just as easily fail to get more than a handful of users. We've worked on such applications both in datacenters and in the cloud. If you're a small company, the cloud can help you hedge against the risk that you'll need to scale larger and faster than your capital can support up front.

Another potentially great use for the cloud is to run noncritical infrastructure, such as integration environments, testbeds for deployment, and evaluations. Suppose your deployment lifecycle is two weeks long. Do you test a deployment every hour of every day, or do you test when you're toward the end of the sprint? Many users need staging and deployment test environments only occasionally. Cloud hosting can help save money in such cases.

Here are two ways we use the cloud ourselves. The first is as part of our interviewing process for technical staff members, where we ask them to solve some real problems. We spin up some "broken" machines with Amazon Machine Images (AMIs) that we created for this purpose, and we ask candidates to log in and perform a variety of tasks on the servers. We don't have to open up access to our own network, and it's unbeatably cheap. Another way we've used cloud hosting is for staging and development servers for new projects. One such project ran on a staging server in the cloud for months and generated a total bill of less than a dollar! There's no way we could do that on our own infrastructure. Just sending an email to our system administrator asking for a staging server would take more than a dollar's worth of time.

On the other hand, cloud hosting can be more expensive over the long term. You should take the time to do the math yourself, if you're in it for the long haul. This will require benchmarking and a full accounting of total cost of ownership (TCO), as well as some guesswork about what future innovations will bring both in cloud computing and in commodity hardware. To get to the heart of the matter and incorporate all the relevant details, you need to boil everything down to a single number: business transactions per dollar. Things change quickly, so we leave this as an exercise for the reader.

MySQL Scaling and HA in the Cloud

As we noted earlier, MySQL doesn't automatically become more scalable in the cloud. In fact, the less powerful machines that are available force you to use horizontal scaling strategies much earlier. And cloud-hosted servers are less reliable and predictable than dedicated hardware, so achieving high availability requires more creativity.

By and large, though, there aren't many differences between scaling MySQL in the cloud and scaling MySQL elsewhere. The biggest difference is the ability to provision servers on demand. However, there are some limitations that make scaling and high availability a bit harder, at least in some cloud environments. For example, in the AWS cloud platform, you can't use the equivalent of virtual IP addresses to perform fast atomic failover. The limited control over resources like this simply means you have to use other approaches, such as proxies. (ScaleBase is one that could be worth looking into.)

The other siren call of the cloud is the dream of auto-scaling—that is, spinning up more instances in response to increased demand, and shutting them down again when demand reduces. Although this is feasible with stateless parts of the stack such as web servers, it's very hard to do with the database server, because it is stateful. For special cases, such as read-mostly applications, you can get a limited form of auto-scaling by adding replicas,[4] but this is not a one-size-fits-all solution. In practice, although many applications use auto-scaling in the web tier, MySQL isn't natively capable of running across a shared-nothing cluster of servers that all assume peer roles. You could do it with a sharded architecture that automatically reshards and grows or shrinks,[5] but MySQL itself just isn't able to auto-scale.

In fact, as it's typically the main or only stateful and persistent component of an application, it's pretty common for people to move an application into the cloud because of the benefits it offers for everything *but* the database—web servers, job queue servers, caches, etc.—and MySQL just has to go where everything else goes.

The database isn't the center of the world, after all. If the benefits to the rest of the application outweigh the additional cost and effort required to make MySQL work as needed, then it's not a question of whether it will happen, but how. To answer this, it's helpful to understand the additional challenges you might face in the cloud. These typically center around the resources available to the database server.

The Four Fundamental Resources

MySQL needs four fundamental resources to do its work: CPU cycles, memory, I/O, and the network. These four resources have characteristic and important differences in most cloud platforms. One helpful way to approach decisions about hosting MySQL in the cloud is to examine these differences and their implications for MySQL:

- CPUs are generally fewer and slower. The largest standard EC2 instances at the time of writing offer eight virtual CPU cores. The virtual CPUs EC2 offers are effectively slower than top-end CPUs (see our benchmarks a bit later in the chapter for the subtleties). This is probably fairly typical of most cloud hosting, although there will be variations. EC2 offers instances with more CPU resources, but they have lower maximum memory sizes. At the time of writing, commodity servers offer dozens of CPU cores—and even more, if you count hardware threads.[6]

---

4. A popular open source service for auto-scaling MySQL replication in the cloud is Scalr (*http://scalr.net*).

5. This is what computer scientists like to call a "non-trivial challenge."

6. Commodity hardware still offers more power than MySQL can use effectively in terms of CPU, RAM, and I/O, so it's not completely fair to compare the cloud with the biggest horsepower available outside the cloud.

- Memory size is limited. The largest EC2 instances currently offer 68.4 GB of memory. In contrast, commodity servers are available with 512 GB to 1 TB of memory.

- I/O performance is limited in throughput, latency, and consistency. There are two options for storage in the AWS cloud.

  The first is using EBS volumes, which are like a cloud SAN. The best practice in the AWS cloud is to build servers on RAID 10 volumes over EBS. However, EBS is a shared resource, as is the network connection between the EC2 server and the EBS server. Latency can be high and unpredictable, even under moderate throughput demands. We've measured I/O latency to EBS devices well into the tenths of seconds. In comparison, directly attached commodity hard drives respond in single-digit milliseconds, and flash devices are orders of magnitude faster even than hard drives. On the other hand, EBS volumes have a lot of nice features, such as integration with other AWS services, fast snapshots, and so on.

  The second storage option is the instance's local storage. Each EC2 server has some amount of local storage, which is actually attached to the underlying server. It can offer more consistent performance than EBS,[7] but it does not persist when the instance is stopped. The ephemeral nature of the local storage makes it unsuitable for most database server use cases.

- Network performance is usually decent, although it is a shared resource and can be variable. Although you can get faster and more consistent network performance in commodity hardware, the CPU, RAM, and I/O tend to be the first bottlenecks, and we haven't had problems with network performance in the AWS cloud.

As you can see, three of the four fundamental resources are limited in the AWS cloud, in some cases significantly so. In general, the underlying resources aren't as powerful as what's available in commodity hardware. We'll discuss the precise consequences of this in the next section.

MySQL Performance in Cloud Hosting

In general, MySQL performance on cloud hosting platforms such as AWS isn't as good as you can get elsewhere, due to weaker CPU, memory, and I/O performance. This varies from cloud platform to cloud platform, but it is still generally true.[8] However, cloud hosting might still be a high-enough performance platform for your needs, and it's better for some needs than for others.

It shouldn't surprise you that with weaker resources to run the database, you can't make MySQL run as fast when you host it in the cloud. What might surprise you is

---

7. Local storage is not actually allocated to the instance until it is written, causing a *first-write penalty* for each block that is written. The trick to avoiding this penalty is to use *dd* to write the device full of data.

8. If you believe *http://www.xkcd.com/908/*, then obviously all clouds have the same weaknesses. We're just sayin'.

that you might not be able to make it run as fast as you can on similarly sized physical hardware. For example, if you have a server with 8 CPU cores, 16 GB of memory, and a midlevel RAID array, you might assume that you can get about the same performance from an EC2 instance with 8 EC2 compute units, 15 GB of memory, and a handful of EBS volumes. That's not guaranteed, however. The EC2 instance's performance is likely to be more variable than that of your physical hardware, especially because it's not one of the super-large instances and is therefore presumably sharing resources with other instances on the same physical hardware.

Variability is a really big deal. MySQL, and InnoDB in particular, doesn't like variable performance—especially not variable I/O performance. I/O operations can acquire mutex locks inside the server, and when these last too long they can cause pileups that manifest as many "stuck" processes, inexplicably long-running queries, and spikes in status variables such as `Threads_running` or `Threads_connected`.

The practical result of inconsistent or unpredictable performance is that queueing becomes more severe. Queueing is a natural consequence of variability in response times and inter-arrival times, and there is an entire branch of mathematics devoted to the study of queueing. All computers are networks of queueing systems, and requests for resources must wait if the desired resource (CPU, I/O, network, etc.) is busy. When resource performance is more variable, requests overlap more often, and they experience more queueing. As a result, it's a bit harder to achieve high concurrency or consistently low response times in most cloud computing platforms. We have a lot of experience observing these limitations on the EC2 platform. In our experience, the most concurrency you can expect from MySQL on the largest instance sizes is a `Threads _running` count of 8 to 12 on typical web OLTP workloads. Anything beyond that, and performance tends to become unacceptable, as a rule of thumb.

Note that we said "typical web OLTP workloads." Not all workloads respond in the same way to the limitations of cloud platforms. It turns out that there are actually some workloads that perform just fine in the cloud, and some that suffer especially badly. Let's take a look at what those are:

- Workloads that need high concurrency, as we just discussed, don't tend to be as well suited to cloud computing. The same is true of applications that demand extremely fast response times. The reason boils down to the limited number and speed of the virtual CPUs. Every query runs on a single CPU inside MySQL, so query response time is limited by the raw speed of the CPU. If you want fast response times, you need fast CPUs. To support higher concurrency, you need more of them. It's true that MySQL and InnoDB don't provide great bang for the buck on many dozens of CPU cores, but they generally scale well out to at least 24 cores these days, and that's more than you can usually get in the cloud.

- Workloads that require a lot of I/O don't tend to perform all that well in the cloud. When I/O is slow and variable, things grind to a halt fairly quickly. On the other hand, if your workload doesn't demand a lot of I/O, either in throughput (operations per second) or bandwidth (bytes per second), MySQL can hum along quite nicely.

The preceding points really follow from the weaknesses of CPU and I/O resources in the cloud. What can you do about them? There's not much you can do about CPU limitations. If you don't have enough, you don't have enough. However, I/O is different. I/O is really the interchange between two kinds of memory: volatile memory (RAM) and persistent memory (disk, EBS, or what have you). As a result, MySQL's I/O demands can be influenced by how much memory the system has. With enough memory, reads can be served from caches, reducing the I/O needed for both reads and writes. Writes can generally be buffered in memory too, and multiple writes to the same bits of memory can be combined and then persisted with a single I/O operation.

That's where the limitations on memory come into the picture. With enough memory to hold the working set of data,[9] I/O demands can be reduced significantly for certain workloads. Larger EC2 instance sizes also offer better network performance, which further helps I/O to EBS volumes. But if your working set is too big to fit into the largest instances available, I/O demands escalate and things start to block and stall, as discussed earlier. The largest high-memory instance sizes in EC2 have enough memory to serve many workloads quite nicely. However, you should be aware that warmup time can be very long; more on that topic later in this section.

What types of workloads can't be fixed by adding more memory? Regardless of buffering, some write-heavy workloads simply require more I/O than you can expect from many cloud computing platforms. If you're executing many transactions per second, for example, that will demand a lot of I/O operations per second to ensure durability, and you can only get so much throughput from systems such as EBS. Likewise, if you're pushing a lot of data into the database, you might exceed the available bandwidth.

You might think that you can improve your I/O performance by striping and mirroring EBS volumes with RAID. That does help, up to a point. The problem is that as you add more EBS volumes, you actually increase the likelihood that one of them is going to be performing badly at any given point in time, and due to the way I/O works inside of InnoDB, the weakest link is often the bottleneck for the whole system. In practice, we've tried RAID 10 sets of 10 and 20 EBS volumes, and the 20-volume RAID had more problems with stalls than the 10-volume one did. When we measured the I/O performance of the underlying block devices, it was clear that only one or two of the EBS volumes was performing slowly, and yet the whole server suffered.

You can change the application and server to reduce the I/O demands, too. Careful logical and physical database design (schema and indexing) goes a long way toward reducing I/O needs, as does application and query optimization. These are the most powerful levers you can apply to reducing I/O. Some workloads, such as insert-heavy workloads, can be helped by judicious use of partitioning to concentrate the I/O on a

---

9. See Chapter 9 for a definition of the working set and a discussion of how it influences I/O demands.

single partition whose indexes fit in memory. You can relax durability, for example by setting `innodb_flush_logs_at_trx_commit=2` and `sync_binlog=0`, or moving the InnoDB transaction logs and binary logs off the EBS volumes and onto the local drives (though this is risky). But the harder you try to squeeze a little bit extra from the server, the more complexity (and thus cost) you inevitably add.

You can also upgrade your MySQL server software. Newer versions of MySQL and InnoDB (recent versions of MySQL 5.1 with the InnoDB plugin, or MySQL 5.5 and newer) offer significantly better I/O performance and fewer internal bottlenecks, and will suffer from stalls and pileups much less than the older code in early 5.1 and previous versions. Percona Server can offer even more benefits in certain workloads. For example, Percona Server's feature to warm up the buffer pool quickly after a restart is enormously helpful in getting a server back up and running quickly, especially if the I/O performance is not great and the server relies on an in-memory workload. This is one of the scenarios we've been discussing as a candidate for good performance in the cloud, where servers tend to fail more often than on-premise hardware. Percona Server can reduce warmup times from hours or even days to just minutes. At the time of writing, a similar warmup feature is available in a MySQL 5.6 development milestone release.

Ultimately, though, a growing application will reach a point where you have to shard the database to stay in the cloud. We really like to avoid sharding when we can, but if you only have so much horsepower, at some point you have to either go elsewhere (leave the cloud), or break things up into smaller pieces whose demands don't exceed the capacity of the virtual hardware that's available. You can generally count on having to shard when your working set doesn't fit in memory anymore, meaning a working set size of around 50 GB to 60 GB on the largest EC2 instances. In contrast, we have lots of experience running multi-terabyte databases on physical hardware. You have to shard much earlier in the cloud.

Benchmarks for MySQL in the Cloud

We performed some benchmarks to illustrate MySQL's performance in the AWS cloud environment. It's virtually impossible to get consistent and reproducible benchmarks in the cloud when a lot of I/O is needed, so we chose an in-memory workload that measures essentially everything except I/O. We used Percona Server version 5.5.16 with a 4 GB buffer pool to run the standard SysBench read-only benchmark on 10 million rows of data. This allowed us to compare results across a variety of instance sizes. We omitted the high-CPU instances because they actually have less CPU power than the *m2.4xlarge* instance does, and we included a Cisco server as a point of reference. The Cisco machine is fairly powerful but aging a bit, with dual Intel Xeon X5670 Nehalem CPUs at 2.93 GHz. Each CPU has six cores with two hardware threads on each, which the operating system sees as 24 CPUs overall. Figure 13-1 shows the results.

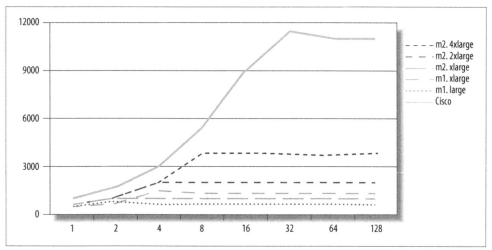

Figure 13-1. SysBench read-only benchmarks for MySQL in the AWS cloud

The results should not be surprising, given the workload and the hardware. For example, the largest EC2 instance tops out at eight threads, because it has eight CPU cores. (A read/write workload would spend some of its time off-CPU doing I/O, so we would be able to achieve more than eight threads of effective concurrency.) This chart might lead you to assume that the Cisco's advantage is in CPU power, which is what we thought. So we benchmarked raw CPU performance to find out, using SysBench's prime-number benchmark. Figure 13-2 shows the results.

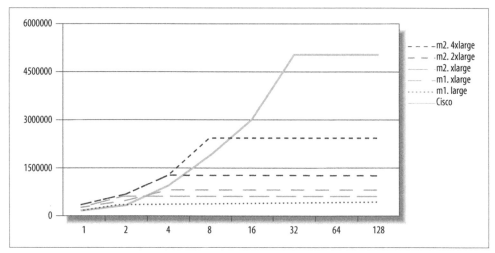

Figure 13-2. SysBench CPU prime-number benchmarks for AWS servers

The Cisco server has lower per-CPU performance than the EC2 servers. Surprised? We were a bit surprised ourselves. The prime-number benchmark is essentially raw CPU instructions, and as such, it shouldn't have a noticeable virtualization overhead or much memory traffic. Thus, the explanation for our results is probably as follows: the Cisco server's CPUs are a couple of years old, and are slower than the EC2 servers. But for more complex tasks such as running a database server, the overhead of virtualization places the EC2 servers at a disadvantage. It's not always easy to distinguish between slow CPUs, slow memory access, and virtualization overhead, but in this instance the differences seem a bit clearer.

MySQL Database as a Service (DBaaS)

Installing MySQL on a cloud-hosted server isn't the only option for using MySQL in the cloud. More and more companies are offering the database itself as a cloud resource, dubbing it Database as a Service (DBaaS, or sometimes DaaS). This means that you can get a database in the cloud somewhere and leave the actual running of the service to others. Although we've spent most of our time examining IaaS in this chapter, the IaaS market is rapidly becoming commoditized, and we expect that in the future a lot of emphasis will shift to DBaaS instead. There are several DBaaS providers at the time of writing.

Amazon RDS

We've seen much more deployment on Amazon's Relational Database Service (RDS) than any of the other DBaaS offerings. Amazon RDS isn't just a MySQL-compatible service; it actually is MySQL, so it's completely compatible with your own MySQL server[10] and can serve as a drop-in replacement. We can't say for sure, but like most people we believe that RDS is hosted on an EC2 machine backed by EBS volumes—Amazon has not officially confirmed the underlying technologies, but when you get to know RDS well, it seems pretty obvious that it's just MySQL, EC2, and EBS.

Amazon does all the system administration for you. You don't have access to the EC2 machine; you have access credentials to log into MySQL, and that's it. You can create databases, insert data, and so on. You're not locked in; if you want to, you can export the data and move it elsewhere, and you can create volume snapshots and mount them on other machines, too.

RDS comes with some restrictions to keep you from inspecting or interfering with Amazon's management of the server or the host instance. There are some privilege restrictions, for example. You can't use SELECT INTO OUTFILE, FILE(), LOAD DATA INFILE, or any other method of accessing the server's filesystem through MySQL. You can't do anything related to replication, and you can't escalate your privileges to grant yourself these rights, either. Amazon has taken measures such as placing triggers on

---

10. Unless you're using an alternative storage engine or some other nonstandard modification to MySQL.

the system tables to prevent that. And as part of the terms of service, you agree not to try to get around these limitations.

The MySQL version installed is slightly modified to prevent you from meddling with the server, but otherwise it seems to be stock MySQL as you know it. We benchmarked RDS against EBS and EC2 and found nothing beyond the variations we'd expect from the platform. That is, it looks like Amazon hasn't done any performance enhancements to the server.

RDS can offer few compelling benefits, depending on your circumstances:

- You can leave the system administration work and even much of the database administration work to Amazon. For example, they handle replication for you and ensure you don't mess it up.

- Depending on your cost structure and staffing resources, RDS can be inexpensive compared to the alternatives.

- The restrictions can be seen as a good thing: Amazon takes away the loaded gun you might otherwise use to shoot yourself in the foot.

However, it does have some potential drawbacks:

- Because you can't access the server, you can't tell what's going on in the operating system. For example, you can't measure I/O response time or CPU utilization. Amazon does provide this through another of its services, CloudWatch. It gives detailed enough metrics to troubleshoot many performance problems, but sometimes you need the raw data to know exactly what's happening. (You can't use functions such as FILE() to access /proc/diskstats, either.)

- You can't get the full slow query log file. You can direct MySQL to log slow queries to a CSV logging table, but this isn't as good. It consumes a lot more server resources, and it doesn't give high-resolution query response times. This makes it a bit harder to profile and troubleshoot SQL.

- If you want the latest and greatest, or some performance enhancements such as those you could get with Percona Server, you're out of luck. RDS doesn't offer them.

- You must rely on Amazon's support team to resolve some problems that you might otherwise be able to fix yourself. For example, suppose queries hang, or your server crashes due to data corruption. You can either wait for Amazon to work on it, or you can take matters into your own hands. But to do the latter, you have to take the data elsewhere; you can't access the instance itself to fix it. You have to spend extra time and pay for additional resources if you want to do this. This isn't just theoretical; we've gotten lots of support requests for help with things that really require access to the system to troubleshoot, and aren't really solvable for RDS users as a result.

In terms of performance, as we said, RDS is pretty comparable to a large high-memory EC2 instance with EBS storage and stock MySQL. You can squeeze a little more performance out of the AWS cloud if you use EC2 and EBS directly and install and tweak a higher-performance version of MySQL, such as Percona Server, but it won't be an order-of-magnitude difference. With that in mind, it makes sense to base your decision to use RDS on your business needs, not on performance. If you really need performance that badly, you should not use the AWS cloud at all.

Other DBaaS Solutions

Amazon RDS isn't the only DBaaS game in town for MySQL users. There are also services such as FathomDB (*http://fathomdb.com*) and Xeround (*http://xeround.com*). We don't have enough firsthand experience to recommend any of them, though, because we haven't had any production deployments on these services. From the limited public information on FathomDB, it appears to be similar to Amazon RDS, although it is available on the Rackspace cloud as well as the AWS cloud. It is in private beta at the time of writing.

Xeround is quite different: it is a distributed cluster of servers, fronted by MySQL with a proprietary storage engine. It seems to have at least some minor incompatibilities with or differences from stock MySQL, but it only recently became generally available (GA), so it's too early to judge it. The storage engine appears to communicate with a clustered backend system that might bear similarities to NDB Cluster. It has the added benefit of resharding automatically to add and subtract nodes (dynamic scaling) as the workload increases and decreases.

There are many other DBaaS services, and new ones are announced pretty frequently. Anything we write about this will be outdated by the time you read it, so we'll let you research the landscape yourself.

Summary

There are at least two mainstream ways to use MySQL in the cloud: install it on cloud servers, or use a DBaaS offering. MySQL runs just fine in cloud hosting, but the limitations of the cloud environment usually result in sharding much earlier than is necessary outside the cloud. And cloud servers that appear comparable to your existing physical hardware are likely to provide reduced performance and quality of service.

Sometimes it seems that people are saying, "The cloud is the answer; what is the question?" That is one extreme, but people who are fervent believers that the cloud is a silver bullet are likely to have corresponding problems. Three of the four fundamental resources the database needs (CPU, memory, and disk) can be significantly weaker and/or less effective in the cloud, and that has a direct impact on MySQL performance.

Nevertheless, MySQL runs great in the cloud for lots of workloads. In general, you'll be fine if you can fit your working set in memory, and if you don't generate a higher write workload than your cloud-based I/O can handle. With careful design and architecture, and by choosing the correct version of MySQL and configuring it properly, you can match your database's workload and capabilities to the cloud's strengths. Still, MySQL isn't a cloud database by nature; that is, it can't really use all of the benefits cloud computing theoretically offers, such as auto-scaling. Alternative technologies such as Xeround are attempting to address these shortcomings.

We've talked a lot about the shortcomings of the cloud, which might give you the impression that we're anti-cloud. We're not. It's just that we're trying to focus on MySQL, instead of listing all of the benefits of cloud computing, which would not be much different from anything you'd read elsewhere. We're trying to point out what's different, and what you really need to know, about running MySQL in the cloud.

The biggest successes we've seen in the cloud have been when decisions are motivated by business reasons. Even if the cost per business transaction is higher in the cloud over the long term, other factors, such as increased flexibility, reduced upfront costs, reduced time to market, and reduced risk, can be more important. And the benefits to the non-MySQL parts of your application could far outweigh any disadvantages you experience with MySQL.

Application-Level Optimization

If you spend a lot of time improving MySQL's performance, it's easy to get tunnel vision and forget to focus on the user's experience. You may step back for a bit and realize that MySQL is so highly optimized that it's contributing only a tiny fraction of the response time the user sees, and it's time to focus elsewhere. This is a great insight (especially for a DBA), and it's exactly the right thing to do. But what is causing problems, if not MySQL? The answer can be found most reliably and quickly by measuring, using the techniques we showed in Chapter 3. If your profiling is thorough and you follow a logical process, it should not be hard to find the source of your problem. Sometimes, though, even when the problem is MySQL, it might be easiest to solve it in another part of the system!

No matter where the problem lies, there's sure to be at least one great tool available to help you measure it, often for free. For example, if you have issues with JavaScript or page rendering, you can use the profiler included with the Firebug extension for the Firefox web browser, or you can use the YSlow tool from Yahoo!. We mentioned several application-level tools in Chapter 3. Some tools even profile the whole stack; New Relic is an example of a tool that profiles the frontend, application, and backend of web applications.

Common Problems

We see the same problems over and over again in applications, often because people have used poorly designed off-the-shelf systems or popular frameworks that simplify development. Although it's sometimes easier and faster to use something you didn't build yourself, it also adds risk if you don't really know what it's doing under the hood. Here's a laundry list of things that we often find to be problems, to stimulate your creative thought processes:

- What's using the CPU, disk, network, and memory resources on each of the machines involved? Do the numbers look reasonable to you? If not, check the basics for the applications that are hogging resources. Configuration is sometimes the simplest way to solve problems. For example, if Apache runs out of memory because it creates 1,000 worker processes that each need 50 MB of memory, you can configure the application to require fewer Apache workers. You can also configure the system to use less memory for each process.

- Is the application really using all the data it's getting? Fetching 1,000 rows but displaying only 10 and throwing away the rest is a common mistake. (However, if the application caches the other 990 rows for later use, it might be an intentional optimization.)

- Is the application doing processing that ought to be done in the database, or vice versa? Two examples are fetching all rows from a table to count them and doing complex string manipulations in the database. Databases are good at counting rows, and application languages are good at regular expressions. Use the best tool for the job.

- Is the application doing too many queries? Object-relational mapping (ORM) query interfaces that "protect programmers from having to write SQL" are often to blame. The database server is designed to match data from multiple tables. Remove the nested loops in the code and write a join instead.

- Is the application doing too few queries? We know, we just said doing too many queries can be a problem. But sometimes "manual joins" and similar practices can be a *good* idea, because they can permit more granular and efficient caching, less locking, and sometimes even faster execution when you emulate a hash join in application code (MySQL's nested loop join method is not always efficient).

- Is the application connecting to MySQL unnecessarily? If you can get the data from the cache, don't connect.

- Is the application connecting too many times to the same MySQL instance, perhaps because different parts of the application open their own connections? It's usually a better idea to reuse the same connection throughout.

- Is the application doing a lot of "garbage" queries? A common example is sending a ping to see if the server is alive before sending the query itself, or selecting the desired database before each query. It might be a good idea to always connect to a specific database and use fully qualified names for tables. (This also makes it easier to analyze queries from the log or via SHOW PROCESSLIST, because you can execute them without needing to change the database.) "Preparing" the connection is another common problem. The Java driver in particular does a lot of things during preparation, most of which you can disable. Another common garbage query is SET NAMES UTF8, which is the wrong way to do things anyway (it does not change the client library's character set; it affects only the server). If your application uses a specific character set for most of its work, you can avoid the need to change the character set by configuring it as the default.

- Does the application use a connection pool? This can be both a good and a bad thing. It helps limit the number of connections, which is good when connections aren't used for many queries (Ajax applications are a typical example). However, it can have side effects, such as applications interfering with each other's transactions, temporary tables, connection-specific settings, and user-defined variables.

- Does the application use persistent connections? These can result in way too many connections to MySQL. They're generally a bad idea, except if the cost of connecting to MySQL is very high because of a slow network, if the connection will be used only for one or two fast queries, or if you're connecting so frequently that you're running out of local port numbers on the client. If you configure MySQL correctly, you might not need persistent connections. Use `skip-name-resolve` to prevent reverse DNS lookups, ensure that `thread_cache` is set high enough, and increase `back_log`. See Chapter 8 and Chapter 9 for more details.

- Is the application holding connections open even when it's not using them? If so—particularly if it connects to many servers—it might be consuming connections that other processes need. For example, suppose you're connecting to 10 MySQL servers. Getting 10 connections from an Apache process isn't a problem, but only one of them will really be doing anything at any given time. The other nine will spend a lot of time in the `Sleep` state. If one server slows down, or there's a long network call, the other servers can suffer because they're out of connections. The solution is to control how the application uses connections. For example, you can batch operations to each MySQL instance in turn, and close each connection before querying the next one. If you're doing time-consuming operations, such as calls to a web service, you can even close the MySQL connection, perform the time-consuming work, then reopen the MySQL connection and continue working with the database.

The difference between persistent connections and connection pooling can be confusing. Persistent connections can cause the same side effects as connection pooling, because a reused connection is stateful in either case.

However, connection pools don't usually result in as many connections to the server, because they queue and share connections among processes. Persistent connections, on the other hand, are created on a per-process basis and can't be shared among processes.

Connection pools also allow more control over connection policies than shared connections. You can configure a pool to autoextend, but the usual practice is to queue connection requests when the pool is completely busy. This makes the connection requests wait on the application server, rather than overload the MySQL server with too many connections.

There are many ways to make queries and connections faster, but the general rule is that avoiding them altogether is better than trying to speed them up.

Web Server Issues

Apache is the most popular server software for web applications. It works well for many purposes, but when used badly it can consume a lot of resources. The most common issues are keeping its processes alive too long, and using it for a mixture of purposes instead of optimizing it separately for each type of work.

Apache is usually used with mod_php, mod_perl, and mod_python in a "prefork" configuration. Preforking dedicates a process for each request. Because the PHP, Perl, and Python scripts can be demanding, it's not uncommon for each process to use 50 or 100 MB of memory. When a request completes, it returns most of this memory to the operating system, but not all of it. Apache keeps the process open and reuses it for future requests. This means that if the next request is for a static file, such as a CSS file or an image, you'll wind up with a big fat process serving a simple request. This is why it's dangerous to use Apache as a general-purpose web server. It is general-purpose, but if you specialize it, you'll get much better performance.

The other major problem is that processes can be kept busy for a long time if you have Keep-Alive enabled. And even if you don't, some of the processes might be staying alive too long, "spoon-feeding" content to a client that is fetching the data slowly.[1]

People also often make the mistake of leaving the default set of Apache modules enabled. You can trim Apache's footprint by removing modules you don't need. It's simple: just review the Apache configuration file and comment out unwanted modules, then restart Apache. You can also remove unused PHP modules from your *php.ini* file.

The bottom line is that if you create an all-purpose Apache configuration that faces the Web directly, you're likely to end up with many heavyweight Apache processes. These will waste resources on your web server. They can also keep a lot of connections open to MySQL, wasting resources on MySQL, too. Here are some ways you can reduce the load on your servers:[2]

- Don't use Apache to serve static content, or at least use a different Apache instance. Popular alternatives are Nginx (*http://www.nginx.com*) and *lighttpd* (*http://www .lighttpd.net*).
- Use a caching proxy server, such as Squid or Varnish, to keep requests from ever reaching your web servers. Even if you can't cache full pages on this level, you might be able to cache most of a page and use technologies such as edge side

---

1. Spoon-feeding occurs when a client makes an HTTP request but then doesn't fetch the result quickly. Until the client fetches the entire result, the HTTP connection—and thus the Apache process—stays alive.

2. A good book on how to optimize web applications is *High Performance Web Sites (http://shop.oreilly.com/ product/9780596529307.do)* by Steve Souders (O'Reilly). Though it's mostly about how to make websites faster from the client's point of view, the practices he advocates are good for your servers, too. Steve's follow-up book, *Even Faster Web Sites (http://shop.oreilly.com/product/9780596522315.do)*, is also a good resource.

includes (ESI; see *http://www.esi.org*) to embed the small dynamic portion of the page into the cached static portion.

- Set an expiration policy on both dynamic and static content. You can use caching proxies such as Squid to invalidate content explicitly. Wikipedia uses this technique to remove articles from caches when they change.

- Sometimes you might need to change the application so that you can use longer expiration times. For example, if you tell the browser to cache CSS and JavaScript files forever and then release a change to the site's HTML, the pages might render badly. You can version the files explicitly with a unique filename for each revision. For example, you can customize your website publishing script to copy the CSS files to */css/123_frontpage.css*, where *123* is the Subversion revision number. You can do the same thing for image filenames—never reuse a filename, and your pages will never break when you upgrade them, no matter how long the browser caches them.

- Don't let Apache spoon-feed the client. It's not just slow; it also makes denial-of-service attacks easy. Hardware load balancers typically do buffering, so Apache can finish quickly and the load balancer can spoon-feed the client from the buffer. You can also use Nginx, Squid, or Apache in event-driven mode in front of the application.

- Enable *gzip* compression. It's very cheap for modern CPUs, and it saves a lot of traffic. If you want to save on CPU cycles, you can cache and serve the compressed version of the page with a lightweight server such as Nginx.

- Don't configure Apache with a Keep-Alive for long-distance connections, because that will keep fat Apache processes alive for a long time. Instead, let a server-side proxy handle the Keep-Alive, and shield Apache from the client. It's OK to configure the connections between the proxy and Apache with a Keep-Alive, because the proxy will use only a few connections to fetch data from Apache. Figure 14-1 illustrates the difference.

These tactics should keep Apache processes short-lived, so you don't end up with more processes than you need. However, some operations might still cause an Apache process to stay alive for a long time and consume a lot of resources. An example is a query to an external resource that has high latency, such as a remote web service. This problem is often unsolvable.

Finding the Optimal Concurrency

Every web server has an *optimal concurrency*—that is, an optimal number of concurrent connections that will result in requests being processed as quickly as possible, without overloading your systems. This is the maximum system capacity we referred to in Chapter 11. A little measurement and modeling, or simply trial and error, can be required to find this "magic number," but it's worth the effort.

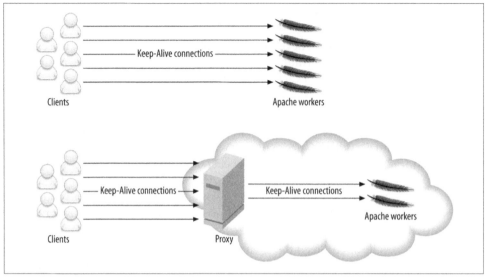

Figure 14-1. A proxy can shield Apache from long-lived Keep-Alive connections, resulting in fewer Apache workers

It's common for a high-traffic website to handle thousands of connections to the web server at the same time. However, only a few of these connections need to be actively processing requests. The others might be reading requests, handling file uploads, spoon-feeding content, or simply awaiting further requests from the client.

As concurrency increases, there's a point at which the server reaches its peak throughput. After that, the throughput levels off and often starts to decrease. More importantly, the response time (latency) starts to increase due to queueing.

To see why, consider what happens when you have a single CPU and the server receives 100 requests simultaneously. Imagine that one second of CPU time is required to process each request. Assuming a perfect operating system scheduler with no overhead, and no context switching overhead, the requests will need a total of 100 CPU seconds to complete.

What's the best way to serve the requests? You can queue them one after another, or you can run them in parallel and switch between them, giving each request equal time before switching to the next. In both cases, the throughput is one request per second. However, the average latency is 50 seconds if they're queued (concurrency = 1), and 100 seconds if they're run in parallel (concurrency = 100). In practice, the average latency would be even higher for parallel execution, because of the switching cost.

For a CPU-bound workload, the optimal concurrency is equal to the number of CPUs (or CPU cores). However, processes are not always runnable, because they make blocking calls such as I/O, database queries, and network requests. Therefore, the optimal concurrency is usually higher than the number of CPUs.

You can estimate the optimal concurrency, but it requires accurate profiling. It's usually easier to either experiment with different concurrency values and see what gives the peak throughput without degrading response time, or measure your real workload and analyze it. Percona Toolkit's *pt-tcp-model* tool can help you measure and model your system's scalability and performance characteristics from a TCP dump.

Caching

Caching is vital for high-load applications. A typical web application serves a lot of content that costs much more to generate than it costs to cache (including the cost of checking and expiring the cache), so caching can usually improve performance by orders of magnitude. The trick is to find the right combination of granularity and expiration policies. You also need to decide what content to cache and where to cache it.

A typical high-load application has many layers of caching. Caching doesn't just happen in your servers: it happens at every step along the way, including the user's web browser (that's what content expiration headers are for). In general, the closer the cache is to the client, the more resources it saves and the more effective it is. Serving an image from the browser's cache is better than serving it from the web server's memory, which is better than reading it from the server's disk. Each type of cache has unique characteristics, such as size and latency; we examine some of them in the following sections.

You can think about caches in two broad categories: *passive caches* and *active caches*. Passive caches do nothing but store and return data. When you request something from a passive cache, either you get the result or the cache tells you "that doesn't exist." An example of a passive cache is *memcached*.

In contrast, an active cache does something when there's a miss. It usually passes your request on to some other part of the application, which generates the requested result. The active cache then stores the result and returns it. The Squid caching proxy server is an active cache.

When you design your application, you usually want your caches to be active (also called *transparent*), because they hide the check-generate-store logic from the application. You can build active caches on top of passive caches.

Caching Below the Application

The MySQL server has its own internal caches, and you can build your own cache and summary tables, too. You can custom-design your cache tables so that they're most useful for filtering, sorting, joining to other tables, counting, or any other purpose. Cache tables are also more persistent than many application-level caches, because they'll survive a server restart.

We wrote about these cache strategies in Chapter 4 and Chapter 5, so in this chapter we focus on caching at the application level and above.

Caching Doesn't Always Help

You need to make sure that caching really improves performance, because it might not help at all. For example, in practice it's often faster to serve content from Nginx's memory than to serve it from a caching proxy. This is especially true if the proxy's cache is on disk.

The reason is simple: caching has its own overhead. There's the overhead of checking the cache, and serving the data from the cache if there's a hit. There's also the overhead of invalidating the cache and storing data in it. Caching is helpful only if these costs are less than the cost of generating and serving the data without a cache.

If you know the costs of all these operations, you can calculate how much the cache helps. The cost without the cache is the cost of generating the data for each request. The cost with the cache is the cost of checking the cache, plus the probability of a cache miss times the cost of generating the data, plus the probability of a cache hit times the cost of serving the data from the cache.

If the cost with the cache is lower than without, it's an improvement, but that's not guaranteed. Also bear in mind that, as in the case of serving data from Nginx's memory rather than from the proxy's on-disk cache, some caches are cheaper than others.

Application-Level Caching

An application-level cache typically stores data in memory on the same machine, or across the network in another machine's memory.

Application-level caching can be more efficient than caching at a lower level, because the application can store partially computed results in the cache. Thus, the cache saves two types of work: fetching the data, and doing computations on it. A good example is blocks of HTML text. The application can generate HTML snippets, such as the top news headlines, and cache them. Subsequent page views can then simply insert this cached text into the page. In general, the more you process the data before you cache it, the more work you save when there's a cache hit.

The disadvantage is that the cache hit rate can be lower, and the cache can use more memory. Suppose you need 50 different versions of the top news headlines, so the user sees different content depending on where she lives. You'll need enough memory to store all 50 of them, fewer requests will hit any given version of the headlines, and invalidation can be more complicated.

There are many types of application caches. Here are a few:

Local caches
> These caches are usually small and live only in the process's memory for the duration of the request. They're useful for avoiding a repeated request for a resource when it's needed more than once. There's nothing fancy about this type of cache: it's usually just a variable or hash table in the application code. For example,

suppose you need to display a user's name, and you know the user's ID. You can build a get_name_from_id() function and add caching to it like this:

```php
<?php
function get_name_from_id($user_id) {
    static $name; // static makes the variable persist
    if ( !$name ) {
        // Fetch name from database
    }
    return $name;
}
?>
```

If you're using Perl, the Memoize module is the standard way to cache the results of function calls:

```perl
use Memoize qw(memoize);
memoize 'get_name_from_id';
sub get_name_from_id {
    my ( $user_id ) = @_;
    my $name = # get name from database
    return $name;
}
```

These techniques are simple, but they can save your application a lot of work.

Local shared-memory caches

These caches are medium-sized (a few GB), fast, and hard to synchronize across multiple machines. They're good for small, semi-static bits of data. Examples include lists of the cities in each state, the partitioning function (mapping table) for a sharded data store, or data that you can invalidate with time-to-live (TTL) policies. The biggest benefit of shared memory is that accessing it is very fast—usually much faster than accessing any type of remote cache.

Distributed memory caches

The best-known example of a distributed memory cache is *memcached*. Distributed caches are much larger than local shared-memory caches and are easy to grow. Only one copy of each bit of cached data is created, so you don't waste memory and introduce consistency problems by caching the same data in many places. Distributed memory is great for storing shared objects, such as user profiles, comments, and HTML snippets.

These caches have much higher latency than local shared-memory caches, though, so the most efficient way to use them is with multiple get operations (i.e., getting many objects in a single round-trip). They also require you to plan how you'll add more nodes, and what to do if one of the nodes dies. In both cases, the application needs to decide how to distribute or redistribute cached objects across the nodes.

Consistent caching is important to avoid performance problems when you add a server to or remove a server from your cache cluster. There's a consistent caching library for *memcached* at *http://www.audioscrobbler.net/development/ketama/*.

On-disk caches

Disks are slow, so caching on disk is best for persistent objects, objects that are hard to fit in memory, or static content (pregenerated custom images, for example).

One very useful trick with on-disk caches and web servers is to use 404 error handlers to catch cache misses. Suppose your web application shows a custom-generated image in the header, based on the user's name ("Welcome back, John!"). You can refer to the image as */images/welcomeback/john.jpg*. If the image doesn't exist, it will cause a 404 error and trigger the error handler. The error handler can generate the image, store it on the disk, and either issue a redirect or just stream the image back to the browser. Further requests will just return the image from the file.

You can use this trick for many types of content. For example, instead of caching the latest headlines as a block of HTML, you can store them in a JavaScript file and then refer to */latest_headlines.js* in the web page's header.

Cache invalidation is easy: just delete the file. You can implement TTL invalidation by running a periodic job that deletes files created more than *N* minutes ago. And if you want to limit the cache size, you can implement a least recently used (LRU) invalidation policy by deleting files in order of their last access time.

Invalidation based on last access time requires you to enable the access time option in your filesystem's mount options. (You actually do this by omitting the noatime mount option.) If you do this, you should use an in-memory filesystem to avoid a lot of disk activity.

Cache Control Policies

Caches create the same problem as denormalizing your database design: they duplicate data, which means there are multiple places to update the data, and you have to figure out how to avoid reading stale data. The following are several of the most common cache control policies:

TTL (time to live)

The cached object is stored with an expiration date; you can either remove the object with a purge process when that date arrives, or leave it until the next time something accesses it (at which time you should replace it with a fresh version). This invalidation policy is best for data that changes rarely or doesn't have to be fresh.

Explicit invalidation

If stale data is not acceptable, the process that updates the source data can invalidate the old version in the cache. There are two variations of this policy: *write-invalidate* and *write-update*. The write-invalidate policy is simple: you just mark the cached data as expired (and optionally purge it from the cache). The write-update policy involves a little more work, because you have to replace the old cache entry with the updated data. However, it can be very beneficial, especially if it is expensive to generate the cached data (which the writer process might already have). If you update the cached data, future requests won't have to wait for the application to generate it. If you do invalidations in the background, such as TTL-based invalidations, you can generate new versions of the invalidated data in a process that's completely detached from any user request.

Invalidation on read

Instead of invalidating stale data when you change the source data from which it's derived, you can store some information that lets you determine whether the data has expired when you read it from the cache. This has a significant advantage over explicit invalidation: it has a fixed cost that you can spread out over time. Suppose you invalidate an object upon which a million cached objects depend. If you invalidate on write, you have to invalidate a million things in the cache in one hit, which could take a long time even if you have an efficient way to find them. If you invalidate on read, the write can complete immediately, and each of a million reads will be delayed slightly. This spreads out the cost of the invalidation and helps avoid spikes of load and long latencies.

One of the simplest ways to do invalidation on read is with *object versioning*. With this approach, when you store an object in the cache, you also store the current version number or timestamp of the data upon which it depends. For example, suppose you're caching statistics about a user's blog posts, including the number of posts the user has made. When you cache the blog_stats object, you store the user's current version number with it, because the statistics are dependent on the user.

Whenever you update some data that also depends on the user, you update the user's version number. Suppose the user's version is initially 0, and you generate and cache the statistics. When the user publishes a blog post, you increase the user's version to 1 (you'd store this with the blog post too, though we don't really need it for this example). Then, when you need to display the statistics, you compare the cached blog_stats object's version to the cached user's version. Because the user's version is greater than the object's version, you know that the statistics are stale and you need to recompute them.

This is a pretty coarse way to invalidate content, because it assumes that every bit of data that's dependent on the user also interacts with all other data. That's not always true. If a user edits a blog post, for example, you'll increment the user's version, and that will invalidate the stored statistics even though the statistics (the number of blog posts) didn't really change. The trade-off is simplicity. A simple cache invalidation policy isn't just easier to build; it might be more efficient, too.

Object versioning is a simplified approach to a *tagged cache*, which can handle more complex dependencies. A tagged cache knows about different kinds of dependencies and tracks versions separately for each of them. To return to the book club example from Chapter 11, you could make the cached comments dependent on the user's version and the book's version by tagging the comments with these version numbers:

user_ver=1234 and book_ver=5678. If either version changes, you'd refresh the cached comments.

Cache Object Hierarchies

Storing objects in a cache hierarchically can help with retrieval, invalidation, and memory usage. Instead of caching just objects, you can cache the object IDs, as well as the groups of object IDs that you commonly retrieve together.

A search result on an ecommerce website is a good example of this technique. A search might return a list of matching products, complete with names, descriptions, thumbnail photos, and prices. Caching the entire list would be inefficient: other searches would be likely to include some of the same products, resulting in duplicate data and wasted memory. That strategy would also make it hard to find and invalidate search results when a product's price changes, because you'd have to look inside each list to see which ones include the updated product.

Instead of caching the list, you can cache minimal information about the search, such as the number of results returned and a list of product IDs. You can then cache each product separately. This solves both problems: it doesn't duplicate any results, and it makes it easy to invalidate the cache at the granularity of individual products.

The drawback is that you have to retrieve multiple objects from the cache, instead of getting the entire search result at once. However, storing the list of product IDs for the search result makes this efficient. Now a cache hit returns the list of IDs, which you can use for a second call to the cache. The second call can return multiple products if the cache lets you get multiple results with a single call (*memcached* supports this through the mget() call).

If you're not careful, though, this approach could cause odd results. Suppose you use a TTL policy to invalidate search results, and you invalidate individual products explicitly when they change. Now imagine that a product's description changes so it no longer contains the keywords that matched a search, but the search isn't old enough to have expired from the cache. Your users will see stale search results, because the cached search will refer to the product even though it no longer matches the search keywords.

This isn't usually a problem for most applications. If your application can't tolerate it, you can use version-based caching and store the product versions with the results when you perform a search. When you find a search result in the cache, you can compare each product's version in the search results to the current (cached) version. If any product is stale, you can repeat the search and recache the results.

It's important to understand how expensive a remote cache access is. Although caches are fast and avoid a lot of work, the network round-trip to a cache server on a LAN typically takes about three tenths of a millisecond. We've seen many cases where a complex web page requires around a thousand cache accesses to assemble. That's a total of three seconds of network latency, which means that your page can be unacceptably slow even if it's served without a single database access! Using a multi-get call to the cache is absolutely vital in these situations. Using a cache hierarchy, with a smaller local cache, can also be very beneficial.

Pregenerating Content

In addition to caching bits of data at the application level, you can prerequest some pages with background processes and store the results as static pages. If your pages are dynamic, you can pregenerate parts of the pages and use a technique such as server-side includes to build the final pages. This can help to reduce the size and cost of the pregenerated content, because you might otherwise duplicate a lot of content due to minor variations in how the constituent pieces are assembled into the final page. You can use a pregeneration strategy for almost any type of caching, including *memcached*.

Pregenerating content has several important benefits:

- Your application's code doesn't have to be complicated with hit and miss paths.
- It works well when the miss path is unacceptably slow, because it ensures that a miss never happens. In fact, anytime you design any type of caching system, you should always consider how slow the miss path is. If the average performance increases a lot but the occasional request becomes extremely slow due to regenerating cached content, it might actually be *worse* than not using a cache. Consistent performance is often as important as fast performance.
- Pregenerating content avoids a stampede to the cache when there's a miss.

Caching pregenerated content can take a lot of space, and it's not always possible to pregenerate everything. As with any form of caching, the most important pieces of content to pregenerate are those that are requested the most or are the most expensive to generate, so you can do on-demand generation with the 404 error handlers we mentioned earlier in this chapter.

Pregenerated content sometimes benefits from being stored on an in-memory filesystem to avoid disk I/O.

The Cache as an Infrastructure Component

A cache is likely to become a vital part of your infrastructure. It can be easy to fall into the trap of thinking of a cache as a nice thing to have, but not something so important that you can't live without it. You might reason that if the cache server goes down, or you lose the cached content, the request will simply go to the database instead. This might be true when you initially add the cache into the application, but the cache can enable the application to grow significantly without increasing the resources dedicated to some portion of the system—typically the database. As a result, you might become dependent on the cache without realizing it.

For example, if your cache hit rate is 90% and you lose the cache for some reason, the load on the database will increase tenfold. It's rather likely that this will exceed the database server's capacity.

To avoid surprises such as this, you should think about some kind of high-availability solution for the cache (the data as well as the service), or at least measure the performance impact of disabling the cache or losing its data. You might need to design the application to degrade its functionality, for example.

Using HandlerSocket and memcached Access

Instead of storing data in MySQL and caching it outside of MySQL, an alternative approach is to create a faster access path to MySQL and then bypass the cache. For small, simple queries, a large portion of the overhead can come from parsing the SQL, checking privileges, generating an execution plan, and so on. If this overhead can be eliminated, MySQL can be very fast at simple queries.

There are currently two solutions that take advantage of this by permitting so-called NoSQL access to MySQL. The first is a daemon plugin called HandlerSocket, which was created at DeNA, a large Japanese social networking site. It permits you to access an InnoDB Handler object through a simple protocol. In effect, you're reaching past the upper layers of the server and connecting directly to InnoDB over the network. There are reports of HandlerSocket achieving over 750,000 queries per second. HandlerSocket is distributed with Percona Server, and the *memcached* access to InnoDB is available in a lab release of MySQL 5.6.

The second option is accessing InnoDB through the *memcached* protocol. The lab releases of MySQL 5.6 have a plugin that permits this.

Both approaches are somewhat limited—especially the *memcached* approach, which doesn't support as many access methods to the data. Why would you ever want to access your data through anything but SQL? Aside from speed, the biggest reason is probably simplicity. It's a big win to get rid of caches, and all of the invalidation logic and additional infrastructure that accompanies them.

Extending MySQL

If MySQL can't do what you need, one possibility is to extend its capabilities. We won't show you how to do that, but we want to mention some of the possibilities. If you're interested in exploring any of these avenues further, there are good resources online, and there are books available on many of the topics.

When we say "MySQL can't do what you need," we mean two things: MySQL can't do it at all, or MySQL can do it, but in a slow or awkward way that's not good enough. Either is a reason to look at extending MySQL. The good news is that MySQL is becoming more and more modular and general-purpose.

Storage engines are a great way to extend MySQL for a special purpose. Brian Aker has written a skeleton storage engine and a series of articles and presentations about how to get started writing your own storage engine. This has formed the basis for several of the major third-party storage engines. Many companies have written their own internal storage engines. For example, some social networking companies use special storage engines for social graph operations, and we know of a company that built a custom engine for fuzzy searches. A simple custom storage engine isn't very hard to write.

You can also use a storage engine as an interface to another piece of software. A good example of this is the Sphinx storage engine, which interfaces with the Sphinx full-text search software (see Appendix F).

Alternatives to MySQL

MySQL is not necessarily the solution for every need. It's often much better to do some work completely outside MySQL, even if MySQL can theoretically do what you want.

One of the most obvious examples is storing data in a traditional filesystem instead of in tables. Image files are the classic case: you can put them into a BLOB column, but this is rarely a good idea.[3] The usual practice is to store images or other large binary files on the filesystem and store the filenames inside MySQL; the application can then retrieve the files from outside of MySQL. In a web application, you accomplish this by putting the filename in the <img> element's src attribute.

Full-text searching is something else that's best handled outside of MySQL—MySQL doesn't perform these searches as well as Lucene or Sphinx.

The NDB API can also be useful for certain tasks. For instance, although MySQL's NDB Cluster storage engine isn't (yet) well suited for storing all of a high-performance web application's data, it's possible to use the NDB API directly for storing website session data or user registration information. You can learn more about the NDB API at *http://dev.mysql.com/doc/ndbapi/en/index.html*. There's also an NDB module for Apache, *mod_ndb*, which you can download at *http://code.google.com/p/mod-ndb/*.

Finally, for some operations—such as graph relationships and tree traversals—a relational database just isn't always the right paradigm. MySQL isn't good for distributed data processing, because it lacks parallel query execution capabilities. You'll probably want to use other tools for this purpose (possibly in combination with MySQL). Examples that come to mind:

---

3. There are advantages to using MySQL replication to distribute images quickly to many machines, and we know of some applications that use this technique.

- We have replaced MySQL with Redis when simple key-value pairs were being stored at such a high rate that the replicas fell behind, even though the master could handle the load just fine. Redis is also popular for queues, due to its nice support for queue operations.
- Hadoop is the elephant in the room, pun intended. Hybrid MySQL/Hadoop deployments are very common for processing large or semistructured datasets.

Summary

Optimization isn't just a database thing. As we suggested in Chapter 3, the highest form of optimization is both business-focused and user-focused. Full-stack performance optimization is what's really needed to achieve this.

The first thing to do is measure, as always. Focus on profiling per-tier. Which tiers are responsible for most of the response time? Concentrate there first. If the user's experience is impacted the most by DOM rendering in the browser, and MySQL contributes only a tiny fraction of the total response time, then optimizing queries further can never help the user experience appreciably. After you've measured, it's usually easy to understand where your efforts should be directed. We recommend reading both of Steve Souders's books (*High Performance Web Sites and Even Faster Web Sites*) and the use of New Relic.

You can often find big, easy wins in web server configuration and caching. There's a stereotypical notion that "it's always a database problem," but that just isn't true. The other tiers in the application are no less important, and they're just as prone to being misconfigured, although sometimes the effects are less obvious. Caches, in particular, can help you deliver a lot of content at a much lower cost than you'd be able to do with MySQL alone. And although Apache is still the world's most popular web server software, it's not always the best tool for the job, so consider alternatives such as Nginx when they make sense.

Backup and Recovery

If you don't plan for backups up front, you might later find that you've ruled out some of the best options. For example, you might set up a server and then wish for LVM so that you can take filesystem snapshots—but it's too late. You also might not notice some important performance impacts of configuring your systems for backups. And if you don't plan for and practice recovery, it won't go smoothly when you need to do it.

In contrast to the first and second editions of this book, we now assume most readers are using primarily InnoDB instead of MyISAM. We won't cover all parts of a well-designed backup and recovery solution in this chapter—just the parts that are relevant to MySQL. Here are some points we decided not to include:

- Security (access to the backup, privileges to restore data, whether the files need to be encrypted)
- Where to store the backups, including how far away from the source they should be (on a different disk, a different server, or offsite), and how to move the data from the source to the destination
- Retention policies, auditing, legal requirements, and related subjects
- Storage solutions and media, compression, and incremental backups
- Storage formats
- Monitoring and reporting on your backups
- Backup capabilities built into storage layers, or particular devices such as prefabricated file servers

These topics are covered in books such as W. Curtis Preston's *Backup & Recovery* (O'Reilly).

Before we begin, let's clarify some key terms. First, you'll often hear about so-called *hot*, *warm*, and *cold* backups. People generally use these terms to denote a backup's impact: "hot" backups aren't supposed to require any server downtime, for example. The problem is that these terms don't mean the same things to everyone. Some tools even use the word "hot" in their names, but definitely don't perform what we consider to be hot backups. We try to avoid these terms and instead tell you how much a specific technique or tool interrupts your server.

Two other confusing words are *restore* and *recover*. We use them in specific ways in this chapter. *Restoring* means retrieving data from a backup and either loading it into MySQL or placing the files where MySQL expects them to be. *Recovery* generally means the entire process of rescuing a system, or part of a system, after something has gone wrong. This includes restoring data from backups as well as all the steps necessary to make a server fully functional again, such as restarting MySQL, changing the configuration, warming up the server's caches, and so on.

To many people, recovery just means fixing corrupted tables after a crash. This is not the same as recovering an entire server. A storage engine's crash recovery reconciles its data and log files. It makes sure the data files contain only the modifications made by committed transactions, and it replays transactions from the log files that have not yet been applied to the data files. This might be part of the overall recovery process, or even part of making backups. However, it's not the same as the recovery you might need to do after an accidental DROP TABLE, for example.

Why Backups?

Here are a few reasons that backups are important:

Disaster recovery
> Disaster recovery is what you do when hardware fails, a nasty bug corrupts your data, or your server and its data become unavailable or unusable for some other reason. You need to be ready for everything from someone accidentally connecting to the wrong server doing an ALTER TABLE,[1] to the building burning down, to a malicious attacker or a MySQL bug. Although the odds of any particular disaster striking are fairly low, taken together they add up.

People changing their minds
> You'd be surprised how often people intentionally delete data and then want it back.

Auditing
> Sometimes you need to know what your data or schema looked like at some point in the past. You might be involved in a lawsuit, for example, or you might discover a bug in your application and need to see what the code used to do (sometimes just having your code in version control isn't enough).

---

1. Baron still remembers his first job after college, where he dropped two columns from the production server's invoice table at an ecommerce site.

Testing

> One of the easiest ways to test on realistic data is to periodically refresh a test server with the latest production data. If you're making backups, it's easy; just restore the backup to the test server.

Check your assumptions. For example, do you assume your shared hosting provider is backing up the MySQL server provided with your account? Many hosting providers don't back up MySQL servers all, and others just do a file copy while the server is running, which probably creates a corrupt backup that's useless.

Defining Recovery Requirements

If all goes well, you'll never need to think about recovery. But when you do, the best backup system in the world won't help. Instead, you'll need a great recovery system.

Unfortunately, it's easier to make your backup systems work smoothly than it is to build good recovery processes and tools. Here's why:

- Backups come first. You can't recover unless you've first backed up, so your attention naturally focuses on backups when building a system.
- Backups are automated with scripts and jobs. It's easy to spend time fine-tuning the backup process, often without thinking of it. Five-minute tweaks to your backup process might not seem important, but are you applying the same attention to recovery, day in and day out?
- Backups are routine, but recovery is usually a crisis situation.
- Security gets in the way. If you're doing offsite backups, you're probably encrypting the backup data or taking other measures to protect it. You know how damaging it would be for your data to be compromised, but how damaging is it when nobody can unlock your encrypted volume to recover your data, or when you need to extract a single file from a monolithic encrypted file?
- One person can plan, design, and implement backups. That person might not be available when disaster strikes. You need to train several people and plan for coverage, so you're not asking an unqualified person to recover your data.

Here's an example we've seen in the real world: a customer reported that backups became lightning fast when the *-d* option was added to *mysqldump*, and wanted to know why no one had mentioned how much that option could speed up the backup process. If this customer had tried to restore the backups, it would have been hard to miss the reason: the *-d* option dumps no data! The customer was focused on backups, not recovery, and was therefore completely unaware of this problem.

There are two Big Important Requirements that are helpful to consider when you're planning your backup and recovery strategy. These are the recovery point objective (RPO) and the recovery time objective (RTO). They define how much data you're comfortable losing, and how long you're comfortable waiting to get it back. Try to answer the following types of questions when defining your RPO and RTO:

- How much data can you lose without serious consequences? Do you need point-in-time recovery, or is it acceptable to lose whatever work has happened since your last regular backup? Are there legal requirements?

- How fast does recovery have to be? What kind of downtime is acceptable? What impacts (e.g., partial unavailability) can your application and users accept, and how will you build in the capability to continue functioning when those scenarios happen?

- What do you need to recover? Common requirements are to recover a whole server, a single database, a single table, or just specific transactions or statements.

It's a good idea to document the answers to these questions, and indeed your entire backup policy, as well as the backup procedures.

Backup Myth #1: "My Replica Is My Backup"

This is a mistake we see quite often. A replica is not a backup. Neither is a RAID array. To see why, consider this: will they help you get back all your data if you accidentally execute DROP DATABASE on your production database? RAID and replication don't pass even this simple test. Not only are they not backups, they're not a substitute for backups. Nothing but backups fill the need for backups.

Designing a MySQL Backup Solution

Backing up MySQL is harder than it looks. At its most basic, a backup is just a copy of the data, but your application's needs, MySQL's storage engine architecture, and your system configuration can make it difficult to make a copy of your data.

Before we go into great detail on all of the available options, here are our recommendations:

- Raw backups are practically a must-have for large databases: logical backups are simply too slow and resource-intensive, and recovery from a logical backup takes way too long. Snapshot-based backups, Percona XtraBackup, and MySQL Enterprise Backup are the best options. For small databases, logical backups can work nicely.

- Keep several backup generations.

- Extract logical backups (probably from the raw backups) periodically.

- Keep binary logs for point-in-time recovery. Set expire_logs_days long enough to recover from at least two generations of raw backups, so that you can create a replica and start it from the running master without applying any binary logs to it.

Back up your binary logs independently of the expiry setting, and keep them in the backup long enough to recover from at least the most recent logical backup.

- Monitor your backups and backup processes independently from the backup tools themselves. You need external verification that they're OK.

- Test your backups and recovery process by going through the entire recovery process. Measure the resources needed for recovery (CPU, disk space, wall-clock time, network bandwidth, etc.).

- Think hard about security. What happens if someone compromises your server—can he then get access to the backup server too, or vice versa?

Knowing your RPO and RTO will guide your backup strategy. Do you need point-in-time recovery capability, or is it enough to recover to last night's backup and lose whatever work has been done since then? If you need point-in-time recovery, you can probably make a regular backup and make sure the binary log is enabled, so you can restore that backup and recover to the desired point by replaying the binary log.

Generally, the more you can afford to lose, the easier it is to do backups. If you have very strict requirements, it's harder to ensure you can recover everything. There are also different flavors of point-in-time recovery. A "soft" point-in-time recovery requirement means you'd like to be able to recreate your data so that it's "close enough" to where it was when the problem happened. A "hard" requirement means you can never tolerate the loss of a committed transaction, even if something terrible happens (such as the server catching fire). This requires special techniques, such as keeping your binary log on a separate SAN volume or using DRBD disk replication.

Online or Offline Backups?

If you can get away with it, shutting down MySQL to make a backup is the easiest, safest, and overall best way to get a consistent copy of the data with minimal risk of corruption or inconsistency. If you shut down MySQL, you can copy the data without any complications from things such as dirty buffers in the InnoDB buffer pool or other caches. You don't need to worry about your data being modified while you're trying to back it up, and because the server isn't under load from the application, you can make the backup more quickly.

However, taking a server offline is more expensive than it might seem. Even if you can minimize the downtime, shutting down and restarting MySQL can take a long time under demanding loads and high data volumes, as discussed in Chapter 8. We showed some techniques for minimizing this impact, but it can't be reduced to zero. As a result, you'll almost certainly need to design your backups so that they don't require the production server to be taken offline. Depending on your consistency requirements, though, making a backup while the server is online can still mean interrupting service significantly.

One of the biggest problems with many backup methods is their use of FLUSH TABLES WITH READ LOCK. This tells MySQL to close and lock all tables, flushes MyISAM's data files to disk (but not InnoDB's!), and flushes the query cache. That can take a very long time to complete. Exactly how long is unpredictable; it will be even longer if the global read lock has to wait for a long-running statement to finish, or if you have many tables. Until the lock is released, you can't change any data on the server, and everything will block and queue.[2] FLUSH TABLES WITH READ LOCK is not as expensive as shutting down, because most of your caches are still in memory and the server is still "warm," but it's very disruptive. Anyone who tells you it's fast probably is trying to sell you something and has never worked on a real MySQL server in production.

The best way to avoid any use of FLUSH TABLES WITH READ LOCK is to use only InnoDB tables. You can't avoid using MyISAM tables for privileges and other system information, but if that data changes rarely (which is the norm) you can flush and lock only those tables without causing trouble.

Here are some performance-related factors to consider when you're planning backups:

Lock time
How long do you need to hold locks, such as the global FLUSH TABLES WITH READ LOCK, while backing up?

Backup time
How long does it take to copy the backup to the destination?

Backup load
How much does it impact the server's performance to copy the backup to the destination?

Recovery time
How long does it take to copy your backup image from its storage location to the MySQL server, replay binary logs, and so on?

The biggest trade-off is backup time versus backup load. You can often improve one at the other's expense; for example, you can prioritize the backup at the expense of causing more performance degradation on the server.

You can also design your backups to take advantage of load patterns. For instance, if your server is only 50% loaded for 8 hours during the night, you can try to design your backups to load the server less than 50% and still complete within 8 hours. You can accomplish this in many ways: for example, you can use *ionice* and *nice* to prioritize the copy or compression operations, use different compression levels, or compress the data on the backup server instead of the MySQL server. You can also use *lzo* or *pigz* for faster compression. You can use O_DIRECT or fadvise() to bypass the operating system's cache for the copy operations, so they don't pollute the server's caches. Tools

---

2. Yes, even SELECT queries will get blocked, because there's bound to be a query that tries to modify some data, and as soon as it starts waiting for a write lock on a table, all of the queries trying to get read locks will have to wait, too.

such as Percona XtraBackup and MySQL Enterprise Backup also have throttling options, and you can use *pv* with the *--rate-limit* option to limit the throughput of scripts you write yourself.

Logical or Raw Backups?

There are two major ways to back up MySQL's data: with a *logical backup* (also called a "dump"), and by copying the *raw files*. A logical backup contains the data in a form that MySQL can interpret either as SQL or as delimited text.[3] The raw files are the files as they exist on disk.

Each type of backup has advantages and disadvantages.

Logical backups

Logical backups have the following advantages:

- They're normal files you can manipulate and inspect with editors and command-line tools such as *grep* and *sed*. This can be very helpful when restoring data, or when you just want to inspect the data without restoring.

- They're simple to restore. You can just pipe them into *mysql* or use *mysqlimport*.

- You can back up and restore across the network—that is, on a different machine from the MySQL host.

- They can work for systems such as Amazon RDS, where you have no access to the underlying filesystem.

- They can be very flexible, because *mysqldump*—the tool most people prefer to use to make them—can accept lots of options, such as a `WHERE` clause to restrict what rows are backed up.

- They're storage engine–independent. Because you create them by extracting data from the MySQL server, they abstract away differences in the underlying data storage. Thus, you can back up from InnoDB tables and restore to MyISAM tables with very little work. You can't do this with raw file copies.

- They can help avoid data corruption. If your disk drives are failing and you copy the raw files, you'll get an error and/or make a partial or corrupt backup, and unless you check the backup, you won't notice it and it'll be unusable later. If the data MySQL has in memory is *not* corrupt, you can sometimes get a trustworthy logical backup when you can't get a good raw file copy.

---

3. Logical backups produced by *mysqldump* are not always text files. SQL dumps can contain many different character sets, and can even include binary data that's not valid character data at all. Lines can be too long for many editors, too. Still, many such files will contain data a text editor can open and read, especially if you run *mysqldump* with the *—hex-blob* option.

Logical backups have their shortcomings, though:

- The server has to do the work of generating them, so they use more CPU cycles.
- Logical backups can be bigger than the underlying files in some cases.[4] The ASCII representation of the data isn't always as efficient as the way the storage engine stores the data. For example, an integer requires 4 bytes to store, but when written in ASCII, it can require up to 12 characters. You can often compress the files effectively and get a smaller backup, but this uses more CPU resources. (Logical backups are typically smaller than raw backups if there are a lot of indexes.)
- Dumping and restoring your data isn't always guaranteed to result in the same data. Floating-point representation problems, bugs, and so on can cause trouble, though this is rare.
- Restoring from a logical backup requires MySQL to load and interpret the statements, convert them to the storage format, and rebuild indexes, all of which is very slow.

The biggest disadvantages are really the cost of dumping the data from MySQL and the cost of loading data back in via SQL statements. If you use logical backups, it is essential to test the time required for restoring the data.

The *mysqldump* included with Percona Server can help when you're working with InnoDB tables, because it formats the output so that it will take advantage of InnoDB's fast index creation code upon reloading it. Our testing shows that this can reduce the restore time by two-thirds or more. The more indexes there are, the more beneficial it is.

Raw backups

Raw backups have the following benefits:

- Raw file backups simply require you to copy the desired files somewhere else for backup. The raw files don't require any extra work to generate.
- Restoring raw backups can be simpler, depending on the storage engine. For MyISAM, it can be as easy as just copying the files into their destinations. InnoDB, however, requires you to stop the server and possibly take other steps as well.
- Raw backups of InnoDB and MyISAM data are very portable across platforms, operating systems, and MySQL versions. (Logical dumps are, too. We're simply pointing this out to alleviate any concerns you might have.)
- It can be faster to restore raw backups, because the MySQL server doesn't have to execute any SQL or build indexes. If you have InnoDB tables that don't fit entirely in the server's memory, it can be *much* faster to restore raw files—an order of

---

4. In our experience, logical backups are generally smaller than raw backups, but they aren't always.

magnitude or more. In fact, one of the scariest things about logical backups is their unpredictable restore time.

Here are some disadvantages of raw backups:

- InnoDB's raw files are often far larger than the corresponding logical backups. The InnoDB tablespace typically has lots of unused space. Quite a bit of space is also used for purposes other than storing table data (the insert buffer, the rollback segment, and so on).

- Raw backups are not always portable across platforms, operating systems, and MySQL versions. Filename case sensitivity and floating-point formats are places where you might encounter trouble. You might not be able to move files to a system whose floating-point format is different (however, the vast majority of processors use the IEEE floating-point format).

Raw backups are generally easier and much more efficient.[5] You should not rely on raw backups for long-term retention or legal requirements, though; you must make logical backups at least periodically.

Don't consider a backup (especially a raw backup) to be good until you've tested it. For InnoDB, that means starting a MySQL instance and letting InnoDB recovery run, then running CHECK TABLES. You can skip this, or just run *innochecksum* on the files, but we don't recommend it. For MyISAM, you should run CHECK TABLES or use *myisamchk*. You can run CHECK TABLES on all tables with the *mysqlcheck* command.

We suggest a blend of the two approaches: make raw copies, then start a MySQL server instance with the resulting data and run *mysqlcheck*. Then, at least periodically, dump the data with *mysqldump* to get a logical backup. This gives you the advantages of both approaches, without unduly burdening the production server during the dump. It's especially convenient if you have the ability to take filesystem snapshots—you can take a snapshot, copy the snapshot to another server and release it, then test the raw files and perform a logical backup.

What to Back Up

Your recovery requirements will dictate what you need to back up. The simplest strategy is to just back up your data and table definitions, but this is a bare-minimum approach. You generally need a lot more to recover a server for use in production. Here are some things you might consider including with your MySQL backups:

Nonobvious data
    Don't forget data that's easy to overlook: your binary logs and InnoDB transaction logs, for example.

---

5. It's worth mentioning that raw backups can be more error-prone; it's hard to beat the simplicity of *mysqldump*.

Code

A modern MySQL server can store a lot of code, such as triggers and stored procedures. If you back up the `mysql` database, you'll back up much of this code, but then it will be hard to restore a single database in its entirety, because some of the "data" in that database, such as stored procedures, will actually be stored in the `mysql` database.

Replication configuration

If you are recovering to a server that is involved in replication, you should include in your backups whatever replication files you'll need for that—e.g., binary logs, relay logs, log index files, and the *.info* files. At a minimum, you should include the output of `SHOW MASTER STATUS` and/or `SHOW SLAVE STATUS`. It's also helpful to issue `FLUSH LOGS` so MySQL starts a new binary log. It's easier to do point-in-time recovery from the beginning of a log file than the middle.

Server configuration

If you have to recover from a real disaster—say, if you're building a server from scratch in a new data center after an earthquake—you'll appreciate having the server's configuration files included in the backup.

Selected operating system files

As with the server configuration, it's important to back up any external configuration that is essential to a production server. On a Unix server, this might include your *cron* jobs, user and group configurations, administrative scripts, and *sudo* rules.

These recommendations quickly translate into "back up everything" in many scenarios. If you have a lot of data, however, this can get expensive, and you might have to be smarter about how you do your backups. In particular, you might want to back up different data into different backups. For example, you can back up data, binary logs, and operating system and system configuration files separately.

Incremental and differential backups

A common strategy for dealing with too much data is to do regular incremental or differential backups. The difference might be a little confusing, so let's clarify the terms: a *differential backup* is a backup of everything that has changed since the last full backup, whereas an *incremental backup* contains everything that has changed since the last backup of any type.

For example, suppose that you do a full backup every Sunday. On Monday, you do a differential backup of everything that has changed since Sunday. On Tuesday, you have two choices: you can back up everything that's changed since Sunday (differential), or you can back up only the data that has changed since Monday's backup (incremental).

Both differential and incremental backups are partial backups: they generally don't contain a full dataset, because some data almost certainly hasn't changed. Partial backups are often desirable for their savings in overhead on the server, backup time, and backup space. Some partial backups don't really reduce the overhead on the server, though. Percona XtraBackup and MySQL Enterprise Backup, for example, still scan every block of data on the server, though, so they don't save a lot of overhead, although they do save a bit of wall-clock time, lots of CPU time for compression, and of course disk space.[6]

You can get pretty fancy with advanced backup techniques, but the more complex your solution is, the more risky it's likely to be. Beware of hidden dangers, such as multiple generations of backups that are tightly coupled to one another, because if one generation contains corruption, it can invalidate all of the others, too.

Here are some ideas:

- Use the incremental backup features of Percona XtraBackup or MySQL Enterprise Backup.
- Back up your binary logs. You can also use FLUSH LOGS to begin a new binary log after each backup, then back up only new binary logs.
- Don't back up tables that haven't changed. Some storage engines, such as MyISAM, record the last time each table was modified. You can see these times by inspecting the files on disk or by running SHOW TABLE STATUS. If you use InnoDB, a trigger can help you keep track of the last changes by recording the change times in a small "last changed time" table. You need to do this only on tables that change infrequently, so the cost should be minimal. A custom backup script can easily determine which tables have changed.

  If you have "lookup" tables that contain data such as lists of month names in various languages or abbreviations for states or regions, it can be a good idea to place them into a separate database, so you don't have to back them up all the time.
- Don't back up rows that haven't changed. If a table is INSERT-only, such as a table that logs hits to a web page, you can add a TIMESTAMP column and back up only rows that have been inserted since the last backup.
- Don't back up some data at all. Sometimes this makes a lot of sense—for example, if you have a data warehouse that's built from other data and is technically redundant, you can merely back up the data you used to build the warehouse, instead of the data warehouse itself. This can be a good idea even if it's very slow to "recover" by rebuilding the warehouse from the original files. Avoiding the backups can add up over time to much greater savings than the potentially faster recovery time you'll gain by having a full backup. You can also opt not to back up some temporary data, such as tables that hold website session data.
- Back up everything, but send it to a destination that has data deduplication features, such as a ZFS filer.

---

6. A "true" incremental backup feature for Percona XtraBackup is in progress. It will be able to back up the blocks that have changed, without needing to scan every block.

The drawbacks of incremental backups include increased recovery complexity, increased risk, and a longer recovery time. If you can do full backups, we suggest that you do so for simplicity's sake.

Regardless, you definitely need to do full backups occasionally—we suggest at least weekly. You can't expect to recover from a month's worth of incremental backups. Even a week is a lot of work and risk.

Storage Engines and Consistency

MySQL's choice of storage engines can make backups significantly more complicated. The issue is how to get a consistent backup with any given storage engine.

There are actually two kinds of consistency to think about: *data consistency* and *file consistency*.

Data consistency

When you do backups, you must consider whether you need the data to be point in time–consistent. For example, in an ecommerce database, you probably need to make sure your invoices and payments are consistent with each other. Recovering a payment without its corresponding invoice, or vice versa, is bound to cause trouble!

If you're making online backups (from a running server), you probably need a consistent backup of all related tables. That means you can't just lock and back up tables one at a time—which in turn means your backups might be more intrusive than you'd like. If you're not using a transactional storage engine, you have no choice but to use LOCK TABLES on all the tables you want to back up together, and release the lock only when all the related tables have been backed up.

InnoDB's MVCC capabilities can help. You can begin a transaction, dump a group of related tables, and commit the transaction. (You should not use LOCK TABLES if you're using a transaction to get a consistent backup, because it commits your transaction implicitly—see the MySQL manual for details.) As long as you're using the REPEATABLE READ transaction isolation level and you don't have any DDL on the server, this will give you a perfectly consistent, point-in-time snapshot of the data that doesn't block further work from happening on your server while the backup is being made.

However, this approach doesn't protect you from poorly designed application logic. Suppose your ecommerce store inserts a payment, commits the transaction, and then inserts the invoice in a different transaction. Your backup process might start between those two operations, backing up the payment and not the invoice. This is why you have to design transactions carefully to group related operations together.

You can also get a consistent logical backup of InnoDB tables with *mysqldump*, which supports a *--single-transaction* option that does what we just described. However, this can cause a very long transaction, which might have an unacceptably high overhead on some workloads.

File consistency

It's also important that each file is internally consistent—e.g., that the backup doesn't reflect a file's state partway through a big UPDATE statement—and that all the files you're backing up are consistent with each other. If you don't get internally consistent files, you'll have a nasty surprise when you try to restore them (they'll probably be corrupt). And if you copy related files at different times, they won't be consistent with each other. MyISAM's *.MYD* and *.MYI* files are an example. InnoDB will log errors or even crash the server intentionally if it detects inconsistency or corruption.

With a nontransactional storage engine such as MyISAM, your only option is to lock and flush the tables. That means using either a combination of LOCK TABLES and FLUSH TABLES, so the server flushes its in-memory changes to disk, or FLUSH TABLES WITH READ LOCK. Once the flush is complete, you can safely do a raw copy of MyISAM's files.

With InnoDB, it's harder to ensure the files are consistent on disk. Even if you do a FLUSH TABLES WITH READ LOCK, InnoDB keeps working in the background: its insert buffer, log, and write threads continue to merge changes to its log and tablespace files. These threads are asynchronous by design—doing this work in background threads is what helps InnoDB achieve high concurrency—so they are independent of LOCK TABLES. Thus, you need to make sure not only that each file is internally consistent, but that you copy the log and tablespace files at the same instant. If you make a backup while a thread is changing a file, or back up the log files at a different point in time from the tablespace files, you can again end up with a corrupt system after recovery. You can avoid this problem in a few ways:

- Wait until InnoDB's purge and insert buffer merge threads are done. You can watch the output of SHOW INNODB STATUS and copy the files when there are no more dirty buffers or pending writes. However, this approach might take a long time; it also involves too much guesswork and might not be safe, because of InnoDB's background threads. Consequently, we don't recommend it.

- Take a consistent snapshot of the data and log files with a system such as LVM. You *must* snapshot the data and log files consistently with respect to each other; it's no good to snapshot them separately. We discuss LVM snapshots later in this chapter.

- Send a STOP signal to MySQL, make the backup, and then send a CONT signal to wake MySQL up again. This might seem like an odd recommendation, but it's worth considering if the only alternative is to shut down the server during the backup. At least this technique won't require you to warm the server up after re-starting it.

After you have copied the files elsewhere, you can release the locks and let the MySQL server run normally again.

Replication

The biggest advantage to backing up from a replica is that it doesn't interrupt the master or place extra load on it. This is a good reason to set up a replica server, even if you don't need it for load balancing or high availability. If money is a concern, you can always use the backup replica for other purposes too, such as reporting—as long as you don't write to it and thus change the data you're trying to back up. The replica doesn't have to be dedicated to backups; it just has to be able to catch up to the master in time to make your next backup in the event that its other roles make it fall behind in replication at times.

When you make a backup from a replica, save all the information about the replication processes, such as the replica's position relative to the master. This is useful for cloning new replicas, reapplying binary logs to the master to get point-in-time recovery, promoting the replica to a master, and more. Also be sure that no temporary tables are open if you stop your replica, because they might keep you from restarting replication.

Intentionally delaying replication on one of your replicas can be very useful for recovering from some disaster scenarios. Suppose you delay replication by an hour. If an unwanted statement runs on the master, you have an hour to notice it and stop the replica before it repeats the event from its relay log. You can then promote the replica to master and replay some relatively small number of log events, skipping the bad statements. This can be much faster than the point-in-time recovery technique we discuss later. The *pt-slave-delay* tool from Percona Toolkit can help with this.

The replica might not have the same data as the master. Many people assume replicas are exact copies of their masters, but in our experience, data mismatches on replicas are common, and MySQL has no way to detect this problem. The only way to detect the problem is with a tool such as Percona Toolkit's *pt-table-checksum*.

Having a replicated copy of your data might help protect you from problems such as disk meltdowns on the master, but there's no guarantee. Replication is *not* a backup.

Managing and Backing Up Binary Logs

Your server's binary logs are one of the most important things you can back up. They are necessary for point-in-time recovery, and because they're usually smaller than your data, they're easier to back up frequently. If you have a backup of your data at some point and all the binary logs since then, you can replay the binary logs and "roll forward" changes made since the last full backup.

MySQL uses the binary log for replication, too. That means that your backup and recovery policy often interacts with your replication configuration.

Binary logs are "special." If you lose your data, you really don't want to lose the binary logs as well. To minimize the chances of this happening, you can keep them on a separate volume. It's OK to do this even if you want to snapshot the binary logs with LVM. For extra safety, you can keep them on a SAN or replicate them to another device with DRBD.

It's a good idea to back up binary logs frequently. If you can't afford to lose more than 30 minutes' worth of data, back them up at least every 30 minutes. You can also use a read-only replica with *--log_slave_updates*, for an extra degree of safety. The log positions won't match the master's, but it's usually not hard to find the right positions for recovery. Finally, MySQL 5.6's version of *mysqlbinlog* has a very handy feature to connect to a server and mirror its binary logs in real time, which is simpler and more lightweight than running an instance of *mysqld*. It's backward-compatible with older server versions.

See Chapter 8 and Chapter 10 for our recommended server configuration for binary logging.

The Binary Log Format

The binary log consists of a sequence of events. Each event has a fixed-size header that contains a variety of information, such as the current timestamp and default database. You can use the *mysqlbinlog* tool to inspect a binary log's contents, and it prints out some of the header information. Here's an example of the output:

```
1  # at 277
2  #071030 10:47:21 server id 3  end_log_pos 369   Query   thread_id=13    exec_time=0
   error_code=0
3  SET TIMESTAMP=1193755641/*!*/;
4  insert into test(a) values(2)/*!*/;
```

Line 1 contains the byte offset within the log file (in this case, 277).

Line 2 contains the following items:

- The date and time of the event, which MySQL also uses to generate the SET TIME STAMP statement.
- The server ID of the originating server, which is necessary to prevent endless loops in replication and other problems.
- The end_log_pos, which is the byte offset of the next event. This value is incorrect for most of the events in a multistatement transaction. MySQL copies the events into a buffer on the master during such transactions, but it doesn't know the next log event's position when it does so.
- The event type. Our sample's type is Query, but there are many different types.
- The thread ID of the thread that executed the event on the originating server, which is important for auditing as well as for executing the CONNECTION_ID() function.

- The `exec_time`, which is the difference between the statement's timestamp and the time at which it was written to the binary log. It's a good idea not to rely on this value, because it can be very wrong on replicas that have fallen behind in replication.

- Any error code the event raised on the originating server. If the event causes a different error when replayed on a replica, then replication will fail as a safety precaution.

Any further lines contain the data needed to replay the modification. User-defined variables and any other special settings, such as the timestamp in effect when the statement executed, also appear here.

 If you're using the row-based logging available in MySQL 5.1, the event won't be SQL. Instead, it's a non-human-readable "image" of the modifications the statement made to the table.

Purging Old Binary Logs Safely

You'll need to decide on a log expiration policy to keep MySQL from filling your disk with binary logs. How large your logs grow depends on your workload and the logging format (row-based logging results in larger log entries). We suggest you keep logs as long as they're useful, if possible. Keeping them is helpful for setting up replicas, analyzing your server's workload, auditing, and point-in-time recovery from your last full backup. Consider all of these needs when you decide how long you want to keep your logs.

A common setup is to use the `expire_logs_days` variable to tell MySQL to purge logs after a while. This variable wasn't available until MySQL 4.1; prior to this version, you had to purge binary logs manually. Thus, you might see advice to remove old binary logs with a *cron* entry such as the following:

```
0 0 * * * /usr/bin/find /var/log/mysql -mtime +N -name "mysql-bin.[0-9]*" | xargs rm
```

Although this was the only way to purge the logs prior to MySQL 4.1, don't do this in newer server versions! Removing the logs with *rm* can cause the *mysql-bin.index* status file to become out of sync with the files on disk, and some statements, such as SHOW MASTER LOGS, can begin failing silently. Changing the *mysql-bin.index* file by hand might not fix the problem, either. Instead, use a *cron* command such as the following:

```
0 0 * * * /usr/bin/mysql -e "PURGE MASTER LOGS BEFORE CURRENT_DATE - INTERVAL N DAY"
```

The `expire_logs_days` setting takes effect upon server startup or when MySQL rotates the binary log, so if your binary log never fills up and rotates, the server will not purge older entries. It decides which files to purge by looking at their modification times, not their contents.

Backing Up Data

As with most things, there are better and worse ways to actually make a backup—and the obvious ways are sometimes not so good. The trick is to maximize your network, disk, and CPU capacity to make backups as fast as possible. This is a balancing act, and you'll have to experiment to find the "sweet spot."

Making a Logical Backup

The first thing to realize about logical backups is that they are not all created equal. There are actually two kinds of logical backups: SQL dumps and delimited files.

SQL dumps

SQL dumps are what most people are familiar with, because they're what *mysqldump* creates by default. For example, dumping a small table with the default options will produce the following (abridged) output:

```
$ mysqldump test t1
-- [Version and host comments]
/*!40101 SET @OLD_CHARACTER_SET_CLIENT=@@CHARACTER_SET_CLIENT */;
-- [More version-specific comments to save options for restore]
--
-- Table structure for table `t1`
--
DROP TABLE IF EXISTS `t1`;
CREATE TABLE `t1` (
  `a` int(11) NOT NULL,
  PRIMARY KEY (`a`)
) ENGINE=MyISAM DEFAULT CHARSET=latin1;
--
-- Dumping data for table `t1`
--
LOCK TABLES `t1` WRITE;
/*!40000 ALTER TABLE `t1` DISABLE KEYS */;
INSERT INTO `t1` VALUES (1);
/*!40000 ALTER TABLE `t1` ENABLE KEYS */;
UNLOCK TABLES;
/*!40103 SET TIME_ZONE=@OLD_TIME_ZONE */;
/*!40101 SET SQL_MODE=@OLD_SQL_MODE */;
-- [More option restoration]
```

The dump file contains both the table structure and the data, all written out as valid SQL commands. The file begins with comments that set various MySQL options. These are present either to make the restore work more efficiently or for compatibility and correctness. Next you can see the table's structure, and then its data. Finally, the script resets the options it changed at the beginning of the dump.

The dump's output is executable for a restore operation. This is convenient, but *mysqldump*'s default options aren't great for making a huge backup (we delve into *mysqldump*'s options in more detail later).

mysqldump is not the only tool that can make SQL logical backups. You can also create them with *mydumper* or phpMyAdmin, for example.[7] What we'd really like to point out here is not so much problems with any particular tool, but rather the shortcomings of doing monolithic SQL logical backups in the first place. Here are the main problem areas:

Schema and data stored together
Although this is convenient if you want to restore from a single file, it makes things difficult if you need to restore only one table or want to restore only the data. You can alleviate this concern by dumping twice—once for data, once for schema—but you'll still have the next problem.

Huge SQL statements
It's a lot of work for the server to parse and execute all of the SQL statements. This is a very slow way to load data.

A single huge file
Most text editors can't edit large files or files with very long lines. Although you can sometimes use command-line stream editors—such as *sed* or *grep*—to pull out the data you need, it's preferable to keep the files small.

Logical backups are expensive
There are more efficient ways to get data out of MySQL than fetching it from the storage engine and sending it over the client/server protocol as a result set.

These limitations mean that SQL dumps quickly become unusable as tables get large. There's another option, though: export data to delimited files.

Delimited file backups

You can use the `SELECT INTO OUTFILE` SQL command to create a logical backup of your data in a delimited file format. (You can dump to delimited files with *mysqldump*'s *--tab* option, which runs the SQL command for you.) Delimited files contain the raw data represented in ASCII, without SQL, comments, and column names. Here's an example that dumps into comma-separated values (CSV) format, which is a good *lingua franca* for tabular data:

```
mysql> SELECT * INTO OUTFILE '/tmp/t1.txt'
    -> FIELDS TERMINATED BY ',' OPTIONALLY ENCLOSED BY '"'
    -> LINES TERMINATED BY '\n'
    -> FROM test.t1;
```

The resulting file is more compact and easier to manipulate with command-line tools than a SQL dump file, but the biggest advantage of this approach is the speed of backing up and restoring. You can load the data back into the table with `LOAD DATA INFILE`, with the same options used to dump it:

---

7. Please do not use Maatkit's *mk-parallel-dump* and *mk-parallel-restore* tools. They are not safe.

```
mysql> LOAD DATA INFILE '/tmp/t1.txt'
    -> INTO TABLE test.t1
    -> FIELDS TERMINATED BY ',' OPTIONALLY ENCLOSED BY '"'
    -> LINES TERMINATED BY '\n';
```

Here's an informal test we did to demonstrate the backup and restore speed difference between SQL files and delimited files. We adapted some production data for this test. The table we're dumping from looks like the following:

```
CREATE TABLE load_test (
    col1 date NOT NULL,
    col2 int NOT NULL,
    col3 smallint unsigned NOT NULL,
    col4 mediumint NOT NULL,
    col5 mediumint NOT NULL,
    col6 mediumint NOT NULL,
    col7 decimal(3,1) default NULL,
    col8 varchar(10) NOT NULL default '',
    col9 int NOT NULL,
    PRIMARY KEY  (col1, col2)
) ENGINE=InnoDB;
```

The table has 15 million rows and uses about 700 MB on disk. Table 15-1 compares the performance of the two backup and restore methods. You can see there's a large speed difference in the restore times for the test.

Table 15-1. Backup and restore times for SQL and delimited dumps

Method	Dump size	Dump time	Restore time
SQL dump	727 MB	102 sec	600 sec
Delimited dump	669 MB	86 sec	301 sec

The SELECT INTO OUTFILE method has some limitations, though:

- You can back up only to a file on the machine on which the MySQL server is running. (You can roll your own SELECT INTO OUTFILE by writing a program that reads a SELECT result and writes it to disk, which is an approach we've seen some people take.)

- MySQL must have permission to write to the directory where the file is written, because the MySQL server—not the user running the SQL command—is what writes the file.

- For security reasons, you can't overwrite an existing file, no matter what the file's permissions are.

- You can't dump directly to a compressed file.

- Some things, such as nonstandard character sets, are hard to get right in either the export or the import step.

Filesystem Snapshots

Filesystem snapshots are a great way to make online backups. Snapshot-capable filesystems can create a consistent image of their contents at an instant in time, which you can then use to make a backup. Snapshot-capable filesystems and appliances include FreeBSD's filesystem, the ZFS filesystem, GNU/Linux's Logical Volume Manager (LVM), and many SAN systems and file-storage solutions, such as NetApp storage appliances.

Don't confuse a snapshot with a backup. Taking a snapshot is simply a way of reducing the time for which locks must be held; after releasing the locks, you must copy the files to the backup. In fact, you can optionally take snapshots on InnoDB without even acquiring locks. We'll show you two ways to use LVM to make backups of an all-InnoDB system, with your choice of minimal or zero locking.

A snapshot can be a great way to make a backup for specific uses. One example is as a fallback in case of a problem during an upgrade. You can take a snapshot, upgrade, and, if there's a problem, just roll back to the snapshot. You can do the same thing for any operation that's uncertain and risky, such as altering a huge table (which will take an unknown amount of time).

How LVM snapshots work

LVM uses copy-on-write technology to create a snapshot—i.e., a logical copy of an entire volume at an instant in time. It's a little like MVCC in a database, except it keeps only one old version of the data.

Notice we didn't say a *physical* copy. A logical copy appears to contain all the same data as the volume you snapshotted, but initially it contains no data. Instead of copying the data to the snapshot, LVM simply notes the time at which you created the snapshot, then it reads the data from the original volume when you request it from the snapshot. So, the initial copy is basically an instantaneous operation, no matter how large a volume you're snapshotting.

When something changes the data in the original volume, LVM copies the affected blocks to an area reserved for the snapshot before it writes any changes to them. LVM doesn't keep multiple "old versions" of the data, so additional writes to blocks that are changed in the original volume don't require any further work for the snapshot. In other words, only the first write to each block causes a copy-on-write to the reserved area.

Now, when you request these blocks in the snapshot, LVM reads the data from the copied blocks instead of from the original volume. This lets you continue to see the same data in the snapshot without blocking anything on the original volume. Figure 15-1 depicts this arrangement.

The snapshot creates a new logical device in the */dev* directory, and you can mount this device just as you would mount any other.

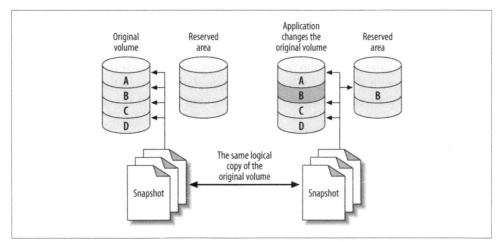

Figure 15-1. How copy-on-write technology reduces the size needed for a volume snapshot

You can theoretically snapshot an enormous volume and consume very little physical space with this technique. However, you need to set aside enough space to hold all the blocks you expect to be updated in the original volume while you hold the snapshot open. If you don't reserve enough copy-on-write space, the snapshot will run out of space, and the device will become unavailable. The effect is like unplugging an external drive: any backup job that's reading from the device will fail with an I/O error.

Prerequisites and configuration

It's almost trivial to create a snapshot, but you need to ensure that your system is configured in such a way that you can get a consistent copy of *all* the files you want to back up at a single instant in time. First, make sure your system meets these conditions:

- All InnoDB files (InnoDB tablespace files and InnoDB transaction logs) must be on a single logical volume (partition). You need absolute point-in-time consistency, and LVM can't take consistent snapshots of more than one volume at a time. (This is an LVM limitation; some other systems do not have this problem.)
- If you need to back up the table definitions too, the MySQL data directory must be in the same logical volume. If you use another method to back up table definitions, such as a schema-only backup into your version control system, you might not need to worry about this.
- You must have enough free space in the volume group to create the snapshot. How much you need will depend on your workload. When you set up your system, leave some unallocated space so that you'll have room for snapshots later.

LVM has the concept of a *volume group*, which contains one or more logical volumes. You can see the volume groups on your system as follows:

```
# vgs
  VG    #PV #LV #SN Attr   VSize   VFree
  vg     1    4   0 wz--n- 534.18G 249.18G
```

This output shows a volume group that has four logical volumes distributed across one physical volume, with about 250 GB free. The *vgdisplay* command gives more detail if you need it. Now let's take a look at the logical volumes on the system:

```
# lvs
  LV    VG  Attr    LSize   Origin Snap% Move Log Copy%
  home  vg  -wi-ao   40.00G
  mysql vg  -wi-ao  225.00G
  tmp   vg  -wi-ao   10.00G
  var   vg  -wi-ao   10.00G
```

The output shows that the mysql volume has 225 GB of space. The device name is /dev/vg/mysql. This is just a name, even though it looks like a filesystem path. To add to the confusion, there's a symbolic link from the file of the same name to the real device node at */dev/mapper/vg-mysql*, which you can see with the *ls* and *mount* commands:

```
# ls -l /dev/vg/mysql
lrwxrwxrwx 1 root root 20 Sep 19 13:08 /dev/vg/mysql -> /dev/mapper/vg-mysql
# mount | grep mysql
/dev/mapper/vg-mysql on /var/lib/mysql
```

Armed with this information, you're ready to create a filesystem snapshot.

Creating, mounting, and removing an LVM snapshot

You can create the snapshot with a single command. You just need to decide where to put it and how much space to allocate for copy-on-write. Don't hesitate to use more space than you think you'll need. LVM doesn't use the space you specify right away; it just reserves it for future use, so there's no harm in reserving lots of space, unless you need to leave space for other snapshots at the same time.

Let's create a snapshot just for practice. We'll give it 16 GB of space for copy-on-write, and we'll call it backup_mysql:

```
# lvcreate --size 16G --snapshot --name backup_mysql /dev/vg/mysql
  Logical volume "backup_mysql" created
```

 We deliberately called the volume backup_mysql instead of mysql _backup so that tab completion would be unambiguous. This helps avoid the possibility of tab completion causing you to accidentally delete the mysql volume group.

Now let's see the newly created volume's status:

```
# lvs
  LV            VG  Attr    LSize   Origin Snap% Move Log Copy%
  backup_mysql  vg  swi-a-  16.00G  mysql   0.01
  home          vg  -wi-ao  40.00G
```

```
mysql       vg    owi-ao  225.00G
tmp         vg    -wi-ao   10.00G
var         vg    -wi-ao   10.00G
```

Notice that the snapshot's attributes are different from the original device's, and that the display shows a little extra information: its origin and how much of the allocated 16 GB is currently being used for copy-on-write. It's a good idea to monitor this as you make your backup, so you can see if the device is getting full and is about to fail. You can monitor your device's status interactively, or with a monitoring system such as Nagios:

```
# watch 'lvs | grep backup'
```

As you saw from the output of *mount* earlier, the mysql volume contains a filesystem. That means the snapshot volume does too, and you can mount and use it just like any other filesystem:

```
# mkdir /tmp/backup
# mount /dev/mapper/vg-backup_mysql /tmp/backup
# ls -l /tmp/backup/mysql
total 5336
-rw-r----- 1 mysql mysql        0 Nov 17  2006 columns_priv.MYD
-rw-r----- 1 mysql mysql     1024 Mar 24  2007 columns_priv.MYI
-rw-r----- 1 mysql mysql     8820 Mar 24  2007 columns_priv.frm
-rw-r----- 1 mysql mysql    10512 Jul 12 10:26 db.MYD
-rw-r----- 1 mysql mysql     4096 Jul 12 10:29 db.MYI
-rw-r----- 1 mysql mysql     9494 Mar 24  2007 db.frm
... omitted ...
```

This is just for practice, so we'll unmount and remove the snapshot now with the *lvremove* command:

```
# umount /tmp/backup
# rmdir /tmp/backup
# lvremove --force /dev/vg/backup_mysql
  Logical volume "backup_mysql" successfully removed
```

LVM snapshots for online backups

Now that you've seen how to create, mount, and remove snapshots, you can use them to make backups. First, let's look at how to back up an InnoDB database without stopping the MySQL server, but with a global read lock. Connect to the MySQL server and flush the tables to disk with a global read lock, then get the binary log coordinates:

```
mysql> FLUSH TABLES WITH READ LOCK; SHOW MASTER STATUS;
```

Record the output from SHOW MASTER STATUS, and make sure you keep the connection to MySQL open so the lock doesn't get released. You can then take the LVM snapshot and immediately release the read lock, either with UNLOCK TABLES or by closing the connection. Finally, mount the snapshot and copy the files to the backup location.

The major problem with this approach is that it might take a while to get the read lock, especially if there are long-running queries. All queries will be blocked while the connection waits for the global read lock, and it's impossible to predict how long this will take.

Filesystem Snapshots and InnoDB

InnoDB's background threads continue to work even if you've locked all tables, so it is probably still writing to its files even as you take the snapshot. Also, because InnoDB hasn't performed its shutdown sequence, the snapshot's InnoDB files will look the way these files would have looked if the server had lost power unexpectedly.

This is not a problem, because InnoDB is an ACID system. At any instant (such as the instant you take the snapshot), every committed transaction is either in the InnoDB data files or in the log files. When you start MySQL after restoring the snapshot, InnoDB will run its recovery process, just as though the server had lost power. It will look in the transaction log for any committed transactions that haven't yet been applied to the data files and apply them, so you won't lose any transactions. This is why it's mandatory to snapshot the InnoDB data and log files together.

This is also why you should test your backups when you make them. Start an instance of MySQL, point it at the new backup, let InnoDB's recovery run, and check all the tables. This way you won't back up corrupted data without knowing it (the files could be corrupt for any number of reasons). Another benefit to this practice is that restoring from the backup will be faster in the future, because you've already run the recovery process.

You can optionally run this process on the snapshot before even copying it to the backup, but that can add quite a bit of overhead. Just be sure you plan for it. (More on this later.)

Lock-free InnoDB backups with LVM snapshots

Lock-free backups are only a little different. The distinction is that you don't do a FLUSH TABLES WITH READ LOCK. This means there won't be any guarantee that your MyISAM files will be consistent on disk, but if you use only InnoDB, that's probably not an issue. You'll still have some MyISAM tables in the mysql system database, but if your workload is typical, they're unlikely to be changing at the moment you take the snapshot.

If you think the mysql system tables might be changing, you can lock and then flush them. You shouldn't have any long-running queries on these tables, so this will normally be very fast:

```
mysql> LOCK TABLES mysql.user READ, mysql.db READ, ...;
mysql> FLUSH TABLES mysql.user, mysql.db, ...;
```

You're not getting a global read lock, so you won't be able to get anything useful from SHOW MASTER STATUS. However, when you start MySQL on the snapshot (to verify your backup's integrity), you'll see something like the following in the log file:

```
InnoDB: Doing recovery: scanned up to log sequence number 0 40817239
InnoDB: Starting an apply batch of log records to the database...
InnoDB: Progress in percents: 3 4 5 6 ...[omitted]... 97 98 99
InnoDB: Apply batch completed
InnoDB: Last MySQL binlog file position 0 3304937, file name
/var/log/mysql/mysql-bin.000001
070928 14:08:42  InnoDB: Started; log sequence number 0 40817239
```

InnoDB logs the MySQL binary log position corresponding to the point to which it has recovered. This is the binary log position you can use for point-in-time recovery.

This approach to lock-free backups with snapshots has a twist in MySQL 5.0 and newer. These MySQL versions use XA to coordinate transactions between InnoDB and the binary log. If you restore the backup to a server with a different server_id from the one on which the backup was made, the server might find prepared transactions from a server whose ID doesn't match its own. In this case, the server can become confused, and it's possible for transactions to become stuck in PREPARED status upon recovery. This rarely happens, but it is possible. This is why you should always verify your backup before you consider it a success. It might not be recoverable!

If you're taking the snapshot from a replica, InnoDB recovery will also print some lines that look like these:

```
InnoDB: In a MySQL replica the last master binlog file
InnoDB: position 0 115, file name mysql-bin.001717
```

This output shows you the master's binary log coordinates (as opposed to the replica's binary log coordinates) at the point to which InnoDB has recovered, which can be very useful for making backups from replicas or cloning replicas from other replicas.

Planning for LVM backups

LVM snapshot backups aren't free. The more your server writes to the original volume, the more overhead they cause. When the server modifies many distinct blocks in random order, the disk head has to seek back and forth to the copy-on-write space and write the old version of the data there. Reading from the snapshot also has overhead, because LVM really reads most of the data from the original volume. It reads from the copy-on-write space only as needed; thus, a logically sequential read from the snapshot actually causes the disk head to move back and forth.

You should plan for this to happen. What it really means is that both the original volume and the snapshot will perform worse than usual for both reads and writes—possibly much worse if you use a lot of copy-on-write space. This can slow down both your MySQL server and the process of copying the files for the backup. We benchmarked and found that the overhead of an LVM snapshot is much greater than it ought to be—we found that performance could be as much as five times slower, depending on the workload and the filesystem. Keep this in mind when you're planning your backups.

The other important thing to plan for is allocating enough space for the snapshot. We take the following approach:

- Remember that LVM needs to copy each modified block to the snapshot only once. When MySQL writes a block in the original volume, it copies the block to the snapshot, then makes a note of the copied block in its exception table. Future writes to this block will not cause any further copies to the snapshot.

- If you use only InnoDB, consider how InnoDB writes data. Because it writes all data twice, at least half of InnoDB's write I/O goes to the doublewrite buffer, log files, and other relatively small areas on disk. These reuse the same disk blocks over and over, so they'll have an initial impact on the snapshot, but after that they'll stop causing writes to the snapshot.

- Next, estimate how much of your I/O will be writing to blocks that haven't yet been copied to the snapshot, as opposed to modifying the same data again and again. Be generous with your estimate.

- Use *vmstat* or *iostat* to gather statistics on how many blocks your server writes per second.

- Measure (or estimate) how long it will take to copy your backup to another location: in other words, how long you need to keep the LVM snapshot open.

Let's suppose you've estimated that half of your writes will cause writes to the snapshot's copy-on-write space, and your server writes 10 MB per second. If it takes an hour (3,600 seconds) to copy the snapshot to another server, you will need 1/2 × 10 MB × 3,600, or 18 GB of space for the snapshot. Err on the side of caution, and add some extra space as well.

Sometimes it's easy to calculate how much data will change while you keep the snapshot open. Let's look at an example. The BoardReader forum search engine has about 1 TB of InnoDB tables per storage node. However, we know the biggest cost is loading new data. About 10 GB of new data is added per day, so 50 GB should be plenty of space for the snapshot. This estimate doesn't always work, though. At one point, we had a long-running ALTER TABLE that changed each shard one after the other, which modified much more than 50 GB of data; while this was running, we weren't able to make the backup. To avoid problems such as this, you can wait a while after creating the snapshot, because the added load is the highest right after creating the snapshot.

Backup Myth #2: "My Snapshot Is My Backup"

A snapshot, whether it's an LVM snapshot, a ZFS snapshot, or a SAN snapshot, isn't a real backup because it doesn't contain a full copy of your data. Because snapshots are copy-on-write, they contain only the differences between the live copy of the data and the data at the point in time when the snapshot happened. If an unmodified block becomes corrupt in the live copy of the data, there's no good copy of that block that you can use for recovery, and every snapshot sees the same corrupted block that the live volume does. Use snapshots to "freeze" your data while you take a backup, but don't rely on the snapshot itself as a backup.

Other uses and alternatives

You can use snapshots for more than just backups. For example, as mentioned previously, they can be a useful way to take a "checkpoint" just before a potentially dangerous action. Some systems let you promote the snapshot to the original filesystem. This makes it easy to roll back to the point at which you took the snapshot.

Filesystem snapshots aren't the only way to get an instantaneous copy of your data, either. Another option is a *RAID split*: if you have a three-disk software RAID mirror, for example, you can remove one disk from the mirror and mount it separately. There's no copy-on-write penalty, and it's easy to promote this kind of "snapshot" to be the master copy if necessary. After adding the disk back to the RAID set, however, it will have to be resynced. There's no free lunch, sadly.

Recovering from a Backup

How you recover your data depends on how you backed it up. You might need to take some or all of the following steps:

- Stop the MySQL server.
- Take notes on the server's configuration and file permissions.
- Move the data from the backup into the MySQL data directory.
- Make configuration changes.
- Change file permissions.
- Restart the server with limited access, and wait for it to start fully.
- Reload logical backup files.
- Examine and replay binary logs.
- Verify what you've restored.
- Restart the server with full access.

We demonstrate how to do each of these steps as needed in the following sections. We also add notes specific to certain backup methods or tools in sections about those methods or tools later in this chapter.

 If there's a chance you'll need the current versions of your files, *don't replace them with the files from the backup*. For example, if your backup includes the binary logs, and you need to replay binary logs for point-in-time recovery, don't overwrite the current binary logs with older copies from the backup. Rename them or move them elsewhere if necessary.

During recovery, it's often important to make MySQL inaccessible to everything except the recovery process. We like to start MySQL with the *--skip-networking* and *--socket=/*

tmp/mysql_recover.sock options to ensure that it is unavailable to existing applications until we've checked it and brought it back online. This is especially important for logical backups, which are loaded in pieces.

Restoring Raw Files

Restoring raw files tends to be pretty straightforward—which is another way of saying there aren't many options. This can be a good or a bad thing, depending on your recovery requirements. The usual procedure is simply to copy the files into place.

Whether you need to shut down MySQL depends on the storage engine. MyISAM's files are generally independent from one another, and simply copying each table's *.frm*, *.MYI*, and *.MYD* files works well, even if the server is running. The server will find the table as soon as anyone queries it or otherwise makes the server look for it (for example, by executing SHOW TABLES). If the table is open when you copy in these files, it'll probably cause trouble, so before doing so you should either drop or rename the table, or use LOCK TABLES and FLUSH TABLES to close it.

InnoDB is another matter. If you're restoring a traditional InnoDB setup, where all tables are stored in a single tablespace, you'll have to shut down MySQL, copy or move the files into place, and then restart. You also need to ensure that InnoDB's transaction log files match its tablespace files. If the files don't match—for example, if you replace the tablespace files but not the transaction log files—InnoDB will refuse to start. This is one reason it's crucial to back up the transaction log along with the data files.

If you're using the InnoDB file-per-table feature (innodb_file_per_table), InnoDB stores the data and indexes for each table in a *.ibd* file, which is like a combination of MyISAM's *.MYI* and *.MYD* files. You can back up and restore individual tables by copying these files, and you can do it while the server is running, but it's not as simple as with MyISAM. The individual files are not independent from InnoDB as a whole. Each *.ibd* file has internal information that tells InnoDB how the file is related to the main (shared) tablespace. When you restore such a file, you have to tell InnoDB to "import" the file.

There are many restrictions on this process, which you can read about in the MySQL manual section on using per-table tablespaces. The biggest is that you can only restore a table to the server from which you backed it up. It's not impossible to back up and restore tables in this configuration, but it's trickier than you might think.

 Percona Server and Percona XtraBackup have some enhancements that lift some of the restrictions on this process, such as the same-server restriction.

All this complexity means that restoring raw files can be very tedious, and it's easy to get it wrong. A good rule of thumb is that the harder and more complex your recovery procedure becomes, the more you need to protect yourself with logical backups as well. It's always a good idea to have a logical backup, in case something goes wrong and you can't convince MySQL to use your raw backups.

Starting MySQL after restoring raw files

There are a few things you'll need to do before you start the MySQL server you're recovering.

The first and most important thing, and one of the easiest to forget, is to check your server's configuration and make sure the restored files have the correct owner and permissions, *before* you try to start the MySQL server. These attributes must be exactly right, or MySQL might not start. The attributes vary from system to system, so check your notes to see exactly what you'll need to set. You typically want the *mysql* user and group to own the files and directories, which you want to be readable and writable by that user and group but no others.

We also suggest watching the MySQL error log while the server starts. On a Unix-style system, you can watch the file like this:

```
$ tail -f /var/log/mysql/mysql.err
```

The exact location of the error log will vary. Once you're monitoring the file, you can start the MySQL server and watch for errors. If all goes well, you'll have a nicely recovered server once MySQL starts.

Watching the error log is even more important in newer MySQL versions. Older versions wouldn't start if InnoDB had an error, but in newer versions the server will start anyway and just disable InnoDB. Even if the server seems to start without trouble, you should run SHOW TABLE STATUS in each database, then check the error log again.

Restoring Logical Backups

If you're restoring logical backups instead of raw files, you need to use the MySQL server itself to load the data back into the tables, as opposed to using the operating system to simply copy files into place.

Before you load that dump file, however, take a moment to consider how large it is, how long it'll take to load, and anything you might want to do before you start, such as notifying your users or disabling part of your application. Disabling binary logging might be a good idea, unless you need to replicate the restoration to a replica: a huge dump file is hard enough for the server to load, and writing it to the binary log adds even more (possibly unnecessary) overhead. Loading huge files also has consequences for some storage engines. For example, it's not a good idea to load 100 GB of data into InnoDB in a single transaction, because of the huge rollback segment that will result. You should load in manageable chunks and commit the transaction after each chunk.

There are two kinds of restoration you might do, which correspond to the two kinds of logical backups you can make.

Loading SQL files

If you have a SQL dump, the file will contain executable SQL. All you need to do is run it. Assuming you backed up the Sakila sample database and schema into a single file, the following is a typical command you might use to restore it:

```
$ mysql < sakila-backup.sql
```

You can also load the file from within the *mysql* command-line client with the SOURCE command. Although this is mostly a different way of doing the same thing, it makes some things easier. For example, if you're an administrative user in MySQL, you can turn off binary logging of the statements you'll execute from within your client connection, and then load the file without needing to restart the MySQL server:

```
mysql> SET SQL_LOG_BIN = 0;
mysql> SOURCE sakila-backup.sql;
mysql> SET SQL_LOG_BIN = 1;
```

If you use SOURCE, be aware that an error won't abort a batch of statements, as it will by default when you redirect the file into *mysql*.

If you compressed the backup, don't separately decompress and load it. Instead, decompress and load it in a single operation. This is much faster:

```
$ gunzip -c sakila-backup.sql.gz | mysql
```

If you want to load a compressed file with the SOURCE command, see the discussion of named pipes in the next section.

What if you want to restore only a single table (for example, the actor table)? If your data has no line breaks, it's not hard to restore the data if the schema is already in place:

```
$ grep 'INSERT INTO `actor`' sakila-backup.sql | mysql sakila
```

Or, if the file is compressed:

```
$ gunzip -c sakila-backup.sql.gz | grep 'INSERT INTO `actor`'| mysql sakila
```

If you need to create the table as well as restore the data, and you have the entire database in a single file, you'll have to edit the file. This is why some people like to dump each table into its own file. Most editors can't deal with huge files, especially if they're compressed. Besides, you don't want to actually edit the file itself—you just want to extract the relevant lines—so you'll probably have to do some command-line work. It's easy to use *grep* to pull out only the INSERT statements for a given table, as we did in the previous commands, but it's harder to get the CREATE TABLE statement. Here's a *sed* script that extracts the paragraph you need:

```
$ sed -e '/./{H;$!d;}' -e 'x;/CREATE TABLE `actor`/!d;q' sakila-backup.sql
```

That's pretty cryptic, we admit. If you have to do this kind of work to restore data, your backups are poorly designed. With a little planning, it's possible to prevent a situation in which you're panicked and trying to figure out how *sed* works. Just back up each table into its own file, or, better yet, back up the data and schema separately.

Loading delimited files

If you dumped the data via `SELECT INTO OUTFILE`, you'll have to use `LOAD DATA INFILE` with the same parameters to restore it. You can also use *mysqlimport*, which is a wrapper around `LOAD DATA INFILE`. It relies on naming conventions to determine where to load a file's data.

We hope you dumped your schema, not just your data. If so, it's a SQL dump, and you can use the techniques outlined in the previous section to load it.

There's a great optimization you can use with `LOAD DATA INFILE`. It must read directly from a file, so you might think you have to decompress the file before loading it, which is very slow and disk-intensive. However, there's a way around that, at least on systems that support FIFO "named pipe" files, such as GNU/Linux. First, create a named pipe and stream the decompressed data into it:

```
$ mkfifo /tmp/backup/default/sakila/payment.fifo
$ chmod 666 /tmp/backup/default/sakila/payment.fifo
$ gunzip -c /tmp/backup/default/sakila/payment.txt.gz
   > /tmp/backup/default/sakila/payment.fifo
```

Notice we're using a greater-than character (>) to redirect the decompressed output into the *payment.fifo* file—not a pipe symbol, which creates anonymous pipes between programs. The *payment.fifo* file is a named pipe, so there's no need for an anonymous one.

The pipe will wait until some program opens it for reading from the other end. Here's the neat part: the MySQL server can read the decompressed data from the pipe, just like any other file. Don't forget to disable binary logging if appropriate:

```
mysql> SET SQL_LOG_BIN = 0; -- Optional
    -> LOAD DATA INFILE '/tmp/backup/default/sakila/payment.fifo'
    -> INTO TABLE sakila.payment;
Query OK, 16049 rows affected (2.29 sec)
Records: 16049  Deleted: 0  Skipped: 0  Warnings: 0
```

Once MySQL is done loading the data, *gunzip* will exit, and you can delete the named pipe. You can use this same technique to load compressed files from within the MySQL command-line client with the `SOURCE` command. The *pt-fifo-split* program in Percona Toolkit can help you load large files in chunks, rather than one large transaction, which can be a lot more efficient.

Point-in-Time Recovery

The most common way to do point-in-time recovery with MySQL is to restore your
last full backup and then replay the binary log from that time forward (sometimes called
"roll-forward recovery"). As long as you have the binary log, you can recover to any
point you wish. You can even recover a single database without too much trouble.

The main drawback is that binary log replay can potentially be a slow process. It's
essentially equivalent to replication. If you have a replica, and you have measured how
heavily utilized the SQL thread is, you'll have a good gauge of how quickly you can
replay binary logs. For example, if your SQL thread is about 50% utilized, recovering
a week's worth of binary logs is probably going to take between three and four days.

A common scenario is undoing the effects of a harmful statement, such as a `DROP`
`TABLE`. Let's look at a simplified example of how to do that, using only MyISAM tables.
Suppose that at midnight, the backup job ran the equivalent of the following state-
ments, which copied the database elsewhere on the same server:

```
mysql> FLUSH TABLES WITH READ LOCK;
    -> server1# cp -a /var/lib/mysql/sakila /backup/sakila;
mysql> FLUSH LOGS;
    -> server1# mysql -e "SHOW MASTER STATUS" --vertical > /backup/master.info;
mysql> UNLOCK TABLES;
```

Then, later in the day, suppose someone ran the following statement:

```
mysql> USE sakila;
mysql> DROP TABLE sakila.payment;
```

For the sake of illustration, we assume that we can recover this database in isolation
(that is, that no tables in this database were involved in cross-database queries). We
also assume that we didn't notice the offending statement until some time later. The
goal is to recover everything that's happened to the database, except for that statement.

That is, we must also preserve all the modifications that have been made to other tables, including after that statement was run.

This isn't all that hard to do. First, we stop MySQL to prevent further modifications and restore just the sakila database from the backup:

```
server1# /etc/init.d/mysql stop
server1# mv /var/lib/mysql/sakila /var/lib/mysql/sakila.tmp
server1# cp -a /backup/sakila /var/lib/mysql
```

We disable normal connections by adding the following to the server's *my.cnf* file while we work:

```
skip-networking
socket=/tmp/mysql_recover.sock
```

Now it's safe to start the server:

```
server1# /etc/init.d/mysql start
```

The next task is to find which statements in the binary log we want to replay, and which we want to skip. As it happens, the server has created only one binary log since the backup at midnight. We can examine this file with *grep* and find the offending statement:

```
server1# mysqlbinlog --database=sakila /var/log/mysql/mysql-bin.000215
| grep -B3 -i 'drop table sakila.payment'
# at 352
#070919 16:11:23 server id 1  end_log_pos 429   Query   thread_id=16    exec_time=0
error_code=0
SET TIMESTAMP=1190232683/*!*/;
DROP TABLE sakila.payment/*!*/;
```

The statement we want to skip is at position 352 in the log file, and the next statement is at position 429. We can replay the log up to position 352, and then from 429 on, with the following commands:

```
server1# mysqlbinlog --database=sakila /var/log/mysql/mysql-bin.000215
--stop-position=352 | mysql -uroot -p
server1# mysqlbinlog --database=sakila /var/log/mysql/mysql-bin.000215
--start-position=429 | mysql -uroot -p
```

Now all we have to do is check the data just to be sure, stop the server and undo the changes to *my.cnf*, and restart the server.

More Advanced Recovery Techniques

Replication and point-in-time recovery use the same mechanism: the server's binary log. This means replication can be a helpful tool during recovery, in some not-so-obvious ways. We show you some of the possibilities in this section. This isn't an exhaustive list, but it should give you some ideas about how to design recovery processes for your needs. Remember to script and rehearse anything you think you'll need to do during recovery.

Delayed replication for fast recovery

As we mentioned earlier in this chapter, having a delayed replica can make point-in-time recovery much faster and easier if you notice the accident before the replica executes the offending statement.

The procedure is a little different from that outlined in the preceding section, but the idea is the same. You stop the replica, then use `START SLAVE UNTIL` to replay events until just before the statement you want to skip. Next, you execute `SET GLOBAL SQL _SLAVE_SKIP_COUNTER=1` to skip the bad statement. Set it to a value higher than 1 if you want to skip several events (or simply use `CHANGE MASTER TO` to advance the replica's position in the log).

All you have to do then is execute `START SLAVE` and let the replica run until it is finished executing its relay logs. Your replica has done all the tedious work of point-in-time recovery for you. Now you can promote the replica to master, and you've recovered with very little interruption.

Even if you don't have a delayed replica to speed recovery, replicas can be useful because they fetch the master's binary logs onto another machine. If your master's disk fails, a replica's relay logs might be the only place you'll have a reasonably up-to-date copy of the master's binary logs.

Recovering with a log server

There's another way to use replication for recovery: set up a log server. We feel that replication is more trustworthy than *mysqlbinlog*, which might have odd bugs or edge cases that cause unexpected behavior. A log server is also more flexible and easier to use for recovery than *mysqlbinlog*, not only because of the `START SLAVE UNTIL` option, but also because of the replication rules you can apply (such as `replicate-do-table`). With a log server, you can do much more complex filtering than you'd be able to do otherwise.

For example, a log server lets you recover a single table easily. This is a lot harder to do correctly with *mysqlbinlog* and command-line tools—in fact, it's hard enough that we advise you not to try.

Let's suppose our careless developer dropped the same table as before, and we want to recover it without reverting the whole server to last night's backup. Here's how to do this with a log server:

1. Let the server you need to recover be called `server1`.
2. Recover last night's backup to another server, called `server2`. Run the recovery process on this server to avoid the risk of making things worse if you make a mistake in recovery.

3. Set up a log server to serve server1's binary logs, following the directions in Chapter 10. (It might be a good idea to copy the logs away to another server and set up the log server there, just to be extra careful.)

4. Change server2's configuration file to include the following:

```
replicate-do-table=sakila.payment
```

5. Restart server2, then make it a replica of the log server with CHANGE MASTER TO. Configure it to read from the binary log coordinates of last night's backup. Don't run START SLAVE yet.

6. Examine the output of SHOW SLAVE STATUS on server2 and verify that everything is correct. Measure twice, cut once!

7. Find the binary log position of the offending statement, and execute START SLAVE UNTIL to replay events until just before that position on server2.

8. Stop the replica process on server2 with STOP SLAVE. It should now have the table as it existed just before it was dropped.

9. Copy the table from server2 to server1.

This process is possible only if the table isn't the target of any multitable UPDATE, DELETE, or INSERT statements. Any such statements will execute against a different database state than the one that existed when the binary log events were logged, so the table will probably end up containing different data than it should. (This applies only if you're using statement-based binary logging; if you use row-based logging, the replay process won't be prone to this error.)

InnoDB Crash Recovery

InnoDB checks its data and log files every time it starts to see whether it needs to perform its recovery process. However, InnoDB's recovery isn't the same thing we've been talking about in the context of this chapter. It's not recovering backed-up data; instead, it's applying transactions from the logs to the data files and rolling back uncommitted modifications to the data files.

Exactly how InnoDB recovery works is a little too complicated to describe here. We focus instead on how to actually perform recovery when InnoDB has a serious problem.

Most of the time InnoDB is very good at fixing problems. Unless there is a bug in MySQL or your hardware is faulty, you shouldn't have to do anything out of the ordinary, even if your server loses power. InnoDB will just perform its normal recovery upon startup, and all will be well. In the log file, you'll see messages like the following:

```
InnoDB: Doing recovery: scanned up to log sequence number 0 40817239
InnoDB: Starting an apply batch of log records to the database...
```

InnoDB prints progress messages in percents into the log file. Some people report not seeing these until the whole process is done. Be patient; there is no way to hurry the process. Killing and restarting will just make it take longer.

If there's a severe problem with your hardware, such as memory or disk corruption, or if you run into a bug in MySQL or InnoDB, you might have to intervene and either force recovery or prevent the normal recovery from happening.

Causes of InnoDB corruption

InnoDB is very robust. It is built to be reliable, and it has a lot of built-in sanity checks to prevent, find, and fix corrupted data—much more so than other MySQL storage engines, and even more than some other databases. However, it can't protect itself against everything.

At a minimum, InnoDB relies on unbuffered I/O calls and `fsync()` calls not returning until the data is safely written to physical media. If your hardware doesn't guarantee this behavior, InnoDB can't protect your data, and a crash can cause corruption.

Many InnoDB corruption problems are hardware-related (e.g., corrupted page writes caused by power failures or bad memory). However, misconfigured hardware is a much bigger source of problems in our experience. Common misconfigurations include enabling the writeback cache on a RAID card that doesn't have a battery backup unit, or enabling the writeback cache on hard drives themselves. These mistakes will cause the controller or drive to lie and say the `fsync()` completed, when the data is in fact only in the writeback cache, not on disk. In other words, the hardware doesn't provide the guarantees InnoDB needs to keep your data safe.

Sometimes machines are configured this way by default, because it gives better performance—which might be fine for some purposes, but not for a transactional database server.

You can also get corruption if you run InnoDB on network-attached storage (NAS), because completing an `fsync()` to such a device might just mean the device received the data. The data is safe if InnoDB crashes, but not necessarily if the NAS device crashes.

Sometimes the corruption is worse than other times. Severe corruption can crash InnoDB or MySQL, but less severe corruption might just mean some transactions are lost because the log files weren't really synced to disk.

How to recover corrupted InnoDB data

There are three major types of InnoDB corruption, and each requires a different level of effort to recover the data:

Secondary index corruption
> You can often fix a corrupt secondary index with `OPTIMIZE TABLE`; alternatively, you can use `SELECT INTO OUTFILE`, drop and recreate the table, then use `LOAD DATA INFILE`. (You can also alter the table to MyISAM and back.) These processes fix the corruption by building a new table, and hence rebuilding the affected index.

Clustered index corruption

In the event of clustered index corruption, you might need to use the `innodb _force_recovery` settings to dump the table (more on this later). Sometimes the dump process crashes InnoDB; if this happens, you might need to dump ranges of rows to skip the corrupted pages that are causing the crash. A corrupt clustered index is a more severe problem than a corrupt secondary index because it affects the data rows themselves, but it's still possible to fix just the affected tables in many cases.

Corrupt system structures

System structures include the InnoDB transaction log, the undo log area of the tablespace, and the data dictionary. This type of corruption is likely to require a complete dump and restore, because much of InnoDB's inner workings might be affected.

You can usually repair a corrupted secondary index without losing any data. However, the other two scenarios often involve at least some data loss. If you have a backup, you're probably better off restoring that backup rather than trying to extract data from corrupt files.

If you must try to extract the data from the corrupted files, the general process is to try to get InnoDB up and running, then use SELECT INTO OUTFILE to dump the data. If your server has already crashed and you can't even start InnoDB without crashing it, you can configure it to prevent the normal recovery and background processes from running. This might let you start the server and make a logical backup with reduced or no integrity checking.

The `innodb_force_recovery` parameter controls which kinds of operations InnoDB will do at startup and during normal operation. The normal value is 0, and you can increase it up to 6. The MySQL manual documents the exact behavior of each option; we won't duplicate that information here, but we will note that you can increase the value to as high as 4 with little danger. At this setting, you might lose some data on pages that have corruption; if you go higher, you might extract bad data from corrupted pages, or increase the risk of a crash during the SELECT INTO OUTFILE. In other words, levels up to 4 do no harm to your data, but they might miss opportunities to fix problems; levels 5 and 6 are more aggressive at fixing problems but risk doing harm.

When you set `innodb_force_recovery` to a value greater than 0, InnoDB is essentially read-only, but you can still create and drop tables. This prevents further corruption, and it makes InnoDB relax some of its normal checks so it doesn't intentionally crash when it finds bad data. In normal operations, this is a safeguard, but you don't want it when you're recovering. If you need to force InnoDB recovery, it's a good idea to configure MySQL not to allow normal connection requests until you're finished.

If InnoDB's data is so corrupt that you can't start MySQL at all, you can use Percona's InnoDB Recovery Toolkit to extract data directly from the files. These tools are freely available at *http://www.percona.com/software/*. Percona Server also has an option that allows the server to run even when some tables are corrupted, rather than the default MySQL behavior of hard-crashing the entire server when a single corrupt page is detected.

Backup and Recovery Tools

A variety of good and not-so-good backup tools are available. Our favorites are *mylvm-backup* for LVM snapshot backups, and Percona XtraBackup (open source) or MySQL Enterprise Backup (proprietary) for hot InnoDB backups. We don't recommend *mysql-dump* for backing up any significant amount of data, due to the impact on the server and the unpredictably long restore times.

There are a few backup tools that should have disappeared over the years, but unfortunately they've stayed around. The most obvious example is Maatkit's *mk-parallel-dump*, which never worked right, even though it was redesigned several times. Another is *mysqlhotcopy*, which sort of worked for MyISAM tables in the olden days. Neither tool is safe to trust with your data in the general case, and can lead you to believe that data is backed up when it isn't. For example, *mysqlhotcopy* will copy your *.ibd* files if you use InnoDB with `innodb_file_per_table`, which has fooled some people into thinking their InnoDB data was backed up. Both tools can have an adverse impact on a running server in some circumstances.

If you were watching MySQL's roadmap around 2008 or 2009, you probably heard about MySQL online backup. This was a feature that let you initiate backups and restores from the server, with SQL commands. It was originally planned for MySQL 5.2, then rescheduled for MySQL 6.0, then canceled forever as far as we know.

MySQL Enterprise Backup

This tool, formerly known as InnoDB Hot Backup or *ibbackup*, is part of a MySQL Enterprise subscription from Oracle. Using it does not require stopping MySQL, setting locks, or interrupting normal database activity (though it will cause some extra load on your server). It supports features such as compressed backups, incremental backups, and streaming backups to another server. It is the "official" backup tool for MySQL.

Percona XtraBackup

Percona XtraBackup is quite similar to MySQL Enterprise Backup in many ways, but it's open source and free. In addition to the core backup tool, there is also a wrapper script written in Perl that enhances its functionality for more advanced tasks. It supports features such as streaming, incremental, compressed, and multithreaded (parallel) backup operations. It also has a variety of special features to reduce the impact of backups on heavily loaded systems.

Percona XtraBackup works by "tailing" the InnoDB log files in a background thread, then copying the InnoDB data files. This is a slightly involved process, with special checks to ensure that data is copied consistently. When all the data files are copied, the log-copying thread finishes, too. The result is a copy of all the data, but at different points in time. The logs can now be applied to the data files, using InnoDB's crash recovery routines, to bring all of the data files into a consistent state. This is referred to as the *prepare* process. Once prepared, the backup is fully consistent and contains all committed transactions as of the ending point of the file copy process. All of this happens completely externally to MySQL, so it doesn't need to connect to or access MySQL in any way.

The wrapper script adds the ability to recover a backup by copying it back to its original location. There's also Lachlan Mulcahy's XtraBackup Manager project for even more functionality; see *http://code.google.com/p/xtrabackup-manager/* for more information.

mylvmbackup

Lenz Grimmer's *mylvmbackup* (*http://lenz.homelinux.org/mylvmbackup/*) is a Perl script to help automate MySQL backups via LVM snapshots. It gets a global read lock, creates a snapshot, and releases the lock. It then compresses the data with *tar* and removes the snapshot. It names the tarball according to the timestamp at which the backup was made. It has a few more advanced options, but in general it's a straightforward tool for performing LVM backups.

Zmanda Recovery Manager

Zmanda Recovery Manager for MySQL, or ZRM (*http://www.zmanda.com*), comes in both free (GPL) and commercial versions. The enterprise edition comes with a management console that provides a graphical web-based interface for configuration, backup, verification, recovery, reporting, and scheduling. The open source edition is not crippled in any way, but it doesn't include some of the extra niceties, such as the web-based console.

True to its name, ZRM is actually a backup and recovery manager, not just a single tool. It wraps its own functionality around standard tools and techniques, such as *mysqldump*, LVM snapshots, and Percona XtraBackup. It automates much of the tedious work of backups and recovery.

mydumper

Several current and former MySQL engineers created *mydumper* as a replacement for *mysqldump*, based on their years of experience. It is a multithreaded (parallel) backup and restore toolset for MySQL and Drizzle with a lot of nice features. Many people will probably find the speed of multithreaded backups and restores to be this tool's most attractive feature. Although we know of some people using it in production, we don't

have any production experience with it ourselves. You can find out more at *http://www*
.mydumper.org.

mysqldump

Most people use the programs that ship with MySQL, so despite its shortcomings, the
most common choice for creating logical backups of data and schemas is *mysqldump*.
It's a general-purpose tool that can be used for many tasks, such as copying a table from
one server to another:

```
$ mysqldump --host=server1 test t1 | mysql --host=server2 test
```

We've shown several examples of how to create logical backups with *mysqldump*
throughout this chapter. By default, it outputs a script containing all the commands
needed to create a table and fill it with data; there are also options to output views,
stored routines, and triggers. Here are some more examples of typical usage:

- To make a logical backup of everything on a server to a single file, with all tables
  in each database backed up at the same logical point in time:

  ```
  $ mysqldump --all-databases > dump.sql
  ```
- To make a logical backup of only the Sakila sample database:

  ```
  $ mysqldump --databases sakila > dump.sql
  ```
- To make a logical backup of only the `sakila.actor` table:

  ```
  $ mysqldump sakila actor > dump.sql
  ```

You can use the *--result-file* option to specify an output file, which can help prevent
newline conversion on Windows:

```
$ mysqldump sakila actor --result-file=dump.sql
```

The default options for *mysqldump* aren't good for most backup purposes. You'll
probably want to specify some options explicitly to change the output. Here are options
we use frequently to make *mysqldump* more efficient and make its output easier to use:

--opt
> Enables a group of options that disable buffering (which could make your server
> run out of memory), write more data into fewer SQL statements in the dump so
> they'll load more efficiently, and do some other useful things. Read your version's
> help for the details. If you disable this group of options, *mysqldump* will store each
> table you dump in its memory before writing it to the disk, which is impractical
> for large tables.

--allow-keywords, --quote-names
> Make it possible to dump and restore tables that use reserved words as names.

--complete-insert
> Makes it possible to move data between tables that don't have identical columns.

--tz-utc
>   Makes it possible to move data between servers in different time zones.

--lock-all-tables
>   Uses `FLUSH TABLES WITH READ LOCK` to get a globally consistent backup.

--tab
>   Dumps files with `SELECT INTO OUTFILE`.

--skip-extended-insert
>   Causes each row of data to have its own `INSERT` statement. This can help you selectively restore certain rows if necessary. The cost is larger files that are more expensive to import into MySQL; you should enable this only if you need it.

If you use the *--databases* or *--all-databases* options to *mysqldump*, the resulting dump's data will be consistent within each database, because *mysqldump* will lock and dump all tables a database at a time. However, tables from different databases might not be consistent with each other. Using the *--lock-all-tables* option solves this problem.

For InnoDB backups, you should add the *--single-transaction* option, which uses InnoDB's MVCC features to create a consistent backup at a single point in time, instead of using `LOCK TABLES`. If you add the *--master-data* option, the backup will also contain the server's binary log coordinates at the moment of the backup, which is very helpful for point-in-time recovery and setting up replicas. However, be aware that it will use `FLUSH TABLES WITH READ LOCK` to freeze the server so it can get the coordinates.

Scripting Backups

It's pretty standard to need to write some scripts for backups. Rather than showing you a sample program, which would necessarily have a lot of scaffolding that just takes up space on the page, we list the ingredients that go into a typical backup script and show you code snippets for a Perl script. You can view these as building blocks that you can snap together to create your own script. We show them in roughly the order you'll need to use them:

Sanity checking
>   Make life easier on yourself and your teammates—turn on strict error checking and use English variable names:

```
use strict;
use warnings FATAL => 'all';
use English qw(-no_match_vars);
```

>   If you script in Bash, you can enable stricter variable checking, too. The following will raise an error when there's an undefined variable in a substitution or when a program exits with an error:

```
set -u;
set -e;
```

Command-line arguments

The best way to add command-line option processing is with the standard libraries, which are included with every Perl installation:

```
use Getopt::Long;
Getopt::Long::Configure('no_ignore_case', 'bundling');
GetOptions( .... );
```

Connecting to MySQL

The standard Perl DBI library is nearly ubiquitous, and it provides a lot of power and flexibility. Read the Perldoc (available online at *http://search.cpan.org*) for details on how to use it. You can connect to MySQL using DBI as follows:

```
use DBI;
$dbh = DBI->connect(
        'DBI:mysql:;host=localhost', 'user', 'p4ssw0rd', {RaiseError => 1 });
```

For command-line scripting, read the *--help* text for the standard *mysql* program. It has a lot of options to make it friendly for scripting. For example, here's how to iterate over a list of databases in Bash:

```
mysql -ss -e 'SHOW DATABASES' | while read DB; do
  echo "${DB}"
done
```

Stopping and starting MySQL

The best way to stop and start MySQL is to use your operating system's preferred method, such as running the */etc/init.d/mysql* init script or the service control (on Windows). It's not the only way, though. You can shut down the database from Perl, with an existing database connection:

```
$dbh->func("shutdown", 'admin');
```

You shouldn't rely on MySQL being shut down when this command completes—it might only be in the process of shutting down. You can also stop MySQL from the command line:

```
$ mysqladmin shutdown
```

Getting lists of databases and tables

Every backup script asks MySQL for a list of databases and tables. Beware of entries that aren't really databases, such as the *lost+found* directory in some journaling filesystems and the INFORMATION_SCHEMA. Make sure your script is ready to deal with views, too, and be aware that SHOW TABLE STATUS can take a really long time when you have lots of data in InnoDB:

```
mysql> SHOW DATABASES;
mysql> SHOW /*!50002 FULL*/ TABLES FROM <database>;
mysql> SHOW TABLE STATUS FROM <database>;
```

Locking, flushing, and unlocking tables

You're bound to need to lock and/or flush one or more tables. You can either lock the desired tables by naming them all, or just lock everything globally:

```
mysql> LOCK TABLES <database.table> READ [, ...];
mysql> FLUSH TABLES;
mysql> FLUSH TABLES <database.table> [, ...];
mysql> FLUSH TABLES WITH READ LOCK;
mysql> UNLOCK TABLES;
```

Be very careful about race conditions when getting lists of tables and locking them. New tables could be created, or tables could be dropped or renamed. If you lock and back them up one at a time, you won't get consistent backups.

Flushing binary logs

It's handy to ask the server to begin a new binary log (do this after locking the tables, but before taking a backup):

```
mysql> FLUSH LOGS;
```

It makes recovery and incremental backups easier if you don't have to think about starting in the middle of a log file. This does have some side effects with regard to flushing and reopening error logs and potentially destroying old log entries, so be careful you're not throwing away data you need.

Getting binary log positions

Your script should get and record both the master and replica status—even if the server is just a master or just a replica:

```
mysql> SHOW MASTER STATUS\G
mysql> SHOW SLAVE STATUS\G
```

Issue both statements and ignore any errors you get, so your script gets all the information possible.

Dumping data

Your best options are to use *mysqldump*, *mydumper*, or SELECT INTO OUTFILE.

Copying data

Use one of the methods we showed throughout the chapter.

These are the building blocks of any backup script. The hard part is to script the management and recovery tasks. If you want inspiration for how to do this, you can take a look at the source code for ZRM.

Summary

Everyone knows that they need backups, but not everyone realizes that they need recoverable backups. There are many ways to design backups that contradict your recovery requirements. To help avoid this problem, we suggest that you define and document your recovery point objective and your recovery time objective, and use those requirements when choosing a backup system.

It's also important to test recovery on a routine basis and ensure that it works. It's easy to set up *mysqldump* and let it run every night, without realizing that your data has grown over time to the point where it might take days or weeks to import again. The worst time to find out how long your recovery will take is when you actually need it. A backup that completes in hours can literally take *weeks* to restore, depending on your hardware, schema, indexes, and data.

Don't fall into the trap of thinking that a replica is a backup. It's a less intrusive source for taking a backup, but it's not a backup. The same is true of your RAID volume, your SAN, and filesystem snapshots. Make sure that your backups can pass the DROP TABLE test (or the "I got hacked" test), as well as the test of losing your datacenter. And if you take backups from a replica, be sure that you verify replication integrity with *pt-table-checksum*.

Our two favorite ways to take backups are to copy the data from a filesystem or SAN snapshot, or to use Percona XtraBackup. Both techniques let you take nonintrusive binary (raw) backups of your data, which you can then verify by starting a *mysqld* instance and checking the tables. Sometimes you can even kill two birds with one stone: test recovery every single day by restoring the backup to your development or staging server. You can also dump the data from that instance to create a logical backup. We also like to back up binary logs, and to keep enough generations of backups and binary logs that we can perform recovery or set up a new replica even if the most recent backup is unusable.

There are good commercial backup tools in addition to the open source ones we've mentioned, foremost among them MySQL Enterprise Backup. Be careful with "backup" tools that are included with GUI SQL editors, server management tools, and the like. Likewise, be careful with "MySQL backup plugins" from companies who make one-size-fits-all backup tools that claim to support MySQL. You really need a first-class backup tool that's designed primarily for MySQL, not one that just happens to support MySQL as well as a hundred other things. A lot of backup tool vendors don't know or acknowledge the impact of practices such as using FLUSH TABLES WITH READ LOCK. The use of this SQL command automatically disqualifies a solution as a "hot" backup in our opinion. If you use only InnoDB tables, you usually don't need it.

Tools for MySQL Users

The MySQL server distribution doesn't include tools for many common tasks, such as monitoring the server or comparing data between servers. Fortunately, Oracle's commercial offerings extend these tools, and MySQL's active open source community and third-party companies also provide a wide variety of tools, reducing the need to roll your own.

Interface Tools

Interface tools help you run queries, create tables and users, and perform other routine tasks. This section gives a brief description of some of the most popular tools for these purposes. You can generally do all or most of the jobs they're used for with SQL queries or commands—the tools we discuss here just add convenience, help you avoid mistakes, and speed up your work:

MySQL Workbench

MySQL Workbench is an all-in-one tool for tasks such as managing your server, writing queries, developing stored procedures, and working with schema diagrams. It features a plugin interface that lets you write your own tools and integrate them into the workbench, and there are Python scripts and libraries that use this plugin interface. MySQL Workbench is available in both community and commercial editions, with the commercial editions adding in some more advanced features. The free version is more than adequate for most needs, though. You can learn more at *http://www.mysql.com/products/workbench/*.

SQLyog

SQLyog is one of the most popular visual tools for MySQL, with many nice features. It's in the same class as MySQL Workbench, but both tools have some checkboxes in their feature matrices that the other doesn't have. It is available only for Microsoft Windows, in a full-featured edition for a price and in a limited-functionality edition for free. More information about SQLyog is available at *http://www.webyog.com*.

phpMyAdmin

phpMyAdmin is a popular administration tool that runs on a web server and gives you a browser-based interface to your MySQL servers. Although browser-based access is nice sometimes, phpMyAdmin is a large and complex tool, and it has been accused of having a lot of security problems. Be extremely careful with it. We recommend not installing it anywhere that's accessible from the Internet. More information is available at *http://sourceforge.net/projects/phpmyadmin/*.

Adminer

Adminer is a lightweight, secure browser-based administration tool that's in the same category as phpMyAdmin. The developer positions it as a better replacement for phpMyAdmin. Although it does seem to be more secure, we still recommend being cautious about installing it in any publicly accessible place. More information is available at *http://www.adminer.org*.

Command-Line Utilities

MySQL comes with some command-line utilities, such as *mysqladmin* and *mysql-check*. These are listed and documented in the MySQL manual. The MySQL community has also created a wide range of high-quality toolkits with good documentation to supplement these utilities:

Percona Toolkit

Percona Toolkit is the must-have toolkit for MySQL administrators. It is the successor to Baron's earlier toolkits, Maatkit and Aspersa, which many people regarded as mandatory for anyone running a serious MySQL deployment. It includes many tools for purposes such as log analysis, replication integrity checking, data synchronization, schema and indexing analysis, query advice, and data archiving. If you're just getting started with MySQL, we suggest that you learn these essential tools first: *pt-mysql-summary*, *pt-table-checksum*, *pt-table-sync*, and *pt-query-digest*. More information is available at *http://www.percona.com/software/*.

Maatkit and Aspersa

These two toolkits have been around since 2006 in one form or another, and both came to be widely regarded as essential for MySQL users. They have now been merged into Percona Toolkit.

The openark kit

Shlomi Noach's openark kit (*http://code.openark.org/forge/openark-kit*) contains Python scripts that you can use for a wide variety of administrative tasks.

MySQL Workbench utilities

Some of the MySQL Workbench utilities are usable as standalone Python scripts. They are available from *https://launchpad.net/mysql-utilities*.

In addition to these tools, there are a variety of others that are less formally packaged and maintained. Many of the prominent MySQL community members have contributed tools at one time or another, mostly hosted on their own websites or on the MySQL Forge (*http://forge.mysql.com*). You can find a great deal of information by watching the Planet MySQL blog aggregator over time (*http://planet.mysql.com*), but unfortunately there is no single central directory for these tools.

SQL Utilities

There are a variety of free add-ons and utilities you can use from within the server itself; some of them are quite powerful indeed:

common_schema
> Shlomi Noach's `common_schema` project (*http://code.openark.org/forge/common _schema*) is a powerful set of routines and views for server scripting and administration. The `common_schema` is to MySQL as jQuery is to JavaScript.

mysql-sr-lib
> Giuseppe Maxia created a library of stored routines for MySQL, which you can find at *http://www.nongnu.org/mysql-sr-lib/*.

UDF repository for MySQL
> Roland Bouman has curated a collection of user-defined functions for MySQL, which is available at *http://www.mysqludf.org*.

MySQL Forge
> At the MySQL Forge (*http://forge.mysql.com*), you'll find hundreds of community-contributed programs, scripts, snippets, utilities, and tips and tricks.

Monitoring Tools

In our experience, most MySQL shops primarily need two kinds of monitoring: tools for health monitoring—detecting and alerting when something goes wrong—and recording metrics for trending, diagnosis, troubleshooting, capacity planning, and so on. Most systems are good at only one of these tasks, and can't do a good job of both. Unfortunately, there are dozens of tools to choose from, making it a very time-intensive process to evaluate the offerings and decide whether a specific one suits you well.

Most monitoring systems are not designed specifically to monitor MySQL servers. Instead, they are general-purpose systems designed to periodically check the status of many kinds of resources, from machines to routers to software (such as MySQL). They usually have some kind of plugin architecture and often come with plugins for MySQL.

You generally install a monitoring system on its own server and use it to monitor other servers. If you're using it to monitor important systems, it will quickly become a critical part of your infrastructure, so you might need to take extra steps, such as making the monitoring system itself redundant with failover.

Open Source Monitoring Tools

The following are some of the most popular open source all-in-one monitoring systems:

Nagios

Nagios (*http://www.nagios.org*) is probably the most popular open source problem detection and alerting system. It periodically checks services you define and compares the results to default or explicit thresholds. If the results are outside the limits, Nagios can execute a program and/or alert someone to the trouble. Nagios's contact and alert system lets you escalate alerts to different contacts, change alerts or send them to different places depending on the time of day and other conditions, and honor scheduled downtime. Nagios also understands dependencies between services, so it won't bother you about a MySQL instance being down when it notices the server is unreachable because a router in the middle is down, or when it finds that the host server itself is down.

Nagios can run any executable file as a plugin, provided it accepts the right arguments and gives the right output. As a result, Nagios plugins exist in many languages, including the shell, Perl, Python, Ruby, and other scripting languages. And if you can't find a plugin that does exactly what you need, it's simple to create your own. A plugin just needs to accept standard arguments, exit with an appropriate status, and optionally print output for Nagios to capture.

Nagios has some serious shortcomings, though. Even after you've learned it well, it is hard to maintain. It also keeps its entire configuration in files, instead of a database. The files have a special syntax that is easy to get wrong, and they are labor-intensive to modify as your systems grow and evolve. Nagios is not very extensible; you can write monitoring plugins easily, but that's about all you can do. Finally, its graphing, trending, and visualization capabilities are limited. Nagios can store some performance and other data in a MySQL server and generate graphs from it, but not as flexibly as some other systems. All of these problems are made worse by politics. Nagios has been forked at least twice due to the real or perceived difficulties of working with the code and people involved. The forks are named Opsview (*http://www.opsview.com*) and Icinga (*http://www.icinga.org*). Many people prefer these systems to Nagios.

There are several books devoted to Nagios; we like Wolfgang Barth's *Nagios System and Network Monitoring* (No Starch Press).

Zabbix

Zabbix is a full-featured system for monitoring and metrics collection. For example, it stores all configuration and other data in a database, not in configuration files. It also stores more types of data than Nagios and can thus generate better trending and history reports. Its network graphing and visualization capabilities are superior to Nagios's, and many people find it easier to configure, more flexible, and more scalable. See *http://www.zabbix.com* for more information.

Zenoss

Zenoss is written in Python and has a browser-based user interface that uses Ajax to make it faster and more productive. It can autodiscover resources on the network, and it folds monitoring, alerting, trending, graphing, and recording historical data into a unified tool. Zenoss uses SNMP to gather data from remote machines by default, but it can also use SSH, and it has support for Nagios plugins. More information is available at *http://www.zenoss.com*.

Hyperic HQ

Hyperic HQ is a Java-based monitoring system that is targeted more toward so-called enterprise monitoring than most of the other systems in its class. Like Zenoss, it can autodiscover resources and supports Nagios plugins, but its logical organization and architecture are different, and it is a little "bulkier." More information can be found at *http://www.hyperic.com*.

OpenNMS

OpenNMS is written in Java and has an active developer community. It has the usual features, such as monitoring and alerting, but adds graphing and trending capabilities as well. Its goals are high performance and scalability, automation, and flexibility. Like Hyperic, it is intended for enterprise monitoring of large, critical systems. For more information, see *http://www.opennms.org*.

Groundwork Open Source

Groundwork Open Source combines Nagios and several other tools into one system with a portal interface. Perhaps the best way to describe it is as the system you might build in-house if you were an expert in Nagios, Cacti, and a host of other tools and had a lot of time to integrate them together. More information is available at *http://www.groundworkopen source.com*.

In addition to the all-in-one systems, there is a variety of software that's focused on collecting metrics and letting you graph and visualize them, rather than performing health checks. Many of these are built on top of RRDTool (*http://www.rrdtool.org*), which stores time-series data in round-robin database (RRD) files. RRD files automatically aggregate incoming data, interpolate missing values in case the incoming values are not delivered when expected, and have powerful graphing tools that generate beautiful, distinctive graphs. Several RRDTool-based systems are available. Here are some of the most popular:

MRTG

The Multi Router Traffic Grapher, or MRTG (*http://oss.oetiker.ch/mrtg/*), is the quintessential RRDTool-based system. It is really designed for recording network traffic, but it can be extended to record and graph other things as well.

Cacti

Cacti (*http://www.cacti.net*) is probably the most popular RRDTool-based system. It is a PHP web interface to RRDTool. It uses a MySQL database to define the servers, plugins, graphs, and so on. It is template-driven, so you can define templates and then apply them to your systems. Baron wrote a very popular set of templates for MySQL and other systems; see *http://code.google.com/p/mysql -cacti-templates/* for more information. These have been ported to Munin, OpenNMS, and Zabbix.

Ganglia

Ganglia (*http://ganglia.sourceforge.net*) is similar to Cacti, but it's designed to monitor clusters and grids of systems, so you can view data from many servers in aggregate and drill down to the individual servers if you wish.

Munin

Munin (*http://munin.projects.linpro.no*) gathers data for you, puts it into RRDTool, and then generates graphs of the data at several levels of granularity. It creates static HTML files from the configuration, so you can browse them and view trends easily. It is easy to define a graph; you just create a plugin script whose command-line help output has some special syntaxes Munin recognizes as graphing instructions.

RRDTool-based systems have some limitations, such as the inability to query the stored data with a standard query language, the inability to keep data forever, problems with kinds of data that don't fit into simple counters or gauges easily, the requirement to predefine metrics and graphs, and so on. Ideally, we'd like to have a system that can just accept any metrics you send to it, with no predefinition of what they are, and draw arbitrary plots of them afterward, again without needing to predefine them. Probably the closest we've seen to such a system is Graphite (*http://graphite.wikidot.com*).

These systems can all be used to gather, record, and graph data and report on MySQL systems, with various degrees of flexibility and for slightly different purposes. They all lack a really flexible means of alerting someone when something is wrong.

The main problem with most of the systems we've mentioned is that they were apparently designed by people who were frustrated that the existing systems didn't quite meet their needs, so they wrote yet another system that doesn't quite meet a lot of other people's needs. Most of these systems have fundamental limitations, such as a strange internal data model that doesn't work well in a lot of situations. It's frustrating, but in many cases, using one of these systems is like trying to fit a round peg into a square hole.

Commercial Monitoring Systems

Although we know a lot of MySQL users who are most interested in using open source tools, we also know many who are perfectly happy to pay for proprietary software as well, if it gets the job done better and saves them time and hassle. Here are some of the available commercial options:

MySQL Enterprise Monitor

The MySQL Enterprise Monitor is included with a MySQL support subscription from Oracle. It combines features such as monitoring, metrics and graphing, advisory services, and query analysis into a single tool. It uses an agent on the servers to monitor their status counters (including key operating system metrics). It can capture queries in two ways: via MySQL Proxy, or by using the appropriate MySQL connectors, such as Connector/J for Java or MySQLi for PHP. Although it's designed to monitor MySQL, it is extensible to some degree. Still, you will probably not find it adequate for monitoring every server and service in your infrastructure. More information is available at *http://www.mysql.com/products/en terprise/monitor.html*.

MONyog
: MONyog (*http://www.webyog.com*) is an agentless browser-based monitoring system that runs on a desktop system. It starts an HTTP server, and you can point your browser at this server to use the system.

New Relic
: New Relic (*http://newrelic.com*) is a hosted, software-as-a-service application performance management system that can analyze your entire application's performance, from the application code (in Ruby, PHP, Java, and other languages) to the JavaScript running in the browser, the SQL calls you make to the database, and even the server's disk space, CPU utilization, and other metrics.

Circonus
: Circonus (*https://circonus.com*) is a hosted SaaS metrics and alerting system from OmniTI. An agent collects metrics from one or more servers and forwards them to Circonus, where you view them through a browser-based dashboard.

Monitis
: Monitis (*http://monitis.com*) is another cloud-hosted SaaS monitoring system. It is designed to monitor "everything," which means that it's slightly generic. It has a free entry-level cousin, Monitor.us (*http://mon.itor.us*), which has a MySQL plugin, too.

Splunk
: Splunk (*http://www.splunk.com*) is a log aggregator and search engine that can help you gain operational insight into all of the machine-generated data in your environment.

Pingdom
: Pingdom (*http://www.pingdom.com*) monitors your website's availability and performance from many locations in the world. There are many services like Pingdom, actually, and we don't necessarily recommend any specific one, but we do recommend that you use some external monitoring service to alert you when your site is unavailable. Many of the services can do a lot more than just "pinging" or fetching a web page.

There are many other commercial monitoring tools—we could tick off a dozen or more from memory. One thing to be careful about with all monitoring systems is their impact on the server. Some tools are pretty intrusive because they're designed by companies who have no practical experience with large, heavily loaded MySQL systems. For example, we have solved more than one emergency by disabling the monitoring system's feature that executed `SHOW TABLE STATUS` in every database once per minute. (This command is extremely disruptive on large I/O-bound systems.) Tools that query some of the `INFORMATION_SCHEMA` tables too often can also tend to have negative impacts.

Command-Line Monitoring with Innotop

There are a few command line–based monitoring tools, most of which emulate the Unix *top* tool in some way. The most sophisticated and capable of these is *innotop* (*http://code.google.com/p/innotop/*), which we'll explore in some detail. There are several others, though, such as *mtop* (*http://mtop.sourceforge.net*), *mytop* (*http://jeremy .zawodny.com/mysql/mytop/*), and some web-based clones of *mytop*.

Although *mytop* is the original *top* clone for MySQL, *innotop* can do everything it can do and much more, which is why we focus on *innotop* instead.

Baron Schwartz, one of this book's authors, wrote *innotop*. It presents a real-time updating view of what's happening in your server. Despite its name, it is not limited to monitoring InnoDB, but can monitor practically any aspect of MySQL. It lets you monitor multiple MySQL instances simultaneously, and it is very configurable and extensible.

Some of its features include:

- A transaction list that displays current InnoDB transactions
- A query list that shows currently running queries
- A list of current locks and lock waits
- Summaries of server status and variables to show the relative magnitudes of values
- Modes to display information about InnoDB internals, such as its buffers, deadlocks, foreign key errors, I/O activity, row operations, semaphores, and more
- Replication monitoring, with master and slave statuses displayed together
- A mode to view arbitrary server variables
- Server grouping to help you organize many servers easily
- Noninteractive mode for use in command-line scripting

It's easy to install *innotop*. You can either install it from your operating system's package repository or download it from *http://code.google.com/p/innotop/*, unpack it, and run the standard `make install` routine:

```
perl Makefile.PL
make install
```

Once you've installed it, execute *innotop* at the command line, and it will walk you through the process of connecting to a MySQL instance. It can read your *~/.my.cnf* option files, so you might not need to do anything but type your server's hostname and press Enter a few times. Once connected, you'll be in T (InnoDB Transaction) mode, and you should see a list of InnoDB transactions, as shown in Figure 16-1.

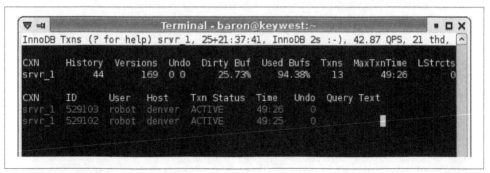

Figure 16-1. innotop in T (Transaction) mode

By default, *innotop* applies filters to reduce the clutter (as with everything in *innotop*, you can define your own or customize the built-in filters). In Figure 16-1, most of the transactions have been filtered out to show only active transactions. You can press the i key to disable the filter and fill the screen with as many transactions as will fit.

innotop displays a header and a main thread list in this mode. The header shows some overall InnoDB information, such as the length of the history list, the number of un-purged InnoDB transactions, the percentage of dirty buffers in the buffer pool, and so forth.

The first key you should press is the question mark (?), to see the help screen. This screen's contents will vary depending on what mode *innotop* is in, but it always displays every active key, so you can see all possible actions. Figure 16-2 shows the help screen in T mode.

We won't go through all of its other modes, but as you can see from the help screen, *innotop* has a lot of features.

The only other thing we cover here is some basic customization to show you how to monitor whatever you please. One of *innotop*'s strengths is its ability to interpret user-defined expressions, such as Uptime/Questions to derive a queries-per-second metric. It can display the result since the server was started and/or incrementally since the last sample.

This makes it easy to add your own columns to its tabular displays. For example, the Q (Query List) mode has a header that shows some overall server information. Let's see how to modify it to monitor how full the key cache is. Start *innotop* and press Q to enter Q mode. The result will look like Figure 16-3.

The screenshot is truncated because we're not interested in the query list for this ex-ercise; we care only about the header.

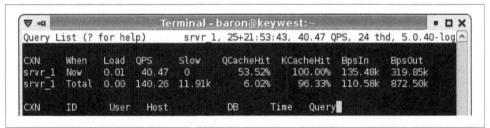

Figure 16-2. innotop help screen

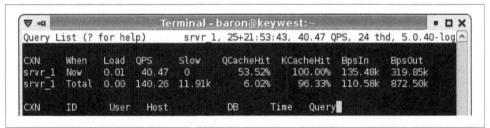

Figure 16-3. innotop in Q (Query List) mode

The header shows statistics for "Now" (which measures incremental activity since the last time *innotop* refreshed itself with new data from the server) and "Total" (which measures all activity since the MySQL server started, in this case 25 days ago). Each column in the header is derived from an equation involving values from SHOW STATUS and SHOW VARIABLES. The default headers shown in Figure 16-3 are built in, but it's easy to add your own. All you have to do is add a column to the header "table." Press the ^ key to start the table editor, then enter q_header at the prompt to edit the header table (Figure 16-4). Tab completion is built in, so you can just press q and then Tab to complete the word.

Figure 16-4. Adding a header (start)

After this, you'll see the table definition for the Q mode header (Figure 16-5). The table definition shows the table's columns. The first column is selected. We could move the selection around, reorder and edit the columns, and do several other things (press ? to see a full list), but we're just going to create a new column. Press the n key and type the column name (Figure 16-6).

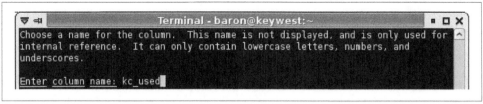

Figure 16-5. Adding a header (choices)

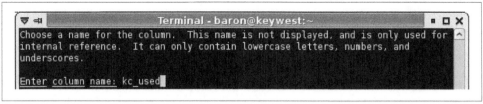

Figure 16-6. Adding a header (naming column)

Next, type the column's header, which will appear at the top of the column (Figure 16-7). Finally, choose the column's source. This is an expression that *innotop* compiles into a function internally. You can use names from SHOW VARIABLES and SHOW STATUS as though they're variables in an equation. We use some parentheses and Perlish "or" defaults to prevent division by zero, but otherwise this equation is pretty straightforward. We also use an *innotop* transformation called percent() to format the resulting column as a percentage; check the *innotop* documentation for more on that. Figure 16-8 shows the expression.

Figure 16-7. Adding a header (text for column)

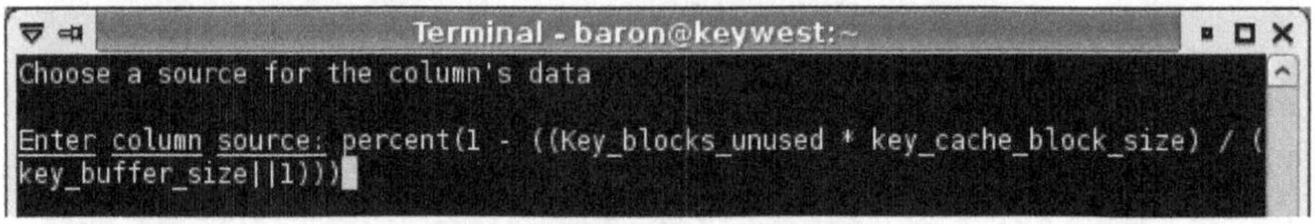

Figure 16-8. Adding a header (expression to calculate)

Press Enter, and you'll see the table definition just as before, but with the new column added at the bottom. Press the + key a few times to move it up the list, next to the key_buffer_hit column, and then press q to exit the table editor. *Voilà*: your new column, nested between KCacheHit and BpsIn (Figure 16-9). It's easy to customize *innotop* to monitor what you want. You can even write plugins if it really can't do what you need. There's more documentation at *http://code.google.com/p/innotop/*.

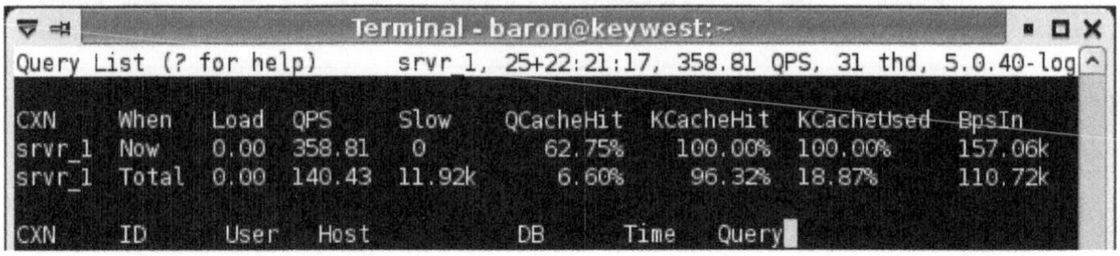

Figure 16-9. Adding a header (result)

Summary

Good tools are essential for administering MySQL. You'd be well advised to use some of the excellent tools that are already available, widely tested, and popular, such as Percona Toolkit (*nee* Maatkit). When we are introduced to new servers, practically the first thing we do is run *pt-summary* and *pt-mysql-summary*. If we're working on a server, we'll probably be watching it and any related servers in another terminal running *innotop*.

Monitoring tools are a more complicated topic, because they're so central to the organization. If you're an open source advocate and you want to use open source monitoring systems, you might try either the combination of Nagios and Cacti with Baron's Cacti templates, or Zabbix if you don't mind its complicated interface. If you want a commercial tool for monitoring MySQL, MySQL Enterprise Monitor is quite well done, and we know a lot of happy users. If you want something capable of monitoring your whole environment, and all of the software and hardware in it, you will need to do your own investigation—that is a bigger topic than we can tackle in this book.

Forks and Variants of MySQL

In Chapter 1, we discussed the history of MySQL's acquisition by Sun Microsystems, then Sun's acquisition by Oracle Corporation, and how the server has fared through these stewardship changes. But there is much more to the story. MySQL isn't available solely from Oracle anymore. In the process of two acquisitions, several variants of MySQL appeared. Although most users are unlikely to want anything but the "official" version of MySQL from Oracle, the variants are genuinely important and have made a big difference to all MySQL users—even those who would never consider using them.

There have been a handful of MySQL variants over the years, but three major variants have stood the test of time so far. These three are Percona Server, MariaDB, and Drizzle. All of them have active user communities and some degree of commercial backing. All are supported by independent service providers.

As the creators of Percona Server, we're biased to some extent, but we think this appendix is fairly objective because we provide services, support, consulting, training, and engineering for all of the variants of MySQL. We also invited Brian Aker and Monty Widenius, who created the Drizzle and MariaDB projects, respectively, to contribute to this appendix, so that it wouldn't just be our version of the story.

Percona Server

Percona Server (*http://www.percona.com/software/*) grew out of our efforts to solve customer problems. In the second edition of this book, we mentioned some patches that we had created to enhance the MySQL server's logging and instrumentation. That was really the genesis of Percona Server. We modified the server's source code when we encountered problems that could not be solved any other way.

Percona Server has three primary goals:

Transparency
> Added instrumentation permits users to inspect the server internals and behavior more closely. This includes features such as counters in SHOW STATUS, tables in the INFORMATION_SCHEMA, and especially added verbosity in the slow query log.

Performance
> Percona Server includes many improvements to performance and scalability. Raw performance is important, but Percona Server also enhances predictability and the stability of performance. Most of the focus is on InnoDB.

Operational flexibility
> Percona Server contains many features that remove limitations. Although some of the limitations seem small, they can make it hard for operations staff and system administrators to run MySQL as a reliable and stable component of their infrastructure.

Percona Server is a backwards-compatible drop-in replacement for MySQL, with minimal changes that do not alter SQL syntax, the client/server protocol, or file formats on disk.[1] Anything that runs on MySQL will run without modification on Percona Server. Switching to Percona Server requires only shutting down MySQL and starting Percona Server, with no need to export and reimport data. Switching back is similarly painless, and this is actually very important: many problems have been solved by switching temporarily, using the improved instrumentation to diagnose the problem, and then reverting to standard MySQL.

We choose enhancements that deviate from standard MySQL only where needed and that provide significant benefit. We believe that most users are best served by sticking to the official version of MySQL as distributed by Oracle, and strive to remain as close to this as possible.

Percona Server includes the Percona XtraDB storage engine, Percona's enhanced version of InnoDB. This is also a backward-compatible replacement. For example, if you create a table with the InnoDB storage engine, Percona Server recognizes it automatically and uses Percona XtraDB instead. Percona XtraDB is also included in MariaDB.

Some of the enhancements in Percona Server have been included into Oracle's version of MySQL, and many others have been reimplemented in slightly different ways. As a result, Percona Server has become a sort of early-access preview to features that sometimes appear later in standard MySQL. Many of the enhancements in Percona Server 5.1 and 5.5 are probably going to be reimplemented in MySQL 5.6.

---

1. Historically, there have been a few changes to file formats, but these are disabled by default and can be enabled if desired.

MariaDB

After Sun's MySQL acquisition Monty Widenius, the cofounder of MySQL, left Sun Microsystems over disagreements about the MySQL development process. He founded Monty Program AB and created MariaDB to foster an "open development environment that would encourage outside participation." MariaDB's goals are community development, along with bug fixes and lots of new features—especially integration of community-developed features. To quote Monty again,[2] "the vision for MariaDB is for it to be user and customer driven, as well as more inclusive of community patches and plugins."

What's different about MariaDB? As compared to Percona Server, it includes much more extensive changes to the server. (Most of Percona Server's big changes are in the Percona XtraDB storage engine, not the server level.) There are many changes to the query optimizer and replication, for example. And it uses the Aria storage engine for internal temporary tables (those used for complex queries, such as DISTINCT or subqueries) instead of MyISAM. Aria was originally named Maria, and was intended as an InnoDB replacement during the uncertain Sun times. It is essentially a crash-safe version of MyISAM.

In addition to Percona XtraDB and Aria, MariaDB also includes a number of community storage engines, such as SphinxSE and PBXT.

MariaDB is a superset of stock MySQL, so existing applications should keep working with no changes, just as with Percona Server. However, MariaDB will work much better for some scenarios, such as complex subqueries or many-table joins. It also features a segmented MyISAM key cache, which makes MyISAM much more scalable on modern hardware.

Perhaps the finest work in MariaDB, however, is in MariaDB 5.3, which is in Release Candidate status at the time of writing. This version includes an enormous amount of work on the query optimizer—probably the biggest optimizer improvements MySQL has seen in a decade. It adds new query execution plans such as hash joins, and fixes many of the things we've pointed out as weaknesses in MySQL throughout this book, such as outside-in subquery execution. It also includes significant extensions to the server, such as dynamic columns, role-based access control, and microsecond timestamp support.

For a more complete list of improvements to MariaDB, you can read the documentation on *http://www.askmonty.org* or these web pages that summarize the changes: *http://askmonty.org/blog/the-2-year-old-mariadb/* and *http://kb.askmonty.org/en/what-is-mariadb-53*.

---

2. The quotes are from *http://monty-says.blogspot.com/2009/02/time-to-move-on.html* and *http://monty-says.blogspot.com/2010/03/time-flies-one-year-of-mariadb.html*.

Drizzle

Drizzle is a true fork of MySQL, not just a variant or enhancement. It is not compatible with MySQL, although it's not so different that it's unrecognizable. In most cases, you won't simply be able to switch out your MySQL backend and replace it with Drizzle, due to changes such as different SQL syntax.

Drizzle was created in 2008 to better serve the needs of MySQL users. It is built to satisfy the core functionality needed by web applications. It is greatly streamlined and simplified compared to MySQL, with many fewer choices; for example, it uses only utf8 for character storage, and there is only one type of BLOB. It is built primarily for 64-bit hardware, and it supports IPv6 networking.

One of the key goals of the Drizzle database server is to eliminate surprises and legacy behaviors that exist in MySQL, such as declaring a column NOT NULL and then finding that the database somehow stored a NULL into it. The poorly implemented or unwieldy features you can find in MySQL, such as triggers, the query cache, and INSERT ON DUPLICATE KEY UPDATE, are simply removed.

At the code level, Drizzle is built on a microkernel architecture with a lean core and plugins. The core of the server has been stripped down to a much smaller codebase than MySQL. Nearly everything is a plugin—even functions such as SLEEP(). This makes Drizzle very easy and productive to work with on the source code level.

Drizzle uses standard open-source libraries such as Boost, and complies to standards in code, build infrastructure, and APIs. It uses the Google Protocol Buffers open messaging format for purposes such as replication, and it uses a modified version of InnoDB as its default storage engine.

The Drizzle team began benchmarking the server very early, using industry-standard benchmarks with up to 1,024 threads to measure performance at high concurrencies. Performance gains at high concurrency are prioritized over low-end gains, and there has been much progress on improving performance.

Drizzle is a community-developed project, and it has attracted more open source contributions than MySQL was ever able to. The server's license is pure GPL, with no dual licensing. However—and this is one of the most important aspects for developing a commercial ecosystem—there is a new client library that speaks the MySQL client-server protocol but is BSD-licensed. This means that you can build a proprietary application that connects to MySQL through the Drizzle client library, and you do not need to purchase a commercial license to the MySQL client library or make your software available under the GPL license. The *libmysql* client library for MySQL was one of the primary reasons that companies purchased commercial licenses for MySQL—without the commercial license that permitted them to link to *libmysql*, they would have been forced to release their software under the GPL. This is no longer necessary, because now they can use the Drizzle library instead.

Drizzle is deployed in some production environments, but not very widely from what we've seen. The Drizzle project's philosophy of casting off the chains of backward-compatibility means that it's probably a better candidate for new applications than for migrating an existing application.

Other MySQL Variants

There are, or have been, many other variants of the MySQL server. Many large companies, such as Google, Facebook, and eBay, maintain modified versions of the server that suit their precise needs and deployment scenarios. Much of this source code has been made available publicly; perhaps the best-known examples are the Facebook and Google patches for MySQL.

In addition, there have been several forks or redistributions, such as OurDelta, DorsalSource, and, for a brief time, a distribution from Henrik Ingo.

Finally, many people don't realize that when they install MySQL from their GNU/Linux distribution's package repositories, they are actually getting a modified version of the server—in some cases, quite heavily modified. Red Hat and Debian (and therefore Fedora and Ubuntu) ship a nonstandard version of MySQL, as does Gentoo and practically every other GNU/Linux distribution. In contrast to the other variants we've mentioned, these distributions don't advertise how much they've changed the server's source code, because they keep the MySQL name.

We've had a lot of problems in the past with such modified versions of MySQL. This is one reason that we tend to advocate using Oracle's version of MySQL unless there is a compelling reason to do otherwise.

Summary

The forks and variants of MySQL have rarely resulted in significant amounts of code being adopted back into the main MySQL source code tree, but they have nevertheless influenced the direction and pace of MySQL development greatly. In some cases they provide a superior alternative.

Should you use a fork instead of Oracle's official MySQL? We don't think this is usually necessary. The choice is usually based on perceptions (which are never completely accurate) or business reasons, such as having an enterprise-wide relationship with Oracle. There are two general categories of people who tend to turn away from the official version of the server:

- Those who are facing a specific problem that can't be solved without a source code modification
- Those who distrust Oracle's stewardship of MySQL[3] and feel happier with a variant that they regard as being truly open-source

Why would you choose any specific fork? We'd summarize it as follows. If you want to stay as close as possible to official MySQL, but get better performance, instrumentation, and helpful features, choose Percona Server. Choose MariaDB if you are more comfortable with big changes to the server, or if you want a broader range of community contributions such as additional storage engines. Choose Drizzle if you want a lean, stripped-down database server and you don't mind that it's not compatible with MySQL, or if you want to be able to make your own enhancements to the database much more easily.

How popular are the forks and variants? Nobody really knows, but one thing we all agree on is that if you add together all the deployments of unofficial MySQL versions, they constitute only a tiny fraction of the number of official MySQL deployments in the world. In terms of relative popularity, we're biased because many of our customers choose to use Percona Server, but from what we've see deployed "in the wild," Percona Server appears to be the most popular, followed by MariaDB.

Speaking of Percona, in general all of the service providers have a lot of experience with the official MySQL, but naturally Percona has the most experts in working with Percona Server, and Monty Program is correspondingly the most familiar with MariaDB. This matters a lot when you're looking for bug-fix support contracts. Only Oracle can guarantee that a bug will be fixed in the official MySQL releases; other vendors can provide fixes but have no power to get them included in the official releases. This is one answer to the question of why to choose a fork: some people choose one of the forks simply because it is the version of MySQL that their service provider controls fully and can conveniently fix and enhance.

---

3. As we explained in Chapter 1, we are actually quite happy with Oracle as MySQL's owner

MySQL Server Status

You can answer many questions about a MySQL server by inspecting its status. MySQL exposes information about server internals in several ways. The newest is the PERFOR MANCE_SCHEMA database in MySQL 5.5, but the standard INFORMATION_SCHEMA database has existed since MySQL 5.0, and there are a series of SHOW commands that have existed practically forever. Some information you can get via SHOW commands isn't found in the INFORMATION_SCHEMA tables.

The challenges for you are determining what is relevant to your problem, how to get the information you need, and how to interpret it. Although MySQL lets you see a lot of information about what's going on inside the server, it's not always easy to use that information. Understanding it requires patience, experience, and ready access to the MySQL manual. Good tools are helpful, too.

This appendix is mostly reference material, but you will also find some information on the functioning of server internals, especially in the sections on InnoDB.

System Variables

MySQL exposes many system variables through the SHOW VARIABLES SQL command, as variables you can use in expressions, or with *mysqladmin variables* at the command line. From MySQL 5.1, you can also access them through tables in the INFORMATION _SCHEMA database.

These variables represent a variety of configuration information, such as the server's default storage engine (storage_engine), the available time zones, the connection's collation, and startup parameters. We explained how to set and use system variables in Chapter 8.

SHOW STATUS

The SHOW STATUS command shows server status variables in a two-column name-value table. Unlike the server variables we mentioned in the previous section, these are read-only. You can view the variables by either executing SHOW STATUS as a SQL command or executing *mysqladmin extended-status* as a shell command. If you use the SQL command, you can use LIKE and WHERE to limit the results; the LIKE does a standard pattern match on the variable name. The commands return a table of results, but you can't sort it, join it to other tables, or do other standard things you can do with MySQL tables. In MySQL 5.1 and newer, you can select values directly from the INFORMATION_SCHEMA.GLOBAL_STATUS and INFORMATION_SCHEMA.SESSION_STATUS tables.

 We use the term "status variable" to refer to a value from SHOW STATUS and the term "system variable" to refer to a server configuration variable.

The behavior of SHOW STATUS changed greatly in MySQL 5.0, but you might not notice unless you're paying close attention. Instead of just maintaining one set of global variables, MySQL now maintains some variables globally and some on a per-connection basis. Thus, SHOW STATUS contains a mixture of global and session variables. Many of them have dual scope: there's both a global and a session variable, and they have the same name. SHOW STATUS also now shows session variables by default, so if you were accustomed to running SHOW STATUS and seeing global variables, you won't see them anymore; now you have to run SHOW GLOBAL STATUS instead.[1]

There are hundreds of status variables. Most either are counters or contain the current value of some status metric. Counters increment every time MySQL does something, such as initiating a full table scan (Select_scan). Metrics, such as the number of open connections to the server (Threads_connected), may increase and decrease. Sometimes there are several variables that seem to refer to the same thing, such as Connections (the number of connection attempts to the server) and Threads_connected; in this case, the variables are related, but similar names don't always imply a relationship.

Counters are stored as unsigned integers. They use 4 bytes on 32-bit builds and 8 bytes on 64-bit builds, and they wrap back to 0 after reaching their maximum values. If you're monitoring the variables incrementally, you might need to watch for and correct the wrap; you should also be aware that if your server has been up for a long time, you might see lower values than you expect simply because the variable's values have wrapped around to zero. (This is very rarely a problem on 64-bit builds.)

---

1. There's a gotcha waiting here: if you use an old version of *mysqladmin* on a new server, it won't use SHOW GLOBAL STATUS, so it won't display the "right" information.

A good way to get a feel for your overall workload is to compare values within a group of related status variables—for example, look at all the `Select_*` variables together, or all the `Handler_*` variables. If you're using *innotop*, this is easy to do in Command Summary mode, but you can also do it manually with a command like *mysqladmin extended -r -i60 | grep Handler_*. Here's what *innotop* shows for the `Select_*` variables on one server we checked:

```
_____ Command Summary _____
Name                     Value    Pct      Last Incr  Pct
Select_scan              756582   59.89%           2  100.00%
Select_range             497675   39.40%           0    0.00%
Select_full_join           7847    0.62%           0    0.00%
Select_full_range_join     1159    0.09%           0    0.00%
Select_range_check            1    0.00%           0    0.00%
```

The first two columns of values are since the server was booted, and the last two are since the last refresh (10 seconds ago, in this case). The percentages are over the total of the values shown in the display, not over the total of all queries.

For a side-by-side view of current and previous snapshots and the differences between them, you can also use the *pt-mext* tool from Percona Toolkit, or this clever query from Shlomi Noach:[2]

```sql
SELECT STRAIGHT_JOIN
    LOWER(gs0.VARIABLE_NAME) AS variable_name,
    gs0.VARIABLE_VALUE AS value_0,
    gs1.VARIABLE_VALUE AS value_1,
    (gs1.VARIABLE_VALUE - gs0.VARIABLE_VALUE) AS diff,
    (gs1.VARIABLE_VALUE - gs0.VARIABLE_VALUE) / 10 AS per_sec,
    (gs1.VARIABLE_VALUE - gs0.VARIABLE_VALUE) * 60 / 10 AS per_min
FROM (
    SELECT VARIABLE_NAME, VARIABLE_VALUE
    FROM INFORMATION_SCHEMA.GLOBAL_STATUS
    UNION ALL
    SELECT '', SLEEP(10) FROM DUAL
) AS gs0
    JOIN INFORMATION_SCHEMA.GLOBAL_STATUS gs1 USING (VARIABLE_NAME)
WHERE gs1.VARIABLE_VALUE <> gs0.VARIABLE_VALUE;
```

variable_name	value_0	value_1	diff	per_sec	per_min
handler_read_rnd_next	2366	2953	587	58.7	3522
handler_write	2340	3218	878	87.8	5268
open_files	22	20	-2	-0.2	-12
select_full_join	2	3	1	0.1	6
select_scan	7	9	2	0.2	12

---

2. First published at *http://code.openark.org/blog/mysql/mysql-global-status-difference-using-single-query*.

It's most useful to look at the values of all these variables and metrics over the course of the last several minutes, as well as over the entire uptime of the server.

The following is an overview—not an exhaustive list—of the different categories of variables you'll see in SHOW STATUS. For full details on a given variable, you should consult the MySQL manual, which helpfully documents them at *http://dev.mysql.com/doc/en/mysqld-option-tables.html*. When we discuss a set of related variables whose name begins with a common prefix, we refer to the group collectively as "the *prefix*_* variables.*"

Thread and Connection Statistics

These variables track connection attempts, aborted connections, network traffic, and thread statistics:

- Connections, Max_used_connections, Threads_connected
- Aborted_clients, Aborted_connects
- Bytes_received, Bytes_sent
- Slow_launch_threads, Threads_cached, Threads_created, Threads_running

If Aborted_connects isn't zero, it might mean that you have network problems or that someone is trying to connect and failing (perhaps a user is specifying the wrong password or an invalid database, or maybe a monitoring system is opening TCP port 3306 to check if the server is alive). If this value gets too high, it can have serious side effects: it can cause MySQL to block a host.

Aborted_clients has a similar name but a completely different meaning. If this value increments, it usually means there's been an application error, such as the programmer forgetting to close MySQL connections properly before terminating the program. This is not usually indicative of a big problem.

Binary Logging Status

The Binlog_cache_use and Binlog_cache_disk_use status variables show how many transactions have been stored in the binary log cache, and how many transactions were too large for the binary log cache and so had their statements stored in a temporary file. MySQL 5.5 also includes Binlog_stmt_cache_use and Binlog_stmt_cache_disk_use, which show corresponding metrics for nontransactional statements. The so-called "binary log cache hit ratio" is not usually useful for configuring the binary log cache size. See Chapter 8 for more on this topic.

Command Counters

The Com_* variables count the number of times each type of SQL or C API command has been issued. For example, Com_select counts the number of SELECT statements, and Com_change_db counts the number of times a connection's default database has been changed, either with the USE statement or via a C API call. The Questions variable[3] counts the total number of queries and commands the server has received. However, it doesn't quite equal the sum of all the Com_* variables, because of query cache hits, closed and aborted connections, and possibly other factors.

The Com_admin_commands status variable might be very large. It counts not only administrative commands, but ping requests to the MySQL instance as well. These requests are issued through the C API and typically come from client code, such as the following Perl code:

```perl
my $dbh = DBI->connect(...);
while ( $dbh && $dbh->ping ) {
    # Do something
}
```

These ping requests are "garbage" queries. They usually don't load the server very much, but they're still a waste and contribute a lot to application response time because of the network round trip time. We've seen ORM systems (Ruby on Rails comes to mind) that ping the server before each query, which is pointless; pinging the server and then querying it is a classic example of the "look before you leap" design pattern, which creates a race condition. We've also seen database abstraction libraries that change the default database before every query, which will show up as a very large number of Com_change_db commands. It's best to eliminate both practices.

Temporary Files and Tables

You can view the variables that count how many times MySQL has created temporary tables and files with:

```
mysql> SHOW GLOBAL STATUS LIKE 'Created_tmp%';
```

This shows statistics about implicit temporary tables and files—those created internally to execute queries. In Percona Server, there is also a command that can show explicit temporary tables, which are created by users with CREATE TEMPORARY TABLE:

```
mysql> SHOW GLOBAL TEMPORARY TABLES;
```

---

3. In MySQL 5.1, this variable was split into Questions and Queries, with slightly different meanings.

Handler Operations

The handler API is the interface between MySQL and its storage engines. The `Handler_*` variables count handler operations, such as the number of times MySQL asks a storage engine to read the next row from an index. You can view these variables with:

```
mysql> SHOW GLOBAL STATUS LIKE 'Handler_%';
```

MyISAM Key Buffer

The `Key_*` variables contain metrics and counters about the MyISAM key buffer. You can view these variables with:

```
mysql> SHOW GLOBAL STATUS LIKE 'Key_%';
```

File Descriptors

If you mainly use the MyISAM storage engine the `Open_*` variables reveal how often MySQL opens each table's *.frm, .MYI,* and *.MYD* files. InnoDB keeps all data in its tablespace files, so if you mainly use InnoDB, these variables aren't accurate. You can view the `Open_*` variables with:

```
mysql> SHOW GLOBAL STATUS LIKE 'Open_%';
```

Query Cache

You can inspect the query cache by looking at the `Qcache_*` status variables, with:

```
mysql> SHOW GLOBAL STATUS LIKE 'Qcache_%';
```

SELECT Types

The `Select_*` variables are counters for certain types of `SELECT` queries. They can help you see the ratio of `SELECT` queries that use various query plans. Unfortunately, there are no such status variables for other kinds of queries, such as `UPDATE` and `REPLACE`; however, you can look at the `Handler_*` status variables (discussed earlier) for insight into the relative numbers of non-`SELECT` queries. To see all the `Select_*` variables, use:

```
mysql> SHOW GLOBAL STATUS LIKE 'Select_%';
```

In our judgment, the `Select_*` status variables can be ranked as follows, in order of ascending cost:

Select_range
> The number of joins that scanned an index range on the first table.

Select_scan
> The number of joins that scanned the entire first table. There is nothing wrong with this if every row in the first table should participate in the join; it's only a bad thing if you don't want all the rows and there is no index to find the ones you want.

`Select_full_range_join`
> The number of joins that used a value from table *n* to retrieve rows from a range of the reference index in table *n* + 1. Depending on the query, this can be more or less costly than `Select_scan`.

`Select_range_check`
> The number of joins that reevaluate indexes in table *n* + 1 for every row in table *n* to see which is least expensive. This generally means no indexes in table *n* + 1 are useful for the join. This query plan has very high overhead.

`Select_full_join`
> The number of cross joins, or joins without any criteria to match rows in the tables. The number of rows examined is the product of the number of rows in each table. This is usually a very bad thing.

The last two variables usually should not increase rapidly, and if they do, it might be an indication that a "bad" query has been introduced into the system. See Chapter 3 for details on how to find such queries.

Sorts

We covered a lot of MySQL's sorting optimizations in several previous chapters, so you should have a good idea of how sorting works. When MySQL can't use an index to retrieve rows presorted, it has to do a filesort, and it increments the `Sort_*` status variables. Aside from `Sort_merge_passes`, you can influence these values only by adding indexes that MySQL can use for sorting. `Sort_merge_passes` depends on the `sort_buffer_size` server variable (not to be confused with the `myisam_sort_buffer_size` server variable). MySQL uses the sort buffer to hold a chunk of rows for sorting. When it's finished sorting them, it merges these sorted rows into the result, increments `Sort_merge_passes`, and fills the buffer with the next chunk of rows to sort. However, it's not a great idea to use this variable as a guide to sort buffer sizing, as shown in Chapter 3.

You can see all the `Sort_*` variables with:

```
mysql> SHOW GLOBAL STATUS LIKE 'Sort_%';
```

MySQL increments the `Sort_scan` and `Sort_range` variables when it reads sorted rows from the results of a filesort and returns them to the client. The difference is merely that the first is incremented when the query plan causes `Select_scan` to increment (see the preceding section), and the second is incremented when `Select_range` increments. There is no implementation or cost difference between the two; they merely indicate the type of query plan that caused the sort.

Table Locking

The `Table_locks_immediate` and `Table_locks_waited` variables tell you how many locks were granted immediately and how many had to be waited for. Be aware, however, that they show only server-level locking statistics, not storage engine locking statistics.

InnoDB-Specific

The `Innodb_*` variables show some of the data included in `SHOW ENGINE INNODB STATUS`, discussed later in this appendix. The variables can be grouped together by name: `Innodb_buffer_pool_*`, `Innodb_log_*`, and so on. We discuss InnoDB's internals more in a moment, when we examine `SHOW ENGINE INNODB STATUS`.

These variables are available in MySQL 5.0 and newer, and they have an important side effect: they create a global lock and traverse the entire InnoDB buffer pool before releasing the lock. In the meantime, other threads will run into the lock and block until it is released. This skews some status values, such as `Threads_running`, so they will appear higher than normal (possibly much higher, depending on how busy your server is). The same effect happens when you run `SHOW ENGINE INNODB STATUS` or access these statistics via the `INFORMATION_SCHEMA` tables (in MySQL 5.0 and newer, `SHOW STATUS` and `SHOW VARIABLES` are mapped to queries against the `INFORMATION_SCHEMA` tables behind the scenes).

These operations can, therefore, be expensive in these versions of MySQL—checking the server status too frequently (e.g., once a second) can cause significant overhead. Using `SHOW STATUS LIKE` doesn't help, because it retrieves the full status and then post-filters it.

There are many more variables in MySQL 5.5 than in 5.1, and even more in Percona Server.

Plugin-Specific

MySQL 5.1 and newer support pluggable storage engines and provide a mechanism for storage engines to register their own status and configuration variables with the MySQL server. You might see some plugin-specific variables if you're using a pluggable storage engine. Such variables always begin with the name of the plugin.

SHOW ENGINE INNODB STATUS

The InnoDB storage engine exposes a lot of information about its internals in the output of `SHOW ENGINE INNODB STATUS`, or its older synonym, `SHOW INNODB STATUS`.

Unlike most of the `SHOW` commands, its output consists of a single string, not rows and columns. It is divided into sections, each of which shows information about a different part of the InnoDB storage engine. Some of the output is most useful for InnoDB developers, but much of it is interesting—or even essential—if you're trying to understand and configure InnoDB for high performance.

 Older versions of InnoDB often print out 64-bit numbers in two pieces: the high 32 bits and the low 32 bits. An example is a transaction ID, such as TRANSACTION 0 3793469. You can calculate the 64-bit number's value by shifting the first number left 32 bits and adding it to the second one. We show some examples later.

The output includes some average statistics, such as fsync() calls per second. These show average activity since the last time the output was generated, so if you're examining these values, make sure you wait 30 seconds or so between samples to give the statistics time to accumulate, and sample multiple times and examine the changes to the counters to understand their behaviors. The output is not all generated at a single point in time, so not all averages that appear in the output are calculated over the same time interval. Also, InnoDB has an internal reset interval that is unpredictable and varies between versions; you should examine the output to see the time over which the averages were generated, because it will not necessarily be the same as the time between samples.

There's enough information in the output to calculate averages for most of the statistics manually if you want. However, a tool such as *innotop*—which does incremental differences and averages for you—is very helpful here.

Header

The first section is the header, which simply announces the beginning of the output, the current date and time, and how long it has been since the last printout. Line 2 shows the current date and time. Line 4 shows the time frame over which the averages were calculated, which is either the time since the last printout or the time since the last internal reset:

```
1  =======================================
2  070913 10:31:48 INNODB MONITOR OUTPUT
3  =======================================
4  Per second averages calculated from the last 49 seconds
```

SEMAPHORES

If you have a high-concurrency workload, you might want to pay attention to the next section, SEMAPHORES. It contains two kinds of data: event counters and, optionally, a list of current waits. If you're having trouble with bottlenecks, you can use this information to help you find the bottlenecks. Unfortunately, knowing what to do about them is a little more complex, but we give some advice later in this appendix. Here is some sample output for this section:

```
 1   ----------
 2   SEMAPHORES
 3   ----------
 4   OS WAIT ARRAY INFO: reservation count 13569, signal count 11421
 5   --Thread 1152170336 has waited at ./../include/buf0buf.ic line 630 for 0.00 seconds
     the semaphore:
 6   Mutex at 0x2a957858b8 created file buf0buf.c line 517, lock var 0
 7   waiters flag 0
 8   wait is ending
 9   --Thread 1147709792 has waited at ./../include/buf0buf.ic line 630 for 0.00 seconds
     the semaphore:
10   Mutex at 0x2a957858b8 created file buf0buf.c line 517, lock var 0
11   waiters flag 0
12   wait is ending
13   Mutex spin waits 5672442, rounds 3899888, OS waits 4719
14   RW-shared spins 5920, OS waits 2918; RW-excl spins 3463, OS waits 3163
```

Line 4 gives information about the operating system wait array, which is an array of "slots." InnoDB reserves slots in the array for semaphores, which the operating system uses to signal threads that they can go ahead and do the work they're waiting to do. This line shows how many times InnoDB has needed to use operating system waits. The reservation count indicates how often InnoDB has allocated slots, and the signal count measures how often threads have been signaled via the array. Operating system waits are costly relative to spin waits, as we'll see momentarily.

Lines 5 through 12 show the InnoDB threads that are currently waiting for a mutex. The example shows two waits, each beginning with the text "-- Thread <num> has waited...." This section should be empty unless your server has a high-concurrency workload that causes InnoDB to resort to operating system waits. The most useful thing to look at, unless you're familiar with InnoDB source code, is the filename at which the thread is waiting. This gives you a hint where the hot spots are inside InnoDB. For example, if you see many threads waiting at a file called *buf0buf.ic*, you have buffer pool contention. The output indicates how long the thread has been waiting, and the "waiters flag" shows how many waiters are waiting for the mutex.

The text "wait is ending" means the mutex is actually free already, but the operating system hasn't scheduled the thread to run yet.

You might wonder what exactly InnoDB is waiting for. InnoDB uses mutexes and semaphores to protect critical sections of code by restricting them to only one thread at a time, or to restrict writers when there are active readers, and so on. There are many critical sections in InnoDB's code, and under the right conditions any of them could appear here. Gaining access to a buffer pool page is one you might see commonly.

After the list of waiting threads, lines 13 and 14 show more event counters. Line 13 shows several counters related to mutexes, and line 14 is for read/write shared and exclusive locks. In each case, you can see how often InnoDB has resorted to an operating system wait.

InnoDB has a multiphase wait policy. First, it tries to spin-wait for the lock. If this doesn't succeed after a preconfigured number of spin rounds (specified by the `innodb _sync_spin_loops` configuration variable), it falls back to the more expensive and complex wait array.[4]

Spin waits are relatively low-cost, but they burn CPU cycles by checking repeatedly if a resource can be locked. This isn't as bad as it sounds, because there are typically free CPU cycles while the processor is waiting for I/O. And even if there aren't any free CPU cycles, spin waits are often much less expensive than the alternative. However, spinning monopolizes the processor when another thread might be able to do some work.

The alternative to a spin wait is for the operating system to do a context switch, so another thread can run while the thread waits, then wake the sleeping thread when it is signaled via the semaphore in the wait array. Signaling via a semaphore is efficient, but the context switch is expensive. These can add up quickly: thousands of them per second can cause a lot of overhead.

You can try to strike a balance between spin waits and operating system waits by changing the `innodb_sync_spin_loops` system variable. Don't worry about spin waits unless you see many (perhaps in the range of hundreds of thousands) spin rounds per second. This is something you usually need to resolve by understanding the source code involved, or by consulting with experts. You can also consider using the Performance Schema, or look at `SHOW ENGINE INNODB MUTEX`.

LATEST FOREIGN KEY ERROR

The next section, `LATEST FOREIGN KEY ERROR`, doesn't appear unless your server has had a foreign key error. There are many places in the source code that can generate this output, depending on the kind of error. Sometimes the problem is to do with a transaction and the parent or child rows it was looking for while trying to insert, update, or delete a record. At other times it's a type mismatch between tables while InnoDB was trying to add or delete a foreign key, or alter a table that already had a foreign key.

This section's output is very helpful for debugging the exact causes of InnoDB's often vague foreign key errors. Let's look at some examples. First, we'll create two tables with a foreign key between them, and insert a little data:

```
CREATE TABLE parent (
   parent_id int NOT NULL,
   PRIMARY KEY(parent_id)
) ENGINE=InnoDB;
CREATE TABLE child (
   parent_id int NOT NULL,
   KEY parent_id (parent_id),
   CONSTRAINT child_ibfk_1 FOREIGN KEY (parent_id) REFERENCES parent (parent_id)
) ENGINE=InnoDB;
```

---

4. The wait array was changed to be much more efficient in MySQL 5.1.

```
INSERT INTO parent(parent_id) VALUES(1);
INSERT INTO child(parent_id) VALUES(1);
```

There are two basic classes of foreign key errors. Adding, updating, or deleting data in a way that would violate the foreign key causes the first class of errors. For example, here's what happens when we delete the row from the parent table:

```
DELETE FROM parent;
ERROR 1451 (23000): Cannot delete or update a parent row: a foreign key constraint
fails (`test/child`, CONSTRAINT `child_ibfk_1` FOREIGN KEY (`parent_id`) REFERENCES
`parent` (`parent_id`))
```

The error message is fairly straightforward, and you'll get similar messages for all errors caused by adding, updating, or deleting nonmatching rows. Here's the output from SHOW ENGINE INNODB STATUS:

```
 1  ------------------------
 2  LATEST FOREIGN KEY ERROR
 3  ------------------------
 4  070913 10:57:34 Transaction:
 5  TRANSACTION 0 3793469, ACTIVE 0 sec, process no 5488, OS thread id 1141152064
    updating or deleting, thread declared inside InnoDB 499
 6  mysql tables in use 1, locked 1
 7  4 lock struct(s), heap size 1216, undo log entries 1
 8  MySQL thread id 9, query id 305 localhost baron updating
 9  DELETE FROM parent
10  Foreign key constraint fails for table `test/child`:
11  '
12    CONSTRAINT `child_ibfk_1` FOREIGN KEY (`parent_id`) REFERENCES `parent` (`parent_
    id`)
13  Trying to delete or update in parent table, in index `PRIMARY` tuple:
14  DATA TUPLE: 3 fields;
15   0: len 4; hex 80000001; asc      ;; 1: len 6; hex 00000039e23d; asc     9 =;; 2: len
    7; hex 000000002d0e24; asc    - $;;
16
17  But in child table `test/child`, in index `parent_id`, there is a record:
18  PHYSICAL RECORD: n_fields 2; compact format; info bits 0
19   0: len 4; hex 80000001; asc      ;; 1: len 6; hex 000000000500; asc      ;;
```

Line 4 shows the date and time of the last foreign key error. Lines 5 through 9 show details about the transaction that violated the foreign key constraint; we explain more about these lines later. Lines 10 through 19 show the exact data InnoDB was trying to change when it found the error. A lot of this output is the row data converted to printable formats; we say more about this later, too.

So far, so good, but there's another class of foreign key error that can be much harder to debug. Here's what happens when we try to alter the parent table:

```
ALTER TABLE parent MODIFY parent_id INT UNSIGNED NOT NULL;
ERROR 1025 (HY000): Error on rename of './test/#sql-1570_9' to './test/parent'
(errno: 150)
```

This is less than clear, but the SHOW ENGINE INNODB STATUS text sheds some light on it:

```
 1  ------------------------
 2  LATEST FOREIGN KEY ERROR
 3  ------------------------
 4  070913 11:06:03 Error in foreign key constraint of table test/child:
 5  there is no index in referenced table which would contain
 6  the columns as the first columns, or the data types in the
 7  referenced table do not match to the ones in table. Constraint:
 8  ,
 9    CONSTRAINT child_ibfk_1 FOREIGN KEY (parent_id) REFERENCES parent (parent_id)
10  The index in the foreign key in table is parent_id
11  See http://dev.mysql.com/doc/refman/5.0/en/innodb-foreign-key-constraints.html
12  for correct foreign key definition.
```

The error in this case is a different data type. Foreign-keyed columns must have *exactly* the same data type, including any modifiers (such as UNSIGNED, which was the problem in this case). Whenever you see error 1025 and don't understand why, the best place to look is in SHOW ENGINE INNODB STATUS.

The foreign key error messages are overwritten every time there's a new error. The *pt-fk-error-logger* tool from Percona Toolkit can help you save these for later analysis.

LATEST DETECTED DEADLOCK

Like the foreign key section, the LATEST DETECTED DEADLOCK section appears only if your server has had a deadlock. The deadlock error messages are also overwritten every time there's a new error, and the *pt-deadlock -logger* tool from Percona Toolkit can help you save these for later analysis.

A deadlock is a cycle in the waits-for graph, which is a data structure of row locks held and waited for. The cycle can be arbitrarily large. InnoDB detects deadlocks instantly, because it checks for a cycle in the graph every time a transaction has to wait for a row lock. Deadlocks can be quite complex, but this section shows only the last two transactions involved, the last statement executed in each of the transactions, and the locks that created the cycle in the graph. You don't see other transactions that might also be included in the cycle, nor do you see the statement that might have really acquired the locks earlier in a transaction. Nevertheless, you can often find out what caused the deadlock by looking at this output.

There are actually two types of InnoDB deadlocks. The first, which is what most people are accustomed to, is a true cycle in the waits-for graph. The other type is a waits-for graph that is too expensive to check for cycles. If InnoDB has to check more than a million locks in the graph, or if it recurses through more than 200 transactions while checking, it gives up and says there's a deadlock. These numbers are hardcoded constants in the InnoDB source, and you can't configure them (though you can change them and recompile InnoDB if you wish). You'll know when exceeding these limits causes a deadlock, because you'll see "TOO DEEP OR LONG SEARCH IN THE LOCK TABLE WAITS-FOR GRAPH" in the output.

InnoDB prints not only the transactions and the locks they held and waited for, but also the records themselves. This information is mostly useful to the InnoDB developers, but there's currently no way to disable it. Unfortunately, it can be so large that it runs over the length allocated for output and prevents you from seeing the sections that follow. The only way to remedy this is to cause a small deadlock to replace the large one, or to use Percona Server, which adds configuration variables to suppress the overly verbose text.

Here's a sample deadlock:

```
1  ------------------------
2  LATEST DETECTED DEADLOCK
3  ------------------------
4  070913 11:14:21
5  *** (1) TRANSACTION:
6  TRANSACTION 0 3793488, ACTIVE 2 sec, process no 5488, OS thread id 1141287232
   starting index read
7  mysql tables in use 1, locked 1
8  LOCK WAIT 4 lock struct(s), heap size 1216
9  MySQL thread id 11, query id 350 localhost baron Updating
10 UPDATE test.tiny_dl SET a = 0 WHERE a <> 0
11 *** (1) WAITING FOR THIS LOCK TO BE GRANTED:
12 RECORD LOCKS space id 0 page no 3662 n bits 72 index `GEN_CLUST_INDEX` of table
   `test/tiny_dl` trx id 0 3793488 lock_mode X waiting
13 Record lock, heap no 2 PHYSICAL RECORD: n_fields 4; compact format; info bits 0
14  0: len 6; hex 000000000501 ...[ omitted ] ...
15
16 *** (2) TRANSACTION:
17 TRANSACTION 0 3793489, ACTIVE 2 sec, process no 5488, OS thread id 1141422400
   starting index read, thread declared inside InnoDB 500
18 mysql tables in use 1, locked 1
19 4 lock struct(s), heap size 1216
20 MySQL thread id 12, query id 351 localhost baron Updating
21 UPDATE test.tiny_dl SET a = 1 WHERE a <> 1
22 *** (2) HOLDS THE LOCK(S):
23 RECORD LOCKS space id 0 page no 3662 n bits 72 index `GEN_CLUST_INDEX` of table
   `test/tiny_dl` trx id 0 3793489 lock mode S
24 Record lock, heap no 1 PHYSICAL RECORD: n_fields 1; compact format; info bits 0
25  0: ... [ omitted ] ...
26
27 *** (2) WAITING FOR THIS LOCK TO BE GRANTED:
28 RECORD LOCKS space id 0 page no 3662 n bits 72 index `GEN_CLUST_INDEX` of table
   `test/tiny_dl` trx id 0 3793489 lock_mode X waiting
29 Record lock, heap no 2 PHYSICAL RECORD: n_fields 4; compact format; info bits 0
30  0: len 6; hex 000000000501 ...[ omitted ] ...
31
32 *** WE ROLL BACK TRANSACTION (2)
```

Line 4 shows when the deadlock occurred, and lines 5 through 10 show information about the first transaction involved in the deadlock. We explain the meaning of this output in detail in the next section.

Lines 11 through 15 show the locks transaction 1 was waiting for when the deadlock happened. We've omitted some of the information that's useful only for debugging InnoDB on line 14. The important thing to notice is line 12, which says this transaction wanted an exclusive (X) lock on GEN_CLUST_INDEX[5] on the test.tiny_dl table.

Lines 16 through 21 show the second transaction's status, and lines 22 through 26 show the locks it held. There are several records listed on line 25, which we've removed for brevity. One of these was the record for which the first transaction was waiting. Finally, lines 27 through 31 show the locks for which it was waiting.

A cycle in the waits-for graph occurs when each transaction holds a lock the other wants and wants a lock the other holds. InnoDB doesn't show all the locks held and waited for, but it often shows enough to help you determine what indexes the queries were using, which is valuable in determining whether you can avoid deadlocks.

If you can get both queries to scan the same index in the same direction, you can often reduce the number of deadlocks, because queries can't create a cycle when they request locks in the same order. This is sometimes easy to do. For example, if you need to update a number of records within a transaction, sort them by their primary key in the application's memory, then update them in that order—then they can't deadlock. At other times, however, it can be infeasible (such as when you have two processes that need to work on the same table but are using different indexes).

Line 32 shows which transaction was chosen as the deadlock victim. InnoDB tries to choose the transaction it thinks will be easiest to roll back, which is the one with the fewest updates.

It's very helpful to examine the general log, find all the queries from the threads involved, and see what really caused the deadlock. Read the next section to see where to find the thread ID in the deadlock output.

TRANSACTIONS

This section contains a little summary information about InnoDB transactions, followed by a list of the currently active transactions. Here are the first few lines (the header):

```
1   ------------
2   TRANSACTIONS
3   ------------
4   Trx id counter 0 80157601
5   Purge done for trx's n:o <0 80154573 undo n:o <0 0
6   History list length 6
7   Total number of lock structs in row lock hash table 0
```

The output varies depending on the MySQL version, but it includes at least the following:

---

5. This is the index InnoDB creates internally when you don't specify a primary key.

- Line 4: the current transaction identifier, which is a system variable that increments for each new transaction.
- Line 5: the transaction ID to which InnoDB has purged old MVCC row versions. You can see how many old versions haven't yet been purged by looking at the difference between this value and the current transaction ID. There's no hard and fast rule as to how large this number can safely get. If nothing is updating any data, a large number doesn't mean there's unpurged data, because all the transactions are actually looking at the same version of the database. On the other hand, if many rows are being updated, one or more versions of each row is staying in memory. The best policy for reducing overhead is to ensure that transactions commit when they're done instead of staying open a long time, because even an open transaction that doesn't do any work keeps InnoDB from purging old row versions.

  Also in line 5: the undo log record number InnoDB's purge process is currently working on, if any. If it's "0 0", as in our example, the purge process is idle.
- Line 6: the history list length, which is the number of pages in the undo space in InnoDB's data files. When a transaction performs updates and commits, this number increases; when the purge process removes the old versions, it decreases. The purge process also updates the value in line 5.
- Line 7: the number of lock structs. Each lock struct usually holds many row locks, so this is not the same as the number of rows locked.

The header is followed by a list of transactions. Current versions of MySQL don't support nested transactions, so there's a maximum of one transaction per client connection at a time, and each transaction belongs to only a single connection. Each transaction has at least two lines in the output. Here's a sample of the minimal information you'll see about a transaction:

```
1   ---TRANSACTION 0 3793494, not started, process no 5488, OS thread id 1141152064
2   MySQL thread id 15, query id 479 localhost baron
```

The first line begins with the transaction's ID and status. This transaction is "not started," which means it has committed and not issued any more statements that affect transactions; it's probably just idle. Then there's some process and thread information. The second line shows the MySQL process ID, which is also the same as the Id column in SHOW FULL PROCESSLIST. This is followed by an internal query number and some connection information (also the same as what you can find in SHOW FULL PROCESSLIST).

Each transaction can print much more information than that, though. Here's a more complex example:

```
1   ---TRANSACTION 0 80157600, ACTIVE 4 sec, process no 3396, OS thread id 1148250464,
    thread declared inside InnoDB 442
2   mysql tables in use 1, locked 0
3   MySQL thread id 8079, query id 728899 localhost baron Sending data
4   select sql_calc_found_rows * from b limit 5
5   Trx read view will not see trx with id>= 0 80157601, sees <0 80157597
```

Line 1 in this sample shows the transaction has been active for four seconds. The possible states are "not started," "active," "prepared," and "committed in memory" (once it commits to disk, the state will change to "not started"). You might also see information about what the transaction is currently doing, though this example doesn't show that. There are over 30 string constants in the source that can be printed here, such as "fetching rows," "adding foreign keys," and so on.

The "thread declared inside InnoDB 442" text on line 1 means the thread is doing some operation inside the InnoDB kernel and has 442 "tickets" left to use. In other words, the same SQL query is allowed to reenter the InnoDB kernel 442 more times. The ticket system limits thread concurrency inside the kernel to prevent thread thrashing on some platforms. Even if the thread's state is "inside InnoDB," the thread might not necessarily be doing all its work inside InnoDB; the query might be processing some operations at the server level and just interacting with the InnoDB kernel in some way. You might also see that the transaction's status is "sleeping before joining InnoDB queue" or "waiting in InnoDB queue."

The next line you might see shows how many tables the current statement has used and locked. InnoDB doesn't normally lock tables, but it does for some statements. Locked tables can also show up if the MySQL server has locked them at a higher level than InnoDB. If the transaction has locked any rows, there will be a line showing the number of lock structs (again, not the same thing as row locks) and the heap size; you can see examples of this in the earlier deadlock output. In MySQL 5.1 and newer, this line also shows the actual number of row locks the transaction holds.

The heap size is the amount of memory used to hold row locks. InnoDB implements row locks with a special table of bitmaps, which can theoretically use as little as one bit per row it locks. Our tests have shown that it generally uses no more than four bits per lock.

The third line in this example has a little more information than the second line in the previous sample: at the end of the line is the thread status, "Sending data." This is the same as what you'll see in the Command column in SHOW FULL PROCESSLIST.

If the transaction is actively running a query, the query's text (or, in some MySQL versions, just an excerpt of it) will come next, in this case in line 4.

Line 5 shows the transaction's read view, which indicates the range of transaction identifiers that are definitely visible and definitely invisible to the transaction because of versioning. In this case, there's a gap of four transactions between the two numbers. These four transactions might not be visible. When InnoDB executes a query, it must check the visibility of any rows whose transaction identifiers fall into this gap.

If the transaction is waiting for a lock, you'll also see the lock information just after the query. There are examples of this in the earlier deadlock sample as well. Unfortunately, the output doesn't say which other transaction *holds* the lock for which this transaction is waiting. You can find that in the INFORMATION_SCHEMA tables in MySQL 5.1 and newer, if you're using the InnoDB plugin.

If there are many transactions, InnoDB might limit the number it prints to try to keep the output from growing too large. You'll see " ...truncated... " if this happens.

FILE I/O

The FILE I/O section shows the state of the I/O helper threads, along with performance counters:

```
 1  --------
 2  FILE I/O
 3  --------
 4  I/O thread 0 state: waiting for i/o request (insert buffer thread)
 5  I/O thread 1 state: waiting for i/o request (log thread)
 6  I/O thread 2 state: waiting for i/o request (read thread)
 7  I/O thread 3 state: waiting for i/o request (write thread)
 8  Pending normal aio reads: 0, aio writes: 0,
 9   ibuf aio reads: 0, log i/o's: 0, sync i/o's: 0
10  Pending flushes (fsync) log: 0; buffer pool: 0
11  17909940 OS file reads, 22088963 OS file writes, 1743764 OS fsyncs
12  0.20 reads/s, 16384 avg bytes/read, 5.00 writes/s, 0.80 fsyncs/s
```

Lines 4 through 7 show the I/O helper thread states. Lines 8 through 10 show the number of pending operations for each helper thread, and the number of pending fsync() operations for the log and buffer pool threads. The abbreviation "aio" means "asynchronous I/O." Line 11 shows the number of reads, writes, and fsync() calls performed. Absolute values will vary with your workload, so it's more important to monitor how they change over time. Line 12 shows per-second averages over the time interval shown in the header section.

The pending values on lines 8 and 9 are good ways to detect an I/O-bound application. If most of these types of I/O have some pending operations, the workload is probably I/O-bound.

On Windows, you can adjust the number of I/O helper threads with the innodb _file_io_threads configuration variable, so you might see more than one read and write thread. And in MySQL 5.1 and newer with the InnoDB plugin, or with Percona Server, you can use innodb_read_io_threads and innodb_write_io_threads to configure multiple threads for reading and writing. However, you'll always see at least these four threads on all platforms:

Insert buffer thread
> Responsible for insert buffer merges (i.e., records being merged from the insert buffer into the tablespace)

Log thread
> Responsible for asynchronous log flushes

Read thread
    Performs read-ahead operations to try to prefetch data InnoDB predicts it will need

Write thread
    Flushes dirty buffers

INSERT BUFFER AND ADAPTIVE HASH INDEX

This section shows the status of these two structures inside InnoDB:

```
1   -------------------------------------
2   INSERT BUFFER AND ADAPTIVE HASH INDEX
3   -------------------------------------
4   Ibuf for space 0: size 1, free list len 887, seg size 889, is not empty
5   Ibuf for space 0: size 1, free list len 887, seg size 889,
6   2431891 inserts, 2672643 merged recs, 1059730 merges
7   Hash table size 8850487, used cells 2381348, node heap has 4091 buffer(s)
8   2208.17 hash searches/s, 175.05 non-hash searches/s
```

Line 4 shows information about the insert buffer's size, the length of its "free list," and its segment size. The text "for space 0" seems to indicate the possibility of multiple insert buffers—one per tablespace—but that was never implemented, and this text has been removed in more recent MySQL versions. There's only one insert buffer, so line 5 is really redundant. Line 6 shows statistics about how many buffer operations InnoDB has done. The ratio of merges to inserts gives a good idea of how efficient the buffer is.

Line 7 shows the adaptive hash index's status. Line 8 shows how many hash index operations InnoDB has done over the time frame mentioned in the header section. The ratio of hash index lookups to non-hash index lookups is advisory information; you can't configure the adaptive hash index.

LOG

This section shows statistics about InnoDB's transaction log (redo log) subsystem:

```
1   ---
2   LOG
3   ---
4   Log sequence number 84 3000620880
5   Log flushed up to   84 3000611265
6   Last checkpoint at  84 2939889199
7   0 pending log writes, 0 pending chkp writes
8   14073669 log i/o's done, 10.90 log i/o's/second
```

Line 4 shows the current log sequence number, and line 5 shows the point up to which the logs have been flushed. The log sequence number is just the number of bytes written to the log files, so you can use it to calculate how much data in the log buffer has not yet been flushed to the log files. In this case, it is 9,615 bytes (13000620880–13000611265). Line 6 shows the last checkpoint (a checkpoint identifies an instant at which the data and log files were in a known state, and can be used for recovery). If the last checkpoint falls too far behind the log sequence number, and the difference becomes close to the size of the log files, InnoDB will trigger "furious flushing," which is very bad for performance. Lines 7 and 8 show pending log operations and statistics, which you can compare to values in the FILE I/O section to see how much of your I/O is caused by your log subsystem relative to other causes of I/O.

BUFFER POOL AND MEMORY

This section shows statistics about InnoDB's buffer pool and how it uses memory:

```
 1  ----------------------
 2  BUFFER POOL AND MEMORY
 3  ----------------------
 4  Total memory allocated 4648979546; in additional pool allocated 16773888
 5  Buffer pool size    262144
 6  Free buffers         0
 7  Database pages          258053
 8  Modified db pages   37491
 9  Pending reads 0
10  Pending writes: LRU 0, flush list 0, single page 0
11  Pages read 57973114, created 251137, written 10761167
12  9.79 reads/s, 0.31 creates/s, 6.00 writes/s
13  Buffer pool hit rate 999 / 1000
```

Line 4 shows the total memory allocated by InnoDB, and how much of that amount is allocated in the additional memory pool. The additional memory pool is just a (typically small) amount of memory it allocates when it wants to use its own internal memory allocator. Modern versions of InnoDB typically use the operating system's memory allocator, but older versions had their own allocator because some operating systems didn't provide a very good implementation.

Lines 5 through 8 show buffer pool metrics, in units of pages. The metrics are the total buffer pool size, the number of free pages, the number of pages allocated to store database pages, and the number of "dirty" database pages. InnoDB uses some pages in the buffer pool for lock indexes, the adaptive hash index, and other system structures, so the number of database pages in the pool will never equal the total pool size.

Lines 9 and 10 show the number of pending reads and writes (i.e., the number of logical reads and writes InnoDB needs to do for the buffer pool). These values will not match values in the FILE I/O section, because InnoDB might merge many logical operations into a single physical I/O operation. LRU stands for "least recently used"; it's a method of freeing space for frequently used pages by flushing infrequently used ones from the buffer pool. The flush list holds old pages that need to be flushed by the checkpoint process, and single page writes are independent page writes that won't be merged.

Line 8 in this output shows that the buffer pool contains 37,491 dirty pages, which need to be flushed to disk at some point (they have been modified in memory but not on disk). However, line 10 shows that no flushes are scheduled at the moment. This is not a problem; InnoDB will flush them when it needs to. If you see a high number of pending I/O operations anywhere in InnoDB's status output, it's typically indicative of a pretty severe problem.

Line 11 shows how many pages InnoDB has read, created, and written. The pages read and written values refer to data that's read into the buffer pool from disk, or vice versa. The pages created value refers to pages that InnoDB allocates in the buffer pool without reading their contents from the data file, because it doesn't care what the contents are (for example, they might have belonged to a table that has since been dropped).

Line 13 reports the buffer pool hit rate, which measures the rate at which InnoDB finds the pages it needs in the buffer pool. It measures hits since the last InnoDB status printout, so if the server has been quiet since then, you'll see "No buffer pool page gets since the last printout." It's not useful as a metric for buffer pool sizing.

In MySQL 5.5, there might be several buffer pools, and each one will print out a section in the output. Percona XtraDB will also print more detailed output—for example, showing exactly where memory is allocated.

ROW OPERATIONS

This section shows miscellaneous InnoDB statistics:

```
 1  --------------
 2  ROW OPERATIONS
 3  --------------
 4  0 queries inside InnoDB, 0 queries in queue
 5  1 read views open inside InnoDB
 6  Main thread process no. 10099, id 88021936, state: waiting for server activity
 7  Number of rows inserted 143, updated 3000041, deleted 0, read 24865563
 8  0.00 inserts/s, 0.00 updates/s, 0.00 deletes/s, 0.00 reads/s
 9  ----------------------------
10  END OF INNODB MONITOR OUTPUT
11  ============================
```

Line 4 shows how many threads are inside the InnoDB kernel (we referred to this in our discussion of the TRANSACTIONS section). Queries in the queue are threads InnoDB is not admitting into the kernel yet to restrict the number of threads concurrently executing. Queries can also be sleeping before they go into the queue to wait, as discussed earlier.

Line 5 shows how many read views InnoDB has open. A read view is a consistent MVCC "snapshot" of the database's contents as of the point the transaction started. You can see whether a specific transaction has a read view in the TRANSACTIONS section.

Line 6 shows the kernel's main thread status. Possible status values are as follows:

- doing background drop tables
- doing insert buffer merge
- flushing buffer pool pages

- flushing log
- making checkpoint
- purging
- reserving kernel mutex
- sleeping
- suspending
- waiting for buffer pool flush to end
- waiting for server activity

You should usually see "sleeping" in most servers, and if you take several snapshots and repeatedly see a different status, such as "flushing buffer pool pages," you should suspect a problem with the related activity—for example, a "furious flushing" problem caused by a version of InnoDB with a poor flushing algorithm, or poor configuration such as too-small transaction log files.

Lines 7 and 8 show statistics on the number of rows inserted, updated, deleted, and read, and per-second averages of these values. These are good numbers to monitor if you want to watch how much work InnoDB is doing.

The SHOW ENGINE INNODB STATUS output ends with lines 9 through 13. If you don't see this text, you probably have a very large deadlock that's truncating the output.

SHOW PROCESSLIST

The process list is the list of connections, or threads, that are currently connected to MySQL. SHOW PROCESSLIST lists the threads, with information about each thread's status. For example:

```
mysql> SHOW FULL PROCESSLIST\G
*************************** 1. row ***************************
     Id: 61539
   User: sphinx
   Host: se02:58392
     db: art136
Command: Query
   Time: 0
  State: Sending data
   Info: SELECT a.id id, a.site_id site_id, unix_timestamp(inserted) AS
inserted,forum_id, unix_timestamp(p
*************************** 2. row ***************************
     Id: 65094
   User: mailboxer
   Host: db01:59659
     db: link84
Command: Killed
   Time: 12931
  State: end
```

```
    Info: update link84.link_in84 set url_to =
replace(replace(url_to,'&amp;','&'),'%20','+'), url_prefix=repl
```

There are several tools (such as *innotop*) that can show you an updating view of the process list.

You can also retrieve this information from a table in the INFORMATION_SCHEMA. Percona Server and MariaDB add more useful information to this table, such as a high-resolution time column or a column that indicates how much work the query has done, which you can use as a progress indicator.

The Command and State columns are where the thread's "status" is really indicated. Notice that the first of our processes is running a query and sending data while the second has been killed, probably because it took a very long time to complete and someone deliberately terminated it with the KILL command. A thread can remain in this state for some time, because a kill might not complete instantly. For example, it might take a while to roll back the thread's transaction.

SHOW FULL PROCESSLIST (with the added FULL keyword) shows the full text of each query, which is otherwise truncated after 100 characters.

SHOW ENGINE INNODB MUTEX

SHOW ENGINE INNODB MUTEX returns detailed InnoDB mutex information and is mostly useful for gaining insight into scalability and concurrency problems. Each mutex protects a critical section in the code, as explained previously.

The output varies depending on the MySQL version and compile options. Here's a sample from a MySQL 5.5 server:

```
mysql> SHOW ENGINE INNODB MUTEX;
+--------+----------------------------+-------------+
| Type   | Name                       | Status      |
+--------+----------------------------+-------------+
| InnoDB | &table->autoinc_mutex      | os_waits=1  |
| InnoDB | &table->autoinc_mutex      | os_waits=1  |
| InnoDB | &table->autoinc_mutex      | os_waits=4  |
| InnoDB | &table->autoinc_mutex      | os_waits=1  |
| InnoDB | &table->autoinc_mutex      | os_waits=12 |
| InnoDB | &dict_sys->mutex           | os_waits=1  |
| InnoDB | &log_sys->mutex            | os_waits=12 |
| InnoDB | &fil_system->mutex         | os_waits=11 |
| InnoDB | &kernel_mutex              | os_waits=1  |
| InnoDB | &dict_table_stats_latches[i] | os_waits=2  |
| InnoDB | &dict_table_stats_latches[i] | os_waits=54 |
| InnoDB | &dict_table_stats_latches[i] | os_waits=1  |
| InnoDB | &dict_table_stats_latches[i] | os_waits=31 |
| InnoDB | &dict_table_stats_latches[i] | os_waits=41 |
| InnoDB | &dict_table_stats_latches[i] | os_waits=12 |
| InnoDB | &dict_table_stats_latches[i] | os_waits=1  |
| InnoDB | &dict_table_stats_latches[i] | os_waits=90 |
| InnoDB | &dict_table_stats_latches[i] | os_waits=1  |
```

```
| InnoDB | &dict_operation_lock        | os_waits=13 |
| InnoDB | &log_sys->checkpoint_lock   | os_waits=66 |
| InnoDB | combined &block->lock       | os_waits=2  |
+--------+-----------------------------+-------------+
```

You can use the output to help determine which parts of InnoDB are bottlenecks, based on the number of waits. Anywhere there's a mutex, there's a potential for contention. You might need to write a script to aggregate the output, which can be very large.

There are three main strategies for easing mutex-related bottlenecks: try to avoid InnoDB's weak points, try to limit concurrency, or try to balance between CPU-intensive spin waits and resource-intensive operating system waits. We discussed this earlier in this appendix, and in Chapter 8.

Replication Status

MySQL has several commands for monitoring replication. On a master server, SHOW MASTER STATUS shows the master's replication status and configuration:

```
mysql> SHOW MASTER STATUS\G
*************************** 1. row ***************************
            File: mysql-bin.000079
        Position: 13847
    Binlog_Do_DB:
Binlog_Ignore_DB:
```

The output includes the master's current binary log position. You can get a list of binary logs with SHOW BINARY LOGS:

```
mysql> SHOW BINARY LOGS
+------------------+-----------+
| Log_name         | File_size |
+------------------+-----------+
| mysql-bin.000044 |     13677 |
...
| mysql-bin.000079 |     13847 |
+------------------+-----------+
36 rows in set (0.18 sec)
```

To view the events in the binary logs, use SHOW BINLOG EVENTS. In MySQL 5.5, you can also use SHOW RELAYLOG EVENTS.

On a replica server, you can view the replica's status and configuration with SHOW SLAVE STATUS. We won't include the output here, because it's a bit verbose, but we will note a few things about it. First, you can see the status of both the replica I/O and replica SQL threads, including any errors. You can also see how far behind the replica is in replication. Finally, for the purposes of backups and cloning replicas, there are three sets of binary log coordinates in the output:

Master_Log_File/Read_Master_Log_Pos
  The position at which the I/O thread is reading in the master's binary logs.

Relay_Log_File/Relay_Log_Pos

    The position at which the SQL thread is executing in the replica's relay logs.

Relay_Master_Log_File/Exec_Master_Log_Pos

    The position at which the SQL thread is executing in the master's binary logs. This is the same logical position as Relay_Log_File/Relay_Log_Pos, but it's in the replica's relay logs instead of the master's binary logs. In other words, if you look at these two positions in the logs, you will find the same log events.

The INFORMATION_SCHEMA

The INFORMATION_SCHEMA database is a set of system views defined in the SQL standard. MySQL implements many of the standard views and adds some others. In MySQL 5.1, many of the views correspond to MySQL's SHOW commands, such as SHOW FULL PROCESSLIST and SHOW STATUS. However, there are also some views that have no corresponding SHOW command.

The beauty of the INFORMATION_SCHEMA views is that you can query them with standard SQL. This gives you much more flexibility than the SHOW commands, which produce result sets that you can't aggregate, join, or otherwise manipulate with standard SQL. Having all this data available in system views makes it possible to write interesting and useful queries.

For example, what tables have a reference to the actor table in the Sakila sample database? The consistent naming convention makes this relatively easy to determine:

```
mysql> SELECT TABLE_NAME FROM INFORMATION_SCHEMA.COLUMNS
    -> WHERE TABLE_SCHEMA='sakila' AND COLUMN_NAME='actor_id'
    -> AND TABLE_NAME <> 'actor';
+------------+
| TABLE_NAME |
+------------+
| actor_info |
| film_actor |
+------------+
```

We needed to find tables with multiple-column indexes for several of the examples in this book. Here's a query for that:

```
mysql> SELECT TABLE_NAME, GROUP_CONCAT(COLUMN_NAME)
    -> FROM INFORMATION_SCHEMA.KEY_COLUMN_USAGE
    -> WHERE TABLE_SCHEMA='sakila'
    -> GROUP BY TABLE_NAME, CONSTRAINT_NAME
    -> HAVING COUNT(*) > 1;
+---------------+---------------------------------------+
| TABLE_NAME    | GROUP_CONCAT(COLUMN_NAME)             |
+---------------+---------------------------------------+
| film_actor    | actor_id,film_id                      |
| film_category | film_id,category_id                   |
| rental        | customer_id,rental_date,inventory_id  |
+---------------+---------------------------------------+
```

You can also write more complex queries, just as you would against any ordinary tables. The MySQL Forge (*http://forge.mysql.com*) is a great place to find and share queries against these views. There are samples to find duplicate or redundant indexes, find indexes with very low cardinality, and much more. There is also a set of useful views written on top of the INFORMATION_SCHEMA views in Shlomi Noach's *common_schema* project (*http://code.openark.org/forge/common_schema*).

The biggest drawback is that the views are sometimes very slow compared to the corresponding SHOW commands. They typically fetch all the data, store it in a temporary table, then make the temporary table available to the query. Querying the INFORMATION_SCHEMA tables on a server with a lot of data or many tables can cause a great deal of load on the server, and can cause the server to stall or become unresponsive to other users, so do be cautious about using it on a heavily loaded, large server in production. The main tables that can be dangerous to query are the ones that contain table metadata: TABLES, COLUMNS, REFERENTIAL_CONSTRAINTS, KEY_COLUMN_USAGE, and so forth. Queries against these tables can cause MySQL to ask the storage engine for data such as index statistics on the tables in the server, which is especially burdensome in InnoDB.

The views aren't updatable. Although you can retrieve server settings from them, you can't update them to influence the server's configuration, so you'll still need to use the SHOW and SET commands for configuration, even though the INFORMATION_SCHEMA views are very useful for other tasks.

InnoDB Tables

In MySQL 5.1 and newer, the InnoDB plugin creates a number of INFORMATION_SCHEMA tables. These are very helpful. There are more in MySQL 5.5, and even more in the unreleased MySQL 5.6.

In MySQL 5.1, the following tables exist:

INNODB_CMP *and* INNODB_CMP_RESET
> These tables show information about data that's compressed in InnoDB's new file format, Barracuda. The second table shows the same information as the first but has the side effect of resetting the data it contains, sort of like using a FLUSH command.

INNODB_CMPMEM *and* INNODB_CMPMEM_RESET
> These tables show information about buffer pool pages used for InnoDB compressed data. The second table is again a reset table.

INNODB_TRX *and* INNODB_LOCKS
> These tables show transactions, and transactions that hold and wait for locks. They are very important for diagnosing lock wait problems and long-running transactions. The MySQL manual contains sample queries you can copy and paste to show which transactions are blocking which others, the queries they're running, and so forth.

In addition to these tables, MySQL 5.5 adds `INNODB_LOCK_WAITS`, which can help diagnose more types of lock-waiting problems more easily. MySQL 5.6 will add tables that show more information about InnoDB's internals, including the buffer pool and data dictionary, and a new table called `INNODB_METRICS`, which will be an alternative to using the Performance Schema.

Tables in Percona Server

Percona Server adds a large number of tables to the `INFORMATION_SCHEMA` database. The stock MySQL 5.5 server has 39 tables, and Percona Server 5.5 has 61 tables. Here's an overview of the additional tables:

The "user statistics" tables
> These tables originated in Google's patches for MySQL. They show activity statistics for clients, indexes, tables, threads, and users. We've mentioned uses for these throughout this book, such as determining when replication is beginning to approach the limit of its ability to keep up with the master.

The InnoDB data dictionary
> A series of tables that expose InnoDB's internal data dictionary as read-only tables: columns, foreign keys, indexes, statistics, and so on. These are very helpful for examining and understanding InnoDB's view of the database, which can differ from MySQL's due to MySQL's reliance on *.frm* files to store the data dictionary. Similar tables will be included with MySQL 5.6 when it is released.

The InnoDB buffer pool
> These tables let you query the buffer pool as though it's a table where each page is a row, so you can see what pages are resident in the buffer pool, what types of pages they are, and so on. These tables have proven useful for diagnosing problems such as a bloated insert buffer.

Temporary tables
> These tables show the same type of information available in the `INFORMATION_SCHEMA.TABLES` table, but for temporary tables instead. There is one for your own session's temporary tables, and one for all temporary tables in the whole server. Both are helpful for gaining visibility into which temporary tables exist, for which sessions, and how much space they're using.

Miscellaneous tables
> There are a handful of other tables that add visibility into query execution times, files, tablespaces, and more InnoDB internals.

The documentation for Percona Server's additional tables is available at *http://www.percona.com/doc/*.

The Performance Schema

The Performance Schema (which resides in the PERFORMANCE_SCHEMA database) is MySQL's new home for enhanced instrumentation, as of MySQL 5.5. We discussed it a bit in Chapter 3.

By default, the Performance Schema is disabled, and you have to turn it on and enable specific instrumentation points ("consumers") that you wish to collect. We benchmarked the server in a few different configurations and found that the Performance Schema caused around an 8% to 11% overhead even when it was collecting no data, and 19% to 25% with all consumers enabled, depending on whether it was a read-only or read/write workload. Whether this is a little or a lot is up to you to decide.

This is slated to improve in MySQL 5.6, especially when the feature itself is enabled but all of the instrumentation points are disabled. This will make it more practical for some users to enable the Performance Schema, but leave it inactive until they want to gather some information.

In MySQL 5.5, the Performance Schema contains tables that instrument instances of condition variables, mutexes, read/write locks, and file I/O. There are also tables that instrument the waits on the instances, and these are what you'll usually be interested in querying first, with joins to the instance tables. These event wait tables come in a few variations that hold current and historical information about server performance and behavior. Finally, there are is a group of "setup tables," which you use to enable or disable the desired consumers.

In MySQL 5.6.3 development milestone release 6, the number of tables in the Performance Schema increases from 17 to 49. That means that there is a lot more instrumentation in MySQL 5.6! Added instrumentation includes SQL statements, stages of statements (basically the same thing as the thread status you can see in SHOW PROCESS LIST), tables, indexes, hosts, threads, users, accounts, and a larger variety of summary and history tables, among other things.

How can you use these tables? With 49 of them, the time has come for someone to write tools to help with this. However, for some good examples of old-fashioned SQL against the Performance Schema tables, you can read some of the articles on Oracle engineer Mark Leith's blog, such as *http://www.markleith.co.uk/?p=471*.

Summary

MySQL's primary means of exposing server internals is the SHOW commands, but that's changing. The introduction in MySQL 5.1 of pluggable INFORMATION_SCHEMA tables permitted the InnoDB plugin to add some very valuable instrumentation, and Percona Server adds many more. However, the ability to read SHOW ENGINE INNODB STATUS output and interpret it remains essential for managing InnoDB. In MySQL 5.5 and newer server versions, the Performance Schema is available, and it will probably become the most powerful and complete means of inspecting the server's internals. The great thing about the Performance Schema is that it's time-based, meaning that MySQL is finally getting instrumented for elapsed time, not just operation counts.

Transferring Large Files

Copying, compressing, and decompressing huge files (often across a network) are common tasks when administering MySQL, initializing servers, cloning replicas, and performing backups and recovery operations. The fastest and best ways to do these jobs are not always the most obvious, and the difference between good and bad methods can be significant. This appendix shows some examples of how to copy a large backup image from one server to another using common Unix utilities.

It's common to begin with an *uncompressed* file, such as one server's InnoDB tablespace and log files. You also want the file to be decompressed when you finish copying it to the destination, of course. The other common scenario is to begin with a *compressed* file, such as a backup image, and finish with a decompressed file.

If you have limited network capacity, it's usually a good idea to send the files across the network in compressed form. You might also need to do a secure transfer, so your data isn't compromised; this is a common requirement for backup images.

Copying Files

The task, then, is to do the following efficiently:

1. (Optionally) compress the data.
2. Send it to another machine.
3. Decompress the data into its final destination.
4. Verify the files aren't corrupted after copying.

We've benchmarked various methods of achieving these goals. The rest of this appendix shows you how we did it and what we found to be the fastest way.

For many of the purposes we've discussed in this book, such as backups, you might want to consider which machine to do the compression on. If you have the network bandwidth, you can copy your backup images uncompressed and save the CPU resources on your MySQL server for queries.

A Naïve Example

We begin with a naïve example of how to send an uncompressed file securely from one machine to another, compress it en route, and then decompress it. On the source server, which we call `server1`, we execute the following:

```
server1$ gzip -c /backup/mydb/mytable.MYD > mytable.MYD.gz
server1$ scp mytable.MYD.gz root@server2:/var/lib/myql/mydb/
```

And then, on `server2`:

```
server2$ gunzip /var/lib/mysql/mydb/mytable.MYD.gz
```

This is probably the simplest approach, but it's not very efficient because it serializes the steps involved in compressing, copying, and decompressing the file. Each step also requires reads from and writes to disk, which is slow. Here's what really happens during each of the above commands: the *gzip* performs both reads and writes on `server1`, the *scp* reads on `server1` and writes on `server2`, and the *gunzip* reads and writes on `server2`.

A One-Step Method

It's more efficient to compress and copy the file and then decompress it on the other end in one step. This time we use SSH, the secure protocol upon which SCP is based. Here's the command we execute on `server1`:

```
server1$ gzip -c /backup/mydb/mytable.MYD | ssh root@server2"gunzip -c - > /var/lib
>/mysql/mydb/mytable.MYD"
```

This usually performs much better than the first method, because it significantly reduces disk I/O: the disk activity is reduced to reading on `server1` and writing on `server2`. This lets the disk operate sequentially.

You can also use SSH's built-in compression to do this, but we've shown you how to compress and decompress with pipes because they give you more flexibility. For example, if you didn't want to decompress the file on the other end, you wouldn't want to use SSH compression.

You can improve on this method by tweaking some options, such as adding *-1* to make the *gzip* compression faster. This usually doesn't lower the compression ratio much, but it can make it much faster, which is important. You can also use different compression algorithms. For example, if you want very high compression and don't care about how long it takes, you can use *bzip2* instead of *gzip*. If you want very fast compression, you can instead use an LZO-based archiver. The compressed data might be about 20% larger, but the compression will be around five times faster.

Avoiding Encryption Overhead

SSH isn't the fastest way to transport data across the network, because it adds the overhead of encrypting and decrypting. If you don't need encryption, you can just copy the "raw" bits over the network with *netcat*. You invoke this tool as *nc* for noninteractive operations, which is what we want.

Here's an example. First, let's start listening for the file on port 12345 (any unused port will do) on server2, and uncompress anything sent to that port to the desired data file:

```
server2$ nc -l -p 12345 | gunzip -c - > /var/lib/mysql/mydb/mytable.MYD
```

On server1, we then start another instance of *netcat*, sending to the port on which the destination is listening. The *-q* option tells *netcat* to close the connection after it sees the end of the incoming file. This will cause the listening instance to close the destination file and quit:

```
server1$ gzip -c - /var/lib/mysql/mydb/mytable.MYD | nc -q 1 server2 12345
```

An even easier technique is to use *tar* so filenames are sent across the wire, eliminating another source of errors and automatically writing the files to their correct locations. The *z* option tells *tar* to use *gzip* compression and decompression. Here's the command to execute on server2:

```
server2$ nc -l -p 12345 | tar xvzf -
```

And here's the command for server1:

```
server1$ tar cvzf - /var/lib/mysql/mydb/mytable.MYD | nc -q 1 server2 12345
```

You can assemble these commands into a single script that will compress and copy lots of files into the network connection efficiently, then decompress them on the other side.

Other Options

Another option is *rsync*. *rsync* is convenient because it makes it easy to mirror the source and destination and because it can restart interrupted file transfers, but it doesn't tend to work as well when its binary difference algorithm can't be put to good use. You might consider using it for cases where you know most of the file doesn't need to be sent—for example, for finishing an aborted *nc* copy operation.

You should experiment with file copying when you're not in a crisis situation, because it will take a little trial and error to discover the fastest method. Which method performs best will depend on your system. The biggest factors are how many disk drives, network cards, and CPUs you have, and how fast they are relative to each other. It's a good idea to monitor *vmstat -n 5* to see whether the disk or the CPU is the speed bottleneck.

If you have idle CPUs, you can probably speed up the process by running several copy operations in parallel. Conversely, if the CPU is the bottleneck and you have lots of disk and network capacity, omit the compression. As with dumping and restoring, it's often a good idea to do these operations in parallel for speed. Again, monitor your servers' performance to see if you have unused capacity. Trying to overparallelize might just slow things down.

File Copy Benchmarks

For the sake of comparison, Table C-1 shows how quickly we were able to copy a sample file over a standard 100 Mbps Ethernet link on a LAN. The file was 738 MB uncompressed and compressed to 100 MB with *gzip*'s default options. The source and destination machines had plenty of available memory, CPU resources, and disk capacity; the network was the bottleneck.

Table C-1. Benchmarks for copying files across a network

Method	Time (seconds)
rsync without compression	71
scp without compression	68
nc without compression	67
rsync with compression (*-z*)	63
gzip, *scp*, and *gunzip*	60 (44 + 10 + 6)
ssh with compression	44
nc with compression	42

Notice how much it helped to compress the file when sending it across the network—the three slowest methods didn't compress the file. Your mileage will vary, however. If you have slow CPUs and disks and a gigabit Ethernet connection, reading and compressing the data might be the bottleneck, and it might be faster to skip the compression.

By the way, it's often much faster to use fast compression, such as *gzip --fast*, than to use the default compression levels, which use a lot of CPU time to compress the file only slightly more. Our test used the default compression level.

The last step in transferring data is to verify that the copy didn't corrupt the files. You can use a variety of methods for this, such as *md5sum*, but it's rather expensive to do a full scan of the file again. This is another reason why compression is helpful: the compression itself typically includes at least a cyclic redundancy check (CRC), which should catch any errors, so you get error checking for free.

Using EXPLAIN

This appendix shows you how to invoke EXPLAIN to get information about the query execution plan, and how to interpret the output. The EXPLAIN command is the main way to find out how the query optimizer decides to execute queries. This feature has limitations and doesn't always tell the truth, but its output is the best information available, and it's worth studying so you can learn how your queries are executed. Learning to interpret EXPLAIN will also help you learn how MySQL's optimizer works.

Invoking EXPLAIN

To use EXPLAIN, simply add the word EXPLAIN just before the SELECT keyword in your query. MySQL will set a flag on the query. When it executes the query, the flag causes it to return information about each step in the execution plan, instead of executing it. It returns one or more rows, which show each part of the execution plan and the order of execution.

Here's the simplest possible EXPLAIN result:

```
mysql> EXPLAIN SELECT 1\G
*************************** 1. row ***************************
           id: 1
  select_type: SIMPLE
        table: NULL
         type: NULL
possible_keys: NULL
          key: NULL
      key_len: NULL
          ref: NULL
         rows: NULL
        Extra: No tables used
```

There's one row in the output per table in the query. If the query joins two tables, there will be two rows of output. An aliased table counts as a separate table, so if you join a table to itself, there will be two rows in the output. The meaning of "table" is fairly broad here: it can mean a subquery, a UNION result, and so on. You'll see later why this is so.

There are two important variations on EXPLAIN:

- EXPLAIN EXTENDED appears to behave just like a normal EXPLAIN, but it tells the server to "reverse compile" the execution plan into a SELECT statement. You can see this generated statement by running SHOW WARNINGS immediately afterward. The statement comes directly from the execution plan, not from the original SQL statement, which by this point has been reduced to a data structure. It will not be the same as the original statement in most cases. You can examine it to see exactly how the query optimizer has transformed the statement. EXPLAIN EXTENDED is available in MySQL 5.0 and newer, and it adds an extra filtered column in MySQL 5.1 (more on that later).

- EXPLAIN PARTITIONS shows the partitions the query will access, if applicable. It is available only in MySQL 5.1 and newer.

It's a common mistake to think that MySQL doesn't execute a query when you add EXPLAIN to it. In fact, if the query contains a subquery in the FROM clause, MySQL actually executes the subquery, places its results into a temporary table, and then finishes optimizing the outer query. It has to process all such subqueries before it can optimize the outer query fully, which it must do for EXPLAIN.[1] This means EXPLAIN can actually cause a great deal of work for the server if the statement contains expensive subqueries or views that use the TEMPTABLE algorithm.

Bear in mind that EXPLAIN is an approximation, nothing more. Sometimes it's a good approximation, but at other times, it can be very far from the truth. Here are some of its limitations:

- EXPLAIN doesn't tell you anything about how triggers, stored functions, or UDFs will affect your query.

- It doesn't work for stored procedures, although you can extract the queries manually and EXPLAIN them individually.

- It doesn't tell you about ad hoc optimizations MySQL does during query execution.

- Some of the statistics it shows are estimates and can be very inaccurate.

- It doesn't show you everything there is to know about a query's execution plan. (The MySQL developers are adding more information when possible.)

- It doesn't distinguish between some things with the same name. For example, it uses "filesort" for in-memory sorts and for temporary files, and it displays "Using temporary" for temporary tables on disk and in memory.

---

1. This limitation will be lifted in MySQL 5.6.

- It can be misleading. For example, it can show a full index scan for a query with a small LIMIT. (MySQL 5.1's EXPLAIN shows more accurate information about the number of rows to be examined, but earlier versions don't take LIMIT into account.)

Rewriting Non-SELECT Queries

MySQL explains only SELECT queries, not stored routine calls or INSERT, UPDATE, DELETE, or any other statements. However, you can rewrite some non-SELECT queries to be EXPLAIN-able. To do this, you just need to convert the statement into an equivalent SELECT that accesses all the same columns. Any column mentioned must be in a SELECT list, a join clause, or a WHERE clause.

For example, suppose you want to rewrite the following UPDATE statement to make it EXPLAIN-able:

```
UPDATE sakila.actor
    INNER JOIN sakila.film_actor USING (actor_id)
SET actor.last_update=film_actor.last_update;
```

The following EXPLAIN statement is *not* equivalent to the UPDATE, because it doesn't require the server to retrieve the last_update column from either table:

```
mysql> EXPLAIN SELECT film_actor.actor_id
    -> FROM sakila.actor
    ->     INNER JOIN sakila.film_actor USING (actor_id)\G
*************************** 1. row ***************************
           id: 1
  select_type: SIMPLE
        table: actor
         type: index
possible_keys: PRIMARY
          key: PRIMARY
      key_len: 2
          ref: NULL
         rows: 200
        Extra: Using index
*************************** 2. row ***************************
           id: 1
  select_type: SIMPLE
        table: film_actor
         type: ref
possible_keys: PRIMARY
          key: PRIMARY
      key_len: 2
          ref: sakila.actor.actor_id
         rows: 13
        Extra: Using index
```

This difference is very important. The output shows that MySQL will use covering indexes, for example, which it can't use when retrieving and updating the last_updated column. The following statement is much closer to the original:

```
mysql> EXPLAIN SELECT film_actor.last_update, actor.last_update
    -> FROM sakila.actor
    ->     INNER JOIN sakila.film_actor USING (actor_id)\G
*************************** 1. row ***************************
           id: 1
  select_type: SIMPLE
        table: actor
         type: ALL
possible_keys: PRIMARY
          key: NULL
      key_len: NULL
          ref: NULL
         rows: 200
        Extra:
*************************** 2. row ***************************
           id: 1
  select_type: SIMPLE
        table: film_actor
         type: ref
possible_keys: PRIMARY
          key: PRIMARY
      key_len: 2
          ref: sakila.actor.actor_id
         rows: 13
        Extra:
```

Rewriting queries like this is not an exact science, but it's often good enough to help you understand what a query will do.[2]

It's important to understand that there is no such thing as an "equivalent" read query to show you the plan for a write query. A SELECT query needs to find only one copy of the data and return it to you. Any query that modifies data must find and modify all copies of it, in all indexes. This will often be much more expensive than what appears to be an equivalent SELECT query.

The Columns in EXPLAIN

EXPLAIN's output always has the same columns (except for EXPLAIN EXTENDED, which adds a filtered column in MySQL 5.1, and EXPLAIN PARTITIONS, which adds a partitions column). The variability is in the number and contents of the rows. However, to keep our examples clear, we don't always show all columns in this appendix.

In the following sections, we show you the meaning of each of the columns in an EXPLAIN result. Keep in mind that the rows in the output come in the order in which MySQL actually executes the parts of the query, which is not always the same as the order in which they appear in the original SQL.

---

2. MySQL 5.6 will permit you to explain non-SELECT queries. Hooray!

The id Column

This column always contains a number, which identifies the SELECT to which the row belongs. If there are no subqueries or unions in the statement, there is only one SELECT, so every row will show a 1 in this column. Otherwise, the inner SELECT statements generally will be numbered sequentially, according to their positions in the original statement.

MySQL divides SELECT queries into simple and complex types, and the complex types can be grouped into three broad classes: simple subqueries, so-called derived tables (subqueries in the FROM clause),[3] and UNIONs. Here's a simple subquery:

```
mysql> EXPLAIN SELECT (SELECT 1 FROM sakila.actor LIMIT 1) FROM sakila.film;
+----+-------------+-------+...
| id | select_type | table |...
+----+-------------+-------+...
|  1 | PRIMARY     | film  |...
|  2 | SUBQUERY    | actor |...
+----+-------------+-------+...
```

Subqueries in the FROM clause and UNIONs add more complexity to the id column. Here's a basic subquery in the FROM clause:

```
mysql> EXPLAIN SELECT film_id FROM (SELECT film_id FROM sakila.film) AS der;
+----+-------------+-----------+...
| id | select_type | table     |...
+----+-------------+-----------+...
|  1 | PRIMARY     | <derived2>|...
|  2 | DERIVED     | film      |...
+----+-------------+-----------+...
```

As you know, this query is executed with an anonymous temporary table. MySQL internally refers to the temporary table by its alias (der) within the outer query, which you can see in the ref column in more complicated queries.

Finally, here's a UNION query:

```
mysql> EXPLAIN SELECT 1 UNION ALL SELECT 1;
+------+--------------+-----------+...
| id   | select_type  | table     |...
+------+--------------+-----------+...
|  1   | PRIMARY      | NULL      |...
|  2   | UNION        | NULL      |...
| NULL | UNION RESULT | <union1,2>|...
+------+--------------+-----------+...
```

Note the extra row in the output for the result of the UNION. UNION results are always placed into an anonymous temporary table, and MySQL then reads the results back out of the temporary table. The temporary table doesn't appear in the original SQL, so its id column is NULL. In contrast to the preceding example (illustrating a subquery in

---

3. The statement "a subquery in the FROM clause is a derived table" is true, but "a derived table is a subquery in the FROM clause" is false. The term "derived table" has a broader meaning in SQL.

the FROM clause), the temporary table that results from this query is shown as the last row in the results, not the first.

So far this is all very straightforward, but mixtures of these three categories of statements can cause the output to become more complicated, as we'll see a bit later.

The select_type Column

This column shows whether the row is a simple or complex SELECT (and if it's the latter, which of the three complex types it is). The value SIMPLE means the query contains no subqueries or UNIONs. If the query has any such complex subparts, the outermost part is labeled PRIMARY, and other parts are labeled as follows:

SUBQUERY
  A SELECT that is contained in a subquery in the SELECT list (in other words, not in the FROM clause) is labeled as SUBQUERY.

DERIVED
  The value DERIVED is used for a SELECT that is contained in a subquery in the FROM clause, which MySQL executes recursively and places into a temporary table. The server refers to this as a "derived table" internally, because the temporary table is derived from the subquery.

UNION
  The second and subsequent SELECTs in a UNION are labeled as UNION. The first SELECT is labeled as though it is executed as part of the outer query. This is why the previous example showed the first SELECT in the UNION as PRIMARY. If the UNION were contained in a subquery in the FROM clause, its first SELECT would be labeled as DERIVED.

UNION RESULT
  The SELECT used to retrieve results from the UNION's anonymous temporary table is labeled as UNION RESULT.

In addition to these values, a SUBQUERY and a UNION can be labeled as DEPENDENT and UNCACHEABLE. DEPENDENT means the SELECT depends on data that is found in an outer query; UNCACHEABLE means something in the SELECT prevents the results from being cached with an Item_cache. (Item_cache is undocumented; it is not the same thing as the query cache, although it can be defeated by some of the same types of constructs, such as the RAND() function.)

The table Column

This column shows which table the row is accessing. In most cases, it's straightforward: it's the table, or its alias if the SQL specifies one.

You can read this column from top to bottom to see the join order MySQL's join optimizer chose for the query. For example, you can see that MySQL chose a different
join order than the one specified for the following query:

```
mysql> EXPLAIN SELECT film.film_id
    -> FROM sakila.film
    ->     INNER JOIN sakila.film_actor USING(film_id)
    ->     INNER JOIN sakila.actor USING(actor_id);
+----+-------------+------------+...
| id | select_type | table      |...
+----+-------------+------------+...
|  1 | SIMPLE      | actor      |...
|  1 | SIMPLE      | film_actor |...
|  1 | SIMPLE      | film       |...
+----+-------------+------------+...
```

Remember the left-deep tree diagrams we showed in Chapter 6? MySQL's query execution plans are always left-deep trees. If you flip the plan on its side, you can read off
the leaf nodes in order, and they'll correspond directly to the rows in EXPLAIN. The plan
for the preceding query looks like Figure D-1.

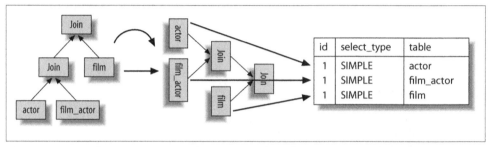

Figure D-1. How the query execution plan corresponds to the rows in EXPLAIN

Derived tables and unions

The table column becomes much more complicated when there is a subquery in the
FROM clause or a UNION. In these cases, there really isn't a "table" to refer to, because the
anonymous temporary table MySQL creates exists only while the query is executing.

When there's a subquery in the FROM clause, the table column is of the form
<derivedN>, where N is the subquery's id. This is always a "forward reference"—in
other words, N refers to a later row in the EXPLAIN output.

When there's a UNION, the UNION RESULT table column contains a list of ids that participate in the UNION. This is always a "backward reference," because the UNION RESULT
comes after all of the rows that participate in the UNION. If there are more than about
20 ids in the list, the table column might be truncated to keep it from getting too long,
and you won't be able to see all the values. Fortunately, you can still deduce which
rows were included, because you'll be able to see the first row's id. Everything that
comes between that row and the UNION RESULT is included in some way.

An example of complex SELECT types

Here's a nonsense query that serves as a fairly compact example of some of the complex SELECT types:

```
1   EXPLAIN
2   SELECT actor_id,
3      (SELECT 1 FROM sakila.film_actor WHERE film_actor.actor_id =
4          der_1.actor_id LIMIT 1)
5   FROM (
6      SELECT actor_id
7      FROM sakila.actor LIMIT 5
8   ) AS der_1
9   UNION ALL
10  SELECT film_id,
11     (SELECT @var1 FROM sakila.rental LIMIT 1)
12  FROM (
13     SELECT film_id,
14         (SELECT 1 FROM sakila.store LIMIT 1)
15     FROM sakila.film LIMIT 5
16  ) AS der_2;
```

The LIMIT clauses are just for convenience, in case you wish to execute the query without EXPLAIN and see the results. Here is the result of the EXPLAIN:

```
+------+---------------------+------------+...
| id   | select_type         | table      |...
+------+---------------------+------------+...
|    1 | PRIMARY             | <derived3> |...
|    3 | DERIVED             | actor      |...
|    2 | DEPENDENT SUBQUERY  | film_actor |...
|    4 | UNION               | <derived6> |...
|    6 | DERIVED             | film       |...
|    7 | SUBQUERY            | store      |...
|    5 | UNCACHEABLE SUBQUERY | rental    |...
| NULL | UNION RESULT        | <union1,4> |...
+------+---------------------+------------+...
```

We've been careful to make each part of the query access a different table, so you can see what goes where, but it's still hard to figure out! Taking it from the top:

- The first row is a forward reference to der_1, which the query has labeled as <derived3>. It comes from line 2 in the original SQL. To see which rows in the output refer to SELECT statements that are part of <derived3>, look forward ...

- ...to the second row, whose id is 3. It is 3 because it's part of the third SELECT in the query, and it's listed as a DERIVED type because it's nested inside a subquery in the FROM clause. It comes from lines 6 and 7 in the original SQL.

- The third row's id is 2. It comes from line 3 in the original SQL. Notice that it comes after a row with a higher id number, suggesting that it is executed afterward, which makes sense. It is listed as a DEPENDENT SUBQUERY, which means its results depend on the results of an outer query (also known as a *correlated subquery*). The outer query in this case is the SELECT that begins in line 2 and retrieves data from der_1.

- The fourth row is listed as a UNION, which means it is the second or later SELECT in a UNION. Its table is <derived6>, which means it's retrieving data from a subquery in the FROM clause and appending to a temporary table for the UNION. As before, to find the EXPLAIN rows that show the query plan for this subquery, you must look forward.

- The fifth row is the der_2 subquery defined in lines 13, 14, and 15 in the original SQL, which EXPLAIN refers to as <derived6>.

- The sixth row is an ordinary subquery in <derived6>'s SELECT list. Its id is 7, which is important...

- ...because it is greater than 5, which is the seventh row's id. Why is this important? Because it shows the boundaries of the <derived6> subquery. When EXPLAIN outputs a row whose SELECT type is DERIVED, it represents the beginning of a "nested scope." If a subsequent row's id is smaller (in this case, 5 is smaller than 6), it means the nested scope has closed. This lets us know that the seventh row is part of the SELECT list that is retrieving data from <derived6>—i.e., part of the fourth row's SELECT list (line 11 in the original SQL). This example is fairly easy to understand without knowing the significance and rules of nested scopes, but sometimes it's not so easy. The other notable thing about this row in the output is that it is listed as an UNCACHEABLE SUBQUERY because of the user variable.

- Finally, the last row is the UNION RESULT. It represents the stage of reading the rows from the UNION's temporary table. You can begin at this row and work backward if you wish; it is returning results from rows whose ids are 1 and 4, which are in turn references to <derived3> and <derived6>.

As you can see, the combination of these complicated SELECT types can result in EXPLAIN output that's pretty difficult to read. Understanding the rules makes it easier, but there's no substitute for practice.

Reading EXPLAIN's output often requires you to jump forward and backward in the list. For example, look again at the first row in the output. There is no way to know just by looking at it that it is part of a UNION. You'll only see that when you read the last row of the output.

The type Column

The MySQL manual says this column shows the "join type," but we think it's more accurate to say the *access type*—in other words, how MySQL has decided to find rows in the table. Here are the most important access methods, from worst to best:

ALL

This is what most people call a table scan. It generally means MySQL must scan through the table, from beginning to end, to find the row. (There are exceptions, such as queries with `LIMIT` or queries that display "Using distinct/not exists" in the `Extra` column.)

index

This is the same as a table scan, except MySQL scans the table in index order instead of the rows. The main advantage is that this avoids sorting; the biggest disadvantage is the cost of reading an entire table in index order. This usually means accessing the rows in random order, which is very expensive.

If you also see "Using index" in the `Extra` column, it means MySQL is using a covering index and scanning only the index's data, not reading each row in index order. This is much less expensive than scanning the table in index order.

range

A range scan is a limited index scan. It begins at some point in the index and returns rows that match a range of values. This is better than a full index scan because it doesn't go through the entire index. Obvious range scans are queries with a `BETWEEN` or `>` in the `WHERE` clause.

When MySQL uses an index to look up lists of values, such as `IN()` and `OR` lists, it also displays it as a range scan. However, these are quite different types of accesses, and they have important performance differences. See the sidebar "What Is a Range Condition?" on page 192 in Chapter 5 for more information.

The same cost considerations apply for this type as for the `index` type.

ref

This is an index access (sometimes called an index lookup) that returns rows that match a single value. However, it might find multiple rows, so it's a mixture of a lookup and a scan. This type of index access can happen only on a nonunique index or a nonunique prefix of a unique index. It's called `ref` because the index is compared to some reference value. The reference value is either a constant or a value from a previous table in a multiple-table query.

The `ref_or_null` access type is a variation on `ref`. It means MySQL must do a second lookup to find `NULL` entries after doing the initial lookup.

eq_ref

This is an index lookup that MySQL knows will return at most a single value. You'll see this access method when MySQL decides to use a primary key or unique index to satisfy the query by comparing it to some reference value. MySQL can optimize this access type very well, because it knows it doesn't have to estimate ranges of matching rows or look for more matching rows after it finds one.

const, system

MySQL uses these access types when it can optimize away some part of the query and turn it into a constant. For example, if you select a row's primary key by placing its primary key into the WHERE clause, MySQL can convert the query into a constant. It then effectively removes the table from the join execution.

NULL

This access method means MySQL can resolve the query during the optimization phase and will not even access the table or index during the execution stage. For example, selecting the minimum value from an indexed column can be done by looking at the index alone and requires no table access during execution.

The possible_keys Column

This column shows which indexes could be used for the query, based on the columns the query accesses and the comparison operators used. This list is created early in the optimization phase, so some of the indexes listed might be useless for the query after subsequent optimization phases.

The key Column

This column shows which index MySQL decided to use to optimize the access to the table. If the index doesn't appear in possible_keys, MySQL chose it for another reason—for example, it might choose a covering index even when there is no WHERE clause.

In other words, possible_keys reveals which indexes can help *make row lookups efficient*, but key shows which index the optimizer decided to use to *minimize query cost* (see Chapter 6 for more on the optimizer's cost metrics). Here's an example:

```
mysql> EXPLAIN SELECT actor_id, film_id FROM sakila.film_actor\G
*************************** 1. row ***************************
           id: 1
  select_type: SIMPLE
        table: film_actor
         type: index
possible_keys: NULL
          key: idx_fk_film_id
      key_len: 2
          ref: NULL
         rows: 5143
        Extra: Using index
```

The key_len Column

This column shows the number of bytes MySQL will use in the index. If MySQL is using only some of the index's columns, you can use this value to calculate which columns it uses. Remember that MySQL 5.5 and older versions can use only the leftmost prefix of the index. For example, sakila.film_actor's primary key covers two SMALLINT columns, and a SMALLINT is two bytes, so each tuple in the index is four bytes. Here's a sample query:

```
mysql> EXPLAIN SELECT actor_id, film_id FROM sakila.film_actor WHERE actor_id=4;
...+------+---------------+---------+---------+...
...| type | possible_keys | key     | key_len |...
...+------+---------------+---------+---------+...
...| ref  | PRIMARY       | PRIMARY | 2       |...
...+------+---------------+---------+---------+...
```

Based on the key_len column in the result, you can deduce that the query performs index lookups with only the first column, the actor_id. When calculating column usage, be sure to account for character sets in character columns:

```
mysql> CREATE TABLE t (
    ->     a char(3) NOT NULL,
    ->     b int(11) NOT NULL,
    ->     c char(1) NOT NULL,
    ->     PRIMARY KEY  (a,b,c)
    -> ) ENGINE=MyISAM DEFAULT CHARSET=utf8 ;
mysql> INSERT INTO t(a, b, c)
    ->     SELECT DISTINCT LEFT(TABLE_SCHEMA, 3), ORD(TABLE_NAME),
    ->         LEFT(COLUMN_NAME, 1)
    ->     FROM INFORMATION_SCHEMA.COLUMNS:
mysql> EXPLAIN SELECT a FROM t WHERE a='sak' AND b = 112;
...+------+---------------+---------+---------+...
...| type | possible_keys | key     | key_len |...
...+------+---------------+---------+---------+...
...| ref  | PRIMARY       | PRIMARY | 13      |...
...+------+---------------+---------+---------+...
```

The length of 13 bytes in this query is the sum of the lengths of the a and b columns. Column a is three characters, which in utf8 require up to three bytes each, and column b is a four-byte integer.

MySQL doesn't always show you how much of an index is really being used. For example, if you perform a LIKE query with a prefix pattern match, it will show that the full width of the column is being used.

The key_len column shows the maximum possible length of the indexed fields, not the actual number of bytes the data in the table used. MySQL will always show 13 bytes in the preceding example, even if column a happens to contain no values more than one character long. In other words, key_len is calculated by looking at the table's definition, not the data in the table.

The ref Column

This column shows which columns or constants from preceding tables are being used to look up values in the index named in the key column. Here's an example that shows a combination of join conditions and aliases. Notice that the ref column reflects how the film table is aliased as f in the query text:

```
mysql> EXPLAIN
    -> SELECT STRAIGHT_JOIN f.film_id
    -> FROM sakila.film AS f
    ->    INNER JOIN sakila.film_actor AS fa
    ->      ON f.film_id=fa.film_id AND fa.actor_id = 1
    ->    INNER JOIN sakila.actor AS a USING(actor_id);
```

...	table	...	key	key_len	ref	...
...	a	...	PRIMARY	2	const	...
...	f	...	idx_fk_language_id	1	NULL	...
...	fa	...	PRIMARY	4	const,sakila.f.film_id	...

The rows Column

This column shows the number of rows MySQL estimates it will need to read to find the desired rows. This number is *per loop in the nested-loop join plan*. That is, it's not just the number of rows MySQL thinks it will need to read from the table; it is the number of rows, on average, MySQL thinks it will have to read to find rows that satisfy the criteria in effect at that point in query execution. (The criteria include constants given in the SQL as well as the current columns from previous tables in the join order.)

This estimate can be quite inaccurate, depending on the table statistics and how selective the indexes are. It also doesn't reflect LIMIT clauses in MySQL 5.0 and earlier. For example, the following query will not examine 1,022 rows:

```
mysql> EXPLAIN SELECT * FROM sakila.film LIMIT 1\G
...
        rows: 1022
```

You can calculate roughly the number of rows the entire query will examine by multiplying all the rows values together. For example, the following query might examine approximately 2,600 rows:

```
mysql> EXPLAIN
    -> SELECT f.film_id
    -> FROM sakila.film AS f
    ->    INNER JOIN sakila.film_actor AS fa USING(film_id)
    ->    INNER JOIN sakila.actor AS a USING(actor_id);
```

...	rows	...
...	200	...
...	13	...
...	1	...

Remember, this is the number of rows MySQL thinks it will examine, not the number of rows in the result set. Also realize that there are many optimizations, such as join buffers and caches, that aren't factored into the number of rows shown. MySQL will probably not have to actually read every row it predicts it will. MySQL also doesn't know anything about the operating system or hardware caches.

The filtered Column

This column is new in MySQL 5.1 and appears when you use EXPLAIN EXTENDED. It shows a pessimistic estimate of the percentage of rows that will satisfy some condition on the table, such as a WHERE clause or a join condition. If you multiply the rows column by this percentage, you will see the number of rows MySQL estimates it will join with the previous tables in the query plan. At the time of this writing, the optimizer uses this estimate only for the ALL, index, range, and index_merge access methods.

To illustrate this column's output, we created a table as follows:

```
CREATE TABLE t1 (
    id INT NOT NULL AUTO_INCREMENT,
    filler char(200),
    PRIMARY KEY(id)
);
```

We then inserted 1,000 rows into this table, with random text in the filler column. Its purpose is to prevent MySQL from using a covering index for the query we're about to run:

```
mysql> EXPLAIN EXTENDED SELECT * FROM t1 WHERE id < 500\G
*************************** 1. row ***************************
           id: 1
  select_type: SIMPLE
        table: t1
         type: ALL
possible_keys: PRIMARY
          key: NULL
      key_len: NULL
          ref: NULL
         rows: 1000
     filtered: 49.40
        Extra: Using where
```

MySQL could use a range access to retrieve all rows with IDs less than 500 from the table, but it won't because that would eliminate only about half the rows. It thinks a table scan is less expensive. As a result, it uses a table scan and a WHERE clause to filter out rows. It knows how many rows the WHERE clause will remove from the result, because of the range access cost estimates. That's why the 49.40% value appears in the filtered column.

The Extra Column

This column contains extra information that doesn't fit into other columns. The MySQL manual documents most of the many values that can appear here; we have referred to many of them throughout this book.

The most important values you might see frequently are as follows:

"Using index"

This indicates that MySQL will use a covering index to avoid accessing the table. Don't confuse covering indexes with the `index` access type.

"Using where"

This means the MySQL server will post-filter rows after the storage engine retrieves them. Many `WHERE` conditions that involve columns in an index can be checked by the storage engine when (and if) it reads the index, so not all queries with a `WHERE` clause will show "Using where." Sometimes the presence of "Using where" is a hint that the query can benefit from different indexing.

"Using temporary"

This means MySQL will use a temporary table while sorting the query's result.

"Using filesort"

This means MySQL will use an external sort to order the results, instead of reading the rows from the table in index order. MySQL has two filesort algorithms, which you can read about in Chapter 6. Either type can be done in memory or on disk. `EXPLAIN` doesn't tell you which type of filesort MySQL will use, and it doesn't tell you whether the sort will be done in memory or on disk.

"Range checked for each record (index map: N)"

This value means there's no good index, and the indexes will be reevaluated for each row in a join. *N* is a bitmap of the indexes shown in `possible_keys` and is redundant.

Tree-Formatted Output

MySQL users often wish they could get `EXPLAIN`'s output to be formatted as a tree, showing a more accurate representation of the execution plan. As it is, `EXPLAIN` is a somewhat awkward way to see the execution plan; a tree structure doesn't fit very well into a tabular output. The awkwardness is highlighted by the large number of possible values for the `Extra` column, as well as by `UNION`. `UNION` is quite unlike every other kind of join MySQL can do, and it doesn't fit well into `EXPLAIN`.

It's possible, with a good understanding of the rules and particularities of `EXPLAIN`, to work backward to a tree-formatted execution plan. This is quite tedious, though, and it's best left to an automated tool. Percona Toolkit contains *pt-visual-explain*, which is such a tool.

Improvements in MySQL 5.6

MySQL 5.6 will include an important enhancement to EXPLAIN: the ability to explain queries such as UPDATE, INSERT, and so on. This is very helpful because although one can convert a DML statement to a quasi-equivalent SELECT statement and EXPLAIN it, the result will not truly reflect how the statement executes. While developing and using tools such as Percona Toolkit's *pt-upgrade* that attempt to use that technique, we've found several cases where the optimizer doesn't follow the code path we expected when converting statements to SELECT. The ability to EXPLAIN a statement without transforming it to a SELECT is thus helpful for understanding what truly happens during execution.

MySQL 5.6 will also include a variety of improvements to the query optimizer and execution engine that allow anonymous temporary tables to be materialized as late as possible, rather than always creating and filling them before optimizing and executing the portions of the query that refer to them. This will allow MySQL to explain queries with subqueries instantly, without having to actually execute the subqueries first.

Finally, MySQL 5.6 will enhance a related area of the optimizer by adding *optimizer trace* functionality to the server. This will permit the user to view the decisions the optimizer made, as well as the inputs (index cardinality, for example) and the reasons for the decisions. This will be very helpful for understanding not just the execution plan that the server chose, but also why it chose that plan.

Debugging Locks

Any system that uses locks to control shared access to resources can be hard to debug when a lock contention issue crops up. Perhaps you're trying to add a column to a table, or just trying to run a query, when suddenly you find that your queries are blocked because something else is locking the table or rows you're trying to use. Often all you will want to do is find out why your query is blocked, but sometimes you will want to know what's blocking it, so you know which process to kill. This appendix shows you how to achieve both goals.

The MySQL server itself uses several types of locks. If a query is waiting for a lock at the server level, you can see evidence of it in the output of SHOW PROCESSLIST. In addition to server-level locks, any storage engine that supports row-level locks, such as InnoDB, implements its own locks. In MySQL 5.0 and earlier versions, the server is unaware of such locks, and they're mostly hidden from users and database administrators. There's more visibility in MySQL 5.1 and later versions.

Lock Waits at the Server Level

A lock wait can happen at either the server level or the storage engine level.[1] (Application-level locks could be a problem too, but we're focusing on MySQL.) Here are the kinds of locks the MySQL server uses:

Table locks

Tables can be locked with explicit read and write locks. There are a couple of variations on these locks, such as local read locks. You can learn about the variations in the LOCK TABLES section of the MySQL manual. In addition to these explicit locks, queries acquire implicit locks on tables for their durations.

---

1. Refer to Figure 1-1 in Chapter 1 if you need to refresh your memory on the separation between the server and the storage engines.

Global locks

> There is a single global read lock that can be acquired with FLUSH TABLES WITH READ LOCK or by setting read_only=1. This conflicts with any table locks.

Name locks

> Name locks are a type of table lock that the server creates when it renames or drops a table.

String locks

> You can lock and release an arbitrary string server-wide with GET_LOCK() and its associated functions.

We examine each of these lock types in more detail in the following sections.

Table Locks

Table locks can be either explicit or implicit. You create explicit locks with LOCK TABLES. For example, if you execute the following command in a *mysql* session, you'll have an explicit lock on sakila.film:

```
mysql> LOCK TABLES sakila.film READ;
```

If you then execute the following command in a different session, the query will hang and not complete:

```
mysql> LOCK TABLES sakila.film WRITE;
```

You can see the waiting thread in the first connection:

```
mysql> SHOW PROCESSLIST\G
*************************** 1. row ***************************
     Id: 7
   User: baron
   Host: localhost
     db: NULL
Command: Query
   Time: 0
  State: NULL
   Info: SHOW PROCESSLIST
*************************** 2. row ***************************
     Id: 11
   User: baron
   Host: localhost
     db: NULL
Command: Query
   Time: 4
  State: Locked
   Info: LOCK TABLES sakila.film WRITE
2 rows in set (0.01 sec)
```

Notice that thread 11's state is Locked. There is only one place in the MySQL server's code where a thread enters that state: when it tries to acquire a table lock and another thread has the table locked. Thus, if you see this, you know the thread is waiting for a lock in the MySQL server, not in the storage engine.

Explicit locks, however, are not the only type of lock that might block such an operation. As we mentioned earlier, the server implicitly locks tables during queries. An easy way to show this is with a long-running query, which you can create easily with the SLEEP() function:

```
mysql> SELECT SLEEP(30) FROM sakila.film LIMIT 1;
```

If you try again to lock `sakila.film` while that query is running, the operation will hang because of the implicit lock, just as it did when you had the explicit lock. You'll be able to see the effects in the process list, as before:

```
mysql> SHOW PROCESSLIST\G
*************************** 1. row ***************************
     Id: 7
   User: baron
   Host: localhost
     db: NULL
Command: Query
   Time: 12
  State: Sending data
   Info: SELECT SLEEP(30) FROM sakila.film LIMIT 1
*************************** 2. row ***************************
     Id: 11
   User: baron
   Host: localhost
     db: NULL
Command: Query
   Time: 9
  State: Locked
   Info: LOCK TABLES sakila.film WRITE
```

In this example, the implicit read lock for the SELECT query blocks the explicit write lock requested by LOCK TABLES. Implicit locks can block each other, too.

You might be wondering about the difference between implicit and explicit locks. Internally, they are the same type of structure, and the same MySQL server code controls them. Externally, you can control explicit locks yourself with LOCK TABLES and UNLOCK TABLES.

When it comes to storage engines other than MyISAM, however, there's one very important difference between them. When you create a lock explicitly, it does what you tell it to, but implicit locks are hidden and "magical." The server creates and releases implicit locks automatically as needed, and it tells the storage engine about them. Storage engines "convert" these locks as they see fit. For example, InnoDB has rules about what type of InnoDB table lock it should create for a given server-level table lock. This can make it hard to understand what locks InnoDB is really creating behind the scenes.

Finding out who holds a lock

If you see a lot of processes in the Locked state, your problem might be that you're trying to use MyISAM or a similar storage engine for a high-concurrency workload. This can block you from performing an operation manually, such as adding an index to a table. If an UPDATE query is queued and waiting for a lock on a MyISAM table, even a SELECT query won't be allowed to run. (You can read more about MySQL's lock queuing and priorities in the MySQL manual.)

In some cases, it can become clear that some connection has been holding a lock on a table for a very long time and just needs to be killed (or a user needs to be admonished not to hold up the works!). But how can you find out which connection that is?

There's currently no SQL command that can show you which thread holds the table locks that are blocking your query. If you run SHOW PROCESSLIST, you can see the processes that are waiting for locks, but not which processes hold those locks. Fortunately, there's a *debug* command that can print information about locks into the server's error log. You can use the *mysqladmin* utility to run the command:

```
$ mysqladmin debug
```

The output in the error log includes a lot of debugging information, but near the end you'll see something like the following. We created this output by locking the table in one connection, then trying to lock it again in another:

```
Thread database.table_name Locked/Waiting    Lock_type
7       sakila.film        Locked - read     Read lock  without concurrent inserts
8       sakila.film        Waiting - write   Highest priority write lock
```

You can see that thread 8 is waiting for the lock thread 7 holds.

The Global Read Lock

The MySQL server also implements a global read lock. You can obtain this lock as follows:

```
mysql> FLUSH TABLES WITH READ LOCK;
```

If you now try to lock a table in another session, it will hang as before:

```
mysql> LOCK TABLES sakila.film WRITE;
```

How can you tell that this query is waiting for the global read lock and not a table-level lock? Look at the output of SHOW PROCESSLIST:

```
mysql> SHOW PROCESSLIST\G
...
*************************** 2. row ***************************
      Id: 22
    User: baron
    Host: localhost
      db: NULL
 Command: Query
```

```
    Time: 9
   State: Waiting for release of readlock
    Info: LOCK TABLES sakila.film WRITE
```

Notice that the query's state is `Waiting for release of readlock`. This is your clue that the query is waiting for the global read lock, not a table-level lock.

MySQL provides no way to find out who holds the global read lock.

Name Locks

Name locks are a type of table lock that the server creates when it renames or drops a table. A name lock conflicts with an ordinary table lock, whether implicit or explicit. For example, if we use `LOCK TABLES` as before, and then in another session try to rename the locked table, the query will hang, but this time not in the `Locked` state:

```
mysql> RENAME TABLE sakila.film2 TO sakila.film;
```

As before, the process list is the place to see the locked query, which is in the `Waiting for table` state:

```
mysql> SHOW PROCESSLIST\G
...
*************************** 2. row ***************************
     Id: 27
   User: baron
   Host: localhost
     db: NULL
Command: Query
   Time: 3
  State: Waiting for table
   Info: rename table sakila.film to sakila.film 2
```

You can see the effects of a name lock in the output of `SHOW OPEN TABLES`, too:

```
mysql> SHOW OPEN TABLES;
+----------+-----------+--------+-------------+
| Database | Table     | In_use | Name_locked |
+----------+-----------+--------+-------------+
| sakila   | film_text |      3 |           0 |
| sakila   | film      |      2 |           1 |
| sakila   | film2     |      1 |           1 |
+----------+-----------+--------+-------------+
3 rows in set (0.00 sec)
```

Notice that both names (the original and the new name) are locked. `sakila.film_text` is locked because there's a trigger on `sakila.film` that refers to it, which illustrates another way locks can insinuate themselves into places you might not expect. If you query `sakila.film`, the trigger causes you to implicitly touch `sakila.film_text`, and therefore to implicitly lock it. It's true that the trigger really doesn't need to fire for the rename, and thus technically the lock isn't required, but that's the way it is: MySQL's locking is sometimes not as fine-grained as you might like.

MySQL doesn't provide any way to find out who holds name locks, but this usually isn't a problem because they're generally held for only a very short time. When there's a conflict, it is generally because a name lock is waiting for a normal table lock, which you can view with *mysqladmin debug*, as shown earlier.

User Locks

The final type of lock implemented in the server is the user lock, which is basically a named mutex. You specify the string to lock and the number of seconds to wait before the lock attempt should time out:

```
mysql> SELECT GET_LOCK('my lock', 100);
+--------------------------+
| GET_LOCK('my lock', 100) |
+--------------------------+
|                        1 |
+--------------------------+
1 row in set (0.00 sec)
```

This attempt returned success immediately, so this thread now has a lock on that named mutex. If another thread tries to lock the same string, it will hang until it times out. This time the process list shows a different state:

```
mysql> SHOW PROCESSLIST\G
*************************** 1. row ***************************
     Id: 22
   User: baron
   Host: localhost
     db: NULL
Command: Query
   Time: 9
  State: User lock
   Info: SELECT GET_LOCK('my lock', 100)
```

The User lock state is unique to this type of lock. MySQL provides no way to find out who holds a user lock.

Lock Waits in InnoDB

Locks at the server level can be quite a bit easier to debug than locks in storage engines. Storage engine locks differ from one storage engine to the next, and the engines might not provide any means to inspect their locks. We focus on InnoDB in this appendix.

InnoDB exposes some lock information in the output of SHOW INNODB STATUS. If a transaction is waiting for a lock, the lock will appear in the TRANSACTIONS section of the output from SHOW INNODB STATUS. For example, if you execute the following commands in one session, you will acquire a write lock on the first row in the table:

```
mysql> SET AUTOCOMMIT=0;
mysql> BEGIN;
mysql> SELECT film_id FROM sakila.film LIMIT 1 FOR UPDATE;
```

If you now run the same commands in another session, your query will block on the lock the first session acquired on that row. You can see the effects in SHOW INNODB STATUS (we've abbreviated the results for clarity):

```
1  LOCK WAIT 2 lock struct(s), heap size 1216
2  MySQL thread id 8, query id 89 localhost baron Sending data
3  SELECT film_id FROM sakila.film LIMIT 1 FOR UPDATE
4  ------- TRX HAS BEEN WAITING 9 SEC FOR THIS LOCK TO BE GRANTED:
5  RECORD LOCKS space id 0 page no 194 n bits 1072 index `idx_fk_language_id` of table
   `sakila/film` trx id 0 61714 lock_mode X waiting
```

The last line shows that the query is waiting for an exclusive (lock_mode X) lock on page 194 of the table's idx_fk_language_id index. Eventually, the lock wait timeout will be exceeded, and the query will return an error:

```
ERROR 1205 (HY000): Lock wait timeout exceeded; try restarting transaction
```

Unfortunately, without seeing who holds the locks, it's hard to figure out which transaction is causing the problem. You can often make an educated guess by looking at which transactions have been open a very long time; alternatively, you can activate the InnoDB lock monitor, which will show up to 10 of the locks each transaction holds. To activate the monitor, you create a magically named table with the InnoDB storage engine:[2]

```
mysql> CREATE TABLE innodb_lock_monitor(a int) ENGINE=INNODB;
```

When you issue this query, InnoDB begins printing a slightly enhanced version of the output of SHOW INNODB STATUS to standard output at intervals (the interval varies, but it's usually several times per minute). On most systems, this output is redirected to the server's error log; you can examine it to see which transactions hold which locks. To stop the lock monitor, drop the table.

Here's the relevant sample of the lock monitor output:

```
 1  ---TRANSACTION 0 61717, ACTIVE 3 sec, process no 5102, OS thread id 1141152080
 2  3 lock struct(s), heap size 1216
 3  MySQL thread id 11, query id 108 localhost baron
 4  show innodb status
 5  TABLE LOCK table `sakila/film` trx id 0 61717 lock mode IX
 6  RECORD LOCKS space id 0 page no 194 n bits 1072 index `idx_fk_language_id` of table
    `sakila/film` trx id 0 61717 lock_mode X
 7  Record lock, heap no 2 PHYSICAL RECORD: n_fields 2; compact format; info bits 0
 8  ... omitted ...
 9
10  RECORD LOCKS space id 0 page no 231 n bits 168 index `PRIMARY` of table `sakila/film`
    trx id 0 61717 lock_mode X locks rec but not gap
11  Record lock, heap no 2 PHYSICAL RECORD: n_fields 15; compact format; info bits 0
12  ... omitted ...
```

---

2. InnoDB honors several "magical" table names as instructions. Current practice is to use dynamically settable server variables, but InnoDB has been around a long time, so it still has some old behaviors.

Notice that line 3 shows the MySQL thread ID, which is the same as the value in the Id column in the process list. Line 5 shows that the transaction has an implicit exclusive table lock (IX) on the table. Lines 6 through 8 show the lock on the index. We've omitted the information on line 8 because it's a dump of the locked record and is pretty verbose. Lines 9 through 11 show the corresponding lock on the primary key (a FOR UPDATE lock must lock the row, not just the index).

When the lock monitor is activated the extra information appears in the output of SHOW INNODB STATUS too, so you don't actually have to look in the server's error log to see the lock information.

The lock monitor is not optimal, for several reasons. The primary problem is that the lock information is very verbose, because it includes hex and ASCII dumps of the records that are locked. It fills up the error log, and it can easily overflow the fixed-size output of SHOW INNODB STATUS. This means you might not get the information you're looking for in later sections of the output. InnoDB also has a hardcoded limit to the number of locks it prints per transaction—after printing 10 locks, it will not print any more, which means you might not even see any information on the lock you want. To top it all off, even if what you're looking for is there, it's hard to find it in all that lock output. (Just try it on a busy server, and you'll see!)

Two things can make the lock output more usable. The first is a patch one of this book's authors wrote for InnoDB and the MySQL server, which is included in Percona Server and MariaDB. The patch removes the verbose record dumps from the output, includes the lock information in the output of SHOW INNODB STATUS by default (so the lock monitor doesn't need to be activated), and adds dynamically settable server variables to control the verbosity and how many locks should be printed per transaction.

The second option is to use *innotop* to parse and format the output. Its Lock mode shows locks, aggregated neatly by connection and table, so you can see quickly which transactions hold locks on a given table. This is not a foolproof method of finding which transaction is blocking a lock, because that would require examining the dumped records to find the precise record that's locked. However, it's much better than the usual alternatives, and it's good enough for many purposes.

Using the INFORMATION_SCHEMA Tables

Using SHOW INNODB STATUS to look at locks is definitely old-school, now that InnoDB has INFORMATION_SCHEMA tables that expose its transactions and locks.

If you don't see the tables, you are not using a new enough version of InnoDB. You need at least MySQL 5.1 and the InnoDB plugin. If you're using MySQL 5.1 and you don't see the INNODB_LOCKS table, check SHOW VARIABLES for the innodb_version variable. If you don't see the variable, you're not using the InnoDB plugin, and you should be! If you see the variable but you don't have the tables, you need to ensure that the `plugin_load` setting in the server configuration file includes the tables explicitly. Check the MySQL manual for details.

Fortunately, in MySQL 5.5 you don't need to worry about all of this; the modern version of InnoDB is built right into the server.

The MySQL and InnoDB manuals have sample queries you can use against these tables, which we won't repeat here, but we'll add a couple of our own. For example, here is a query that shows who's blocking and who's waiting, and for how long:

```
SELECT r.trx_id AS waiting_trx_id,  r.trx_mysql_thread_id AS waiting_thread,
       TIMESTAMPDIFF(SECOND, r.trx_wait_started, CURRENT_TIMESTAMP) AS wait_time,
       r.trx_query AS waiting_query,
       l.lock_table AS waiting_table_lock,
       b.trx_id AS blocking_trx_id, b.trx_mysql_thread_id AS blocking_thread,
       SUBSTRING(p.host, 1, INSTR(p.host, ':') - 1) AS blocking_host,
       SUBSTRING(p.host, INSTR(p.host, ':') +1) AS blocking_port,
       IF(p.command = "Sleep", p.time, 0) AS idle_in_trx,
       b.trx_query AS blocking_query
FROM INFORMATION_SCHEMA.INNODB_LOCK_WAITS  AS w
INNER JOIN INFORMATION_SCHEMA.INNODB_TRX   AS b ON  b.trx_id = w.blocking_trx_id
INNER JOIN INFORMATION_SCHEMA.INNODB_TRX   AS r ON  r.trx_id = w.requesting_trx_id
INNER JOIN INFORMATION_SCHEMA.INNODB_LOCKS AS l ON  w.requested_lock_id = l.lock_id
LEFT JOIN  INFORMATION_SCHEMA.PROCESSLIST  AS p ON  p.id      = b.trx_mysql_thread_id
ORDER BY wait_time DESC\G
*************************** 1. row ***************************
    waiting_trx_id: 5D03
    waiting_thread: 3
        wait_time: 6
     waiting_query: select * from store limit 1 for update
waiting_table_lock: `sakila`.`store`
   blocking_trx_id: 5D02
   blocking_thread: 2
     blocking_host: localhost
     blocking_port: 40298
       idle_in_trx: 8
    blocking_query: NULL
```

The result shows that thread 3 has been waiting for 6 seconds to lock a row in the store table. It is blocked on thread 2, which has been idle for 8 seconds.

If you're suffering from a lot of locking due to threads that are idle in a transaction, the following variation can show you how many queries are blocked on which threads, without all the verbosity:

```
SELECT CONCAT('thread ', b.trx_mysql_thread_id, ' from ', p.host) AS who_blocks,
       IF(p.command = "Sleep", p.time, 0) AS idle_in_trx,
       MAX(TIMESTAMPDIFF(SECOND, r.trx_wait_started, NOW())) AS max_wait_time,
       COUNT(*) AS num_waiters
FROM INFORMATION_SCHEMA.INNODB_LOCK_WAITS  AS w
INNER JOIN INFORMATION_SCHEMA.INNODB_TRX   AS b ON  b.trx_id = w.blocking_trx_id
INNER JOIN INFORMATION_SCHEMA.INNODB_TRX   AS r ON  r.trx_id = w.requesting_trx_id
LEFT JOIN  INFORMATION_SCHEMA.PROCESSLIST  AS p ON  p.id      = b.trx_mysql_thread_id
GROUP BY who_blocks ORDER BY num_waiters DESC\G
*************************** 1. row ***************************
```

```
    who_blocks: thread 2 from localhost:40298
   idle_in_trx: 1016
 max_wait_time: 37
   num_waiters: 8
```

The result shows that thread 2 has now been idle for a much longer time, and at least one thread has been waiting for up to 37 seconds for it to release its locks. There are eight threads waiting for thread 2 to finish its work and commit.

We've found that idle-in-transaction locking is a common cause of emergency problems, and is sometimes difficult for people to diagnose. The *pt-kill* tool from Percona Toolkit can be configured to kill long-running idle transactions to prevent this situation. Percona Server itself also supports an idle transaction timeout parameter to accomplish the same thing.

Using Sphinx with MySQL

Sphinx (*http://www.sphinxsearch.com*) is a free, open source, full-text search engine, designed from the ground up to integrate well with databases. It has DBMS-like features, is very fast, supports distributed searching, and scales well. It is also designed for efficient memory and disk I/O, which is important because they're often the limiting factors for large operations.

Sphinx works well with MySQL. It can be used to accelerate a variety of queries, including full-text searches; you can also use it to perform fast grouping and sorting operations, among other applications. It speaks MySQL's wire protocol and a mostly MySQL-compatible SQL-like dialect, so you can actually query it just like a MySQL database. Additionally, there is a pluggable storage engine that lets a programmer or administrator access Sphinx directly through MySQL. Sphinx is especially useful for certain queries that MySQL's general-purpose architecture doesn't optimize very well for large datasets in real-world settings. In short, Sphinx can enhance MySQL's functionality and performance.

The source of data for a Sphinx index is usually the result of a MySQL SELECT query, but you can build an index from an unlimited number of sources of varying types, and each instance of Sphinx can search an unlimited number of indexes. For example, you can pull some of the documents in an index from a MySQL instance running on one remote server, some from a PostgreSQL instance running on another server, and some from the output of a local script through an XML pipe mechanism.

In this appendix, we explore some use cases where Sphinx's capabilities enable enhanced performance, show a summary of the steps needed to install and configure it, explain its features in detail, and we discuss several examples of real-world implementations.

A Typical Sphinx Search

We start with a simple but complete Sphinx usage example to provide a starting point for further discussion. We use PHP because of its popularity, although APIs are available for a number of other languages, too.

Assume that we're implementing full-text searching for a comparison-shopping engine. Our requirements are to:

- Maintain a searchable full-text index on a product table stored in MySQL
- Allow full-text searches over product titles and descriptions
- Be able to narrow down searches to a given category if needed
- Be able to sort the result not only by relevance, but by item price or submission date

We begin by setting up a data source and an index in the Sphinx configuration file:

```
source products
{
    type        = mysql
    sql_host    = localhost
    sql_user    = shopping
    sql_pass    = mysecretpassword
    sql_db      = shopping
    sql_query   = SELECT id, title, description, \
                    cat_id, price, UNIX_TIMESTAMP(added_date) AS added_ts \
                    FROM products
    sql_attr_uint       = cat_id
    sql_attr_float      = price
    sql_attr_timestamp  = added_ts
}

index products
{
    source  = products
    path    = /usr/local/sphinx/var/data/products
    docinfo = extern
}
```

This example assumes that the MySQL `shopping` database contains a `products` table with the columns we request in our `SELECT` query to populate our Sphinx index. The Sphinx index is also named `products`. After creating a new source and index, we run the *indexer* program to create the initial full-text index data files and then (re)start the *searchd* daemon to pick up the changes:

```
$ cd /usr/local/sphinx/bin
$ ./indexer products
$ ./searchd --stop
$ ./searchd
```

The index is now ready to answer queries. We can test it with Sphinx's bundled *test.php* sample script:

```
$ php -q test.php -i products ipod
```

```
Query 'ipod ' retrieved 3 of 3 matches in 0.010 sec.
Query stats:
    'ipod' found 3 times in 3 documents
Matches:
1. doc_id=123, weight=100, cat_id=100, price=159.99, added_ts=2008-01-03 22:38:26
2. doc_id=124, weight=100, cat_id=100, price=199.99, added_ts=2008-01-03 22:38:26
3. doc_id=125, weight=100, cat_id=100, price=249.99, added_ts=2008-01-03 22:38:26
```

The final step is to add searching to our web application. We need to set sorting and filtering options based on user input and format the output nicely. Also, because Sphinx returns only document IDs and configured attributes to the client—it doesn't store any of the original text data—we need to pull additional row data from MySQL ourselves:

```
1  <?php
2  include ( "sphinxapi.php" );
3  // ... other includes, MySQL connection code,
4  // displaying page header and search form, etc. all go here
5
6  // set query options based on end-user input
7  $cl = new SphinxClient ();
8  $sortby = $_REQUEST["sortby"];
9  if ( !in_array ( $sortby, array ( "price", "added_ts" ) ) )
10     $sortby = "price";
11 if ( $_REQUEST["sortorder"]=="asc" )
12     $cl->SetSortMode ( SPH_SORT_ATTR_ASC, $sortby );
13 else
14     $cl->SetSortMode ( SPH_SORT_ATTR_DESC, $sortby );
15 $offset = ($_REQUEST["page"]-1)*$rows_per_page;
16 $cl->SetLimits ( $offset, $rows_per_page );
17
18 // issue the query, get the results
19 $res = $cl->Query ( $_REQUEST["query"], "products" );
20
21 // handle search errors
22 if ( !$res )
23 {
24     print "<b>Search error:</b>" . $cl->GetLastError ();
25     die;
26 }
27
28 // fetch additional columns from MySQL
29 $ids = join ( ",", array_keys ( $res["matches"] ) );
30 $r = mysql_query ( "SELECT id, title FROM products WHERE id IN ($ids)" )
31     or die ( "MySQL error: " . mysql_error() );
32 while ( $row = mysql_fetch_assoc($r) )
33 {
34     $id = $row["id"];
35     $res["matches"][$id]["sql"] = $row;
36 }
37
38 // display the results in the order returned from Sphinx
39 $n = 1 + $offset;
40 foreach ( $res["matches"] as $id=>$match )
```

```
41  {
42      printf ( "%d. <a href=details.php?id=%d>%s</a>, USD %.2f<br>\n",
43          $n++, $id, $match["sql"]["title"], $match["attrs"]["price"] );
44  }
45
46  ?>
```

Even though the snippet just shown is pretty simple, there are a few things worth highlighting:

- The SetLimits() call tells Sphinx to fetch only the number of rows that the client wants to display on a page. It's cheap to impose this limit in Sphinx (unlike in MySQL's built-in search facility), and the number of results that would have been returned without the limit are available in $result['total_found'] at no extra cost.

- Because Sphinx only *indexes* the title column and doesn't *store* it, we must fetch that data from MySQL.

- We retrieve data from MySQL with a single combined query for the whole document batch using the clause WHERE id IN (...), instead of running one query for each match (which would be inefficient).

- We inject the rows pulled from MySQL into our full-text search result set, to keep the original sorting order. We explain this more in a moment.

- We display the rows using data pulled from both Sphinx and MySQL.

The row injection code, which is PHP-specific, deserves a more detailed explanation. We couldn't simply iterate over the result set from the MySQL query, because the row order can (and in most cases actually will) be different from that specified in the WHERE id IN (...) clause. PHP hashes (associative arrays), however, keep the order in which the matches were inserted into them, so iterating over $result["matches"] will produce rows in the proper sorting order as returned by Sphinx. To keep the matches in the proper order returned from Sphinx (rather than the semirandom order returned from MySQL), therefore, we inject the MySQL query results one by one into the hash that PHP stores from the Sphinx result set of matches.

There are also a few major implementation and performance differences between MySQL and Sphinx when it comes to counting matches and applying a LIMIT clause. First, LIMIT is cheap in Sphinx. Consider a LIMIT 500,10 clause. MySQL will retrieve 510 semirandom rows (which is slow) and throw away 500, whereas Sphinx will return the IDs that you will use to retrieve the 10 rows you actually need from MySQL. Second, Sphinx will always return the exact number of matches it actually found in the result set, no matter what's in the LIMIT clause. MySQL can't do this efficiently, although in MySQL 5.6 it will have partial improvements for this limitation.

Why Use Sphinx?

Sphinx can complement a MySQL-based application in many ways, bolstering performance where MySQL is not a good solution and adding functionality MySQL can't provide. Typical usage scenarios include:

- Fast, efficient, scalable, relevant full-text searches
- Optimizing `WHERE` conditions on low-selectivity indexes or columns without indexes
- Optimizing `ORDER BY ... LIMIT N` queries and `GROUP BY` queries
- Generating result sets in parallel
- Scaling up and scaling out
- Aggregating partitioned data

We explore each of these scenarios in the following sections. This list is not exhaustive, though, and Sphinx users find new applications regularly. For example, one of Sphinx's most important uses—scanning and filtering records quickly—was a user innovation, not one of Sphinx's original design goals.

Efficient and Scalable Full-Text Searching

MyISAM's full-text search capability is fast for smaller datasets but performs badly when the data size grows. With millions of records and gigabytes of indexed text, query times can vary from a second to more than 10 minutes, which is unacceptable for a high-performance web application. Although it's possible to scale MyISAM's full-text searches by distributing the data in many locations, this requires you to perform searches in parallel and merge the results in your application.

Sphinx works significantly faster than MyISAM's built-in full-text indexes. For instance, it can search over 1 GB of text within 10 to 100 milliseconds—and that scales well up to 10–100 GB per CPU. Sphinx also has the following advantages:

- It can index data stored with InnoDB and other engines, not just MyISAM.
- It can create indexes on data combined from many source tables, instead of being limited to columns in a single table.
- It can dynamically combine search results from multiple indexes.
- In addition to indexing textual columns, its indexes can contain an unlimited number of numeric *attributes*, which are analogous to "extra columns." Sphinx attributes can be integers, floating-point numbers, and Unix timestamps.
- It can optimize full-text searches with additional conditions on attributes.
- Its phrase-based ranking algorithm helps it return more relevant results. For instance, if you search a table of song lyrics for "I love you, dear," a song that contains

that exact phrase will turn up at the top, before songs that just contain "love" or "dear" many times.

- It makes scaling out much easier.

Applying WHERE Clauses Efficiently

Sometimes you'll need to run SELECT queries against very large tables (containing millions of records), with several WHERE conditions on columns that have poor index selectivity (i.e., return too many rows for a given WHERE condition) or could not be indexed at all. Common examples include searching for users in a social network and searching for items on an auction site. Typical search interfaces let the user apply WHERE conditions to 10 or more columns, while requiring the results to be sorted by other columns. See the indexing case study in Chapter 5 for an example of such an application and the required indexing strategies.

With the proper schema and query optimizations, MySQL can work acceptably for such queries, as long as the WHERE clauses don't contain too many columns. But as the number of columns grows, the number of indexes required to support all possible searches grows exponentially. Covering all the possible combinations for just four columns strains MySQL's limits. It becomes very slow and expensive to maintain the indexes, too. This means it's practically impossible to have all the required indexes for many WHERE conditions, and you have to run the queries without indexes.

More importantly, even if you can add indexes, they won't give much benefit unless they're selective. The classic example is a gender column, which isn't much help because it typically selects around half of all rows. MySQL will generally revert to a full table scan when the index isn't selective enough to help it.

Sphinx can perform such queries much faster than MySQL. You can build a Sphinx index with only the required columns from the data. Sphinx then allows two types of access to the data: an indexed search on a keyword or a full scan. In both cases, Sphinx applies *filters*, which are its equivalent of a WHERE clause. Unlike MySQL, which decides internally whether to use an index or a full scan, Sphinx lets you choose which access method to use.

To use a full scan with filters, specify an empty string as the search query. To use an indexed search, add pseudokeywords to your full-text fields while building the index and then search for those keywords. For example, if you wanted to search for items in category 123, you'd add a "category123" keyword to the document during indexing and then perform a full-text search for "category123." You can either add keywords to one of the existing fields using the CONCAT() function, or create a special full-text field for the pseudokeywords for more flexibility. Normally, you should use filters for nonselective values that cover over 30% of the rows, and fake keywords for selective ones that select 10% or less. If the values are in the 10–30% gray zone, your mileage may vary, and you should use benchmarks to find the best solution.

Sphinx will perform both indexed searches and scans faster than MySQL. Sometimes Sphinx actually performs a full scan faster than MySQL can perform an index read.

Finding the Top Results in Order

Web applications frequently need the top *N* results in order. As we discussed previously, this is hard to optimize in MySQL 5.5 and older versions.

The worst case is when the WHERE condition finds many rows (let's say 1 million) and the ORDER BY columns aren't indexed. MySQL uses the index to identify all the matching rows, reads the records one by one into the sort buffer with semirandom disk reads, sorts them all with a filesort, and then discards most of them. It will temporarily store and process the entire result, ignoring the LIMIT clause and churning RAM. And if the result set doesn't fit in the sort buffer, it will need to go to disk, causing even more disk I/O.

This is an extreme case, and you might think it happens rarely in the real world, but in fact the problems it illustrates happen often. MySQL's limitations on indexes for sorting—using only the leftmost part of the index, not supporting loose index scans, and allowing only a single range condition—mean many real-world queries can't benefit from indexes. And even when they can, using semirandom disk I/O to retrieve rows is a performance killer.

Paginated result sets, which usually require queries of the form SELECT ... LIMIT *N*, *M*, are another performance problem in MySQL. They read *N* + *M* rows from disk, causing a large amount of random I/O and wasting memory resources. Sphinx can accelerate such queries significantly by eliminating the two biggest problems:

Memory usage
> Sphinx's RAM usage is always strictly limited, and the limit is configurable. Sphinx supports a result set offset and size similar to the MySQL LIMIT *N*, *M* syntax, but it also has a max_matches option. This controls the equivalent of the "sort buffer" size, on both a per-server and a per-query basis. Sphinx's RAM footprint is guaranteed to be within the specified limits.

I/O
> If attributes are stored in RAM, Sphinx does not do any I/O at all. And even if attributes are stored on disk, Sphinx will perform sequential I/O to read them, which is much faster than MySQL's semirandom retrieval of rows from disks.

You can sort search results by a combination of relevance (weight), attribute values, and (when using GROUP BY) aggregate function values. The sorting clause syntax is similar to a SQL ORDER BY clause:

```php
<?php
$cl = new SphinxClient ();
$cl->SetSortMode ( SPH_SORT_EXTENDED, 'price DESC, @weight ASC' );
// more code and Query() call here...
?>
```

In this example, `price` is a user-specified attribute stored in the index, and `@weight` is a special attribute, created at runtime, that contains each result's computed relevance. You can also sort by an arithmetic expression involving attribute values, common math operators, and functions:

```php
<?php
$cl = new SphinxClient ();
$cl->SetSortMode ( SPH_SORT_EXPR, '@weight + log(pageviews)*1.5' );
// more code and Query() call here...
?>
```

Optimizing GROUP BY Queries

Support for everyday SQL-like clauses would be incomplete without GROUP BY functionality, so Sphinx has that, too. But unlike MySQL's general-purpose implementation, Sphinx specializes in solving a practical subset of GROUP BY tasks efficiently. This subset covers the generation of reports from big (1–100 million row) datasets when one of the following cases holds:

- The result is only a "small" number of grouped rows (where "small" is on the order of 100,000 to 1 million rows).
- Very fast execution speed is required and approximate COUNT(*) results are acceptable, when many groups are retrieved from data distributed over a cluster of machines.

This is not as restrictive as it might sound. The first scenario covers practically all imaginable time-based reports. For example, a detailed per-hour report for a period of 10 years will return fewer than 90,000 records. The second scenario could be expressed in plain English as something like "as quickly and accurately as possible, find the 20 most important records in a 100-million-row sharded table."

These two types of queries can accelerate general-purpose queries, but you can also use them for full-text search applications. Many applications need to display not only full-text matches, but some aggregate results as well. For example, many search result pages show how many matches were found in each product category, or display a graph of matching document counts over time. Another common requirement is to group the results and show the most relevant match from each category. Sphinx's group-by support lets you combine grouping and full-text searching, eliminating the overhead of doing the grouping in your application or in MySQL.

As with sorting, grouping in Sphinx uses fixed memory. It is slightly (10% to 50%) more efficient than similar MySQL queries on datasets that fit in RAM. In this case, most of Sphinx's power comes from its ability to distribute the load and greatly reduce the latency. For huge datasets that could never fit in RAM, you can build a special disk-based index for reporting, using inline attributes (defined later). Queries against such indexes execute about as fast as the disk can read the data—about 30–100 MB/sec on modern hardware. In this case, the performance can be many times better than MySQL's, though the results will be approximate.

The most important difference from MySQL's GROUP BY is that Sphinx may, under certain circumstances, yield approximate results. There are two reasons for this:

- Grouping uses a fixed amount of memory. If there are too many groups to hold in RAM and the matches are in a certain "unfortunate" order, per-group counts might be smaller than the actual values.

- A distributed search sends only the aggregate results, not the matches themselves, from node to node. If there are duplicate records in different nodes, per-group distinct counts might be greater than the actual values, because the information that can remove the duplicates is not transmitted between nodes.

In practice, it is often acceptable to have fast approximate group-by counts. If this isn't acceptable, it's often possible to get exact results by configuring the daemon and client application carefully.

You can generate the equivalent of COUNT(DISTINCT <attribute>), too. For example, you can use this to compute the number of distinct sellers per category in an auction site.

Finally, Sphinx lets you choose criteria to select the single "best" document within each group. For example, you can select the most relevant document from each domain, while grouping by domain and sorting the result set by per-domain match counts. This is not possible in MySQL without a complex query.

Generating Parallel Result Sets

Sphinx lets you generate several results from the same data simultaneously, again using a fixed amount of memory. Compared to the traditional SQL approach of either running two queries (and hoping that some data stays in the cache between runs) or creating a temporary table for each search result set, this yields a noticeable improvement.

For example, assume you need per-day, per-week, and per-month reports over a period of time. To generate these with MySQL you'd have to run three queries with different GROUP BY clauses, processing the source data three times. Sphinx, however, can process the underlying data once and accumulate all three reports in parallel.

Sphinx does this with a *multi-query* mechanism. Instead of issuing queries one by one, you batch several queries and submit them in one request:

```
<?php
$cl = new SphinxClient ();
$cl->SetSortMode ( SPH_SORT_EXTENDED, "price desc" );
$cl->AddQuery ( "ipod" );
$cl->SetGroupBy ( "category_id", SPH_GROUPBY_ATTR, "@count desc" );
$cl->AddQuery ( "ipod" );
$cl->RunQueries ();
?>
```

Sphinx will analyze the request, identify query parts it can combine, and parallelize the queries where possible.

For example, Sphinx might notice that only the sorting and grouping modes differ, and that the queries are otherwise the same. This is the case in the sample code just shown, where the sorting is by `price` but the grouping is by `category_id`. Sphinx will create several sorting queues to process these queries. When it runs the queries, it will retrieve the rows once and submit them to all queues. Compared to running the queries one by one, this eliminates several redundant full-text search or full scan operations.

Note that generating parallel result sets, although it's a common and important optimization, is only a particular case of the more generalized multi-query mechanism. It is not the *only* possible optimization. The rule of thumb is to combine queries in one request where possible, which generally allows Sphinx to apply internal optimizations. Even if Sphinx can't parallelize the queries, it still saves network round-trips. And if Sphinx adds more optimizations in the future, your queries will use them automatically with no further changes.

Scaling

Sphinx scales well both horizontally (scaling out) and vertically (scaling up).

Sphinx is fully distributable across many machines. All the use cases we've mentioned can benefit from distributing the work across several CPUs.

The Sphinx search daemon (*searchd*) supports special *distributed indexes*, which know which local and remote indexes should be queried and aggregated. This means scaling out is a trivial configuration change. You simply partition the data across the nodes, configure the master node to issue several remote queries in parallel with local ones, and that's it.

You can also scale up, as in using more cores or CPUs on a single machine to improve latency. To accomplish this, you can just run several instances of *searchd* on a single machine and query them all from another machine via a distributed index. Alternatively, you can configure a single instance to communicate with itself so that the parallel "remote" queries actually run on a single machine, but on different CPUs or cores.

In other words, with Sphinx a single query can be made to use more than one CPU (multiple concurrent queries will use multiple CPUs automatically). This is a major difference from MySQL, where one query always gets one CPU, no matter how many are available. Also, Sphinx does not need any synchronization between concurrently running queries. That lets it avoid mutexes (a synchronization mechanism), which are a notorious MySQL performance bottleneck on multi-CPU systems.

Another important aspect of scaling up is scaling disk I/O. Different indexes (including parts of a larger distributed index) can easily be put on different physical disks or RAID volumes to improve latency and throughput. This approach has some of the same benefits as MySQL 5.1's partitioned tables, which can also partition data into multiple locations. However, distributed indexes have some advantages over partitioned tables. Sphinx uses distributed indexes both to distribute the load and to process all parts of a query in parallel. In contrast, MySQL's partitioning can optimize some queries (but not all) by pruning partitions, but the query processing will not be parallelized. And even though both Sphinx and MySQL partitioning will improve query throughput, if your queries are I/O-bound, you can expect linear latency improvement from Sphinx on all queries, whereas MySQL's partitioning will improve latency only on those queries where the optimizer can prune entire partitions.

The distributed searching workflow is straightforward:

1. Issue remote queries on all remote servers.
2. Perform sequential local index searches.
3. Read the partial search results from the remote servers.
4. Merge all the partial results into the final result set, and return it to the client.

If your hardware resources permit it, you can search through several indexes on the same machine in parallel, too. If there are several physical disk drives and several CPU cores, the concurrent searches can run without interfering with each other. You can pretend that some of the indexes are remote and configure *searchd* to contact itself to launch a parallel query on the same machine:

```
index distributed_sample
{
    type = distributed
    local = chunk1 # resides on HDD1
    agent = localhost:3312:chunk2 # resides on HDD2, searchd contacts itself
}
```

From the client's point of view, distributed indexes are absolutely no different from local indexes. This lets you create "trees" of distributed indexes by using nodes as proxies for sets of other nodes. For example, the first-level node could proxy the queries to a number of the second-level nodes, which could in turn either search locally themselves or pass the queries to other nodes, to an arbitrary depth.

Aggregating Sharded Data

Building a scalable system often involves *sharding* (partitioning) the data across different physical MySQL servers. We discussed this in depth in Chapter 11.

When the data is sharded at a fine level of granularity, simply fetching a few rows with a selective WHERE (which should be fast) means contacting many servers, checking for errors, and merging the results together in the application. Sphinx alleviates this problem, because all the necessary functionality is already implemented inside the search daemon.

Consider an example where a 1 TB table with a billion blog posts is sharded by user ID over 10 physical MySQL servers, so a given user's posts always go to the same server. As long as queries are restricted to a single user, everything is fine: we choose the server based on user ID and work with it as usual.

Now assume that we need to implement an archive page that shows the user's friends' posts. How are we going to display "Other sysbench features," with entries 981 to 1000, sorted by post date? Most likely, the various friends' data will be on different servers. With only 10 friends, there's about a 90% chance that more than 8 servers will be used, and that probability increases to 99% if there are 20 friends. So, for most queries, we will need to contact all the servers. Worse, we'll need to pull 1,000 posts from *each* server and sort them all in the application. Following the suggestions we've made previously in this book, we'd trim down the required data to the post ID and timestamp only, but that's still 10,000 records to sort in the application. Most modern scripting languages consume a lot of CPU time for that sorting step alone. In addition, we'll either have to fetch the records from each server sequentially (which will be slow) or write some code to juggle the parallel querying threads (which will be difficult to implement and maintain).

In such situations, it makes sense to use Sphinx instead of reinventing the wheel. All we'll have to do in this case is set up several Sphinx instances, mirror the frequently accessed post attributes from each table—in this example, the post ID, user ID, and timestamp—and query the master Sphinx instance for entries 981 to 1000, sorted by post date, in approximately three lines of code. This is a much smarter way to scale.

Architectural Overview

Sphinx is a standalone set of programs. The two main programs are:

indexer
> A program that fetches documents from specified sources (e.g., from MySQL query results) and creates a full-text index over them. This is a background batch job, which sites usually run regularly.

searchd
> A daemon that serves search queries from the indexes *indexer* builds. This provides the runtime support for applications.

The Sphinx distribution also includes native *searchd* client APIs in a number of programming languages (PHP, Python, Perl, Ruby, and Java, at the time of this writing), and SphinxSE, which is a client implemented as a pluggable storage engine for MySQL 5.0 and newer. The APIs and SphinxSE allow a client application to connect to *searchd*, pass it the search query, and fetch back the search results.

Each Sphinx full-text index can be compared to a table in a database; in place of rows in a table, the Sphinx index consists of *documents*. (Sphinx also has a separate data structure called a *multivalued attribute*, discussed later.) Each document has a unique 32-bit or 64-bit integer identifier that should be drawn from the database table being indexed (for instance, from a primary key column). In addition, each document has one or more full-text fields (each corresponding to a text column from the database) and numerical attributes. Like a database table, the Sphinx index has the same fields and attributes for all of its documents. Table F-1 shows the analogy between a database table and a Sphinx index.

Table F-1. Database structure and corresponding Sphinx structure

Database structure	Sphinx structure
`CREATE TABLE documents (`	`index documents`

`    id int(11) NOT NULL auto_increment,`
`    title varchar(255),`
`    content text,`
`    group_id int(11),`
`    added datetime,`
`    PRIMARY KEY  (id)`
`);`
	`    document ID`
	`    title field, full-text indexed`
	`    content field, full-text indexed`
	`    group_id attribute, sql_attr_uint`
	`    added attribute, sql_attr_timestamp`

Sphinx does not store the text fields from the database but just uses their contents to build a search index.

Installation Overview

Sphinx installation is straightforward and typically includes the following steps:

1. Building the programs from sources:

   ```
   $ configure && make && make install
   ```
2. Creating a configuration file with definitions for data sources and full-text indexes
3. Initial indexing
4. Launching *searchd*

After that, the search functionality is immediately available for client programs:

```
<?php
include ( 'sphinxapi.php' );
$cl = new SphinxClient ();
$res = $cl->Query ( 'test query', 'myindex' );
// use $res search result here
?>
```

The only thing left to do is run *indexer* regularly to update the full-text index data. Indexes that *searchd* is currently serving will stay fully functional during reindexing: *indexer* will detect that they are in use, create a "shadow" index copy instead, and notify *searchd* to pick up that copy on completion.

Full-text indexes are stored in the filesystem (at the location specified in the configuration file) and are in a special "monolithic" format, which is not well suited for incremental updates. The normal way to update the index data is to rebuild it from scratch. This is not as big a problem as it might seem, though, for the following reasons:

- Indexing is fast. Sphinx can index plain text (without HTML markup) at a rate of 4–8 MB/sec on modern hardware.
- You can partition the data in several indexes, as shown in the next section, and reindex only the updated part from scratch on each run of *indexer*.
- There is no need to "defragment" the indexes—they are built for optimal I/O, which improves search speed.
- Numeric attributes can be updated without a complete rebuild.

A future version will offer an additional index backend, which will support real-time index updates.

Typical Partition Use

Let's discuss partitioning in a bit more detail. The simplest partitioning scheme is the *main + delta* approach, in which two indexes are created to index one document collection. *main* indexes the whole document set, while *delta* indexes only documents that have changed since the last time the main index was built.

This scheme matches many data modification patterns perfectly. Forums, blogs, email and news archives, and vertical search engines are all good examples. Most of the data in those repositories never changes once it is entered, and only a tiny fraction of documents are changed or added on a regular basis. This means the delta index is small and can be rebuilt as frequently as required (e.g., once every 1–15 minutes). This is equivalent to indexing just the newly inserted rows.

You don't need to rebuild the indexes to change attributes associated with documents—you can do this online via *searchd*. You can mark rows as deleted by simply setting a "deleted" attribute in the main index. Thus, you can handle updates by marking this attribute on documents in the main index, then rebuilding the delta index. Searching for all documents that are not marked as "deleted" will return the correct results.

Note that the indexed data can come from the results of any SELECT statement; it doesn't have to come from just a single SQL table. There are no restrictions on the SELECT statements. That means you can preprocess the results in the database before they're indexed. Common preprocessing examples include joins with other tables, creating additional fields on the fly, excluding some fields from indexing, and manipulating values.

Special Features

Besides "just" indexing and searching through database content, Sphinx offers several other special features. Here's a partial list of the most important ones:

- The searching and ranking algorithms take word positions and the query phrase's proximity to the document content into account.
- You can bind numeric attributes to documents, including multivalued attributes.
- You can sort, filter, and group by attribute values.
- You can create document snippets with search query keyword highlighting.
- You can distribute searching across several machines.
- You can optimize queries that generate several result sets from the same data.
- You can access the search results from within MySQL using SphinxSE.
- You can fine-tune the load Sphinx imposes on the server.

We covered some of these features earlier. This section covers a few of the remaining features.

Phrase Proximity Ranking

Sphinx remembers word positions within each document, as do other open source full-text search systems. But unlike most other ones, it uses the positions to rank matches and return more relevant results.

A number of factors might contribute to a document's final rank. To compute the rank, most other systems use only keyword frequency: the number of times each keyword occurs. The classic BM25 weighting function[1] that virtually all full-text search systems use is built around giving more weight to words that either occur frequently in the particular document being searched or occur rarely in the whole collection. The BM25 result is usually returned as the final rank value.

In contrast, Sphinx also computes query phrase proximity, which is simply the length of the longest verbatim query subphrase contained in the document, counted in words. For instance, the phrase "John Doe Jr" queried against a document with the text "John Black, John White Jr, and Jane Dunne" will produce a phrase proximity of 1, because no two words in the query appear together in the query order. The same query against "Mr. John Doe Jr and friends" will yield a proximity of 3, because three query words occur in the document in the query order. The document "John Gray, Jane Doe Jr" will produce a proximity of 2, thanks to its "Doe Jr" query subphrase.

---

1. See *http://en.wikipedia.org/wiki/Okapi_BM25* for details.

By default, Sphinx ranks matches using phrase proximity first and the classic BM25 weight second. This means that verbatim query quotes are guaranteed to be at the very top, quotes that are off by a single word will be right below those, and so on.

When and how does phrase proximity affect results? Consider searching 1,000,000 pages of text for the phrase "To be or not to be." Sphinx will put the pages with verbatim quotes at the very top of the search results, whereas BM25-based systems will first return the pages with the most mentions of "to," "be," "or," and "not"—pages with an exact quote match but only a few instances of "to" will be buried deep in the results.

Most major web search engines today rank results with keyword positions as well. Searching for a phrase on Google will likely result in pages with perfect or near-perfect phrase matches appearing at the very top of the search results, followed by the "bag of words" documents.

However, analyzing keyword positions requires additional CPU time, and sometimes you might need to skip it for performance reasons. There are also cases when phrase ranking produces undesired, unexpected results. For example, searching for tags in a cloud is better without keyword positions: it makes no difference whether the tags from the query are next to each other in the document.

To allow for flexibility, Sphinx offers a choice of ranking modes. Besides the default mode of proximity plus BM25, you can choose from a number of others that include BM25-only weighting, fully disabled weighting (which provides a nice optimization if you're not sorting by rank), and more.

Support for Attributes

Each document might contain an unlimited number of numeric attributes. Attributes are user-specified and can contain any additional information required for a specific task. Examples include a blog post's author ID, an inventory item's price, a category ID, and so on.

Attributes enable efficient full-text searches with additional filtering, sorting, and grouping of the search results. In theory, they could be stored in MySQL and pulled from there every time a search is performed. But in practice, if a full-text search locates even hundreds or thousands of rows (which is not many), retrieving them from MySQL is unacceptably slow.

Sphinx supports two ways to store attributes: inline in the document lists or externally in a separate file. Inlining requires all attribute values to be stored in the index many times, once for each time a document ID is stored. This inflates the index size and increases I/O, but reduces use of RAM. Storing the attributes externally requires preloading them into RAM upon *searchd* startup.

Attributes normally fit in RAM, so the usual practice is to store them externally. This makes filtering, sorting, and grouping very fast, because accessing data is a matter of quick in-memory lookup. Also, only the externally stored attributes can be updated at runtime. Inline storage should be used only when there is not enough free RAM to hold the attribute data.

Sphinx also supports *multivalued attributes* (MVAs). MVA content consists of an arbitrarily long list of integer values associated with each document. Examples of good uses for MVAs are lists of tag IDs, product categories, and access control lists.

Filtering

Having access to attribute values in the full-text engine allows Sphinx to filter and reject candidate matches as early as possible while searching. Technically, the filter check occurs after verification that the document contains all the required keywords, but before certain computationally intensive calculations (such as ranking) are done. Because of these optimizations, using Sphinx to combine full-text searching with filtering and sorting can be 10 to 100 times faster than using Sphinx for searching and then filtering results in MySQL.

Sphinx supports two types of filters, which are analogous to simple WHERE conditions in SQL:

- An attribute value matches a specified range of values (analogous to a BETWEEN clause, or numeric comparisons).
- An attribute value matches a specified set of values (analogous to an IN( ) list).

If the filters will have a fixed number of values ("set" filters instead of "range" filters), and if such values are selective, it makes sense to replace the integer values with "fake keywords" and index them as full-text content instead of attributes. This applies to both normal numeric attributes and MVAs. We'll see some examples of how to do this later.

Sphinx can also use filters to optimize full scans. Sphinx remembers minimum and maximum attribute values for short continuous row blocks (128 rows, by default) and can quickly throw away whole blocks based on filtering conditions. Rows are stored in the order of ascending document IDs, so this optimization works best for columns that are correlated with the ID. For instance, if you have a row-insertion timestamp that grows along with the ID, a full scan with filtering on that timestamp will be very fast.

The SphinxSE Pluggable Storage Engine

Full-text search results received from Sphinx almost always require additional work involving MySQL—at the very least, to pull out the text column values that the Sphinx index does not store. As a result, you'll frequently need to JOIN search results from Sphinx with other MySQL tables.

Although you can achieve this by sending the result's document IDs to MySQL in a query, that strategy leads to neither the cleanest nor the fastest code. For high-volume situations, you should consider using SphinxSE, a pluggable storage engine that you can compile into MySQL 5.0 or newer, or load into MySQL 5.1 or newer as a plugin.

SphinxSE lets programmers query *searchd* and access search results from within MySQL. The usage is as simple as creating a special table with an `ENGINE=SPHINX` clause (and an optional `CONNECTION` clause to locate the Sphinx server if it's at a nondefault location), and then running queries against that table:

```
mysql> CREATE TABLE search_table (
    ->    id        INTEGER NOT NULL,
    ->    weight    INTEGER NOT NULL,
    ->    query     VARCHAR(3072) NOT NULL,
    ->    group_id  INTEGER,
    ->    INDEX(query)
    -> ) ENGINE=SPHINX CONNECTION="sphinx://localhost:3312/test";
Query OK, 0 rows affected (0.12 sec)

mysql> SELECT * FROM search_table WHERE query='test;mode=all' \G
*************************** 1. row ***************************
      id: 123
  weight: 1
   query: test;mode=all
group_id: 45
1 row in set (0.00 sec)
```

Each `SELECT` passes a Sphinx query as the `query` column in the `WHERE` clause. The Sphinx *searchd* server returns the results. The SphinxSE storage engine then translates these into MySQL results and returns them to the `SELECT` statement.

Queries might include `JOIN`s with any other tables stored using any other storage engines.

The SphinxSE engine supports most searching options available via the API, too. You can specify options such as filtering and limits by plugging additional clauses into the query string:

```
mysql> SELECT * FROM search_table WHERE query='test;mode=all;
    -> filter=group_id,5,7,11;maxmatches=3000';
```

Per-query and per-word statistics that are returned by the API are also accessible through `SHOW STATUS`:

```
mysql> SHOW ENGINE SPHINX STATUS \G
*************************** 1. row ***************************
  Type: SPH INX
  Name: stats
Status: total: 3, total found: 3, time: 8, words: 1
*************************** 2. row ***************************
  Type: SPHINX
  Name: words
Status: test:3:5
2 rows in set (0.00 sec)
```

Even when you're using SphinxSE, the rule of thumb still is to allow *searchd* to perform sorting, filtering, and grouping—i.e., to add all the required clauses to the query string rather than use `WHERE`, `ORDER BY`, or `GROUP BY`. This is especially important for `WHERE` conditions. The reason is that SphinxSE is only a client to *searchd*, not a full-blown built-in search library. Thus, you need to pass everything that you can to the Sphinx engine to get the best performance.

Advanced Performance Control

Both indexing and searching operations could impose a significant additional load on either the search server or the database server. Fortunately, a number of settings let you limit the load coming from Sphinx.

An undesired database-side load can be caused by *indexer* queries that either stall MySQL completely with their locks or just occur too quickly and hog resources from other concurrent queries.

The first case is a notorious problem with MyISAM, where long-running reads lock the tables and stall other pending reads and writes—you can't simply do `SELECT * FROM big_table` on a production server, because you risk disrupting all other operations. To work around that, Sphinx offers *ranged queries*. Instead of configuring a single huge query, you can specify one query that quickly computes the indexable row ranges and another query that pulls out the data step by step, in small chunks:

```
sql_query_range   = SELECT MIN(id),MAX(id) FROM documents
sql_range_step    = 1000
sql_query         = SELECT id, title, body FROM documents \
                    WHERE id>=$start AND id<=$end
```

This feature is extremely helpful for indexing MyISAM tables, but it should also be considered when using InnoDB tables. Although InnoDB won't just lock the table and stall other queries when running a big `SELECT *`, it will still use significant machine resources because of its MVCC architecture. Multiversioning for a thousand transactions that cover a thousand rows each can be less expensive than a single long-running million-row transaction.

The second cause of excessive load happens when *indexer* is able to process the data more quickly than MySQL provides it. You should also use ranged queries in this case. The `sql_ranged_throttle` option forces *indexer* to sleep for a given time period (in milliseconds) between subsequent ranged query steps, increasing indexing time but easing the load on MySQL.

Interestingly enough, there's a special case where you can configure Sphinx to achieve exactly the opposite effect: that is, you can improve indexing time by placing *more* load on MySQL. When the connection between the *indexer* box and the database box is 100 Mbps, and the rows compress well (which is typical for text data), the MySQL compression protocol can improve overall indexing time. The improvement comes at a cost of more CPU time spent on both the MySQL and *indexer* sides to compress and uncompress the rows transmitted over the network, respectively but the overall indexing time could be up to 20–30% less because of greatly reduced network traffic.

Search clusters can suffer from occasional overload, too, so Sphinx provides a few ways to help avoid *searchd* going off on a spin.

First, a `max_children` option simply limits the total number of concurrently running queries and tells clients to retry when that limit is reached.

Then there are query-level limits. You can specify that query processing stop either at a given threshold of matches found or a given threshold of elapsed time, using the `SetLimits()` and `SetMaxQueryTime()` API calls, respectively. This is done on a per-query basis, so you can ensure that more important queries always complete fully.

Finally, periodic *indexer* runs can cause bursts of additional I/O that will in turn cause intermittent *searchd* slowdowns. To prevent that, options that limit *indexer* disk I/O exist. `max_iops` enforces a minimal delay between I/O operations that ensures that no more than `max_iops` disk operations per second will be performed. But even a single operation could be too much; consider a 100 MB `read()` call as an example. The `max_iosize` option takes cares of that, guaranteeing that the length of every disk read or write will be under a given boundary. Larger operations are automatically split into smaller ones, and these smaller ones are then controlled by `max_iops` settings.

Practical Implementation Examples

Each of the features we've described can be found successfully deployed in production. The following sections review several of these real-world Sphinx deployments, briefly describing the sites and some implementation details.

Full-Text Searching on Mininova.org

A popular torrent search engine, Mininova (*http://www.mininova.org*) provides a clear example of how to optimize "just" full-text searching. Sphinx replaced several MySQL replicas using MySQL built-in full-text indexes, which were unable to handle the load. After the replacement, the search servers were underloaded; the current load average is now in the 0.3–0.4 range.

Here are the database size and load numbers:

- The site has a small database, with about 300,000–500,000 records and about 300–500 MB of index.
- The site load is quite high: about 8–10 million searches per day at the time of this writing.

The data mostly consists of user-supplied filenames, frequently without proper punctuation. For this reason, prefix indexing is used instead of whole-word indexing. The resulting index is several times larger than it would otherwise be, but it is still small enough that it can be built quickly and its data can be cached effectively.

Search results for the 1,000 most frequent queries are cached on the application side. About 20–30% of all queries are served from the cache. Because of the "long tail" query distribution, a larger cache would not help much more.

For high availability, the site uses two servers with complete full-text index replicas. The indexes are rebuilt from scratch every few minutes. Indexing takes less than one minute, so there's no point in implementing more complex schemes.

The following are lessons learned from this example:

- Caching search results in the application helps a lot.
- There might be no need to have a huge cache, even for busy applications. A mere 1,000 to 10,000 entries can be enough.
- For databases on the order of 1 GB in size, simple periodic reindexing instead of more complicated schemes is OK, even for busy sites.

Full-Text Searching on BoardReader.com

Mininova is an extreme high-load project case—there's not that much data, but there are a lot of queries against that data. BoardReader (*http://www.boardreader.com*) is just the opposite: a forum search engine that performs many fewer searches on a much larger dataset. Sphinx replaced a commercial full-text search engine that took up to 10 seconds per query to search through a 1 GB collection. Sphinx allowed BoardReader to scale greatly, both in terms of data size and query throughput.

Here's some general information:

- There are more than 1 billion documents and 1.5 TB of text in the database.
- There are about 500,000 page views and between 700,000 and 1 million searches per day.

At the time of this writing, the search cluster consists of six servers, each with four logical CPUs (two dual-core Xeons), 16 GB of RAM, and 0.5 TB of disk space. The database itself is stored on a separate cluster. The search cluster is used only for indexing and searching.

Each of the six servers runs four *searchd* instances, so all four cores are used. One of the four instances aggregates the results from the other three. That makes a total of 24 *searchd* instances. The data is distributed evenly across all of them. Every *searchd* copy carries several indexes over approximately 1/24 of the total data (about 60 GB).

The search results from the six "first-tier" *searchd* nodes are in turn aggregated by another *searchd* instance running on the frontend web server. This instance carries several purely distributed indexes, which reference the six search cluster servers but have no local data at all.

Why have four *searchd* instances per node? Why not have only one *searchd* instance per server, configure it to carry four index chunks, and make it contact itself as though it's a remote server to utilize multiple CPUs, as we suggested earlier? Having four instances instead of just one has its benefits. First, it reduces startup time. There are several gigabytes of attribute data that need to be preloaded in RAM; starting several daemons at a time lets us parallelize that. Second, it improves availability. In the event of *searchd* failures or updates, only 1/24 of the whole index is inaccessible, instead of 1/6.

Within each of the 24 instances on the search cluster, we used time-based partitioning to reduce the load even further. Many queries need to be run only on the most recent data, so the data is divided into three disjoint index sets: data from the last week, from the last three months, and from all time. These indexes are distributed over several different physical disks on a per-instance basis. This way, each instance has its own CPU and physical disk drive and won't interfere with the others.

Local *cron* jobs update the indexes periodically. They pull the data from MySQL over the network but create the index files locally.

Using several explicitly separated "raw" disks proved to be faster than a single RAID volume. Raw disks give control over which files go on which physical disk. That is not the case with RAID, where the controller decides which block goes on which physical disk. Raw disks also guarantee fully parallel I/O on different index chunks, but concurrent searches on RAID are subject to I/O stepping. We chose RAID 0, which has no redundancy, because we don't care about disk failures; we can easily rebuild the indexes on the search nodes. We could also have used several RAID 1 (mirror) volumes to give the same throughput as raw disks while improving reliability.

Another interesting thing to learn from BoardReader is how Sphinx version updates are performed. Obviously, the whole cluster cannot be taken down. Therefore, backward compatibility is critical. Fortunately, Sphinx provides it—newer *searchd* versions usually can read older index files, and they are always able to communicate to older clients over the network. Note that the first-tier nodes that aggregate the search results look just like clients to the second-tier nodes, which do most of the actual searching. Thus, the second-tier nodes are updated first, then the first-tier ones, and finally the web frontend.

Lessons learned from this example are:

- The Very Large Database Motto: partition, partition, partition, parallelize.
- On big search farms, organize *searchd* in trees with several tiers.
- Build optimized indexes with a fraction of the total data where possible.
- Map files to disks explicitly rather than relying on the RAID controller.

Optimizing Selects on Sahibinden.com

Sahibinden (*http://www.sahibinden.com*), a leading Turkish online auction site, had a number of performance problems, including full-text search performance. After deploying Sphinx and profiling some queries, we found that Sphinx could perform many of the frequent application-specific queries with filters faster than MySQL—even when there was an index on one of the participating columns in MySQL. Besides, using Sphinx for non-full-text searches resulted in unified application code that was simpler to write and support.

MySQL was underperforming because the selectivity on each individual column was not enough to reduce the search space significantly. In fact, it was almost impossible to create and maintain all the required indexes, because too many columns required them. The product information tables had about 100 columns, each of which the web application could technically use for filtering or sorting.

Active insertion and updates to the "hot" products table slowed to a crawl, because of too many index updates.

For that reason, Sphinx was a natural choice for *all* the SELECT queries on the product information tables, not just the full-text search queries.

Here are the database size and load numbers for the site:

- The database contains about 400,000 records and 500 MB of data.
- The load is about 3 million queries per day.

To emulate normal SELECT queries with WHERE conditions, the Sphinx indexing process included special keywords in the full-text index. The keywords were of the form _ _CATN_ _ _, where N was replaced with the corresponding category ID. This replacement happened during indexing with the CONCAT() function in the MySQL query, so the source data was not altered.

The indexes needed to be rebuilt as frequently as possible. We settled on rebuilding them every minute. A full reindexing took 9–15 seconds on one of many CPUs, so the *main + delta* scheme discussed earlier was not necessary.

The PHP API turned out to spend a noticeable amount of time (7–9 milliseconds per query) parsing the result set when it had many attributes. Normally, this overhead would not be an issue because the full-text search costs, especially over big collections, would be higher than the parsing cost. But in this specific case, we also needed non-full-text queries against a small collection. To alleviate the issue, the indexes were separated into pairs: a "lightweight" one with the 34 most frequently used attributes, and a "complete" one with all 99 attributes.

Other possible solutions would have been to use SphinxSE or to implement a feature to pull only the specified columns into Sphinx. However, the workaround with two indexes was by far the fastest to implement, and time was a concern.

The following are the lessons learned from this example:

- Sometimes, a full scan in Sphinx performs better than an index read in MySQL.
- For selective conditions, use a "fake keyword" instead of filtering on an attribute, so the full-text search engine can do more of the work.
- APIs in scripting languages can be a bottleneck in certain extreme but real-world cases.

Optimizing GROUP BY on BoardReader.com

An improvement to the BoardReader service required counting hyperlinks and building various reports from the linking data. For instance, one of the reports needed to show the top *N* second-level domains linked to during the last week. Another counted the top *N* second- and third-level domains that linked to a given site, such as YouTube. The queries to build these reports had the following common characteristics:

- They always group by domain.
- They sort by count per group or by the count of distinct values per group.
- They process a lot of data (up to millions of records), but the result set with the best groups is always small.
- Approximate results are acceptable.

During the prototype-testing phase, MySQL took up to 300 seconds to execute these queries. In theory, by partitioning the data, splitting it across servers, and manually aggregating the results in the application, it would have been possible to optimize the queries to around 10 seconds. But this is a complicated architecture to build; even the partitioning implementation is far from straightforward.

Because we had successfully distributed the search load with Sphinx, we decided to implement an approximate distributed GROUP BY with Sphinx, too. This required pre-processing the data before indexing to convert all the interesting substrings into stand-alone "words." Here's a sample URL before and after preprocessing:

```
source_url      = http://my.blogger.com/my/best-post.php
processed_url   = my$blogger$com, blogger$com, my$blogger$com$my,
                  my$blogger$com$my$best, my$blogger$com$my$best$post.php
```

Dollar signs ($) are merely a unified replacement for URL separator characters so that searches can be conducted on any URL part, be it domain or path. This type of pre-processing extracts all "interesting" substrings into single keywords that are the fastest to search. Technically, we could have used phrase queries or prefix indexing, but that would have resulted in bigger indexes and slower performance.

Links are preprocessed at indexing time using a specially crafted MySQL UDF. We also enhanced Sphinx with the ability to count distinct values for this task. After that, we were able to move the queries completely to the search cluster, distribute them easily, and reduce query latency greatly.

Here are the database size and load numbers:

- There are about 150–200 million records, which becomes about 50–100 GB of data after preprocessing.
- The load is approximately 60,000–100,000 GROUP BY queries per day.

The indexes for the distributed GROUP BY were deployed on the same search cluster of 6 machines and 24 logical CPUs described previously. This is a minor complementary load to the main search load over the 1.5 TB text database.

Sphinx replaced MySQL's exact, slow, single-CPU computations with approximate, fast, distributed computations. All of the factors that introduce approximation errors are present here: the incoming data frequently contains too many rows to fit in the "sort buffer" (we use a fixed RAM limit of 100K rows), we use COUNT(DISTINCT), and the result sets are aggregated over the network. Despite that, the results for the first 10 to 1000 groups—which are actually required for the reports—are from 99% to 100% correct.

The indexed data is very different from the data that would be used for an ordinary full-text search. There are a huge number of documents and keywords, even though the documents are very small. The document numbering is nonsequential, because a special numbering convention (source server, source table, and primary key) that does not fit in 32 bits is used. The huge amount of search "keywords" was also causing frequent CRC32 collisions (Sphinx uses CRC32 to map keywords to internal word IDs). For these reasons, we were forced to use 64-bit identifiers everywhere internally.

The current performance is satisfactory. For the most complex domains, queries normally complete in 0.1 to 1.0 seconds.

The following are the lessons learned from this example:

- For GROUP BY queries, some precision can be traded for speed.
- With huge textual collections or moderately sized special collections, 64-bit identifiers might be required.

Optimizing Sharded JOIN Queries on Grouply.com

Grouply (*http://www.grouply.com*) built a Sphinx-based solution to search its multi-million-record database of tagged messages, using Sphinx's MVA support. The database is split across many physical servers for massive scalability, so it might be necessary to query tables that are located on different servers. Arbitrary large-scale joins are impossible because there are too many participating servers, databases, and tables.

Grouply uses Sphinx's MVA attributes to store message tags. The tag list is retrieved from a Sphinx cluster via the PHP API. This replaces multiple sequential SELECTs from several MySQL servers. To reduce the number of SQL queries as well, certain presentation-only data (for example, a small list of users who last read the message) is also stored in a separate MVA attribute and accessed through Sphinx.

Two key innovations here are using Sphinx to prebuild JOIN results and using its distributed capabilities to merge data scattered over many shards. This would be next to impossible with MySQL alone. Efficient merging would require partitioning the data over as few physical servers and tables as possible, but that would hurt both scalability and extensibility.

Lessons learned from this example are:

- Sphinx can be used to aggregate highly partitioned data efficiently.
- MVAs can be used to store and optimize prebuilt JOIN results.

Summary

We've discussed the Sphinx full-text search system only briefly in this appendix. To keep it short, we intentionally omitted discussions of many other Sphinx features, such as HTML indexing support, ranged queries for better MyISAM support, morphology and synonym support, prefix and infix indexing, and CJK indexing. Nevertheless, this appendix should give you some idea of how Sphinx can solve many different real-world problems efficiently. It is not limited to full-text searching; it can solve a number of difficult problems that would traditionally be done in SQL.

Sphinx is neither a silver bullet nor a replacement for MySQL. However, in many cases (which are becoming common in modern web applications), it can be used as a very useful complement to MySQL. You can use it to simply offload some work, or even to create new possibilities for your application.

Download it at *http://www.sphinxsearch.com—and* don't forget to share your own usage ideas!

Index

Symbols

32-bit architecture, 390
404 errors, 614, 617
451 Group, 549
64-bit architecture, 390
:= assign operator, 249
@ user variable, 253
@@ system variable, 334

A

ab tool, Apache, 51
Aborted_clients variable, 688
Aborted_connects variable, 688
access time, 398
access types, 205, 727
ACID transactions, 6, 551
active caches, 611
active data, keeping separate, 554
active-active access, 574
Adaptec controllers, 405
adaptive hash indexes, 154, 703
Adaptive Query Localization, 550, 577
Address Resolution Protocol (ARP), 560, 584
Adminer, 666
admission control features, 373
advanced performance control, 763
after-action reviews, 571
aggregating sharded data, 755
Ajax, 607
Aker, Brian, 296, 679
Akiban, 549, 552
algebraic equivalence rules, 217
algorithms, load-balancing, 562
ALL_O_DIRECT variable, 363

ALTER TABLE command, 11, 28, 141–144, 266, 472, 538
Amazon EBS (Elastic Block Store), 589, 595
Amazon EC2 (Elastic Compute Cloud), 589, 595–598
Amazon RDS (Relational Database Service), 589, 600
Amazon Web Services (AWS), 589
Amdahl scaling, 525
Amdahl's Law, 74, 525
ANALYZE TABLE command, 195
ANSI SQL isolation levels, 8
Apache ab, 51
application-level optimization
    alternatives to MySQL, 619
    caching, 611–618
    common problems, 605–607
    extending MySQL, 618
    finding the optimal concurrency, 609
    web server issues, 608
approximations, 243
Archive storage engine, 19, 220
Aria storage engine, 23, 681
ARP (Address Resolution Protocol), 560, 584
Aslett, Matt, 549
Aspersa (see Percona Toolkit)
asynchronous I/O, 702
asynchronous replication, 447
async_unbuffered, 364
atomicity, 6
attributes, 749, 760
audit plugins, 297
auditing, 622
authentication plugins, 298
auto-increment keys, 578

We'd like to hear your suggestions for improving our indexes. Send email to *index@oreilly.com*.

PURGE MASTER LOGS command, 369, 464, 486
purging old binary logs, 636
pushdown joins, 550, 577

Q

Q mode, 673
Q4M storage engine, 23
Qcache_lowmem_prunes variable, 325
query cache, 214, 315, 330, 690
    alternatives to, 328
    configuring and maintaining, 323–325
    InnoDB and the, 326
    memory use, 318
    optimizations, 327
    when to use, 320–323
query execution
    MySQL client/server protocol, 210–213
    optimization process, 214
    query cache, 214, 315–328
query execution engine, 228
query logging, 95
query optimization, 214–227
    complex queries versus many queries, 207
    COUNT() aggregate function, 241
    join decomposition, 209
    limitations of MySQL, 229–238
    optimizing data access, 202–207
    reasons for slow queries, 201
    restructuring queries, 207–209
query states, 213
query-based splits, 557
querying across shards, 537
query_cache_limit variable, 324
query_cache_min_res_unit value variable, 324
query_cache_size variable, 324, 336
query_cache_type variable, 323
query_cache_wlock_invalidate variable, 324
queue scheduler, 434
queue tables, 256
queue time, 204
quicksort, 226

R

R-Tree indexes, 157
Rackspace Cloud, 589
RAID
    balancing hardware and software, 418

configuration and caching, 419–422
failure, recovery, and monitoring, 417
moving files from flash to, 411
not for backup, 624
performance optimization, 415–417
splits, 647
with SSDs, 405
RAND() function, 160, 724
random read-ahead, 412
random versus sequential I/O, 394
RANGE COLUMNS type, 268
range conditions, 192
raw file
    backup, 627
    restoration, 648
RDBMS technology, 400
RDS (Relational Database Service), 589, 600
read buffer size, 343
READ COMMITTED isolation level, 8, 13
read locks, 4, 189
read threads, 703
READ UNCOMMITTED isolation level, 8, 13
read-ahead, 412
read-around writes, 353
read-mostly tables, 26
read-only variable, 26, 382, 459, 479
read-write splitting, 557
read_buffer_size variable, 336
Read_Master_Log_Pos, 491
read_rnd_buffer_size variable, 336
real number data types, 118
rebalancing shards, 544
records_in_range() function, 195
recovery
    from a backup, 647–658
    defined, 622
    defining requirements, 623
    more advanced techniques, 653
recovery point objective (RPO), 623, 625
recovery time objective (RTO), 623, 625
Red Hat, 432, 683
Redis, 620
redundancy, replication-based, 580
Redundant Array of Inexpensive Disks (see RAID)
redundant indexes, 185–187
ref column, 730

Y

YEAR() function, 268, 270

Z

Zabbix, 668
Zenoss, 669
ZFS filer, 631, 640
ZFS filesystem, 408, 431
zlib, 19, 511
Zmanda Recovery Manager (ZRM), 659

About the Authors

Baron Schwartz is a software engineer who lives in Charlottesville, Virginia, and goes by the online handle of "Xaprb," which is his first name typed in QWERTY on a Dvorak keyboard. When he's not busy solving a fun programming challenge, he relaxes with his wife, Lynn, and dog, Carbon. He blogs about software engineering at *http://www .xaprb.com/blog/*.

A former manager of the High Performance Group at MySQL AB, **Peter Zaitsev** now runs the mysqlperformanceblog.com (*http://www.mysqlperformanceblog.com/*) site. He specializes in helping administrators fix issues with websites handling millions of visitors a day, dealing with terabytes of data using hundreds of servers. He is used to making changes and upgrades both to hardware and to software (such as query optimization) in order to find solutions. He also speaks frequently at conferences.

Vadim Tkachenko was a Performance Engineer in at MySQL AB. As an expert in multithreaded programming and synchronization, his primary tasks were benchmarks, profiling, and finding bottlenecks. He also worked on a number of features for performance monitoring and tuning, and getting MySQL to scale well on multiple CPUs.

Colophon

The animal on the cover of *High Performance MySQL* is a sparrow hawk (*Accipiter nisus*), a small woodland member of the falcon family found in Eurasia and North Africa. Sparrow hawks have a long tail and short wings; males are bluish-gray with a light brown breast, and females are more brown-gray and have an almost fully white breast. Males are normally somewhat smaller (11 inches) than females (15 inches).

Sparrow hawks live in coniferous woods and feed on small mammals, insects, and birds. They nest in trees and sometimes on cliff ledges. At the beginning of the summer, the female lays four to six white eggs, blotched red and brown, in a nest made in the boughs of the tallest tree available. The male feeds the female and their young.

Like all hawks, the sparrow hawk is capable of bursts of high speed in flight. Whether soaring or gliding, the sparrow hawk has a characteristic flap-flap-glide action; its large tail enables the hawk to twist and turn effortlessly in and out of cover.

The cover image is a nineteenth-century engraving from the Dover Pictorial Archive. The cover font is Adobe ITC Garamond. The text font is Linotype Birka; the heading font is Adobe Myriad Condensed; and the code font is LucasFont's TheSansMono-Condensed.

Have it your way.

Get even more for your money.

Join the O'Reilly Community, and register the O'Reilly books you own. It's free, and you'll get:

- $4.99 ebook upgrade offer
- 40% upgrade offer on O'Reilly print books
- Membership discounts on books and events
- Free lifetime updates to ebooks and videos
- Multiple ebook formats, DRM FREE
- Participation in the O'Reilly community
- Newsletters
- Account management
- 100% Satisfaction Guarantee

Signing up is easy:

1. **Go to: oreilly.com/go/register**
2. **Create an O'Reilly login.**
3. **Provide your address.**
4. **Register your books.**

Note: English-language books only

To order books online:

oreilly.com/store

For questions about products or an order:

orders@oreilly.com

To sign up to get topic-specific email announcements and/or news about upcoming books, conferences, special offers, and new technologies:

elists@oreilly.com

For technical questions about book content:

booktech@oreilly.com

To submit new book proposals to our editors:

proposals@oreilly.com

O'Reilly books are available in multiple DRM-free ebook formats. For more information:

oreilly.com/ebooks

O'REILLY®

Spreading the knowledge of innovators

oreilly.com

CPSIA information can be obtained at www.ICGtesting.com
Printed in the USA
BVOW09s1111220814

363831BV00010B/92/P